INTERNATIONAL
POLITICAL
ECONOMY

SIXTH EDITION

SIXTH EDITION

INTERNATIONAL POLITICAL ECONOMY

Perspectives on Global Power and Wealth

Jeffry A. Frieden

HARVARD UNIVERSITY

David A. Lake

UNIVERSITY OF CALIFORNIA, SAN DIEGO

J. Lawrence Broz

UNIVERSITY OF CALIFORNIA, SAN DIEGO

W. W. Norton & Company ■ New York ■ London

W. W. Norton & Company has been independent since its founding in 1923, when William Warder Norton and Mary D. Herter Norton first published lectures delivered at the People's Institute, the adult education division of New York City's Cooper Union. The firm soon expanded its program beyond the Institute, publishing books by celebrated academics from America and abroad. By midcentury, the two major pillars of Norton's publishing program—trade books and college texts—were firmly established. In the 1950s, the Norton family transferred control of the company to its employees, and today—with a staff of four hundred and a comparable number of trade, college, and professional titles published each year—W. W. Norton & Company stands as the largest and oldest publishing house owned wholly by its employees.

The text of this book is composed in New Aster
with the display set in Akzidenz Grotesk
Project supervised by Westchester Publishing Services / Susan Baker.
Manufacturing by Sheridan Books—Ann Arbor, MI.
Associate Director of Production, College: Benjamin Reynolds.

ISBN 13: 978-0-393-60388-0

W. W. Norton & Company, Inc., 500 Fifth Avenue, New York, N.Y. 10110-0017
www.wwnorton.com

W. W. Norton & Company Ltd., Castle House, 75/76 Wells Street, London W1T 3QT

1 2 3 4 5 6 7 8 9 0

CONTENTS

PREFACE

The readings in *International Political Economy: Perspectives on Global Power and Wealth* are primarily intended to introduce the study of international political economy to those with little or no prior knowledge of it. The book is designed for use in courses in international political economy, international relations, and international economics. The selections present both clear and identifiable theoretical arguments and important substantive material. Twenty-two of the thirty-three articles are new to this sixth edition of our book.

Although the selections can be read in any order, they are grouped into eight parts that reflect some of the more common organizing principles used in international political economy courses. Each part begins with an introduction by the editors that provides background information and highlights issues raised in the readings. Each reading is preceded by an abstract summarizing its specific arguments and contributions. The readings have been edited to eliminate extraneous or dated information, and most footnotes were removed.

The introduction defines the study of international political economy, summarizes major analytical frameworks in the field, and identifies several current debates. To capture the most important work and current debates in the international political economy, we highlight the three analytic tools common to virtually all explanations: interests, interactions, and institutions. We then present an integrated framework using these tools that starts with individuals or corporate groups pursuing their interests and interacting within domestic political institutions, and then bargaining with other states possibly within international institutions. We also show, however, that while interests, interactions, and institutions are all necessary for any complete explanation, different authors may choose to focus on one or the other of these tools. We also provide a brief overview of the various paradigms that have informed scholarship on international political economy in the past.

Part I presents examples of research that focus more or less heavily on the interests, interactions, and institutions in the formulation of policy and international outcomes. The readings in this part are intended to suggest the underlying logic and types of arguments used by those who emphasize a particular tool. Although they are representative of their respective approach, they do not necessarily capture the wide range of opinion within each.

Part II, which reviews the history of the international economy since the nineteenth century and provides the background and perspective necessary to understand the contemporary international political economy. The selections describe the major developments in the history of the modern international economy from a variety of different theoretical viewpoints.

The remainder of the book is devoted to the modern international political economy. Separate sections on production, money and finance, trade, and migration look at the principal issue areas associated with the politics of international economic relations. Part VII focuses on the particular political and economic problems of developing economies. Finally, Part VIII examines current problems in the politics of international economics.

The selections in this volume have been used successfully in our courses on international political economy at Harvard University and the University of California, San Diego. In our own research, we approach the study of international political economy from very different perspectives. Yet, we find that this set of readings accommodates our individual approaches to the subject matter while simultaneously covering the major questions of the field.

For this edition, we thank Ann Shin, our editor at W. W. Norton & Company, for helping prepare the manuscript for publication. We also thank our respective spouses, Anabela Costa, Wendy K. Lake, and Rebecca L. Webb, for their continuing encouragement.

JEFFRY A. FRIEDEN
DAVID A. LAKE
J. LAWRENCE BROZ

ABOUT THE EDITORS

JEFFRY A. FRIEDEN (Ph.D., Columbia University) is professor of government at Harvard University. He specializes in the political economy of international monetary and financial relations. His book publications include *Currency Politics: The Political Economy of Exchange Rate Policy* (2015), *Lost Decades: The Making of America's Debt Crisis and the Long Recovery* (with Menzie Chinn, 2011), *Global Capitalism: Its Fall and Rise in the Twentieth Century* (2006), *Debt, Development, and Democracy: Modern Political Economy and Latin America, 1965–1985* (1991), and *Banking on the World: The Politics of American International Finance* (1987).

DAVID A. LAKE (Ph.D., Cornell University) is the Gerri-Ann and Gary E. Jacobs professor of social sciences and distinguished professor of political science at the University of California, San Diego. He has published widely in the field of international relations and international political economy. His principal book publications include *The Statebuilder's Dilemma: On the Limits of External Intervention* (2016), *Hierarchy in International Relations* (2009), *Entangling Relations: American Foreign Policy in Its Century* (1999), and *Power, Protection, and Free Trade: International Sources of U.S. Commercial Strategy, 1887–1939* (1988).

J. LAWRENCE BROZ (Ph.D., University of California, Los Angeles) is professor of political science at the University of California, San Diego. He studies the institutions that regulate national and international monetary and financial relations: central banks, exchange rate regimes, and international financial institutions. He is the author of *International Origins of the Federal Reserve System* (1997) and a series of articles on the congressional politics of financing the International Monetary Fund.

INTRODUCTION

International Politics and International Economics

International political economy is the study of the interplay of economics and politics in the world arena. In the most general sense, the economy can be defined as the system of producing, distributing, and using wealth; politics is the struggle between actors with divergent interests to make collective decisions, whether inside or outside of formal governments. *Political economy* has a variety of meanings. For some, it refers primarily to the study of the political basis of economic actions—the ways that government policies affect market operations. For others, the principal preoccupation is the economic basis of political action—the ways that economic forces mold government policies. The two focuses are, in a sense, complementary, for politics and markets are in a constant state of mutual interaction.

Most markets are governed by certain fundamental laws that operate more or less independently of the will of firms and individuals. Any shopkeeper knows that an attempt to raise the price of a readily available and standardized product—a pencil, for example—above that charged by nearby and competing shopkeepers will rapidly cause customers to stop buying pencils at the higher price. Unless the shopkeeper wants to be left with piles of unsold pencils, he or she will have to bring the price back into line with "what the market will bear." The shopkeeper will have learned a microcosmic lesson in what economists call *market-clearing equilibrium,* the price at which the number of goods supplied equals the number demanded—the point at which supply and demand curves intersect.

At the base of all modern economics is the general assertion that, within certain carefully specified parameters, markets operate in and of themselves to maintain balance between supply and demand. Other things being equal, if the supply of a good increases far beyond the demand for it, the good's price will be driven down until demand rises to meet supply, supply falls to meet demand, and market-clearing equilibrium is restored. By the same token, if demand exceeds supply, the good's price will rise, thus causing demand to decline and supply to increase until the two are in balance.

If the international and domestic economies functioned as perfectly competitive markets, they would be relatively easy to describe and comprehend. But such markets are only highly stylized or abstract models, which are rarely reproduced in the real world. A variety of factors influence the workings of domestic and international markets in ways that a focus on perfectly competitive and unchanging market forces does not fully capture. Consumer tastes can change—how large is the American market for spats or sarsaparilla today?—as can the technology needed to make products more cheaply, or even to make entirely new goods that displace others (stick shifts for horsewhips, computers for slide rules). Producers, sellers, or buyers of goods can band together to try to raise or lower prices unilaterally, as the Organization of Petroleum Exporting Countries (OPEC) has done with petroleum since 1973. And governments can act, consciously or inadvertently, to alter patterns of consumption, supply, demand, prices, and virtually all other economic variables.

This last fact—the impact of policy and politics on economic trends—is the most visible, and probably the most important, reason to look beyond market-based, purely economic explanations of social behavior. Indeed, many market-oriented economists are continually surprised by the ability of governments or of powerful groups pressuring governments to contravene economic tendencies. When OPEC first raised oil prices in December 1973, some market-minded pundits, and even a few naive economists, predicted that such naked manipulation of the forces of supply and demand could last only a matter of months. However, what has emerged from almost fifty years' experience with oil prices is the recognition that they are a function of both market forces and the ability of OPEC's member states to organize concerted intervention in the oil market.

Somewhat less dramatic are the everyday operations of local and national governments, which affect prices, production, profits, wages, and almost every other aspect of the economy. Wage, price, and rent controls; taxation; incentives and subsidies; tariffs and other barriers to trade; and government spending all serve to mold modern economies and the functioning of markets themselves. Who could understand the suburbanization of the United States after World War II without taking into account government tax incentives to home mortgage holders, government-financed highway construction, and politically driven patterns of local educational expenditures? How many American (or Japanese or European) farmers would be left if agricultural subsidies were eliminated? How many Americans would have college educations were it not for public universities, government scholarships and publicly subsidized student loans, and tax exemptions for private universities? Who could explain the proliferation of nonprofit groups in the United States without knowing the tax incentives given to charitable donations?

In these instances, and many more, political pressure groups, politicians, and government bureaucrats have at least as much effect on economic outcomes as do the laws of the marketplace. Social scientists, especially political scientists, have spent decades trying to understand how these political pressures interact to produce government policy. Many of the results provide as elegant and stylized a view of politics as the economics profession has developed of markets. As in economics, however, social science models of political behavior are little more than didactic devices whose accuracy depends on a wide variety of unpredictable factors, including underlying economic trends. If an economist would be foolish to dismiss the possibilities of intergovernmental producers' cartels (such as OPEC) out of hand, a political scientist would be equally foolish not to realize that the economic realities of modern international commodity markets ensure that successful producers' cartels will be few and far between.

It is thus no surprise that political economy is far from new. Indeed, until a century ago, virtually all thinkers concerned with understanding human society wrote about political economy. For individuals as diverse as Adam Smith, John Stuart Mill, and Karl Marx, the economy was eminently political and politics was obviously tied to economic phenomena. Few scholars before 1900 would have taken seriously any attempt to describe and analyze politics and economics independently of each other.

Around the turn of the last century, however, professional studies of economics and politics became increasingly divorced from one another. Economic investigation began to focus on understanding more fully the operation of specific markets and their interaction; the development of new mathematical techniques permitted the formalization of, for example, laws of supply and demand. By the time of World War I, an economics profession per se was in existence, and its attention was focused on understanding the operation of economic activities in and of themselves. At the same time, other scholars were looking increasingly at the political realm in isolation from the economy. The rise of modern representative political institutions, mass political parties, more politically informed populations, and modern bureaucracies all seemed to justify the study of politics as an activity that had a logic of its own.

With the exception of a few isolated individuals and an upsurge of interest during the politically and economically troubled Depression years, the twentieth century saw an increasing separation of the study of economics from that of politics. Economists developed ever more elaborate and sophisticated models of how economies work, and similarly, political scientists spun out ever more complex theories of political development and activity.

The resurgence of political economy in the last half century has had two interrelated sources. The first was dissatisfaction among academics with the gap between abstract models of political and economic behavior, on the one hand, and the actual behavior of polities and economies, on the other. Theory had become more ethereal and seemed less realistic. Many scholars therefore questioned the intellectual justifications for a strict analytic division between politics and economics. Second, as the stability and prosperity of the first twenty-five postwar years started to disintegrate in the early 1970s, economic issues became politicized while political systems became increasingly preoccupied with economic affairs. In August 1971, President Richard Nixon ended the gold-dollar standard, which had formed the basis for postwar monetary relations; two and a half years later, OPEC, a previously little-known group, succeeded in substantially raising the price of oil. In 1974 and 1975, the industrial nations of Western Europe, North America, and Japan fell into the first worldwide economic recession since the 1930s; unemployment and inflation were soon widespread realities and explosive political issues. In the world arena, the underdeveloped countries—most of them recently independent—burst onto center stage as the third world and demanded a fairer division of global wealth and power. If, in the 1950s and 1960s, economic growth was taken for granted and politics occupied itself with other matters, in the 1970s and 1980s, economic stagnation fed political strife while political conflict exacerbated economic uncertainty. The politicization of international economics has continued ever since, especially after the Great Recession in 2008 with new demands for financial market reform, less economic inequality, and greater trade protection.

For both intellectual and practical reasons, then, social scientists once again began seeking to understand how politics and economics interact in modern society. To be sure, today's political economists have not simply reproduced the studies of earlier (and perhaps neglected) generations of scholars in the discipline. The professionalization of both economics and political science led to major advances in both fields, and scholars now understand both economic and political phenomena far better than they did a generation or two ago. It is on this improved basis that the new political economy has been constructed, albeit with some long-standing issues in mind.

Just as in the real world, where politicians pay close attention to economic trends and economic actors keep track of political tendencies, those who would understand the political process must take the economy into account, and vice versa. A much richer picture of social processes emerges from an integrated understanding of both political and economic affairs than from the isolated study of politics and economics as separate realms. This much is, by now, hardly controversial; it is in application that disagreements arise. Government actions may influence economic trends, but these actions themselves may simply reflect the pressures of economic interest groups. Economic interest groups may be central in determining government policy, yet political institutions—democratic or totalitarian, two-party or multiparty, parliamentary or presidential—may crucially color the outlook and influence of economic interests. Although they may emphasize different forces, international political economists have moved toward a common framework for understanding the interaction of politics and economics.

INTERESTS, INTERACTIONS, INSTITUTIONS, AND THE INTERNATIONAL POLITICAL ECONOMY

Analysts of the international political economy must understand the complex interplay of many disparate forces. Globalization affects the employment, purchasing power, and quality of life of individuals, as well as the prosperity, level of economic inequality, and competitive success of nations. As the financial crisis of 2008 and the political instability that continues to roil both developed and developing countries makes clear, countries in the international economy are highly interdependent and closely integrated. To understand this complexity, international political economists frequently begin with three core concepts: interests, interactions, and institutions.

- Interests are actors' goals, usually defined in terms of the outcomes they hope to obtain through political action. Businesses generally have an interest in maximizing profits, just as workers have an interest in maximizing wages; environmental activists typically have interests in protecting the atmosphere, the oceans, or endangered species; states may have interests in protecting citizens, expanding national wealth, or acquiring new territory.
- Interactions are the ways in which the choices of two or more actors combine to produce political outcomes. The outcomes we observe—trade disputes, financial stabilization, or international cooperation to protect the environment—reflect the choices of many actors, each looking out for its own interest, but also taking into account the interests and likely actions of others. All forms of international cooperation, for instance, require multiple states to coordinate their policy choices toward a common goal.
- Institutions are sets of rules, known and shared by the relevant community, that structure political interactions. Institutions define the "rules of the game," often embodied in constitutions, statutes, treaties, and global forums like the World Trade Organization. Institutions create procedures for making joint decisions, such as voting rules; they also lay out standards of acceptable behavior and often include provisions for monitoring compliance and punishing those that violate the rules.

There are many different types of actors in the international political economy. Individuals have interests as consumers, workers, shareholders, and in other roles. Many actors are collectives, such as firms, unions, business associations, and even states. Which actor an analyst focuses on is determined by the problem under investigation and the theory relevant to understanding that problem. For some questions, like trade policy preferences, we might start with individuals and their dual roles as consumers and producers working in a particular economic sector. For other questions, such as international financial negotiations, it might make sense to distinguish between creditor and debtor nations. There is no right or wrong way to specify the actors in any set of events. We judge different assumptions about who the relevant actors are by whether they are useful in helping us understand outcomes.

Having identified the relevant actors, the first task is to determine the actor's interest. Interests can be many and varied, depending on the specific policy or event under examination. In identifying the interests of an actor, analysts sometimes draw on prior theories of human nature or behavior; at other times, they simply assume the actors have a particular goal. In international political economy, it is common to assume that actors are motivated by material conditions and economic welfare, though exactly how welfare is defined and understood may well be the product of prevailing ideas and social norms—a point we return to below in our discussion of Constructivism in the next section.

We often use economic theory to deduce what types of individuals can be reasonably assumed to share identical interests. A key divide is between the Ricardo-Viner or specific factors theory of international trade, which assumes that capital and labor are fixed in particular occupations and, thus, will tend to have similar interests over trade policy, and the Heckscher-Ohlin theory of international trade, which assumes that all factors are mobile across occupations and, therefore, capital, land, and labor will possess opposing interests. A recent approach, sometimes known as new new trade theory, argues that only the most productive firms are capable of exporting, which implies that trade policy interests will differ between firms even in the same economic sector.

Having defined the relevant unit of analysis, we can then derive preferences over alternative policies from the distributional implications of different economic policies and, in turn, how an actor is located relative to others in the international economy. Firms vary by whether they are productive enough to compete with imports, export finished goods, or engage in foreign direct investment. By knowing a firm's productivity profile, we can then predict how it will be helped or harmed by policies to increase international openness. Sectors vary by similar characteristics. Factors of production, in turn, vary by their scarcity relative to the world economy. Since flows of goods and factors across international borders are equivalent in their distributional effects, we can use these same theories to derive expectations about how factors will be affected by a large range of economic policies and, thus, identify their interests over foreign direct and portfolio investment or migration.

Interests are essential in analyzing any event in international political economy because they capture how the actors assess alternative outcomes. But to account for these outcomes, we must examine the choices of all relevant actors and how their choices interact to produce a particular result. When outcomes result from an interaction, actors have to anticipate the likely choices of others and take those choices into account when making their own decisions. A low-productivity firm might prefer trade protection for its products, but if it cannot form a coalition with other firms to successfully lobby Congress, it might decide simply to close down and sell off its assets. Its choice depends crucially on what it anticipates would be the likely choices of other actors within the policy-making process. Similarly, states might prefer a global environmental compact, but unless they expect that most other states will cooperate, they might aim to negotiate only a smaller regional agreement or free ride on the efforts of others entirely.

Institutions play a major role in the international political economy, both domestically and internationally. Institutions are sets of rules that often determine how interactions play out and, thus, the choices actors make. The U.S. Constitution gives the right to set tariffs to Congress, which tends to be more responsive to local industries and their interests than the Senate or the president. The result is that for much of its history, Congress has created large "logrolls" that have produced high tariffs that protected nearly all industries in the United States. In the midst of the Great Depression of the 1930s, however, Congress delegated authority to the president to negotiate bilateral trade agreements in an effort to expand U.S. exports (see Bailey, Goldstein, and Weingast, Reading 8). The president could now offer to reduce tariffs on foreign products imported into the United States in exchange for reductions in tariffs on U.S. goods exported to other countries. This institutional change fundamentally altered the politics of trade protection by pitting exporters who desired access to foreign markets against importers who wanted to protect the domestic market. Over time, as a consequence of this institutional change, tariffs were greatly reduced in the United States and in countries that were its trading partners. The reciprocal reduction in tariffs, in turn, was later codified in the international institutions of the General Agreement on Tariffs and Trade (GATT) and eventually in the World Trade Organization (WTO).

However, institutions themselves are the product of political struggle. Precisely because they matter for how actors choose to interact, and the outcomes that result, actors will seek to negotiate the rules of politics in ways that favor their interests. In the example of U.S. trade policy, Congress delegated authority to the president to negotiate international agreements only under pressure from exporters who understood that such an institutional change would be to their benefit. Thus, institutions are often part of the political "game" itself, conditioned by even deeper rules about how institutions are themselves changed.

These concepts of interests, interactions, and institutions suggest a model of the politics of international economy policy that begins with individuals, firms, sectors, or factors of production as the units of analysis and derives their interests over economic policy from each unit's position within the international economy. This approach, sometimes referred to as "Open Economy Politics," conceives of domestic political institutions as mechanisms that aggregate interests (with more or less bias) and structure the bargaining of competing societal groups. Finally, it introduces, when necessary, strategic bargaining between states with different interests. Analysis within the approach can proceed from the micro to the macro level in a linear and orderly fashion, reflecting an implicit unidirectional conception of politics as flowing up from individuals to interstate bargaining. The overall image, though, is one of groups within countries struggling within domestic political institutions over policies that will favor their interests, and then states—representing those preferred policies—bargaining sometimes within international institutions and sometimes without any rules over international outcomes.

Few theorists give equal weight to all steps in this analysis. As the selections in the remainder of this volume indicate, most focus on one step—for instance, how institutions aggregate societal interests—and treat others as analytic simplifications that are often left implicit in the specific theory at hand. For tractability, scholars focus on one or another step in the process and bracket many obviously varying features of a political-economic environment by treating them as exogenous for purposes of studying a single characteristic of the policy-making process. One might, for instance, bracket where interests "come from" and study how domestic institutions aggregate these interests in different ways. Alternatively, one might simplify the domestic political process and assume it produces some "national interest" or aggregated social welfare function and focus on how states then bargain over more or less favorable policies. In reality, of course, all else is not constant. Institutions often embody different sets of interests, the goals actors pursue are affected by the institutional setting in which they are embedded, and both interests and institutions at home are influenced by interactions between states. Yet, in practice, analysts must narrow the lens through which they view the world and concentrate on understanding particular steps in the political process that produce outcomes of concern. In most cases, the author's focus on interests, interactions, and institutions will be obvious, but our section introductions and summaries of each reading presented below highlight their contribution and explain why it is integral to understanding the problem emphasized in the study.

FOUR ALTERNATIVE VIEWS OF INTERNATIONAL POLITICAL ECONOMY

In addition to tools of interests, interactions, and institutions just discussed, some scholars attempt to classify interpretations of global political and economic developments in a somewhat different manner. Many theories of international political economy can also be categorized into one of four perspectives: Liberalism, Marxism, Realism, and Constructivism. Note that in international political economy, advocates of free trade and free markets are still referred to as Liberals. In twentieth-century American domestic politics, however, the term has come to mean something different. In the United States today, whereas "conservatives" traditionally support free markets and less government intervention, "liberals" typically advocate greater governmental intervention in the market to stimulate growth and mitigate inequalities. These contradictory usages of the term *Liberal* may seem confusing, but the context will usually make an author's meaning clear. Although little research in international political economy now occurs strictly within these four perspectives, they have helped structure past debates in the field, and students should be familiar with their broad contours.

The Liberal argument emphasizes how both the market and politics are environments in which all parties can benefit by entering into voluntary exchanges with others. If there are no impediments to trade among individuals, Liberals reason, everyone can be made as well-off as possible, given the existing stocks of goods and services. All participants in the market, in other words, will be at their highest possible level of utility. Neoclassical economists, who are generally Liberals, believe firmly in the superiority of the market—as both a set of interactions and an institution—as a mechanism for allocating scarce resources. Liberals therefore reason that the economic role of government should be quite limited. Many forms of government intervention in the economy, they argue, intentionally or unintentionally restrict the market and thereby prevent potentially rewarding trades from occurring.

Liberals do generally support the provision by government of certain "public goods"—goods and services that benefit society and that would not be provided by private markets.[1] The government, for example, plays an important role in supplying the conditions necessary for the maintenance of a free and competitive market. Governments must provide for the defense of the country, protect property rights, and prevent any unfair collusion or concentration of power within the market. The government should also, according to most Liberals, educate its citizens, build infrastructure, and provide and regulate a common currency. The proper role of government, in other words, is to provide the necessary foundation for the market.

At the level of the international economy, Liberals assert that a fundamental harmony of interests exists between, as well as within, countries. Focusing mostly on interests defined in terms of material consumption, they argue that all countries are best off when goods and services move freely across national borders in mutually rewarding exchanges. If universal free trade were to exist, all countries would enjoy the highest level of utility and there would be no economic basis for international conflict or war. Liberals also believe that governments should manage the international economy in much the same way as they manage their domestic economies. They should establish institutions, often referred to as "international regimes," to govern exchanges between different national currencies and to ensure that no country or domestic group is damaged by "unfair" international competition.

Marxism originated with the writings of Karl Marx, a nineteenth-century political economist and perhaps the severest critic of capitalism and its Liberal supporters. Marx saw capitalism and the market as creating extremes of wealth for capitalists and poverty for workers. While the entire populace may have been better-off than before, the capitalists were clearly expanding their wealth more rapidly than everyone else. Marx rejected the assertion that exchange between individuals necessarily maximizes the welfare of the whole society. Accordingly, he perceived capitalism as an inherently conflictual system that both should, and will, be inevitably overthrown and replaced by socialism.

Marxists believe that classes are the dominant actors in the political economy. Specifically, they identify as central two economically determined aggregations of individuals or classes: capital, or the owners of the means of production, and labor, or the workers. Marxists assume that classes act in their economic interests—that is, to maximize the economic well-being of the class as a whole. Accordingly, the basis of the capitalist economy is the exploitation of labor by capital: capitalism, by its very nature, denies labor the full return for its efforts.

Marxists see the political economy as necessarily conflictual, since the relationship between capitalists and workers is essentially antagonistic. Because the means of production are controlled by a minority within society—the capitalists—labor does not receive its full return; conflict between the classes is inevitably caused by this exploitation. Marxists also believe that capitalism is inherently prone to periodic economic crises, which will, they believe, ultimately lead to the overthrow of capitalism by labor and the erection of a socialist society in which the means of production will be owned jointly by all members of society and exploitation will cease.

V. I. Lenin, the Russian revolutionary who founded the Soviet Union, extended Marx's ideas to the international political economy to explain imperialism and war. Imperialism, Lenin argued, was endemic to modern capitalism. As capitalism decayed in the most developed nations, capitalists would attempt to solve their problems by exporting capital abroad. As this capital required protection from both local and foreign challengers, governments would colonize regions to safeguard the interests of their foreign investors. Eventually, capitalist countries would compete for control over these areas and intracapitalist wars would follow.

Today, Marxists who study the international political economy are primarily concerned with two issues. The first is the fate of labor in a world of increasingly internationalized capital. The growth of multinational corporations and the rise of globally integrated financial markets appear to have weakened labor's economic and political power. If workers in a particular country demand higher wages or improved health and safety measures, for example, the multinational capitalist can simply shift production to another country where labor is more compliant. As a result, many Marxists fear that labor's ability to negotiate with capital for a more equitable division of wealth has been significantly undermined.

Second, Marxists are concerned with the poverty and continued underdevelopment of the third world. Some Marxists argue that development is blocked by domestic ruling classes, which pursue their own narrow interests at the expense of national economic progress. Others, known as "dependency" theorists, extend class analysis to the level of the international economy. According to these Marxists, the global system is stratified into a wealthy area (the "core," or first world) and a region of oppression and poverty (the "periphery," or third world). International capitalism, in this view, exploits the periphery and benefits the core, just as capitalists exploit workers within a single country. The principal questions here focus on the mechanisms of exploitation—whether they be multinational corporations, international financial markets and organizations, or trade—and the appropriate strategies for stimulating autonomous growth and development in the periphery.

Realism traces its intellectual roots back to Thucydides' writings in 400 B.C.E., as well as those of Niccolò Machiavelli, Thomas Hobbes, and the mercantilists Jean-Baptiste Colbert and Friedrich List. Realists believe that nation-states pursue power and shape the economy to this end. Moreover, they also believe states are the dominant actors within the international political economy. According to Realists, the international system is anarchical, a condition under which nation-states are sovereign, the sole judges of their own behaviors, and subject to no higher authority. If no authority is higher than the nation-state, Realists believe, then all actors must be subordinate to it. While private citizens can interact with their counterparts in other countries, Realists assert that the basis for this interaction is legislated by the nation-state. Thus, where Liberals focus on individuals and Marxists on classes, Realists concentrate on nation-states.

Realists also argue that nation-states have a fundamental interest in maximizing international power or, at least, the chances for national survival. Because the international system is based on anarchy, the use of force or coercion by other nation-states is always a possibility and no higher authority is obligated to come to the aid of a nation-state under attack. Nation-states are thus ultimately dependent on their own resources for protection. For Realists, then, each nation-state must always be prepared to defend itself to the best of its ability. For Realists, politics is largely a zero-sum game and by necessity conflictual. In other words, if one nation-state is to win, another must lose.

Realists also believe that nation-states can be thought of as rational actors in the same sense that other theorists assume individuals to be rational. Nation-states are assumed to operate according to cost-benefit analyses and choose the option that yields the greatest value, especially regarding the nation's international geopolitical and power positions.

The emphasis on power is what gives Realism its distinctive approach to international political economy. While economic considerations may often complement power concerns, the former are, in the Realist view, subordinate to the latter. Realists allow for circumstances in which nation-states sacrifice economic gain to weaken their opponents or strengthen themselves in military or diplomatic terms. Thus, trade protection, which might reduce a country's overall income by restricting the market, may nonetheless be adopted for reasons of national political power.

Realist political economy is primarily concerned with how changes in the distribution of international power affect the form and type of international economy. The best-known Realist approach to this question is the *theory of hegemonic stability*, which holds that an open international economy—that is, one characterized by the free exchange of goods, capital, and services—is most likely to exist when a single dominant or hegemonic power is present to stabilize the system and construct a strong regime (see Krasner, Reading 3). For Realists, then, the pursuit of power by nation-states shapes the international economy.

Each of these first three perspectives features different assumptions and assertions. Liberals assume that individuals are the proper unit of analysis, while Marxists and Realists make similar assumptions regarding classes and nation-states, respectively. The three perspectives also differ on the inevitability of conflict within the political economy. Liberals believe economics and politics are largely autonomous spheres, Marxists maintain that economics determines politics, and Realists argue that politics determines economics.

Constructivism, a fourth and relatively recent approach to international political economy, has roots in critical theory and sociology. Unlike the first three approaches, Constructivism is more of a method of analysis than a set of alternative assumptions and assertions. Constructivists believe that actors in the international political economy and their interests are not innate but are produced or constructed through social interactions. Sectors, factors of production, classes, and especially nation-states are not fixed and immutable in this view, but are themselves produced by their social environments. Rather than pursuing wealth over power, or vice versa, individuals, classes, and states vary in their interests and contain the potential for both conflict and cooperation in different social settings.

Constructivists also believe that norms play an important role in international political economy. The other approaches all assume implicitly that actors are purposive and select among possible courses of action by their anticipated effects. This is sometimes referred to as a "logic of consequences." Constructivists assume that actors select roles and actions by what is right, just, or socially expected. In other words, actors choose according to a "logic of appropriateness." In this view, countries may open themselves to trade or international investment not because, as Liberals assert, this improves their welfare in any instrumental sense, but because this is what responsible or "developed" states understand as appropriate in the modern international political economy.

In addition, Constructivists assert that actors and their interactions can be transformed through the introduction of new norms or understandings of their interests or identities. The rough-and-tumble international political economy described by Realists, for example, is not, according to Constructivists, foreordained by the condition of anarchy. If actors come to understand the world differently, the conception of appropriate behavior could also change dramatically. As the "Washington Consensus" took hold internationally during the 1990s, for instance, countries liberalized their economies and held to this policy long after its promised effects failed to materialize.

This fourfold division of international political economy is useful in many ways, especially as it highlights differing evaluations of the importance of economic efficiency, class conflict, and geostrategic and normative considerations. However, the lines between these views are easily blurred. Some Marxists agree with the Realist focus on interstate conflict, while others concur with the Liberal emphasis on economic interests, while still others agree with Constructivists on the role of norms. Likewise, there are many Liberals who use neoclassical tools to analyze interstate strategic interaction in much the same way Realists do or to investigate the clash of classes as do the Marxists. Nearly all Liberals, Marxists, and Realists have come to a deeper understanding of the role of norms, emphasized by Constructivists. Such substantial overlap, in our view, suggests that instead of adhering to a particular paradigm, scholars instead should think seriously about the interests, interactions, and institutions that motivate actors, influence their choices, and determine the outcomes we observe within the international political economy.

THE CONTEMPORARY INTERNATIONAL POLITICAL ECONOMY: AN OVERVIEW

Following initial sections on theoretical perspectives and historical background, the remainder of this book concerns the politics of international economic relations since World War II, with an emphasis on current issues and debates. Developments since 1945 have, indeed, raised a wide variety of theoretical, practical, and policy issues.

The contemporary international political economy is characterized by unprecedented levels of multinational production (Section III), cross-border financial flows (Section IV), and international trade (Section V). It is also plagued by increasing political conflict as individuals, groups, classes, and countries clash over the meaning and implications of these economic transactions. International migration (Section VI) is lower than in the early twentieth century, the prior period of globalization, and is perhaps the most controversial issue of all. The contradiction between increasing economic integration and the wealth it produces, on the one hand, and the desire for political control and national autonomy, on the other, defines much of what happens in the global political economy.

For the first thirty years after World War II, the general pattern of relations among noncommunist nations was set by American leadership, and this pattern continues to influence the international political economy today. In the political arena, formal and informal alliances tied virtually every major noncommunist nation into an American-led network of mutual support and defense. In the economic arena, a wide-ranging set of international economic organizations—including the International Monetary Fund (IMF), the GATT, and the International Bank for Reconstruction and Development (World Bank)—grew up under a protective American "umbrella" and often as a direct American initiative. The world economy itself was heavily influenced by the rise of modern multinational corporations and banks, whose contemporary form is largely of U.S. origin.

American plans for a reordered world economy go back to the mid-1930s. After World War I, the United States retreated into relative economic insularity, for reasons explored in Part II, "Historical Perspectives." When the Great Depression hit, American political leaders virtually ignored the possibility of international economic cooperation in their attempts to stabilize the domestic economy. Yet, even as the Franklin Roosevelt administration looked inward for recovery, by 1934 new American initiatives were signaling a shift in America's traditional isolation. Roosevelt's secretary of state, Cordell Hull, was a militant free trader, and in 1934 he convinced Congress to pass the Reciprocal Trade Agreements Act, which allowed the executive to negotiate tariff reductions with foreign nations. This important step toward trade liberalization and international economic cooperation was deepened as war threatened in Europe and the United States drew closer to Great Britain and France.

The seeds of the new international order, planted in the 1930s, began to grow even as World War II came to an end. The Bretton Woods agreement, reached among the Allied powers in 1944, established a new series of international economic organizations that became the foundation for the postwar American-led system. As the wartime American–Soviet alliance began to shatter, a new economic order emerged in the noncommunist world. At its center were the three pillars of the Bretton Woods system: international monetary cooperation under the auspices of the IMF, international trade liberalization negotiated within the GATT, and investment in the developing countries stimulated by the World Bank. All three pillars were essentially designed by the United States and dependent on its support.

As it developed, the postwar capitalist world reflected American foreign policy in many of its details. One principal concern of the United States was to build a bulwark of anti-Soviet allies; this was done with a massive inflow of American aid under the Marshall Plan and the encouragement of Western European cooperation within a new Common Market. At the same time, the United States dramatically lowered its barriers to foreign goods and American corporations began to invest heavily in foreign nations. Of course, the United States was not acting altruistically: European recovery, trade liberalization, and booming international investment helped ensure great prosperity within its own borders as well.

American policies, whatever their motivation, had an undeniable impact on the international political economy. Trade liberalization opened the huge American market to foreign producers. American overseas investment provided capital, technology, and expertise for both Europe and the developing world. American governmental economic aid, whether direct or channeled through such institutions as the World Bank, helped finance economic growth abroad. In addition, the American military umbrella allowed anti-Soviet governments in Europe, Japan, and the developing world to rely on the United States for security and to turn their attentions to encouraging economic growth.

All in all, the noncommunist world's unprecedented access to American markets and American capital provided a major stimulus to world economic growth, not to mention the profits of American businesses and general prosperity within the United States. For more than twenty-five years after World War II, the capitalist world experienced impressive levels of economic growth and development, all within a general context of international cooperation under American political, economic, and military tutelage.

This period is often referred to as the Pax Americana because of its broad similarity to the British-led international economic system that operated from about 1820 until World War I, which was known as the Pax Britannica. In both instances, general political and economic peace prevailed under the leadership of an overwhelming world power—the United Kingdom in one case, the United States in the other.

Just as the Pax Britannica eventually ended, however, the Pax Americana gradually eroded. By the early 1970s, strains were developing in the postwar system. Between 1971 and 1975, the postwar international monetary system, which had been based on a gold-backed U.S. dollar, fell apart and was replaced by a new, improvised pattern of floating exchange rates in which the dollar's role was still strong but no longer quite so central. At the same time, pressures for trade protection from uncompetitive industries in North America and Western Europe began to mount; and although tariff levels remained low, a variety of nontariff barriers to world trade, such as import quotas, soon proliferated. In the political arena, détente between the United States and the Soviet Union seemed to make the American security umbrella less relevant for the Japanese and Western Europeans; in the less-developed countries, North–South conflict appeared more important than East–West strife. In short, during the 1970s, as American economic strength declined, the Bretton Woods institutions weakened, and the cold war thawed, the Pax Americana drew to a close.

The quickening pace of change in the Soviet Union and among its allies eventually culminated in the collapse of former Soviet bloc nations in the late 1980s and early 1990s, and ultimately in the disintegration of the former Soviet Union. The end of the cold war did not, of course, mean an end to international conflict, but it did put an end to the East–West divide that had dominated global politics for so long.

As the cold war wound down, international economic issues grew in importance, along with a greater willingness on the part of many nations to integrate with the rest of the world economy. Over the course of the 1980s, a wave of trade liberalization and privatization swept many countries in the developing world, so that by the early 1990s they were clearly committed to global economic integration. Then came the most striking development, the collapse of the centrally planned economies and their startling change in direction toward domestic and world markets. The process started in China and Vietnam, but when the Soviet Union disintegrated and the countries of Eastern and Central Europe joined the European Union, the resurgence of an integrated global economy seemed complete.

Since the mid-1990s, the world economy has continued on the general path of globalization. All of the indicators of integration have trended upward—some of them, such as international financial flows, at a very rapid pace. Yet, concern has grown about globalization in many quarters, and the generalized enthusiasm of the early 1990s is now waning.

The principal issue facing analysts of the international political economy today has to do with the future of this era of globalization. Despite continued conflict over the international economy, most people—especially in the industrialized nations—appear to accept that an international system in which goods and capital can move quite freely among countries has become the normal state of affairs and is likely to continue for the foreseeable future. Nonetheless, there is widespread unease about the current state of international economic relations. Activists worry that footloose corporations may undermine attempts to protect the environment, labor, and human rights. Beleaguered businesses are troubled by foreign competitors. Nationalists and religious traditionalists fear that globalization will undermine cultural and other norms. With growing economic inequality, low-skilled workers in the developed countries are turning increasingly against trade and immigration—feeding nationalist parties across Europe and North America.

All of these apprehensions were heightened by the global economic crisis that began at the end of 2007. Difficulties in the American financial system were quickly transmitted around the world, and within months the entire international economy was in recession. There were even fears that the recession might deepen into depression. The economic downturn raised the specter of economic conflicts among the world's major powers, as each nation focused its efforts on defending itself and its citizens from the fallout of the economic collapse. National governments and international economic institutions were confronted with problems of unprecedented breadth and scope. In this uncertain and rapidly changing environment, the United States remains the most important country within the international political economy, but it is no longer dominant. The era of American hegemony has been replaced by a new, multilateral order based on the joint leadership of Western Europe, Japan, and the United States. So far, these countries have successfully managed—or, some would say, muddled through—the "oil shocks" of the 1970s, the debt crisis of the early 1980s, the transition to the market of the former centrally planned economies after 1989, the currency crises and other financial volatility of the 1990s, and the Great Financial Crisis of 2007–2009.

Despite greater success than many thought possible, multilateral leadership and the liberal international order remain fragile. Conflicts of interest and economic tensions remain muted, but they could erupt at any time. The politics of international economic relations are made more complex by the new involvement of such countries as China, India, and Russia. These nations played virtually no role in international economic affairs for fifty years after World War II, but they are now actors to be reckoned with on the world economic scene—especially China, now the world's second-largest economy and an export powerhouse. It is unclear whether, and how, the developed nations will work together with these newly resurgent developing countries in confronting the economic and political problems of the twenty-first century.

The remainder of this book is devoted to understanding the contemporary international political economy and its likely future. In the sections that follow, a variety of thematic issues are addressed; in each cluster of issues, alternative theoretical and analytical perspectives compete. The selections in this reader serve both to provide information on broad trends in the politics of international economic relations and to give an overview of the contending approaches to be found within the discipline.

NOTE

1. More specifically, a public good is one that, in its purest form, is *nonrival in consumption* and *nonexcludable*. The first characteristic means that consumption of the good by one person does not reduce the opportunities for others to consume that good; for example, clean air can be breathed by one individual without reducing its availability to others. The second characteristic means that nobody can be prevented from consuming the good: those who do not contribute to pollution control are still able to breathe clean air. These two conditions are fully met only rarely, but goods whose characteristics come close to meeting them are generally considered public goods.

I

CONTENDING PERSPECTIVES ON INTERNATIONAL POLITICAL ECONOMY

As outlined in the Introduction, three principal theoretical concepts structure analyses of the international political economy: interests, interactions, and institutions. Interests represent the stakes that actors (i.e., individuals, firms, sectors, factors of production, and states) have in a given policy area. Some actors may favor a certain policy, such as free trade, while others may oppose this policy. In other words, actors have interests in policies because such policies usually create winners and losers. Interactions represent the interplay of actors with distinct interests. Sometimes actors find allies that share their policy goals while at other times actors' interests will conflict. Either way, policy outcomes usually require interaction and bargaining between two or more sets of interested actors. Institutions are the stable sets of rules that structure interactions among the relevant actors. At the domestic level, constitutions lay out the rules by which policies are made; at the international level, states interact strategically within rules established by treaties, agreements, and international organizations. Ronald Rogowski (Reading 1) examines how changing exposure to international trade influences political cleavages within nations. With a focus on interests, he shows how domestic political coalitions are a product of a country's position within the international division of labor and of exogenous changes in the costs of trade. Jeffry A. Frieden (Reading 2) explores political interactions during international debt crises like the Eurozone crisis. He examines strategic bargaining between debtor and creditor countries as well as bargaining between interested domestic actors over who will bear the costs of adjustment. Stephen D. Krasner (Reading 3) examines patterns of trade openness within the international economy over the nineteenth and twentieth centuries and finds that openness hinges on both the interests and the interactions of the most powerful states in the system. Christina L. Davis (Reading 4) focuses on the institutional context of international trade negotiations to show that the rules of the game can determine whether trade negotiations succeed or fail. As exemplars of their respective approaches, these selections are intended only to illustrate basic themes and arguments; all three approaches contain a rich diversity of styles and conclusions, and these readings are only a sample. Nonetheless, they serve to highlight key analytic debates and provide a useful empirical introduction to critical trends and cases in international political economy.

1

Commerce and Coalitions: How Trade Affects Domestic Political Alignments

RONALD ROGOWSKI

According to the Stolper-Samuelson theorem, free trade benefits locally abundant factors of production—such as land, labor, or capital—and harms locally scarce factors of production. This insight is useful because it helps us understand the interests of factor owners like farmers, capitalists, and workers. Ronald Rogowski offers a compelling theoretical and empirical account of political cleavages within countries. He extends the Stolper-Samuelson theorem to reason that increasing exposure to trade—say, because of falling transportation costs—will benefit and empower locally abundant factors, whereas decreasing exposure to trade will hurt these factors. Although not seeking to explain trade policy outcomes (such as the level of protection within a country), Rogowski provides a powerful explanation of the political interests and the coalitions that surround trade policy. This reading shows how international economic forces can exert a profound effect on domestic politics.

THE STOLPER-SAMUELSON THEOREM

In 1941, Wolfgang Stolper and Paul Samuelson solved conclusively the old riddle of gains and losses from protection (or, for that matter, from free trade). In almost any society, they showed, protection benefits (and liberalization of trade harms) owners of factors in which, relative to the rest of the world, that society is *poorly* endowed, as well as producers who use that scarce factor intensively. Conversely, protection harms (and liberalization benefits) those factors that—again, relative to the rest of the world—the given society holds *abundantly*, and the producers who use those locally abundant factors intensively. Thus, in a society rich in labor but poor in capital, protection benefits capital and harms labor; and liberalization of trade benefits labor and harms capital.

So far, the theorem is what it is usually perceived to be, merely a statement, albeit an important and sweeping one, about the effects of tariff policy. The picture is altered, however, when one realizes that *exogenous* changes can have exactly the same effects as increases or decreases in protection. A cheapening of transport costs, for example, is indistinguishable in its impact from an across-the-board decrease in every affected state's tariffs; so is any change in the international regime that decreases the risks or the transaction costs of trade. The converse is of course equally true: when a nation's external transport becomes dearer or its trade less secure, it is affected exactly as if it had imposed a higher tariff.

The point is of more than academic interest because we know, historically, that major changes in the risks and costs of international trade have occurred: notoriously, the railroads and steamships of the nineteenth century brought drastically cheaper transportation; so, in their day, did the improvements in shipbuilding and navigation of the fifteenth and sixteenth centuries; and so, in our own generation, have supertankers, cheap oil, and containerization. According to the familiar argument, . . . international hegemony decreases both the risks and the transaction costs of international trade; and the decline of hegemonic power makes trade more expensive, perhaps—as, some have argued, in the 1930s—prohibitively so. . . .

Global changes of these kinds, it follows, should have had global consequences. The "transportation revolutions" of the sixteenth, the nineteenth, and scarcely less of the mid-twentieth century must have benefited in each affected country owners and intensive employers of locally abundant factors and must have harmed owners and intensive employers of locally scarce factors. The events of the 1930s should have had exactly the opposite effect. What, however, will have been the *political* consequences of those shifts of wealth and income? To answer that question, we require a rudimentary model of the political process and a somewhat more definite one of the economy.

SIMPLE MODELS OF THE POLITY AND THE ECONOMY

Concerning domestic political processes, I shall make only three assumptions: that the beneficiaries of a change will try to continue and accelerate it, while the victims of the same change will endeavor to retard or halt it; that those who enjoy a sudden increase in wealth and income will thereby be enabled to expand their political influence as well; and that, as the desire and the means for a particular political preference increase, the likelihood grows that political entrepreneurs will devise mechanisms that can surmount the obstacles to collective action.

For our present concerns, the first assumption implies that the beneficiaries of safer or cheaper trade will support yet greater openness, while gainers from dearer or riskier trade will pursue even greater self-sufficiency. Conversely, those who are harmed by easier trade will demand protection or imperialism; and the victims of exogenously induced constrictions of trade will seek offsetting reductions in barriers. More important, the second assumption implies that the beneficiaries, potential or actual, of any such exogenous change will be strengthened politically (although they may still lose); the economic losers will be weakened politically as well. The third assumption gives us reason to think that the resultant pressures will not remain invisible but will actually be brought to bear in the political arena.

The issue of potential benefits is an important one, and a familiar example may help to illuminate it. In both great wars of this century, belligerent governments have faced an intensified demand for industrial labor and, because of the military's need for manpower, a reduced supply. That situation has positioned workers—and, in the U.S. case, such traditionally disadvantaged workers as blacks and women—to demand greatly increased compensation: these groups, in short, have had large *potential* gains. Naturally, governments and employers have endeavored to deny them those gains; but in many cases—Germany in World War I, the United States in World War II, Britain in both world wars—the lure of sharing in the potential gains has induced trade union leaders, and workers themselves, to organize and demand more. Similarly, when transportation costs fall, governments may at first partially offset the effect by imposing protection. Owners of abundant factors nonetheless still have substantial *potential* gains from trade, which they may mortgage, or on which others may speculate, to pressure policy toward lower levels of protection.

So much for politics. As regards the economic aspect, I propose to adopt with minor refinements the traditional three-factor model—land, labor, and capital—and to assume . . . that the land-labor ratio informs us fully about any country's endowment of those two factors. . . . No country, in other words, can be rich in both land and labor: a high land-labor ratio implies abundance of land and scarcity of labor; a low ratio signifies the opposite. Finally, I shall simply define an *advanced* economy as one in which capital is abundant.

This model of factor endowments . . . permits us in theory to place any country's economy into one of four cells (see Figure 1), according to whether it is advanced or backward and whether its land-labor ratio is high or low. We recognize, in other words, only economies that are: (1) capital rich, land rich, and labor poor; (2) capital rich, land poor, and labor rich; (3) capital poor, land rich, and labor poor; or (4) capital poor, land poor, and labor rich.

POLITICAL EFFECTS OF EXPANDING TRADE

The Stolper-Samuelson theorem, applied to our simple model, implies that increasing exposure to trade must result in *urban-rural conflict* in two kinds of economies, and in *class conflict* in the two others. Consider first the upper right-hand cell of Figure 1: the advanced (therefore capital-rich) economy endowed abundantly in labor but poorly in land. Expanding trade must benefit both capitalists and workers; it harms only landowners and the pastoral and agricultural enterprises that use land intensively. Both capitalists and workers—which is to say, almost the entire urban sector—should favor free trade; agriculture should on the whole be protectionist. Moreover, we expect the capitalists and the workers to try, very likely in concert, to expand their

FIGURE 1 Four Main Types of Factor Endowments

Land-Labor Ratio

	High	**Low**
Economy Advanced	ABUNDANT: Capital Land SCARCE: Labor	ABUNDANT: Capital Labor SCARCE: Land
Economy Backward	ABUNDANT: Land SCARCE: Capital Labor	ABUNDANT: Labor SCARCE: Capital Land

political influence. Depending on preexisting circumstances, they may seek concretely an extension of the franchise, a reapportionment of seats, a diminution in the powers of an upper house or of a gentry-based political elite, or a violent "bourgeois" revolution.

Urban-rural conflict should also arise in backward, land-rich economies (the lower left-hand cell of Figure 1) when trade expands, albeit with a complete reversal of fronts. In such "frontier" societies, both capital and labor are scarce; hence both are harmed by expanding trade and, normally, will seek protection. Only land is abundant, and therefore only agriculture will gain from free trade. Farmers and pastoralists will try to expand their influence in some movement of a "populist" and antiurban stripe.

Conversely, in backward economies with low land-labor ratios (the lower right-hand cell of Figure 1), land and capital are scarce and labor is abundant. The model therefore predicts *class conflict*: labor will pursue free trade and expanded political power (including, in some circumstances, a workers' revolution); landowners, capitalists, and capital-intensive industrialists will unite to support protection, imperialism, and a politics of continued exclusion.

The reverse form of class conflict is expected to arise in the final case, that of the advanced but land-rich economy (the upper left-hand cell of Figure 1) under increasing exposure to trade. Because both capital and land are abundant, capitalists, capital-intensive industries, and agriculture will all benefit from, and will endorse, free trade; labor being scarce, workers and labor-intensive industries will resist, normally embracing protection and (if need be) imperialism. The benefited sectors will seek to expand their political power, if not by disfranchisement then by curtailment of workers' economic prerogatives and suppression of their organizations.

These implications of the theory of international trade (summarized in Figure 2) seem clear, but do they in any way describe reality? . . . [I]t is worth observing how closely the experience of three major countries—Germany, Britain, and the United States—conforms to this analysis in the period of rapidly expanding trade in the last third of the nineteenth century; and how far it can go to explain otherwise puzzling disparities in those states' patterns of political evolution.

Germany and the United States were both relatively backward (i.e., capital-poor) societies: both imported considerable amounts of capital in this period, and neither had until late in the century anything like the per capita industrial capacity of the United Kingdom or Belgium. Germany, however, was rich in labor and poor in land; the United States, of course, was in exactly the opposite position. (Again, we observe that the United States imported, and Germany exported—not least to the United States—workers, which is not surprising since, at midcentury, Prussia's labor-land ratio was fifteen times that of the United States.)

FIGURE 2 Predicted Effects of Expanding Exposure to Trade

Land-Labor Ratio

	High	Low
Economy Advanced	CLASS CLEAVAGE: Land and Capital free-trading, assertive; Labor defensive, protectionist	URBAN-RURAL CLEAVAGE: Capital and Labor free-trading, assertive; Land defensive, protectionist **Radicalism**
Economy Backward	URBAN-RURAL CLEAVAGE: Land free-trading, assertive; Labor and Capital defensive, protectionist **U.S. Populism**	CLASS CLEAVAGE: Labor free-trading, assertive; Land and Capital defensive, protectionist **Socialism**

The theory predicts class conflict in Germany, with labor the "revolution-ary" and free-trading element, and with land and capital united in support of protection and imperialism. Surely this description will not ring false to any student of German socialism or of Germany's infamous "marriage of iron and rye." For the United States, conversely, the theory predicts—quite accurately, I submit—urban-rural conflict, with the agrarians now assuming the "revolu-tionary" and free-trading role; capital and labor unite in a protectionist and imperialist coalition. . . .

Britain, on the other hand, was already an advanced economy in the nine-teenth century. Its per capita industrial output far exceeded that of any other nation, and it exported capital in vast quantities. That it was also rich in labor is suggested by its extensive exports of that factor to the United States, Can-ada, Australia, New Zealand, and Africa; in fact, Britain's labor-land ratio then exceeded Japan's by 50 percent and was over thirty times that of the United States. Britain therefore falls into the upper right-hand quadrant of Figure 1 and is predicted to exhibit a rural-urban cleavage whose fronts are opposite those found in the United States: capitalists and labor unite in support of free trade and in demands for expanded political power, while landowners and agriculture support protection and imperialism.

Although this picture surely obscures important nuances, it illuminates cru-cial differences—between, for example, British and German political devel-opment in this period. In Britain, capitalists and labor united in the Liberal party and forced an expanded suffrage and curtailment of (still principally land-owning) aristocratic power. In Germany, liberalism shattered, the suf-frage at the crucial level of the individual states was actually contracted, and—far from eroding aristocratic power—the bourgeoisie grew more and more *verjunkert* in style and aspirations.

POLITICAL EFFECTS OF DECLINING TRADE

When rising costs or declining security substantially increases the risks or costs of external trade, the gainers and losers in each situation are simply the reverse of those under increasing exposure to trade. Let us first consider the situation of the highly developed (and therefore by definition capital-rich) economies.

In an advanced economy with a high land-labor ratio (the upper left-hand cell of Figure 1), we should expect intense *class conflict* precipitated by a newly aggressive working class. Land and capital are both abundant in such an econ-omy; hence, under declining trade owners of both factors (and producers who use either factor intensively) lose. Moreover, they can resort to no such simple remedy as protection or imperialism. Labor being the only scarce resource, workers and labor-intensive industries are well positioned to reap a significant windfall from the "protection" that dearer or riskier trade affords; and, accord-ing to our earlier assumption, like any other benefited class they will soon endeavor to parlay their greater economic power into greater political power. Capitalists and landowners, even if they were previously at odds, will unite to oppose labor's demands.

Quite to the contrary, declining trade in an advanced economy that is labor rich and land poor (the upper right-hand cell of Figure 1) will entail renewed *urban-rural* conflict. Capital and labor are both abundant, and both are harmed by the contraction of external trade. Agriculture, as the intense exploiter of the only scarce factor, gains significantly and quickly tries to translate its gain into greater political control.

Urban-rural conflict is also predicted for backward, land-rich countries under declining trade; but here agriculture is on the defensive. Labor and capital being both scarce, both benefit from the contraction of trade; land, as the only locally abundant factor, is threatened. The urban sectors unite, in a parallel to the "radical" coalition of labor-rich developed countries under expanding trade discussed previously, to demand an increased voice in the state.

Finally, in backward economies rich in labor rather than land, class conflict resumes, with labor this time on the defensive. Capital and land, as the locally scarce factors, gain from declining trade; labor, locally abundant, suffers economic reverses and is soon threatened politically.

Observe again, as a first test of the plausibility of these results—summarized in Figure 3—how they appear to account for some prominent disparities of political response to the last precipitous decline of international trade, the depression of the 1930s. The U.S. New Deal represented a sharp turn to the left and occasioned a significant increase in organized labor's political power. In Germany, a depression of similar depth (gauged by unemployment rates and declines in industrial production) brought to power first Hindenburg's and then Hitler's dictatorship. Landowners exercised markedly greater influence than they had under Weimar; and indeed a credible case can be made that the rural sector was the principal early beneficiary of the early Nazi regime. Yet this is exactly the broad difference that the model would lead us to anticipate, if we accept that by 1930 both countries were economically advanced— although Germany, after physical reparations and cessions of industrial regions, was surely less rich in capital than the United States—but the United States held land abundantly, which in Germany was scarce (respectively, the left- and right-hand cells of the upper half of Figure 3). Only an obtuse observer would claim that such factors as cultural inheritance and recent defeat in war played no role; but surely it is also important to recognize the sectoral impact of declining trade in the two societies.

As regards the less developed economies of the time, it may be profitable to contrast the depression's impact on such South American cases as Argentina and Brazil with its effects in the leading Asian country, Japan. In Argentina and Brazil, it is usually asserted, the depression gave rise to, or at the least strengthened, "populist" coalitions that united labor and the urban middle classes in opposition to traditional, landowning elites. In Japan, growing

FIGURE 3   Predicted Effects of Declining Exposure to Trade

Land-Labor Ratio

	High	Low
Economy Advanced	CLASS CLEAVAGE: Labor assertive, Land and Capital defensive **U.S. New Deal**	URBAN-RURAL CLEAVAGE: Land assertive, Labor and Capital defensive **W. European Fascism**
Economy Backward	URBAN-RURAL CLEAVAGE: Labor and Capital assertive, Land defensive **South American Populism**	CLASS CLEAVAGE: Land and Capital assertive, Labor defensive **Asian & East European Fascism**

military influence suppressed representative institutions and nascent workers' organizations, ruling in the immediate interest—if hardly under the
domination—of landowners and capitalists. (Similar suppressions of labor
occurred in China and Vietnam.) In considering these contrasting responses,
should we not take into account that Argentina and Brazil were rich in land
and poor in labor, while in Japan (and, with local exceptions, in Asia generally) labor was abundant and land was scarce? . . .

POSSIBLE OBJECTIONS

Several objections can plausibly be raised to the whole line of analysis that I
have advanced here. . . .

1. It may be argued that the effects sketched out here will not obtain in
   countries that depend only slightly on trade. Belgium, where external
   trade (taken as the sum of exports and imports) roughly equals gross
   domestic product (GDP), can indeed be affected profoundly by changes
   in the risks or costs of international commerce; but a state like the
   United States in the 1960s, where trade amounted to scarcely a tenth
   of GDP, will have remained largely immune.

   This view, while superficially plausible, is incorrect. The Stolper-
   Samuelson result obtains at any margin; and in fact holders of scarce
   factors have been quite as devastated by expanding trade in almost

autarkic economies—one need think only of the weavers of India or of Silesia, exposed in the nineteenth century to the competition of Lancashire mills—as in ones previously more dependent on trade.

2. Given that comparative advantage always assures gains from trade, it may be objected that the cleavages described here need not arise at all: the gainers from trade can always compensate the losers and have something left over; trade remains the Pareto-superior outcome. As Stolper and Samuelson readily conceded in their original essay, this is perfectly true. To the student of politics, however, and with even greater urgency to those who are losing from trade in concrete historical situations, it remains unobvious that such compensation will in fact occur. Rather, the natural tendency is for gainers to husband their winnings and to stop their ears to the cries of the afflicted. Perhaps only unusually strong and trustworthy states, or political cultures that especially value compassion and honesty, can credibly assure the requisite compensation . . . and even in those cases, substantial conflict over the nature and level of compensation will usually precede the ultimate agreement.

3. Equally, one can ask why the cleavages indicated here should persist. In a world of perfectly mobile factors and rational behavior, people would quickly disinvest from losing factors and enterprises (e.g., farming in Britain after 1880) and move to sectors whose auspices were more favorable. Markets should swiftly clear; and a new, if different, political equilibrium should be achieved.

   To this two answers may be given. First, in some cases trade expands or contracts so rapidly and surprisingly as to frustrate rational expectations. Especially in countries that experience a steady series of such exogenous shocks—the case in Europe, I would contend, from 1840 to the present day—divisions based on factor endowments (which ordinarily change only gradually) will be repeatedly revived. Second, not infrequently some factors' privileged access to political influence makes the extraction of rents and subsidies seem cheaper than adaptation: Prussian *Junkers* familiarly, sought (and easily won) protection rather than adjustment. In such circumstances, adaptation may be long delayed, sometimes with ultimately disastrous consequences.

   At the same time, it should be conceded that, as improved technology makes factors more mobile . . . and anticipation easier, the theory advanced here will likely apply less well. Indeed, this entire analysis may be a historically conditioned one, whose usefulness will be found to have entered a rapid decline sometime after 1960. . . .

4. This analysis, some may contend, reifies such categories as "capital," "labor," and "land," assuming a unanimity of preference that most countries' evidence belies. In fact, a kind of shorthand and a testable hypothesis are involved: a term like "capital" is the convenient abbreviation of

"those who draw their income principally from investments, plus the most capital-intensive producers"; and I indeed hypothesize that individuals' political positions will vary with their derivation of income—or, more precisely, of present value of all anticipated future income—from particular factors.

A worker, for example, who derives 90 percent of her income from wages and 10 percent from investments will conform more to the theory's expectation of "labor"'s political behavior than one who depends half on investments and half on wages. An extremely labor-intensive manufacturer will behave less like a "capitalist" than a more capital-intensive one. And a peasant (as noted previously) who depends chiefly on inputs of his own labor will resemble a "worker," whereas a more land-intensive neighbor will behave as a "landowner."

5. Finally, it may be objected that I have said nothing about the outcome of these conflicts. I have not done so for the simple reason that I cannot: history makes it all too plain, as in the cases of nineteenth-century Germany and America, that the economic losers from trade may win politically over more than the short run. What I have advanced here is a speculation about *cleavages*, not about outcomes. I have asserted only that those who gain from fluctuations in trade will be strengthened and emboldened politically; nothing guarantees that they will win. Victory or defeat depends, so far as I can see, both on the relative size of the various groups and on those institutional and cultural factors that this perspective so resolutely ignores.

CONCLUSION

It is essential to recall what I am *not* claiming to do. . . . I do not contend that changes in countries' exposure to trade explain all, or even most, of their varying patterns of political cleavage. It would be foolish to ignore the importance of ancient cultural and religious loyalties, of wars and migrations, or of such historical memories as the French Revolution and the *Kulturkampf.* Other cleavages antedate, and persist through, the ones I discuss here, shaping, crosscutting, complicating, and indeed sometimes dominating their political resolution. . . .

In the main, I am presenting here a theoretical puzzle, a kind of social-scientific "thought experiment" in Hempel's original sense: a teasing out of unexpected, and sometimes counterintuitive, implications of theories already widely accepted. For the Stolper-Samuelson theorem *is* generally, indeed almost universally, embraced; yet, coupled with a stark and unexceptionable model of the political realm, it plainly implies that changes in exposure to trade must profoundly affect nations' internal political cleavages. Do they do so? If they do not, what conclusions shall we draw, either about our theories of international trade, or about our understanding of politics?

2

The Political Economy of Adjustment and Rebalancing

JEFFRY A. FRIEDEN

International debt and balance of payments crises are politically controversial. Jeffry A. Frieden examines the interactions that typically break out in the aftermath of such crises over how the burden of adjustment will be distributed. There are conflictual international interactions, between debtor nations and creditor nations over how outstanding debts will be resolved. And there are conflictual interactions within nations over who will make the sacrifices necessary to get economies back on track. These political interactions often become so bitter and protracted that they impede productive bargaining over the adjustment process. The characteristics of socioeconomic and political divisions within societies affect the battles over economic adjustment, as well as who will emerge victorious from these battles and how difficult it may be to arrive at a productive resolution of the crisis.

The world's recovery from the Global Financial Crisis (GFC) was extraordinarily slow and difficult. In the United States, it took some fifty months for employment to return to pre-crisis levels. This contrasts dramatically with the norm in American recessions: since the 1930s, employment has on average taken about ten months to return to pre-recession levels. Output, similarly, regained its pre-crisis levels far more slowly than in other post-Depression recessions. And five years after the crisis began, median household income was still over 8 percent below its pre-crisis level.

Recovery in Europe was even slower and more difficult. The region fell into a second recession soon after the first one ended; unemployment soared in many countries, and has remained extremely high for a very long time.

The painful recovery was due in part to the severity of the crisis itself. The Global Financial Crisis was, after all, the longest downturn since the 1940s, and the steepest downturn since the Great Depression. But the principal reason for the different experience in the aftermath of this crisis was that this was not a typical cyclical recession, such as developed economies have experienced periodically for hundreds of years. It was, instead, a debt crisis—in fact, a series of inter-related debt crises. We are familiar with debt crises, of course, as they have afflicted developing economies and emerging markets on a regular basis since the 1820s. But the GFC was the first debt crisis in a rich country in decades, at least since Germany in the 1930s. And it was the first debt crisis in history to hit a whole host of rich countries at once.

Debt crises are different from garden-variety recessions, and recovery from them is much more troubled. . . . The differences are both economic and political. Economically, debt crises leave the affected societies with a debt overhang that exercises a serious drag on the economy. Both creditors and debtors focus on restoring their damaged balance sheets rather than on lending and spending, respectively. This much is well-known, and helps explain why recovery from the average debt crisis takes . . . , on the order of five to seven years rather than a few months.

But the intractability of debt crises is not only economic, for every debt crisis leads to political conflicts. These conflicts impede recovery both in and of themselves, and their continuation impedes the ability of policymakers to address the crisis. As an example, a quick look at a recent . . . listing of the 30 most serious systemic (national) banking crises since 1857 (not including the GFC) indicates that at least half of them were associated with major political upheavals: revolutions, civil wars, the collapse of democracy into authoritarianism or vice versa. Recent work . . . shows empirically that financial crises are associated with increased political polarization. Causation is never obvious—did the severity of the crisis cause political turmoil or did the political turmoil make the crisis more severe?—and probably the arrows point in both directions. Nonetheless, the connection between debt crises and political unrest is clear.

Debt crises typically dissolve into political conflicts over how the burden of adjustment will be distributed. Conflict erupts on two dimensions. Internationally, creditor countries face off against debtor countries over the division of the costs of cleaning up bad debts. Domestically, both within debtor countries and within creditor countries, groups struggle over who will be asked to make the sacrifices necessary to resolve the debt problem. These international and domestic political struggles seriously constrain attempts to arrive at productive and constructive policies that might facilitate a more rapid recovery.

In what follows, I analyze the domestic and international politics of economic adjustment to a debt crisis. These regularities also apply to related balance of payments crises, and to current discussions over "rebalancing," which have to do with the international dimension of adjustment. First, I suggest and analyze the kinds of socio-economic and political divisions we can expect to emerge in the battles over economic adjustment, as well as the factors that help determine who will emerge victorious from these battles. Then I discuss why it is that the political conflicts often become so bitter and protracted that they impede a sensible resolution to the crisis. I start with international conflicts over adjustment, then move on to domestic political battles. In much of what follows, I elide adjustment by debtor and deficit countries; although there are differences between the two categories, they are close enough to warrant being lumped together for ease of exposition.

1. THE INTERNATIONAL POLITICAL ECONOMY OF ADJUSTMENT

In debt conflicts among countries, the interests at stake are clear: creditors want to be repaid, and debtors want relief. In the case of balance of payments adjustment, the analogous issue is whether the principal adjustments will be undertaken by deficit countries or surplus countries. Deficit-country adjustment typically involves imposing austerity to reduce consumption and increase exports; for surplus countries adjustment requires increasing consumption and imports. Since the GFC began there has been analogous attention to whether, and how, countries will "rebalance," that is, act to avoid a recurrence of the very large current account surpluses and deficits that played a central role in the crisis.

Standard macroeconomic analysis points to the asymmetry of the adjustment process, favoring surplus over deficit countries (and creditors over debtors). Deficit countries are under substantial pressure to adjust, especially if they find it expensive, difficult, or impossible to borrow to finance their deficits. In the limiting case of a "sudden stop" in foreign lending, the deficit country must adjust more or less immediately. Surplus countries are under no such inherent pressure to adjust.

But this asymmetry is purely economic, and debtor and deficit nations usually react to it with political efforts to redress the imbalance. For debtors have powerful weapons in their arsenal, in particular the threat of suspending service on their debts—of defaulting. Creditors can threaten to cut borrowers off from financing, but debtors can threaten to cut creditors off from their earnings.

Creditors and debtors are thus drawn into explicit or implicit negotiations, in which each side has powerful weapons and powerful incentives to use them to obtain a favorable outcome. Standard bargaining approaches point out that effective bargaining power is largely a function of how attractive each protagonist's exit option is. The party better able to make a credible commitment to find an alternative to the debtor–creditor relationship in which it finds itself is better able to drive a hard bargain with the other. A related factor is the relative patience of the bargainers, with the more patient of them having an advantage (as in a typical divide-the-dollar game) . . . This is linked to the existence of an exit option, to the extent that the option allows the party to be patient; in debt negotiations patience might be regarded as a function of the financial reserves at the disposal of each party.

This dynamic can be seen in a wide variety of historical settings. In the 1930s, as the world economy crumbled, virtually every debtor country defaulted on its debts, and eventually received very favorable terms from creditors. The threat to default was eminently credible, for the international financial system had collapsed and the threat of being frozen out of it was entirely empty. "Exiting" from effectively non-existent international financial markets was not very costly to debtors, while foregoing debt service payments was very costly to creditors. The debtors held virtually all the bargaining power.

The Depression-era bargaining relationship contrasts with the situation in the early 1980s. In this episode, international financial markets remained vibrant despite serious debt problems in the developing world. Developing countries were reluctant to risk losing access to external financing, and found themselves in a much weaker bargaining position. While many did default, they were usually only able to restructure their debts after a long delay and at great cost. The creditors, on the other hand, were typically able to emerge from the debt crisis without too much damage.

Prominent historical examples of bargaining over balance of payments adjustment also help illustrate the point. In the late 1960s and early 1970s, the United States was at the center of a fixed-rate monetary order, and its monetary policy was out of step with that of its partners. For several years threats and promises went back and forth, with the major European nations attempting to get the Nixon Administration to undertake the adjustment measures necessary to restore balance to American payments. In this case, however, asymmetry or no, the deficit country had most of the bargaining power: the United States had a readily available alternative, which was to destroy the Bretton Woods fixed-rate system rather than adjust to its requirements. And this is exactly what it did, showing how a deficit country could force adjustment costs onto the rest of the world if it were powerful enough.

Twenty years later, the members of another fixed-rate system were in similar disagreement. In 1991 Germany was the anchor of the European Monetary System. In the aftermath of German unification, with Germany running a current account deficit, the Bundesbank adopted a highly restrictive monetary policy that drove much of the rest of Europe into recession. Again, the monetary policy of an anchor-currency country was at odds with the preferences of its partners, as Germany attempted to shift some of the adjustment costs onto its neighbors; again the partners were vocal in their disagreement with German policy. This time, however, the other EMS members had an alternative available: they could violate their commitments to the EMS and let their currencies depreciate, which many of them did. In each case, the anchor-currency country had substantial bargaining power, but in the EMS case so too did other countries, so that the outcome after 1991 was more of a compromise.

In the context of the European component of the GFC, similar battles have been underway among the member states of the Eurozone. Creditors in Northern Europe want their loans to be serviced; debtors on the periphery, inside or outside the Eurozone, want their debts to be restructured. With the exception of Greece, which was in such dire straits that there was no hope of anything like full recovery, there has been no debt relief. This is quite unusual, and quite remarkable given the circumstances. It is almost certainly due, at least in part, to the nature of the bargaining problem. Spain and other peripheral debtors had few alternatives available to them, unless they wanted to exit the Eurozone (and perhaps the European Union), while Germany and the other Northern European creditors were in no hurry to address the debt problem. With bargaining power heavily weighted toward the creditors, the Eurozone crisis so far seems to have been managed in ways that were extremely favorable to them.

The resolution of debt and balance of payments adjustment problems at the international level is highly political. This is certainly true of "rebalancing," the current variant of attempts to address global payments imbalances seen as dangerous. One of the more politically contentious aspects of rebalancing has been the fate of China's large current account surplus. The United States, in particular, has insisted that it is largely the job of the Chinese to reduce this surplus—by allowing the *renminbi* to appreciate, increasing domestic consumption, or other means. China, on the other hand, insists that the United States has a responsibility to pursue more sustainable patterns of consumption and production. In this case, again, asymmetry or no, most of the bargaining power would appear to be with the deficit country, and most of the adjustment has been undertaken by the Chinese.

A second contentious instance of conflicts over rebalancing is within the Eurozone, already alluded to in the context of intra-EU debt problems. Here, as with debts, the surplus countries have seemed to be largely in control, and most of what adjustment has taken place has been in the deficit and debtor countries. This is especially evident in the case of nations on the European periphery that were not members of the Eurozone but had hard pegs with the euro. While such Eurozone members as Spain and Portugal could appeal to their Eurozone partners for support in the interests of Eurozone stability, such countries as Latvia and Estonia had no such negotiating leverage. The former have adjusted, true, but at a much slower and less painful rate than the latter. This undoubtedly has much to do with the relative ability of the two sorts of deficit countries to bargain effectively with the creditor states. The interests in play are clear, and the bargaining power of the various sides seems to explain much of the outcome we observe.

I leave aside for now one important, related, aspect of this problem, which is why it often seems difficult for the parties to arrive at a deal that would be mutually beneficial. After all, even the most nakedly self-interested creditor would rather find a way to permit debtors to service their debts, even in part, than to lose everything to default. Yet it often seems that protracted bargaining makes the problem worse, and that arrangements that would make both parties better off are not arrived at. Some might argue that current trends in Europe resemble this. Inasmuch as German growth depends on the country's commercial and financial relations with the European periphery (both in and outside the Eurozone), it might be in the interest of Germany to oversee enough debt relief to allow the heavily indebted countries to start growing again, at which point they would be more attractive markets for German goods and sites for German investments. This problem—of the difficulty for countries to arrive at negotiated settlements that are advantageous to all—is important, and I return to it below. First, I discuss the domestic political economy of adjustment, which is substantially more complicated than that at the international level.

2. THE DOMESTIC POLITICAL ECONOMY OF ADJUSTMENT

Domestic politics is ever-present in the adjustment process, even at the international level, for governments attempting to address international adjustment problems are answerable to domestic political constituents. This can be an important constraint on the international politics of adjustment. Indeed, many of the more spectacular instances of political conflict over debt and balance of payments adjustment are more or less purely domestic, as the experiences of East Asia in 1997–1998, Argentina in 2000–2001, and many others demonstrate. How, then, can we think about the domestic political economy of adjustment?

We start by outlining the battle lines we expect to see in domestic political struggles over adjustment to a foreign debt burden, or to a serious balance of payments crisis. This is perhaps most simply addressed by reviewing the macroeconomic impact of such adjustment.

A country experiencing a substantial capital inflow—in the run-up to a debt or payments crisis—is thereby able to consume more than it produces, invest more than it saves, and/or import more than it exports; its government can, if it does some of the borrowing, spend more than it takes in. Once borrowing becomes difficult or impossible and the adjustment process begins, all of these relationships have to reverse: the country needs to produce more than it consumes, save more than it invests, and export more than it imports, and a debtor government needs to take in more than it spends in (non-debt service) expenditures. To understand the distributional implications of these trends, it is instructive to consider the associated relative price effects, for socio-economic actors are expected to respond to changes in relative prices that affect them rather than abstract terms in national income accounting.

The relevant relative price movements necessary to the adjustment process in a debtor or deficit country are straightforward, but hardly easy. They can be simplified for the sake of illustration and clarity. In order to compress consumption and increase production, real wages and incomes need to decline. In order to increase savings and reduce investment, real interest rates must rise. To increase exports and reduce imports, the currency has to depreciate in real terms. And for the government to service its debts, it needs to increase taxes or reduce non-debt-service spending, or both. None of these measures is likely to be popular, but some groups are likely to be harder hit by each of them than others (and some may be helped).

Attempts to increase revenue and reduce spending hurt taxpayers and beneficiaries of government programs. A depreciating currency is good for exporters and import competers, but harms consumers by reducing their real purchasing power. Of great political importance is the fact that depreciation can be disastrous for households or firms with substantial debts denominated in foreign currency. Higher real interest rates harm debtors but help savers. And the compression of real wages and incomes, of course, hurts workers and consumers directly while it helps employers. These expectations help us understand who would expect to be on the barricades—and on which side—in political battles over adjustment.

The central issue in contention in the domestic political economy of adjustment, as at the international level, is who will bear the principal burden of adjustment. One set of choices, relevant to discussion of the Eurozone crisis and that of countries on the European periphery, is between what has come to be called "external devaluation" and "internal devaluation." The former is simply a nominal devaluation of the currency, changing the exchange rate to help encourage adjustment. As above, this is particularly threatening to households and firms with foreign-currency liabilities but helps exporters and import-competers; it was the approach taken by Poland in the aftermath of the GFC. What Europeans have taken to calling an "internal devaluation" is simply domestic adjustment while keeping the nominal exchange rate fixed, typically by austerity measures to put downward pressure on wages and prices. This places the principal burden on workers, and can threaten the competitive position of tradables producers as wages and prices adjust slowly, but it protects those with foreign-currency obligations and also sustains a fixed exchange rate that may be favored by economic actors with important cross-border economic ties.

Domestic political factors of this sort may help explain the relatively limited attempts by such debtor countries as Spain to use their bargaining power to extract better conditions from creditors. While the adjustment process was extremely painful, there were powerful groups in Spain, especially in finance and industry, that did not want a debt restructuring to damage their relationship with European partners. This highlights the potential for *domestic* conflict between those who stand to lose from adjustment, on the one hand, and those who would be harmed by interference with the country's international financial relations.

Other choices in the adjustment process are equally contentious, as whatever path is chosen is sure to ignite opposition from some group or other. In the aftermath of the GFC, the peripheral European debtor nations were riven over whether sacrifices would be made by taxpayers, beneficiaries of government programs, financial institutions, or others. In the United States, there was substantial controversy over the response to the mortgage debt crisis. Policy could have concentrated on relieving indebted homeowners or bailing out troubled financial institutions; in the event, virtually all efforts went to the financial institutions, and almost nothing to homeowners. Meanwhile, battles over fiscal policy pitted taxpayers against beneficiaries, while conflicts over monetary policy saw divisions between heavily indebted homeowners who appreciated near-zero interest rates, on the one hand, and savers—especially retirees—who had come to rely on interest income.

While divisions within debtor societies receive the most attention—everyone understands that austerity is unpopular—creditor or surplus societies can also be divided by conflicts. When the issue is how to deal with outstanding debts of a creditor nation, the most directly relevant conflict has to do with whether the creditors will give up something in order to restructure debts. And this issue could easily divide creditor-country financial institutions from creditor-country taxpayers who resist paying for the bad decisions of their banks. This is especially the case where debt restructuring may be better for the society as a whole, for example by restoring health to an important export market, while it imposes important costs on the creditor financial institutions themselves.

Many of the Northern European creditor nations in the Eurozone debt crisis have been torn by debates over whether, and to what extent, to force the creditor institutions themselves to shoulder some of the burden of adjustment, rather than putting it on creditor-country taxpayers or debtor-country citizens. In the run-up to the Eurozone sovereign debt crisis, in fact, many Northern European financial institutions loaded up on debt to peripheral borrowers, including sovereigns, in the expectation of a bail-out. And, in fact, the bail-out was forthcoming, at the expense of Northern taxpayers: Northern European banks received government bail-outs worth nearly 2.3 trillion euro in the aftermath of the crisis.

The European experience also demonstrates that the "public diplomacy" of a crisis response can have a powerful impact on its politics. The emergency operations put together by member states of the European Union were often presented, especially in Germany, as the result of irresponsible borrowing by profligate Southern European governments and their lazy citizens. In fact, in most of the troubled peripheral nations, loans had been made predominantly to the private sector and the rescue programs largely benefited the Northern European banks that had been just as irresponsible in their lending as the borrowers were in their borrowing. The rescues were as much about bailing out Northern European banks as they were about supporting peripheral European governments, but few Northern Europeans would have known that—a fact that undoubtedly colored public opinion on the matter. If German citizens had been clearer about the true beneficiaries of the bail-outs, they might have been more favorably inclined to policies to require German financial institutions to restructure intra-European debts and pay some of the price themselves, rather than shunting it onto taxpayers.

A similar dynamic to that present in debtor–creditor conflicts can be seen in debates over "rebalancing," as countries in surplus come under pressure to reduce their surpluses by reorienting economic activity. In such export-led economies as Germany, Japan, and China, this involves directing resources away from the export sector and into domestic economic activity for domestic consumption. This almost certainly means that previously favored sectors—such as export-oriented manufacturers—will lose some of their previous favors. The economic importance of the export sector in such societies is usually mirrored by its political influence, which is likely to make it extremely difficult to point the economy in a new direction without giving rise to howls of protest.

The task of analytical political economy in these circumstances starts with tracking the expected divisions in society, and how they are reflected in the political arena. I have attempted to provide a general sense of how to think about a map of the actors in play, of how their interests translate into their policy preferences, and of how this affects the politics of adjustment. In this context, the impact of adjustment policies on relative prices, hence on the economic interests of groups in society, gives us a first cut into the kinds of political divisions to expect. Of course, governments have choices about the kinds of policies to pursue in order to adjust, and these policies are likely to reflect the relative political influence of the groups expected to be affected by various approaches. However, simply knowing the likely political cleavages tells us little or nothing about who will prevail in the political process. For this we can turn to some of the same features of bargaining models that were relevant to international negotiations over adjustment and rebalancing.

Bargaining power in domestic politics, as internationally, is in large part a function of the existence of exit options. Groups or individuals that have more readily accessible, or more credible, alternatives to current circumstances are better able to insist on more favorable terms in negotiations over adjustment. A firm that can easily pick up shop rather than pay higher taxes is in a much stronger bargaining position than one with substantial fixed assets that cannot easily be redeployed. Citizens who can move easily elsewhere to avoid wage compression are more likely to be able to avoid it—or simply to evade it by in fact moving.

Patience is closely related to better exit options. A group that can wait out its challengers will be better able to withstand conflict over adjustment: in the case of firms, those with more financial resources in reserve will be able to outlast those with less. This can be interpreted as simply a restatement of available exit—waiting is an alternative (exit) option. The same is true of longer time horizons on the part of firms, groups, or individuals—those that discount the future less will be more patient, and have more and better alternatives, hence greater bargaining power. This may help explain, both in the United States and in Europe, why debtors typically lost out to creditors. Whether they were heavily mortgaged households or sovereign governments, debtors were in no position to wait out creditors in negotiations. . . .

The availability of other alternatives to the *status quo*—exit, waiting, procrastinating—generally increases the political power of those involved in battles over adjustment. To be sure, the definition of alternatives can be endlessly flexible in the political sphere: exit could mean fomenting a coup, or creating a new political party, or withdrawing capital. In any case, focusing on the choices available to the protagonists in domestic political battles over adjustment and rebalancing helps clarify the analysis of who is likely to predominate in such battles.

The domestic and international political economy of adjustment are closely linked. Domestic political considerations often constrain international negotiations, restricting bargaining positions in ways that can make compromise difficult. In the case of the crisis of the Bretton Woods monetary order, for example, many feasible settlements could be imagined, involving some adjustment by both the European surplus nations and the United States. But American domestic politics ruled out adjustment in the deficit country, at least in the view of the Nixon Administration, and the U.S. held the whip hand in the relationship; the collapse of Bretton Woods was, in this sense, almost entirely the result of the domestic politics of adjustment in the United States. In the Eurozone crisis, many observers anticipated that negotiations between debtors and creditors would, as is almost always the case, lead to some debt restructuring. However, it would appear that domestic political constraints in the creditor countries, Germany in particular, may have ruled out concessions of this type. Because in this case it was the surplus countries that held the whip hand, no compromise was forthcoming. It may also be the case that there were important groups in the European debtor nations that did not want to press too hard for debt relief, so as not to endanger their economic ties to European partners.

We can go a long way toward understanding the factors that affect the domestic and international political economy of adjustment by analyzing how adjustment measures would affect socio-economic interests, and how their characteristics and those of national and international political institutions affect relative bargaining influence. This is abstract and general, of course, and its value depends on specific applications; but at least it gives analysts a framework to work with. However, all this leaves to one side a crucially important question, alluded to earlier in the context of international adjustment problems: why is adjustment so commonly delayed, to the detriment of all concerned?

3. EXPLAINING DELAYED ADJUSTMENT

It is easy to understand that there are important conflicts of interest in the adjustment process. Especially in a heavily indebted economy, or one facing a major current account deficit that is difficult to finance, adjustment can—at least in the short run—be a negative-sum game. A contested and controversial outcome of a battle over economic adjustment is a terrible thing that can tear societies apart; but no outcome at all is even worse. In many cases, conflict is prolonged, with no consistent policy resolution. Especially in the case of financial crises, delay can be extremely costly. Bad debts accumulate, dragging the economy further and further down and retarding a possible recovery.

The cost of delay implies that a Pareto improvement is available, inasmuch as a clear resolution to the crisis is better than continued conflict and prolonged uncertainty. This leads us to shift our attention away from the distributional specifics of the contours of the conflict to a different question: why are some distributional conflicts so much harder to resolve than others? Why, and when, does bargaining break down? What are the factors that might lead the protagonists of such conflict to dig their heels in so hard so to make resolution difficult or impossible? This is as true of the GFC as it has been of previous crises. This much seems obvious from the extraordinary costs Europeans have had to bear for the EU's inability to deal effectively with the Eurozone crisis. . . . The United States paid a massive price for the U.S. government's unwillingness to push aggressively for private debt restructuring, relying instead almost entirely on bailing out the affected financial institutions. What, then, stands in the way of governments adopting policies that could, in the final analysis, make everyone better off?

This question has typically been asked in terms of understanding the eruption of a war of attrition. Theory and history can tell us a great deal about what might in fact prolong (or shorten) such a war of attrition, both in general and in the case of economic adjustment. We can point to four principal factors. There is a certain amount of overlap among them, and they are not mutually exclusive, but each addresses a somewhat different potential cause of delay.

3.1. Patience

While the ability to wait out the other side gives one party greater bargaining power, there are instances in which both sides can be patient. When each participant recognizes that the loser will pay a stiffer price, and is unsure of how long others can last, the best strategy can be to delay in anticipation that one of the others will "blink" first. Groups that think they may be able to outwait others have powerful incentives to resist any settlement that is not strongly in their favor. . . . Governments that are new to office, or that are particularly strong—and therefore almost certainly better able to force through a settlement—are more likely to do so, using their position to end the war of attrition quickly. But it is common for governments to confront powerful actors—opposition parties, interest groups, public employees—that have both the resources and the time to wait out their opponents.

3.2. Uncertainty

When economic actors are unsure as to what the impact of an adjustment policy will be on them, they may have reasons to avoid the implementation of the policy. Fernandez and Rodrik 1991 present a model in which adjustment is welfare-improving, but large numbers of citizens are unsure as to whether they will end up on the winning or losing side of the process. This gives the potential losers a strong bias in favor of the *status quo*, in which at least they will not be seriously harmed—and this can impart a powerful *status quo* bias to the political process more generally. While Fernandez and Rodrik apply the model to trade liberalization, it is easy to see how a leap into the unknown of a major stabilization program could induce delay on the part of major groups that believed that they could end up losing a lot in the process.

3.3. Asymmetric Information

One of the forces that can make a war of attrition better than the alternatives is the absence of reliable information on the true preferences, resolve, or resources of opponents. If one party in the conflict is unsure about how hard the other is willing to fight, then prolonging the bargaining is one way of testing the waters. In this setting, delay is a potentially valuable strategy in pursuit of information revelation, in particular about the true intentions and power of other parties to the negotiation. Strategically valuable or no, asymmetric information can contribute to serious delays in arriving at a negotiated settlement that is, in the final analysis, in the best interests of all parties.

3.4. Commitment Problems

It is almost certainly the case that failures to arrive at an adjustment policy are Pareto sub-optimal; however, achieving a Pareto improvement can be difficult if the commitments made by the various actors are not credible. Put differently, most Pareto improvements—including in the adjustment process—involve some measure of compensation for those who would be losers in its absence. But if those who need to be compensated do not believe that the promises made to them will be carried out, they have little or no incentive to go along with the bargain. And all involved are well aware of the fact that promises made in the process of negotiating over a major adjustment package are not time-consistent. Features of social relations, or of political institutions, that make commitments more or less credible, can be expected to affect the ease or difficulty with which compromises to settle adjustment-related disputes are reached.

Each of these considerations suggests comparative statics drawn from national socio-economic and political conditions, and the respective literature on them is replete with illustrations. Examples, or at least working hypotheses, are relatively easy to come by. Strong governments unlikely to be removed from office should be better able make credible commitments, hence quicker to arrive at agreement. Left governments are likely to be able to make more credible commitments to labor, so if this would otherwise be an obstacle they should be more successful in the adjustment process (which may explain why so many successful stabilization and adjustment programs in Latin America are under the auspices of Left governments). The more information parties have about each other's preferences and resources, the more quickly they should be able to arrive at a compromise.

Similar considerations should also apply internationally. The persistence of drawn-out conflicts over adjustments—such as the prolonged quagmire involving Latin American foreign debts in the 1980s—is due to some or all of these factors. In the context of the Eurozone conflict, two considerations appear to have been fundamental, at least as a first approximation. The first is that neither side's commitments were credible to the other. The debtors' promises to adjust were not believed by the creditors, and the creditors' promises to restore normal capital flows were not believed by the debtors. The second is that the creditors, and in particular Germany, seemed quite willing to wait as long as necessary to prevail. This helps explain both why the conflict was so drawn out, and why it tended to be resolved in favor of the creditors.

4. CONCLUSION

It is common for analysts to invoke "politics" to explain the proliferation of conflict, delay, and policy twists and turns as societies deal with the aftermath of debt or payments crises. We can do better than to appeal to so vague a putative explanation. There are reasons why people, groups, parties, and countries fight so hard, and so long, to affect the nature of adjustment policies. And there are reasons why the fighting is so often inconclusive, drawn-out, and eventually counter-productive. The implications of the analysis here are perhaps depressing, inasmuch as it demonstrates that there are powerful forces that can lead rational actors to drive their societies toward very undesirable outcomes. In this sense, political economy may well be the truly dismal science. And to be sure, Europe in the aftermath of the Eurozone crisis has given us many, varied, and vivid examples of just how many things can go so wrong. Nonetheless, as always, understanding the sources of policy disasters is the first, necessary, step to avoiding them.

REFERENCE

Fernandez, Raquel, and Dani Rodrik. December 1991. Resistance to reform: status quo bias in the presence of individual-specific uncertainty. Am. Econ. Rev. 81 (5), 1146–55.

3

State Power and the Structure
of International Trade

STEPHEN D. KRASNER

In this reading, Stephen D. Krasner argues that the level of trade openness in the international economy hinges on the interests and the interactions of the most powerful states in the system. He begins by identifying four principal goals of state action: political power, aggregate national income, economic growth, and social stability. He then combines these goals with different national abilities to pursue them, relating the international distribution of economic power to alternative trade regimes. Krasner maintains, most significantly, that the hegemony of a leading power is necessary for the creation and continuance of free trade. He applies his model to six periods. Krasner's analysis in this 1976 article is a well-known attempt to use Realism to explain international economic outcomes. The theory he propounds, which has been dubbed the "theory of hegemonic stability," has influenced many subsequent analyses.

INTRODUCTION

In recent years, students of international relations have multinationalized, transnationalized, bureaucratized, and transgovernmentalized the state until it has virtually ceased to exist as an analytic construct. Nowhere is that trend more apparent than in the study of the politics of international economic relations. The basic conventional assumptions have been undermined by assertions that the state is trapped by a transnational society created not by sovereigns, but by nonstate actors. Interdependence is not seen as a reflection of state policies and state choices (the perspective of balance-of-power theory), but as the result of elements beyond the control of any state or a system created by states.

This perspective is at best profoundly misleading. It may explain developments within a particular international economic structure, but it cannot explain the structure itself. That structure has many institutional and behavioral manifestations. The central continuum along which it can be described is openness. International economic structures may range from complete autarky (if all states prevent movements across their borders), to complete openness (if no restrictions exist). In this paper I will present an analysis of one aspect of the international economy—the structure of international trade; that is, the degree of openness for the movement of goods as opposed to capital, labor, technology, or other factors of production. Since the beginning of the nineteenth century, this structure has gone through several changes. These can be explained, albeit imperfectly, by a state-power theory: an approach that begins with the assumption that the structure of international trade is determined by the interests and power of states acting to maximize national goals. The first step in this argument is to relate four basic state interests—aggregate national income, social stability, political power, and economic growth—to the degree of openness for the movement of goods. The relationship between these interests and openness depends upon the potential economic power of any given state. Potential economic power is operationalized in terms of the relative size and level of economic development of the state. The second step in the argument is to relate different distributions of potential power, such as multipolar and hegemonic, to different international trading structures. The most important conclusion of this theoretical analysis is that a hegemonic distribution of potential economic power is likely to result in an open trading structure. That argument is largely, although not completely, substantiated by empirical data. For a fully adequate analysis it is necessary to amend a state-power argument to take account of the impact of past state decisions on domestic social structures as well as on international economic ones. The two major organizers of the structure of trade since the beginning of the nineteenth century, Great Britain and the United States, have both been prevented from making policy amendments in line with state interests by particular societal groups whose power had been enhanced by earlier state policies.

THE CAUSAL ARGUMENT: STATE INTERESTS, STATE POWER, AND INTERNATIONAL TRADING STRUCTURES

Neoclassical trade theory is based upon the assumption that states act to maximize their aggregate economic utility. This leads to the conclusion that maximum global welfare and Pareto optimality are achieved under free trade. While particular countries might better their situations through protectionism, economic theory has generally looked askance at such policies. . . . Neoclassical theory recognizes that trade regulations can . . . be used to correct domestic distortions and to promote infant industries, but these are exceptions or temporary departures from policy conclusions that lead logically to the support of free trade.

State Preferences

Historical experience suggests that policy makers are dense, or that the assumptions of the conventional argument are wrong. Free trade has hardly been the norm. Stupidity is not a very interesting analytic category. An alternative approach to explaining international trading structures is to assume that states seek a broad range of goals. At least four major state interests affected by the structure of international trade can be identified. They are: political power, aggregate national income, economic growth, and social stability. The way in which each of these goals is affected by the degree of openness depends upon the potential economic power of the state as defined by its relative size and level of development.

Let us begin with aggregate national income because it is most straightforward. Given the exceptions noted above, conventional neoclassical theory demonstrates that the greater the degree of openness in the international trading system, the greater the level of aggregate economic income. This conclusion applies to all states regardless of their size or relative level of development. The static economic benefits of openness are, however, generally inversely related to size. Trade gives small states relatively more welfare benefits than it gives large ones. Empirically, small states have higher ratios of trade to national product. They do not have the generous factor endowments or potential for national economies of scale that are enjoyed by larger—particularly continental—states.

The impact of openness on social stability runs in the opposite direction. Greater openness exposes the domestic economy to the exigencies of the world market. That implies a higher level of factor movements than in a closed economy, because domestic production patterns must adjust to changes in international prices. Social instability is thereby increased, since there is friction in moving factors, particularly labor, from one sector to another. The impact will be stronger in small states than in large, and in relatively less developed than in more developed ones. Large states are less involved in the international economy: a smaller percentage of their total factor endowment is affected by the international market at any given level of openness. More developed states are better able to adjust factors: skilled workers can more easily be moved from one kind of production to another than can unskilled laborers or peasants. Hence social stability is, *ceteris paribus*, inversely related to openness, but the deleterious consequences of exposure to the international trading system are mitigated by larger size and greater economic development.

The relationship between political power and the international trading structure can be analyzed in terms of the relative opportunity costs of closure for trading partners. The higher the relative cost of closure, the weaker the political position of the state. Hirschman has argued that this cost can be measured in terms of direct income losses and the adjustment costs of reallocating factors. These will be smaller for large states and for relatively more developed states. Other things being equal, utility costs will be less for large states because they generally have a smaller proportion of their economy engaged in the international economic system. Reallocation costs will be less for more advanced states because their factors are more mobile. Hence a state that is relatively large and more developed will find its political power enhanced by an open system because its opportunity costs of closure are less. The large state can use the threat to alter the system to secure economic or noneconomic objectives. Historically, there is one important exception to this generalization—the oil-exporting states. The level of reserves for some of these states, particularly Saudi Arabia, has reduced the economic opportunity costs of closure to a very low level despite their lack of development.

The relationship between international economic structure and economic growth is elusive. For small states, economic growth has generally been empirically associated with openness. Exposure to the international system makes possible a much more efficient allocation of resources. Openness also probably furthers the rate of growth of large countries with relatively advanced technologies because they do not need to protect infant industries and can take advantage of expanded world markets. In the long term, however, openness for capital and technology, as well as goods, may hamper the growth of large, developed countries by diverting resources from the domestic economy, and by providing potential competitors with the knowledge needed to develop their own industries. Only by maintaining its technological lead and continually developing new industries can even a very large state escape the undesired consequences of an entirely open economic system. For medium-size states, the relationship between international trading structure and growth is impossible to specify definitively, either theoretically or empirically. On the one hand, writers from the mercantilists through the American protectionists and the German historical school, and more recently analysts of *dependencia*, have argued that an entirely open system can undermine a state's effort to develop, and even lead to underdevelopment. On the other hand, adherents of more conventional neoclassical positions have maintained that exposure to international competition spurs economic transformation. The evidence is not yet in. All that can confidently be said is that openness furthers the economic growth of small states and of large ones so long as they maintain their technological edge.

From State Preferences to International Trading Structures

The next step in this argument is to relate particular distributions of potential economic power, defined by the size and level of development of individual states, to the structure of the international trading system, defined in terms of openness.

Let us consider a system composed of a large number of small, highly developed states. Such a system is likely to lead to an open international trading structure. The aggregate income and economic growth of each state are increased by an open system. The social instability produced by exposure to international competition is mitigated by the factor mobility made possible by higher levels of development. There is no loss of political power from openness because the costs of closure are symmetrical for all members of the system.

Now let us consider a system composed of a few very large, but unequally developed states. Such a distribution of potential economic power is likely to lead to a closed structure. Each state could increase its income through a more open system, but the gains would be modest. Openness would create more social instability in the less developed countries. The rate of growth for more backward areas might be frustrated, while that of the more advanced ones would be enhanced. A more open structure would leave the less developed states in a politically more vulnerable position, because their greater factor rigidity would mean a higher relative cost of closure. Because of these disadvantages, large but relatively less developed states are unlikely to accept an open trading structure. More advanced states cannot, unless they are militarily much more powerful, force large backward countries to accept openness.

Finally, let us consider a hegemonic system—one in which there is a single state that is much larger and relatively more advanced than its trading partners. The costs and benefits of openness are not symmetrical for all members of the system. The hegemonic state will have a preference for an open structure. Such a structure increases its aggregate national income. It also increases its rate of growth during its ascendency—that is, when its relative size and technological lead are increasing. Further, an open structure increases its political power, since the opportunity costs of closure are least for a large and developed state. The social instability resulting from exposure to the international system is mitigated by the hegemonic power's relatively low level of involvement in the international economy, and the mobility of its factors.

What of the other members of a hegemonic system? Small states are likely to opt for openness because the advantages in terms of aggregate income and growth are so great, and their political power is bound to be restricted regardless of what they do. The reaction of medium-size states is hard to predict; it depends at least in part on the way in which the hegemonic power utilizes its resources. The potentially dominant state has symbolic, economic, and military capabilities that can be used to entice or compel others to accept an open trading structure.

At the symbolic level, the hegemonic state stands as an example of how economic development can be achieved. Its policies may be emulated, even if they are inappropriate for other states. Where there are very dramatic asymmetries, military power can be used to coerce weaker states into an open structure. Force is not, however, a very efficient means for changing economic policies, and it is unlikely to be employed against medium-size states.

Most importantly, the hegemonic state can use its economic resources to create an open structure. In terms of positive incentives, it can offer access to its large domestic market and to its relatively cheap exports. In terms of negative ones, it can withhold foreign grants and engage in competition, potentially ruinous for the weaker state, in third-country markets. The size and economic robustness of the hegemonic state also enable it to provide the confidence

FIGURE 1 Probability of an Open Trading Structure with Different Distributions of Potential Economic Power

Level of Development of States	Size of States		
	Relatively Equal		Very Unequal
	Small	Large	
Equal	Moderate-High	Low-Moderate	High
Unequal	Moderate	Low	Moderate-High

necessary for a stable international monetary system, and its currency can offer the liquidity needed for an increasingly open system.

In sum, openness is most likely to occur during periods when a hegemonic state is in its ascendency. Such a state has the interest and the resources to create a structure characterized by lower tariffs, rising trade proportions, and less regionalism. There are other distributions of potential power where openness is likely, such as a system composed of many small, highly developed states. But even here, that potential might not be realized because of the problems of creating confidence in a monetary system where adequate liquidity would have to be provided by a negotiated international reserve asset or a group of national currencies. Finally, it is unlikely that very large states, particularly at unequal levels of development, would accept open trading relations.

These arguments, and the implications of other ideal typical configurations of potential economic power for the openness of trading structures, are summarized in [Figure 1].

THE DEPENDENT VARIABLE: DESCRIBING THE STRUCTURE OF THE INTERNATIONAL TRADING SYSTEM

The structure of international trade has both behavioral and institutional attributes. The degree of openness can be described both by the *flow* of goods and by the *policies* that are followed by states with respect to trade barriers and international payments. The two are not unrelated, but they do not coincide perfectly.

In common usage, the focus of attention has been upon institutions. Openness is associated with those historical periods in which tariffs were substantially lowered: the third quarter of the nineteenth century and the period since the Second World War.

Tariffs alone, however, are not an adequate indicator of structure. They are hard to operationalize quantitatively. Tariffs do not have to be high to be effective. If cost functions are nearly identical, even low tariffs can prevent trade. Effective tariff rates may be much higher than nominal ones. Non-tariff barriers to trade, which are not easily compared across states, can substitute for duties. An undervalued exchange rate can protect domestic markets from foreign competition. Tariff levels alone cannot describe the structure of international trade.

A second indicator, and one which is behavioral rather than institutional, is trade proportions—the ratios of trade to national income for different states. Like tariff levels, these involve describing the system in terms of an agglomeration of national tendencies. A period in which these ratios are increasing across time for most states can be described as one of increasing openness.

A third indicator is the concentration of trade within regions composed of states at different levels of development. The degree of such regional encapsulation is determined not so much by comparative advantage (because relative factor endowments would allow almost any backward area to trade with almost any developed one), but by political choices or dictates. Large states, attempting to protect themselves from the vagaries of a global system, seek to maximize their interests by creating regional blocs. Openness in the global economic system has in effect meant greater trade among the leading industrial states. Periods of closure are associated with the encapsulation of certain advanced states within regional systems shared with certain less developed areas.

A description of the international trading system involves, then, an exercise that is comparative rather than absolute. A period when tariffs are falling, trade proportions are rising, and regional trading patterns are becoming less extreme will be defined as one in which the structure is becoming more open.

Tariff Levels

The period from the 1820s to 1879 was basically one of decreasing tariff levels in Europe. The trend began in Great Britain in the 1820s, with reductions of duties and other barriers to trade. In 1846 the abolition of the Corn Laws ended agricultural protectionism. France reduced duties on some intermediate goods in the 1830s, and on coal, iron, and steel in 1852. The *Zollverein* established fairly low tariffs in 1834. Belgium, Portugal, Spain, Piedmont, Norway, Switzerland, and Sweden lowered imposts in the 1850s. The golden age of free trade began in 1860, when Britain and France signed the Cobden-Chevalier Treaty, which virtually eliminated trade barriers. This was followed by a series of bilateral trade agreements between virtually all European states. It is important to note, however, that the United States took little part in the general movement toward lower trade barriers.

The movement toward greater liberality was reversed in the late 1870s. Austria-Hungary increased duties in 1876 and 1878, and Italy also in 1878; but the main breach came in Germany in 1879. France increased tariffs modestly in 1881, sharply in 1892, and raised them still further in 1910. Other countries followed a similar pattern. Only Great Britain, Belgium, the Netherlands, and Switzerland continued to follow free-trade policies through the 1880s. Although Britain did not herself impose duties, she began establishing a system of preferential markets in her overseas Empire in 1898. The United States was basically protectionist throughout the nineteenth century. The high tariffs imposed during the Civil War continued with the exception of a brief period in the 1890s. There were no major duty reductions before 1914.

During the 1920s, tariff levels increased further. Western European states protected their agrarian sectors against imports from the Danube region, Australia, Canada, and the United States, where the war had stimulated increased output. Great Britain adopted some colonial preferences in 1919, imposed a small number of tariffs in 1921, and extended some wartime duties. The successor states of the Austro-Hungarian Empire imposed duties to achieve some national self-sufficiency. The British dominions and Latin America protected industries nurtured by wartime demands. In the United States the Fordney-McCumber Tariff Act of 1922 increased protectionism. The October Revolution removed Russia from the Western trading system.

Dramatic closure in terms of tariff levels began with the passage of the Smoot-Hawley Tariff Act in the United States in 1930. Britain raised tariffs in 1931 and definitively abandoned free trade at the Ottawa Conference of 1932, which introduced extensive imperial preferences. Germany and Japan established trading blocs within their own spheres of influence. All other major countries followed protectionist policies.

Significant reductions in protection began after the Second World War; the United States had foreshadowed the movement toward greater liberality with the passage of the Reciprocal Trade Agreements Act in 1934. Since 1945 there have been seven rounds of multilateral tariff reductions. The first, held in 1947 at Geneva, and the Kennedy Round, held during the 1960s, have been the most significant. They have substantially reduced the level of protection.

The present situation is ambiguous. There have recently been some new trade controls. In the United States these include a voluntary import agreement for steel, the imposition of a 10 percent import surcharge during four months of 1971, and export controls on agricultural products in 1973 and 1974. Italy imposed a deposit requirement on imports during parts of 1974 and 1975. Britain and Japan have engaged in export subsidization. Non-tariff barriers have become more important. On balance, there has been movement toward greater protectionism since the end of the Kennedy Round, but it is not decisive. The outcome of the multilateral negotiations that began in 1975 remains to be seen.

In sum, after 1820 there was a general trend toward lower tariffs (with the notable exception of the United States), which culminated between 1860 and

1879; higher tariffs from 1879 through the interwar years, with dramatic increases in the 1930s; and less protectionism from 1945 through the conclusion of the Kennedy Round in 1967.

Trade Proportions

With the exception of one period, ratios of trade to aggregate economic activity followed the same general pattern as tariff levels. Trade proportions increased from the early part of the nineteenth century to about 1880. Between 1880 and 1900 there was a decrease, sharper if measured in current prices than constant ones, but apparent in both statistical series for most countries. Between 1900 and 1913—and here is the exception from the tariff pattern—there was a marked increase in the ratio of trade to aggregate economic activity. This trend brought trade proportions to levels that have generally not been reattained. During the 1920s and 1930s the importance of trade in national economic activity declined. After the Second World War it increased.

. . . There are considerable differences in the movement of trade proportions among states. They hold more or less constant for the United States; Japan, Denmark, and Norway . . . are unaffected by the general decrease in the ratio of trade to aggregate economic activity that takes place after 1880. The pattern described in the previous paragraph does, however, hold for Great Britain, France, Sweden, Germany, and Italy.

. . . Because of the boom in commodity prices that occurred in the early 1950s, the ratio of trade to gross domestic product was relatively high for larger states during these years, at least in current prices. It then faltered or remained constant until about 1960. From the early 1960s through 1972, trade proportions rose for all major states except Japan. Data for 1973 and 1974 show further increases. For smaller countries the trend was more erratic, with Belgium showing a more or less steady increase, Norway vacillating between 82 and 90 percent, and Denmark and the Netherlands showing higher figures for the late 1950s than for more recent years. There is then, in current prices, a generally upward trend in trade proportions since 1960, particularly for larger states. This movement is more pronounced if constant prices are used.

Regional Trading Patterns

The final indicator of the degree of openness of the global trading system is regional bloc concentration. There is a natural affinity for some states to trade with others because of geographical propinquity or comparative advantage. In general, however, a system in which there are fewer manifestations of trading within given blocs, particularly among specific groups of more and less developed states, is a more open one. Over time there have been extensive changes in trading patterns between particular areas of the world whose relative factor endowments have remained largely the same.

Richard Chadwick and Karl Deutsch have collected extensive information on international trading patterns since 1890. Their basic datum is the relative acceptance indicator (RA), which measures deviations from a null hypothesis in which trade between a pair of states, or a state and a region, is precisely what would be predicted on the basis of their total share of international trade. When the null hypothesis holds, the RA indicator is equal to zero. Values less than zero indicate less trade than expected, greater than zero more trade than expected. For our purposes the critical issue is whether, over time, trade tends to become more concentrated as shown by movements away from zero, or less as shown by movements toward zero. . . .

There is a general pattern. In three of the four cases, the RA value closest to zero—that is the least regional encapsulation—occurred in 1890, 1913, or 1928; in the fourth case (France and French West Africa), the 1928 value was not bettered until 1964. In every case there was an increase in the RA indicator between 1928 and 1938, reflecting the breakdown of international commerce that is associated with the depression. Surprisingly, the RA indicator was higher for each of the four pairs in 1954 than in 1938, an indication that regional patterns persisted and even became more intense in the postwar period. With the exception of the Soviet Union and Eastern Europe, there was a general trend toward decreasing RAs for the period after 1954. They still, however, show fairly high values even in the late 1960s.

If we put all three indicators—tariff levels, trade proportions, and trade patterns—together, they suggest the following periodization.

> Period I (1820–1879): Increasing openness—tariffs are generally lowered; trade proportions increase. Data are not available for trade patterns. However, it is important to note that this is not a universal pattern. The United States is largely unaffected: its tariff levels remain high (and are in fact increased during the early 1860s) and American trade proportions remain almost constant.
>
> Period II (1879–1900): Modest closure—tariffs are increased; trade proportions decline modestly for most states. Data are not available for trade patterns.
>
> Period III (1900–1913): Greater openness—tariff levels remain generally unchanged; trade proportions increase for all major trading states except the United States. Trading patterns become less regional in three out of the four cases for which data are available.
>
> Period IV (1918–1939): Closure—tariff levels are increased in the 1920s and again in the 1930s; trade proportions decline. Trade becomes more regionally encapsulated.
>
> Period V (1945–c. 1970): Great openness—tariffs are lowered; trade proportions increase, particularly after 1960. Regional concentration decreases after 1960. However, these developments are limited to non-Communist areas of the world.

THE INDEPENDENT VARIABLE: DESCRIBING THE DISTRIBUTION OF POTENTIAL ECONOMIC POWER AMONG STATES

Analysts of international relations have an almost pro forma set of variables designed to show the distribution of potential power in the international *political* system. It includes such factors as gross national product, per capita income, geographical position, and size of armed forces. A similar set of indicators can be presented for the international economic system.

Statistics are available over a long time period for per capita income, aggregate size, share of world trade, and share of world investment. They demonstrate that, since the beginning of the nineteenth century, there have been two first-rank economic powers in the world economy—Britain and the United States. The United States passed Britain in aggregate size sometime in the middle of the nineteenth century and, in the 1880s, became the largest producer of manufactures. America's lead was particularly marked in technologically advanced industries turning out sewing machines, harvesters, cash registers, locomotives, steam pumps, telephones, and petroleum. Until the First World War, however, Great Britain had a higher per capita income, a greater share of world trade, and a greater share of world investment than any other state. The peak of British ascendance occurred around 1880, when Britain's relative per capita income, share of world trade, and share of investment flows reached their highest levels. Britain's potential dominance in 1880 and 1900 was particularly striking in the international economic system, where her share of trade and foreign investment was about twice as large as that of any other state.

It was only after the First World War that the United States became relatively larger and more developed in terms of all four indicators. This potential dominance reached new and dramatic heights between 1945 and 1960. Since then, the relative position of the United States has declined, bringing it quite close to West Germany, its nearest rival, in terms of per capita income and share of world trade. The devaluations of the dollar that have taken place since 1972 are reflected in a continuation of this downward trend for income and aggregate size.

The relative potential economic power of Britain and the United States is shown in [Tables 1 and 2].

In sum, Britain was the world's most important trading state from the period after the Napoleonic Wars until 1913. Her relative position rose until about 1880 and fell thereafter. The United States became the largest and most advanced state in economic terms after the First World War, but did not equal the relative share of world trade and investment achieved by Britain in the 1880s until after the Second World War.

TABLE 1 Indicators of British Potential Power (ratio of British value to next highest)

	Per capita income	Aggregate size	Share of world trade	Share of world investment*
1860	.91(US)	.74(US)	2.01(FR)	n.a.
1880	1.30(US)	.79(1874–83 US)	2.22(FR)	1.93(FR)
1900	1.05(1899 US)	.58(1899 US)	2.17(1890 GERM)	2.08(FR)
1913	.92(US)	.43(US)	1.20(US)	2.18(1914 FR)
1928	.66(US)	.25(1929 US)	.79(US)	.64(1921–1929 US)
1937	.79(US)	.29(US)	.88(US)	.18(1930–1938 US)
1950	.56(US)	.19(US)	.69(US)	.13(1951–1955 US)
1960	.49(US)	.14(US)	.46(1958 US)	.15(1956–1961 US)
1972	.46(US)	.13(US)	.47(1973 US)	n.a.

*Stock 1870–1913; Flow 1928–1950.

NOTE: Years are in parentheses when different from those in first column.

Countries in parentheses are those with the largest values for the particular indicator other than Great Britain. n.a. = not available.

TABLE 2 Indicators of U.S. Potential Power (ratio of U.S. value to next highest)

	Per capita income	Aggregate size	Share of world trade	Share of world investment flows
1860	1.10(GB)	1.41(GB)	.36(GB)	Net debtor
1880	.77(GB)	1.23(1883 GB)	.37(GB)	Net debtor
1900	.95(1899 GB)	1.73(1899 GB)	.43(1890 GB)	n.a.
1913	1.09(GB)	2.15(RUS)	.83(GB)	Net debtor
1928	1.51(GB)	3.22(USSR)	1.26(GB)	1.55(1921–1920 UK)
1937	1.26(GB)	2.67(USSR)	1.13(GB)	5.53(1930–1938 UK)
1950	1.78(GB)	3.15(USSR)	1.44(GB)	7.42(1951–1955 UK)
1960	2.05(GB)	2.81(USSR)	2.15(1958 GB)	6.60(1956–1961 UK)
1972	1.31(GERM)	n.a.	1.18(1973 GERM)	n.a.

NOTE: Years are in parentheses when different from those in first column.

Countries in parentheses are those with the largest values for the particular indicator other than the United States. n.a. = not available.

TESTING THE ARGUMENT

The contention that hegemony leads to a more open trading structure is fairly well, but not perfectly, confirmed by the empirical evidence presented in the preceding sections. The argument explains the periods 1820 to 1879, 1880 to 1900, and 1945 to 1960. It does not fully explain those from 1900 to 1913, 1919 to 1939, or 1960 to the present.

1820–1879

The period from 1820 to 1879 was one of increasing openness in the structure of international trade. It was also one of rising hegemony. Great Britain was the instigator and supporter of the new structure. She began lowering her trade barriers in the 1820s, before any other state. The signing of the Cobden-Chevalier Tariff Treaty with France in 1860 initiated a series of bilateral tariff reductions. It is, however, important to note that the United States was hardly involved in these developments, and that America's ratio of trade to aggregate economic activity did not increase during the nineteenth century.

Britain put to use her internal flexibility and external power in securing a more open structure. At the domestic level, openness was favored by the rising industrialists. The opposition of the agrarian sector was mitigated by its capacity for adjustment: the rate of capital investment and technological innovation was high enough to prevent British agricultural incomes from falling until some thirty years after the abolition of the Corn Laws. Symbolically, the Manchester School led by Cobden and Bright provided the ideological justification for free trade. Its influence was felt throughout Europe where Britain stood as an example to at least some members of the elite.

Britain used her military strength to open many backward areas: British interventions were frequent in Latin America during the nineteenth century, and formal and informal colonial expansion opened the interior of Africa. Most importantly, Britain forced India into the international economic system. British military power was also a factor in concluding the Cobden-Chevalier Treaty, for Louis Napoleon was more concerned with cementing his relations with Britain than he was in the economic consequences of greater openness. Once this pact was signed, however, it became a catalyst for the many other treaties that followed.

Britain also put economic instruments to good use in creating an open system. The abolition of the Corn Laws offered continental grain producers the incentive of continued access to the growing British market. Britain was at the heart of the nineteenth-century international monetary system which functioned exceptionally well, at least for the core of the more developed states and the areas closely associated with them. Exchange rates were stable, and countries did not have to impose trade barriers to rectify cyclical payments difficulties. Both confidence and liquidity were, to a critical degree, provided by Britain. The use of sterling balances as opposed to specie became increasingly widespread, alleviating the liquidity problems presented by the erratic production of gold and silver. Foreign private and central banks increasingly placed their cash reserves in London, and accounts were cleared through changing bank balances rather than gold flows. Great Britain's extremely sophisticated financial institutions, centered in the City of London, provided the short-term financing necessary to facilitate the international flow of goods. Her early and somewhat fortuitous adherence to the gold—as opposed to the silver or bimetallic—standard proved to be an important source of confidence as all countries adopted at least a *de facto* gold standard after 1870 because of the declining relative value of silver. In times of monetary emergency, the confidence placed in the pound because of the strength of the British economy allowed the Bank of England to be a lender of last resort.

Hence, for the first three-quarters of the nineteenth century, British policy favored an open international trading structure, and British power helped to create it. But this was not a global regime. British resources were not sufficient to entice or compel the United States (a country whose economy was larger than Britain's by 1860 and whose technology was developing very rapidly) to abandon its protectionist commercial policy. As a state-power argument suggests, openness was only established within the geographical area where the rising economic hegemony was able to exercise its influence.

1880–1900

The last two decades of the nineteenth century were a period of modest closure which corresponds to a relative decline in British per capita income, size, and share of world trade. The event that precipitated higher tariff levels was the availability of inexpensive grain from the American Midwest, made possible by the construction of continental railways. National responses varied. Britain let her agricultural sector decline, a not unexpected development given her still dominant economic position. Denmark, a small and relatively well-developed state, also refrained from imposing tariffs and transformed its farming sector from agriculture to animal husbandry. Several other small states also followed open policies. Germany, France, Russia, and Italy imposed higher tariffs, however. Britain did not have the military or economic power to forestall these policies. Still, the institutional structure of the international monetary system, with the city of London at its center, did not crumble. The decline in trade proportions was modest despite higher tariffs.

1945–1960

The third period that is neatly explained by the argument that hegemony leads to an open trading structure is the decade and a half after the Second World War, characterized by the ascendancy of the United States. During these years the structure of the international trading system became increasingly open. Tariffs were lowered; trade proportions were restored well above interwar levels. Asymmetrical regional trading patterns did begin to decline, although not until the late 1950s. America's bilateral rival, the Soviet Union, remained—as the theory would predict—encapsulated within its own regional sphere of influence.

Unlike Britain in the nineteenth century, the United States after the Second World War operated in a bipolar political structure. Free trade was preferred, but departures such as the Common Market and Japanese import restrictions were accepted to make sure that these areas remained within the general American sphere of influence. Domestically the Reciprocal Trade Agreements Act, first passed in 1934, was extended several times after the war. Internationally the United States supported the framework for tariff reductions provided by the General Agreement on Tariffs and Trade. American policy makers used their economic leverage over Great Britain to force an end to the imperial preference system. The monetary system established at Bretton Woods was basically an American creation. In practice, liquidity was provided by the American deficit; confidence by the size of the American economy. Behind the economic veil stood American military protection for other industrialized market economies—an overwhelming incentive for them to accept an open system, particularly one which was in fact relatively beneficial.

The argument about the relationship between hegemony and openness is not as satisfactory for the years 1900 to 1913, 1919 to 1939, and 1960 to the present.

1900–1913

During the years immediately preceding the First World War, the structure of international trade became more open in terms of trade proportions and regional patterns. Britain remained the largest international economic entity, but her relative position continued a decline that had begun two decades earlier. Still, Britain maintained her commitment to free trade and to the financial institutions of the city of London. A state-power argument would suggest some reconsideration of these policies.

Perhaps the simplest explanation for the increase in trade proportions was the burst of loans that flowed out of Europe in the years before the First World War, loans that financed the increasing sale of goods. Germany and France as well as Britain participated in this development. Despite the higher tariff levels imposed after 1879, institutional structures—particularly the monetary system—allowed these capital flows to generate increasing trade flows. Had Britain reconsidered her policies, this might not have been the case.

1919–1939

The United States emerged from the First World War as the world's most powerful economic state. Whether America was large enough to have put an open system in place is a moot question. As Table 2 indicates, America's share of world trade and investment was [respectively] only 26 and 55 percent greater than that of any other state, while comparable figures for Great Britain during the last part of the nineteenth century are 100 percent. What is apparent, though, is that American policy makers made little effort to open the structure of international trade. The call for an open door was a shibboleth, not a policy. It was really the British who attempted to continue a hegemonic role.

In the area of trade, the U.S. Fordney-McCumber Tariff of 1922 increased protection. That tendency was greatly reinforced by the Smoot-Hawley Tariff of 1930 which touched off a wave of protective legislation. Instead of leading the way to openness, the United States led the way to closure.

In the monetary area, the American government made little effort to alter a situation that was confused and often chaotic. During the first half of the 1920s, exchange rates fluctuated widely among major currencies as countries were forced, by the inflationary pressures of the war, to abandon the gold standard. Convertibility was restored in the mid-twenties at values incompatible with long-term equilibrium. The British pound was overvalued, and the French franc undervalued. Britain was forced off the gold standard in September 1931, accelerating a trend that had begun with Uruguay in April 1929. The United States went off gold in 1933. France's decision to end convertibility in 1936 completed the pattern. During the 1930s the monetary system collapsed.

Constructing a stable monetary order would have been no easy task in the political environment of the 1920s and 1930s. The United States made no effort. It refused to recognize a connection between war debts and reparations, although much of the postwar flow of funds took the form of American loans to Germany, German reparations payments to France and Britain, and French and British war-debt payments to the United States. The Great Depression was in no small measure touched off by the contraction of American credit in the late 1920s. In the deflationary collapse that followed, the British were too weak to act as a lender of last resort, and the Americans actually undercut efforts to reconstruct the Western economy when, before the London Monetary Conference of 1933, President Roosevelt changed the basic assumptions of the meeting by taking the United States off gold. American concern was wholly with restoring the domestic economy.

That is not to say that American behavior was entirely obstreperous; but cooperation was erratic and often private. The Federal Reserve Bank of New York did try, during the late 1920s, to maintain New York interest rates below those in London to protect the value of the pound. Two Americans, Dawes and Young, lent their names to the renegotiations of German reparations payments, but most of the actual work was carried out by British experts. At the official level, the first manifestation of American leadership was President Hoover's call for a moratorium on war debts and reparations in June 1931; but in 1932 the United States refused to participate in the Lausanne Conference that in effect ended reparations.

It was not until the mid-thirties that the United States asserted any real leadership. The Reciprocal Trade Agreements Act of 1934 led to bilateral treaties with twenty-seven countries before 1945. American concessions covered 64 percent of dutiable items, and reduced rates by an average of 44 percent. However, tariffs were so high to begin with that the actual impact of these agreements was limited. There were also some modest steps toward tariff liberalization in Britain and France. In the monetary field, the United States, Britain, and France pledged to maintain exchange-rate stability in the Tripartite Declaration of September 1936. These actions were not adequate to create an open international economic structure. American policy during the interwar period, and particularly before the mid-thirties, fails to accord with the

predictions made by a state-power explanation of the behavior of a rising hegemonic power.

1960–Present

The final period not adequately dealt with by a state-power explanation is the
last decade or so. In recent years, the relative size and level of development of
the U.S. economy has fallen. This decline has not, however, been accompanied
by a clear turn toward protectionism. The Trade Expansion Act of 1962 was
extremely liberal and led to the very successful Kennedy Round of multilateral tariff cuts during the mid-sixties. The protectionist Burke-Hartke Bill did
not pass. The 1974 Trade Act does include new protectionist aspects, particularly in its requirements for review of the removal of non-tariff barriers by
Congress and for stiffer requirements for the imposition of countervailing
duties, but it still maintains the mechanism of presidential discretion on tariff cuts that has been the keystone of postwar reductions. While the Voluntary Steel Agreement, the August 1971 economic policy, and restrictions on
agricultural exports all show a tendency toward protectionism, there is as yet
no evidence of a basic turn away from a commitment to openness.

In terms of behavior in the international trading system, the decade of the
1960s was clearly one of greater openness. Trade proportions increased, and
traditional regional trade patterns became weaker. A state-power argument
would predict a downturn or at least a faltering in these indicators as American power declined.

In sum, although the general pattern of the structure of international trade
conforms with the predictions of a state-power argument—two periods of openness separated by one of closure—corresponding to periods of rising British
and American hegemony and an interregnum, the whole pattern is out of
phase. British commitment to openness continued long after Britain's position had declined. American commitment to openness did not begin until well
after the United States had become the world's leading economic power and
has continued during a period of relative American decline. The state-power
argument needs to be amended to take these delayed reactions into account.

AMENDING THE ARGUMENT

The structure of the international trading system does not move in lockstep
with changes in the distribution of potential power among states. Systems are
initiated and ended, not as a state-power theory would predict, by close assessments of the interests of the state at every given moment, but by external
events—usually cataclysmic ones. The closure that began in 1879 coincided
with the Great Depression of the last part of the nineteenth century. The final
dismantling of the nineteenth-century international economic system was not
precipitated by a change in British trade or monetary policy, but by the First
World War and the Depression. The potato famine of the 1840s prompted

abolition of the Corn Laws; and the United States did not assume the mantle of world leadership until the world had been laid bare by six years of total war. Some catalytic external event seems necessary to move states to dramatic policy initiatives in line with state interests.

Once policies have been adopted, they are pursued until a new crisis demonstrates that they are no longer feasible. States become locked in by the impact of prior choices on their domestic political structures. The British decision to opt for openness in 1846 corresponded with state interests. It also strengthened the position of industrial and financial groups over time, because they had the opportunity to operate in an international system that furthered their objectives. That system eventually undermined the position of British farmers, a group that would have supported protectionism if it had survived. Once entrenched, Britain's export industries, and more importantly the City of London, resisted policies of closure. In the interwar years, the British rentier class insisted on restoring the prewar parity of the pound—a decision that placed enormous deflationary pressures on the domestic economy—because they wanted to protect the value of their investments.

Institutions created during periods of rising ascendancy remained in operation when they were no longer appropriate. For instance, the organization of British banking in the nineteenth century separated domestic and foreign operations. The Court of Directors of the Bank of England was dominated by international banking houses. Their decisions about British monetary policy were geared toward the international economy. Under a different institutional arrangement more attention might have been given after 1900 to the need to revitalize the domestic economy. The British state was unable to free itself from the domestic structures that its earlier policy decisions had created, and continued to follow policies appropriate for a rising hegemony long after Britain's star had begun to fall.

Similarly, earlier policies in the United States begat social structures and institutional arrangements that trammeled state policy. After protecting import-competing industries for a century, the United States was unable in the 1920s to opt for more open policies, even though state interests would have been furthered thereby. Institutionally, decisions about tariff reductions were taken primarily in congressional committees, giving virtually any group seeking protection easy access to the decision-making process. When there were conflicts among groups, they were resolved by raising the levels of protection for everyone. It was only after the cataclysm of the Depression that the decision-making processes for trade policy were changed. The presidency, far more insulated from the entreaties of particular societal groups than congressional committees, was then given more power. Furthermore, the American commercial banking system was unable to assume the burden of regulating the international economy during the 1920s. American institutions were geared toward the domestic economy. Only after the Second World War, and in fact not until the late 1950s, did American banks fully develop the complex institutional structures commensurate with the dollar's role in the international monetary system.

Having taken the critical decisions that created an open system after 1945, the American government is unlikely to change its policy until it confronts some external event that it cannot control, such as a worldwide deflation, drought in the great plains, or the malicious use of petrodollars. In America perhaps more than in any other country "new policies," as E. E. Schattschneider wrote in his brilliant study of the Smoot-Hawley Tariff in 1935, "create new politics,"[1] for in America the state is weak and the society strong. State decisions taken because of state interests reinforce private societal groups that the state is unable to resist in later periods. Multinational corporations have grown and prospered since 1950. International economic policy making has passed from the Congress to the Executive. Groups favoring closure, such as organized labor, are unlikely to carry the day until some external event demonstrates that existing policies can no longer be implemented.

The structure of international trade changes in fits and starts; it does not flow smoothly with the redistribution of potential state power. Nevertheless, it is the power and the policies of states that create order where there would otherwise be chaos or at best a Lockean state of nature. The existence of various transnational, multinational, transgovernmental, and other nonstate actors that have riveted scholarly attention in recent years can only be understood within the context of a broader structure that ultimately rests upon the power and interests of states, shackled though they may be by the societal consequences of their own past decisions.

NOTE

1. E. E. Schattschneider, *Politics, Pressures and the Tariff: A Study of Free Enterprise in Pressure Politics as Shown in the 1929–1930 Revision of the Tariff* (New York: Prentice-Hall, 1935).

4

International Institutions and Issue Linkage: Building Support for Agricultural Trade Liberalization

CHRISTINA L. DAVIS

In this reading, Christina L. Davis explains how the institutions that structure international trade negotiations influence trade policy outcomes. She argues that issue linkage counteracts domestic obstacles to trade liberalization by broadening the negotiation stakes, but institutions play the key role of bolstering the credibility of the linkage. She tests the argument in the agricultural sector, which is one of the most difficult sectors to liberalize. Her analysis of U.S. negotiations with Japan and the EU from 1970 to 1999 indicates that an institutionalized linkage between agricultural and industrial issues encouraged agricultural liberalization in both Japan and Europe. Through case studies of key negotiations, she examines why countries choose to link issues, and how the linkage then changes interest group mobilization and shifts the policy process to promote liberalization.

Why do some international economic negotiations bring major policy changes while others end in deadlock? The difference between success and failure in these negotiations often amounts to billions of dollars and the seeds of economic disorder or cooperation. A successful negotiation can establish rules that open markets and promote coordination of policies. For example, the Bretton Woods conference of 1944 established the framework for postwar economic cooperation that promoted greater interdependence. Fifty years later, the Uruguay Round Agreement reduced agricultural and industrial trade barriers and expanded trade rules to regulate services and investment. On the other hand, failed negotiations often leave both sides worse off as relations between participants deteriorate. One such setback was the World Economic Conference of 1933, which ended without agreement and was followed by retaliatory trade protectionism and competitive currency devaluations. Failures on a smaller scale can also have significant consequences. For example, inability to reach agreement on wheat support policies in the Tokyo Round led to a subsidy war between the United States and Europe during the 1980s that drained their budgets and undercut the sales of developing country farmers. While the consequences of a negotiation may be far-reaching, the source of successful negotiation strategies lies in the details of the institutions that shape the negotiation process.

To explain negotiation outcomes, one must look closer at how the agenda, rules, and procedures of a negotiation influence state choices. Power and interests alone fail to account for the variation across negotiations. Strong states sometimes are unable to persuade weaker states to open their markets, and influential lobby groups are not always able to prevent their government from signing a liberalizing agreement. This article focuses on issue linkage, which is a common negotiation strategy that involves combining multiple issues to change the balance of interests in favor of a negotiated agreement. Only when the institutional context supports a linkage strategy, however, will it appear credible. Once established, the institutionalized issue linkage applies greater pressure for liberalization than threats or domestic political and financial constraints. Moreover, issue linkage can bring liberalization even when it would be least expected in sensitive sectors.

Using agricultural trade as a hard case that has been a frequent source of trade disputes, I present evidence that linking negotiations on agriculture and other sectors brings more agricultural liberalization than other strategies. Historically, agriculture stands out as a sector where countries stubbornly defend domestic programs. Farm lobbies represent the classic example of an influential pressure group. Indeed, nearly all industrialized countries raise the levels of protection on farming as the sector's size in the economy shrinks. Collective action incentives motivate farmers to organize, and both strong lobbies and electoral rules favoring rural districts guarantee that farmers wield political strength beyond their numbers. As a result, while bound tariffs on industrial goods have fallen to an average rate of 5% for OECD countries, agricultural protection has remained high, with bound tariffs averaging 60%. Nontariff barriers remained common in the agricultural sector long after they were eliminated for most industrial goods. Japan and Europe stand out among those giving the most protection to agriculture.[1]

Agricultural protection brings high costs in terms of financial expenditures, lost export opportunities, and increased trade friction. Agriculture exporters, which include the United States and the developing countries, demand liberalization because protection closes off valuable markets. A study by the U.S. Department of Agriculture (2001) indicates that elimination of agricultural protection and support could increase global economic welfare by 56 billion dollars annually, which would be in addition to the direct budget savings. In Japan and Europe, on the other hand, where many producers are not competitive in world markets, liberalization threatens the welfare of rural society. Politicization and high economic stakes make for an explosive combination that threatens the stability of the trade system. Japan and Europe both have risked trade wars with the United States over food fights. Agricultural issues have nearly blocked the conclusion of successive trade rounds and generated half of all GATT trade disputes over the period 1960–1989 (Hudec 1993, 327).

1. OECD producer subsidy estimates for 2001 show that 59% of the value of farm production resulted directly from government policies in Japan, while the corresponding figure was 35% for the EU—both above the OECD average of 31% and the U.S. levels of 21% (OECD 2002b, 160–61).

Agriculture continues to present a central challenge for the successful conclusion of the new WTO trade round launched in November 2001 in Doha,
Qatar. The large share of agriculture in the economies of developing countries
makes further liberalization of agricultural trade essential if the Doha Round
is to fulfill its development agenda.

Although agriculture remains protected in comparison to other sectors,
liberalization has occurred. Over the past 30 years, even Japan and Europe
have agreed to reduce many trade barriers, and the share of imports in total
consumption has increased. According to the OECD measures of agricultural protection, the total support for agriculture as a share of GDP has
declined from 2.4% for Japan and 2.6% for the EU in 1986 to 1.4% for both in
2001. In specific policy changes, market price support has been reduced,
Japan dismantled its system of quota restrictions one by one, and the EU
replaced its trade-distorting variable levy with a more transparent tariff
system. Thus, negotiations on agricultural trade policy have included both
dramatic negotiation failures and negotiations that brought substantial
liberalization.

FRAMEWORK FOR NEGOTIATION ANALYSIS

In negotiations that bring liberalization, what has allowed governments to
overcome domestic interests that will be harmed? The literature on trade
politics highlights the importance of distributional stakes for interest groups.
I emphasize how the institutional context of the international negotiation
changes the aggregation of these interests. Negotiations that link issues across
multiple sectors have a different impact on domestic politics than single sector negotiations. An institutionalized linkage of negotiations on multiple sectors broadens interest group lobbying and bureaucratic jurisdiction to counter
the domestic bias that favors protection.

Putnam (1988) introduced the analogy of *two-level games* to characterize the
observation that a leader negotiates simultaneously over domestic goals and
the international bargain. Since then, a growing literature has attempted to
explain how interest groups, domestic political institutions, or the bargaining
strategies of negotiators determine the range of possible negotiation agreements. While two-level game analysis has improved our understanding of
how domestic politics affect outcomes, many studies treat the international
level as an undifferentiated bargaining arena. Milner (1997, 70), for example,
writes, "The international game adopted does not have a well-defined institutional structure; politics on that level are assumed to be anarchic, and international negotiations are generally conducted without a constitutionally
mandated sequence of moves." This disregards the dense network of international institutions that shapes the conduct of any given negotiation.

The institutions of the negotiation structure—the agenda, rules, and procedures that guide the interaction between states in a policy dispute—influence

the negotiation outcome because they establish which alternatives are considered and how they are decided. As with other institutional constraints, such as international treaties or legislative committee rules, the institutions of the negotiation structure favor certain actors and policy options. In trade negotiations, institutions change both the mobilization by interest groups and the policy track for decision making.

First, the negotiation agenda sets the negotiation stakes and policy scope. Publicly announcing the issues that are up for discussion informs domestic actors of the potential gains and losses. Interest groups are involved in the process of creating the agenda as they lobby for the inclusion or exclusion of their own issue. Few, however, lobby beyond their own issue. Governments must aggregate diverse demands from domestic interests while also trying to accommodate other governments to produce a single agenda. The final agenda reveals the full array of issues that then become important for all groups with a stake in any one issue. Likewise, the issues on the agenda determine the scope of bureaucratic and political committee jurisdictions that will address the negotiation. This matters given the importance of who initiates policy proposals and who makes the last decision.

Second, the negotiation procedures guide the sequence of decisions. If there are multiple issues on the agenda, for example, the negotiation could culminate in a single decision on all the issues or separate decisions on each one. As shown by the literature on institutions in American politics, outcomes often differ according to which alternatives are presented to the legislature.

Third, the nature of the rules determines the form of commitments that are reached in the negotiation. Specifically, the rule framework creates the expectation for whether a negotiated agreement will represent a binding legal commitment with a monitoring mechanism. This raises the costs of later defection from agreements. Greater legalization adds the value of the rule system and future cooperation as new incentives. Taken altogether, the institutions of the negotiation structure have a direct impact on the distributional consequences of the negotiation.

There are multiple venues for trade negotiations, and the institutional context influences the potential for effective issue linkage. The General Agreement on Tariffs and Trade (GATT) and its successor, the World Trade Organization (WTO), form the core international institution for trade policy. Within the GATT/WTO framework, negotiations consist of comprehensive trade rounds or legalistic dispute settlement procedures (DSP). The former bring together all members and are launched with an opening declaration that sets forth an agenda for discussion of liberalization across sectors. Rounds proceed as a mix of informal bargaining and consensus decisions that culminate in a multilateral agreement with binding commitments. Issue linkages are integral to producing agreement among the diverse economic interests of members. The Uruguay Round formalized more than any prior negotiation the explicit commitment to a package approach, which continues in the Doha Round.

In contrast, linkages are more difficult to sustain in other institutional contexts. The DSP negotiations resemble adjudication and begin with the filing of a legal complaint against a specific policy that leads to either plea bargaining or a negotiated settlement after a panel of judges provides a legal ruling. The narrow focus on the legal status of a trade barrier tends to exclude linkage among issues even while it raises normative pressure. Outside of the GATT/WTO framework, other types of trade negotiations include bilateral talks on either a single policy or a broad agenda of issues. In addition, meetings of regional trade associations share the comprehensive character of trade rounds, but follow different procedures. Asia-Pacific Economic Cooperation (APEC), for example, emphasizes the voluntary nature of participation in nonbinding agreements. In bilateral and regional trade negotiations, linkages are possible, but not always present.

Interests and the Choice to Link Issues

I first consider the domestic and international politics that shape negotiation structures. Since states design institutions in order to address particular policy problems, "institutions are both the objects of state choice and consequential" (Martin and Simmons 2001, 451). In addition to the anticipated functions performed by an institution, path dependency can make the initial choice of rules constrain policy choices even after it no longer serves those interests. For example, in an historical irony, the United States shaped GATT rules in 1947 to create special exceptions to fit protection programs for U.S. agriculture. Later, when U.S. agricultural interests had shifted to favor exports and other countries had developed entrenched agricultural protection, the United States could not easily change these rules.

The decision to establish a linkage in a negotiation agenda raises the possibility of a selection effect. Skeptics caution that international institutions cannot change state behavior on hard issues that raise distributional concerns or strong domestic interest group opposition. From this perspective, states would only agree to link issues in a negotiation agenda when there is no strong opposition to any individual component of the agreement. To address these concerns empirically, I investigate whether institutional linkages promote agreements even when they involve an issue where cooperation is unlikely on that issue alone—agricultural liberalization by Japan and Europe faces opposition by strong domestic lobby groups. In order to account for variation among the agricultural negotiations, I include measures for other characteristics, such as budget and economic conditions, that could make liberalization more or less likely for a given case.

Several factors facilitate the acceptance of issue linkage even when there is strong opposition to agricultural liberalization. First, governments realize that a broad agenda encourages wider participation and greater potential gains from liberalization. Indeed, negotiations over the agendas that launched past trade rounds have consistently added more issues in order to gain the consent of all members. Second, protectionist interests face higher costs to mobilize early in the negotiation. The broad diplomatic coordination required for the meetings that set the negotiation agenda privileges foreign policy elites and national leaders more than sectoral representatives. Although farm lobbies and agriculture ministries in Japan and Europe are likely to resist the inclusion of agriculture on the agenda, they will find it difficult to veto agenda items because the foreign policy decisions at this stage of the negotiation lie outside of their jurisdiction. Moreover, the decisions that shape the structure of the negotiation occur amidst uncertainty about the timing and shape of the future agreement. This is particularly true for trade rounds, which bring together many countries and often last five to eight years. For politically sensitive cases, linkage in a multilateral setting will be more appealing than a bilateral negotiation or legal dispute. The longer time frame as well as the broader context avoids placing the spotlight on a single product, which makes it easier for protectionist interests and diplomats to reluctantly agree to talk about the issue. Facing strong U.S. demands, the EU and Japan may prefer to negotiate their most vulnerable products in a linkage setting rather than in a bilateral or DSP negotiation.

The Uruguay Round illustrates how these factors helped persuade governments to accept an agenda calling for liberalization across all sectors. When negotiators tried to formulate the agenda for a new trade round in 1986, developing countries such as Brazil and India were reluctant to discuss service sector liberalization and intellectual property rights as part of the Uruguay Round. Eventually, however, they agreed to participate because they expected to benefit from liberalization in other areas to be included on the agenda, namely, agricultural and textiles trade. For France and other European states, the incentives were the opposite; potential gains from service sector liberalization persuaded governments to agree to a negotiation agenda including agriculture. During EC decision making for the acceptance of the Uruguay Round agenda, the scope of jurisdiction favored foreign affairs officials over the representatives of specific sectoral interests. The Commission Directorate for External Relations produced initial proposals, and all of the important decisions were discussed in the trade committee and COREPER (the committee composed of heads of delegations) and then forwarded to the General Affairs Council for approval. Nevertheless, agriculture interests were not shut out entirely. Their consent reflected that many in the Commission and national delegations believed that the final agreement would not require substantial changes of the Common Agricultural Policy (CAP). A Commission negotiator for the agriculture group negotiations of the Uruguay Round said, "We knew agriculture might be a problem, but this was not really clear until the mid-term review in 1988. Nobody in Europe thought there could be a negotiation that left out agriculture, but it was hoped that there might not have to be major reforms—like in the Tokyo Round."

Similar logic led Japanese government officials to plead with the U.S. government to address rice market access as an issue in the Uruguay Round rather than in a bilateral negotiation. Yet at the same time, the Diet passed a unanimous resolution against any liberalization of the ban against rice imports. An official from an agricultural interest group explained in an interview that his organization did not oppose the government promise to discuss rice liberalization in the Uruguay Round because his group hoped to get support from France and other countries and thought the talks would go better than if Japan faced the United States alone in bilateral talks. Yet in the end, the Uruguay Round did bring substantial reforms in the agricultural sector as well as in the industrial and service sectors, leading to both an overhaul of CAP and the partial opening of Japan's rice market. In sum, economic interests, the costs of mobilization, and uncertainty about outcomes encourage acceptance of the issue linkage in the agenda despite resistance to liberalization of one component.

Package Negotiations: Institutionalized Cross-Sector Linkage

Issue linkage has long served as a basic tool for political bargains and diplomatic deals. Sebenius (1983, 287) provides the definition that issues are linked "when they are simultaneously discussed for joint settlement." This definition encompasses side-payments, log-rolling bargains, or a formal agenda on a broad range of issues. The focus of this article is on tactical linkages, which combine issues that do not substantively require joint settlement. In such cases, multiple issues are included in the final settlement in an effort to create a balance where both sides gain enough to accept the costs. Trade liberalization, in particular, has relied upon negotiating across a range of products as countries exchange reciprocal concessions. Under what conditions will issue linkage promote agreement?

One challenge for successful linkage is finding complementary issues. Sebenius (1983) points out that simply adding issues does not necessarily promote agreement. Rather, adding a nonnegotiable issue to the agenda can cause the collapse of the entire negotiation. Much of the study of issue linkage focuses on combining issues so that all participants gain from the agreement. A second challenge is the difficulty of convincing all actors to believe that agreement on one issue is conditional on agreement on the other issue. Tactical linkages can be unstable when some participants resist the linkage. Several scholars voice skepticism about issue linkage because of this added credibility problem. Lohmann (1997) counters that it is possible for issue linkage to promote cooperation if actors care sufficiently about future interaction on one of the issue dimensions for this "credibility surplus" to spill over and increase incentives for cooperation across issues. While issue linkage can promote cooperation in some cases, either the wrong combination of issues or an inability to credibly commit to the linkage may undermine the effectiveness of a linkage strategy.

I examine how a particular kind of linkage, *a package negotiation structure*, addresses these two problems. Package negotiations have a formal agenda that combines distinct issues for joint approval or rejection. . . . I focus on the use of package negotiation structure to institutionalize cross-sector issue linkages. These negotiations address agriculture and industry sectoral issues along with other trade topics in a single negotiation. The cross-sector scope of the agenda combines issues to produce overall gains, while the institutional context promotes the credibility of the linkage.

CROSS-SECTOR INTERESTS. Liberalization depends on overcoming the collective action problems and institutional biases at the domestic level that favor protection. For trade policies in general and agricultural issues in particular, those who demand protection have strong incentives and high levels of organization, while those who pay the costs are loosely organized taxpayers and consumers. Protection policies also persist because policy makers with a vested interest in the status quo retain control over decision making. The closed policy communities formed by the ties among farm groups, agriculture ministries, and political committees in Japan, the EU, and France have been described as forming a corporatist relationship. Using issue linkage to mobilize industry groups and to broaden the policy jurisdiction helps to counter both problems.

Cross-sector issue linkage offsets the influence of farmers by engaging interests important to other powerful lobby groups. Japan and the EU must offer concessions in agriculture, while both can gain much from liberalization in the industrial and service sectors. When there is a credible cross-sector linkage, industry lobbies also advocate agricultural liberalization in order to achieve specific gains for industry from conclusion of an overall agreement. Finding domestic allies to support foreign demands has been a critical factor in explaining variation in outcomes across different U.S.–Japan bilateral negotiations. The importance of the expansion of actors has also been widely commented on in studies of European and American politics. . . . In the case of agricultural liberalization, farmers represent the entrenched interest group, and issue expansion offers one route to dilute their influence by forcing competition with other interests.

Not only does issue linkage lead to competition among interest groups, but also among actors across jurisdictional boundaries. The framing of issues in the negotiation shifts the policy discussion from one venue to another in the domestic arena. Studies of domestic institutions have long emphasized the importance of agenda setting given the substantive impact of differences between domestic actors. . . . The view of the problem and preference for a solution will reflect the particular ministry's own bias and interests—the agriculture ministry favors farmer interests, the trade ministry favors industry interests, and the foreign ministry tries to balance national interests with concern for maintaining better foreign relations. Similar differences occur across the boundaries of political committees. To the extent that the negotiation lifts decision making outside of the corporatist ties in the agricultural policy setting, it will create new opportunities to promote agricultural liberalization.

Evidence confirms that the international setting has an impact on the domestic policy jurisdiction. With regard to Japanese trade negotiations, for example, Fukui (1978) argues that the Foreign Ministry influence was greater in the Tokyo Round, while the domestic ministries such as the Ministry of Agriculture had more influence in bilateral negotiations on narrow issues. Similarly, Japanese government decision making during the Uruguay Round brought top officials from five ministries together to coordinate policies. This enabled ministries such as the Ministry of International Trade and Industry (MITI) that typically have no voice on agricultural trade issues to play a role in agricultural policy decisions because these decisions also affected the progress of the entire negotiation.

In the EU, the comparable question centers on which officials in the Council of Ministers shape the negotiation mandate. Although the agriculture ministers meeting in the Agriculture Council dominate decision making for issues directly related to CAP, broader trade policy issues related to negotiations are likely to be addressed by the foreign and trade ministers meeting in the General Affairs Council. Member states opposing agricultural reform prefer to maintain control within the Agriculture Council, while those favoring reform try to push issues into the trade committee or the General Affairs Council. The scope of issues in the negotiation influences which council is likely to take the lead role and which procedures are followed under EU treaty provisions.

INSTITUTIONS AND CREDIBILITY.   Many have pointed to the role of international institutions in facilitating positive linkages that promote cooperation. First, as Keohane (1984, 91) writes, more *quids* make it easier to reach agreement in *quid pro quo* deal making. The institutional context of the GATT/WTO promotes the kind of cross-sector issue linkages discussed above. Equally important, the institutional context adds credibility to the decision to link issues because it makes the decision represent a commitment in an ongoing process of repeated negotiations. Martin (1993, 129) explains, "Deals cut within an institution rather than outside one gain stability because members put increased value on their reputations for living up to agreements." The costs of backing down from a commitment to link issues are greater because such action damages their "ability to reach mutually beneficial cross-issue deals" in the future. The institutional context also endows the linkage with greater legitimacy by providing a common set of procedures and norms that justify use of the linkage strategy.

Publicizing the issue linkage as a formal agenda accomplishes two purposes: first, it creates a focal point from which negotiators are reluctant to retreat; second, it signals to domestic groups that the success of any part of the negotiation will depend upon reaching an overall agreement. The formal agenda of the negotiation establishes whether talks will address multiple sectors and whether agreement on the entire range of issues will form a single package. Considerable time and hard bargaining go behind the creation of the agenda, and this inhibits frequent renegotiation. Subsequent behavior by states reinforces the linkage. By obstructing discussions in one negotiating group to match the deadlock in another negotiating group, a state can force parallel progress on different issues. The combination of the formal agenda and the support for each agenda issue by some participating states creates a more credible cross-sector linkage. Information that liberalization for any sector is conditional on agreement on all issues provides an incentive for interest groups and officials to closely follow all parts of the negotiation rather than just the part related to their own sector. As a credible signal, the institutionalization of the issue linkage in the agenda and procedures of the negotiation strengthens the incentives for those who gain from free trade to lobby against protectionist interests.

LINKAGE HYPOTHESIS. *The more institutionalized the linkage among multiple sectors in a negotiation, the more likely that the negotiation will liberalize agricultural trade barriers.*

Different levels of institutionalization form a weak or strong linkage among issues. The two key institutional features concern whether the agenda commits to liberalization of multiple sectors and whether procedures call for a single agreement with binding commitments on all of the agenda issues. An agenda that only calls for liberalization of one sector does not have any institutionalized cross-sector issue linkage. An agenda that includes multiple issues but provides for flexibility to reach settlements on each issue separately forms a weak linkage. In contrast, a package negotiation structure establishes a strong linkage by explicitly mandating that the negotiation will proceed in an all-or-nothing approach that ties together deals on multiple sectors and issues to culminate in signing a single agreement. Comparison of two GATT trade rounds and one APEC negotiation illustrates these differences. The agendas for the two GATT negotiations, the Tokyo Round (1973–1979) and the Uruguay Round (1986–1994), as well as the Kuala Lumpur APEC ministerial meeting in 1998, gave a mandate for talks on a wide range of issues including both primary and industrial sectors and other rules related to economic activities, such as investment regulations and product standards. Nevertheless, the agenda and procedures of each negotiation present observable differences in the commitment to the cross-sector linkage.

Weak institutionalization of the cross-sector linkage characterized the APEC "*Early Voluntary Sectoral Liberalization*" agenda. APEC trade liberalization talks jointly address trade sectors ranging from agriculture to automobiles. The principles of voluntarism and flexibility, however, explicitly allowed countries to set their own pace for the timing and scope of liberalization in any particular sector. Likewise, bilateral negotiations may also address multiple issues, but they often do not bind them together with a formal agenda. For both APEC and comprehensive bilateral negotiations, tradeoffs across issues in the negotiation are possible. The lack of a formal commitment to the linkage, however, makes it more difficult to signal that concessions in one area are necessary for gains in another.

There was a moderate linkage between agricultural and industrial issues in the Tokyo Round. The declaration that set the agenda for the Tokyo Round stated that the negotiation "shall cover . . . both industrial and agricultural products," but also added flexibility by urging that the negotiations should "take account of the special characteristics and problems in this [agricultural] sector." It established several negotiation groups that produced agreements from which nations could pick and choose. . . . The agricultural group had a particularly weak linkage with the rest of the round. Subgroups for dairy, meat, and grains discussed separate commodity agreements rather than general principles for agricultural policy. Moreover, at the U.S. initiative, which wanted to include the Soviet Union (a major purchaser on grains markets that was not a GATT member), the talks on grains were primarily conducted outside the Tokyo Round in the context of the International Wheat Council. These talks ultimately failed to produce a new commodity agreement on grains, and states were able choose whether to join the dairy and meat commodity agreements regardless of their position on other issues in the round. In sum, the agenda statement and the procedures that allowed stand-alone agreements provided only moderate institutionalization of an issue linkage.

In contrast, a strong cross-sector linkage characterized the Uruguay Round. The Punta del Este Declaration that set the agenda for the Uruguay Round called for 15 groups to negotiate issues ranging from industrial goods to agricultural goods to reform of GATT trade rules. In the declaration, the term *single undertaking* referred to the commitment to decide jointly on all the parts of the negotiation and supported the refrain among negotiators that "nothing is agreed until everything is agreed." Two later events further strengthened the linkage credibility. First, some Latin American states walked out of the 1990 Brussels meeting, declaring that they would not negotiate anything if the United States, EU, and Japan would not agree to a substantive agricultural liberalization package. Then, at the end of 1991, the GATT Director-General Arthur Dunkel independently produced a draft agreement binding all parts of the negotiations into a single text. A procedural step reinforced the concept of a single undertaking: the final agreement texts would form a single charter for a new trade organization such that accepting all agreements was a condition of membership. Given this strong linkage, one would expect more liberalization in the Uruguay Round than in other negotiation fora.

On the other hand, less liberalization is expected when there is no cross-sector linkage. The U.S.–Japan talks on beef and citrus in 1983 and the U.S.–EU talks on wine in 1991 are examples of single-sector negotiations that focused exclusively on agricultural products. This observable variation in the agenda, rules, and procedures across negotiations in terms of the sectoral scope and institutionalization of the commitment to a linkage approach facilitates testing the linkage hypothesis. . . .

Qualitative Evidence for Cross-Sector Linkage

A closer look at a few key negotiations supports the aggregate evidence that a strong cross-sector issue linkage promotes liberalization by broadening the mobilization of industry and expanding the policy jurisdiction. In the Uruguay Round negotiation, Japan tried to argue that the need for food security should justify price supports and import quotas for staple foods. The government adamantly refused to consider allowing rice imports, even when U.S. and GATT officials made a special plea in the fall of 1990 before a critical meeting of the trade round. More than half of Japanese farmers grow rice, and it had been considered a political taboo to discuss market opening. After the failure of this meeting, however, export industries began lobbying for agricultural trade liberalization as the credibility of the cross-sector linkage increased. In December 1991, when Dunkel put forward his draft agreement calling for joint conclusion of negotiations on all sectors, Japan's leading business association endorsed it in its entirety and urged the government to be more flexible on agricultural talks. Senior LDP politicians began to issue public statements that Japan would have to accept some kind of partial liberalization. In government discussions, MITI became concerned about the agricultural negotiations blocking the round and urged concessions for the sake of the Uruguay Round. Faced with internal divisions over the gains promised by the round and the necessity to accept agricultural liberalization as part of the package, Japan made concessions on even the most important agricultural item—rice.

The rice-opening agreement was the result of a compromise proposal submitted by the GATT official heading the agriculture negotiating group. Although rice would remain heavily protected, the government agreed to end the ban against imports and to guarantee the purchase of five percent of domestic consumption as imports, with provisions for a gradual increase and tariffication plan. Prior to making the decision to accept rice imports, Prime Minister Morihiro Hosokawa said to his staff, "Japan cannot become the criminal that wrecks the Uruguay Round" (Karube 1997, 104). In his public announcement, he called for Japan to endure sacrifices in difficult areas such as agriculture for the sake of the free trade system and successful conclusion to the Uruguay Round. Similar arguments were used in Diet debates as well. The following exchange during a Diet committee meeting is illustrative: a senior LDP politician, Kōsuke Hori, argued that even partial liberalization would violate the Diet resolutions for complete self-sufficiency in rice. He urged the government to renegotiate the proposal with a tougher position. Hosokawa responded that it was necessary to evaluate the Uruguay Round negotiation as a whole and that, in a multilateral negotiation, it was unreasonable for Japan to insist that it could not import even a grain of rice.

The reforms achieved in the context of the Uruguay Round also demonstrate the influence of issue linkage to promote liberalization in Europe. In 1986, the EU only agreed to discuss agricultural liberalization because of its strong interest in the financial and service sector. Thereafter, the linkage of agricultural talks with service and industrial goods talks, which was reinforced by the long deadlock over agricultural issues, persuaded EU ministers that internal reform of CAP was necessary to conclude the round. A veto of the agriculture agreement was narrowly avoided as the EU followed the package approach in its own decision making by not voting on the agricultural component separately from the Uruguay Round. France would not invoke a veto in the Council of Ministers without German support, which was not forthcoming. German industrial groups, along with the EU-level industry association UNICE (Union of Industrial and Employers' Confederations of Europe), strongly advocated an agricultural agreement for the sake of successful conclusion of the trade round. Moreover, French interests in the industrial and service sector agreements also favored the successful conclusion of the Uruguay Round, and employer groups began to pressure the French government to compromise. The package approach helped gain EU acceptance of an agricultural agreement that had faced initial public rejection and threat of a veto by France.

In contrast, a weakly institutionalized cross-sector linkage contributed to the inability of the United States to persuade Japan to make any concession for fish or forestry liberalization during the 1998 Kuala Lumpur meeting of APEC. Based on the principle of voluntarism and lacking any kind of dispute mechanism, APEC is widely viewed as a negotiation forum with low levels of institutionalization. The agenda for the 1998 meeting included a cross-sector linkage calling for liberalization of nine priority sectors and a pledge to pursue liberalization of six additional sectors the following year. The linkage was weak, however, because the package was labeled "early voluntary sectoral liberalization," and the agenda made explicit reference to flexibility for the liberalization of any given sector with difficult circumstances. The United States along with several Southeast Asian nations insisted that Japan must contribute to liberalization on all nine sectors, including fisheries and forestry. Rising trade dependence made Japan especially vulnerable to U.S. pressure in 1998 as declining demand in recession-struck Asia and Japan left the U.S. market as a crucial outlet for Japanese exports.

Resistance from the forestry and fisheries lobbies in Japan was strong, however, and the negotiation did not force tradeoffs with other interests. The Ministry of Foreign Affairs along with a top Cabinet official backed the Ministry of Agriculture's opposition to any concession. Protests from business groups that had been heard during the Uruguay Round, when rice stood as an obstacle to agreement, did not materialize. Taking a unified position, the common refrain by Japanese officials and politicians was that the appropriate forum for discussing tariffs was the WTO, where binding commitments could be made, not APEC. The voluntary nature of commitments reduced expectations for the likely gains from the negotiation and any sense of necessity for painful cuts. In the end, no agreement was reached. Although the agenda lacked an institutionalized all-or-nothing approach, in fact, the choice came down to moving forward on the package as a whole or not at all. The U.S. government reported that Japan had blocked the agreement by refusing to participate in fishery and forestry liberalization, while officials of Japan and some of the other member governments emphasized that the provisions for flexibility and voluntarism in APEC meant that there was no obligation to participate. The weakly institutionalized linkage allowed for different interpretations over which sectors had to be included, dooming any chance for liberalization of a sensitive sector. . . .

CONCLUSION

Institutionalized cross-sector linkages promote liberalization in the face of strong opposition from perhaps the most powerful interest groups—Japanese and European farmers. For both Japan and the EU, a strong linkage changes the predicted negotiation outcome from an expectation of minor or no policy change to an expectation of major liberalization. Case study evidence shows that linking agricultural and industrial issues builds the prospects for liberalization by shifting the aggregation of domestic interests. Without a strong issue linkage, the united strength of the farm lobby and jurisdictional autonomy of the agriculture ministries reinforce the status quo protection policies. Presence of a linkage increases negotiation stakes, and this leads to more lobbying by industrial export interests against agricultural protection as well as a greater role for bureaucrats and politicians outside of the agricultural policy community. Even while taking into account other factors such as threats and budget constraints, negotiation structure remains one of the most important determinants of policy outcomes.

When narrow interests defend the status quo, broadening the scope of actors and interests can provide the impetus for change. A cross-sector issue linkage that is institutionalized as a package deal combines issues with a credible linkage to make it politically possible for leaders to choose liberalization over the protests of influential lobbies. This highlights the possibility for the structure of an international negotiation to compensate for the political market for protection in the domestic arena.

The advanced industrial nations spend over $300 billion a year subsidizing their farmers. Consumers in rich countries and farmers in poor countries are among the leading beneficiaries of liberalization, but they have been unable to bring change on their own. International negotiations represent a critical venue for adding pressure to reduce the subsidies and trade barriers. While it is unlikely that any negotiation will bring an end to agricultural protection, understanding what leverage is more effective will help to reform some of the most trade distortionary policies in the world economy.

REFERENCES

Fukui, Haruhiro. 1978. "The GATT Tokyo Round: The Bureaucratic Politics of Multilateral Diplomacy." In *The Politics of Trade: U.S. and Japanese Policymaking for the GATT Negotiations*, ed. Michael Blaker. New York: Columbia University East Asian Institute, 75–169.

Hudec, Robert. 1993. *Enforcing International Trade Law: The Evolution of the Modern GATT Legal System*. Salem, NH: Butterworth.

Karube, Kensuke. 1997. *Nichibei kome kōshō [U.S.–Japan Rice Negotiations]*. Tokyo: Chukō shinshō.

Keohane, Robert. 1984. *After Hegemony: Cooperation and Discord in the World Political Economy*. Princeton, NJ: Princeton University Press.

Lohmann, Susanne. 1997. "Linkage Politics." *Journal of Conflict Resolution* 41 (1): 38–67.

Martin, Lisa. 1993. "International and Domestic Institutions in the EMU Process." *Economics and Politics* 5 (2): 125–44.

Martin, Lisa, and Beth Simmons. 2001. "Theories and Empirical Studies of International Institutions." In *International Institutions: An International Organization Reader*. Cambridge, MA: MIT Press, 437–65.

Milner, Helen. 1997. *Interests, Institutions, and Information: Domestic Politics and International Relations*. Princeton, NJ: Princeton University Press.

Putnam, Robert. 1988. "Diplomacy and Domestic Politics: The Logic of Two-Level Games." *International Organization* 42 (3): 427–60.

Sebenius, James. 1983. "Negotiation Arithmetic: Adding and Subtracting Issues and Parties." *International Organization* 37 (2): 281–316.

II

HISTORICAL
PERSPECTIVES

A truly international economy first emerged during the "long sixteenth century," the period from approximately 1480 to 1650. In its earliest form, the modern international economy was organized on the basis of mercantilism, a doctrine asserting that power and wealth were closely interrelated and were legitimate national interests. Thus, wealth was necessary for power, and power could be used to obtain wealth. Power is a relative concept because one country can gain it only at the expense of another; thus, mercantilist nations perceived themselves to be locked in zero-sum interactions in the international economy.

During this period, countries pursued their interests with a variety of policies intended to expand production and wealth at home while denying similar capabilities to others. Six policies were of nearly universal importance. First, countries sought to prevent gold and silver, common mercantilist measures of wealth, from being exported. At the beginning of the sixteenth century, Spain declared the export of gold or silver punishable by death. Similarly, France declared the export of coined gold and silver illegal in 1506, 1540, 1548, and 1574, thereby demonstrating the difficulty of enforcing such laws. Second, regulations (typically, high tariffs) were adopted to limit imports to necessary raw materials. Importing raw materials was desirable because it lowered prices at home and thereby reduced costs for manufacturers. By limiting imports of manufactured and luxury items, countries sought to stimulate production at home while reducing it abroad. Third, exports of manufactured goods were encouraged for similar reasons. Fourth, just as they sought to encourage imports of raw materials, countries aimed to limit the export of these goods so as to both lower prices at home and limit the ability of others to develop a manufacturing capability of their own. Fifth, exports of technology—including both machinery and skilled artisans—were restricted in order to inhibit potential foreign competitors. Finally, many countries adopted navigation laws mandating that a certain percentage of their foreign trade had to be carried in native ships. This last trade regulation was intended to stimulate the domestic shipping and shipbuilding industries—both of which were necessary resources for successful war making.

By the early nineteenth century, mercantilist trade restrictions were coming under widespread attack, particularly in Great Britain. Drawing on the writings of Adam Smith and David Ricardo, Richard Cobden and other Manchester industrialists led the fight for free trade, which culminated in 1846 in the abolition of the "Corn Laws" (restrictions on grain imports), the last major mercantilist impediment to free trade in Britain (see Schonhardt-Bailey, Reading 5). Other countries soon followed England's example. Indeed, under Britain's leadership, Europe entered a period of free trade that lasted from 1860 to 1879. However, this trend toward freer trade was reversed in the last quarter of the nineteenth century. The purported causes of this reversal are many, including the decline of British hegemony, the onset of the first Great Depression (of 1873–1896), and the new wave of industrialization on the Continent, which led to protection for domestic manufacturers from British competition (see Gourevitch, Reading 6). For whatever reason—and the debate continues even today—by 1890, nearly all the major industrialized countries except Great Britain had once again imposed substantial restrictions on imports.

Coupled with this trend toward increased protection was a new wave of international investment and formal colonialism (see Acemoglu, Reading 7). Britain had already begun to expand its holdings of foreign territory during the period of free trade, and after 1880, it was joined by Germany and France. In 1860, Great Britain possessed 2.5 million square miles of colonial territory, and France, only .2 million square miles; Germany had not yet entered the colonial race. By 1899, Britain's holdings had expanded to 9.3 million square miles, France's to 3.7 million, and Germany's to 1.0 million, an expansion that occurred primarily in Africa and the Pacific. In 1876, slightly less than 11 percent of Africa and nearly 57 percent of Polynesia were colonized, yet by 1900, more than 90 percent of Africa and almost 99 percent of Polynesia were controlled by European colonial powers and the United States.

World War I, which many analysts believe to have been stimulated by the race for colonies, and in particular by Germany's aggressive attempt to catch up with Great Britain, destroyed the remaining elements of the Pax Britannica. The mantle of leadership, which had previously been borne by Britain, was now divided between Britain and the United States. Yet neither country could—or desired to—play the leadership role previously performed by Britain.

World War I was indeed a watershed in American international involvement. The terrible devastation caused by the war in Europe served to weaken the traditional world powers, while it brought the United States a period of unexpected prosperity. The Allies, which were short of food and weapons, bought furiously from American suppliers. To finance their purchases, they borrowed heavily from American banks and, once the United States entered the war, from the U.S. government. As a result, American factories and farms hummed as the war dragged on; industrial production nearly doubled during the war years. Moreover, because the war forced the European powers to neglect many of their overseas economic activities, American exporters and investors were also able to move into areas they had never before influenced. When the war began, the United States was a net debtor of the major European nations; by the time it ended, however, it was the world's principal lender and all the Allies were deeply in debt to American banks and the U.S. government.

Despite the position of political and economic leadership that the United States shared with Great Britain after World War I, Washington rapidly retreated into its traditional inward orientation. To be sure, many American banks and corporations continued to expand abroad very rapidly in the 1920s and the country remained an important world power, but the United States refused to join the League of Nations or any of the other international organizations created in the period. American tariff levels, which had been reduced on the eve of World War I, were once again raised. The reasons for the country's post–World War I isolationism, as it is often called, are many and controversial. Chief among them were the continued insularity of major segments of the American public, which was traditionally inward-looking in political and economic matters; the resistance to American power of such European nations as Great Britain and France; and widespread revulsion at the apparently futile deaths that had resulted from involvement in the internecine strife of the Old World.

Whatever the reasons for the isolationism of the 1920s, these tendencies were heightened as the world spiraled downward into depression after 1929. In the Smoot-Hawley Act of 1930, the United States dramatically increased its tariffs, and by 1933 the world was engulfed in bitter trade and currency conflicts. In 1933, desperate to encourage domestic economic recovery, U.S. president Franklin Roosevelt significantly devalued the dollar, thus effectively sounding the death knell of what remained of the nineteenth-century international economic order.

Even as the Depression wore on, interactions among some of the world's major economic powers began to change. One of the more dramatic changes took place in the United States in the 1930s, as the Roosevelt administration began attempting to reverse the country's protectionist tendencies. One of the more important ways in which this was accomplished was by changing the institutions that make American trade policy in such a way as to give them a less protectionist bias (see reading 8, Bailey, Goldstein, and Weingast). This change in American trade policy-making institutions was but the beginning of a much broader trend, both in the United States and in the rest of the world, away from protectionism and toward a more open international economy. The trend was interrupted by World War II, but it began with the recasting of interests, interactions, and institutions of the 1930s.

During the nearly four centuries summarized here, the international economy underwent several dramatic transformations. From a closed and highly regulated mercantilist system, the international economy evolved toward free trade in the middle of the nineteenth century. However, after a relatively brief period of openness, the international economy reversed direction and, starting with the resurgence of formal imperialism and accelerating after World War I, once again drifted toward closure. This historical survey highlights the uniqueness of the contemporary international political economy, which is the focus of the rest of this book. This survey also raises a host of analytic questions, many of which appear elsewhere in the book as well. Particularly important here is the question of what drives change in the international economy. In the readings that follow, Cheryl Schonhardt-Bailey highlights the role of interest group lobbying and electoral politics; Peter Alexis Gourevitch examines interest groups and domestic institutions; Daron Acemoglu emphasizes how interactions between colonizers and colonized could have lasting effects on development; and Michael Bailey, Judith Goldstein, and Barry R. Weingast explore the impact of both institutions and interests in the remaking of American trade policy after the Great Depression.

5

Free Trade: The Repeal of the Corn Laws

CHERYL SCHONHARDT-BAILEY

In 1846, England unilaterally dismantled its mercantilist trade restrictions (known as the Corn Laws) and adopted free trade in what is broadly recognized as the single most important economic liberalization in modern world history. Cheryl Schonhardt-Bailey presents an interest-based argument to explain the repeal of the Corn Laws by the world's first industrial nation. She documents a struggle for political power between a rising manufacturing and export industry and a declining agricultural sector controlled by the landed aristocracy. Industrialists wanted to repeal the Corn Laws to increase foreign consumption of British manufactured products; if foreigners were allowed to sell grain to Great Britain, they could earn the foreign exchange to buy British manufactured goods. Agricultural elites, by contrast, saw repeal of the Corn Laws as a direct threat to their interests because the trade barriers kept the price of the grain they produced artificially high. With each side cloaking its interests in terms of national welfare and national security, it took a gifted leader, Prime Minister Robert Peel, to maneuver through Britain's political institutions in order to craft a workable compromise.

150 YEARS ON, WHY REPEAL REMAINS RELEVANT

At four o'clock in the morning of Saturday, 16 May 1846, Members of the British House of Commons voted 327 to 229 to abolish tariff protection for agriculture. Economists, political scientists, historians and sociologists have spilled much ink attempting to explain this historic decision. That the repeal of the protectionist Corn Laws was a crucially significant event in British history is undisputed, but exactly *why* repeal was significant is a question that produces a variety of responses. Britain's unilateral move to free trade is said to have signified the triumph of Manchester School liberal thinking; marked the birth of its international economic hegemony; launched a new form of British imperialism; paved the way for the disintegration of the Conservative party for a generation; been the catalyst for class conflict between the rising industrial middle class and the politically dominant landed aristocracy; given testimony to the organization, political astuteness and tenacity of the pro-repeal lobby, the Anti-Corn Law League; been an inevitable outcome of changes in the financial system and industrial structure; and illustrated the dramatic and abrupt change of mind of one absolutely pivotal individual—Prime Minister

Sir Robert Peel. Researchers will undoubtedly continue to debate the significance of repeal, as well as its causes and consequences. Indeed, over the past twenty years researchers have applied a number of new methods and new theories to explain Britain's move to free trade, and this renewed interest shows no sign of abating. At its core, the question that continues to puzzle and intrigue us is, why did Britain unilaterally open its domestic market to free trade—and particularly free trade in agriculture? . . .

THE CORN LAWS, IN BRIEF

Government regulation of exports and imports of corn was well-established long before the nineteenth century. The Corn Laws of the seventeenth and eighteenth centuries had a dual purpose—they sought to prevent "grain from being at any time, either so dear that the poor cannot subsist, or so cheap that the farmer cannot live by growing of it."[1] The Napoleonic Wars brought a fundamental change in the history of the Corn Laws. During the war years, agriculturists had enjoyed high grain prices, but with the peace, prices fell dramatically. In response, Parliament enacted the Corn Law of 1815, which allowed free entry when the price of corn was above 80s. per quarter, and prohibited entry when the price fell below 80s. Some argue that this new legislation, unlike that of the earlier Corn Laws, was "defiantly protective." 'It sought to fasten on a country at peace the protection furnished by a generation of war."[2] However, others maintain that fear of scarcity drove government policy. Rapid population growth and a dependence upon foreign corn are said to have justified a policy of self-sufficiency based on concerns for national security. Evidence for both interpretations may be found, . . . as we shall see below. . . .

In brief, 1815, 1828 and 1842 were the years of significant changes in the Corn Laws, although numerous other minor (and often temporary) modifications were also made in the regulation of corn during the early nineteenth century. Paralleling the history of Corn Law legislation were major demographic and economic changes that cut against the fabric of protection for food. From 1811 to 1841 the population of Great Britain increased from 12.6 million to 18 million and British farmers were becoming less able to provide sufficient supplies for the home market. This said, while Britain had not been self-sufficient in corn since the early 1760s, British agriculturists "still managed to feed every year on the average all except about 700,000 and as late as

---

1. C. Smith, *Tracts on the Corn Trade and Corn Laws*, II.72, as quoted in C.R. Fay, *The Corn Laws and Social England* (Cambridge University Press, 1932), p. 34.
2. Fay, p. 35.

1831–1840, all except about 1,050,000 of the population."[3] A second factor proved more fatal to the Corn Laws—the growth of British manufacturing industry and export trade, particularly in textiles. More particularly, as the industrial prosperity and export boom of the early 1830s began to crack, industrialists became increasingly vocal about "unfair" protection enjoyed by the agriculturists. Beginning in 1836, an economic downturn together with a series of poor harvests, sparked the industrialists into action. High food prices and unemployment gave impetus both to the middle and working classes, the former organized as the Anti-Corn Law League and the latter as the Chartist movement.

THE LEAGUE MACHINE

The Anti-Corn Law League was the first modern and national-level political pressure group to emerge in Britain. It began in London in 1836 as the Anti-Corn Law Association, but by 1838 had found its natural base in Manchester. The leaders of the League were manufacturers and professionals engaged in export trade, most of whom were concentrated in the county of Lancashire. Foremost among its leaders were two cotton textile manufacturers—Richard Cobden and John Bright. In the course of the struggle against the Corn Laws, both were to become Members of Parliament, Cobden for Stockport and Bright for Rochdale. Another key MP in the Corn Law struggle was Charles Villiers, Member for Wolverhampton. It was Villiers who became famous for his annual motions for repeal of the Corn Laws, which began in 1838 and continued through 1846.

Historians refer to the League as "the most impressive of nineteenth-century pressure groups, which exercised a distinct influence on the repeal of the Corn Laws in 1846."[4] It was called the *league machine*, whose organization "presents one of the first examples of a recurring feature of modern political life, the highly organized political pressure group with its centralized administration and its formidable propaganda apparatus."[5] . . . The two key features of the League's operational strategy were its nation-wide propaganda and electoral registration campaigns. The League raised substantial subscriptions to finance its propaganda campaign. It maintained a small army of workers and speakers, who toured the country distributing numerous tracts (most notably, the famous *Anti-Corn Law Circular*) and giving thousands of speeches on the virtues of free trade and the evils of protection. The registration campaign

3. W. H. Chaloner, "Introduction to the Second Edition," in Archibald Prentice, *History of the Anti-Corn Law League*, vols. I & II (London: Frank Cass & Co. [1853], 1968). p. x.

4. Anthony Howe, *The Cotton Masters, 1830–1860* (Oxford University Press, 1984).

5. Norman McCord, *The Anti-Corn Law League 1838–1846* (London: George Allen & Unwin, 1958), p. 187.

was, however, the League's tool for replacing protectionist landowners in Parliament with free trade supporters. After electoral losses in 1841–1842, the League focused its energy and resources on returning a free trade majority in the anticipated general parliamentary election of 1848. Its leaders' tactical strategy included manipulating the voter registers and employing propaganda devices on existing voters. Looking toward the 1848 election, the League sought to add as many free traders and delete as many protectionists from these registers as possible. The latter they accomplished by making objections against thousands of protectionists at the annual revisions of the registers. The former required a different tactic—exploiting a loophole in the 1832 Electoral Reform Act (which effectively enfranchised the middle class). This loophole was the forty-shilling county property qualification, which Bright referred to as "the great constitutional weapon which we intend to wield."[6] . . . While the 40s. qualification had been a feature of the system since 1430, the increase in county seats from 188 to 253 (an increase from roughly 29% to 38% of the total seats) magnified the importance of this overlooked loophole in the 1832 Reform Act. The League used the 40s. qualification to create several thousand new free trade voters in county constituencies with large urban electorates, constituencies whose representation was increased by the Reform Act. Leaguers went so far as to urge parents, wanting to create a nest egg for a son, to make him a freeholder: in Cobden's words, "it is an act of duty, for you make him thereby an independent freeman, and put it in his power to defend himself and his children from political oppression." . . . In spite of the Appeal Court ruling in February 1845 and January 1846 that votes created by the 40s. freehold qualification were valid, protectionists continued to challenge the constitutionality of the League's registration campaign, . . . and Leaguers continued to defend their activities. . . .

The propaganda and registration campaigns, moreover, were brought together to further the political success of the League. As its agents distributed propaganda tracts to every elector in 24 county divisions and 187 boroughs, they submitted to the League headquarters consistent and complete reports on the electorate in their districts. These reports provided the League with a comprehensive picture of the electoral scene throughout England, thereby allowing it much greater knowledge of, and control over, electoral districts than either the Conservatives or Liberals possessed. . . . The earlier distribution of propaganda tracts thus provided the League with an extensive database from which they could inflict political pressure on Members of Parliament, who were concerned with their bids for re-election in the anticipated 1848 election.

6. Unless otherwise noted, all quotes are from writings and statements reprinted in Cheryl Schonhardt-Bailey, ed., *Free Trade: The Repeal of the Corn Laws* (London: Thoemmes Continuum, 1995).

In 1844, as the League's success—particularly that of its registration campaign in the counties—became more conspicuous, a defensive Anti-League (or, Agricultural Protection Society) emerged. . . . This group of protectionist landowners and farmers did not, however, ever obtain the momentum or backing of the League. . . . In financial terms, while the League grew from a £5,000 annual fund in 1839 to one of £250,000 in 1845, the latter year saw the core of the Anti-League (the Essex Agricultural Protection Society) scraping together the paltry sum of £2,000 to fund its campaign. . . .

THE ISSUES AT STAKE

From today's perspective, the high drama and intense conflict that surrounded the question of protection for grain seems a bit exaggerated. One must bear in mind, however, that during the early nineteenth century the working and middle classes spent a large percentage of their income on food, and central to their food consumption was bread. The price of bread was therefore key to the cost of living. Yet the importance of the price of bread, in itself, does not reveal why the Corn Laws created such fury in British political life. Underlying the cry for a "cheap loaf" was the economic tension between a rising manufacturing and export industry and a declining agricultural sector, which translated into a struggle for political power between the industrial middle class and the landed aristocracy. The language of the debates, not surprisingly, focused predominantly on the economic issues and the "interests" who gained or lost from protection—although, ample evidence exists of middle class resentment towards the landed aristocracy for their "political oppression." To the industrialists, the Corn Laws were a form of pilfering by the landed aristocracy. They argued that high food prices, the direct consequence of restrictions on food imports, resulted in near-famine conditions among the poor. Manufacturing districts were particularly hard hit since foreigners, limited in their capacity to export grain to Britain, were unable to import British manufactured goods. Free traders provided widely varying estimates of the cost of protection for agriculture—in 1838, Villiers estimated the annual cost at £15.6 million . . . and in 1839, James Deacon Hume (Secretary to the Board of Trade) estimated the annual cost at £36 million . . . G. R. Porter's estimate for 1840 (including duties for silk) was £53.6 million, . . . while an Anti-Corn Law League circular calculated the total cost of the Corn Laws from 1815 to 1841 as £1,365 million. . . . It was argued that landowners, as rentiers, were the primary if not sole beneficiaries of this legislated protection. Defenders of the Corn Laws retorted that cheap bread (the effect of repeal) would result in lower wages for workers, thus revealing that the "true" motive of the industrialists was to obtain cheaper labour. Additionally, they argued that agriculture was a unique and ultimately essential industry and therefore deserved to be protected from destruction. Overlaying this clash of interests were arguments concerning aggregate national welfare, such as the effect of repeal on government revenue and the nation's security.

One way to lend order to the arguments for and against repeal is to group them into two broad categories—those relating to aggregate national welfare, and those associated with the interests of groups or classes.

The Corn Laws and National Welfare

The debate over the nation's welfare highlighted four main issues: (1) unilateralism versus reciprocity; (2) the threat of foreign competition in manufactures; (3) self-sufficiency as a national security concern; and (4) the effect of repeal on government revenue.

The theory of free trade in the 1840s was, it should be emphasized, just that—*theory*. No hard evidence existed as to its effects, particularly on its trading partners. While Britain had, after Peel's 1842 tariff reforms, liberalized most of its trade in manufactures, it had not endorsed a universal policy of free trade. One critical question of repeal, then, was—would other countries follow Britain's lead and open their home markets to British manufacturing exports? That is, what would be the effect of unilateral free trade, with no demands for reciprocal tariff reductions? Free traders such as Hume maintained that others would indeed follow Britain's lead: "I feel the strongest confidence that if we were to give up our protective system altogether, it would be impossible for other countries to retain theirs much longer." Protectionists challenged this claim, arguing that because foreign countries saw infant industry protection as the road to industrialization, reciprocal free trade would never emerge. . . .

Some historians have imputed a more sinister motive to Britain's move to free trade—that of staving off the competition in manufactures from other countries. Statements from contemporaries lend some weight to this hypothesis. For instance, Nassau Senior wrote that free trade would "increase the productiveness of our labour" and "diminish, or perhaps destroy, the rivalry of many of our competitors in third markets," . . . and Hume noted that "(al) together, I conceive that the reduction in the price of food, and particularly the admission of it from abroad, must tend to prevent other countries from being able to surpass us in manufactures."

Because free trade meant relying on foreigners for Britain's food supply, the nation's security became a topic of concern. National security remains to this day one of the more compelling arguments for protection for agriculture, since many countries (island nations perhaps more than most) strongly resist forfeiting food self-sufficiency. Anti-Leaguers argued that international specialization of production—with Britain producing manufactures and other countries producing food—was too risky. . . . If export markets were to dry up or agricultural exporters were to withhold supplies (such as during time of war), how would Britain obtain its food? Free traders responded by labelling this a bogus argument for protection: a League spokesman retorted that "(i)n

1810, when we were engaged in war with almost every European power, we imported 1,491,000 quarters of wheat, nearly half a million of which were obtained from France alone" . . . and Porter wrote that "(t)he dread of dependence upon foreigners for food is, indeed, a childish dread; and we act like children in our choice of a remedy for the evil." . . .

The final argument which related to the nation as a whole centers on the contribution of duties to the government's revenue. Although Peel instituted the first peace time income tax in 1842, the government still relied on customs for 38% of its revenue in 1846. The question then became, to what extent would the repeal of duties on corn harm the public purse? Some protectionists pointed to the £800 million national debt, claiming that free trade would put Britain at risk of failing to meet the interest payments on its debt. . . . J. R. McCulloch and Senior, both defenders of free trade, were sensitive to the reliance of the government on customs revenue. . . . Senior advocated levying duties only for the purposes of revenue, while McCulloch argued for the replacement of the sliding scale with a moderate, fixed duty. A fixed duty would prevent speculation and would protect agriculture as a "business," but it would also bolster the government's revenue. Villiers, a strong advocate of repeal, argued that the Corn Laws actually operated to reduce revenue from customs by increasing the cost of production (presumably by increasing wage costs) and thereby limiting foreign trade. The Corn Laws therefore reduced excise duties by limiting consumption through higher prices. Insofar as customs and excise provided 75% of government revenue, Villiers maintained that savings would be had by repeal. Free traders also tended to link the revenue issue to the importance of bolstering British exports, and thereby ensuring the future prosperity of the country—a topic to be discussed below.

In Whose Interests?

Both the industrialists and the landowners claimed to be defending the interests of the workers and farmers. Both sought to present their case in terms of the common man and concern for public welfare. Morality and ethics were often woven into their economic arguments in an effort to pitch the battle in terms of good versus evil. Free traders were particularly adept at this form of argumentation, while the protectionists found the morality of protection a difficult case to defend, except by treating agriculture as a "unique" industry (see below). Villiers set the tone in 1838 by speaking of the principle of freedom in trade: "For what is this freedom, but liberty for persons to provide, and the community to enjoy, that which is needful and desired at the lowest cost and at the greatest advantage?" Some free traders carried the morality of free trade further, arguing that free trade constituted (1) a "civil liberty," as it insured the right to buy in the cheapest market and sell in the dearest, (2) "political justice," or a justice which shows no favouritism or partisanship, (3) "peace" in bringing peace between nations and peace between classes, and (4) "civilization," or the bringing of man near man, for mutual help and solace. . . .

The League, moreover, sought and obtained the backing of the religious community. . . . In an effort to regain the moral high ground, protectionists lamely argued that the League denied "the liberty . . . of expressing publicly a difference of opinion," endangered the peace of society, and failed to tell the "truth." . . .

Yet, however persuaded the common man may have been by these appeals to a higher order, economic interests lay at the heart of the arguments for and against repeal. These arguments centred on six distinct issues: (1) the relationship between bread prices and wages; (2) class conflict; (3) the taxation of landowners relative to other groups; (4) the extent to which farmers, as opposed to landowners, benefited from protection; (5) agriculture as a "unique" industry deserving of protection; and (6) the effect of the Corn Laws on the export trade.

If one topic could be labelled as central to the debates between free traders and protectionists, it was the relationship between bread prices and wages. Chartists suspected that the true motive of the industrialists was to obtain lower wages through repeal, and the protectionists were happy to feed this suspicion. League circulars and Anti-League pamphlets were filled with claims and counter-claims about the effect of bread prices on workers wages. . . . Villiers, in a House of Commons speech in 1845, remarked that he had looked "over all the publications of the Protection Society, and he found that the leading topic, from beginning to end, was that if you made food cheap you would reduce the wages of the people, and that if you made it dear you would increase their wages. Was he to understand, then, that there were still some persons in that house who maintained this doctrine?" The writings of the political economists were more informative on the price/wage issue. According to Torrens, . . . the Corn Laws prevented workers from obtaining higher wages, which would reflect their higher productivity relative to foreign labour, thereby dismissing the claim of the protectionists. On the same lines, Porter argued that high food prices did not yield high wages, but just the reverse. . . . High prices for food were said to have lessened the demand for labour and therefore lessened wages (which rests on the argument that demand for food is price inelastic, and that the demand for other goods—notably manufactured goods—is more elastic with respect to food prices). James Pennington rejected the hoopla associated with this issue, arguing that free traders and protectionists alike exaggerated the effects of repeal on corn prices (and on domestic agriculture more generally). . . . He doubted that the quantity of foreign grain available to Britain would be great enough to bring about any significant fall in prices. In defence of the protectionist case, Alison argued that repeal would not lower food prices, but rather food prices would initially fall but subsequently rise when foreigners became monopoly suppliers of grain to Britain. . . . Moreover, labourers would not benefit from lower grain prices because the increased labour supply (resulting from agricultural decline) would release labour into industry and thereby force wages down.

A second issue—indeed, for some historians, the *key* issue—was class conflict between the industrial middle class and the landed aristocracy. While Chartism raised the pitch of class conflict . . . , further Parliamentary reform was so remote at this time as to place working class conflict in the shadow of the main struggle. Perhaps one of the clearest statements of the class conflict between the industrialists and the aristocracy was in a speech by Bright in Covent Garden. . . . According to the *Times*, the theatre was filled to overflowing and the popular speaker was received "with deafening cheers." Bright's incendiary speech spoke of the free trade struggle as "a struggle between the numbers, wealth, comforts, the all in fact, of the middle and industrious classes, and the wealth, the union, and the sordidness of a large section of the aristocracy of this empire." The League presented itself as a defender not only of the middle class but also the working class, and even tenant farmers, against the landed interest. Landowners, in turn, maintained that the manufacturing class constituted only a small percentage of the population, and it was only by enjoying an innate skill at organization that this class had acquired influence beyond their share. Free traders vehemently rejected that the battle for repeal was for the sole benefit of industry. . . . A more sophisticated variant of the landowners' counter-attack is seen in E. S. Cayley's address in 1844. . . . Cayley called upon Adam Smith to argue that because land is (internationally) immobile and capital is (internationally) mobile, landowners had an "abiding interest in the country in which they live" since they could not pack up their land and move it to another country. Thus, the landowners were able to turn on its head the industrialists' implicit threat of capital flight to the continent if repeal was not forthcoming. . . .

A third issue is closely related to class conflict—namely, the supposed heavy tax burden incurred by the landowners. Defenders of the Corn Laws suggested that because landowners paid disproportionately large taxes, they were entitled to protection as compensation for their tax burden. . . . Free traders challenged landowners to demonstrate this "excessive tax burden," and claimed instead that landowners paid less than their fair share of taxes. League circulars repeatedly pointed out that the land tax had not increased since 1692, while land values (and therefore, rents) had increased seven-fold. . . .

As mentioned earlier, the League endeavoured to present itself as a national movement, one that included the interests not only of industrialists but also of farmers and farm labourers. To this end, Cobden shifted the focus of the League away from the theme of urban distress (with Peel shouldering "individual responsibility" for the present distress of the country) to an attack on the rental income of landowners. . . . Cobden asserted that "if the corn law operates to cause a profit at all, it also operates to put that profit into the pockets of the landlord." The argument put to tenant farmers was that it was the landlord, not the farmer, who benefited from high food prices. As food prices rose, so too would the value of land. Thus, while in the short term farmers may enjoy the benefits of higher prices for their produce, in the longer term, as they renewed their leases, these benefits would evaporate with higher rental charges. . . . One protectionist attempted to use the League's own data (presented to manufacturers to illustrate the high prices they were forced to pay because of the Corn Laws) to demonstrate the inconsistency in its argument. Ignoring the question of rents, George Game Day argued that the League could not, on the one hand, tell manufacturers about the high prices they paid as a result of food tariffs, and on the other hand persuade farmers that they did not benefit from the high prices associated with the Corn Laws. . . . Other landowners challenged the rent argument directly, claiming that landowners received only three-percent return (rent) while capitalists received from 20% to 50% interest on their investments. . . .

A fifth argument was often used as a fallback position by the agriculturists. Not unlike farmers in present day Japan, Europe and the United States, British farmers and landowners wholly believed that agriculture was a unique industry, and thereby entitled to special privileges. Its status as producer of the nation's food supply meant that it could not be allowed to decline, since this would create a dangerous reliance on untrustworthy foreigners for food (thus relating back to the earlier national security argument). Protectionists argued that agriculture provided employment for a large share of the workforce, in addition to providing a constant and reliable food supply. They defended their stance by quoting Adam Smith: "The land is the greatest, most important, and most durable part of the wealth of every extensive country," whereas "capital . . . is . . . a very precarious and uncertain possession, till some part of it has been secured and realised in the cultivation . . . of its lands." . . . Free traders decried the basis of this claim, maintaining that agriculture was no more and no less than any other business, which, if unprofitable, closes up shop and reallocates its resources elsewhere. . . . Responding to the question of whether free trade ought to apply equally to food as it does to manufactures, Hume responded bluntly, "I conceive myself, if I were compelled to choose, that food is the last thing upon which I would attempt to place any protection."

A final issue of interests touches on the core feature of industrialization—a rising industrial sector and a declining agricultural sector. The middle classes, and eventually many MPs, recognized that the present and future of the country's wealth depended on industry, and not on agriculture. When asked, "Do you consider the wealth of England to be caused and maintained by her commercial and manufacturing industry?" Hume replied, "Certainly: if meant as in contradistinction from the produce of the soil. . . . (H)aving always had the land, but not the trade, I must conceive that the increase of our riches arises from the trade and not from the land." Landowners were, however, undeterred. They argued that home trade was more important than export trade. Because foreign trade was often the victim of other countries' tariffs on British goods, it could not be relied upon for the future welfare of the country. In the meantime, since the export industry employed only a fraction of the workforce, the merits of a policy which served predominantly the interests of this fraction would be unfair to the rest of the population. . . .

CONCLUSION

. . . Peel argued that the principle of free trade was welfare-enhancing because it would: (1) allow Britain to retain its pre-eminence in world trade (thereby staving off foreign competition); (2) be a winning strategy, regardless of whether or not other countries reciprocated with lower duties; and (3) not result in a loss to public revenue, as the trade and industrial prosperity combined with the new income tax would offset the lost income from duties. Quoting League sources, Peel explained why he believed that the prosperity following the 1842 reduction of duties could not continue without further liberalization.

At the heart of Peel's speech was a plea to the opposing manufacturing and agricultural interests to accept a policy of mutual concessions. He urged manufacturers to forfeit their remaining protective duties on woollens, linen, silks, and other manufactured goods, in order to adhere to the general rule that no duty should exceed 10% (15% for silks). He introduced a further simplification of the tariff code and reduced tariffs on a number of other items (shoes, spirits, sugar). His greatest hurdle, however, was to gain the support of the agriculturists. Duties on certain foods (butter, cheese, hops and fish) would be reduced while those on others (meat, beef, port, potatoes, vegetables, bacon, and other non-grains) would be abolished. And, of course, grain protection would be abolished as of 1849. After discounting the link between bread prices and wages, Peel sought to address two issues associated with the clash of interests. First, in regard to class conflict, Peel argued that agitation had grown to such an extent that the government had no option but to act to appease the industrial and working classes. Second, the "heavy" financial burden of the landowning classes was lessened by a number of incentives to agriculturists—a consolidation of the highways system, relief to rural districts from pauperism, a number of expenses shifted from the counties to the consolidated fund, and finally loans for agricultural improvements at moderate interest rates.

If one were to view each of the issues associated with national welfare and economic interests as potentially competing explanations for repeal, one would find evidence to support almost every one of them in Peel's speech. It is therefore not surprising that modern interpretations of repeal show no signs of converging on a single explanation.

6

International Trade, Domestic Coalitions, and Liberty: Comparative Responses to the Crisis of 1873–1896

PETER ALEXIS GOUREVITCH

Peter Alexis Gourevitch examines the impact of the Great Depression of 1873–1896 on the trade policies and political coalitions of four countries. During this time period, Germany and France adopted high tariffs on both agricultural and industrial products, Great Britain maintained its historic policy of free trade, and the United States protected industry but not agriculture. In attempting to explain this pattern of response, Gourevitch compares four alternative hypotheses: economic explanations, emphasizing domestic interests; political system explanations, focusing on domestic institutions; international system explanations, emphasizing interactions among countries; and economic ideology explanations. He concludes that domestic interests and domestic institutions provide the most persuasive account of these four cases. Gourevitch not only gives a detailed and informative history of the trade policies of the four great economic powers of the late nineteenth century, he also provides a useful evaluation of the relative importance of some crucial factors in international political economy.

For social scientists who enjoy comparisons, happiness is finding a force or event which affects a number of societies at the same time. Like test-tube solutions that respond differently to the same reagent, these societies reveal their characters in divergent responses to the same stimulus. One such phenomenon is the present worldwide inflation/depression. An earlier one was the Great Depression of 1873–1896. Technological breakthroughs in agriculture (the reaper, sower, fertilizers, drainage tiles, and new forms of wheat) and in transportation (continental rail networks, refrigeration, and motorized shipping) transformed international markets for food, causing world prices to fall. Since conditions favored extensive grain growing, the plains nations of the world (the United States, Canada, Australia, Argentina, and Russia) became the low cost producers. The agricultural populations of Western and Central Europe found themselves abruptly uncompetitive.

In industry as well, 1873 marks a break. At first the sharp slump of that year looked like an ordinary business-cycle downturn, like the one in 1857. Instead, prices continued to drop for over two decades, while output continued to rise. New industries—steel, chemicals, electrical equipment, and shipbuilding—sprang up, but the return on capital declined. As in agriculture, international competition became intense. Businessmen everywhere felt the crisis, and most of them wanted remedies.

The clamour for action was universal. The responses differed: vertical integration, cartels, government contracts, and economic protection. The most visible response was tariffs. . . .

Although the economic stimuli were uniform, the political systems forced to cope with them differed considerably. Some systems were new or relatively precarious: Republican France, Imperial Germany, Monarchical Italy, Reconstruction America, Newly Formed Canada, Recently Autonomous Australia. Only Britain could be called stable. Thirty years later when most of these political systems had grown stronger, most of the countries had high tariffs. The importance of the relation between the nature of the political system and protection has been most forcefully argued by Gershenkron in *Bread and Democracy in Germany*. The coalition of iron and rye built around high tariffs contributed to a belligerent foreign policy and helped to shore up the authoritarian Imperial Constitution of 1871. High tariffs, then, contributed to both world wars and to fascism, not a minor consequence. It was once a commonly held notion that free trade and democracy, protection and authoritarianism, went together. . . .

These basic facts about tariff levels and political forms have been discussed by many authors. What is less clear, and not thoroughly explored in the literature, is the best way to understand these outcomes. As with most complex problems, there is no shortage of possible explanations: interest groups, class conflict, institutions, foreign policy, ideology. Are these explanations all necessary though, or equally important? This essay seeks to probe these alternative explanations. It is speculative; it does not offer new information or definitive answers to old questions. Rather, it takes a type of debate about which social scientists are increasingly conscious (the comparison of different explanations of a given phenomenon) and extends it to an old problem that has significant bearing on current issues in political economy—the interaction of international trade and domestic politics. The paper examines closely the formation of tariff policy in late nineteenth-century Germany, France, Britain, and the United States, and then considers the impact of the tariff policy quarrel on the character of each political system.

EXPLAINING TARIFF LEVELS

Explanations for late nineteenth-century tariff levels may be classified under four headings, according to the type of variable to which primacy is given.

1. *Economic Explanations.* Tariff levels derive from the interests of economic groups able to translate calculations of economic benefit into public policy. Types of economic explanations differ in their conceptualization of groups (classes vs. sectors vs. companies) and of the

strategies groups pursue (maximizing income, satisficing, stability, and class hegemony).

2. *Political System Explanations.* The "statement of the groups" does not state everything. The ability of economic actors to realize policy goals is affected by political structures and the individuals who staff them. Groups differ in their access to power, the costs they must bear in influencing decisions, prestige, and other elements of political power.

3. *International System Explanations.* Tariff levels derive from a country's position in the international state system. Considerations of military security, independence, stability, or glory shape trade policy. Agriculture may be protected, for example, in order to guarantee supplies of food and soldiers, rather than to provide profit to farmers (as explanation 1 would suggest).

4. *Economic Ideology Explanations.* Tariff levels derive from intellectual orientations about proper economic and trade policies. National traditions may favor autarchy or market principles; faddishness or emulation may induce policy makers to follow the lead given by successful countries. Such intellectual orientations may have originated in calculations of self-interest (explanation 1), or in broader political concerns (explanation 2) or in understandings of international politics (explanation 3), but they may outlive the conditions that spawned them.

These explanations are by no means mutually exclusive. The German case could be construed as compatible with all four: Junkers and heavy industry fought falling prices, competition, and political reformism; Bismarck helped organize the iron and rye coalition; foreign policy concerns over supply sources and hostile great powers helped to create it; and the nationalist school of German economic thought provided fertile ground for protectionist arguments. But were all four factors really essential to produce high tariffs in Germany? Given the principle that a simple explanation is better than a complex one, we may legitimately try to determine at what point we have said enough to explain the result. Other points may be interesting, perhaps crucial for other outcomes, but redundant for this one. It would also be useful to find explanations that fit the largest possible number of cases.

Economic explanation offers us a good port of entry. It requires that we investigate the impact of high and low tariffs, both for agricultural and industrial products, on the economic situation of each major group in each country. We can then turn to the types of evidence—structures, interstate relations, and ideas—required by the other modes of reasoning. Having worked these out for each country, it will then be possible to attempt an evaluation of all four arguments.

GERMANY

Economic Explanations

What attitude toward industrial and agricultural tariffs would we predict for each of the major economic groups in German society, if each acted according to its economic interests? A simple model of German society contains the following groups: small peasants; Junkers (or estate owners); manufacturers in heavy, basic industries (iron, coal, steel); manufacturers of finished goods; workers in each type of industry; shopkeepers and artisans; shippers; bankers; and professionals (lawyers, doctors). What were the interests of each in relation to the new market conditions after 1873?

Agriculture, notes Gerschenkron, could respond to the sharp drop in grain prices in two ways: modernization or protection. Modernization meant applying the logic of comparative advantage to agriculture. Domestic grain production would be abandoned. Cheap foreign grain would become an input for the domestic production of higher quality foodstuffs such as dairy products and meat. With rising incomes, the urban and industrial sectors would provide the market for this type of produce. Protection, conversely, meant maintaining domestic grain production. This would retard modernization, maintain a large agricultural population, and prolong national self-sufficiency in food.

Each policy implied a different organization for farming. Under late nineteenth-century conditions, dairy products, meats, and vegetables were best produced by high quality labor, working in small units, managed by owners, or long-term leaseholders. They were produced least well on estates by landless laborers working for a squirearchy. Thus, modernization would be easier where small units of production already predominated, as in Denmark, which is Gerschenkron's model of a modernizing response to the crisis of 1873. The Danish state helped by organizing cooperatives, providing technology, and loaning capital.

In Germany, however, landholding patterns varied considerably. In the region of vast estates east of the Elbe, modernization would have required drastic restructuring of the Junkers' control of the land. It would have eroded their hold over the laborers, their dominance of local life, and their position in German society. The poor quality of Prussian soil hindered modernization of any kind; in any case it would have cost money. Conversely, western and southern Germany contained primarily small- and medium-sized farms more suited to modernization.

Gerschenkron thinks that the Danish solution would have been best for everyone, but especially for these smaller farmers. Following his reasoning, we can impute divergent interests to these two groups. For the Junkers, protection of agriculture was a dire necessity. For the small farmers, modernization optimized their welfare in the long run, but in the short run protection would keep them going; their interests, therefore, can be construed as ambivalent.

What were the interests of agriculture concerning industrial tariffs? Presumably the agricultural population sought to pay the lowest possible prices for the industrial goods that it consumed, and would be opposed to high industrial tariffs. Farmers selling high quality produce to the industrial sector prospered, however, when that sector prospered, since additional income was spent disproportionately on meat and eggs. Modernizing producers might therefore be receptive to tariff and other economic policies which helped industry. For grain, conversely, demand was less elastic. Whatever the state of the industrial economy, the Junkers would be able to sell their output provided that foreign sources were prevented from undercutting them. Thus, we would expect the Junkers to be the most resolutely against high industrial tariffs, while the smaller farmers would again have a less clear-cut interest.

Neither were the interests of the industrial sector homogenous. Makers of basic materials such as iron and steel wanted the producers of manufactured products such as stoves, pots and pans, shovels, rakes, to buy supplies at home rather than from cheaper sources abroad. Conversely the finished goods manufacturers wanted cheap materials; their ideal policy would have been low tariffs on all goods except the ones that they made.

In theory, both types of industries were already well past the "infant industry" stage and would have benefited from low tariffs and international specialization. Indeed, German industry competed very effectively against British and American products during this period, penetrating Latin America, Africa, Asia, and even the United States and United Kingdom home markets. Low tariffs might not have meant lower incomes for industry, but rather a shift among companies and a change in the mix of items produced.

Nevertheless, tariffs still offered certain advantages even to the strong. They reduced risk in industries requiring massive investments, like steel; they assured economies of scale, which supported price wars or dumping in foreign markets; and to the extent that cartels and mergers suppressed domestic production, they allowed monopoly profits. Finally, iron and steel manufacturers everywhere faced softening demand due to the declining rate of railroad building, not wholly offset by shipbuilding. As we shall see, steelmen were in the vanguard of protectionist movements everywhere, including Britain (their only failure).

All industrialists (except those who sold farm equipment) had an interest in low agricultural tariffs. Cheap food helped to keep wages down and to conserve purchasing power for manufactured goods.

The interests of the industrial work force were pulled in conflicting directions by the divergent claims of consumer preoccupations and producer concerns. As consumers, workers found any duties onerous, especially those on food. But as producers, they shared an interest with their employers in hav-

TABLE 1 Interests of Different Groups in Relation to Industrial and Agricultural Tariffs (Germany)

AGRICULTURAL TARIFFS

		HIGH	LOW
INDUSTRIAL TARIFFS	HIGH	The Outcome: High Tariffs Small Farmers	Heavy Industry Workers in Heavy Industry
	LOW	Junkers	Workers in FM Finished Manufacturers

ing their particular products protected, or in advancing the interests of the industrial sector as a whole.

Shippers and their employees had an interest in high levels of imports and exports and hence in low tariffs of all kinds. Bankers and those employed in finance had varied interests according to the ties each had with particular sectors of the economy. As consumers, professionals and shopkeepers, along with labor, had a general interest in keeping cost down, although special links (counsel to a steel company or greengrocer in a steel town) might align them to a high-tariff industry.

This pattern of group interests may be represented diagrammatically. Table 1 shows each group's position in relation to four policy combinations, pairing high and low tariffs for industry and agriculture. The group's intensity of interest can be conveyed by its placement in relation to the axis: closeness to the origin suggests ambiguity in the group's interest; distance from the intersection suggests clarity and intensity of interest.

Notice that no group wanted the actual policy outcome in Germany—high tariffs in both sectors. To become policy, the law of 1879 and its successors required trade-offs among members of different sectors. This is not really surprising. Logrolling is expected of interest groups. Explanation 1 would therefore find the coalition of iron and rye quite normal.

Nevertheless, a different outcome—low tariffs on both types of goods—also would have been compatible with an economic interest group explanation. Logrolling could also have linked up those parts of industry and agriculture that had a plausible interest in low tariffs: finished goods manufacturers, shippers and dockworkers, labor, professionals, shopkeepers, consumers, and farmers of the West and South. This coalition may even have been a majority of electorate, and at certain moments managed to impose its policy preferences. Under Chancellor Georg von Caprivi (1890–1894), reciprocal trade treaties were negotiated and tariffs lowered. Why did this coalition lose over the long run? Clearly because it was weaker, but of what did this weakness consist?

Political Explanations

One answer looks to aspects of the political system which favored protectionist forces at the expense of free traders: institutions (weighted voting, bureaucracy); personalities who intervened on one side or another; the press of other issues (socialism, taxation, constitutional reform, democratization); and interest group organization.

In all these domains, the protectionists had real advantages. The Junkers especially enjoyed a privileged position in the German system. They staffed or influenced the army, the bureaucracy, the judiciary, the educational system, and the Court. The three-class voting system in Prussia, and the allocation of seats, helped overrepresent them and propertied interests in general.

In the late 1870s, Bismarck and the emperor switched to the protectionists' side. Their motives were primarily political. They sought to strengthen the basic foundations of the conservative system (autonomy of the military and the executive from parliamentary pressure; a conservative foreign policy; dominance of conservative social forces at home; and preservation of the Junkers). For a long time, industry and bourgeois elements had fought over many of these issues. Unification had helped to reconcile the army and the middle classes, but many among the latter still demanded a more liberal constitution and economic reforms opposed by the Junkers. In the 1870s Bismarck used the Kulturkampf to prevent a revisionist alliance of Liberals, Catholics, and Federalists. In the long run, this was an unsatisfactory arrangement because it made the government dependent on unreliable political liberals and alienated the essentially conservative Catholics.

Tariffs offered a way to overcome these contradictions and forge a new, conservative alliance. Industrialists gave up their antagonism toward the Junkers, and any lingering constitutionalist demands, in exchange for tariffs, anti-Socialist laws, and incorporation into the governing majority. Catholics gave way on constitutional revision in exchange for tariffs and the end of the Kulturkampf (expendable because protection would now carry out its political function). The Junkers accepted industry and paid higher prices for industrial goods, but maintained a variety of privileges, and their estates. Peasants obtained a solution to their immediate distress, less desirable over the long run than modernization credits, but effective nonetheless. Tariff revenues eased conflicts over tax reform. The military obtained armaments for which the iron and steel manufacturers received the contracts. The coalition excluded everyone who challenged the economic order and/or the constitutional settlement of 1871. The passage of the first broad protectionist measure in 1879 has aptly been called the "second founding" of the Empire.

Control of the Executive allowed Bismarck to orchestrate these complex trade-offs. Each of the coalition partners had to be persuaded to pay the price, especially that of high tariffs on the goods of the other sector. Control of foreign policy offered instruments for maintaining the bargain once it had been struck. . . . The Chancellor used imperialism, nationalism, and overseas crises to obscure internal divisions, and particularly, to blunt middle-class criticism. Nationalism and the vision of Germany surrounded by enemies, or at least harsh competitors, reinforced arguments on behalf of the need for self-sufficiency in food and industrial production, and for a powerful military machine. . . .

The protectionists also appear to have organized more effectively than the free traders. In the aftermath of 1848, industry had been a junior partner, concerned with the elimination of obstacles to a domestic German free market (such as guild regulations and internal tariffs). Its demands for protection against British imports were ignored. . . . The boom of the 1860s greatly increased the relative importance of the industrialists. After 1873, managers of heavy industry, mines and some of the banks formed new associations and worked to convert old ones: in 1874 the Association of German Steel Producers was founded; in 1876, the majority of the Chambers of Commerce swung away from free trade, and other associations began to fall apart over the issue. These protectionist producers' groups were clear in purpose, small in number, and intense in interest. Such groups generally have an easier time working out means of common action than do more general and diffuse ones. Banks and the state provided coordination among firms and access to other powerful groups in German society.

The most significant of these powerful groups—the Junkers—became available as coalition allies after the sharp drop in wheat prices which began in 1875. Traditionally staunch defenders of free trade, the Junkers switched very quickly to protection. They organized rapidly, adapting with remarkable ease, as Gerschenkron notes, to the *ère des foules*. Associations such as the Union of Agriculturalists and the Conservative Party sought to define and represent the collective interest of the whole agricultural sector, large and small, east and west. Exploiting their great prestige and superior resources, the Junkers imposed their definition of that interest—protection as a means of preserving the status quo—on the land. To legitimate this program, the Junker-led movements developed many of the themes later contained in Nazi propaganda: moral superiority of agriculture; organic unity of those who work the land; anti-Semitism; and distrust of cities, factories, workers, and capitalists. . . .

The alternative (Low/Low) coalition operated under several political handicaps. It comprised heterogeneous components, hence a diffuse range of interests. In economic terms, the coalition embraced producers and consumers, manufacturers and shippers, owners and workers, and city dwellers and peasants. Little in day to day life brought these elements together, or otherwise facilitated the awareness and pursuit of common goals; much kept them apart—property rights, working conditions, credit, and taxation. The low tariff groups also differed on other issues such as religion, federalism, democratization of the Constitution, and constitutional control of the Army and Executive. Unlike the High/High alliance, the low tariff coalition had to overcome its diversity without help from the Executive. Only during the four years of Caprivi was the chancellor's office sympathetic to low tariff politics, and Caprivi was very isolated from the court, the kaiser, the army, and the bureaucracy.

Despite these weaknesses, the low tariff alliance was not without its successes. It did well in the first elections after the "re-founding" (1881), a defeat for Bismarck which . . . drove him further toward social imperialism. From 1890, Caprivi directed a series of reciprocal trade negotiations leading to tariff reductions. Caprivi's ministry suggests the character of the programmatic glue needed to keep a low-tariff coalition together: at home, a little more egalitarianism and constitutionalism (the end of the antisocialist laws); in foreign policy, a little more internationalism—no lack of interest in empire or prestige, but a greater willingness to insert Germany into an international division of labor.

International System Explanations

A third type of explanation for tariff levels looks at each country's position in the international system. Tariff policy has consequences not only for profit and loss for the economy as a whole or for particular industries, but for other national concerns, such as security, independence, and glory. International specialization means interdependence. Food supplies, raw materials, manufactured products, markets become vulnerable. Britain, according to this argument, could rely on imports because of her navy. If Germany did the same, would she not expose her lifeline to that navy? If the German agricultural sector shrank, would she not lose a supply of soldiers with which to protect herself from foreign threats? On the other hand, were there such threats? Was the danger of the Franco-British-Russian alliance an immutable constituent fact of the international order, or a response to German aggressiveness? This brings us back to the Kehr-Wehler emphasis on the importance of domestic interests in shaping foreign policy. There were different ways to interpret the implications of the international system for German interests: one view, seeing the world as hostile, justified protection; the other, seeing the world as benevolent, led to free trade. To the extent that the international system was ambiguous, we cannot explain the choice between these competing foreign policies by reference to the international system alone.

A variant of international system explanations focuses on the structure of bargaining among many actors in the network of reciprocal trade negotiations. Maintenance of low tariffs by one country required a similar willingness by others. One could argue that Germany was driven to high tariffs by the protectionist behavior of other countries. A careful study of the timing of reciprocal trade treaties in this period is required to demonstrate this point, a type of study I have been unable to find. The evidence suggests that at least in Germany, the shift from Caprivi's low tariff policy to Bernhard Bülow's solidarity bloc (protection, naval-building, nationalism, antisocialism) did not come about because of changes in the behavior of foreign governments. Rather, the old Bismarckian coalition of heavy industry, army, Junkers, nationalists, and conservatives mobilized itself to prevent further erosion of its domestic position.

Economic Ideology

A fourth explanation for the success of the protectionist alliance looks to economic ideology. The German nationalist school, associated with Friedrich List, favored state intervention in economic matters to promote national power and welfare. Free trade and laissez-faire doctrines were less entrenched than they were in Britain. According to this explanation, when faced with sharp competition from other countries, German interests found it easier to switch positions toward protection than did their British counterparts. This interpretation is plausible. The free trade policies of the 1850s and 1860s were doubtless more shallowly rooted in Germany and the tradition of state interventionism was stronger.

All four explanations, indeed, are compatible with the German experience: economic circumstances provided powerful inducements for major groups to support high tariffs; political structures and key politicians favored the protectionist coalition; international forces seemed to make its success a matter of national security; and German economic traditions helped justify it. Are all these factors really necessary to explain the protectionist victory, or is this causal overkill? I shall reserve judgement until we have looked at more examples.

FRANCE

The French case offers us a very different political system producing a very similar policy result. As with Germany, the causes may explain more than necessary. The High/High outcome (Table 1) is certainly what we would expect to find looking at the interests of key economic actors. French industry, despite striking gains under the Second Empire and the Cobden-Chevalier Treaty, was certainly less efficient than that of other "late starters" (Germany and the United States). Hence manufacturers in heavy industry, in highly capitalized ones, or in particularly vulnerable ones like textiles had an intense interest in protection. Shippers and successful exporters opposed it.

Agriculture, as in Germany, had diverse interests. France had no precise equivalent to the Junkers; even on the biggest farms the soil was better, the labor force freer, and the owners less likely to be exclusively dependent on the land for income. Nonetheless, whether large or small, all producing units heavily involved in the market were hard hit by the drop in prices. The large proportion of quasi-subsistence farmers, hardly in the market economy, were less affected. The prevalence of small holdings made modernization easier than in Prussia, but still costly. For most of the agricultural sector, the path of least resistance was to maintain past practice behind high tariff walls.

As we would expect, most French producer groups became increasingly protectionist as prices dropped. In the early 1870s Adolphe Thiers tried to raise tariffs, largely for revenue purposes, but failed. New associations demanded tariff revision. In 1881, the National Assembly passed the first general tariff measure, which protected industry more than agriculture. In the same year American meat products were barred as unhealthy. Sugar received help in 1884, grains and meats in the tariffs of 1885 and 1887. Finally, broad coverage was given to both agriculture and industry in the famous Méline Tariff of 1892. Thereafter, tariffs drifted upwards, culminating in the very high tariff of 1910.

This policy response fits the logic of the political system explanation as well. Universal suffrage in a society of small property owners favored the protection of units of production rather than consumer interests. Conflict over non-tariff issues, although severe, did not prevent protectionists from finding each other. Republican, Royalist, Clerical, and anti-Clerical protectionists broke away from their free trade homologues to vote the Méline Tariff. Méline and others even hoped to reform the party system by using economic and social questions to drive out the religious and constitutional ones. This effort failed but cross-party majorities continued to coalesce every time the question of protection arose and high tariffs helped reconcile many conservatives to the Republic.

In France, protection is the result we would expect from the international system explanation: international political rivalries imposed concern for a domestic food supply and a rural reservoir of soldiers. As for the economic ideology explanation, ideological traditions abound with arguments in favor of state intervention. The Cobden-Chevalier Treaty had been negotiated at the top. The process of approving it generated no mass commitment to free trade as had the lengthy public battle over the repeal of the Corn Laws in Britain. The tariffs of the 1880s restored the *status quo ante*.

Two things stand out in the comparison of France with Germany. First, France had no equivalent to Bismarck, or to the state mechanism which supported him. The compromise between industry and agriculture was organized without any help from the top. Interest groups and politicians operating through elections and the party system came together and worked things out. Neither the party system, nor the constitution, nor outstanding personalities can be shown to have favored one coalition over another.

Second, it is mildly surprising that this alliance took so long to come about— perhaps the consequence of having no Bismarck. It appears that industry took the lead in fighting for protection, and scored the first success. Why was agriculture left out of the Tariff of 1881 (while in Germany it was an integral part of the Tariff of 1879), when it represented such a large number of people? Why did it take another eleven years to get a general bill? Part of the answer may lie in the proportion of people outside the market economy; the rest may lie in the absence of leaders with a commanding structural position working to effect a particular policy. In any case, the Republic eventually secured a general bill, at about the same time that the United States was also raising tariffs.

GREAT BRITAIN

Britain is the only highly industrialized country which failed to raise tariffs on either industrial or agricultural products in this period. Explanation 1 appears to deal with this result quite easily. British industry, having developed first, enjoyed a great competitive advantage over its rivals and did not need tariffs. International specialization worked to Britain's advantage. The world provided her with cheap food; she supplied industrial products in exchange and made additional money financing and organizing the exchange. Farmers could make a living by modernizing and integrating their units into this industrial order. Such had been the logic behind the repeal in the Corn Laws in 1846.

Upon closer inspection, British policy during the Great Depression seems less sensible from a materialist viewpoint. Conditions had changed since 1846. After 1873, industry started to suffer at the hands of its new competitors, especially American and German ones. Other countries began to substitute their own products for British goods, compete with Britain in overseas markets, penetrate the British domestic market, and erect tariff barriers against British goods. Britain was beginning that languorous industrial decline which has continued uninterrupted to the present day.

In other countries, industrial producers, especially in heavy industry, led agitation for protection in response to the dilemma of the price slump. Although some British counterparts did organize a Fair Trade league which sought protection within the context of the Empire (the policy adopted after World War I), most industrialists stayed with free trade.

If this outcome is to be consistent with explanation 1, it is necessary to look for forces which blunted the apparent thrust of international market forces. British producers' acceptance of low tariffs was not irrational if other ways of sustaining income existed. In industry, there were several. Despite Canadian and Australian tariff barriers, the rest of the Empire sustained a stable demand for British goods; so did British overseas investment, commercial ties, and prestige. International banking and shipping provided important sources of revenue which helped to conceal the decline in sales. Bankers and shippers also constituted a massive lobby in favor of an open international economy.

To some degree, then, British industry was shielded from perceiving the full extent of the deterioration of her competitive position.

In agriculture, the demand for protection was also weak. This cannot be explained simply by reference to 1846. Initially the repeal of the Corn Laws affected farming rather little. Although repeal helped prevent sharp price increases following bad harvests, there was simply not enough grain produced in the world (nor enough shipping capacity to bring it to Europe) to provoke a major agricultural crisis. The real turning point came in the 1870s, when falling prices were compounded by bad weather. Why, at this moment, did the English landowning aristocracy fail to join its Junker or French counterpart in demanding protection? The aristocrats, after all, held a privileged position in the political system; they remained significantly overrepresented in the composition of the political class, especially in the leadership of Parliament; they had wealth and great prestige.

As with industry, certain characteristics of British agriculture served to shield landowners from the full impact of low grain prices. First, the advanced state of British industrial development had already altered the structure of incentives in agriculture. Many landowners had made the change from growing grain to selling high quality foodstuffs. These farmers, especially dairymen and meat producers, identified their interests with the health of the industrial sector, and were unresponsive to grain growers' efforts to organize agriculture for protection.

Second, since British landowners derived their income from a much wider range of sources than did the Junkers, the decline of farming did not imply as profound a social or economic disaster for them. They had invested in mining, manufacturing, and trading, and had intermarried with the rising industrial bourgeoisie. Interpenetration of wealth provided the material basis for their identification with industry. This might explain some Tories' willingness to abandon protection in 1846, and accept that verdict even in the 1870s.

If repeal of the Corn Laws did not immediately affect the British economy, it did profoundly influence politics and British economic thought in ways, following the logic of explanations 2 and 4, that are relevant for explaining policy in the 1870s. The attack on the Corn Laws mobilized the Anti-Corn Law League (which received some help from another mass movement, the Chartists). Over a twenty-year period, the League linked the demand for cheap food to a broader critique of landed interest and privilege. Its victory, and the defection of Peel and the Tory leadership, had great symbolic meaning. Repeal affirmed that the British future would be an industrial one, in which the two forms of wealth would fuse on terms laid down for agriculture by industry. By the mid-1850s even the backwoods Tory rump led by Disraeli had accepted this; a decade later he made it the basis for the Conservative revival. To most of the ever larger electorate, free trade, cheap food, and the reformed political system were inextricably linked. Protection implied an attack on all the gains realized since 1832. Free trade meant freedom and prosperity. These identifications inhibited the realization that British economic health might no longer be served by keeping her economy open to international economic forces.

Finally, British policy fits what one would expect from analysis of the international system (explanation 3). Empire and navy certainly made it easier to contemplate dependence on overseas sources of food. It is significant that protection could be legitimated in the long run only as part of empire. People would do for imperialism what they would not do to help one industry or another. Chamberlain's passage from free trade to protection via empire foreshadows the entire country's actions after World War I.

UNITED STATES

Of the four countries examined here, only the United States combined low-cost agriculture and dynamic industry within the same political system. The policy outcome of high industrial tariffs and low agricultural ones fits the logic of explanation 1. Endowed with efficient agriculture, the United States had no need to protect it; given the long shadow of the British giant, industry did need protection. But despite its efficiency (or rather because of it) American agriculture did have severe problems in this period. On a number of points, it came into intense conflict with industry. By and large, industry had its way.

> *Monetary policy* The increasing value of money appreciated the value of debt owed to Eastern bankers. Expanding farm production constantly drove prices downward, so that a larger amount of produce was needed to pay off an ever increasing debt. Cheap money schemes were repeatedly defeated.
>
> *Transportation* Where no competition among alternative modes of transport or companies existed, farmers were highly vulnerable to rate manipulation. Regulation eventually was introduced, but whether because of the farmers' efforts or the desire of railroad men and other industrialists to prevent ruinous competition—as part of their "search for order"—is not clear. Insurance and fees also helped redistribute income from one sector to the other.
>
> *Tariffs* The protection of industrial goods required farmers to sell in a free world market and buy in a protected one.
>
> *Taxation* Before income and corporate taxes, the revenue burden was most severe for the landowner. Industry blocked an income tax until 1913.
>
> *Market instability* Highly variable crop yields contributed to erratic prices, which could have been controlled by storage facilities, government price stabilization boards, and price supports. This did not happen until after World War I.
>
> *Monopoly pricing practices* Differential pricing (such as Pittsburgh Plus, whereby goods were priced according to the location of the head office rather than the factory) worked like an internal tariff, pumping money

from the country into the Northeast. The antitrust acts addressed some
of these problems, but left many untouched.

Patronage and pork-barrel   Some agrarian areas, especially the South, fared
badly in the distribution of Federal largesse.

In the process of political and industrial development, defeat of the agricultural sector appears inevitable. Whatever the indicator (share of GNP, percentage of the work force, control of the land) farmers decline; whether
peasants, landless laborers, family farmers, kulaks, or estate owners, they fuel
industrialization by providing foreign exchange, food, and manpower. In the
end they disappear.

This can happen, however, at varying rates: very slowly, as appears to be the
case in China today, slowly as in France, quickly as in Britain. In the United
States, I would argue, the defeat of agriculture as a *sector* was swift and thor-
ough. This may sound strange in light of the stupendous agricultural output
today. Some landowners were successful. They shifted from broad attacks on
the system to interest group lobbying for certain types of members. The mass
of the agricultural population, however, lost most of its policy battles and left
the land.

One might have expected America to develop not like Germany, . . . but like
France: with controlled, slower industrial growth, speed sacrificed to balance,
and the preservation of a large rural population. For it to have happened,
the mass of small farmers would have to have found allies willing to battle the
Eastern banking and industrial combine which dominated American policy-
making. To understand their failure it is useful to analyze the structure of
incentives among potential alliance partners as was done for the European
countries. If we take farmers' grievances on the policy issues noted above (such
as money and rates) as the functional equivalent of tariffs, the politics of coalition formation in the United States become comparable to the equivalent process in Europe.

Again two alliances were competing for the allegiance of the same groups.
The protectionist core consisted of heavy industry, banks, and textiles. These
employers persuaded workers that their interests derived from their roles as
producers in the industrial sector, not as consumers. To farmers selling in
urban markets, the protectionists made the familiar case for keeping industry strong.

The alternative coalition, constructed around hostility toward heavy industry and banks, appealed to workers and farmers as consumers, to farmers as
debtors and victims of industrial manipulation, to the immigrant poor and
factory hands against the tribulations of the industrial system . . . and to shippers and manufacturers of finished products on behalf of lower costs. Broadly
this was a Jackson-type coalition confronting the Whig interest—the little man
versus the man of property. Lower tariffs and more industrial regulation (of
hours, rates, and working conditions) were its policies.

The progressive, low tariff alliance was not weak. Agriculture employed by far the largest percentage of the workforce. Federalism should have given it considerable leverage: the whole South, the Midwest, and the trans-Mississippi West. True, parts of the Midwest were industrializing, but then much of the Northeast remained agricultural. Nonetheless the alliance failed: the explanation turns on an understanding of the critical realignment election of 1896. The defeat of Populism marked the end of two decades of intense party competition, the beginning of forty years of Republican hegemony and the turning point for agriculture as a sector. It will be heuristically useful to work backwards from the conjuncture of 1896 to the broader forces which produced that contest.

The battle of 1896 was shaped by the character and strategy of William Jennings Bryan, the standard bearer of the low-tariff alliance. Bryan has had a bad historical press because his Populism had overtones of bigotry, anti-intellectualism, archaicism, and religious fundamentalism. Politically these attributes were flaws because they made it harder to attract badly needed allies to the farmers' cause. Bryan's style, symbols, and program were meaningful to the trans-Mississippi and Southern farmers who fueled Populism, but incomprehensible to city dwellers, immigrants, and Catholics, to say nothing of free-trade oriented businessmen. In the drive for the Democratic nomination and during the subsequent campaign, Bryan put silver in the forefront. Yet free coinage was but a piece of the Populist economic analysis and not the part with the strongest appeal for nonfarmers (nor even the most important element to farmers themselves). The city dweller's grievances against the industrial economy were more complex. Deflation actually improved his real wages, while cheap money threatened to raise prices. In the search for allies other criticisms of the industrial order could have been developed, but Bryan failed to prevent silver from overwhelming them.

Even within the agrarian sector, the concentration on silver and the fervid quality of the campaign worried the more prosperous farmers. By the 1890s, American agriculture was considerably differentiated. In the trans-Mississippi region, conditions were primitive; farmers were vulnerable, marginal producers: they grew a single crop for the market, had little capital, and no reserves. For different reasons, Southern agriculture was also marginal. In the Northeast and the Midwest farming had become much more diversified; it was less dependent on grain, more highly capitalized, and benefited from greater competition among railroads, alternative shipping routes, and direct access to urban markets. These farmers related to the industrial sector, rather like the dairymen in Britain, or the Danes. Bryan frightened these farmers as he frightened workers and immigrants. The qualities which made him attractive to one group antagonized others. Like Sen. Barry Goldwater and Sen. George McGovern, he was able to win the nomination, but in a manner which guaranteed defeat. Bryan's campaign caused potential allies to define their interests in ways which seemed incompatible with those of the agricultural sector. It drove farmers away rather than attracting them. Workers saw Bryan not as an ally against their bosses but as a threat to the industrial sector of the economy of which they were a part. To immigrants, he was a nativist xenophobe. Well-to-do Midwestern farmers, Southern Whigs, and Northeast shippers all saw him as a threat to property.

The Republicans, on the other hand, were very shrewd. Not only did they have large campaign funds, but, as Williams argues, James G. Blaine, Benjamin Harrison, and William McKinley understood that industrial interests required allies the support of which they must actively recruit. Like Bismarck, these Republican leaders worked to make minimal concessions in order to split the opposition. In the German coalition the terms of trade were social security for the workers, tariffs for the farmers and the manufacturers, guns and boats for the military. In America, McKinley, et al., outmaneuvred President Grover Cleveland and the Gold Democrats on the money issue; when Cleveland repealed the Silver Purchase Act, some of the Republicans helped pass the Sherman Silver Purchase Act. The Republican leaders then went after the farmers. Minimizing the importance of monetary issues, they proposed an alternative solution in the form of overseas markets: selling surpluses to the Chinese or the Latin Americans, negotiating the lowering of tariff levels, and policing the meat industry to meet the health regulations Europeans had imposed in order to keep out American imports. To the working class, the Republicans argued that Bryan and the agrarians would cost them jobs and boost prices. Social security was never mentioned—McKinley paid less than Bismarck.

In 1896, the Republican candidate was tactically shrewd and the Democratic one was not. It might have been the other way around. Imagine a charismatic Democrat from Ohio, with a Catholic mother, traditionally friendly to workers, known for his understanding of farmers' problems, the historical equivalent of Senator Robert Kennedy in the latter's ability to appeal simultaneously to urban ethnics, machine politicians, blacks, and suburban liberals. Unlikely but not impossible: had he existed, such a candidate would still have labored under severe handicaps. The difference between Bryan and McKinley was more than a matter of personality or accident. The forces which made Bryan the standard bearer were built into the structure of American politics. First, McKinley's success in constructing a coalition derives from features inherent in industrial society. As in Germany, producers' groups had a structural advantage. Bringing the farmers, workers, and consumers together was difficult everywhere in the industrial world during that period. In America, ethnic, geographic, and religious differences made it even harder.

Second, the industrialists controlled both political parties. Whatever happened at the local level, the national Democratic party lay in the firm grip of Southern conservatives and Northern businessmen. Prior to 1896, they wrote their ideas into the party platforms and nominated their man at every convention. The Gold Democrats were not a choice but an echo. . . . A Bryan-type crusade was structurally necessary. Action out of the ordinary was required to wrest the electoral machine away from the Gold Democrats. But the requirements of that success also sowed seeds for the failure of November, 1896.

Why, in turn, did the Industrialists control the parties? The Civil War is crucial. At its inception, the Republican party was an amalgam of entrepreneurs, farmers, lawyers, and professionals who believed in opportunity, hard work, and self-help; these were people from medium-sized towns, medium-sized enterprises, medium-sized farms. These people disliked the South not because they wished to help the black race or even eliminate slavery, but because the South and slavery symbolized the very opposite of "Free Soil, Free Labor, Free Men." By accelerating the pace of industrialization, the Civil War altered the internal balance of the Party, tipping control to the industrialists. By mobilizing national emotions against the South, the Civil War fused North and West together, locking the voter into the Republican Party. Men who had been antibusiness and Jacksonian prior to 1860 were now members of a coalition dominated by business.

In the South, the Old Whigs, in desperate need of capital, fearful of social change, and contemptuous of the old Jacksonians, looked to the northern industrialists for help in rebuilding their lands and restoring conservative rule. What would have been more natural then to have joined their northern allies in the Republican Party? In the end, the hostility of the Radical Republicans made this impossible, and instead the Old Whigs went into the Democratic Party where they eventually helped sustain the Gold Democrats and battled with the Populists for control of the Democratic organization in the South.

There were, then, in the American system certain structural obstacles to a low-tariff coalition. What of economic ideology (explanation 4) and the international system (explanation 3)? Free trade in the United States never had the ideological force it had in the United Kingdom. Infant industries and competition with the major industrial power provided the base for a protectionist tradition, as farming and distrust of the state provided a base for free trade. Tariffs had always been an important source of revenue for the Federal government. It is interesting that the "Free Soil, Labor and Men" coalition did not add Free Trade to its program.

Trade bore some relation to foreign policy. . . . Nonetheless, it is hard to see that the international political system determined tariff policy. The United States had no need to worry about foreign control of resources or food supply. In any case the foreign policy of the low-tariff coalition was not very different from the foreign policy of the high-tariff coalition.

In conclusion, four countries have been subjected to a set of questions in an attempt to find evidence relevant to differing explanations of tariff levels in the late nineteenth century. In each country, we find a large bloc of economic interest groups gaining significant economic advantages from the policy decision adopted concerning tariffs. Hence, the economic explanation has both simplicity and power. But is it enough? It does have two weaknesses. First, it presupposes a certain obviousness about the direction of economic pressures upon groups. Yet, as the argumentation above has sought to show, other economic calculations would also have been rational for those groups. Had farmers supported protection in Britain or opposed it in Germany and France, we could also offer a plausible economic interpretation for their behavior. The same is true for industrialists: had they accepted the opposite policy, we could find ways in which they benefited from doing so. We require an explanation, therefore, for the choice between two economic logics. One possibility is to look at the urgency of economic need. For protectionists, the incentive for high tariffs was intense and obvious. For free traders, the advantages of their policy preference, and the costs of their opponents' victory, were more ambiguous. Those who wanted their goals the most, won.

Second, the economic explanation fails to flesh out the political steps involved in translating a potential alliance of interest into policy. Logrolling does take some organization, especially in arranging side payments among the partners. The iron-rye bargain seems so natural that we forget the depth of animosity between the partners in the period preceding it. To get their way, economic groups had to translate their economic power into political currency.

The political structures explanation appears to take care of this problem. Certain institutions and particular individuals helped to organize the winning coalition and facilitate its victory. Looking at each victory separately, these structures and personalities bulk large in the story. Yet viewed comparatively, their importance washes out. Bismarck, the Junkers, the authoritarian constitution, the character of the German civil service, the special connections among the state, banking, and industry—these conspicuous features of the German case have no equivalents elsewhere. Méline was no Bismarck and the system gave him no particular leverage. Mobilization against socialism did not occur in the United States, or even in Britain and France. Yet the pattern of policy outcomes in these countries was the same, suggesting that those aspects of the political system which were *idiosyncratic* to each country (such as Bismarck and regime type) are not crucial in explaining the result. In this sense the political explanation does not add to the economic one.

Nonetheless, some aspects of the relation between economic groups and the political system are *uniform* among the countries examined here and do help explain the outcome. There is a striking similarity in the identity of victors and losers from country to country: producers over consumers, heavy industrialists over finished manufacturers, big farmers over small, and property owners over laborers. In each case, a coalition of producers' interests defined by large-scale basic industry and substantial landowners defeated its opponent. It is probable, therefore, that different types of groups from country to country are systematically not equal in political resources. Rather, heavy industrialists and landowners are stronger than peasants, workers, shopkeepers, and consumers. They have superior resources, access to power, and compactness. They would have had these advantages even if the regimes had differed considerably from their historical profiles. Thus a republicanized or democratized Germany would doubtless have had high tariffs (although it might have taken longer for this to come about, as it did in France). A monarchist France (Bourbon, Orleanist, or Bonapartist) would certainly have had the same high tariffs as Republican France. An authoritarian Britain could only have come about through repression of the industrialists by landowners, so it is possible a shift in regime might have meant higher tariffs; more likely, the industrialists would have broken through as they did in Germany. Certainly Republican Britain would have had the same tariff policy. In the United States, it is possible (although doubtful) that without the critical election of 1896, or with a different party system altogether, the alternation between protectionist Republicans and low-tariff Democrats might have continued.

Two coalitions faced each other. Each contained a variety of groups. Compared to the losers, the winners comprised: (1) groups for which the benefits of their policy goal were intense and urgent, rather than diffuse; (2) groups occupying strategic positions in the economy; and (3) groups with structurally superior positions in each political system. The uniformity of the winners' economic characteristics, regardless of regime type, suggests that to the extent that the political advantages derive from economic ones, the political explanation is not needed. The translation of economic advantage into policy does require action, organization, and politics; to that extent, and to varying degrees, the economic explanation by itself is insufficient. It is strongest in Germany, where the rapidity of the switch from free trade to protection is breathtaking, and in France where economic slowness made the nation especially vulnerable to competition. It works least well for Britain where the policy's advantages to the industrialists seem the least clear, and for the United States, where the weakness of agriculture is not explicable without the Civil War. Note that nowhere do industrialists fail to obtain their preferences.

In this discussion, we have called the actors groups, not classes, for two reasons. First, the language of class often makes it difficult to clarify the conflicts of interest (e.g., heavy industry vs. manufacture) which exist within classes, and to explain which conception of class interest prevails. Second, class analysis is complex. Since interest group reasoning claims less, and works, there is no point in going further.

The international system and economic ideology explanations appear the least useful. Each is certainly compatible with the various outcomes, but has drawbacks. First, adding them violates the principle of parsimony. If one accepts the power of the particular economic-political explanation stated above, the other two explanations become redundant. Second, even if one is not attracted by parsimony, reference to the international system does not escape the difficulty inherent in any "unitary actor" mode of reasoning: why does a particular conception of the national interest predominate? In the German case, the low tariff coalition did not share Bismarck's and Bülow's conception of how Germany should relate to the world. Thus the international system explanation must revert to some investigation of domestic politics.

Finally, the economic ideology explanation seems the weakest. Whatever its strength in accounting for the Free Trade Movement of the 1850s and 1860s, this explanation cannot deal with the rapid switch to protection in the 1870s. A national culture argument cannot really explain why two different policies are followed within a very short span of time. The flight away from Free Trade by Junkers, manufacturers, farmers, and so on was clearly provoked by the price drop. For the United Kingdom, conversely, the continuity of policy makes the cultural argument more appropriate. Belief in free trade may have blunted the receptivity of British interest groups toward a protectionist solution of their problems. The need for the economic ideology explanation here depends on one's evaluation of the structure of economic incentives facing industry: to whatever extent empire, and other advantages of having been first, eased the full impact of the depression, ideology was superfluous. To whatever extent industry suffered but avoided protection, ideology was significant.

7

Root Causes: A Historical Approach to Assessing the Role of Institutions in Economic Development

DARON ACEMOGLU

There are enormous differences in the wealth of nations and living standards across the globe, and the causes of these differences are hotly debated. In this selection, economist Daron Acemoglu develops the empirical and theoretical case that differences in domestic political institutions are the fundamental cause of differences in economic development. The author builds his case by conducting a "natural experiment" from history in which variation in the early colonization experiences of developing countries is considered the "treatment." In colonies where European settlers established institutions that constrained the political power of elites, protected property rights for investors, and provided incentives to develop new technologies, growth rates were high regardless of initial geographic conditions. By contrast, today's development failures are often former colonies that were rich in the fifteenth and sixteenth centuries. But because Europeans installed extractive institutions to plunder resources or exploit the indigenous population, these countries have underperformed their potential. In short, the author claims that political institutions are most important for understanding the wealth of nations.

Tremendous differences in incomes and standards of living exist today between the rich and the poor countries of the world. Average per capita income in sub-Saharan Africa, for example, is less than one-twentieth that in the United States. Explanations for why the economic fortunes of countries have diverged so much abound. Poor countries, such as those in sub-Saharan Africa, Central America, or South Asia, often lack functioning markets, their populations are poorly educated, and their machinery and technology are outdated or nonexistent. But these are only *proximate* causes of poverty, begging the question of why these places don't have better markets, better human capital, more investments, and better machinery and technology. There must be some *fundamental* causes leading to these outcomes, and via these channels, to dire poverty.

The two main candidates to explain the fundamental causes of differences in prosperity between countries are geography and institutions. The *geography hypothesis*, which has a large following both in the popular imagination and in academia, maintains that the geography, climate, and ecology of a society shape both its technology and the incentives of its inhabitants. It emphasizes forces of nature as a primary factor in the poverty of nations. The alternative, the *institutions hypothesis,* is about human influences. According to this view, some societies have good institutions that encourage investment in machinery, human capital, and better technologies, and, consequently, these countries achieve economic prosperity.

Good institutions have three key characteristics: enforcement of property rights for a broad cross section of society, so that a variety of individuals have incentives to invest and take part in economic life; constraints on the actions of elites, politicians, and other powerful groups, so that these people cannot expropriate the incomes and investments of others or create a highly uneven playing field; and some degree of equal opportunity for broad segments of society, so that individuals can make investments, especially in human capital, and participate in productive economic activities. These good institutions contrast with conditions in many societies of the world, throughout history and today, where the rule of law is applied selectively: property rights are nonexistent for the vast majority of the population; the elites have unlimited political and economic power; and only a small fraction of citizens have access to education, credit, and production opportunities.

GEOGRAPHY'S INFLUENCE

If you want to believe that geography is the key, look at a world map. Locate the poorest places in the world where per capita incomes are less than one-twentieth those in the United States. You will find almost all of them close to the equator, in very hot regions that experience periodic torrential rains and where, by definition, tropical diseases are widespread.

However, this evidence does not establish that geography is a primary influence on prosperity. It is true there is a *correlation* between geography and prosperity. But correlation does not prove causation. Most important, there are often omitted factors driving the associations we observe in the data.

Similarly, if you look around the world, you'll see that almost no wealthy country achieves this position without institutions protecting the property rights of investors and imposing some control over the government and elites. Once again, however, this correlation between institutions and economic development could reflect omitted factors or reverse causality.

To make progress in understanding the relative roles of geographic and institutional factors, we need to find a source of exogenous variation in institutions—in other words, a natural experiment where institutions change for reasons unrelated to potential omitted factors (and geographic factors remain constant, as they almost always do).

The colonization of much of the globe by Europeans starting in the fifteenth century provides such a natural experiment. The colonization experience transformed the institutions in many lands conquered or controlled by Europeans but, by and large, had no effect on their geographies. Therefore, if geography is the key factor determining the economic potential of an area or a country, the places that were rich before the arrival of the Europeans should have remained rich after the colonization experience and, in fact, should still be rich today. In other words, since the key determinant of prosperity remains the same, we should see a high degree of persistence in economic outcomes. If, on the other hand, it is institutions that are central, then those places where good institutions were introduced or developed should be richer than those in which Europeans introduced or maintained extractive institutions to plunder resources or exploit the non-European population.

Historical evidence suggests that Europeans indeed pursued very different colonization strategies, with very different associated institutions, in various colonies. At one extreme, Europeans set up exclusively extractive institutions, exemplified by the Belgian colonization of the Congo slave plantations in the Caribbean, and forced labor systems in the mines of Central America. These institutions neither protected the property rights of regular citizens nor constrained the power of elites. At the other extreme, Europeans founded a number of colonies where they created settler societies, replicating—and often improving—the European form of institutions protecting private property. Primary examples of this mode of colonization include Australia, Canada, New Zealand, and the United States. The settlers in these societies also managed to place significant constraints on elites and politicians, even if they had to fight to achieve this objective.

REVERSAL OF FORTUNE

So what happened to economic development after colonization? Did places that were rich before colonization remain rich, as suggested by the geography hypothesis? Or did economic fortunes change systematically as a result of the changes in institutions?

The historical evidence shows no evidence of the persistence suggested by the geography hypothesis. On the contrary, there is a remarkable *reversal of fortune* in economic prosperity. Societies like the Mughals in India and the Aztecs and the Incas in America that were among the richest civilizations in 1500 are among the poorer societies of today. In contrast, countries occupying the territories of the less developed civilizations in North America, New Zealand, and Australia are now much *richer* than those in the lands of the Mughals, the Aztecs, and the Incas. Moreover, the reversal of fortune is not confined to this comparison. Using various proxies for prosperity before modern times, we can show that the reversal is a much more widespread phenomenon. For example, before industrialization, only relatively developed societies could sustain significant urbanization, so urbanization rates are a relatively good proxy for prosperity before European colonization. The chart here shows a strong negative relationship between urbanization rates in 1500 and income per capita today. (See Figure 1.) That is, the former European

FIGURE 1 Shifting Prosperity: Countries That Were Rich in 1500 Are Among the Less Well Off Societies Today

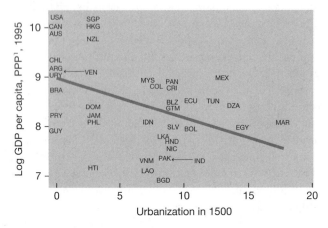

NOTE: ARG=Argentina, AUS=Australia, BGD=Bangladesh, BLZ=Belize, BOL= Bolivia, BRA=Brazil, CAN=Canada, CHL=Chile, COL=Colombia, CRI=Costa Rica, DOM=Dominican Republic, DZA=Albania, ECU=Ecuador, EGY=Egypt, GTM= Guatemala, GUY=Guyana, JAM=Jamaica, HKG=Hong Kong SAR, HND=Honduras, HTI=Haiti, IDN=Indonesia, IND=India, LAO=Lao People's Democratic Republic, LKA=Sri Lanka, MAR=Morocco, MEX=Mexico, MYS=Malaysia, NIC=Nicaragua, NZL=New Zealand, PAK=Pakistan, PAN=Panama, PER=Peru, PHL=Philippines, PRY=Paraguay, SGP=Singapore, SLV=El Salvador, TUN=Tunisia, URY=Uruguay, USA=United States, VEN=Venezuela, VNM=Vietnam.

[1]Purchasing power parity.

SOURCE: Author.

colonies that are relatively rich today are those that were poor before the Europeans arrived.

This reversal is prima facie evidence against the most standard versions of the geography hypothesis discussed above: it cannot be that the climate, ecology, or disease environments of the tropical areas have condemned these countries to poverty today, because these same areas with the same climate, ecology, and disease environment were richer than the temperate areas 500 years ago. Although it is possible that the reversal may be related to geographic factors whose effects on economic prosperity vary over time—for example, certain characteristics that first cause prosperity then condemn nations to poverty—there is no evidence of any such factor or any support for sophisticated geography hypotheses of this sort.

Is the reversal of fortune consistent with the institutions hypothesis? The answer is yes. In fact, once we look at the variation in colonization strategies, we see that the reversal of fortune is exactly what the institutions hypothesis predicts. European colonialism made Europeans the most politically powerful group, with the capability to influence institutions more than any indigenous group was able to at the time. In places where Europeans did not settle and cared little about aggregate output and the welfare of the population, in places where there was a large population that could be coerced and employed cheaply in mines or in agriculture or simply taxed, in places where there were resources to be extracted, Europeans pursued the strategy of setting up extractive institutions or taking over existing extractive institutions and hierarchical structures. In those colonies, there were no constraints on the power of the elites (which were typically the Europeans themselves and their allies) and no civil or property rights for the majority of the population; in fact, many of them were forced into labor or enslaved. Contrasting with this pattern, in colonies where there was little to be extracted, where most of the land was empty, where the disease environment was favorable, Europeans settled in large numbers and developed laws and institutions to ensure that they themselves were protected, in both their political and their economic lives. In these colonies, the institutions were therefore much more conducive to investment and economic growth.

This evidence does not mean that geography does not matter at all, however. Which places were rich and which were poor before Europeans arrived might have been determined by geographic factors. These geographic factors also likely influenced the institutions that Europeans introduced. For example, the climate and soil quality in the Caribbean made it productive to grow sugar there, encouraging the development of a plantation system based on slavery. What the evidence shows instead is that geography neither condemns a nation to poverty nor guarantees its economic success. If you want to understand why a country is poor today, you have to look at its institutions rather than its geography.

NO NATURAL GRAVITATION

If institutions are so important for economic prosperity, why do some societies choose or end up with bad institutions? Moreover, why do these bad institutions persist long after their disastrous consequences are apparent? Is it an accident of history or the result of misconceptions or mistakes by societies or their policymakers? Recent empirical and theoretical research suggests that the answer is no: there are no compelling reasons to think that societies will naturally gravitate toward good institutions. Institutions not only affect the economic prospects of nations but are also central to the distribution of income among individuals and groups in society—in other words, institutions not only affect the size of the social pie, but also how it is distributed.

This perspective implies that a potential change from dysfunctional and bad institutions toward better ones that will increase the size of the social pie may nonetheless be blocked when such a change significantly reduces the slice that powerful groups receive from the pie and when they cannot be credibly compensated for this loss. That there is no natural gravitation toward good institutions is illustrated by the attitudes of the landed elites and the emperors in Austria-Hungary and in Russia during the nineteenth century. These elite groups blocked industrialization and even the introduction of railways and protected the old regime because they realized capitalist growth and industrialization would reduce their power and their privileges.

Similarly, European colonists did not set up institutions to benefit society as a whole. They chose good institutions when it was in their interests to do so, when they would be the ones living under the umbrella of these institutions, as in much of the New World. In contrast, they introduced or maintained existing extractive institutions when it was in their interest to extract resources from the non-European populations of the colonies, as in much of Africa, Central America, the Caribbean, and South Asia. Furthermore, these extractive institutions showed no sign of evolving into better institutions, either under European control or once these colonies gained independence. In almost all cases, we can link the persistence of extractive institutions to the fact that, even after independence, the elites in these societies had a lot to lose from institutional reform. Their political power and claim to economic rents rested on the existing extractive institutions, as best illustrated by the Caribbean plantation owners whose wealth directly depended on slavery and extractive institutions. Any reform of the system, however beneficial for the country as a whole, would be a direct threat to the owners.

European colonialism is only one part of the story of the institutions of the former colonies, and many countries that never experienced European colonialism nonetheless suffer from institutional problems (while certain other former European colonies have arguably some of the best institutions in the world today). Nevertheless, the perspective developed in this article applies to these cases as well: institutional problems are important in a variety of instances, and, in most of these, the source of institutional problems and the difficulty of institutional reform lie in the fact that any major change creates winners and losers, and the potential losers are often powerful enough to resist change.

The persistence of institutions and potential resistance to reform do not mean that institutions are unchanging. There is often significant institutional evolution, and even highly dysfunctional institutions can be successfully transformed. For example, Botswana managed to build a functioning democracy after its independence from Britain and become the fastest-growing country in the world. Institutional change will happen either when groups that favor change become powerful enough to impose it on the potential losers, or when societies can strike a bargain with potential losers so as to credibly compensate them after the change takes place or, perhaps, shield them from the most adverse consequences of these changes. Recognizing the importance of institutions in economic development and the often formidable barriers to beneficial institutional reform is the first step toward significant progress in jump-starting rapid growth in many areas of the world today.

8

The Institutional Roots of American Trade Policy: Politics, Coalitions, and International Trade

MICHAEL BAILEY, JUDITH GOLDSTEIN, AND BARRY R. WEINGAST

Before 1934, U.S. trade policy was protectionist and partisan. When Republicans were in control of Congress and the presidency, they raised tariffs, culminating in the infamous Smoot-Hawley Tariff of 1930. Shortly thereafter, free-trading Democrats took control of government and passed the Reciprocal Trade Agreements Act (RTAA) of 1934. According to Michael Bailey, Judith Goldstein, and Barry R. Weingast, the RTAA fundamentally changed the institutions by which the United States made its trade policy in such a way as to facilitate the reduction of trade barriers. In passing the RTAA, Congress delegated to the executive branch the authority to reduce tariffs through reciprocal trade agreements with other countries. These institutional changes generated broader bipartisan support for freer trade, and the RTAA went on to serve as the basis for more than half a century of U.S. trade liberalization.

While economists are unanimous in their agreement that free trade yields significant welfare gains, no consensus exists on the political conditions that will support such a policy. According to conventional views, even if politicians recognize that society gains from trade, they are constrained because of an organizational bias in society: those who lose from increased trade have a greater incentive to organize than those who benefit from the policy. The outcome is an overrepresentation of protectionist interests and constant pressure on governments to close markets. Although logically consistent, the conventional view suffers from the empirical problem that democracies have and continue to support free-trade policies. We argue that political institutions, by structuring conflict over trade policy, provide an explanation for the divergence between analyses that predict economic closure and the empirical reality of relatively free trade.

The importance of institutional rules is no more apparent than in the case of the creation and sustenance of a liberal trade policy in the United States. For most of the nineteenth century, protectionist interests successfully pressured Congress to maintain high barriers to trade. Although the interest of manufacturers in cheap raw materials periodically led Congress to enact a "free list" for such products, the interests of consumers and exporters were largely ignored. This situation changed dramatically with the passage of the

Reciprocal Trade Agreements Act (RTAA) in 1934, which changed the way trade policy was determined and set the stage for American leadership in efforts to expand international trade.

Trade liberalization in the United States was neither inevitable nor irrevocable; the structure of American politics in the middle of the twentieth century made trade policy still vulnerable to protectionist impulses that were difficult to contain. Hence, any explanation of American trade policy must account not only for the passage of the RTAA but also for how and why Congress sustained the trade liberalization program in the ensuing decades.

This essay offers an explanation for the timing, form, and efficacy of this institutional innovation. The argument has two parts. First, we ask what explains the choice of the rules and procedures that characterized the 1934 foundational legislation. Two rule changes distinguished the Reciprocal Trade Agreements Act from its predecessors: (1) it mandated reciprocal, not unilateral, tariff reductions, and (2) it authorized trade agreements on the basis of a simple majority vote instead of the supermajority mandated in the Constitution. We argue that these changes in trade rules reflected efforts by the Democratic Party to build support for free trade within the party and to insulate trade policy from a future Republican Congress.

Second, the essay demonstrates how these two institutional changes shifted American policy to a more liberal equilibrium. The real significance of the RTAA was not just that it was passed; had it been overturned a few years later, after all, it would be nothing but a footnote to American trade history. Rather, the RTAA had an impact because it created a dynamic of political support for free trade. In contrast to perspectives in which Congress is seen to have abdicated control of trade policy, we focus on how presidential agreements affected congressional preferences. The president's "bundling" of international and domestic tariffs made low tariffs politically durable. The ensuing increases in world trade made members of Congress more willing to trade off the political risk of reducing U.S. tariffs for the political benefits of gaining access to foreign markets. This change in preference enabled presidents to ask for and receive ever broader authority to negotiate tariff reductions.

We divide this essay into three sections. Section I begins with the empirical observation of the breakdown of partisan divisions on trade and the emergence of a free-trade coalition, a puzzling occurrence given the previous decades of trade closure and continued congressional involvement in trade policy. Section II explains the origins of the RTAA and shows how political factors changed the institutional environment of trade policy. We offer a model in which members of Congress, the president, and a generic foreign government interact on trade policy. Section III examines the dynamic effects of the RTAA and shows how its institutional structure changed the political environment of trade policy. Not only did the RTAA dramatically increase the political durability of low tariffs, but, as we show through an empirical examination of congressional voting in 1953 and 1962, the rise in exports that it brought about also led to changes in congressional preferences on trade.

I. BIPARTISAN SUPPORT FOR TRADE POLICY

One of the anomalies in the history of U.S. politics involves the relatively rapid change in the political salience of trade policy. Where trade policy was a defining issue of partisan politics in the late nineteenth and early twentieth centuries, it all but disappeared from the political arena by the 1950s. Indicative of the charged political climate of early tariff policy-making were policy shifts that followed changes in control of government. . . . Trade policy through 1934 shows tremendous predictability. In general, when Democrats took office, they lowered tariffs; when Republicans held office, they did the opposite. This ability to predict policy based on party control disappears in mid-century. After World War II the parties look increasingly similar in their voting behavior. (See Figures 1 and 2.) What explains this change in congressional preferences?

There is an impressive body of literature suggesting that change occurred because Congress abdicated its control over trade policy when the RTAA transferred authority for setting tariffs to the president. By one account, the work associated with tariff legislation had become so onerous that members of Congress chose to remove themselves from the process. While revision of tariff schedules had never been a simple matter, the process had degenerated into a frenzy of special-interest lobbying and deal making with the Smoot-Hawley Tariff Bill of 1930. Schattschneider wrote of the "truly Sisyphean labor" to which the legislation condemned Congress—eleven thousand pages of testimony

FIGURE 1 Voting in Senate on Passage of Major Trade Legislation by Party 1913–1962

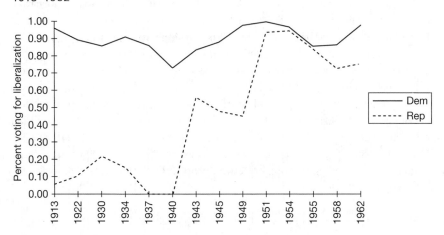

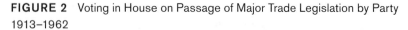

FIGURE 2 Voting in House on Passage of Major Trade Legislation by Party 1913–1962

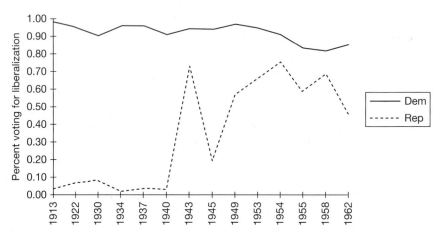

and briefs collected over forty-three days and five nights of hearings.[1] Many therefore viewed the congressional move to delegate authority to change tariffs as a means of avoiding months of tedious hearings and negotiations.

Several factors make it difficult to accept that the fundamental motivation for the RTAA was a desire to reduce workload. First, the easiest way to reduce workload is to do nothing. Clearly this was not the choice of Congress. Second, there were many other ways to streamline the process than by delegating to the president: existing organizations could have been used differently, new committees and commissions could have been created, and rules and formulas could have been established. There is no specific reason to choose delegation to the president over these other possibilities.

An alternative explanation, the "lesson thesis," suggests that the disastrous results of the Smoot-Hawley Tariff led members of Congress to the realization that they were politically incapable of passing a rational tariff policy. Destler, for example, states that members of Congress chose to delegate in order to "protect themselves from the direct one-sided pressure from producer interests that had led them to make bad law."

This perspective, too, is problematic. First, one should be wary of models of congressional behavior in which members of Congress act against one-sided political pressure in the interest of good public policy for no political reason. If such behavior were the norm, one would expect Congress to "protect" itself from the American Association of Retired People, the National Rifle Association,

1. E. E Schattschneider, *Politics, Pressure and the Tariff: A Study of Free Private Enterprise in Pressure Politics as Shown in the 1929–1930 Revision of the Tariff* (Hamden, Conn.: Archon Books, 1935), 29, 36.

farmers, oil producers, and almost all other interests as well. Needless to say, this is not generally the case; even on trade, Congress has continued to represent producer interests on more than a few occasions.

Second, problems with the process in 1930 do not prove that Congress was incapable of getting the process back under control. A new set of congressional leaders with different priorities could have organized procedures differently so as to achieve a better outcome than that of 1930. Congress had gone through such reorganizations in 1894, 1909, and 1913; and it did it again in 1934, when the Senate defeated many amendments seeking exemptions for particular industries, precisely the type of amendments that had spun the process out of control in 1930.[2]

Third, . . . if congressional learning did in fact occur between 1930 and 1934, one would expect to see a substantial number of members who voted for the Smoot-Hawley Tariff coming around to support the RTAA. To the contrary, however, voting on *both* the Smoot-Hawley Tariff and the RTAA was almost wholly partisan: Republicans favored the former and opposed the latter, whereas Democrats opposed the former and favored the latter. Of 225 representatives and senators who voted on both bills, only nine voted in a manner consistent with the lesson thesis. The remaining 96 percent voted either along party lines or in a manner inconsistent with the lesson thesis. The difference between 1930 and 1934 is therefore not that protariff members of Congress learned from their mistake, but rather that there were too few Republicans in 1934 to oppose the Democrats' initiative.

As well as disagreeing on why Congress would grant new tariff-setting powers to the president, analyses differ over the actual effect of the RTAA on American policy. One view, consistent with the deflection and lesson theses, holds that the RTAA allowed Congress to wash its hands of tariffs, leaving the president free to pursue rational liberalization of U.S. trade policy unburdened by members of Congress or the special interests they represented.

This view is overstated. While congressional activity on tariffs declined dramatically after the RTAA, it still remained substantial; Congress continued to play a central role at every step along the path to trade liberalization. Congress extended the RTAA ten times between 1934 and 1962, debating and often modifying the legislation. In 1937, for example, an amendment to limit reductions on agricultural duties to whatever level would be necessary to equalize production costs initially passed the Senate and was only defeated on a revote. In 1948, 1951, and 1955, Congress added peril-point provisions that tied duties to the minimum rates necessary to protect domestic producers against imports. In 1953 Republicans in Congress agreed to a one-year renewal only when the president promised not to enter into any new trade negotiations.

2. Stephan Haggard, "The Institutional Foundations of Hegemony: Explaining the Reciprocal Trade Agreements Act of 1934," in G. John Ikenberry, David Lake, and Michael Mastanduno, eds., *The State and American Foreign Economic Policy* (Ithaca, N.Y.: Cornell University Press, 1988), 113.

While Congress never overturned the RTAA, members were clearly always ready to make significant changes if they thought them necessary. . . .

What does explain the passage of the RTAA in 1934 if not that Congress abdicated control or sought to deflect political pressure? Our answer is simple: the Democratic leadership wanted lower tariffs that would pass an increasingly skeptical Congress and would be able to outlive Democratic control of Congress. The institutions they designed met this goal. In that the Democrats chose to lower tariffs through reciprocal "bundled" agreements with other nations, some delegation to the president to negotiate these agreements was necessary. The significant change, however, was not delegation to the president per se. Rather, the RTAA marks a turning point in American trade history because first, it moved Congress away from legislating unilateral tariffs, and second, it granted these bilateral agreements the status of treaties without a two-thirds supermajority.

II. THE POLITICAL ORIGINS OF THE RTAA

With its passage of the RTAA in 1934, Congress ushered in a new era of trade policy. The legislation amended the 1930 Smoot-Hawley Tariff Act to allow the president to negotiate reciprocal trade agreements with foreign governments. In exchange for increased access to foreign markets, the president was authorized to reduce U.S. duties by up to 50 percent. No specific duties were established or changed by the act and no congressional approval of agreements was required.

That such legislation was passed in 1934 is somewhat surprising in light of the fact that there was no groundswell of support for tariff reductions. Although highly critical of Hoover's tariff policy during the 1932 campaign, Roosevelt was no staunch free trader. While he associated himself with the Wilsonian international wing of the Democratic Party, at times he sounded very much like a protectionist. In the 1932 presidential campaign he announced that his trade doctrine was "not widely different from that preached by Republican statesmen and politicians" and that he favored "continuous protection for American agriculture as well as American industry."[3]

In addition, many in the Roosevelt administration, including leading members of Roosevelt's brain trust, such as Rexford Tugwell, Raymond Moley, and Adolf Berle, placed a low priority on trade liberalization. They considered America's problems to be domestic in nature, requiring domestic solutions. Many members of the administration were thus willing to impose higher duties in the interests of insulating the domestic economy from the world economy. Such sentiment manifested itself in provisions of the National Industrial Recovery Act (NIRA) and the Agriculture Assistance Act (AAA), which

3. Haggard (fn. 2), 106–7.

allowed the government to limit imports if they were deemed to be interfering with the operation of the programs.

Rank-and-file Democrats also were not united in favor of lower tariffs. The increase in blue-collar and immigrant labor in the party proved a counterweight to southern preferences for lower tariffs. Led by Al Smith, 1928 presidential nominee and 1932 contender for the nomination, a major wing of the party supported high tariffs. Indicatively, during the debate on the Smoot-Hawley Tariff of 1930, most Democrats tempered their opposition to high tariffs.

The Great Depression did little to enhance the appeal of lower tariffs for these Democrats. During this period, efforts to cut tariffs unilaterally were dismissed as politically foolhardy. In 1931 Democratic representative and future speaker Henry Rainey of Illinois argued that such a unilateral reduction of tariffs would trigger a flood of imports. During the 1932 presidential campaign, Roosevelt's advisers roundly criticized Hull's proposal of unilateral reductions, and when Roosevelt was given a draft of a speech calling for a flat 10 percent reduction in tariffs, Democratic senators Pittman (Nevada) and Walsh (Montana) warned him that support for such a measure would be politically dangerous. Even after the election, reciprocal cuts were so politically risky that Roosevelt delayed introducing the RTAA to Congress for a year, out of fear that controversy over trade would derail high-priority items like NIRA.

Thus, the Democratic Party faced two constraints in fashioning a trade policy. First, its old platform of unilateral tariff reductions had questionable support, both within and outside the party. Roosevelt's promise of tariff reform would need to be fulfilled some other way. Second, Democrats wanted to provide some durability for their preferred policies. . . . Democratic tariffs had lasted only as long as the Democrats' tenure in power. Although we now consider 1932 as a watershed election in American history, it was not perceived as such at the time. In 1934 the electoral future looked highly uncertain to Democrats. The Republicans after all had dominated national elections for the previous seventy years, and were it not for the depression, they would probably still have been in office. Given this uncertainty, Democrats were looking for a way to make their tariff policy last beyond their tenure. House members were facing midterm elections in November and the president was in the second year of what could be a single four-year term. Party members had not forgotten their last effort at tariff reform, in 1913, when Woodrow Wilson fought long and hard for the Tariff Act, only to see it scuttled when the Republicans regained office.

The institutional form of the legislation introduced in 1934 should be understood as serving dual purposes. The key innovation—coupling liberalization of U.S. tariffs with reductions in foreign tariffs—accomplished two tasks. First, the form of tariff reduction served to broaden the range of tariff cuts acceptable to a majority in Congress. As shown below, it is easier to build majority support for reductions (and harder to form a coalition to negate an

agreement) when tariffs are coupled with changes in access to foreign markets. Second, it provided durability for the reform efforts. Granting the president the right to negotiate "bundled" tariff treaties increased the costs to
Republicans of increasing tariffs. Under the RTAA, even small adjustments
could unravel many agreements and harm U.S. export interests. We take up
each of these points in turn.

Building a Coalition in Favor of Free Trade

We begin with a spatial model to show how the RTAA enabled the Democrats
to ensure domestic political support for lower tariffs. The preferences of political actors in a two-dimensional policy space are shown in Figure 3. The horizontal axis represents the level of domestic tariffs, ranging from low to high.
The vertical axis represents the level of foreign tariffs. Political actors have
ideal policies, that is, tariff rates they prefer over all others. They prefer policies closer to their ideal policy to those farther away. To simplify matters, we
consider the rest of the world to be one nation that sets the foreign tariff levels. For simplicity, we also assume Congress is unicameral.

The historical record is clear about the location of actors in this space. First,
all American political actors prefer foreign tariffs to be as low as possible.
Therefore their ideal points line the horizontal axis in Figure 3. Second, in the
late nineteenth and early twentieth centuries the parties had distinct preferences, with Republicans the party of high tariffs and Democrats the party of
low tariffs. The median in Congress (the "floor median") is located between
the Democratic median and the Republican median. During periods of Republican majority, the median was among the Republicans with the lowest ideal

FIGURE 3   Actor Preferences and Predicted Tariff under Pre-RTAA System

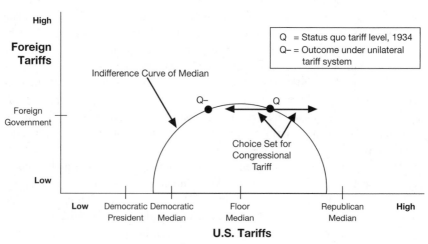

rates; during Democratic majorities, it was among the Democrats with the highest ideal rates.

While presidents shared the partisan inclinations on trade, their national constituencies and their more direct concern with international diplomacy made them less protectionist than the median member of their parties. The foreign government is assumed to be a unitary actor with an ideal point along the vertical axis, preferring U.S. tariffs to be as low as possible.

We also need an assumption about who controls the agenda in Congress. The literature on Congress propounds various views on the question—that committee, party, or the median controls the agenda. Because committee and party leaders took a leading role in the passage of the RTAA, we assume here that the agenda setter is some party leader who is distinct from the floor median. For convenience, we refer to this actor as the Democratic or Republican median.

To analyze congressional choice on the RTAA, we compare outcomes with and without the RTAA. We assume that the Democrats control the presidency and Congress, as they did in 1934. First, consider the situation without the RTAA. Under the existing tariff system, the Democratic median proposes unilateral changes in U.S. tariffs that are passed or rejected by the floor median. Because the tariff changes are unilateral, the Democratic median is constrained to making proposals along a horizontal line extending in both directions from the status quo Q. In other words, the Democratic median treats the foreign tariff level as fixed and makes a proposal affecting only U.S. tariff levels.

The Democratic median will propose a policy that makes it better off than the current status quo and is preferred by the median to the current status quo. In this situation, the status quo is the protectionist level of the Smoot-Hawley tariff. The Democratic median would maximize its utility by proposing Q–, the policy closest to the Democratic median among those preferred by the floor median to the status quo. Figure 3 illustrates the Democratic median's choice.

Such an outcome is suboptimal for many actors. There is a range of policies that would make the Democratic median, the floor median, and the foreign government better off than Q–. In Figure 4 we have drawn the preferred sets of the floor median and the foreign government to Q–; all points in the interior of the indifference curves are preferred to Q–. The shaded region at the intersection of the two preferred sets is an area of potential mutual gain; both of those actors and the Democratic median would be better off at any other outcome in the region than at Q–. When decision making is unilateral, however, Congress cannot move outcomes into this region.

Next consider outcomes under the RTAA. First, the president proposes an agreement to the foreign government subject to the minimum tariff provisions enacted by Congress. The foreign government then accepts or rejects the

FIGURE 4 Gains from Reciprocity

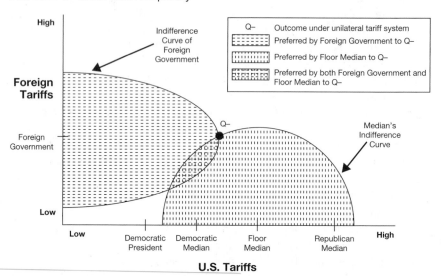

proposal. Even if there is no agreement, Congress still has the option of passing tariff legislation. The criterion for the foreign government is whether the proposal would leave it better off than if there were no proposal. From above we know that if there is no agreement, Congress will pass a unilateral tariff bill and the outcome will be Q–. The foreign government will therefore accept the proposal if the proposal makes it better off than Q–.

In making the proposal, the president seeks to bring the policy as close as possible to his ideal point. If the president proposes an agreement that is rejected by the foreign government, Congress would then set tariffs as if there were no agreement and choose Q–. Since the president is to the left of the Democratic median and the median, he would seek larger reductions, if possible. In particular, he would choose the point closest to his ideal point among policies above the congressional minimum tariff level and preferred to Q–by the foreign government. Agreement A* in Figure 5 is such a point: of the points above the minimum tariff level and preferred by the foreign government to Q–, it is the point closest to the president's ideal policy.

It is essential, then, that the Democratic median choose an appropriate minimum tariff level. If the minimum tariff level is too low—that is, if the president is able to choose a policy that makes the median worse off than the status quo—the floor median will not support the RTAA. Therefore, the Democratic median will set the minimum tariff level such that policy chosen by the president is as close as possible to its ideal point given that the policy is still preferred by the floor median to the status quo. As in Figure 5, such a minimum tariff level will go through the point of tangency between an indifference curve

FIGURE 5 Predicted Tariff under the RTAA

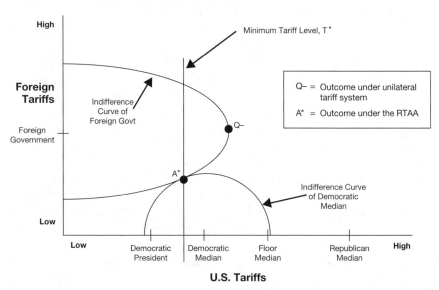

of the Democratic median and the indifference curve of the foreign govern-ment through Q–. The floor median will prefer the outcome chosen by the pres-ident, A*, to Q–.

The result is that under the RTAA, the Democratic median maintains a min-imum tariff level of T*, the floor median supports the RTAA, and the presi-dent proposes an agreement at A* that is accepted by the foreign government. The implication is that the RTAA makes perfect sense given the preferences of American political actors and an assumption of strategic behavior. No extra assumptions about congressional laziness or congressional antipathy toward special interests are necessary. Moreover, it is not a story of congressional abdication.

This framework can also be used to explain why other means of trade lib-eralization were not chosen. First, we can see why congressional Democrats were not satisfied with letting the president use existing treaty-making pow-ers. The Constitution requires that a treaty must be approved by a two-thirds vote in the Senate. Hence, the president would be constrained to please the member at the sixty-seventh percentile of protectionists in order to achieve mutual reduction in tariffs. In fact, the inability to garner a two-thirds major-ity in the Senate had repeatedly nullified trade treaties negotiated in the nine-teenth century. Under the RTAA, by contrast, the process was structured to require only a simple majority to pass tariff reductions—a clever institutional innovation that allowed the Democrats to sidestep the constraints of the exist-ing institutional structure.

A second possible alternative to the RTAA was that Congress could have tried to devise a strategy to induce foreign reductions in tariffs. However, the sequential nature of tariff making could undermine such efforts. Consider first the commitment problems in trying to effect mutual lowering of tariffs. Suppose the status quo is Q and Democrats take over Congress and are considering tariff reductions. We know Congress can pass Q–. Suppose, however, that the Democrats propose some reduction beyond Q–and argue that this large cut in U.S. tariffs will be accompanied by a cut in foreign tariffs. It would be difficult for such a strategy to work. First, the foreign country will be sorely tempted not to lower tariffs, because it favors low U.S. tariffs and high foreign tariffs over low U.S. tariffs and low foreign tariffs. To avoid this outcome, the Democrats would have to commit to raising tariffs if foreign tariffs were not lowered. But here, the temptation would be on the Democrats. Would they be willing to raise tariffs even though they prefer low tariffs? How credible would their threat be? Both the foreign country and the median in Congress would have good reason to doubt that the Democrats would carry out their threat.

These commitment problems would be exacerbated by problems associated with political uncertainty. Even if the Democrats were to lower tariffs beyond Q–and the foreign country responded in kind, the Democrats could lose an election and the incoming Republicans could raise tariffs back to Q. The foreign country would be forced to retreat from its reduction of tariffs. This possibility could make the foreign government reluctant to lower tariffs in the first place.

The RTAA and Political Durability

The second need for congressional Democrats was to provide some political durability for the tariff cuts. To demonstrate the increase in durability of trade liberalization under the RTAA, we first model the extreme volatility of trade policy under the pre-RTAA institutional structure. Under that regime, changes in trade policy followed the classic American legislative process. Parties originated legislation in Congress. If Congress passed a tariff bill, it went to the president. If the president signed the legislation, it became law; if he vetoed it, it went back to Congress where a two-thirds majority was required to override the veto.

Given this framework, we can determine equilibrium outcomes for different states of the world. Because tariffs were set unilaterally by each country, choices can be represented in one dimension. Consider a period in which there is a Republican majority in Congress, a Republican president, and a status quo tariff rate of Q, as in Figure 3. As long as the Republicans maintain their majority, Q is stable. While the median prefers all points between Q and Q–, defined to be a point equidistant from the median as Q but on the left side of the median, the congressional Republicans prefer none of these points.

Now suppose that after an election, the Democrats become the majority party. The status quo, Q, is no longer an equilibrium, as there are points that both the Democratic agenda setters and the median prefer to such a policy. In order for the Democrats to get as close to the Democratic median as possible, given that the bill must be approved by the median, they will introduce and pass the policy Q–. The Democratic president will prefer Q–to Q and will not veto the legislation. Once at this point, policy remains stable as long as the Democrats remain in power. As soon as the Republicans recapture Congress and the presidency, however, the status quo inherited from the Democrats is no longer an equilibrium. By similar reasoning as above, the Republicans would pass Q.

According to this logic, tariff shifts should occur when a new party obtains control of government. In fact, this is what occurred. In 1860, 1897, and 1920 the Republicans gained unified control of government after periods of unified Democratic control. Every time, they raised tariffs. In 1845, 1892, 1912, and 1930 the Democrats gained unified control of government after periods of unified Republican control. Every time, they lowered tariffs.

The dynamics of trade policy under the RTAA provide a stark contrast. To demonstrate the implications of the RTAA for the durability of low tariffs, we analyze two situations, one in which preferences are constant and one in which preferences change. First, we assume that the ideal point of the floor median remains constant, even as parties change. This is plausible if, say, moderate Democrats are replaced by moderate Republicans. We have already seen that the status quo after the passage of the RTAA is A*.

What happens after an election? If Democrats retain the presidency and Congress, there is no change: the minimum tariff level prevents the president from negotiating further tariff reductions, and congressional agenda setters desire no change. If the Republicans win control of both the presidency and Congress, change will be possible only if the median prefers the unilateral tariff of the foreign country to A*. However, since the RTAA moved the median to an outcome preferred over Q (and Q–), this will not be the case and no change will be possible.

Of course, members of Congress are likely to change their preferences after an election. We therefore consider the kind of changes in preferences that would be necessary to allow Congress to overturn the RTAA and resume unilateral tariff making. The president's preferences play a key role. If a protectionist president were elected, the floor median would have to shift to the right to the extent that he or she prefers some point along the foreign unilateral tariff line to the RTAA outcome, A*. In Figure 6 the floor median would have to shift to a point equidistant from A* and the foreign unilateral tariff line. To determine this point, we find an ideal point, C', at which the indifference curve through A* touches the foreign unilateral tariff line. If the change were any smaller, no protectionist legislation would be possible, as the floor median would not be satisfied with any possible unilateral tariff legislation.

On the other hand, if a Democratic or internationalist Republican president were elected, protectionist legislation would have to overcome a presidential

FIGURE 6   Stability of Tariffs under the RTAA

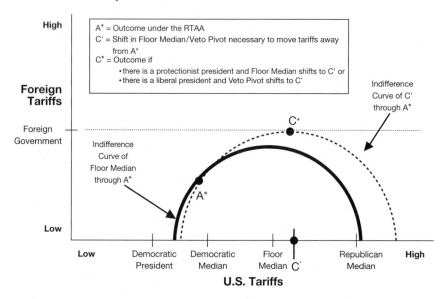

veto. Hence legislative success would depend, not on the floor median, but on the veto pivot. The veto pivot in this case is the member at the sixty-sixth percentile (ranked from least to most liberal); if this member and all more protectionist members prefer a bill to the status quo, then Congress can pass the legislation over the veto of the president. In this case, then, preferences in Congress would have to change such that the veto pivot—one of the more liberal members of Congress—would shift to C' on the right of the current median (as in Figure 6). In other words, if the president is a free trader, Congress would almost certainly not be able to raise tariffs, even if the Republicans were to take power.

Could we expect the president to be liberal on trade? Two factors indicate yes. First, being elected from a national constituency makes a president less susceptible to narrow demands for protection and more interested in policies that benefit the whole country. Second, the president's international role often inclines him to use trade liberalization as a tool in achieving geopolitical goals.

III. LONG-TERM EFFECTS OF THE RTAA

The importance of the RTAA was more than simply creating the mechanism for short-term tariff reform. More important, it set up a self-reinforcing dynamic that led to increasingly lower tariffs. In this section, we discuss the effects of RTAA-induced increases in trade on congressional and foreign preferences. We argue that congressional support for the expansion of presidential authority to negotiate cuts in American and foreign tariffs was forthcoming because the RTAA increased the importance of exports to constituents in congressional districts, which, in turn, changed the trade policy preferences of key congressional representatives. This section illustrates how RTAA structures influenced support for free trade. First, we show that trade did expand under the RTAA. Second, we model how expanding trade affects political preferences. Third, we present empirical evidence that increasing exports were a significant factor in transforming trade from a partisan to a bipartisan issue.

Tariffs declined precipitously and trade expanded dramatically during the tenure of the RTAA. In 1934 American duties averaged over 46 percent; by 1962 they had fallen to 12 percent. World trade increased from 97 trillion dollars at the war's end to 270 trillion at the time of the 1962 Trade Act. U.S. exports grew from $2.1 billion in 1934 to $3.3 billion in 1937 and from $9.8 billion in 1945 to over $20 billion in 1962.

While much of this increase in world trade can be attributed to the emergence of the world economy out of depression and war, two factors point to the substantial role of the RTAA. First, the RTAA allowed the president to take the lead in fighting for increased international openness. After the Smoot-Hawley Tariff Act of 1930, a retaliatory spiral of beggar-thy-neighbor policies had left the world with monumentally high tariffs. Given protectionist pressures inherent in democracies, we have good reason to believe that without the RTAA, tariffs would have moved downward at a far slower pace. Second, there is evidence that U.S. trade with treaty nations increased more rapidly than with nontreaty nations. For example, in the first three years of the program, exports to twenty-two nations with which agreements existed increased by 61 percent as compared with a 38 percent increase to other nations.

There are two ways such changes in trade flows could change political preferences. First, the ideal points could shift. Since we assume that all members of Congress prefer zero foreign tariffs, the only room for movement would be along the horizontal axis. For any given level of foreign tariffs, that is, a member's ideal level of U.S. tariffs could shift. Such a shift could mean members of Congress would prefer unilateral reductions in U.S. tariffs.

A second possible change is that the relative weight members put on the two dimensions may change. Consider a generic situation in which a political actor has preferences over a two-dimensional policy space, with a level of X on the horizontal axis and a level of Y on the vertical axis. If the actor places equal weight on each dimension, the actor's indifference curves will be circular; the actor is willing to trade off loss of units of X in equal proportion to gain in units of Y. Suppose the actor comes to place greater weight on the X dimension such that she is willing to exchange a small gain in X for a larger loss in Y. The indifference curves would then become vertical ellipses; small changes in X would require large changes in Y in order to make her indifferent. By contrast, if the actor comes to place a greater weight on dimension Y, her indifference curves will be horizontal ellipses; small changes in Y would require large changes in X to make the actor indifferent.

We emphasize this latter process; that is, changing weights on issue dimensions allowed the president to expand the coalition in favor of free trade. Increasing trade flows increased the size and profits of export interests but had a lesser effect on import-competing interest (as some industries facing import competition disappeared). A similar effect occurred abroad, as exports to the U.S. activated foreign export interests. The net effect was that the importance placed on foreign access increased relative to the importance of protecting domestic industry. Indifference curves of actors in each nation changed, with American curves being transformed from circles to flat horizontal ellipses and foreign indifference curves becoming vertical ellipses.

Consider Figure 7 in which A* (from Figure 5) is the status quo. The only way that Congress will lower the minimum tariff level is if doing so makes congressional agenda setters (the Democratic median) better off. If the preferences of the Democratic leaders—both in terms of the location and relative weights—remain the same, no such policy will exist. If, however, increasing trade has led the foreign government and members of Congress to place relatively more weight on export interests, the indifference curves will shift. The indifference curves of U.S. actors will flatten and those of the foreign government will broaden, as indicated by the dotted lines in Figure 7. This means that the set of policies preferred over the status quo by the agenda setters will no longer be empty and a new equilibrium at a point such as A** will be possible.

The implication for the dynamics of trade liberalization is now apparent: increasing trade leads members of Congress and foreign actors to place more

FIGURE 7 How Tariffs Shift in Response to Changes in Preferences

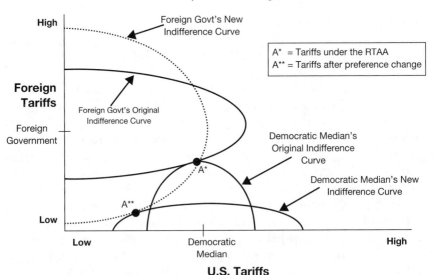

weight on access to foreign markets, indifference curves then shift, and greater liberalization is possible.

Changing Congressional Preferences

We can now return to our original query: what explains the depoliticization of American trade policy after World War II? We noted that trade was a highly partisan issue in the pre-RTAA period. Historically, Democrats voted for tariff reductions; Republicans voted for tariff increases. Figures 1 and 2 indicate that voting in Congress on trade measures before the RTAA generally followed party lines.

As the RTAA program progressed, the partisan composition of trade voting began to change in important ways. In 1943 some Republicans voted for the program for the first time, and by the mid-1950s many Republicans supported the program. Of course, Republicans were still more protectionist than Democrats and many voted for protectionist amendments to the RTAA renewal legislation. Nevertheless, their support for the general principles of the RTAA was no longer in doubt. In our empirical analysis, we concentrate on the period from 1953 to 1962, a time that saw the beginnings of substantial changes in partisan voting patterns on trade.

The logic we offer above suggested that changes in votes will be a function of export interests in congressional districts. With passage of increasing numbers of trade agreements, highly competitive American products were pouring into foreign markets. This increased flow of trade led to growth in the size, number, and profitability of export industries. Import competition was more than offset by increased opportunities in the export sector, so at least until the mid-1960s the overall effect was that producers and their representatives placed increased importance on foreign access relative to the importance of protecting domestic industry.

To explore the relationship between exports and congressional preferences, we estimated probit models on congressional voting on major trade bills in 1953 and 1962. . . .

In the estimations, we controlled for party and ideology, recognizing that these factors have traditionally been important determinants of a representative's trade preferences. . . .

We analyzed votes that occurred in 1953 and 1962, years that spanned the important development of bipartisan support for free trade. For 1953 we considered three votes: the Curtis Motion to recommit an RTAA alternative trade bill; the Smith Motion to recommit the RTAA; and the renewal of the RTAA. Of the three, the most controversial, and thus the most divisive, was the Curtis Motion. The motion recommitted a protectionist trade bill that had been introduced as a substitute for the renewal of the trade agreements program. (The vote on final passage of the renewal was very lopsided [363–34] and is therefore not amenable to probit analysis. To compensate for the skewed vote, we used ordered probit analysis, combining the vote on passage and the Smith Motion.) For 1962 we analyzed the Mason Motion, a protectionist effort to substitute a one-year extension of the RTAA for the Trade Expansion Act and the vote on the final passage of the bill. . . .

Because the estimated coefficients from probit analysis are not directly interpretable, we provide estimates of the effect of change in exports on the probability of liberal trade voting for different groups within Congress. Table 1 does this for the 1953 vote on the Curtis Motion and Table 2 does this for the 1962 vote on final passage. The first column is the predicted probability of voting for trade liberalization by an "average" representative, computed as someone with average levels of all independent variables for the whole subgroup. The second column is the predicted probability of voting for trade liberalization when exports are increased by one standard deviation and all other variables are held constant at their average levels. The third column repeats the exercise for an increase of two standard deviations in exports.

From Tables 1 and 2 we see that exports explain why—for the first time in a century—members of the Republican Party abandoned their party's traditional stance on trade. Table 1 shows for 1953 that a two standard deviation increase in export share of production increased the probability of a free trade

TABLE 1 Estimated Probabilities of Liberal Trade Voting in 1953 by Group and Change in Exports

	Probability of voting for trade liberalization		
	Average Exports	Average exports plus 1 standard deviations	Average exports plus 2 standard deviations
All	0.65	0.75	0.84
Republicans	0.49	0.63	0.75
Democrats	0.78	0.85	0.90

TABLE 2 Estimated Probabilities of Liberal Trade Voting in 1962 by Group and Change in Exports

	Probability of voting for trade liberalization		
	Average exports	Average exports plus 1 standard deviations	Average exports plus 2 standard deviations
All	0.78	0.85	0.90
Republicans	0.47	0.58	0.68
Democrats	0.90	0.94	0.96

vote from 65 percent to 84 percent for an "average" representative. The effect is stronger for Republicans, moving them from a 49 percent probability of voting for free trade at average levels of exports to a 75 percent probability of a free-trade vote when export shares increased by two standard deviations. The effect of exports was less important for Democrats, but most Democrats were already committed to free trade.

Table 2 reveals a similar story for the 1962 vote. An increase in two standard deviations of export shares of production raised the probability of a free-trade vote by 12 percent for all members. For Republicans, those least likely to vote for free trade in 1962, the effect was an increase of 21 points. Democrats in 1962 were still highly likely to vote for free trade, but an increase of two standard deviations in export share of production increased their likelihood to vote for free trade by 6 percent.

The general conclusion that emerges from this analysis is that exports affect congressional voting on trade. Higher levels of exports led to increased support for free trade. Although analysts have often suggested that exports should play such a role, the effect has been difficult to demonstrate. It is hard to get export data on the district level, and often the effects are overwhelmed by the more traditional variables of party, region, and ideology. By extrapolating export shares of production from district-level industrial data and using probit simulations, we have shown that an export effect was felt by congressional representatives. Members of Congress do vote based on constituent interests, and their views on American trade policy shifted as exports grew.

CONCLUSION

Through detailed analysis of both the logic and empirical effects of liberalization, this paper provides a new interpretation of the transformation of U.S. trade policy in the middle of the century. By examining both the causes and economic ramifications of the RTAA, we are able to explain how political factors shaped the institutional environment and, in turn, how the institutional factors shaped the political environment.

Two sets of puzzles have driven the analysis. The first set revolves around the initial legislation. Why would Congress ever agree to forfeit so much power to the president? And, more curiously, why would Congress choose to do so at a time when the commitment to free trade was not particularly strong? The second puzzle revolves around the expansion of the RTAA, especially after the Second World War. What was the mechanism that allowed trade liberalization to move continuously forward throughout the twenty-eight-year life span of the RTAA? Liberalization goes counter to a conventional logic that assumes that pro-protection interests should have been overrepresented in the policy process because of the distributional inequalities obtained from a liberal trade policy.

The existing literature provides incomplete answers to both puzzles. Many analyses of the original delegation emphasize congressional efforts to reduce its workload or to avoid serving special interests. In contrast, we argue that a model positing only policy-oriented, strategic political actors can explain the initial delegation. The RTAA allowed congressional Democrats to satisfy reluctant free traders and to durably reduce tariffs by coupling U.S. tariff cuts with foreign cuts. Further, it created a mechanism for lowering tariffs without having to meet the demanding constitutional requirement for two-thirds support that had undermined previous treaty efforts.

Many analyses of the effects of the RTAA are also suspect. Some claim that the RTAA removed trade policy from the constraints of a protectionist Congress; others argue that delegating authority and its accompanying agenda-setting power to the president was the key to trade liberalization in the period. But neither of these views can explain the clear and continued congressional involvement in tariff policy, even under the RTAA.

We agree with the consensus that congressional delegation to the president was an important element of the trade liberalization program. Nevertheless, the president's involvement in lowering trade barriers should not be exaggerated. Once Congress eschewed unilateral tariff reductions, presidential involvement was inevitable—it is the president's constitutional prerogative to negotiate treaties with foreign nations. But presidents had negotiated trade treaties throughout American history. Few, however, made it past a congressional veto. The RTAA should be remembered not because it delegated power to the president but because it mandated reciprocal tariff cuts under an innovative voting rule that bypassed the need for ex post approval by a supermajority in Congress.

The radical change in underlying preferences that allowed the liberalization of American trade policy cannot be explained either by the insulation of trade policy making or by presidential agenda control. Rather, trade liberalization endured because the RTAA changed the strategic environment of policy setting and later, the optimal policy choices of elected officials. First, the RTAA increased support for trade liberalization by "bundling" domestic and foreign reductions into one package. This not only garnered a larger base of support than did unilateral tariff reductions, but it also made it more difficult to change policy, even with an alteration in political control of government. By tying domestic reductions to foreign reductions, a greater pool of representatives found themselves in the proliberalization coalition. The existence of treaty obligations and the direct loss of foreign markets in response to a tariff hike made tariff reform far more durable than in any previous period of U.S. history. The RTAA was not simply a bill to lower tariffs; it was as well, an attempt to institutionalize a low tariff policy.

Second, and as important, tariff reform under the RTAA began an endogenous process of tariff reduction. Tariff reductions were matched with export growth. Increased export dependence in districts led to a more fundamental and enduring change in the political preferences of key actors in Congress. Although not the only factor, the RTAA was instrumental in increasing world trade, which spurred political interest in increasing access to foreign markets. This made increasing numbers of politicians willing to trade off support from import-competing interests that stood in the way of trade liberalization in exchange for support from export groups.

Empirical analysis of voting on trade bills supports our argument. Before the RTAA, voting on trade was almost wholly partisan, with Democrats in favor of and Republicans opposed to reductions in U.S. tariffs. After World War II partisan voting broke down, as more Democrats voted for protection and many more Republicans voted for trade liberalization.

Overall, the shift in American policy exceeded everyone's expectations. Trade increased dramatically, and the U.S. sustained a policy of relatively open borders. Our analysis strongly suggests that part of this shift should be attributed to an increase in the importance of exports at the district level.

In summary, the early history of liberalization in the U.S. provides a picture of how domestic politics, institutional choice, and the international economy are interlinked. Domestic politics led to an institutional innovation, the RTAA. The institutional innovation led both directly and indirectly to increased world trade. And, in turn, increased world trade led members of Congress and foreign actors to put more weight on increasing access to international markets. These preference changes expanded the coalition supporting free trade and allowed trade liberalization to continue to move forward.

FOREIGN DIRECT
INVESTMENT

Productive activity is at the center of any economy. Agriculture, mining, and manufacturing are the bases on which domestic and international commerce, finance, and other services rest. No society can survive without producing. Thus, production is crucial to both the domestic and international political economies.

In the international arena, production abroad by large corporations gained enormous importance after World War I. The establishment of productive facilities in foreign lands was nothing new, however. The planters who settled the southern portion of the thirteen colonies under contract to, and financed by, British merchant companies were engaging in foreign direct investment in plantation agriculture. Indeed, before the twentieth century, foreign investment in primary production—mining and agriculture—was quite common. In particular, European and North American investors financed copper mines in Chile and Mexico, tea and rubber plantations in India and Indochina, and gold mines in South Africa and Australia, among other endeavors.

Around the turn of the twentieth century, and especially after World War I, a relatively novel form of foreign direct investment (FDI) arose: the establishment of overseas branch factories of manufacturing corporations. In its origin the phenomenon was largely North American, and it remained so until the 1960s, when European, and then Japanese, manufacturers also began investing in productive facilities abroad. These internationalized industrial firms were called multinational or transnational corporations or enterprises (MNCs/ TNCs or MNEs/TNEs), usually defined as firms with productive facilities in three or more countries. Such corporations have been extraordinarily controversial for both scholars and politicians.

By 2015 the foreign affiliates of MNCs were worth over $105 trillion. They employ nearly 80 million people, and they account for more than one-third of world exports and a very substantial proportion of world output. Most MNCs are relatively small, but the top several hundred are so huge and so globe-straddling as to dominate major portions of the world economy.[1] Indeed, the largest MNCs have annual sales larger than the gross national product (GNP) of all but a few of the world's nations.

One major analytic task is to explain the very existence of multinational manufacturing corporations. It is, of course, simple to understand why English investors would finance tea plantations in Ceylon—they could hardly have grown tea in Manchester. Yet, in the abstract, there is little logic in Bayer producing aspirin in the United States. If the German aspirin industry were more efficient than the American, Bayer could simply produce the pills in its factories at home and export them to the United States. Why, then, does Ford make cars in England, Volkswagen make cars in the United States, and both companies make cars in Mexico instead of simply shipping them, respectively, across the Atlantic or the Rio Grande?

For the answer, students of the MNC have examined both economic and political factors. The political spurs to overseas direct investment are straight-forward. Many countries maintain trade barriers in order to protect local industry; this makes exporting to these nations difficult, and MNCs choose to "jump trade barriers" and produce inside protected markets. Similar considerations apply where the local government uses such policies as "Buy American" regulations, which favor domestic products in government purchases, or where, as in the case of Japanese auto investment in the United States, overseas producers fear the onset of protectionist measures.

Economic factors in the spread of MNCs are many and complex. The simplest explanation is that FDI moves capital from more-developed regions, where it is abundant and cheap, to less-developed nations, where it is scarce and expensive. This captures some of the story, but it also leaves much unexplained. Why, for example, does this transfer of capital not take the form of foreign lending rather than the (much more complex) form of FDI? Furthermore, why is most FDI among developed countries with similar endowments of capital rather than between developed and developing nations?

Economists have often explained foreign direct investment by pointing to certain size-related characteristics of multinational corporations. Because MNCs are very large in comparison to local firms in most countries, they can mobilize large amounts of capital more easily than local enterprises. Foreign corporations may then, simply by virtue of their vast wealth, buy up local firms in order to eliminate competitors. In some lines of business, such as large-scale production of appliances or automobiles, the initial investment necessary to begin production may be prohibitive for local firms, giving MNCs a decisive advantage. Similarly, MNC access to many different currencies from the many markets in which they operate may give them a competitive advantage over firms doing business in only one nation and currency. Moreover, the widespread popularity of consumption patterns formed in North America and Western Europe and then transplanted to other nations—a process that often leads to charges of "cultural imperialism"—may lead local consumers to prefer foreign brand names to local ones: for example, much of the third world population brushes their teeth with Colgate and drinks Coke, American brands popularized by literature, cinema, television, and advertising. However, though these points may be accurate, they do not amount to a systematic explanation of FDI.

The first step in the search for a more rigorous explanation of FDI was the "product cycle theory," developed by Raymond Vernon.[2] Vernon pointed out that products manufactured by MNCs typically follow similar patterns or cycles. A firm begins by introducing a new product that it manufactures and sells at home; over time, it expands exports to foreign markets; as the product becomes more widely known, it eventually engages in foreign investment; and finally, as production of the good is standardized, the firm begins exporting back to the home market. This jibes with observations that MNCs tend to operate in oligopolistic markets (those dominated by a few firms); that their products often are produced with new technologies; and that they tend to have important previous exporting experience.

The product cycle theory did not answer all the economic questions, however. There was still no explanation of why firms would invest abroad instead of simply exporting from their (presumably more congenial) home base or licensing the production technology, trademark, or other distinguishing market advantage to local producers. In the past thirty-five years, most economists have come to regard the multinational corporation as a special case of the vertically or horizontally integrated corporation. In this view, large companies come to organize certain activities inside the firm rather than through the marketplace because some transactions are difficult to carry out by normal market means—especially in cases where prices are hard to calculate or contracts are hard to enforce. When applied to MNCs, this approach suggests that FDI takes place because these firms have access to unique technologies, managerial skills, or marketing expertise that is more profitable when maintained within the corporate network than when sold on the open market. In Reading 9, economist Richard E. Caves surveys the modern economic theories of MNCs.

If the origins of MNCs are analytically controversial, their effects are debated with even more ferocity. In the 1950s and 1960s, as American-based corporations expanded rapidly into Western Europe, protests about foreigners buying up the European economies were common. At the time, most Americans regarded these protests as signs of retrograde nationalism, as they had traditionally taken MNCs for granted—few even realized that such firms as Shell, Universal Studios, Bayer, Saks Fifth Avenue, Nestle, and Firestone tires were foreign-owned. However, as investment in the United States by firms from the rest of the world grew, some critics began to argue that this represented a threat to American control over the U.S. economy. Thus, even in the United States, the most important home base of MNCs, the role of FDI is hotly debated. American MNCs employ 12 million people around the world, while foreign firms employ nearly 6 million Americans,[3] which means that FDI is, directly or indirectly, relevant to many people at home and abroad.

While FDI is controversial in the developed countries, it is far more contentious in the third world. Developed nations, after all, have technically advanced regulatory agencies and relatively large economies. However, most of the less-developed countries (LDCs) have economies smaller than the largest MNCs, with governmental regulatory bureaucracies that are no match for MNC executives. In many LDCs, then, the very presence of MNCs is viewed with suspicion. MNCs have been known to interfere in local politics, and local businesspeople often resent the competition created by huge foreign enterprises. Over the years, many LDCs have imposed stringent regulations on foreign direct investors, although most of them continue to believe that on balance, MNCs have a beneficial impact on national economic and political development. In the section that follows, Sonal Pandya (Reading 10) delves into the politics of FDI in developing countries and identifies the interests that strongly support investments by multinational corporations.

Since the 1990s, the growth of FDI by multinational corporations has outpaced the growth of international trade. FDI is now the largest type of capital inflow for many developing countries. But unlike international trade, virtually no multilateral rules exist to govern and promote FDI. In Reading 11, Beth A. Simmons examines the interactions and bargaining that led to the recent spread of Bilateral Investment Treaties—the primary legal mechanisms by which host and home governments regulate the investments of multinationals. Simmons argues that this decentralized system of regulation serves to protect investors' interests but is ill-suited to democratic governance.

If democratic governance and investor interests are at loggerheads, developing countries face a trade-off between competing for FDI and democratization. Quan Li and Adam Resnick (Reading 12) examine this trade-off and find that democratic institutions encourage FDI inflows by protecting investors' property rights but tend to reduce FDI inflows once the positive effect of democracy on property rights is taken into account.

NOTES

1. United Nations Conference on Trade and Development, *World Investment Report 2016* (New York and Geneva: United Nations, 2016), p. 9.

2. Raymond Vernon, "International Investment and International Trade in the Product Cycle," *Quarterly Journal of Economics* 80, 2 (1966): 190–207.

3. "Summary Estimates for Multinational Companies: Employment, Sales, and Capital Expenditures for 2011," U.S. Bureau of Economic Analysis, http://www.bea.gov /newsreleases/international/mnc/mncnewsrelease.htm (accessed 8/31/2016).

9

The Multinational Enterprise as an Economic Organization

RICHARD E. CAVES

Richard E. Caves, an economist, provides a survey of economic explanations of the multinational corporation (MNC). He focuses on how certain circumstances can make it difficult to carry out transactions in the marketplace. For example, it is hard to measure or establish a "fair" price for assets such as new technologies or managerial expertise. In these cases, firms, including MNCs, can overcome the problems of market transactions involving such hard-to-price assets by carrying out transactions internally, within the corporation. This reading presents the predominant economic explanation for the rise and existence of MNCs.

The multinational enterprise (MNE) is defined here as an enterprise that controls and manages production establishments—plants—located in at least two countries. It is simply one subspecies of multiplant firm. We use the term "enterprise" rather than "company" to direct attention to the top level of coordination in the hierarchy of business decisions; a company, itself multinational, may be the controlled subsidiary of another firm. The minimum "plant" abroad needed to make an enterprise multinational is, as we shall see, judgmental. The transition from a foreign sales subsidiary or a technology licensee to a producing subsidiary is not always a discrete jump, for good economic reasons. What constitutes "control" over a foreign establishment is another judgmental issue. Not infrequently a MNE will choose to hold only a minor fraction of the equity of a foreign affiliate. Countries differ in regard to the minimum percentage of equity ownership that they count as a "direct investment" abroad, as distinguished from a "portfolio investment," in their international-payments statistics.

. . . The definition does identify the MNE as essentially a multiplant firm. We are back to Coase's (1937) classic question of why the boundary between the administrative allocation of resources within the firm and the market allocation of resources between firms falls where it does. In a market economy, entrepreneurs are free to try their hands at displacing market transactions by increasing the scope of allocations made administratively within their firms. The Darwinian tradition holds that the most profitable pattern of enterprise organization should ultimately prevail: where more profit results from placing plants under a common administrative control, multiplant enterprises will predominate, and single-plant firms will merge or go out of business. In order to explain the existence and prevalence of MNEs, we require models that predict where the multiplant firm enjoys advantages from displacing the arm's-length market and where it does not. In fact, the prevalence of multiplant (multinational) enterprises varies greatly from sector to sector and from country to country, affording a ready opportunity to test models of the MNE.

The models of the multiplant firm potentially relevant to explaining the presence of MNEs are quite numerous and rather diverse in their concerns. It proves convenient to divide them into three groups: (1) One type of multiplant firm turns out broadly the same line of goods from its plants in each geographic market. Such firms are common in domestic industries with fragmented local markets such as metal containers, bakeries, and brewing. Similarly, the many MNEs that establish plants in different countries to make the same or similar goods can be called horizontally integrated. (2) Another type of multiplant enterprise produces outputs in some of its plants that serve as inputs to its other activities. Actual physical transfer of intermediate products from one of the firm's plants to another is not required by the definition; it needs only to produce at adjacent stages of a vertically related set of production processes. (3) The third type of multiplant firm is the diversified company whose plants' outputs are neither vertically nor horizontally related to one another. As an international firm it is designated a diversified MNE.

1. HORIZONTAL MULTIPLANT ENTERPRISES AND THE MNE

We start by equating the horizontal MNE to a multiplant firm with plants in several countries. Its existence requires, first, that *locational forces* justify dispersing the world's production so that plants are found in different national markets. Given this dispersion of production, there must be some *governance* or *transaction-cost advantage* to placing the plants (some plants, at least) under common administrative control. This abstract, static approach provides the most general and satisfying avenue to explaining the multinational company. . . . We assume at first that plant A was located in southeast England because that was the lowest-cost way to serve the market it in fact serves. We also assume that this locational choice was not essentially influenced by whether the plant was built by an MNE, bought by an MNE, or not owned by an MNE at all. The static approach also puts aside the vital question of why a company grows into MNE status—something more readily explained after the static model is in hand.

The transaction-cost approach asserts, quite simply, that horizontal MNEs will exist only if the plants they control and operate attain lower costs or higher revenue productivity than the same plants under separate managements. Why should this net-revenue advantage arise? Some of the reasons have to do with minimizing costs of production and associated logistical activities of the firm. The more analytically interesting reasons—and, we shall see, the more important ones empirically—concern the complementary nonproduction activities of the firm.

Proprietary Assets

The most fruitful concept for explaining the nonproduction bases for the MNE is that of assets having these properties: the firm owns or can appropriate the assets or their services; they can differ in productivity from comparable assets possessed by competing firms; the assets or their productivity effects are mobile between national markets; they may be depreciable (or subject to augmentation), but their lifespans are not short relative to the horizon of the firm's investment decision. Successful firms in most industries possess one or more types of such assets. An asset might represent knowledge about how to produce a cheaper or better product at given input prices, or how to produce a given product at a lower cost than competing firms. The firm could possess special skills in styling or promoting its product that make it such that the buyer differentiates it from those of competitors. Such an asset has a revenue productivity for the firm because it signifies the willingness of some buyers to pay more for that firm's product than for a rival firm's comparable variety. Assets of this type are closely akin to product differentiation a market condition in which the distinctive features of various sellers' outputs cause each competing firm to face its own downward-sloping demand curve. The proprietary asset might take the form of a specific property—a registered trademark or brand—or it might rest in marketing and selling skills shared among the firm's employees. Finally, the distinctiveness of the firm's marketing-oriented assets might rest with the firm's ability to come up with frequent innovations; its proprietary asset then might be a patented novelty, or simply some new combination of attributes that its rivals cannot quickly or effectively imitate. This asset might vary greatly in tangibility and specificity. It could take the specific form of a patented process or design, or it might simply rest on know-how shared among employees of the firm. It is important that the proprietary asset, however it creates value, might rest on a set of skills or repertory of routines possessed by the firm's team of human (and other) inputs. . . .

The proprietary assets described by these examples evidently share the necessary conditions to support foreign investment. They are things that the firm can use but not necessarily sell or contract upon. Either the firm can hold legal title (patents, trademarks) or the assets are shared among the firm's employees and cannot be easily copied or appropriated (by other firms or by the employees themselves). They possess either the limitless capacities of public goods (the strict intangibles) or the flexible capacities of the firm's repertory of routines. Especially important for the MNE, while the productive use of these assets is not tightly tied to single physical sites or even nations, arm's-length transfers of them between firms are prone to market failures. These failures deter a successful one-plant firm from selling or renting its proprietary assets to other single-plant firms and thereby foster the existence of multiplant (and multinational) firms. Proprietary assets are subject to a daunting list of infirmities for being detached and transferred by sale or lease:

1. They are, at least to some degree, *public goods*. Once a piece of knowledge has been developed and applied at a certain location, it can be put to work elsewhere at little extra cost and without reducing the capacity available at the original site. From society's point of view, the marginal conditions for efficient allocation of resources then require that the price of the intangible asset be equal to its marginal cost, zero or approximately zero. But no one gets rich selling bright ideas for zero. Therefore, intangible assets tend to be underprovided or to be priced inefficiently (at a net price exceeding their marginal cost) or both.
2. Transactions in intangibles suffer from *impactedness* combined with *opportunism*. This problem is best explained by examples: I have a piece of knowledge that I know will be valuable to you. I try to convince you of this value by describing its general nature and character. But I do not reveal the details, because then the cat would be out of the bag, and you could use the knowledge without paying for it unless I have a well-established property right. But you therefore decline to pay me as much as the knowledge would in fact be worth to you, because you suspect that I am opportunistic and overstate my claims.
3. A proprietary asset might be diffuse and therefore incapable of an enforceable lease or sale contract. The owning firm might readily contract with a customer to achieve a specific result using some competence that it possesses, but be unable to contract to install that competence within another firm. Even with well-defined intangibles, various sources of uncertainty can render contractual transfers infeasible or distort the terms of viable deals.

This application of modern transaction-cost analysis underlies a framework widely used in research on the MNE. It asserts the existence of three necessary conditions for the appearance of horizontal foreign investments: (1) The firm can appropriate some value-creating proprietary asset ("ownership"); (2) production processes that employ or apply the value-creating asset are efficiently dispersed among several national markets ("location"); and (3) the decentralized application of the proprietary asset is more efficiently managed within the owning firm than by renting it at arm's length to another firm ("internalization"). . . .

Empirical Evidence: Prevalence of Horizontal Foreign Investment

Hypotheses about horizontal MNEs have received many statistical tests. The usual strategy of research involves relating the prevalence of MNEs in an industry to structural traits of that industry: if attribute x promotes the formation of MNEs, and successful firms in industry A have a lot of x, then MNEs should be prevalent in industry A. These tests have been performed on two dependent variables: foreign operations of firms in a source country's industries normalized by their total activity level in those industries (hereafter "outbound" foreign investment), and foreign subsidiaries' share of activity in a host country's markets normalized by total transactions in those markets (hereafter "inbound" foreign investment). The exogenous variables are chosen to represent features of industries' structures that should either promote or deter foreign direct investment. . . .

. . . There is considerable agreement on the major results among studies of both outbound and inbound investment, among studies of a given type for each country, and among studies based on different countries. Therefore we offer here some generalizations about the principal conclusions without referring extensively to the conclusions reached in individual studies or about particular countries. . . .

. . . [Research] results confirm, first and foremost, the role of proprietary assets inferred from the outlays that firms make to create and maintain these assets. Research and development intensity (R&D sales ratio) is a thoroughly robust predictor. Advertising intensity has proved nearly as robust, even though most studies have lacked an appropriately comprehensive measure of firms' sales-promotion outlays. The literature also consistently finds a significant positive influence for an industry's intensive use of skilled managerial labor; this variable seems to confirm the "repertory of routines" basis for foreign investment, independent of the strictly intangible proprietary assets. . . . A third result that also supports a role for the firm's general coordinating capacity is the positive influence of multiplant operation within large countries such as the United States. . . .

Multinationals in Service Industries

Horizontal MNEs in banking and other services have received increased attention from researchers. The proprietary-assets hypothesis again makes a good showing—especially when extended to the transaction-specific assets of an ongoing semicontractual relationship between the service enterprise and its customer. A bank, advertising agency, or accounting firm acquires a good deal of specific knowledge about its client's business, and the parties' sustained relationship based on trust lowers the cost of contracting and the risks of opportunistic behavior. The service firm enjoying such a quasi-contractual relation with a parent MNE holds a transaction-cost advantage for supplying the same service to the MNE's foreign subsidiaries. If the service must be supplied locally, the service firm goes multinational to follow its customer.

Much casual evidence reveals this transaction-specific asset behind service industries' foreign investments . . . , especially in the banking sector. . . . Some banks acquire particular product-differentiating skills analogous to those found in some goods-producing industries; they can explain banks' foreign investments in less-developed countries . . . and in countries with large populations of migrants from the source country. Also, national banking markets commonly appear somewhat noncompetitive because of cartelization or regulation or both, and foreign banks are well-equipped potential entrants. The Eurocurrency markets' rise can be largely explained on this basis. The traits of foreign banks' operations in the United States affirm these propositions. . . .

The prominence of transaction-specific assets as a factor driving foreign investment is apparently matched in other service industries such as advertising agencies, accounting, and consulting firms. . . . Studies of other multinational service industries, however, bring out different factors. . . .

2. VERTICALLY INTEGRATED MNES

The vertically integrated MNE is readily regarded as a vertically integrated firm whose production units lie in different nations. Theoretical models that explain vertical integration should therefore be directly applicable. Again, we assume that production units are dispersed in different countries due to conventional locational pressures—the bauxite mine where the bauxite is, bauxite converted to alumina at the mine because the process is strongly weight-losing, and the smelter that converts alumina into aluminum near a source of low-cost electric power. The question is, why do they come under common administrative control? The proprietary-assets model is not necessary, because neither upstream nor downstream production unit need bring any distinctive qualification to the parties' vertical consolidation. Some proprietary advantage of course *could* explain which producer operating at one stage undertakes an international forward or backward vertical integration.

Models of Vertical Integration

Until the rise of transaction-cost economics the economic theory of vertical integration contained a large but unsatisfying inventory of special-case models. Some dealt with the physical integration of production processes: if you make structural shapes out of the metal ingot before it cools, you need not incur the cost of reheating it. Such gains from physical integration explain why sequential processes are grouped in a single plant, but they neither preclude two firms sharing that plant nor explain the common ownership of far-flung plants. Another group of traditional models regard vertical integration as preferable to a stalemate between a monopolistic seller and a monopsonistic buyer, or to an arm's-length relation between a monopolistic seller and competitive buyers whose activities are distorted due to paying the monopolist's marked-up price for their input. Some models explain vertical integration as a way around monopolistic distortions, while others explain it as a way to profit by fostering such distortions.

The theory of vertical integration has been much enriched by the same transaction-cost approach that serves to explain horizontal MNEs. Vertical integration occurs, the argument goes, because the parties prefer it to the ex ante contracting costs and ex post monitoring and haggling costs that would mar the alternative state of arm's-length transactions. The vertically integrated firm internalizes a market for an intermediate product, just as the horizontal MNE internalizes markets for proprietary assets. Suppose that there were pure competition in each intermediate-product market, with large numbers of buyers and sellers, the product homogeneous (or its qualities costlessly evaluated by the parties), information about prices and availability in easy access to all parties in the market. Neither seller nor buyer would then have reason to transact repeatedly with any particular party on the other side of the market. When these assumptions do not hold, however, both buyers and sellers acquire motives to make long-term alliances. The two can benefit mutually from investments that each makes suited to special attributes of the other party. Each then incurs a substantial fixed cost upon shifting from one transaction partner to another. Each seller's product could be somewhat different, and the buyer incurs significant costs of testing or adapting to new varieties, or merely learning the requirements and organizational routines of new partners. The buyer and seller gain an incentive to enter into some kind of long-term arrangement.

If transaction-specific assets deter anonymous spot-market transactions, they leave open the choice between long-term contracts and vertical integration. Contracts, however, encounter the costs of negotiation and of monitoring and haggling previously mentioned. These ex ante and ex post costs trade off against one another—a comprehensive contract can reduce subsequent haggling—but the overall cost remains. The problem is compounded because, even in a market with many participants, unattached alternative transaction partners tend to be few *at any particular time* when a party might wish to recontract. Fewness compounds the problems of governance in arm's-length vertical relationships.

One special case of the transaction-cost theory of vertical integration holds promise for explaining MNEs involved in processing natural resources. Vertical integration can occur because of failings in markets for information, as analyzed earlier in the context of proprietary assets. A processing firm must plan its capacity on some assumption about the future price and availability of its key raw material. The producers of that raw material have the cheapest access (perhaps exclusive) to that information. But they have an incentive to overstate availability to the prospective customer: the more capacity customers build, the higher they are likely to bid in the future for any given quantity of the raw material. Therefore, vertical integration could occur in order to evade problems of impacted information. . . .

To summarize, intermediate-product markets can be organized in a spectrum of ways stretching from anonymous spot-market transactions through a variety of long-term contractual arrangements at arm's length to vertical integration. Switching costs and durable, specialized assets discourage spot transactions and favor one of the other modes. If, in addition, the costs of negotiating and monitoring arm's-length contracts are high, the choice falls on vertical integration. These empirical predictions address both where vertical MNEs will appear and how they will trade off against contractual relationships.

Empirical Evidence

Far fewer statistical studies address these hypotheses than the ones concerned with horizontal MNEs. . . .

A great deal of information exists on individual extractive industries in which MNEs operate on a worldwide basis, and this case-study evidence merits a glance in lieu of more systematic findings. For example, Stuckey . . . found the international aluminum industry to contain not only MNEs integrated from the mining of bauxite through the fabrication of aluminum projects but also a network of long-term contracts and joint ventures. Market participants are particularly unwilling to settle for spot transactions in bauxite (the raw ore) and alumina (output of the first processing stage). The problem is not so much the small number of market participants worldwide as the extremely high switching costs. Alumina refining facilities need to be located physically close to bauxite mines (to minimize transportation costs), and they are constructed to deal with the properties of specific ores. Likewise, for technical and transportation-cost reasons, aluminum smelters are somewhat tied to particular sources of alumina. Therefore, arm's-length markets tend to be poisoned by the problems of small numbers and switching costs. And the very large specific and durable investments in facilities also invoke the problems of long-term contracts that were identified earlier. Finally, Stuckey gave some weight to Arrow's model of vertical integration as a route to securing information: nobody knows more about future bauxite supplies and exploration than an existing bauxite producer.

A good deal of evidence also appears on vertical integration in the oil industry. The ambitious investigations have addressed the U.S. segment of the industry, but there appears to be no strong difference between the forces traditionally affecting vertical integration in national and international oil companies. These studies give considerable emphasis to the costs of supply disruption faced by any nonintegrated firm in petroleum extraction or refining. Refineries normally operate at capacity and require a constant flow of crude-oil inputs. Storing large inventories of input is quite costly, and so backward integration that reduces uncertainty about crude supplies can save the refiner a large investment in storage capacity. It also reduces risks in times of "shortages" and "rationing," when constraints somewhere in the integrated system (crude-oil supplies are only the most familiar constraint) can leave the unintegrated firm out in the cold. The hazard of disrupted flows translates into a financial risk, as vertically integrated firms have been found to be able to borrow long-term funds more cheaply than those with exposure to risk. . . .

Country-based studies of the foreign-investment process have also underlined vertical MNEs as the outcome of failed arm's-length market transactions. Japanese companies became involved with extractive foreign investments only after the experience of having arm's-length suppliers renege on long-term contracts; and they also experimented with low-interest loans to independent foreign suppliers as a way to establish commitment. . . .

Vertical Integration: Other Manifestations

The identification of vertically integrated foreign investment with extractive activities is traditional and no doubt faithful to the pattern accounting for the bulk of MNE assets. However, it gives too narrow an impression of the role of vertically subdivided transactions in MNEs.

First of all, it neglects a form of backward integration that depends not on natural resources but on subdividing production processes and placing abroad those that are both labor-intensive and footloose. For example, semiconductors are produced by capital-intensive processes and assembled into electronic equipment by similarly mechanized processes, both undertaken in the industrial countries. But, in between, wires must be soldered to the semiconductors by means of a labor-intensive technology. Because shipping costs for the devices are low relative to their value, it pays to carry out the labor-intensive stage in a low-wage country. The relationship of the enterprises performing these functions in the United States and abroad must obviously be a close one, involving either detailed contractual arrangements or common ownership. This subdivision of production processes should occur through foreign investment to an extent that depends again on the transactional bases for vertical integration.

Writers on offshore procurement and the associated international trade always refer to the role of foreign investment in transplanting the necessary know-how and managerial coordination. . . . [Scholars have] explored statistically both the structural determinants of this type of trade and the role of MNEs in carrying it out. . . . [The] data pertain to imports under a provision of the U.S. tariff whereby components exported from the United States for additional fabrication abroad can be reimported with duty paid only on the value added abroad. . . . [S]tatistical analysis explains how these activities vary both among U.S. industries and among countries taking part in this trade. . . . [The] results confirm the expected properties of the industries that make use of vertically disintegrated production: their outputs have high value per unit of weight, possess reasonably mature technology (so are out of the experimental stage), are produced in the United States under conditions giving rise to high labor costs, and are easily subject to decentralized production. Among overseas countries, U.S. offshore procurement favors those not too far distant (transportation costs) and with low wages and favorable working conditions. With these factors controlled, the component flows increase with the extent of U.S. foreign investment, both among industries and among foreign countries.

A considerable amount of vertical integration is also involved in the "horizontal" foreign investments described earlier in this chapter, and the behavior of horizontal MNEs cannot be fully understood without recognizing the complementary vertical aspects of their domestic and foreign operations. Many foreign subsidiaries do not just produce their parents' goods for the local market; they process semifinished units of that good, or package or assemble them according to local specifications. Pharmaceuticals, for example, are prepared in the locally desired formulations using basic preparations imported from the parent. The subsidiary organizes a distribution system in the host-country market, distributing partly its own production, but with its line of goods filled out with imports from its parent or other affiliates. Or the subsidiary integrates forward to provide local servicing facilities. These activities are bound up with the development and maintenance of the enterprise's goodwill asset, as described earlier, through a commitment of resources to the local market. The firm can thereby assure local customers, who are likely to incur fixed investments of their own in shifting their purchases to the MNE, that the company's presence is not transitory. This consideration helps explain foreign investment in some producer-goods industries for which the proprietary-assets hypothesis otherwise seems rather dubious. . . . All of these activities represent types of forward integration by the MNE, whether into final-stage processing of its goods or into ancillary services.

The evidence of this confluence of vertical and horizontal foreign investments mainly takes the form of case studies rather than systematic data. . . . It is implied by the extent of intracorporate trade among MNE affiliates—flows that would be incompatible with purely horizontal forms of intracorporate relationships. Imports of finished goods by Dutch subsidiaries from their U.S. parents . . . are high (as percentages of the affiliates' total sales) in just those sectors where imports might complement local production for filling out a sales line—chemicals (24.9 percent), electrical equipment (35.4 percent), and transportation equipment (65.5 percent). The prevalence of intracorporate trade in engineering industries also suggests the importance of components shipments. . . .

Statistical evidence on U.S. exports and imports passing between corporate affiliates sheds light on this mixture of vertical and horizontal foreign investment. Lall . . . analyzed the factors determining the extent of U.S. MNEs' exports to their affiliates (normalized either by their total exports or by their affiliates' total production). He could not discriminate between two hypotheses that together have significant force: (1) that trade is internalized where highly innovative and specialized goods are involved, and (2) that trade is internalized where the ultimate sales to final buyers must be attended by extensive customer engineering and after-sales services. Jarrett . . . confirmed these hypotheses with respect to the importance in U.S. imports of interaffiliate trade, which in his data includes exports by foreign MNEs to their manufacturing and marketing subsidiaries in the United States as well as imports by U.S. MNEs from their overseas affiliates. Jarrett also found evidence that interaffiliate trade in manufactures reflects several conventional forms of vertical integration: more of it occurs in industries populated (in the United States) by large plants and companies, capable of meeting the scale-economy problems that arise in the international disintegration of production, and in industries that carry out extensive multiplant operations in the United States. . . .

3. PORTFOLIO DIVERSIFICATION AND THE DIVERSIFIED MNE

This section completes the roster of international multiplant firms by accounting for those whose international plants have no evident horizontal or vertical relationship. An obvious explanation of this type of MNE (though not the only one, it turns out) lies in the spreading of business risks. Going multinational in any form brings some diversification gains to the enterprise, and these reach their maximum when the firm diversifies across "product space" as well as geographical space. . . .

Now we consider empirical evidence on diversification as a motive for the MNE. Within a national economy, many shocks affect all firms rather similarly—recessions, major changes in macroeconomic policy. Between countries, such disturbances are more nearly uncorrelated. Also, changes in exchange rates and terms of trade tend to favor business profits in one country while worsening them elsewhere. Statistical evidence confirms that MNEs enjoy gains from diversification: the larger the share of foreign operations in total sales, the lower the variability of the firm's rate of return on equity capital. . . . MNEs also enjoy lower levels of risk in the sense relevant to the stock market—financial risk (beta). . . . In general, this evidence supports the hypothesis that the MNE attains appreciable international diversification. However, the diversification might result from investments that were propelled by other motives. . . .

4. SUMMARY

The existence of the MNE is best explained by identifying it as a multiplant firm that sprawls across national boundaries, then applying the transaction-cost approach to explain why dispersed plants should fall under common ownership and control rather than simply trade with each other (and with other agents) on the open market. This approach is readily applied to the horizontal MNE (its national branches produce largely the same products), because the economies of multiplant operation can be identified with use of the firm's proprietary assets, which suffer many infirmities for trade at arm's length. This hypothesis receives strong support in statistical studies, with regard both to intangible assets and to capabilities possessed by the firm.

A second major type of MNE is the vertically integrated firm, and several economic models of vertical integration stand ready to explain its existence. Once again, the transaction-cost approach holds a good deal of power, because vertical MNEs in the natural-resources sector seem to respond to the difficulties of working out arm's-length contracts in small-numbers situations where each party has a transaction-specific investment at stake. Evading problems of impacted information also seems to explain some vertical foreign investment. The approach also works well to explain the rapid growth of offshore procurement by firms in industrial countries, which involves carrying out labor-intensive stages of production at foreign locations with low labor costs. Although procurement occurs through arm's-length contracts as well as foreign investment, the role of foreign investment is clearly large. Finally, numerous vertical transactions flow between the units of apparently horizontal MNEs as the foreign subsidiary undertakes final fabrication, fills out its line with imports from its corporate affiliates, or provides ancillary services that complement these imports.

Diversified foreign investments, which have grown rapidly in recent decades, suggest that foreign investment serves as a means of spreading risks to the firm. Foreign investment, whether diversified from the parent's domestic product line or not, apparently does offer some diversification value. Diversified foreign investments can be explained in part by the parent's efforts to utilize its diverse R&D discoveries, and certain other influences as well. However, other diversified investments appear specifically aimed at spreading risks through international diversification, especially among geographic markets.

10

Labor Markets and Demand for Foreign Direct Investment

SONAL PANDYA

In this reading, Sonal Pandya explains the interests that support and oppose for-eign direct investment (FDI) in developing countries. She argues that FDI raises wages in recipient countries, especially for highly skilled workers, because for-eign firms require more skilled labor than their local counterparts. Accordingly, support for FDI inflows should increase with a person's skill level. Using three years of public opinion data from eighteen Latin American countries, she pro-vides robust evidence that individual attitudes toward FDI are consistent with FDI's effects on wages.

Political economy research has only begun to tap into the richness and com-plexity of foreign direct investment (FDI). FDI plays a central role in many aspects of international economic integration. It is the single largest source of global capital, in some years worth more than all other forms of capital flows. It drives other types of economic flows. For example, intrafirm trade—trade between subsidiaries of a single multinational firm—constitutes over one-third of total world trade. FDI can also foster economic development by creating jobs and introducing new technologies. Existing political economy scholarship on FDI emphasizes how political risk influences where multina-tional firms choose to invest. For example, current research shows that coun-tries with lower risk receive higher volumes of FDI; debate in this literature centers on which domestic political conditions make markets appealing to for-eign investors. These studies model the choices of multinational firms to pro-vide political economy explanations for the supply of FDI inflows. Although this is an important topic, it is only one dimension of FDI's politics.

In this article I focus on the demand for FDI. Specifically, I develop and test a theory of individual preferences for FDI inflows, arguing that preferences are a function of FDI's distributional effects. In FDI, multinational firms estab-lish foreign subsidiaries to produce goods and services abroad. These activi-ties redistribute income within recipient countries by driving up labor demand. FDI increases the supply of productive capital. Foreign firms create additional labor demand by hiring local labor; consequently wages rise. Skilled labor wages, in particular, rise because multinational firms are typically more tech-nologically advanced and require more skilled labor than equivalent local firms. Given these distributional effects of FDI inflows, I hypothesize that labor supports FDI inflows and that this support is greater among individuals at higher skill levels.

I test these claims with three years of data from the Latinobarometer, a public opinion survey covering eighteen Latin American countries and perhaps the only major, multicountry survey project that inquires about attitudes toward FDI. These data allow me to test the observable implications of FDI's distributional effects for individuals' preferences. I show that FDI preferences are indeed consistent with FDI's expected effect on individual income. Specifically, support for FDI inflows increases with respondents' skill level. Respondents with a university education are between 7 to 10 percentage points more likely to support FDI inflows than respondents with less than a secondary school education. This finding is robust to a variety of alternate explanations including the socializing and informational effects of education, job insecurity, and opposition to privatization.

By opening up a new dimension to FDI research, these findings make two broader scholarly contributions. First, they build the foundation for a broader theory of FDI demand. Preferences underlie more aggregate phenomena including lobbying for FDI policies, the existence and form of national FDI regulation, and choices about international cooperation on investment. These are all aspects of FDI's political economy about which little is known, even though these are central questions in the study of other types of international economic flows. Awareness of the demand side of FDI's politics may prompt a reassessment of extant findings on FDI supply; the volume of FDI inflows may have as much to do with demand for FDI as with investors' willingness to supply investment. More generally, existing accounts of the political economy of international economic integration are, at best, incomplete without greater attention to the politics of FDI support.

Second, these findings contribute to research on individual preferences for international economic flows. The use of survey data to validate theories of distributional effects is increasingly common and has already provided new insights on preferences for trade, immigration, macroeconomic policy, and social spending. Existing research identifies a role for nonmaterial sources of trade policy preferences including national pride and socialization through higher education. FDI likely has even more potential to ignite nationalist opposition than trade. It can give foreigners a high profile in the national economy as large employers and custodians of natural resources and national infrastructure. Recent years have seen takeovers by multinational firms singled out as affronts to national identity in countries from Bolivia and South Korea to the United States. As such, FDI is a particularly apt policy area in which to test the relative importance of material and nonmaterial sources of international economic policy preferences.

The remainder of this article is organized into three main parts. The next section develops hypotheses about the sources of individual preferences of FDI inflows. I then describe the empirical test of these hypotheses and a series of robustness checks. The article concludes with the implications of the article's findings for public policy and a broader research program on the politics of FDI regulation.

SOURCES OF FOREIGN DIRECT INVESTMENT PREFERENCES

Three facts about FDI help to establish FDI's economic implications for recipient countries. First, FDI is the international flow of firm-specific capital. These firm-specific assets include proprietary production technologies, managerial and organizational practices, and trademarked brands. Multinational corporations arise when firms encounter incomplete contracting problems in directly selling or licensing these assets. Additionally, holdup risk is high when a separate firm is an exclusive inputs supplier. FDI avoids these pitfalls by keeping assets within the firm and expanding the firm itself into multiple markets.

Second, FDI is so expensive that only the world's most productive firms undertake it. FDI requires firms to establish and monitor multiple subsidiaries, often in distant and initially unfamiliar markets. FDI is efficient for only those firms whose exceptionally high productivity offsets the costs of multinational production. For example . . . multinationals are 15 percent more productive than purely domestic, exporting firms. I make use of this fact in deriving FDI's distributional effects by assuming that multinational firms are more productive than local firms in the host market.

Third, there are two distinct strategies for organizing multinational production. Like all forms of capital flow, FDI is a way for firms to earn higher returns on their capital. Owners of firm-specific capital, however, are unable to "lend" their capital due to various incomplete contracting problems. Instead, these firms earn returns to their assets indirectly via product markets. There are two different ways in which firms can organize production to realize these returns. Firms lower production costs by pursuing *export-oriented FDI* that fragments the production process. Firms usually retain headquarter functions such as research and development in the home country and relocate production to foreign countries abundant in necessary inputs, typically labor. *Market-oriented FDI* sees firms entering countries that are potential product markets. This form of investment replicates production facilities in multiple host countries to produce goods and services for local sale. Firms pursue this strategy when trade barriers or transport costs make cross-border trade prohibitive. For example, American restrictions on Japanese auto imports in the 1980s prompted major Japanese carmakers to establish manufacturing plants within the United States. Market-oriented FDI accounts for the majority of FDI flows. In the late 1990s, foreign subsidiaries of U.S.-based multinationals sold approximately two-thirds of their output in the same host country in which they produced it. This figure is actually a historic low, because export-oriented FDI grew considerably in the 1990s. Any account of FDI's distributional effects has to make sense of both its factor price effects and, when relevant, product price effects.

FDI's Distributional Effects

. . . Consider the distributional effects of firm-specific capital inflows. To isolate this effect, assume that FDI does not affect local product prices. This is true of export-oriented FDI in which multinationals export goods rather than selling them locally. In the context of the model, FDI introduces new capital into one of the two local industries. Local workers become more productive because their marginal revenue product increases with additional capital inputs. The exceptionally high productivity of multinational firms magnifies this effect because these firms typically introduce more efficient production technologies than do local firms. At this higher marginal revenue product the multinational firm expands production, hiring workers away from local firms by offering a higher wage. Firms re-establish the equality of wages and marginal revenue product at this higher wage. Since labor is mobile across industries, these gains accrue to all labor, not just those employed by multinational firms. These wage increases represent gains in real income because product prices are unchanged. Returns to domestic capital owners decline because a portion of capital income is redistributed to labor in the form of higher wages.

A wealth of evidence demonstrates that FDI increases wages. That foreign-owned firms pay higher wages than their domestic counterparts is an exceptionally robust finding in the context of both developed and less developed economies. Most studies find between a 10 and 30 percent wage premium for unskilled workers in foreign-owned manufacturing firms. Additionally, wages paid by local firms increase after the entry of multinationals. Blonigen and Figlio examine the effects of FDI on local wages in South Carolina and find that the entry of a single average-sized, foreign-owned plant, employing about 190 workers, increases by 2.3 percent the real wages of all workers employed in the plant's industry and county.[1] This wage increase, they argue, reflects an overall increase in labor demand. Similarly, Feenstra and Hanson identify a close association between FDI inflows and wage increases in Mexico in the 1990s, with the highest wage increases observed in those states receiving the highest volumes of investment.[2] In many developing countries, local firms pay higher wages after the entry of a foreign-owned firm despite constant or even decreasing productivity. These results support the theoretical claim that FDI inflows lead to higher wages via its effect of raising labor demand.

Market-oriented FDI has the additional effect of introducing competition into the local product market. Given that multinational producers are typically

---

1. Blonigen and Figlio 2000.
2. Feenstra and Hanson 1997.

more productive than their host country counterparts, market-oriented FDI can result in lower product prices through greater market competition. The precise effect can range from neutral (that is, FDI has no influence on product prices), to price reductions whose magnitude depends on the degree of market competition that FDI introduces. For labor, any price reductions are an additional channel through which FDI increases real income.

There is considerable evidence that returns to FDI increase with skill level. Recall that firms' fundamental motivation to undertake FDI is to protect firm-specific production technologies. By virtue of these technologies, production processes in multinational firms tend to be more advanced than those of equivalent domestic firms. For this reason, multinational firms systematically demand more highly skilled labor than do local firms. From this fact follows the prediction that labor's gains from FDI inflows increase with skills. Extensive evidence shows that, consistent with this hypothesis, FDI inflows have a particularly large effect on skilled labor wages. Estimates of FDI's effects on skilled labor wages are as high as 50 to 70 percent above skilled wages paid by local firms. . . . Feenstra and Hanson conclude that FDI was the single largest source of increases in skilled labor wages in Mexico during the 1980s.[3]

The theoretical and empirical findings on FDI inflows have clear implications for labor's FDI preferences. Both factor price and product price effects suggest that labor will support FDI. FDI increases wages by increasing labor demand; wage increases are higher for skilled labor due to the relatively high skill intensity of multinational firms' production processes. Accordingly, labor is likely to support FDI inflows because it increases labor's real income through higher labor demand and, sometimes, lower product prices. Skilled workers have a higher probability, all else equal, of supporting FDI inflows since skilled wages receive the largest gains from FDI.

Alternate Mechanisms

Preferences are, of course, complex and multidimensional. Empirical tests must account for other potential sources of FDI preferences. Recent research on trade and immigration attitudes suggests that preferences are not exclusively a function of expected income effects. Mayda and Rodrik find a robust positive relationship between national pride and protectionist preferences.[4] Hiscox and Hainmueller propose that higher education uniquely socializes individuals to have more cosmopolitan preferences by fostering an awareness and appreciation of foreign cultures and influences. Higher education, they continue, also provides the requisite economic literacy to appreciate the welfare gains to free trade independent of the narrow effects on indi-

3. Ibid.
4. See Mayda and Rodrik 2005.

vidual income.[5] These proposed effects of higher education on preferences are independent of the effect of higher education on skills.

Another possible influence on preferences is perceived job insecurity. Scheve and Slaughter argue that FDI can increase the elasticity of labor demand in host countries, thereby fueling job insecurity.[6] Although they do not address FDI preferences directly, their finding suggests that individuals who perceive their jobs to be less secure may be less favorable toward FDI. This mechanism is distinct from the distributional one but it is not necessarily inconsistent.

The finding may not generalize because FDI can also be a source of job stability, especially in times of economic crisis. Multinational firms are more resilient to economic shocks than purely domestic firms in the host country. As part of a larger multinational organization, affiliates have easier access to credit and more diversified portfolios that make them more likely to stay in operation than domestic firms who cannot call upon the resources of a parent firm. Indeed, FDI flows often increase following currency devaluations. In short, the role of job security in the formation of FDI preferences is an open empirical question. . . .

EXPLAINING FDI PREFERENCES: EMPIRICAL TESTS

A growing body of research in comparative and international political economy utilizes public opinion data to test the consistency of preferences with predicted distributional effects. Individual policy preferences can be directly linked to salient demographic information regarding education, employment, and geographic location. By contrast, indirect measures of preferences based on political behavior are much noisier due to the influence of interest groups and political institutions on observed behavior. Following this research I use survey data to test whether preferences for FDI inflows are consistent with FDI's predicted effects on individual income. Data are from the Latinobarometer, an annual public opinion survey conducted in eighteen Latin American countries. This survey is unique among the prominent multicountry survey projects in that it regularly includes questions on attitudes toward FDI inflows. The surveys draw representative samples in each country and inquire about a wide range of political and social topics. Surveys from 1995, 1998, and 2001 included questions about FDI preferences. The 1995 and 1998 surveys ask: *"Do you consider that foreign investment, in general, is beneficial or is it harmful to the economic development of the country?"* Respondents replied "beneficial" or "harmful." FDI BENEFICIAL is a binary variable equal to 1 if the respondent answered "beneficial."

5. Hainmueller and Hiscox 2006.
6. Scheve and Slaughter 2004.

The 1998 and 2001 surveys ask a different but related question: *"Do you strongly agree, agree, disagree, or strongly disagree with the phrase: foreign investment should be encouraged?"* PROMOTE FDI is equal to 1 if the respondent replied agree or strongly agree. The use of two different questions, both of which are present in the 1998 sample, mitigates concerns about framing effects by allowing comparisons across the two questions for the same sample.

Labor's skill level is the central source for FDI preferences. As is standard in empirical work on economic preferences, I use respondents' level of education as a proxy for skill. There is, however, some disagreement over the most appropriate measure of educational attainment. Rather than choose among them, I use three distinct measures of education, each of which captures a somewhat different aspect of the same underlying concept. YEARS OF EDUCATION measures the respondents' number of years of schooling (up to sixteen years). This measure assumes a strictly linear effect of education on skill level. By construction each additional year of education is assumed to have the same effect on the probability of FDI support. Scheve and Slaughter measure educational attainment in this way. A different approach is to use the highest level of education completed as the proxy for skills. I construct two variables on this basis. EDUCATION LEVEL is a four-category variable that is equal to 0 for less than a primary school education (including illiterate), 1 for completed primary school, 2 for compulsory secondary education, and 3 for completed higher education. This measure collapses educational attainment into ordered categories but preserves the assumption that a shift between any two categories has the same effect. Finally, I construct four separate indicator variables for whether the respondent's highest level of education is: a university degree, a partial university education (ended without a degree), postsecondary vocation training, and secondary school completed. The omitted group is all educational attainment less than secondary school completion. . . .

I examine the influence of job security on FDI preferences using responses to the question: *"Which is your degree of concern about being without a job or being unemployed in the next 12 months?"* JOB INSECURITY is a four-category variable for which higher values correspond to greater concern about job security. The expected sign is *ex ante* unclear; there are plausible theoretical arguments that yield opposite predictions. The coefficient represents FDI's net effect on employment volatility, controlling for FDI's effects on wages.

Occupational information provides proxies for additional alternate explanations. PUBLIC EMPLOYEE is a binary variable equal to 1 for respondents employed in the public sector. Privatization and FDI are tightly linked because governments often sell state-owned firms to foreign firms who have the requisite capital and expertise to operate these firms as profitable enterprises. Respondents employed in the public sector are more likely to oppose FDI on these grounds.

I estimate a series of probit models to consider the relationship between these variables and the probability of support for FDI inflows. All models include controls for respondents' basic demographic characteristics: FEMALE, equal to 1 if the respondent is a woman; AGE, the respondent's age; and MARRIED, equal to 1 if the respondent is married or cohabitating. Models also include country-fixed effects to control for the myriad of country-level factors that can influence preferences. I first estimate a set of baseline models to test core hypotheses using all three years' data. I then exploit the richness of individual surveys to test the robustness of core propositions to different measures of key variables and additional sources of FDI preferences. . . .

Empirical Results

The baseline model estimates, summarized in Table 1 demonstrate a consistently positive and statistically significant relationship between skill level and support for FDI. This relationship is robust to the use of different measures of educational attainment as a proxy for the expected return to FDI inflows. Models with separate estimates for different levels of education show that the probability of supporting FDI inflows increases with more education, often quite dramatically. Respondents who have completed university are, depending on the sample, between 7 and 10 percentage points more likely to support FDI inflows than those who have not completed secondary school. Those who have completed secondary school and have no further education are 3 to 4 percentage points more likely to support FDI relative to those who have not completed this level of schooling.

The significant findings for educational attainment below a university degree support an income-based explanation over an information or socialization explanation. Recall that Hiscox and Hainmueller single out a university education as a source of both socialization and information about economic flows. A positive and significant coefficient for only the university completed variable would have supported a nonmaterial explanation. A factor income explanation is more likely given that the support for FDI is robust across educational levels.

The results are mixed for the alternate channels of FDI's income effects. JOB SECURITY is statistically significant for only the 1998 sample, for which it has a negative effect on the probability of support for FDI. The substantive effect of job insecurity is quite small compared to educational attainment. Similarly, public employment has the predicted negative effect but it is statistically significant in only some specifications. The negative sign on the coefficient is consistent with the theoretical claim that public employees are vulnerable to a loss of rents when FDI occurs in conjunction with privatization.

Although a control variable, FEMALE merits brief discussion given its consistently negative and statistically significant coefficient. Across the three sample years, women are between 4 to 6 percentage points less likely than men to support FDI inflows. There are no theoretical reasons to suggest why women are consistently opposed to FDI inflows. This result echoes findings on trade policy preferences that women are consistently more protectionist. . . .

TABLE 1 Baseline Results

| | 1995 | | | 1998 | | | | | | 2000 | | |
| | P(FDI Beneficial=Y) | | | P(FDI Beneficial=Y) | | | P(FDI Encouraged=Y) | | | P(FDI Encouraged=Y) | | |
Variables	Model (1)	Model (2)	Model (3)	Model (4)	Model (5)	Model (6)	Model (7)	Model (8)	Model (9)	Model (10)	Model (11)	Model (12)
Years of Education	0.029**			0.032**			0.028**			0.014**		
	(0.003)			(0.005)			(0.005)			(0.003)		
Education Level		0.149**			0.146**			0.120**			0.075**	
		(0.014)			(0.024)			(0.021)			(0.019)	
University Completed			0.286**			0.375**			0.276**			0.201**
			(0.055)			(0.063)			(0.069)			(0.066)
Vocational Training			0.242**			0.187**			0.153*			-0.031
			(0.075)			(0.045)			(0.068)			(0.053)
Incomplete University			0.197**			0.206**			0.260**			0.109
			(0.054)			(0.061)			(0.065)			(0.061)
Secondary Completed			0.156**			0.116**			0.103**			0.090**
			(0.044)			(0.041)			(0.036)			(0.034)
Job Insecurity	-0.007	-0.003	-0.003	-0.063**	-0.062**	-0.063**	-0.044**	-0.045**	-0.044**	-0.022	-0.022	-0.022
	(0.015)	(0.014)	(0.014)	(0.017)	(0.017)	(0.017)	(0.016)	(0.015)	(0.016)	(0.014)	(0.014)	(0.013)
Public Employee	-0.013	-0.034	0.000	-0.045	-0.038	-0.049	-0.094	-0.088	-0.092	-0.097**	-0.114**	-0.108**
	(0.073)	(0.089)	(0.082)	(0.042)	(0.040)	(0.038)	(0.051)	(0.049)	(0.048)	(0.033)	(0.036)	(0.036)
Female	-0.193**	-0.173**	-0.186**	-0.161**	-0.162**	-0.162**	-0.163**	-0.164**	-0.163**	-0.121**	-0.122**	-0.122**
	(0.050)	(0.049)	(0.048)	(0.038)	(0.038)	(0.038)	(0.039)	(0.039)	(0.039)	(0.027)	(0.027)	(0.027)
Age	0.002	0.002	0.001	0.001	-0.000	-0.001	0.003**	0.002*	0.002*	0.001	0.001	0.001
	(0.001)	(0.001)	(0.001)	(0.001)	(0.001)	(0.001)	(0.001)	(0.001)	(0.001)	(0.001)	(0.001)	(0.001)
Married	0.132**	0.101*	0.138**	0.054	0.049	0.054	0.012	0.007	0.017	0.026	0.026	0.027
	(0.045)	(0.047)	(0.052)	(0.036)	(0.036)	(0.036)	(0.029)	(0.028)	(0.031)	(0.033)	(0.033)	(0.033)
Observations	6759	7199	6427	15011	15011	15011	15220	15220	15220	16526	16526	16526

NOTES: Probit coefficients with robust standard errors clustered by country in parentheses. All models include country fixed effects. * significant at 5% level; ** significant at 1% level.

CONCLUSION

This article has illuminated a new dimension of the political economy of FDI: the sources of individual preferences for FDI inflows. Using three years of extensive public opinion data from eighteen Latin American countries, I have shown that FDI preferences are consistent with FDI's distributional effects: support for FDI inflows increases with respondents' skill level. This finding is robust to a variety of alternate explanations for preferences including concerns about job security and opposition to privatization; evidence for these alternatives is, at best, limited. These findings also speak directly to the role of ideas in the formation of preferences for international economic flows. Previous work on trade and immigration preferences shows that education informs and socializes individuals to be more receptive to international influences, independent of the expected effects of these flows on income. By contrast, I find no evidence to support these alternate mechanisms by which education could influence preferences.

These findings have clear implications for how politicians in emerging markets can build support for greater international economic integration. They show that, at least for FDI, individuals are persuaded by the economic benefits of openness. This robust support for FDI belies causal accounts of opposition to FDI rooted in populism and xenophobia. To be sure, there are instances of such opposition but they are the exception rather than the rule. Efficiency-minded politicians can tap into the broad support for FDI among labor to build a constituency in support of economic integration with the world. In particular, any government efforts to expand education will have the additional payoff of building support for integration. By securing this support for initial inflows of FDI, politicians can pave the way for the realization of long-term potential benefits of FDI including economic growth and development.

These findings suggest some new lines of inquiry into the sources of international economic policy preferences. For the study of FDI preferences, the next step includes testing nuanced hypotheses about different types of FDI using disaggregated data on individuals' exposure to investments. This is a formidable task given the paucity of accurate data on FDI flows but a worthwhile one that would yield many useful insights into the relative importance of ideas and income in the formation of preferences. For example, exposure to FDI into natural resource extraction is likely to elicit very different preferences than FDI into technologically advanced, export-oriented manufacturing industries. Another aspect ripe for study is how the substantive relationship between different kinds of economic flows influences preferences. As noted in the introduction, trade and FDI flows are linked. Sometimes they are complements, as in the case of export-oriented FDI, and other times they are substitutes, as seen in market-oriented FDI. Survey work can uncover how much voters perceive these interdependencies and internalize the consequences of one type of economic policy for other forms of international economic activity.

Finally, the theory and findings presented in this article establish the analytical foundation for a larger research program on the political economy of FDI demand. This broader research agenda includes explanations for special interest coalitions and lobbying activities related to FDI, patterns in formal FDI regulations, and international cooperation pertaining to FDI. Why should international relations scholars be interested in the politics of FDI demand? The study of FDI speaks powerfully to the foundational questions of the discipline, including who comprise the winners and losers from international economic integration and variation in how countries balance the opportunities and risks of international economic integration in their policy choices. FDI occupies a central role in the international economy and drives other prominent forms of economic activity like international trade. To claim that one understands the politics of global integration, one needs to be able to explain the politics of FDI demand, which is still overlooked in the current understanding of international affairs. This research is also necessary to specify more accurate models of trade, finance, and other types of economic activity that intersect with FDI. Perhaps the greatest promise of this research is that it illuminates the political choices that inform how to harness the potential of international economic integration to fuel economic development. By deploying the well-established analytical traditions of international political economy to the politics of FDI demand, scholars stand to gain tremendous new insight into international economic integration more generally.

REFERENCES

Blonigen, Bruce A., and David M. Figlio. 2000. The Effects of Foreign Direct Investment on Local Communities. *Journal of Urban Economics* 48 (2): 338–63.

Hainmueller, Jens, and Michael J. Hiscox. 2006. Learning to Love Globalization: Education and Individual Attitudes Toward International Trade. *International Organization* 60 (2): 469–98.

Mayda, Anna Maria, and Dani Rodrik. 2005. Why Are Some People (and Countries) More Protectionist Than Others? *European Economic Review* 49 (6): 1393–430.

Scheve, Kenneth F., and Matthew J. Slaughter. Economic Insecurity and the Globalization of Production. *American Journal of Political Science* 48 (4): 662–74.

11

Bargaining over BITs, Arbitrating Awards: The Regime for Protection and Promotion of International Investment

BETH A. SIMMONS

In this reading, Beth A. Simmons explores the interactions between MNCs and host governments that led to the rise of the Bilateral Investment Treaty (BIT)— the primary legal institution for regulating the investments of MNCs. She argues that this decentralized, bilateral system of regulation is driven by competitive forces that put developing nations in a weak bargaining position: either they accept a dispute settlement system that is biased in favor of foreign investors or MNCs will take their investments elsewhere. A key conclusion is that it is important not only to consider whether BITs attract foreign investment—which has been the focus of nearly all the empirical research on BIT effects—but also to investigate the governance consequences of the international investment regime generally.

The past three decades have seen the spectacular development and spread of international rules governing foreign direct investment (FDI). Research on why states have signed on to these rules and their effect on investment flows abounds. This article takes a more critical approach than most to the development and consequences of the "regime" for international investment. It examines the bargaining dynamics that have led to broad and asymmetrical rights for private economic agents, considers some of the consequences of such rights, and documents states' efforts to renegotiate some of the central aspects of the regime. It also speaks to the conditions under which states make exceptionally constraining legal commitments and some of the governance consequences of such commitments. States have begun to push back against the investment regime, often attempting to guard their policy space in the face of the legal arrangements that constrain them. Credible commitment making is not exclusively about attracting capital; it is also a choice about economic governance more generally.

The nature and operation of this international legal regime is potentially relevant to global flows of foreign direct investment, estimated to reach $1.45 trillion in 2013 and applicable to a worldwide stock of FDI in 2012 of about $20 trillion. Yet, little research in international relations has taken a close look at it. Investment treaties should be examined in a broader context and be compared with, for example, institutions for the protection and promotion of trade. Bilateralism and a private right of standing for private corporate actors imbues the international investment regime with a peculiar character that stimulates competition for capital, weakens the bargaining position of states when they are in a vulnerable economic position, and exposes them to legal liabilities that they may not have anticipated when they "tied their hands" under these agreements in the first place. While investment treaties may indeed have facilitated some capital imports, researchers have neglected the other side of the coin: pushback from public actors who increasingly view the investment regime as currently constituted as not in their interest. A result has been, as one legal scholar puts it, "one of the most dynamic and controversial areas of international law today."[1]

This article focuses on the international investment regime—from the negotiation of treaties to dispute settlement. By "international investment regime," I mean the collection of often decentralized (even sometimes incoherent) rules about the promotion and protection of foreign direct investment. The first section puts the investment regime in context by comparing it with the regime for international trade. While space constraints do not allow for full testing of a range of explanations here, I suggest one reason for the differences between the two may be differences in dynamic contracting for trade and investment. Section II reviews existing explanations for the spread of bilateral investment agreements. It supplements existing research that characterizes the ratification of bilateral agreements as competition for capital and hard bargaining. . . . Section III explores the sovereignty consequences of the spread of BITs. Evidence suggests that they may have underdelivered investment and served up an unexpectedly large wave of litigation. Moreover, new evidence is beginning to suggest that this litigation is contributing to expansion of the already asymmetrical legal rights of investors. In Section IV, I present evidence that states are beginning to resist and renegotiate the rules that seem increasingly to threaten their sovereignty. The international investment regime is under pressure to change, reflecting pushback from states who feel the balance of advantages favoring investors has gone a little too far.

I. BACKGROUND: A TALE OF TWO REGIMES—TRADE AND INVESTMENT

International economic cooperation is characterized by one obvious fact without a clear explanation: even though international trade and international investment agreements both purport to facilitate economic relations across borders, and even though they are sometimes even addressed in the same treaties, these two clusters of law are *substantially* different. The differences are hardly appreciated by social scientists largely because the legal regime for FDI has developed under the radar of most international relations and international political economy scholars. There are at least two stark contrasts

1. Yackee 2012.

between the international institutions governing trade and investment: their respective degrees of centralization and the nature of rights given to private actors.

Decentralization of the Investment Regime

The international investment regime has no single institutional core; rather, it is comprised of a relatively decentralized system of rules, norms, and dispute resolution procedures. In contrast to international laws governing trade, which are influenced overwhelmingly by the laws of the General Agreement on Tariffs and Trade/World Trade Organization (GATT/WTO), investment rules developed first through customary international law, and more recently through a system of bilateral and regional treaties whose primary purpose is to encourage international investment by protecting property rights of investors in foreign jurisdictions.

These institutional differences are puzzling. As Allee and Peinhart show, at the level of individual treaties the design of the international investment regime is not completely explicable from a rational design point of view.[2] One might think that uncertainty about the security of investment and coordination problems among investors and hosts could encourage centralization. One might also expect a higher degree of centralization in investment rules, since the major players are multinational and would benefit from consistent rules around the world. But these conjectures do not explain why the investment regime tends to be more decentralized than is the case for the trade regime (although the latter is decentralizing as preferential and regional trade agreements become more common).

Despite the fact that the major capital-exporting countries have historically converged on general principles of customary international law, they have not been able to agree on multilateral treaty provisions among themselves, and certainly not with developing countries. Twice in modern history (in discussions of the International Trade Organization in 1947 and the Multilateral Agreement on Investment in 1995–1998), notable efforts were made to multilateralize the international investment regime, and both failed. Even the GATT's Uruguay Round (1986–1994), noted for its sweeping accomplishments codified in fifty major new agreements, touched on investment in a relatively minor way. By the end of the Uruguay Round, attention to FDI amounted to little more than a patchwork of international rules.

While multilateralism languished, bilateral investment agreements flourished. Capital-exporting countries did not respond to the growing risks to investment in the 1950s and 1960s and to ITO and Organization for Economic Cooperation and Development (OECD) failures by sitting on their diplomatic hands. The governments of these countries began quietly at first to negotiate

---

2. Allee and Peinhardt 2014.

a series of agreements with potential host states to address any ambiguity in the law of investment protection. BITs were innovative in a number of respects. In general, they offer a wider array of substantive protections than the customary rule. For example, BITs typically require national treatment and most-favored-nation (MFN) treatment of foreign investments in the host country. They usually protect contractual rights, guarantee the right to transfer profits in hard currency, and prohibit or restrict the use of performance requirements. Perhaps most importantly, BITs provide for international arbitration of disputes between the investor and the host country. This is an unusual arrangement in international law and is discussed in greater detail below.

Judged by their spread, BITs appear to have been spectacularly successful. Today there are some 2,600 known bilateral agreements governing foreign investment in every region of the world and an increasing number of free trade agreements that include analogous investment provisions as well. Their growth was exceptionally explosive in the 1990s. But clearly, an international consensus has never existed for the development of a "World Investment Organization." Rather, rules are negotiated largely bilaterally and disputes settled in a much more ad hoc fashion than is the case with trade in goods and services. Arguably, bilateralism has exacerbated the competitive rush to sign BITs and contributed to bargaining concessions by developing countries when and where their bargaining power has been weakest.

The Privileged Position of Private Actors: A Private Right of Standing in the Investment Regime

The trade regime and the investment regime have another interesting difference. Trade agreements are generally enforced by official state actions through public mechanisms such as sanctions, while investment rules—at least as they have developed in the past fifty years of treaty law—are generally enforced by firms exercising a private right of action, typically granted in the treaties themselves, which may result in monetary compensation for damages.

Giving investors a right to sue states for compensatory damages directly before an international tribunal represented a paradigm shift from the prevailing customary international law (CIL) relating to foreign direct investment. The state-to-state system of dispute settlement on which CIL was premised was replaced by a system in which investors could seek compensation for losses due to host government actions without the support or even the approval of their home governments. This private right to sue a government for damages and to choose the forum in which to do so constitutes the most revolutionary aspect of the international law relating to foreign investment in the past half-century. It is reflected not only in almost all BITs, but also in several important regional and sector-specific investment agreements, such as the Energy Charter Treaty (ECT), the North American Free Trade Agreement (NAFTA), and the Central American Free Trade Agreement (CAFTA).

The comparison between BITs and the WTO and the trade provisions of CAFTA and NAFTA is stark. These latter agreements allow *states only* to initiate disputes over trade practices, although firms can of course lobby their governments to take up their cause. Outside of the EU, trade treaties do not provide for monetary remedies for firms in case of trade law violation. Trade and investment rules are sharply different with respect to their duration as well: whereas a state can exit the WTO with a mere six months' notice of intent to withdraw, BITs typically continue to bind for ten to fifteen years after their termination.

While it is beyond the scope of this article to test fully a satisfying explanation, the basic distinctions between these regimes may result in part from the different risks faced by traders and investors. One possibility is that investment poses a greater credibility problem for potential hosts than trade in goods does for potential importers. It might be necessary for hosts to tie their hands more tightly to attract investment because they are likely to have more time-inconsistent preferences than importing countries, with respect to trade liberalization. It may be rational to promise investors special tax, zoning, or regulatory concessions to encourage them to make an investment that would be costly to withdraw. But once the investment is made, it may be rational for the host country to withdraw those concessions and to impose other costs up to and including expropriation. As has long been recognized in the obsolescing bargaining literature, the greater the sunk cost of investment, the greater the dynamic risk for investors. Time-inconsistent preferences are far less acute in the trade area: once allowed entry, competitive goods are likely to weaken domestic producers, erode their political opposition, and develop a consumer-based constituency. Once goods are imported, changing political pressures may actually make importing governments' ex ante and ex post preferences more consistent over time.

Furthermore, the logic of credible commitment making is reinforced by a weaker logic of reciprocity in the investment area than in trade. Traditionally, investment flows have been lopsided: developing countries want to attract capital but they are rarely capital exporters themselves on a significant scale. That is one reason why investor protections contained in BITs historically may have tended to involve a highly developed and developing dyad (though this is changing), and why defendants in the trade regime (GATT and WTO cases) are overwhelmingly rich developed states while defendants in the investment regime (cases registered with the International Center for Settlement of Investment Disputes [ICSID]) are overwhelmingly middle or lower income states. . . . Reciprocity is most useful as an enforcement mechanism where the players' interactions are symmetrical: where reciprocity is weak (across the developmental divide), legal hands-tying may be useful.

In short, private investing actors have special privileges in international law compared to any other private actors, and they are increasingly exercising these privileges against developing and middle income countries, many of whom may lack the legal capacity and experience to counter the claims effectively. Interestingly, over the past three decades, the number of cases registered with the ICSID has grown much more rapidly than the number of cases registered with the WTO. New disputes registered with the GATT/WTO grew 96 percent from the 1980s to the 1990s but fell about 16 percent from the 1990s to the 2000s. New mixed (firm-state) arbitration cases registered with the ICSID grew 153 percent and a whopping 449 percent, respectively, over the same decades. Keep in mind that private actors' access to enforceable compensatory damages, typically without the need to first exhaust domestic remedies, is unusual in public international law. Private traders have no such rights, nor do noncommercial individuals whose human rights (as opposed to property rights) have been violated, at least not outside of Europe.

II. WHY RATIFY BITS? THE COMPETITIVE AND CYCLICAL ROOTS OF HANDS-TYING

In the absence of multilateral rules, states have proceeded to construct a distinctive regime for investment, treaty by bilateral treaty. Decentralized regime creation has enhanced competitive dynamics as potential host states have attempted to attract capital in the context of stagnating bank lending. Bilateral negotiations have been affected by the relative bargaining power of host states: the weaker their bargaining power, the tighter they may be willing to tie their hands to satisfy investors. . . . This section explores the competitive pressures to ratify BITs and then tests the proposition that hands-tying has been influenced by an important source of eroding bargaining power—weak economic growth in the potential host country.

The Setting: Competing for Capital

The late 1980s and first half of the 1990s was a time of extremely slow growth in international bank lending, which, on the heels of the debt crisis of the 1980s, was contracting in many parts of the world. Foreign direct investment was a potential way to borrow internationally in this period of stagnant bank finance. . . . As the pool of available global FDI increased and international bank loans held steady or in some cases decreased, the ratification of BITs followed. This context suggests that many governments were likely motivated to sign BITs in order to compete more successfully for FDI at a time when alternative forms of international borrowing were stagnant or on the decline.

Patterns of BIT signings seem to confirm the plausibility of a competitive dynamic among developing countries seeking a share of FDI. Such capital could potentially be wooed away from investment venues in which governments refused to provide investors the advantages contained in BITs. Zachary Elkins, Andrew Guzman, and Beth Simmons find that controlling for a broad range of other factors, developing countries were far more willing to sign a BIT with a richer country if close competitors—those with similar infrastructures, similarly skilled work forces, and comparable export profiles—had done so.[3] A dynamic of competition may not only reduce the marginal ability of each additional BIT to attract capital, . . . it also has the potential to encourage countries to concede more sovereign prerogatives than they otherwise might have done.

Hard Economic Times

In addition to the competitive pressures documented in other studies, economic pressures may have also contributed to the turn toward BITs. . . .

. . . Elkins, Guzman, and Simmons find . . . that the more positive a developing country's gross domestic product (GDP) growth, the less likely it was to ratify a bilateral investment treaty with another country, given that it had not done so already. Every percentage point increase in growth in the potential host reduced the likelihood that a given country pair would conclude a bilateral investment agreement by about 3 percentage points. To put that finding in perspective, the more than 11 percent drop in the Czech Republic's growth rate between 1990 and 1991 . . . would correspond with a 33 percent increase in its eagerness to conclude a BIT. (The Czechs, in fact, concluded eight BITs in 1991. In 1993, while still hovering around zero growth, they were up to twenty-eight.) In contrast, Botswana, which averaged nearly 7 percent growth from the mid-1990s to the mid-2000s was, according to these estimates, about 21 percent less likely to ratify a BIT each year. By 2006, Botswana had in fact concluded only eight bilateral investment treaties. This evidence is consistent with the proposition that hard economic times lead to concessions to investors that governments might otherwise not make when economic growth is strong.

If BITs are in fact negotiated and concluded under stressful economic conditions—a situation that would naturally tend to reduce potential hosts' bargaining power vis-à-vis capital-exporting states—then it might be expected that the more unfavorable the conditions, the more significant the concessions governments are willing to make in order to conclude a treaty. Moreover, slow economic growth can be expected to increase the impatience of the potential host country, lowering time horizons and making a government more willing to relinquish increments of sovereignty for the ability to attract economic activity in hopes of stimulating the economy.

Allee and Peinhardt's data on dispute settlement make it possible to test the proposition that BIT dispute settlement provisions reflect the eroding bargaining position of would-be host governments in periods of weak economic growth.[4] Simply stated, developing countries in dire economic conditions are expected to concede more of their sovereignty in these agreements than they might otherwise. The following indicators are useful: (1) Is ICSID mentioned

---

3. Elkins, Guzman, and Simmons 2006.
4. Allee and Peinhardt 2014.

at all as an option for international arbitration between the investor and the contracting party? Is it the sole option mentioned in the treaty? and (2) Is the United Nations Commission on International Trade Law (UNCITRAL) mentioned as an option? From this information one can infer whether either of the two major institutions for international arbitration is mentioned in the treaty. Allee and Peinhardt code whether there is any explicit mention of investors' ability to choose a local tribunal or court to settle a dispute. They also code whether or not there is a requirement for local remedies for dispute settlement to be fully pursued before submission to international arbitration, and whether or not the treaty contains an explicit statement to the effect that the parties are consenting in advance to international arbitration. If potential host governments make more concessions to investors in their BITs when growth is weak, then as economic conditions in the host country deteriorate, the expected tilt would be in favor of international arbitration and away from local remedies. . . .

The results are quite striking; in almost every case, the stronger the economic growth in the less developed BIT partner, the stronger the domestic provisions and the weaker the international provisions contained in the dispute settlement section of a BIT. The lone exception is a provision to use the ICSID for dispute settlement, which has no consistent relationship with the developing country's business cycle. . . . In addition, strong economic growth in the less developed partner is strongly and consistently correlated with a much lower likelihood that the signed BIT will contain a provision to use UNCITRAL rules should a dispute erupt. . . . Treaties that do not contain references to the ICSID or to UNCITRAL rules . . . are also convincingly correlated with positive growth in the less developed partner (but there are relatively few of these). Conversely, slow growth in a developing country makes it less likely to negotiate a treaty without any references to one or more of these dispute settlement institutions/ rules. Pre-consent clauses—general but explicit statements that commit the parties in advance to arbitrate a dispute—may be mildly associated with stronger developing country growth rates during the negotiation phase, . . . but the result is not statistically significant. . . .

To get a substantive sense of the effect of the business cycle on the probability of negotiating an agreement without any ICSID or UNCITRAL clauses, imagine two states, a high-growth state and a low-growth state at two different points in time, 1985 and 2000. The results . . . work out to a probability that a high-growth (10 percent per annum) developing country in 1985 stood about a 31 percent chance of signing a BIT without any references to the ICSID or to UNCITRAL. A low-growth country suffering a –10 percent growth rate for the three years leading to the signing of a BIT had only about a 15 percent chance of that outcome. Over time, however (and consistent with theories that emphasize intensification of competition for capital) progressively fewer states were able to secure such clauses. By 2000, a country with 10 percent growth had only about a 7 percent chance of negotiating a BIT without such a clause, but a country with –10 percent growth had only a miniscule chance (less than 2 percent) of achieving this result. . . .

. . . The likelihood that a BIT will contain some reference to the investor's ability to choose a local tribunal or court is positively associated with growth in the less developed BIT partner. . . . A provision that requires an investor to exhaust local remedies is also positively associated with the developing country's business cycle. . . . Taken together, these results support the general tendency for developing countries with strong positive growth to maintain somewhat greater national control over how investment disputes will be settled. Downturns in the business cycle, by contrast, are consistently associated with much greater delegation to international tribunals in the event of a dispute. Figure 1 (a–c) illustrates the substantive impact of the business cycle when a potential host experiences 10 percent growth versus –10 percent growth, holding all other conditions constant (that is, at their means).

Slower growth is associated with tighter hands-tying, even when several other conditions are controlled for. Democratic countries tend to negotiate agreements with ICSID clauses and avoid concluding treaties that contain neither ICSID nor UNCITRAL provisions. They are also much more likely, according to these results, to agree to treaties that contain explicit clauses that pre-commit them to arbitration in the event of a dispute. Somewhat surprisingly, democracies do not tend to insist on local remedies. . . . Consistent with studies on other areas of international law, democracies tend to delegate authority with greater regularity to international institutions than do nondemocratic states.

A bargaining framework might lead one to suspect that the greater the developmental difference between partners, the greater the tendency for BITs to reflect international delegation for the settlement of disputes. The evidence . . . is consistent with that hypothesis. When the difference between treaty partners is greater, there is a slight tendency for greater delegation to the ICSID . . . and a fairly convincing reduction in local provisions. . . . In this case "developmental difference" is defined as the difference in World Bank categories: (1) high income, (2) high-middle income, (3) low-middle income, and (4) low income. Taking the absolute value of the difference, this measure ranges from 0, when countries are from the same category, to 3, when they are from opposite extremes.

Finally, capital-exporting countries may also have clear preferences over the kind of dispute settlement provisions they include in their BITs. A US dummy variable suggests the United States favors the ICSID and is also likely to negotiate treaties with UNCITRAL provisions, but tends to eschew agreements that contain neither. China has been less willing than other countries to delegate explicitly to either the ICSID or the UNCITRAL and is more likely to conclude treaties that make no reference to either and include localist provisions, and to not require pre-consent agreements in their BITs. China's preferences would appear to be closer to those of a capital-importing country than

FIGURE 1 Impact of Growth Rates on Three Types of BIT Dispute Settlement Clauses

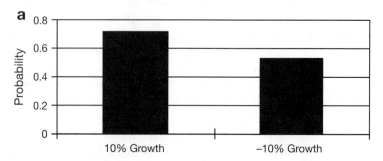

Effect of Growth Rate on Probability of
Clause Relating to Local Recourse

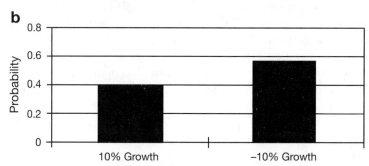

Effect of Growth Rate on Probability of
an UNCITRAL Clause

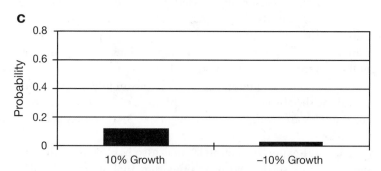

Effect of Growth Rate on Probability of
No ICSID or UNCITRAL Clauses

a capital-exporting country, even when changes in dispute resolution provisions over time are controlled for.

Overall, Allee and Peinhardt's model of structural bargaining power can be supplemented with one based on economic cycles. Developing countries not only make more concessions on dispute settlement provisions the more powerful their negotiating partners are, as Allee and Peinhart have found, but they may also make more concessions when the economic tide begins to turn against them.

III. THE CONSEQUENCES OF RATIFICATION: FIELD OF DREAMS OR LITIGATION NIGHTMARE?

The Consequences of Hands-Tying

The evidence discussed so far suggests that host states sign BITs and accept stronger constraints on their freedom of action when they are in a weak bargaining position. Such constraints on sovereign decision making may be worth it if BITs work—that is, if they attract capital. On this point, the jury is still out. Early studies were able to document very little increased FDI in response to the ratification of BITs. Other studies attribute positive impacts on investments flows to BIT ratifications. And yet the empirical findings are not entirely consistent. Some researchers have found that BITs seem to increase foreign investment in countries that already have fairly good domestic institutions in place, which suggests that BITs alone are not a quick fix for weak domestic institutions. Other scholars seem to have found precisely the opposite, that BITs have their strongest effects where states are most likely to lack credibility. Disagreement exists over whether BITs with the United States have been beneficial to developing countries, with some researchers noting their importance for fixed capital investments for US firms but not for other measures of multinational corporate activity.

One consequence of ratifying bilateral investment treaties that contain dispute settlement provisions seems quite clear: they have led to a burst of litigation, especially since the late 1990s. In addition, they have, in many cases, been quite costly ex post. . . . The more bilateral investment treaties a country signs, the more likely it will be sued in this venue. "If you build (sign) it, they will come (litigate)."

Litigation seems to come at the worst possible time for many countries—when macroeconomic conditions generally are unstable. Inflationary pressures, a deteriorating external position, and flagging investor confidence in a country's economic performance generally are all correlated with litigation. The higher the (log of) inflation, the greater the probability of arbitration is two years later. A country's deteriorating external position is signaled by reserve losses as a proportion of imports, the outflow of foreign direct investment, and a worsening capacity to service foreign debt. Although it is not quite statistically significant by traditional standards, a country's risk premium—the excess in government bond yields over the London Interbank Offer Rate (LIBOR)—is also positively associated with increased litigation. This evidence suggests that litigation may very well be dangerously procyclical. That is, it may flow from broader economic conditions over which governments that have opened up to financial liberalization have little direct ability to control, and aggravate those conditions in the process. Litigation may further complicate the very conditions it is responding to by encouraging further capital flight.

The Consequences of Legal Asymmetry: The Potential for Regime Reinforcement

That litigation can be costly is of course the core dynamic of credible commitment making. As Tim Büthe and Helen Milner point out, if BITs attract capital—it is "precisely *because* they bite." Moreover, "[t]his constraint—on the governments of the FDI host countries that sign them—is not an accidental by-product but *intended* by both sides"[5] [emphases added]. This is where the asymmetry built into the architecture of most BITs becomes quite important. Giving investors a private right of action allows them to decide when, where, and on what basis to sue public entities for damages. It therefore gives them extraordinary agenda-setting power in future law development. . . . Moreover, investment treaty arbitration is nonreciprocal: it gives investors the right to sue, but does not give states a similar right. This allows for the possibility that law development—interpretation of the rules going forward—will be lopsided, trending toward the interests of the parties with the right to choose the forum, rules, and legal issues, and without the traditional safeguards of judicial independence that are built in to most credible domestic legal systems. Even if states could anticipate that they would be sued by private actors in the case of breach—and the history of negotiations for a sophisticated country such as the Czech Republic suggests this eventuality was not well understood—it might be quite difficult to assess how the treaties they signed would be interpreted by arbitration panels over time.

Evidence on the actual pattern of arbitral decision making is very suggestive in this regard. Gus Van Harten, a legal scholar specializing in mixed arbitration between investors and states, has examined trends in legal interpretation to test hypotheses about systemic bias in how contentious claims are resolved in known arbitration cases. These claims over jurisdiction provide an opportunity to analyze the drift of legal interpretation over time. They are issues that by definition could go either way and are litigated precisely because the parties care about them and cannot easily anticipate the outcome. Van Harten's painstaking coding of all publicly available awards in English—some 140

5. Büthe and Milner 2009.

cases under investment treaties handed down as of 2010—suggests a clear tendency toward the expansion of investor's rights where jurisdictional matters were at stake. Van Harten considered how broadly and flexibly arbitrators interpreted the terms "corporate person investor" (69 instances); "natural person investor" (6 instances); "investment" (116 instances); "minority shareholder interest" (72 instances); "permissibility of investment" (27 instances); "parallel claims" (165 instances); and "scope of MFN" (60 instances). He finds that more than 76 percent of the time tribunals chose to interpret these contested terms broadly so as to advantage investors over states. Moreover, the primary nationality of the claimant matters as well. Claimant firms from the US, UK, and France were more likely to win expansive interpretations of investor's rights than were firms from Latin America, the European periphery (Cyprus and Turkey) or the Far East (Singapore). This evidence of lopsided law development is consistent with the broader literature that notes that arbitrators have incentives to favor the interests of those who have the power to invoke the use of the system (in this case, the private investor).[6] . . .

Finally, there is some evidence consistent with a claim that bilateralism has paid handsome dividends for investors in terms of monetary damages. While very little information is available on the terms of monetary awards, twenty-eight of the cases in Van Harten's database include information on their monetary outcome. It is important to note that these are a subset of cases, and hardly a random one at that: arbitral awards are only made public when both the investor and the state agree to do so. When the nationality of the claimant and the income level of the respondent are controlled for, . . . the magnitude of the monetary damages awarded in a particular case shows that complaints based on BITs are much more likely to be associated with larger monetary awards than cases based on multilateral agreements (NAFTA and the ECT, for example). Compared to the non-bilateral treaties, BITs reduced the probability that the monetary award would be zero by about 60 percent and increased the probability that an award would be in the $100 million range or the $500 million range by 20 and 30 percent, respectively. . . .

The choice of commercial rules—those of business groups such as the ICC or the SCC—is also associated with larger awards. Indeed, investors were about 60 percent less likely to receive an award of less than $1 million and 80 percent more likely to get an award over $500 million when commercial venues, such as the ICC or SCC, were used (for example, compared to the ICSID or UNCITRAL). While causal inference is difficult to assign in this case—the choice of tribunal itself is likely to be quite strategic—it is an interesting finding in light of the fact that in almost all international investment agreements, it is the investor who has the right to choose the rules that govern the case.

6. Van Harten 2012.

IV. PUSH-BACK: ANNULMENTS AND RENEGOTIATION

The international investment regime differs from the trade regime in its degree of centralization and the special protections afforded to private actors who invest. The dispute settlement mechanism contained in most BITs is quite different from those contained in trade agreements in another important way as well: *it is a one-shot deal.* There is no provision in the most widely used arbitration rules for appeal; decisions of the tribunals are final and binding. Annulment is the only option, other than noncompliance, available to a party if it does not like the decision of the arbitration tribunal. This is in obvious contrast with the way disputes are settled among WTO states: the appellate body can correct tribunal decisions, giving an unhappy litigant some satisfaction if the decision was a bad one and also helping to provide some degree of uniformity to decisions made under WTO rules.

The investment regime has no such mechanism; it grew out of a commercial arbitration model, the results of which are typically held to be both binding and final. Only a very narrow set of conditions can be used as the basis for annulling an award of an ICSID tribunal, for example, including the complete absence of proper reasoning or the finding that a tribunal had manifestly exceeded its powers. An award is not supposed to be overturned just because the decision was "bad" or "wrong." In general, there is no way to correct the poor judgment of a mixed arbitration investment tribunal.

And yet, there has been an explosion in the registration of cases seeking annulment of ICSID awards. . . . Surprisingly, in 2008 there were more new registrations for ICSID annulment proceedings than there were awards on the merits in original cases. Interestingly, to date, only one country in the high income category, the United Arab Emirates, has sought to annul an ICSID award. For the most part, annulments have been sought by middle-income countries concentrated in Latin America. Argentina, a country that has experienced its share of hard economic times in the last decade, alone accounts for about one-quarter of all annulment requests.

Why do these countries seek to have awards of duly constituted ICSID tribunals annulled? To be clear, the restrictive conditions on annulment make it almost impossible to succeed in this endeavor. Only about 8 percent of ICSID awards have been annulled in whole or in part. One possibility is that annulment proceedings are a symbolic action to express growing frustration with the regime. . . . They are a way for governments to signal that an award is not acceptable and to make a principled argument as to why not. Governments usually choose to take this stand on awards that are of special significance to crucial sectors of their economies and their polities. About a quarter of the annulments sought relate to the provision of basic utilities—water, gas, and electric power. These sectors have particular public significance. They impact the daily lives of thousands, even millions, of people in a very real, ongoing way and are the kind of cases where governments have decided to take their stand for sovereignty over "policy space."

One other trend is quite interesting with respect to annulments. There has been a sharp shift in the type of regime that has sought to annul the decisions of investment arbitration panels over time. In the 1980s and 1990s, they were mostly defiant autocracies that were loath to relinquish their interests in the name of law. But increasingly, the annulment seekers are relatively highly democratic countries with clear lines of accountability to their domestic publics. In fact, when comparing the registrations for annulment before and after 2008, it is stunning to realize that the polity score for all annulment seekers before 2008 was a paltry 2 (on a scale of 0 to 10). Since 2008, the number of new annulments not only exceeds the number for the entire history of the ICSID from its entry into force in 1966 up to 2008, but the polity scores of the governments seeking to turn back a decision of an ICSID tribunal jumped to 6 on the same scale. Increasingly, relatively accountable democratically elected governments are trying to overturn awards that are arguably closely connected to the broader public good—awards flowing from treaties signed during highly constrained periods of significant economic downturn. If the investment regime cannot accommodate the legitimate policy space of democratic governments navigating hard economic times, it may prove quite brittle indeed.

V. CONCLUSIONS

The codification of international economic relations, including rules for international trade and international investments, has been one of the hallmarks of the post–World War II era. However, the trade and investment regimes are surprisingly different in crucial ways, especially in their degree of centralization (which has implications for the competitive dynamics among developing countries signing BITs) and the extent to which private actors are privileged and protected (which has consequences for the regulatory space in which states operate). Familiar political economy theories, quite likely involving the dynamic contracting issues surrounding investing, may account for these differences. Ex post, governments have an incentive to renege, skim rents from sunk investments, and reclaim their sovereign regulatory space. In the case of trade, domestic resistance eventually is likely to be competed away. If the logic of Ronald Rogowki's *Commerce and Coalitions* underlies the domestic political dynamics of trade, then Raymond Vernon's *Sovereignty at Bay* underlies that of international direct foreign investing.

The purpose of this article has not been to test an explanation of these differences, but rather to explore the consequences for governance. Whether BITs attract capital is an important question, but it is not the only question one might raise about the investment regime. The literature shows theoretically and empirically that the need to make credible commitments in the context of bilateral negotiations has led to a competitive ratification dynamic. Power asymmetries imply pressures on developing countries to make concessions to powerful exporting countries, and I show that business cycles contribute to patterns in concession making as well.

The natural question is, *so what?* If BITs attract capital, this is a win-win outcome. It is not obvious, however, that BITs are responsible for greater investment flows to the countries that have ratified them. The explosion of arbitration suggests some kind of breakdown in expectations: whether BITs have failed to tie the hands of rapacious governments, or whether investors have incentives to gamble on a tribunal that they alone can invoke, few governments anticipated the expansion in investors' rights or the number and size of claims they would soon face as a result of ratifying BITs. Arguably, these are not the results many developing countries anticipated when they signed these agreements.

In addition, it is not clear that many states thought through the possible consequences of acquiescing to asymmetrical arbitration in which the market for legal decisions is driven largely by one side of the dispute. Other scholars have explored the incentives this creates for arbitrators, and especially for repeat arbitrators, who gain financially when selected by firms to represent their interests. While a causal test has yet to be done, arbitrators in mixed investment disputes have been much more likely to accept the broad jurisdictional claims of investors than the narrower arguments of states. About a third of the time, mixed arbitration panels award no money at all to the complainant, but an ICSID arbitration panel's recent award of $1.67 billion to the complainant in the case of Occidental Oil Company v. The Republic of Ecuador, decided October 5, 2012, is a good reminder that the stakes in investment disputes are potentially significant.

The outcome of decentralized rule making and asymmetrical dispute settlement over the past three decades has contributed to a strong pro-investment regime. The array of rights and protections for a specific class of private actors in public international law is quite extraordinary. In contrast to the trade area, where rights and benefits are based on reciprocity among the WTO members party to an agreement, the international investment regime is largely unidirectional in its allocation of rights between private actors and public authorities. Only the former are protected by BITs. If a private contractor breaches a contract with a government, the latter need not look through its dossier of BITs for legal succor; it won't be forthcoming. No other category of private individuals—not traders (who do not invest), not human beings in their capacity as human rights holders, not even national investors in their home state—is given such expansive rights in international law as are private actors investing across borders.

It is becoming clear that this system is great for investors but may be ill-suited to democratic governance generally. . . . Early BITs may have originally been designed to constrain capricious autocrats, but more and more, BITs, and, as a result, more of the cases dealt with by mixed arbitral tribunals, are directly related to the difficulties democratic yet sometimes fragile regimes have had coping with various macroeconomic shocks. Modern investment risks have more to do with currency convertibility and capital transfers and with efforts to regulate health, safety, and the environment than they do with the blatant expropriation of foreign extractive interests (the Occidental award noted above notwithstanding). A growing number of investor-state disputes center on the sectors for which modern governments are most clearly required by their people to be held accountable: water, power, gas, and basic infrastructure. To what extent BIT-like hands-tying mechanisms can (or should) constrain public policies in these areas is increasingly a matter of debate. . . .

The investment regime described in this article is experiencing some pressures to change. The explosion of efforts to annul awards is one indicator of resistance. A growing number of countries are beginning to renegotiate or even to terminate their BIT obligations. Norway has had to shelve negotiations on new BITs due to growing domestic polarization about the proper balance between investor protection and the ability of states to regulate in the public interest. Australia will no longer agree to mixed arbitration provisions in its new trade and investment agreements, largely because of the difficulties it foresees in maintaining its regulatory prerogatives. Most importantly, having been on the respondent end of the arbitration system much more than anticipated, the United States government itself has begun to plot out a more balanced approach to the protection of foreign direct investments. The US Model BIT of 2004 has many more state protections than its predecessors, and the 2012 model stipulates that parties must not waive labor and environmental laws in order to encourage investment. The ability to make credible commitments has been central to the investment regime, but the terms of such commitment are and always have been determined by the interests and bargaining power of the parties.

REFERENCES

Allee, Todd L., and Clint Peinhardt. 2014. "Evaluating Three Explanations for the Design of Bilateral Investment Treaties." *World Politics* 66, no. 1 (January): 47–87.

Büthe, Tim, and Helen V. Milner. 2009. "Bilateral Investment Treaties and Foreign Direct Investment: A Political Analysis." In *The Effect of Treaties on Foreign Direct Investment: Bilateral Investment Treaties, Double Taxation Treaties and Investment Flows*, eds. Karl P. Sauvant and Lisa E. Sachs. New York, N.Y.: Oxford University Press: 171–24.

Elkins, Zachary, Andrew T. Guzman, and Beth A. Simmons. 2006. "Competing for Capital: The Diffusion of Bilateral Investment Treaties, 1960–2000." *International Organization* 60, no. 4: 811–46.

Van Harten, Gus. 2012. "Arbitrator Behaviour in Asymmetrical Adjudication: An Empirical Study of Investment Treaty Arbitration." *Osgoode Hall Law Journal* 50, no. 1: 211–68.

Yackee, Jason Webb. 2012. "Controlling the International Investment Law Agency." *Harvard International Law Journal* 53, no. 2: 392–448.

12

Reversal of Fortunes: Democratic Institutions and Foreign Direct Investment Inflows to Developing Countries

QUAN LI AND ADAM RESNICK

Do democratic institutions promote or hinder FDI inflows to developing countries? Quan Li and Adam Resnick argue that democracy has conflicting effects on FDI. On the one hand, democratic institutions promote FDI inflows because they tend to ensure more credible property rights protection, reducing risks for foreign investors. On the other hand, democratic institutions hinder FDI inflows by facilitating indigenous businesses' pursuit of protection from foreign MNCs. Hence, the net effect of democracy on FDI inflows is contingent on the relative strength of these two competing forces. Using data from fifty-three developing countries from 1982 to 1995, Li and Resnick find evidence for both effects: after controlling for the positive effect of democracy on FDI inflows through the property rights protection channel, democratic institutions reduce FDI inflows.

Increasing economic globalization and the diffusion of political democracy are arguably the two most important characteristics of contemporary international political economy. As a salient dimension of globalization, foreign direct investment (FDI) inflows have grown faster than world income since the 1960s, multinational enterprises (MNEs) now account for about 70 percent of world trade, and the sales of their foreign affiliates have exceeded total global exports. Foreign production capital has dispersed to almost all developing countries since the 1980s, and the number of foreign affiliates located in developing economies has reached 129,771, compared with 93,628 in the developed world. Paralleling this economic structural change is the spread of liberal or representative democracy. A growing number of less-developed countries (LDCs) have experienced increased political participation, open competition for elected office, and expanding civil society. The proportion of democratic and partially democratic countries rose from about 31 percent in 1975 to about 73 percent in 1995.

The flood of FDI and the diffusion of democratic governance have come to an inevitable encounter. While the effect of FDI on democracy has long attracted both scholarly attention and public interest, the effect of democracy on FDI is surprisingly understudied and poorly understood. Explaining the effect of democratic institutions on FDI, however, has clear significance for both theory and policy. Many countries that are democratizing also happen to be developing economies pursuing foreign capital. If democratic governance hurts a country's attractiveness to foreign investors, the developing country faces a trade-off between competing for limited FDI and democratization. If, on the other hand, deepening democratic governance enhances a country's ability to attract FDI, then democratization helps to deliver the economic benefits from foreign capital. The stakes for leaders in the LDCs are high given the potential consequences. Theoretically, the lack of an adequate explanation for the effect of democracy on FDI suggests an important gap in how scholars explain interactions between economic globalization and political democracy. In this article, we set out to fill this gap by focusing on the causality from democratic institutions to FDI inflows. More specifically, does increased democracy lead to more FDI inflows to LDCs?

Previous theoretical work, while providing a broad framework for our question, suggests conflicting answers. Olson argues that in well-established democracies, independent judiciaries and electoral challenges help to guarantee property rights, ensuring that investments are secure for the long haul.[1] Investors favor such regimes because their assets are shielded from predatory banditry by dictators. Following this argument, one concludes that higher levels of democracy should be associated with more FDI inflows. O'Donnell presents a contrasting view, arguing that investors and autocrats often share a cozy relationship.[2] Because of political leaders' interest in the economic benefits of FDI, the autocrats shield foreign capital from popular pressure for higher wages, stronger labor protection, or less capital-friendly taxation. Olson and O'Donnell each suggest plausible yet contradictory answers to the democracy-FDI relationship. Olson tells us that property rights make stable democracies fertile territory for investment; O'Donnell illustrates how investor-state collusion favors foreign capital in highly autocratic countries. . . .

While Olson, O'Donnell and others offer useful insights about the expected effect of democratic institutions on FDI inflows to the developing countries, they disagree on the direction of the effect. In this article, we offer a theoretical synthesis and extension. Basing our theory on the logic of why firms invest abroad, we argue that democratic institutions have conflicting effects on FDI inflows. On one hand, democratic institutions hinder FDI inflows through three avenues. First, democratic constraints over elected politicians tend to weaken the oligopolistic or monopolistic positions of MNEs. Second, these constraints further prevent host governments from offering generous financial and fiscal incentives to foreign investors. Third, broad access to elected officials and wide political participation offer institutionalized avenues through which indigenous businesses can seek protection. In each case, the increased pluralism ensured by democratic institutions generates policy outcomes that reduce the MNE's degree of freedom in the host developing country.

1. Olson 1993.
2. O'Donnell 1978 and 1988.

On the other hand, democratic institutions promote FDI inflows by strengthening property rights protection. The representation of the interests of common citizens in the legislature prevents the state from predatory rent seeking. Constraints over elected politicians further guarantee contract enforcement for businesses. These effects generate credible property rights protection, reducing risks for foreign investors and encouraging foreign investment. Hence, the net effect of democratic institutions on FDI inflows to the developing countries is contingent on the relative strength of these two competing forces. . . .

Our theory identifies the causal avenues through which democratic institutions promote or hinder FDI inflows. We assess quantitatively both the positive and negative effects of democratic institutions on FDI inflows with empirical tests covering fifty-three developing countries from 1982 to 1995. We find that both property rights protection and democracy-related property rights protection encourage FDI inflows while democratic institutions improve private property rights protection. After controlling for the positive effect of democracy via property rights protection, democratic institutions reduce FDI inflows. These results support our theoretical claims and are robust against alternative model specifications, statistical estimators, and variable measurements.

The article proceeds as follows. We first elaborate our theory on the effects of democratic institutions on FDI inflows. Next, we discuss the research design and the results of our empirical analyses. We conclude with a discussion of implications of our findings.

A THEORY ON HOW DEMOCRATIC INSTITUTIONS AFFECT FDI INFLOWS

Our theory on the effects of democratic institutions on FDI inflows is based on the logic of why firms invest abroad. As shown below, the level of FDI inflows hinges on the interactions between MNEs and host countries. By affecting these interactions, democratic institutions encourage or deter foreign direct investors.

Why Do Firms Invest Abroad?

As widely accepted, FDI implies that a multinational enterprise organizes production of goods and services in more than one country, involving the transfer of assets or intermediate products within the investing enterprise and without any change in ownership. It involves additional costs of setting up and operating factories in foreign lands. Given the disadvantages of operating overseas, why do some firms locate their production abroad instead of at home? Why do they own foreign production facilities instead of serving the intended market with such alternative means as trade or licensing? Why do they invest in one country instead of another? The logic of international production behind these questions holds the answer to how political institutions affect FDI inflows to the developing countries. Our discussion draws heavily from John Dunning's eclectic paradigm of international production,[3] which encompasses various competing explanations, including those based on the industrial organization approach, transaction cost economics, and trade and location theory.

Dunning explains that international production is motivated by three sets of advantages perceived by firms. The first set is a firm's ownership-specific advantages. These include its ownership of intangible assets and common governance of cross-border production. Some examples of intangible assets are product innovations, management practices, marketing techniques, and brand names. Diversification across borders allows a firm to exploit economies of scale and to develop monopoly power based on its size and established position. The foreign investor's ownership-specific advantages are sensitive to property rights protection in the host country. In other words, an MNE's success is tied to the security of its intellectual and physical property in multiple countries.

The second set of advantages concerns the firm's internalization advantages deriving from its hierarchical control of cross-border production. Internalization refers to a firm's direct control over its value-added activities in multiple countries, as opposed to outsourcing, trade, or licensing. The size of a firm's internalization advantages correlates with the degree of transnational market failure. For example, where the risks of opportunism by foreign buyers and sellers are high, such as disrupting supplies and violating property rights in primary product and high technology industries, the firm has an incentive to claim hierarchical control of cross-border production. Where economic rents from exploiting oligopolistic or monopolistic market structures or large-scale production are high, the firm is also likely to exert hierarchical control of transnational production. The greater the internalization advantages, the more likely a firm is to pursue international production—hierarchical control of its assets, instead of trading or leasing. The exploitation of these advantages is affected by the antitrust or competition-oriented regulation in the host country.

The third set of advantages refers to the location-specific advantages perceived by firms or the characteristics of host countries in terms of their economic environment or government policies. They may include scarce natural resources, abundant labor, high economic development, or favorable macroeconomic, microeconomic, and FDI-specific government policies. For instance, oil companies have to produce overseas where required resources are available. Export-processing firms typically shift production based on labor cost. Firms also consider government policies on tariffs, domestic corporate taxation, investment or tax regulation of foreign firms, profit repatriation or transfer pricing, royalties on extracted natural resources, antitrust regulation, technology transfer requirements, intellectual property protections, and labor market regulation.

---

3. Dunning 1993.

In the context of our analysis, the connection between politics and FDI inflows hinges on the interaction between host governments and MNEs. Firms select investment sites based on how well their ownership-specific and internalization advantages mesh with location-specific benefits. Host government policies create location-specific conditions that affect how well a firm can exploit its advantages.

The logic of international production discussed above suggests the following implications that set the stage for our analysis of the effects of democratic institutions on FDI inflows. First, the MNE's ownership-specific and internalization advantages often result from, and are further enhanced by, the oligopolistic or monopolistic market structures. Host government regulatory policies can limit the use of these advantages, particularly through the application of antitrust and other competition-oriented legislation. Second, endowed with the ownership-specific and internalization advantages, the MNE is more competitive than, and often displaces, indigenous firms in the host country. The host government may adopt industrial policy that either protects indigenous businesses from the MNE or favors the MNE. Third, expecting FDI to bring about managerial skills and production technology beneficial to economic growth, the host government may offer foreign investors financial and fiscal incentives. Such incentives not only affect the choice of FDI location, but also strengthen the competitiveness of foreign investors. Finally, the MNE must rely on the host government for protection of its property rights in proprietary assets, without which its ownership-specific advantages would disappear.

These implications depict a contrast between a good and a bad investment climate for MNEs. A good climate is one in which the location-specific advantages existing in the host country facilitate the MNE's exploitation of its ownership-specific and internalization advantages. For example, the host government provides favorable regulation, preferential treatment for MNEs, and sound property rights protection. Conversely, a bad investment climate is one where the conditions in the host country hinder the MNE from exploiting its ownership-specific and internalization advantages. Firms that enjoy monopolistic or oligopolistic positions may shy away from host countries with strong antitrust regulation. MNEs may also balk at weak property rights protection and strong preferences of the host government for domestic firms. Domestic political institutions, because they define the policymaking environment, have significant effects on the quality of the investment climate.

Suppressive Effect of Democratic Institutions on FDI Inflows

The nature of domestic political institutions is defined largely by the relative strength of democratic versus autocratic characteristics of a country's political system. Generally speaking, it depends on the degree to which citizens are able to choose how and by whom they are governed. Democratic institutions under a representative democracy or "polyarchy" typically include free and fair elections of the executive and legislative offices, the right of citizens to vote and compete for public office, and institutional guarantees for the freedom of association and expression such as an independent judiciary and the absence of censorship. . . . Under democratic institutions, politicians have incentives to develop public policies reflecting the popular sentiment. Representative democracy also allows various interests to be represented in the legislature, thereby constraining executive power. In addition, the stronger a country's democratic characteristics, the more likely its social interests are to get organized and participate in political competition. Even in fledgling democracies, the state is subject to a broad spectrum of political interests as it attempts to broker compliance with democratic rules, offering relevant political actors welfare improvements to induce their consent. Hence, democratic political processes are characterized by the influence of diverse opinions over electoral and public policymaking outcomes.

In contrast, autocratic characteristics derive from "limited pluralism" as opposed to "almost unlimited pluralism" under a representative democracy. They may include government co-optation of civil society leadership or legal limitation of pluralism, a single leader or small ruling clique, and weak political mobilization. Regardless of the methods rulers use to enhance their legitimacy, autocratic politics is biased in favor of narrow elite control over public policy.

Countries exhibit heterogeneity in how and to what extent they conform to democratic or autocratic properties. Despite such cross-sectional and temporal heterogeneity, regime characteristics within the democratic or autocratic category tend to correlate with and reinforce each other. For example, free elections are sustainable only if leaders are constrained through some mechanism by the citizenry; free election can effectively reflect the will of the people only if citizens participate actively in political competition. To a great extent, the relative strength of democratic and autocratic characteristics defines the nature of political institutions. The manner in which these competing democratic and autocratic characteristics are manifested in democratic institutions has implications for foreign direct investors. Below we suggest three mechanisms through which these institutions hinder FDI inflows.

EFFECT ON MNE EXPLOITATION OF MONOPOLISTIC OR OLIGOPOLISTIC POSITION. Democratic institutions in host countries attenuate many MNEs' ability to exploit and enhance their monopolistic or oligopolistic positions. As discussed earlier, firms invest abroad to take advantage of their ownership-specific and internalization advantages, advantages that often result from, and further result in, oligopolistic or monopolistic market structures. Such large MNEs constitute the bulk of FDI, possess enormous market power, and have significantly shaped trade patterns and the location of economic activities in the global economy. In the host countries, such MNEs seek to create and strengthen their oligopolistic or monopolistic positions that result in higher returns. The associated imperfect market structures, however, lead to less optimal allocation of resources in the host economy than perfect competition. While MNEs consider the pursuit of monopolistic or oligopolistic positions a legitimate corporate strategy for greater returns, their desire to create, maintain and increase their monopoly or oligopoly positions sets them at odds with host country governments, particularly democratic ones.

In more democratic host governments, elected politicians presumably encourage and manage inward investment to improve national economic performance, benefit their electoral constituencies, and increase their odds of being reelected. That many MNEs may decrease market competition motivates elected politicians to limit the monopoly or oligopoly positions of the relevant MNEs through public policy. In reaction, the MNEs may seek to bribe and collude with the host government to influence domestic politics of the host country. However, freedom of expression and open media bring about relatively better monitoring of elected politicians and allow the opponents of FDI to access the public policymaking process relatively more easily. Hence, democratic characteristics of the host country collectively constrain the pursuit by many MNEs of monopoly or oligopoly.

Conversely, more autocratic host governments are less likely to clash and more likely to collude with the oligopoly or monopoly-seeking MNEs. By definition, the size of the winning coalition for autocratic leaders is smaller than for democratic leaders because autocratic rulers depend less on broad popular support to stay in power. While such rulers are happy if FDI improves national economic performance, their primary focus is to generate more revenues for the ruling clique. As long as they obtain increased revenues and benefits from foreign capital, these rulers would tolerate the imperfect competition and concentrated market power of oligopolistic or monopolistic foreign firms. Narrow elite control further allows rulers to subdue dissenting voices within or outside of the regime. As a result, the weaker the host country's democratic institutions, the less likely the host government is to limit the monopoly or oligopoly position of the MNEs.

EFFECT ON HOST COUNTRY INDUSTRIAL POLICY. Industrial policy is another arena in which democratic institutions in the host country degrade conditions for MNEs. Because of their ownership-specific and internalization advantages and exposure to international competition, MNEs are typically more competitive than indigenous firms in the developing host country. While inward investment raises competition in the host country and may improve the allocation of resources, foreign firms typically displace local businesses and even compete for loans in the host country. Just as with trade, the growing presence of more-competitive foreign firms often turns less-competitive local firms into losers. Local business owners and the unemployed, suffering concentrated losses, are likely to get organized and lobby for protective industrial policy from the government. While MNEs also bring about new jobs and resources, such benefits do not directly go to the displaced capital and workers.

Grievances are likely to be more pronounced in developing countries, where social welfare systems are not well developed and provide limited compensation for displacement. Where democratic institutions are strong, the opponents of FDI have multiple avenues to influence public policymaking. Domestic interests that lose out to the MNEs can resort to elections, campaign finance, interest groups, public protests, and media exposure. Under such pressures, the host government is compelled to cushion the blow to domestic losers by subsidizing less competitive indigenous firms, imposing more restrictive entry conditions on MNEs such as joint ownership, limiting the sectors open to foreign capital, or demanding solely foreign financing of initial investments. It also could pose more restrictive operating requirements in terms of local purchases of capital goods and raw materials, local employment, the proportion of output to be exported, and the use of technology. These policies reduce the MNE's degree of control over its overseas production and weaken its competitiveness.

This is not to say that MNEs in more democratic countries do not have access to host governments, but MNEs' influence is likely to be balanced and diluted by various opposing groups in these countries. Conversely, where democratic institutions are weak and autocratic characteristics are strong, the host government is exposed to pressures of only limited social interests and, as Evans suggests, may resolve the dilemma by forming an alliance of the state, local, and multinational capital. Restrictions on political participation further prevent the losing groups from getting organized and affecting the policymaking process.

EFFECT ON FISCAL AND FINANCIAL INCENTIVES TO FOREIGN CAPITAL.   Democratic institutions also limit the generosity of the fiscal and financial incentives host countries often offer to attract foreign investors, placing more-democratic LDCs at a comparative disadvantage in the hunt for FDI. Inducements are one of many factors affecting the choice of FDI location. Examples of such inducements include tax holidays, exemptions from import duties, deductions from social security contributions, accelerated depreciation allowances, investment grants, subsidized loans, donations of land or site facilities, and wage subsidies. During the past two decades, various developing countries, regardless of their regime type, have used these fiscal and financial incentives to lure foreign capital in an increasingly vigorous competition. . . .

Democratic politics matters for the design of various incentive programs. Any inducement to foreign capital, such as tax breaks or subsidies, represents a transfer of benefits from domestic taxpayers or firms to foreign investors. As noted earlier, where democratic institutions are strong, domestic players have various ways to pressure elected executives and legislators and influence policymaking. Hence, the host government is limited in its degree of freedom to supply or upgrade such incentives. Compared with more autocratic countries, more democratic host governments have a harder time obtaining the acquiescence of opposing domestic interests to the provision of generous incentives to foreign capital.

Conditions particular to the LDCs also suggest that opposition by domestic interests to generous fiscal and financial incentives is stronger in more democratic host countries than in less democratic ones. FDI stock, inflows, and the associated financial openness tend to increase income inequality. FDI also concentrates in certain sectors, industries, and regions, leading to dual economies and with the backward sectors unlikely to take advantage of the beneficial spillovers from MNEs. Furthermore, as Oman suggests, because fiscal and financial incentives to foreign capital often occur in an insulated, bureaucratic context to facilitate successful negotiation with foreign investors, the process inherently lacks transparency and accountability and often leads to graft, corruption, and rent seeking.

In more-democratic countries, critics of FDI have greater access to political participation and hence, are more able to limit the generosity of incentives their governments offer to foreign capital. Regularly held elections, freedom of speech and association, political representation of local interests by legislators—all constitute venues through which executives' and legislatures' policies toward foreign investors can be questioned, criticized, and rejected. As voters evaluate politicians based on their competence and performance in a well-functioning democracy, voters scrutinize and quite possibly oppose overly generous incentives that do not appear to benefit the community at large. Conversely, in more-autocratic countries, social groups suffering adverse effects from FDI may be inhibited by the lack of institutionalized access to "veto" officeholders through election or through other open and regular channels of participation and representation found in democracies.

Positive Effect of Democratic Institutions on FDI Inflows

Democratic institutions in developing host countries also exert a positive effect on FDI inflows. Because democratic institutions lead to legislative representation of a wide range of social interests and facilitate political mobilization of these groups, government encroachment on private property rights is minimized. Such property rights protection is extended to MNEs, reducing risks for foreign investors and encouraging FDI inflows.

PROPERTY RIGHTS PROTECTION AND FDI. North defines property rights as "the rights individuals appropriate over their own labor and the goods and services they possess. Appropriation is a function of legal rules, organizational forms, enforcement, and norms of behavior—that is, the institutional framework."[4] Take, for example, an MNE that owns a bicycle factory in a foreign country and sells its bicycles to retail outlets in the host or home country.

---

4. North 1990, 33.

The host government recognizes the firm's ownership of tangible and intellectual property through legal title and protects it from a variety of threats including theft or trespass. The government also recognizes contracts between the factory and the retailers as legally binding, intervening to protect the rights of both parties through administrative or judicial action in cases of contract violation. Without having these rights secured, the foreign business is unlikely to invest in a host country. In general, foreign direct investors face several types of threats to their property that the host government can mitigate or exacerbate.

Expropriation, which causes investors to lose their sunken assets, falls at the extreme of the spectrum. Though the likelihood of expropriation declined significantly by the early 1980s, theft of intellectual property is perhaps the most prevalent form of seizure in the contemporary world, with entertainment, software, pharmaceutical, and publishing firms facing significant losses. Foreign investors also worry about contract enforcement. While foreign investors could request state assistance to enforce contracts in countries lacking independent judiciaries, most firms would prefer to operate in a more transparent legal system. Government corruption in a country also hinders FDI inflows. While some MNEs offer side payments to government officials to avoid costly government regulation or to obtain preferential treatment, rent-seeking behaviors by government officials impose costs of unpredictable magnitude on firms, undermining not just their ability to budget or account for costs, but also the rule of law.

Expropriation, seizures of assets, contract repudiation, ineffective rule of law, and government corruption all constitute violations of property rights that deter foreign direct investors. Conversely, the expectations of long-term asset security, regulatory stability and transparency, and institutionalized legal process imply less uncertainty and lower risks for foreign businesses. Better property rights protection should encourage more FDI inflows.

REGIME TYPE AND PROPERTY RIGHTS PROTECTION. Democratic institutions are on average more effective at securing private property rights than autocratic institutions. Typically, the state offers to protect the property rights of firms and individuals in exchange for their tax payments. The state monopoly on coercive power that makes property rights protection possible, however, simultaneously endangers the credibility of the state in the eyes of private agents, rendering the state's *ex post* compliance questionable. Why should the state follow through on its promise to respect or protect assets when no other domestic actor has access to the use of force? Protection by the state is not self-enforcing in that the state has an incentive not to abide by the agreement *ex post* under various contingencies (for example, war). Therefore, the provision of effective property rights protection relies on a constrained state—a state with a transparent, codified legal structure and institutionalized access to enforcement mechanisms.

Olson and others argue that more democratic governments offer better protection of private property rights. North and Weingast show how England's commitment to secure private rights became credible, as the British Parliament gained greater control vis-à-vis the Crown over fiscal policy (borrowing and taxation) and legislative and judicial power. "Increasing the number of veto players implied that a larger set of constituencies could protect themselves against political assault, thus markedly reducing the circumstances under which opportunistic behavior by the government could take place."[5] In addition, because the diversity of interests in the legislature and a politically independent judiciary raised the cost of supplying private benefits, the Parliament did not elapse into another rent-seeking Crown. It is the representative institutions that make the property rights institutions credible. . . .

While stable autocracies with a long-time horizon, like the stationary bandit, also may offer secure property rights, their credibility is weakened by the fact that their leaders are accountable merely to the ruling elite and exercise power out of their own volition. New democracies may do a poor job protecting private property, as new regimes often violate preexisting property rights to secure popular support. The establishment of democracy, particularly the conduct of an election itself, does not necessarily lead to secure property rights. Where democratic institutions are secure and developed, however, governments are more likely to protect private property rights, enforce contracts, and refrain from predation. As Olson argues, lasting democracy inherently implies secure property rights, because the same institutional mechanisms—such as limited executive, the independent judiciary, and respect for law—that are needed for the survival of democracy also imply secure private property rights. . . .

Therefore, the set of democratic institutions, including the dispersion of power, the limited executive, the large number of veto players over public policy, legislative and judicial power, the diversity of interests in the legislature, and the independent judiciary, collectively serve to secure private property rights and lower the risks of expropriation, contract repudiation, ineffective rule of law, and government corruption for domestic citizens as well as foreign investors.

Our theory as a whole suggests that democratic institutions in host countries exert conflicting effects on FDI inflows. On one hand, democratic institutions tend to limit the oligopolistic or monopolistic behaviors of multinational enterprises, facilitate indigenous businesses to pursue protection against foreign capital, and constrain the host government's ability to offer generous financial and fiscal incentives to foreign investors. Hence, they discourage FDI inflows. On the other hand, more-democratic countries offer better property rights protection, reducing risks and attracting more FDI inflows. The empirical analysis below tests these two competing effects.

---

5. North and Weingast 1989.

RESEARCH DESIGN

The empirical analysis covers fifty-three countries . . . from 1982 to 1995. These countries exhibit temporal and spatial variations in the level of FDI inflows and democratic characteristics, enabling a discriminating statistical assessment. Because our arguments are applicable to comparisons both cross-nationally and over time for individual countries, the pooled time-series cross-section (TSCS) design is appropriate for uncovering relationships persistent across time and over space. We use the one-tailed t-test for hypothesis testing because our hypotheses are directional.

Dependent Variable

The dependent variable is the level of FDI net inflows into a country each year, measured in billions of current U.S. dollars. The measure is compatible with our central research question: "Does increased democracy promote or jeopardize foreign direct investment inflows to less-developed countries?" . . . FDI net inflows refer to those investments that acquire a lasting management interest (10 percent or more of voting stock) in an enterprise operating in an economy other than that of the investor. Because of possible divestment, the level of FDI net inflows can appear as a negative value. Data are from the World Bank's *World Development Indicators*.

Negative Effect of Democratic Institutions

We separate empirically the positive and negative effects of democratic institutions on FDI inflows to the developing countries. We use two different methods to capture the negative effect of democratic institutions on FDI because of host country policies on market regulation, industrial protection, and fiscal and financial incentives. The first method is to use a composite measure of democracy, while the second method is to include different components of democratic institutions as separate variables. For both methods, we expect that these variables take on the negative sign. The inclusion of separate measures of democratic institutions in the model controls for the heterogeneity of different countries in terms of conforming to the democratic ideal. While different aspects of democratic institutions should correlate with and reinforce each other, as discussed earlier, their effects may differ in size. Furthermore, countries differ in the strength and content of their democratic institutions while their regime characteristics change over time.

The composite measure of democratic institutions, denoted as LEVEL OF DEMOCRACY, is drawn from the Polity IV database. . . . The Polity IV data set operationalizes institutionalized democracy and autocracy along five dimensions: competitiveness of political participation, regulation of political participation, competitiveness of executive recruitment, openness of executive recruitment, and constraints on the chief executive. The composite measure of democratic institutions from Polity IV is the difference between

DEMOC and AUTOC, ranging from 10 (strongly autocratic) to +10 (strongly democratic). . . .

The separate measures of democratic institutions are also based on the Polity IV database. . . . Democratic institutions consist of three essential, inter-related conceptual elements: institutions and procedures through which citizens choose alternative policies and leaders, institutional constraints on the exercise of decision-making power by the executive, and the guarantee of civil liberties to all citizens in their daily lives and political participation. In Polity IV, these three elements are measured as three variables: executive recruitment (covering regulation of executive transfers, competitiveness of executive selection, and openness of executive recruitment), executive constraints, and political competition (covering regulation of political competition and government restrictions on political competition). We denote the three variables as SELECTION, CONSTRAINT, and COMPETITION.

Positive Effect of Democratic Institutions

The positive effect of democratic institutions works via the causal link of property rights protection. We test the positive effect of democratic institutions with two methods. The first method includes both the LEVEL OF DEMOCRACY and the level of PROPERTY RIGHTS PROTECTION in one model, where PROPERTY RIGHTS PROTECTION captures the positive effect of democratic institutions on FDI inflows while LEVEL OF DEMOCRACY captures the leftover, negative effect only. With this method, the estimate of the PROPERTY RIGHTS PROTECTION variable contains the effects of both democracy and other variables such as ECONOMIC DEVELOPMENT. We use the property rights protection index, constructed by Stephen Knack and Philip Keefer for the IRIS Center at the University of Maryland with risk-rating data from the International Country Risk Guide.[6] The index is based on five components: rule of law, bureaucratic quality, government corruption, contract repudiation by government, and expropriation risk. Rule of law, government corruption, and contract repudiation are on a 6-point scale while bureaucratic quality and expropriation risk on a 10-point scale. Like Knack and Keefer, we build a 50-point index of property rights protection by rescaling the 6-point variables to 10-point scale and then summing the five 10-point measures. . . .

Our second method separates the effect of democracy on property rights protection from the effects of other variables. We estimate a Tobit model in which the dependent variable is PROPERTY RIGHTS PROTECTION. We use Tobit for estimation because the index is bounded between 0 and 50 and ordinary least squares (OLS) generate predicted values beyond this range. The independent variables include the level of PROPERTY RIGHTS PROTECTION in the previous year, ECONOMIC DEVELOPMENT, REGIME DURABILITY, and POLITICAL INSTABILITY but

---

6. Knack and Keefer 1995.

exclude the LEVEL OF DEMOCRACY. We expect that previous PROPERTY RIGHTS PROTECTION, REGIME DURABILITY, and ECONOMIC DEVELOPMENT affect PROPERTY RIGHTS PROTECTION positively, and POLITICAL INSTABILITY negatively. We lag the independent variables one year to control for possible reciprocal effects of PROPERTY RIGHTS PROTECTION on the independent variables. . . . We use the predicted values of PROPERTY RIGHTS PROTECTION from this Tobit model to measure DEMOCRACY-EXCLUDED PROPERTY RIGHTS PROTECTION, that is, the effect of causal determinants other than democracy on property rights protection. DEMOCRACY-RELATED PROPERTY RIGHTS PROTECTION is the difference between the actual level of property rights protection and the democracy-excluded level, normalized to non-negative values. This difference variable captures the positive effect of democracy independent of other factors on property rights protection.

Control Variables

REGIME DURABILITY.   We expect that the volatility of regime change increases investors' uncertainty about the host country's future economic policies, such as interest rates, government budget deficits, or taxation. Conversely, stable domestic political institutions reduce the risks for foreign capital. We use the measure of regime durability from Polity IV. According to the Polity IV manual, regime durability is the number of years since the most recent regime change, defined by a three-point change in the Polity score over a period of three years or less, with the end of transition period defined by either the lack of stable political institutions or the year 1900, whichever comes last. The first year during which a new (postchange) polity is established is coded as the baseline "year zero" (value=0) and each subsequent year increases the value of the variable by one. We expect REGIME DURABILITY to encourage FDI inflows.

POLITICAL INSTABILITY.   Investors are generally less interested in entering a country with high political instability. . . . To measure POLITICAL INSTABILITY, we use Banks's event counts of assassinations, strikes, guerilla wars, government crises, purges, riots, revolts and antigovernment demonstrations, and sum them into an index of POLITICAL INSTABILITY.[7] We expect POLITICAL INSTABILITY to reduce FDI inflows.

MARKET SIZE.   The size of the host market affects the amount of FDI inflows. Large markets are more likely to attract FDI because of an expected stream of future returns, for which China is often cited as an example. Conversely, small market size attracts less FDI. Studies of FDI inflows typically control for market size. We follow this convention, using gross domestic product (GDP) to measure market size. The variable is converted to international dollars using purchasing power parity (PPP)

7. Banks 1999.

rates for intercountry comparability and is logged to deal with its skewed distribution. Data are from the World Bank's *World Development Indicators*. MARKET SIZE is expected to affect FDI inflows positively.

ECONOMIC DEVELOPMENT. Economic development should affect FDI inflows positively. More-developed countries often attract more FDI than less-developed ones, because of differences in consumer purchasing power, capital endowment, and infrastructure. Hence, we include ECONOMIC DEVELOPMENT as a control variable. The variable is measured as GDP per capita based on PPP, . . . logged to deal with its skewed distribution. Data are from the World Bank's *World Development Indicators*.

GROWTH. Economic growth is often found to induce more FDI inflows to a country. Profit-maximizing foreign investors are attracted to fast-growing economies to take advantage of future market opportunities. We measure GROWTH using the annual percentage growth rate of GDP at market prices based on constant local currency. Data are from the World Bank's *World Development Indicators*. GROWTH is expected to affect FDI inflows positively.

LABOR COST CHANGE. Large increases in labor cost are argued to suppress expected returns, causing FDI investors to shy away. The effect is particularly important for developing countries with concentrated labor-intensive industries. We measure LABOR COST CHANGE with the annual percentage change in the real manufacturing wage index for each country. Data are from the International Labor Organization's *1999 Key Indicators of the Labor Market* (KILM). LABOR COST CHANGE should affect FDI inflows into a country negatively.

CAPITAL FLOW RESTRICTIONS. Capital flow restrictions erect barriers to entry into a country, barriers to exit from a country, or both. Under various restrictions, a foreign investor may have difficulty getting into a country, be trapped on shore after investing, or both. As Gastanaga et al. have found, fewer capital flow restrictions are associated with greater capital inflows. The variable is a summed index of eight types of state restrictions on foreign exchange, current and capital accounts. Data are from International Monetary Fund's *Annual Reports on Exchange Arrangements and Exchange Controls*. CAPITAL FLOW RESTRICTIONS should reduce FDI inflows.

EXCHANGE-RATE VOLATILITY. Exchange-rate risk may also affect FDI inflows. Large movements in the exchange rate inhibit long-term planning and disrupt local markets, reducing FDI inflows. We measure EXCHANGE-RATE VOLATILITY as the mean absolute deviation from the mean of the official exchange rate of local currency units per U.S. dollar. Data are from the World Bank's *World Development Indicators*.

WORLD FDI INFLOWS. The variable is the total world FDI inflows in a given year. It controls for changes in the supply of FDI available to recipient countries. We expect WORLD FDI INFLOWS to have a positive effect on the amount of FDI inflows to individual countries.

TABLE 1 Effect of Democratic Institutions on FDI Inflows to Developing Countries 1982–1995

	Model 1	Model 2	Model 3	Model 4
Democracy-Related Property Rights Protection			0.0757** (1.67)	0.0761** (1.67)
Democracy-Excluded Property Rights Protection			0.0435*** (3.01)	0.0437*** (3.08)
Property Rights Protection	0.0522*** (3.16)	0.0519*** (3.33)		
Level of Democracy	−0.0878*** (3.45)		−0.0943*** (3.48)	
Selection		−0.0714 (0.72)		−0.0798 (0.77)
Constraint		−0.0935 (1.05)		−0.0921* (1.33)
Competition		−0.0896 (1.06)		−0.0976 (1.17)
Joint F-Test		28.5***		42.2***
Regime Durability	0.0229*** (2.53)	0.0230*** (2.93)	0.0232*** (2.62)	0.0230*** (2.97)
Political Instability	−0.0172 (0.90)	−0.0201 (1.00)	−0.0163 (0.82)	−0.0184 (0.89)
Labor Cost Change	−0.0007 (0.30)	−0.0007 (0.28)	−0.0019 (0.76)	−0.0019 (0.73)
Economic Size	1.0299*** (3.61)	1.0289*** (3.72)	1.0775*** (3.68)	1.0759*** (3.76)
Economic Development	−0.0973 (0.34)	−0.0858 (0.32)	−0.0047 (0.02)	0.0074 (0.02)
Economic Growth	0.0227** (1.82)	0.0240** (1.87)	0.0189* (1.51)	0.0195* (1.54)
Exchange-rate Volatility	−0.0001** (2.24)	−0.0001*** (2.12)	−0.0001** (2.05)	−0.001** (1.95)
Capital flow Restrictions	−0.0854** (1.88)	−0.0877** (1.95)	−0.0801** (1.69)	−0.0815** (1.72)
World FDI Inflows	0.0036*** (3.81)	0.0037*** (4.05)	0.0037*** (3.32)	0.0037*** (3.42)
Contant	−25.3194*** (4.58)	−24.1824*** (4.72)	−27.3675*** (4.82)	−26.1584*** (4.96)
Observations	483	483	458	458
R^2	0.21	0.22	0.22	0.22

NOTE: OLS estimates and *t*-statistics in parentheses are based on panel-corrected standard errors (PCSE) with AR(1) correction.

***p < .01.

**p < .05.

*p < .10.

FINDINGS

Table 1 presents the statistical results from four model specifications. Model 1 includes PROPERTY RIGHTS PROTECTION, LEVEL OF DEMOCRACY, and control variables while Model 2 replaces LEVEL OF DEMOCRACY in Model 1 with its component measures. Model 3 includes DEMOCRACY-RELATED PROPERTY RIGHTS PROTECTION, DEMOCRACY-EXCLUDED PROPERTY RIGHTS PROTECTION, LEVEL OF DEMOCRACY, and control variables, while Model 4 is the same as Model 3 but uses the component measures of democracy instead. . . .

Effects of Independent Variables

Statistical results for the key variables offer strong support for our theoretical arguments. In Model 1, PROPERTY RIGHTS PROTECTION is statistically significant at the 1 percent level and positive, as expected. LEVEL OF DEMOCRACY is statistically significant at the 1 percent level and negative. As expected, PROPERTY RIGHTS PROTECTION encourages FDI inflows; as we capture the positive effect of democratic institutions via PROPERTY RIGHTS PROTECTION in the model, the LEVEL OF DEMOCRACY reduces FDI inflows.

In Model 2, PROPERTY RIGHTS PROTECTION is still positive and statistically significant. The three measures of different dimensions of democratic institutions (SELECTION, CONSTRAINT, and COMPETITION) are all negative as expected, but none is statistically significant. The statistical insignificance may result from high collinearity among the three measures, with their pairwise correlation ranging from 0.78 to 0.95. . . . A joint F-test rejects, at the 1 percent level with F statistic 28.5, the hypothesis that all three measures in Model 2 are jointly equal to zero. As we discussed in the theory section, different dimensions of democratic institutions—executive recruitment, constraints over executive policymaking, and regulation of political competition and participation—appear to reinforce each other in affecting FDI inflows.

In Model 3, DEMOCRACY-RELATED PROPERTY RIGHTS PROTECTION is included to capture explicitly the positive effect of democracy on FDI via strengthening property rights protection. DEMOCRACY-EXCLUDED PROPERTY RIGHTS PROTECTION is also included to control for the effect of property rights protection on FDI beyond the influence of democracy. Both variables are statistically significant and positive, as expected. These results support the claims that better property rights protection allows a country to attract more FDI inflows and that democracy improves property rights protection in a country, hence making it more attractive to foreign investors. Model 3 also shows that the LEVEL OF DEMOCRACY is statistically significant and negative, as expected. With the positive effect of democracy on FDI via property rights protection controlled for, democratic institutions reduce the amount of FDI flowing into a developing country.

In Model 4, DEMOCRACY-RELATED PROPERTY RIGHTS PROTECTION and DEMOCRACY-EXCLUDED PROPERTY RIGHTS PROTECTION remain statistically significant and

TABLE 2 Effects of Democracy and Property Rights Protection on FDI Inflows

Democracy-related property rights protection	Level of democracy	
	−6 (20%)	6 (50%)
3.85 (20%)	0.86	−0.27
4.82 (50%)	0.93	−0.20

positive. Similar to Model 2, the three measures of different dimensions of democratic institutions (SELECTION, CONSTRAINT, and COMPETITION) are all negative as expected, but none is statistically significant except for CONSTRAINT. A joint F-test rejects, at the 1 percent level with F statistic 42, the hypothesis that all three measures are jointly equal to zero.

Strength of Effects of Democratic Institutions

Based on Models 1 and 3, a 1-point increase in the LEVEL OF DEMOCRACY causes a decline of about 88 and 94 million dollars, respectively, in FDI inflows to a country. In contrast, a 1-point increase in PROPERTY RIGHTS PROTECTION leads to an increase of about 52 million dollars in FDI inflows to a country, and a 1-point increase in the DEMOCRACY-RELATED PROPERTY RIGHTS PROTECTION leads to an increase of about 76 million dollars in FDI inflows to a country. For better illustration, we present some scenarios of how the level of democracy and the democracy-related property rights protection affect FDI inflows in Table 2. We use the coefficients for the LEVEL OF DEMOCRACY and the DEMOCRACY-RELATED PROPERTY RIGHTS PROTECTION variables in Model 3 Table 1 to compute the level of FDI inflows, holding all other variables at zero.

In Table 2, at the sample 20th percentile values of both democracy and the democracy-related property rights protection, FDI inflows are about 0.86 billion dollars. The combination of 20th percentile property rights protection and 50th percentile democracy level results in an FDI divestment of 0.27 billion dollars. At the 50th percentile property rights protection and 20th percentile democracy level, FDI inflows are about 0.93 billion dollars. At the 50th percentile values of both property rights and democracy, there is an FDI divestment of about 0.2 billion dollars.

These scenarios, though hypothetical, are illustrative. Ceteris paribus, countries with strong democracy-related property rights always outperform those with weak property rights. More FDI flows to countries with better democracy-related property rights protection. Holding the democracy-related property rights protection constant, a less democratic country receives more FDI inflows than a more democratic one. Democracy has positive and negative effects on FDI inflows.

Effects of Control Variables

Now we discuss the results of the control variables. REGIME DURABILITY is positive and statistically significant in all models in Table 1. We expect that regime stability is conducive to attracting FDI inflows by reducing risks for foreign capital; frequent large swings in a country's regime reduce FDI inflows by increasing uncertainty. The statistical evidence in Table 1 supports this expectation.

POLITICAL INSTABILITY has the expected negative sign in all four models in Table 1, but is not statistically significant in any of them. We expect that political assassinations, general strikes, guerrilla warfare, purges, riots, revolutions, and anti-government demonstrations contribute to growing political instability and reduce FDI inflows to a country. The statistical test does not offer enough evidence supporting this claim, not inconsistent with the fact that previous studies have produced mixed evidence regarding this variable. Indeed foreign investors may worry about political unrest most when it threatens their property rights. . . .

MARKET SIZE is statistically significant and positive as expected in all four models in Table 1. Larger economies are likely to attract more FDI inflows, as they have large markets and more investment opportunities. ECONOMIC GROWTH is positive as expected and statistically significant in all models as well. Fast-growing economies attract more FDI than slowly-growing economies.

ECONOMIC DEVELOPMENT is statistically insignificant in all four models in Table 1. Its statistical insignificance appears to be an artifact of high collinearity with other variables. Its correlation within the sample is 0.50 with property rights protection, 0.37 with level of democracy, and −0.42 with capital flow restrictions. One may interpret the result for economic development as meaning that its positive effect on FDI works through better property rights protection, high level of democracy, and low capital flow restrictions.

LABOR COST CHANGE is negative as expected, but statistically insignificant in all four models. Many analysts believe that as labor cost rises quickly in a developing host country, foreign investors will balk or divest. The claim does not appear supported by our evidence. The effect of large changes in labor cost on capital flight may have been exaggerated.

EXCHANGE-RATE VOLATILITY is negative and statistically significant in all four models of Table 1. As expected, volatile exchange-rate movements raise transaction costs and decrease FDI inflows into a country. CAPITAL FLOW RESTRICTIONS are negative and statistically significant as expected in all four models. High barriers to entry and exit may reduce a country's ability to attract FDI. Capital control liberalization, on the other hand, may reduce the transaction costs for foreign investors, promoting FDI inflows. WORLD FDI INFLOWS are statistically significant and positive in all four models of Table 1. The level of individual-country FDI inflows tends to move together with the level of WORLD

FDI INFLOWS. A host country can expect to attract more FDI when more foreign capital seeks investment opportunities in the world economy. . . .

CONCLUSION

Previous studies related to the connections between investor behaviors and regime characteristics have produced conflicting theoretical expectations as to whether democratic or autocratic characteristics encourage FDI inflows. These studies also have placed more emphasis on the preferences of the host state and paid less attention to the motivations of foreign investors. In this analysis, we offer a theory that synthesizes and extends the conflicting expectations in previous studies. Instead of starting with the state analytically, we build our theory on the logic of why firms invest abroad. The phenomenon we study, foreign capital inflows, suggests that the logic of international production is the right place to begin our inquiry. How political institutions affect FDI inflows should mesh with why firms go abroad. Based on this premise, we derive a theory suggesting that democratic institutions affect FDI inflows both positively and negatively.

The empirical findings based on . . . a sample of fifty-three developing countries from 1982 to 1995 support our central argument that democratic institutions affect FDI inflows to developing countries via competing causal avenues. Increases in democracy yield improved property rights protection, which encourages FDI inflows. Meanwhile, increases in democracy also reduce FDI received by this set of LDCs. Our sensitivity analysis demonstrates that our findings are robust against alternative measurements of key variables and various statistical methods. With that in mind, we turn to the theoretical and policy implications of our research.

Confirming our argument that democratic institutions affect FDI in a complex manner, our theory and empirical findings offer qualified support for previous explanations. While Olson and many others argue that well-established democracies offer secure property rights and the optimal environment for investors, these analysts fail to recognize that central aspects of democratic politics can attenuate the effect via property rights. While increasing levels of democracy help to produce better judicial systems and rule of law, these higher levels of democracy also drive foreign investors away by imposing constraints on foreign capital and the host government. Similarly, while O'Donnell and several others illustrate that close alignment between states and MNEs often plays a central role in attracting FDI, they fail to take into account that property rights protection and democracy go hand in hand. While foreign investors may fear state exposure to popular will, they welcome restrictions on banditry provided by more democratic governments. Hence, our theory moves substantially further in understanding the interactions of economic globalization and political democracy.

This study also advances the stalled discussion on the effect of democracy on economic growth. Our narrower focus on FDI, a measure reflecting the combined wisdom of world investors on a country's economic prospects, avoids certain problems associated with measuring economic success with GDP. What we have discovered is that a source of economic growth, FDI, has a complex relationship with regime type, suggesting the difficulty of unpacking a direct relationship between democracy and growth. Our results are consistent with other studies arguing that property rights protection may be more important to growth than democracy or that democracy promotes growth by improving property rights protection.

Our findings have policy implications for developing countries in search of FDI. Incremental improvements in property rights protection are likely to induce a more attractive environment for foreign direct investors without requiring wholesale restructuring of state-society relationships. For instance, attempts to increase bureaucratic competence or provide enhanced contract enforcement could go a long way toward setting a country apart from competitors for FDI. Conversely, states that are unable to improve property rights protection may have to amend that weakness with more incentives in tax holidays, discounts on land purchases, or exclusive access to natural resources. Superior property rights provision may thus provide an avenue for attracting investors with less sacrifice of state resources, not to mention the benefits that other actors in the economy would enjoy under a system with clearer costs and incentives.

Our findings also hold implications for transitional economies. As new democracies set up democratic institutions that may adversely affect their ability to attract FDI, these democracies may not yet be ready to provide offsetting improvements in property rights protection because they need to consolidate power and avoid conflicts with powerful domestic actors. Over time, however, the consolidation of democratic governance should bring about better property rights protection, improving the prospect of getting more FDI inflows. Countries experiencing a transition from democracy to autocracy would face the challenge of persuading foreign investors into believing the credibility of their property rights protection.

REFERENCES

Banks, Arthur S. 1999. *Cross-National Time-Series Data Archive*. Binghamton, N.Y.: Banner Software.

Dunning, John H. 1993. *Multinational Enterprises and the Global Economy*. Reading, Mass.: Addison-Wesley.

Knack, Stephen, and Philip Keefer. 1995. Institutions and Economic Performance: Cross-Country Tests Using Alternative Institutional Measures. *Economics and Politics* 7 (3): 207–27.

North, Douglass C. 1990. *Institutions, Institutional Change, and Economic Performance*. Cambridge: Cambridge University Press.

North, Douglass C., and Barry R. Weingast. 1989. Constitutions and Commitment: The Evolution of Institutions Governing Public Choice in Seventeenth-Century England. *Journal of Economic History* 49 (4): 803–32.

O'Donnell, Guillermo. 1978. Reflections on the Patterns of Change in the Bureaucratic Authoritarian State. *Latin American Research Review* 13 (1): 3–38.

———. 1988. *Bureaucratic Authoritarianism: Argentina, 1966–1973 in Comparative Perspective.* Berkeley: University of California Press.

Olson, Mancur. 1993. Dictatorship, Democracy, and Development. *American Political Science Review* 87 (3): 567–76.

IV

MONEY AND FINANCE

The international economy, like domestic economies, requires a common monetary standard to function smoothly. For individuals and firms to buy and sell and to save and invest, they need some generally acceptable and predictable unit of account against which other goods can be measured, a medium of exchange with which transactions can be carried out, and a store of value in which wealth can be held. National currencies serve this purpose within countries: for example, Americans buy, sell, save, and invest in dollars. In international trade and payments, a variety of possible common measures can be imagined; in practice, however, the two pure cases are a commodity standard and an international currency standard. Economic actors could use a widely traded commodity, such as gold or pork bellies, against which to measure other goods; or they might arrive at some fictitious unit in which goods can be priced. The former approximates the classical gold standard; the latter, present-day special drawing rights, which are a sort of "paper gold" issued by the International Monetary Fund and equal to a mix of national currencies. Because reaching agreement on a fictitious international currency is difficult, such national currencies as the dollar or the euro are often used as the basis for international payments.

If the international monetary system provides the measures needed to conduct world trade and payments, the international financial system provides the means to carry out trade and payments. For many hundreds of years, financial institutions—especially banks—have financed trade among clients in different nations, sold and bought foreign currencies, transferred money from one country to another, and lent capital for overseas investment. If, as is often averred, the international monetary system is the "Great Wheel" that enables goods to move in international trade, the international financial system is the grease that allows the wheel itself to turn.

In the modern era (since 1820 or so), there have been, essentially, four well-functioning international monetary systems; each has had corresponding international financial characteristics. From about 1820 until World War I, the world was on or near the classical gold standard, in which many major national currencies were tied to gold at a legally fixed rate. In principle, the gold standard was self-regulating; should any national currency (and economy) move out of balance, it would be forced back into equilibrium by the very operation of the system. In practice, the pre–World War I system was actually a gold-sterling standard; the British pound sterling, backed by a strong government and the world's leading financial center, was "as good as gold," and most international trade and payments were carried out in sterling.

The world financial system in the century before World War I was indeed dominated by British banks, which financed much of world trade and channeled enormous amounts of investment capital to such rapidly developing countries as the United States, Australia, Argentina, and South Africa. As time wore on, the financial institutions of other European powers, especially France and Germany, also began to expand abroad. The result was a highly integrated system of international monetary and financial interactions under the Pax Britannica. Even before World War I, however, strains and rivalries were beginning to test the system. Once the war started, in 1914, international trade and payments collapsed: of all the world's major financial markets, only New York stayed open for the duration of the conflict. Indeed, by the time World War I ended, the center of international finance had shifted from London to New York, and Wall Street remained the world's principal lender until the Great Depression of the 1930s.

As might be expected, given the reduced economic might of Great Britain, the prewar gold-sterling standard could not be rebuilt. Yet neither was the United States, which was beset by the isolationist-internationalist conflict at home, willing to simply replace Great Britain at the apex of the world monetary system. What emerged was the so-called gold exchange standard, whereby most countries went back to tying their currencies to gold but no single national currency came to dominate the others. Dollars, sterling, and French francs were all widely used in world trade and payments, yet, given the lack of lasting international monetary cooperation in the period, the arrangement was quite unstable and short-lived. Normal international economic conditions were not restored until 1924, and within a few years, the Depression had brought the system crashing down. With the collapse of the gold exchange standard and the onset of the Depression and World War II, the international monetary and financial systems remained in disarray until after 1945.

As World War II came to an end, the Allied powers, led by the United States, began reconstructing an international monetary system under the Bretton Woods agreement. This system was based, in the monetary sphere, on an American dollar tied to gold at the rate of thirty-five dollars an ounce; other Western currencies were, in turn, tied to the dollar. This was a modified version of the pre-1914 gold standard, with the dollar at its center rather than sterling. As in the Pax Britannica, massive flows of capital from the leading nation—Great Britain, in the first instance; the United States, in the second—were crucial to the proper functioning of the mechanism. Whereas in the British case these capital flows were primarily private loans, from 1945 to 1965 they were essentially government or multilateral loans and foreign direct investment. After 1965, private international finance once again become significant, rapidly reaching historically unprecedented proportions and developing new characteristics.

Even as the new international financial system was gathering steam, the Bretton Woods monetary system was beginning to weaken. In particular, it was becoming more and more difficult to maintain the dollar's price of thirty-five dollars an ounce. As pressure built on the dollar and attempts at reform stagnated, the Richard Nixon administration finally decided that the system was unsustainable. In August 1971, President Nixon "closed the gold window," ending the dollar's free convertibility into gold. The dollar was soon devalued, and by 1975, the gold-dollar standard had been replaced by the current floating-rate system.

Under the current system of floating exchange rates, the value of most currencies is set, more or less freely, by private traders in world currency markets. Thus, the values of the dollar, the yen, the euro, and so on fluctuate on international currency markets. This has led to frequent and rapid changes in the relative prices of major currencies, as well as to frequent complaints about the unplanned nature of the new system. Because of the central role of the U.S. dollar, even in today's floating-rate system, changes in American economic policy can drive the dollar up and down dramatically, in ways that have important effects on the economy of the United States and of the rest of the world.

The "impossible trinity" or "trilemma" of a fixed exchange rate, capital mobility, and autonomous monetary policy—and the necessary trade-offs engendered by the pursuit of these three goals—is central to understanding the current floating-rate system and the potential for cooperation among the world's leading nations in international monetary affairs. This problem is examined by Joshua Aizenman (Reading 13). In Reading 14, Jeffry A. Frieden discusses how globalization has heightened political controversies over exchange rates. He goes on to explore the domestic economic interests implicated by the trade-offs involved, arguing that interest groups and voters vary in their views on the desirability of one exchange rate policy or another.

In the 1970s, as American inflation rates rose, the dollar's value dropped relative to other major currencies. From 1979 to 1985, American monetary policy concentrated on fighting inflation while fiscal policy was expansionary, leading to a dramatic rise in the dollar's value. Although inflation was brought down, the strong dollar wreaked havoc with the ability of many American industries to compete internationally. In the mid-1980s, the dollar dropped back down to its lowest levels in nearly forty years, and, since the 1990s, it has gone up and down continually.

Through all these fluctuations, there was dissatisfaction in many quarters about the underlying uncertainty concerning international monetary and financial trends. Today, currencies fluctuate widely, many of the world's major nations are experiencing unprecedented trade surpluses or deficits, and capital flows across borders in enormous quantities.

Monetary uncertainty has led some nations to seek security in a variety of alternative institutions. Some governments have relied on establishing independent central banks, while others have chosen stable currency policies to signal monetary stability. In Reading 17, J. Lawrence Broz explores the reasons for these choices, arguing that the institutional differences between democracies and dictatorships lead to different policy outcomes.

In addition to nationally specific policies, there have been a number of measures to alter the nature of the international currency system. Some countries and observers support the development of a new international money, of which special drawing rights might be a precursor. Others desire a return to the gold standard and the monetary discipline that this system implied. The principal strategy has been to seek stability through cooperative regional agreements.

The most important of these regional monetary agreements is Europe's Economic and Monetary Union (EMU). In 1999 the members of the EMU introduced a single currency, the euro, which quickly gained a place as one of the world's three leading currencies. However, as Reading 16 makes clear, the Eurozone has more recently fallen into a devastating debt crisis. In this case, a financial crisis has come to threaten the very existence of Europe's attempt at monetary unification.

In international finance, the period since 1965 has been extraordinarily eventful. International financial markets have grown to over a hundred trillion dollars, and international banking has become one of the great growth industries in the world economy. The recent explosion of international finance is unprecedented. Net international bond and bank lending amounted to $865 billion in 1997, having risen from just $245 billion five years earlier. Capital outflows from the advanced economies were $4,148 billion in 2007, in contrast to $52 billion in the late 1970s; moreover, almost two-thirds of such outflows currently consist of portfolio investment, while only one-third is foreign direct investment, the reverse of forty years ago. Indeed, in the late 1970s, total global outflows of portfolio capital averaged $15 billion a year, whereas between 2004 and 2007, they averaged $2,509 billion a year, a nearly 170-fold increase.

To put these annual flows in perspective, capital outflows were equivalent to 7 percent of world merchandise trade in the late 1970s but averaged 15 percent in the 1990s and 19 percent between 2000 and 2007. Likewise, in 1980, cross-border transactions in stocks and bonds were equal to less than 10 percent of the gross domestic product (GDP) of all major industrial countries, whereas by 2007 they were equivalent to more than twice the GDP of the United States and Germany, and three times the GDP of France and Canada.[1]

However, the extraordinary growth of international finance has been accompanied by reminders that global financial markets—like domestic financial markets—are prone to crisis. Indeed, in 2007, the world was hit by a massive financial crisis, which led to the most serious international economic downturn since the 1930s. Menzie Chinn and Jeffry Frieden, in Reading 15, describe how the United States and other countries borrowed trillions of dollars in less than a decade, and how these debts eventually went bad. The financial crisis in the United States and in the European Union (Reading 16) reminds us that international borrowing and lending has long been prone to crises, and that these crises typically give rise to powerful political conflicts between debtor and creditor countries.

Among scholars, the nature of international monetary and financial relations raises important analytical issues. As in other arenas, the very rapid development of globe-straddling international financial markets has led some to believe that the rise of supranational financial actors has eroded the power of national states. In this view, international financial relations essentially serve the interests of global investors and their allies. For others, such international institutions as the International Monetary Fund (IMF), along with national governments, are the primary determinants of international monetary and financial trends. The tension between a monetary and financial system that is, in a sense, beyond the reach of individual states and currencies and banks that clearly have home countries gives rise to a fundamental tension in world politics and in the study of the international political economy.

NOTE

1. These figures are from the International Monetary Fund's *Balance of Payments Yearbook and International Financial Statistics*; Bank for International Settlements, *Annual Report* (Basel: Bank for International Settlements [BIS], various issues); and Jeffry A. Frieden, "Invested Interests: The Politics of National Economic Policies in a World of Global Finance," *International Organization* 45, 4 (1991): 428.

13

The Impossible Trinity (aka the Policy Trilemma)

JOSHUA AIZENMAN

Governments in an open world economy face what macroeconomists call an "impossible trinity" or "trilemma." They can choose two, but not all three, of the following: financial integration with the rest of the world, a stable exchange rate, and an independent monetary policy. Inasmuch as all three of these goals are generally regarded as desirable, governments have to decide which one they are willing to forego. This reading surveys international trends and experiences with trying to address this trilemma, and new challenges that have arisen in the wake of the Great Financial Crisis of 2008–2009. It highlights the difficulties governments confront in a world in which the choice of monetary policies and monetary institutions can have enduring effects on subsequent economic and political developments.

THE TRILEMMA AND MUNDELL–FLEMING'S FRAMEWORK

A fundamental contribution of the Mundell–Fleming framework is the impossible trinity, or the trilemma. The trilemma states that a country may simultaneously choose any two, but not all, of the following three policy goals—monetary independence, exchange-rate stability, and financial integration. The "trilemma triangle" is illustrated in Figure 1. Each of the three sides of the triangle, representing monetary independence, exchange-rate stability, and financial integration, depicts a potentially desirable policy goal. However, it is not possible to be on all three sides of the triangle simultaneously. The top vertex, labeled "closed financial markets," is associated with monetary policy autonomy and a fixed exchange-rate regime. But it represents financial autarky—the preferred choice of most developing countries in the mid- to late 1980s. The left vertex, labeled "floating exchange-rate regime," is associated with monetary independence and financial integration—the preferred choice of the United States during the last three decades. The right vertex, labeled "giving up monetary independence," is associated with exchange-rate stability (a pegged exchange-rate regime) and financial integration but no monetary independence—the preferred choice of the countries forming the euro block (a currency union) and of Argentina during the 1990s (choosing a currency-board exchange-rate regime).

. . . The model considers a small country choosing its exchange-rate regime and its financial integration with the global financial market. Analysis is considerably simplified by focusing on polarized binary choices, that is, credibly fixed exchange rate or pure float, and perfect capital mobility or financial autarky. To illustrate the resultant trade-off, consider first a fixed exchange-rate system with perfect capital mobility. This policy configuration corresponds to the policy pair associated with the right side of the trilemma triangle. In circumstances where domestic and foreign government bonds are perfect substitutes, credible fixed exchange rate implies that the domestic interest rate equals the foreign interest rate, as follows from the uncovered interest rate parity condition. If the central bank increases the supply of money, the incipient downward pressure on the domestic interest rate triggers the sale of domestic bonds, in search for a higher yield of foreign bonds. As a result of these arbitrage forces, the central bank is faced with an excess demand for foreign currency aimed at purchasing foreign bonds (and a matching excess supply of domestic currency). Under the fixed exchange rate, the central bank must intervene in the currency market in order to satisfy the public's demand for foreign currency at the official exchange rate. As a result, the central bank sells foreign currency to the public. In the process, the central bank buys back the excess supply of domestic currency that is triggered by its own attempt to increase the supply of money. The net effect is that the central bank loses control of the money supply, which passively adjusts to the money demand. Thus, the policy configuration of perfect capital mobility and fixed exchange rate implies giving up monetary policy. . . . This pair of policy choices implies that, in a small open economy, determination of the domestic interest rate is relegated to the country to which its exchange rate is pegged (corresponding to the right vertex of the trilemma triangle).

A small open economy wishing to maintain financial integration can regain its monetary autonomy by giving up the fixed exchange rate. Under a flexible

FIGURE 1   The Trilemma "Textbook Framework"

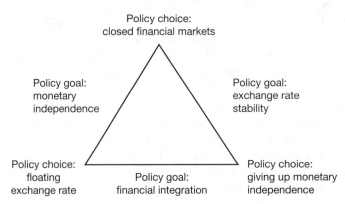

exchange rate regime, expansion of the domestic money supply reduces the interest rate, resulting in capital outflows in search of the higher foreign yield. The incipient excess demand for foreign currency depreciates the exchange rate. Hence, in a flexible exchange-rate regime with financial integration, monetary policy is potent. A higher supply of money reduces the interest rate, thereby increasing domestic investment, and weakens the domestic currency, which in turn expands the economy through increased net exports. This policy configuration corresponds to the policy pair associated with the left and the lower side of the trilemma triangle, attainable under a flexible exchange-rate regime. However, achieving monetary independence requires the small open economy to give up exchange-rate stability, implying a shift from the right vertex of the trilemma triangle to the left.

An alternative way for the small open economy to regain its monetary independence is to give up financial integration and opt for exchange-rate stability and monetary independence. Giving up financial integration prevents arbitrage between domestic and foreign bonds, thereby delinking the domestic interest rate from the foreign interest rate. Monetary policy operates in ways similar to the closed economy, where, in the short run, the central bank controls the supply of money and monetary expansion reduces the domestic interest rate. This policy configuration corresponds to the policy pair associated with the left and the right side of the trilemma triangle, attainable under closed financial markets and a pegged exchange rate, that is, the top vertex. Monetary independence in this case gets traded off with financial integration.

The sharp predictions of the trilemma and its crisp intuitive interpretation made it the Holy Grail of the open-economy neo-Keynesian paradigm. The *impossible trinity* has become self-evident for most academic economists. Today, this insight is also shared by practitioners and policy makers alike. A lingering challenge is that, in practice, most countries rarely face the binary choices articulated by the trilemma. Instead, countries chose the degree of financial integration and exchange-rate flexibility. Even in rare cases of adoption of a strong version of a fixed exchange-rate system (like the currency-board regime chosen by Argentina in the early 1990s), the credibility of the fixed exchange rate changes over time, and the central bank rarely follows the strict version of currency board. Similarly, countries choosing a flexible exchange-rate regime, occasionally (some frequently) actively intervene in foreign currency markets, and end up implementing different versions of a managed float system. Furthermore, most countries operate in the gray range of partial financial integration, where regulations restrict flows of funds. Understanding these mixed regimes remains a challenge.

Testing the predictions of the trilemma paradigm remains [a] work in progress, as there is no unique way to define and measure the degree of exchange-rate flexibility, monetary autonomy, and financial integration. Proper modeling of limited financial integration and limited substitutability of assets remains debatable. Yet, even in this murky situation, the trilemma remains a potent paradigm. A key message of the trilemma is scarcity of policy instruments. Policy makers face a trade-off, where increasing one trilemma variable (such as higher financial integration) would induce a drop in the weighted average of the other two variables (lower exchange-rate stability, or lower monetary independence, or a combination of the two). We continue with a review of the changing trilemma configurations of countries during recent decades, then discuss the empirical literature dealing with the evolving trilemma configurations, and finally interpret challenges facing countries that have been navigating the trilemma throughout the globalization process.

THE TRILEMMA CHOICES OF COUNTRIES— TRENDS AND TRADE-OFFS

Figure 2 summarizes the changing patterns of [the] trilemma during the 1970–2006 period. It reports the trilemma indices for 50 countries (32 of which are developing countries) during the 1970–2006 period, for which there is a balanced dataset. Figure 2(a) vividly shows that, after the breakup of the Bretton Woods system, industrial countries significantly reduced the extent of exchange-rate stability until the early 1980s. Overall, for the industrial countries, financial openness accelerated after the beginning of the 1990s and exchange-rate stability rose after the end of the 1990s, reflecting the introduction of the euro in 1999. In line with the trilemma predictions, monetary independence experienced a declining trend, especially since the early 1990s.

Looking at the group of developing countries, we can see that, not only do these countries differ from industrial ones, but there are also differences between emerging and nonemerging market developing countries. Comparing Figure 2(b) and 2(c) reveals that emerging markets (EMs) moved toward relatively more flexible exchange-rate regimes, higher financial integration, and lower monetary independence than developing non-EMs. The figure shows that EMs have experienced convergence to some middle ground among all three indices. In contrast, non-EMs, on average, have not exhibited such convergence. For both groups, while the degree of exchange-rate stability declined from the early 1970s to the early 1990s, it increased during the last 15 years. However, the 2008 global financial crisis may induce some countries to move toward higher exchange-rate flexibility. By the end of this sample period, non-EMs exhibit a greater degree of exchange-rate stability and monetary independence, but a lower degree of financial integration compared to EMs.

The original formulation of the trilemma focused on polar trilemma configuration at the vertex of the trilemma triangle. However, Figure 2 implies that most of the action has been happening in the middle ground, with countries shifting their configuration to adapt to new challenges and changing economic and global structures. Looking at the time series of the trilemma variables supports the conjecture that major events are associated with structural breaks. After the breakdown of the Bretton Woods system, the mean of

FIGURE 2 The evolution of trilemma indices: (a) industrial countries; (b) emerging market countries; (c) nonemerging market developing countries. Definitions: The index for the extent of monetary independence (MI); $MI = 1 - 0.5[corr(i_j, i) - (-1)]$, where i refers to home countries and j to the base country. By construction, higher values of the index mean higher monetary policy independence. Exchange-rate stability (ERS), ERS=Annual standard deviations of monthly exchange-rate series between the home country and the base country calculated and included in the following formula to normalize the index between 0 and 1: $ERS = 0.01/[0.01 + st\ dev(\Delta(log(exch\_rate)))]$. Financial openness (KAOPEN): KAOPEN = A *de jure* index of capital account openness constructed by Chinn and Ito (2006), normalized between 0 and 1. Higher values of this index indicate that a country is more open to cross-border capital transactions.

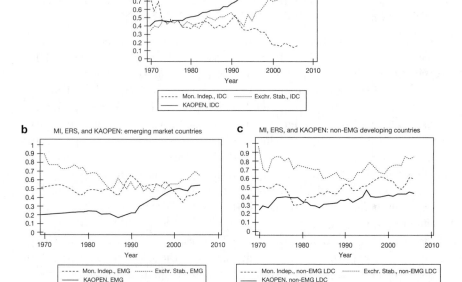

Reproduced from J. Arzenman, M.D. Chinn, H. Ito, 2008. The emerging global finan-cial architecture: Tracing and evaluating new patterns of the trilemma configuration. Journal of International Money and Finance 29 (4), 615–41.

the exchange-rate stability index for the industrial country group fell signifi-cantly, while the mean of financial openness fell only slightly. Nonemerging developing countries, however, did not significantly decrease the level of fixity of their exchange rates over the same time period. However, they became less monetarily independent and more financially open. The external debt crisis of the 1980s led *all* developing countries to pursue higher exchange-rate flex-ibility, most likely reflecting the fact that countries affected by the crisis could not sustain fixed exchange-rate arrangements. Moreover, these countries also simultaneously pursued higher monetary independence, while tightening capital controls in the early 1980s, as a result of the debt crisis.

The level of industrial countries' monetary independence dropped significantly during the 1990s, while their exchange rates became more stable and their efforts of capital account liberalization continued. These trends reflect the European countries' movement toward economic and monetary union. For financial openness, the year 1990 is identified with a major structural break—the beginning of the wave of financial integration of developing countries. For nonemerging developing and EM countries, the debt crisis is found to be a major structural break for exchange-rate stability. The Asian crisis of 1997–1998 is also a major structural break for EM countries. . . .

BEYOND THE TRILEMMA TRIANGLE: INTERNATIONAL RESERVES AND THE IMPOSSIBLE TRINITY

Pertinent developments that modify the context of the trilemma comprise large-scale financial globalization of almost all countries during 1990s–2000s. Concurrently, the economic takeoff of EMs, including the most populous countries (China and India), gradually led to a structural shift, such that by 2010 more than half of the global gross domestic product (GDP; purchasing power parity adjusted) is produced by developing and EMs. An unintended consequence of financial globalization is the growing exposure of developing countries to financial instabilities associated with sudden stops of inflows of capital, capital flights, and deleveraging crises. The significant output and social costs associated with financial crises, on average estimated to be about 10% of GDP, added financial stability to the three policy goals framed by the original trilemma.

Pursuing financial integration while maintaining financial stability of EMs may explain intriguing developments in the three decades since the 1980s—despite the proliferation of greater exchange-rate flexibility, international reserves/GDP ratios increased substantially. Most of the increase in reserve holding has taken place in developing countries, especially in emerging East Asia. The dramatic increase of international reserve hoarding has been lopsided. While the international reserves/GDP ratio of industrial countries was overall stable hovering around 4%, the reserves/GDP ratio of developing countries increased dramatically, from about 5% to about 27%. . . . By 2007, about two-thirds of the global international reserves were held by developing countries. Most of this increase has been in Asia, where the reserves/GDP increased from about 5% in 1980 to about 37% in 2006 (32% in Asia excluding China). The most dramatic changes occurred in China, increasing its reserve/GDP from about 1% in 1980 to about 41% in 2006. Econometric evaluations suggest several structural changes in the patterns of reserves hoarded by developing countries. A notable change occurred in the 1990s, a decade when the international reserves/GDP ratios shifted upward. The trend that intensified shortly after the East Asian crisis of 1997–1998 subsided by 2000. Another structural change took place in early 2000s, mostly driven by an unprecedented increase in the hoarding of international reserves in China. China's reserve/GDP ratio almost tripled within 6 years, from about 14% during 1997–2000 to 41% in 2006. . . .

A probable interpretation for the unprecedented hoarding of international reserves . . . deals with the unintended consequences of financial globalization. . . . While the international reserves/GDP ratios followed similar patterns in the 1980s, a remarkable takeoff in reserve hoarding by developing countries occurs from [the] early 1990s, coinciding with the takeoff of financial integration of developing countries. The hoarding of international reserves/GDP by developing countries accelerated dramatically in the aftermath of the East Asian crisis. The evidence is consistent with the conjecture that financial integration of developing countries led to drastic changes in the demand for international reserves. Prior to the financial integration, the demand for reserves provided self-insurance against volatile trade flows. However, financial integration of developing countries also added the need to self-insure against volatile financial flows. By the nature of financial markets, the exposure to rapidly increasing demands for foreign currency triggered by financial volatility exceeds by a wide margin the one triggered by trade volatility. Consequently, the financial self-insurance motive associated with the growing exposure to sudden stops and deleveraging crises accounts well for the international reserves takeoff in the 1990s. The East Asian crisis was a watershed event, as it impacted high saving countries with overall balanced fiscal accounts. These countries were viewed as [being] less exposed to sudden stop events as compared to other developing countries prior to the crisis. With a lag, the affected countries reacted by massive increases in their stock of reserves.

The link between hoarding reserves and financial integration adds a fourth dimension to the trilemma. In the short run, countries came to expect that hoarding and managing international reserves may increase their financial stability and capacity to run independent monetary policies. This development seems to be important for EMs that are only partially integrated with the global financial system and where sterilization is heavily used to manage the potential inflationary effects of hoarding reserves (China and India being prime examples of these trends). In contrast, most of the industrial countries kept their international reserves/GDP ratios low. This could have reflected the easy access of industrial countries to bilateral swap lines in case of urgent needs for foreign currencies as well as their ability to borrow externally in their currencies.

The research during [the] 2000s links the reserve hoarding trend to three key factors associated with the shifting positions in the trilemma configuration since 1990. The first factor is the "fear of floating," manifested in the desire to tightly manage the exchange rate (or to keep fixing it). The desire to stabilize the exchange rate reflects a hybrid of factors—to boost trade, to mitigate destabilizing balance sheet shocks in the presence of dollarized liabilities, to provide a transparent nominal anchor used to stabilize inflationary expectations, etc. The second factor is the adoption of active policies to develop and increase the depth of domestic financial intermediation through a larger domestic banking and financial system relative to GDP. The third factor is complementing the deepening of domestic financial intermediation with an increase in the financial integration of the developing country with international financial markets.

The combination of these three elements increases the exposure of the economy to financial storms, in the worst case leading to financial meltdowns, as was vividly illustrated by the Mexican 1994–95 crisis, the East Asian 1997–1998 crisis, and the Argentinean 2001–2002 financial collapse. The recent history of EMs implies that the macro challenges facing them are probably more complex than navigating the trilemma triangle. Short of the easy access to institutional swap lines available to mature OECD (Organization for Economic Cooperator and Development) countries, EMs self-insure against financial instability associated with their growing financial integration with the global financial system. Recent studies validate the importance of "financial factors" as determinants in addition to the traditional factors in accounting for increased international reserves/GDP ratios. Indeed, recent research has revealed that the role of financial factors has increased in tandem with growing financial integration.

More financially open, financially deep countries with greater exchange-rate stability tend to hold more reserves. Within the EM sample, the fixed exchange-rate effect is weaker, but financial depth (potentially measured by M2/GDP) is highly significant and growing in importance over time. Trade openness is the other robust determinant of reserve demand, though its importance seems to have diminished over time. The growing importance of financial factors helps in accounting for a greater share of the international reserves/GDP ratios. However, even with the inclusion of the new variables, China's and Japan's international reserves/GDP ratios seem to be outliers. These results are in line with a broader self-insurance view, where reserves provide a buffer, both against deleveraging initiated by foreign parties as well as the sudden wish of domestic residents to acquire new external assets, that is, "sudden capital flight." . . .

The experience of EMs suggests that the trilemma triangle, while useful, overlooks the possibility that, with limited but growing financial integration, countries hoarding international reserves may loosen in the short run some of the trilemma constraints. This possibility may be illustrated by contrasting the trilemma trends of Latin American and Asian EMs. Latin American EM economies liberalized their financial markets rapidly since the 1990s, after some retrenchment during the 1980s, while reducing the extent of monetary independence and maintaining a lower level of exchange-rate stability in recent years. Emerging Asian economies, on the other hand, stand out by achieving comparable levels of exchange-rate stability and growing financial openness while consistently displaying greater monetary independence. These two groups of economies are most differentiated from each other by their high levels of international reserves holding. Without giving up its exchange-rate stability and monetary independence, China has increased its international reserves holding while slowly increasing financial openness. This evidence is consistent with the view that countries' efforts to "relax the trilemma" in the short run can involve an increase in international reserves holding.

THE TRILEMMA AND THE FUTURE FINANCIAL ARCHITECTURE

We conclude with remarks dealing with the relevance of the trilemma five decades after Mundell's seminal contributions. The trilemma is among the few macroeconomic frameworks that have passed the test of time and remains as pertinent today as it was in the past. The main developments that modify the context of the trilemma are the massive financial globalization of almost all countries of the world, and the fast deepening of domestic and international financial markets. Unlike the 1960s, today the private sector dominates financial intermediation. The sheer volume of potential arbitrage in the presence of misaligned exchange rate is huge relative to the resources of a typical central bank. These developments imply that the viability of the fixed exchange rate is limited, like the viability of a promising *Mirage*.

During the 1990s, there was significant discussion about the "disappearing middle"—the hypothesis that everybody was adopting hard pegs or fully flexible exchange-rate regimes. Evidence suggests that, with the exception of the formation of the euro and few currency boards that survived beyond a decade (mostly in small open economies, like Hong Kong), there has been no obvious global trend that implies the disappearance of the middle ground. Indeed, there are no clear-cut reasons to expect any convergence toward the polar choices of pure float or pure fixed exchange-rate regimes. Figure 2 suggests that, while developing countries keep exhibiting preferences toward exchange-rate stability, the growing class of EMs seems to move toward greater exchange-rate flexibility. Beyond these trends, one expects that countries will keep adjusting their policy choices in the extended trilemma framework in ways that reflect the changing economic circumstances, without displaying permanent patterns. Similarly, the large increase in the depth of international trade implies that the viability of financial autarky is vanishing, as trade in goods offers channels leading to *de facto* financial integration by means of trade misinvoicing. These developments do not impact the relevance of the trilemma, but imply that most of [the] action is not in the vertices of the trilemma but in the middle ground of limited exchange-rate flexibility, partial integration of financial markets, and viable though constrained monetary autonomy.

The enormous challenges associated with rapid financial globalization have been vividly illustrated by the global financial crisis of 2008–09, when, to the surprise of the global financial system, the epic center of the crisis was the United States. This crisis happened against the background of a remarkable decline in macroeconomic volatility and cost of risk during the 1990s and early 2000s, a trend that has hence been referred to as "the great moderation." The great moderation induced observers to presume the beginning of the end of costly business cycles. Practitioners and markets got convinced about the durability of this moderation trend, and about the superior financial intermediation of the United States. This reflected the spirit of late 1990s and early 2000s, when the presumption of key policy makers in the United States was that private intermediation with minimal regulatory oversight provides superior results. The alleged superior intermediation of the United States provided the intellectual explanation for the growing global imbalances of the 1990s–2000s, when expanding US current account deficits, ranging between 0.5 and 1% of the global GDP, were financed mostly by EMs and commodities exporters. During this period, EMs channeled a growing portion of financial inflows to hoarding international reserves. The 2008–09 global crisis has been a watershed event, shifting the global patterns of trilemma configurations toward new configurations. . . .

Extending the policy trilemma by adding financial stability to the macropolicy goals is one of the consequences of the global liquidity crisis of 2008–09. While our discussion has focused on the EMs, it applies to the OECD countries as well. The logic of our discussion may be viewed as an open-economy extension of the growing recognition that the current global financial crisis calls for changes in the operations of central banks and treasuries, and in the global financial architecture. By force of history and by virtue of learning by doing, the pendulum is shifting toward a more nuanced view, recognizing central banks' and treasuries' responsibility in implementing prudential regulations and policies aimed at reducing volatility and susceptibility of economies to crises. . . .

These developments illustrate the thorny problems faced by countries as they navigate between the macroeconomic policy trilemma and the goal of maintaining financial stability at times of deepening globalization. Modifying the global financial architecture to deal with the challenges of the twenty-first century remains a work in progress. At the same time, the extended trilemma framework keeps providing useful insights about the trade-offs and challenges facing policy makers, investors, and central banks.

14

Globalization and Exchange Rate Policy

JEFFRY A. FRIEDEN

As economic globalization increases, exchange rates become more politicized and more subject to mass and special-interest political pressures. Jeffry A. Frieden argues that this is because currency policies differentially affect the interests of consumers and powerful economic interest groups, and that globalization intensifies these societal conflicts. He then identifies the domestic winners and losers of policies that affect the stability and the level of the exchange rate. Special interests that are heavily involved in foreign commerce and investment are more likely to desire a fixed exchange rate than are domestically oriented interest groups. By the same token, consumers and nontradables producers are more likely to want a strong (relatively appreciated) currency than are tradables producers. Evidence from Latin America supports these predictions. Policy makers also seem to engineer an "exchange rate electoral cycle" in which they boost voters' incomes via currency appreciation in the run-up to an election and impose costs on voters by devaluing only after a new government is in office.

Exchange rates powerfully affect cross-border economic transactions. Trade, investment, finance, tourism, migration, and more are all profoundly influenced by international monetary policies. Many developing-country governments have searched for alternatives to the uncertainty that can prevail on international currency markets. Policy entrepreneurs have rushed to peddle currency nostrums, urging a turn toward dollarization, managed floating, nominal anchors, target bands, or other options.

There are both theoretical and empirical reasons to expect globalization to heighten the importance of the exchange rate. Theoretically, open-economy macroeconomic principles imply that capital mobility profoundly affects exchange rate policy choices. As Robert Mundell showed more than forty years ago, the government of a financially integrated economy faces a choice between monetary policy autonomy and a fixed exchange rate (Mundell 1963). If the government opts for a fixed rate, capital mobility makes impossible a monetary stance different from that of the anchor currency; alternatively, if the government opts to sustain an independent monetary policy, it must allow the currency to move. These constraints mean that the economics and politics of monetary and exchange rate policy are likely to be very different in an economy that is financially open than in an economy that is not. By the same token, inasmuch as international economic integration involves increased exposure to international financial and commercial flows, it heightens the concerns of those involved in or exposed to international trade and finance. In a relatively closed economy, few economic actors care about currency movements. But as economies become "globalized" more firms, investors, and workers find their fortunes linked to the exchange rate, and to its impact on trade and financial flows. This concentrates attention on the exchange rate.

Empirically, the impact of "globalization" on exchange rate politics can be seen both over time and across countries. The exchange rate was an important policy problem in the previous era of high globalization. Between 1870 and 1914, the gold standard was one of the major political controversies of the era. In the economies that first approximated globalized conditions today—the small open economies of Western Europe—the exchange rate was so prominent an issue that monetary unification became the top priority of many Europeans over a twenty-year period. And, in the many economies that have now liberalized commercial and financial relations with the rest of the world, currency policy has similarly become central.

The policy advice that governments receive on exchange rates has typically been presented as technical solutions to technical economic problems. Yet exchange rate policy is highly political. It is chosen by policy-makers often concerned about the impact of currency policy on electoral conditions, and pressures from special interests and mass public opinion can affect its course profoundly. The gap between exchange-rate policy advice and the actual policy environment resembles the gap often found in discussions of policy towards the rule of law, investor protection, and corruption: the recommendations assume away interest groups, mass public opinion, and electoral coalitions—in a word, politics. And this is more than an academic concern. Recommendations that ignore the political economy of policy implementation can have disastrous outcomes. A first-best policy whose implementation is subverted by political realities may well be far worse than a feasible second-best solution.

In this chapter, I set out a rudimentary picture of the political economy of exchange rate policy in developing countries. I start by outlining prevailing approaches to the analysis of currency policy, highlighting the argument that ignoring politics leads to poor policy advice. I then discuss the choices policy-makers face with regard to exchange rate regimes and exchange rate levels, and the tradeoffs among different values that these choices entail. I analyze the political-economy pressures—special-interest, mass political, electoral—faced by policy-makers, with evidence drawn from recent Latin American experiences, before reaching my conclusion.

POLITICS AND THE EXCHANGE RATE

The events of the past twenty years demonstrate the importance of understanding the political economy of currency policy. The European Monetary Union, debates over dollarization in Latin America, currency crises in Mexico, East Asia, Russia, Brazil, Turkey, and Argentina—all are impossible to understand without incorporating the role of pressures from interest groups, from mass publics, and from politicians concerned about their re-election. (The same, of course, is true of the gold standard in the nineteenth and early twentieth centuries.)

Currency policy is made in an intensely political environment. Even apparently apolitical observations often embody political assumptions or assertions. For example, allusions to the unsustainability of a particular exchange rate must be based on some model of political constraints on policy. Technically, no exchange rate is unsustainable; the real economy can be made to fit any nominal exchange rate. Analysts who refer to an unsustainable exchange rate must have in mind that local political conditions will not allow the government to defend the level of the currency. These conditions might include opposition from exporters or import competitors clamoring for a devaluation, or more general concern that a devaluation might reduce local purchasing power in unpopular ways. Whatever the reality, allegations of unsustainability presume something about the political system and the structure of interests within it.

These presumptions are worth making explicit. Yet prevailing analyses of currency policy largely ignore politics, with the result that practical policy discussions tend to abstract from the real and powerful pressures that are brought to bear on exchange rate policy choices.

Two common explanations of exchange rate policy choice focus on optimal currency area criteria and on the currency as an anchor for inflation expectations. The former . . . arguments are well known: currency union between two countries is welfare-improving where factors are mobile between them, or when the countries are subject to correlated exogenous shocks, or when their economic structures are very similar. This reasoning has been extended to explain the choice of a fixed exchange rate, on the principle that currency union is simply an extreme form of fixing.

The second broad category of currency policy explanations emphasizes the use of the exchange rate as a way of overcoming the time-inconsistency of monetary authorities' anti-inflationary commitments. A government attempting to signal its seriousness about non-inflationary policy can peg the exchange rate to a nominal anchor currency. When a government commits to a peg it makes an easily verifiable promise: either it follows macroeconomic policies consistent with the peg, or it does not, in which case the peg collapses. Most contemporary supporters of fixed rates, including dollarization, point to the disciplining characteristics of this policy stance as its main attraction.

There are both theoretical and empirical problems with these two approaches. Theoretically, they presuppose that policy is made on welfare grounds. A welfare-driven policy could be the result of many things, such as that:

- policy-makers do not depend on support from domestic political actors;
- the relevant political pressures are for improvements in aggregate social welfare; or that
- domestic political actors do not have preferences over exchange rate policies other than that they enhance aggregate social welfare.

Needless to say, these theoretical propositions are at odds with decades of theoretical work in political economy.

There is also little or no empirical support for the supposition that policy follows normative welfare principles. For example, there is little evidence that existing currency unions—from Europe's Economic and Monetary Union to dollarized countries—met optimal currency area criteria when they were created. And most empirical work indicates that, except in the extreme case of hyperinflation, it is rare for countries to use nominal anchors for anti-inflationary credibility.

Exchange rate policy motivates the same sorts of special and mass, particularistic and electoral, interests that are to be found in every other realm of economic policy. Recent analyses incorporate the role of interest group and partisan pressures, political institutions, and the electoral incentives of politicians.

CHOICES AND TRADEOFFS

The first analytical task is to understand the tradeoffs faced by politicians and their constituents as they consider national currency policies. Governments making currency policy face decisions on two basic dimensions: on the *regime* by which the currency is managed (fixed or floating, for example), and on the *level* of the currency (strong or weak). In the first instance, policy-makers have to decide whether to float or fix the exchange rate—and if to float, in which of the many possible ways. In the second instance, assuming the currency is not fixed, they need to determine what the preferred level of the exchange rate is. They can, of course, decide to let the currency float completely freely, but in developing countries policy-makers have shown themselves reluctant to do this. Policy-makers often act to avoid a substantial appreciation or depreciation of the currency, which implies that they have preferences over the currency's level.

Regime

FIXED OR FLOATING: STABILITY AND CREDIBILITY OR POLICY FLEXIBILITY? The traditional case for stable exchange rates hinges on the benefits of economic integration. In an open economy, the main advantage of a fixed rate regime is to lower exchange rate risk and transaction costs that can impede international trade and investment. Volatile exchange rates create uncertainty about international transactions, adding a risk premium to the costs of goods and assets traded across borders. By stabilizing the currency, a government can encourage greater trade and investment. More recent analyses emphasize the possibility that an exchange rate peg can enhance monetary-policy credibility, as mentioned above. Both theory and evidence suggest that fixing the exchange rate to the currency of a low-inflation country both promotes international trade and investment and disciplines monetary policy by providing an observable nominal anchor.

But fixing the exchange rate has costs. To gain the benefits of greater economic integration through fixing, governments must sacrifice their capacity to run an independent monetary policy. The "impossible trinity" principle explains that governments must choose two of three goals: capital mobility, exchange rate stability, or monetary independence (Mundell 1963). In a financially integrated economy, domestic interest rates cannot long differ from world interest rates (capital flows induced by arbitrage opportunities quickly eliminate the differential). There is strong evidence that financial integration has progressed so far that capital mobility can be taken more or less as given—which reduces the choice to sacrificing exchange rate stability versus sacrificing monetary independence. Fixed rates require the subordination of domestic monetary policy to currency and balance of payments considerations.

A floating exchange rate, on the other hand, has the great advantage of allowing a government to pursue its own independent monetary policy. This independence is valuable because it provides flexibility to accommodate foreign and domestic shocks, including changes in the terms of trade and world financial conditions. Floating allows the exchange rate to be used as a policy tool: for example, policy-makers can adjust the nominal exchange rate to affect the competitiveness of the tradeable goods sector. In some countries, especially those with a history of high and variable inflation, policy-makers may place an overriding value on monetary stability. But for other countries, achieving monetary stability at the cost of flexibility may involve too great a sacrifice; an autonomous monetary policy might be the best way to cope with the external shocks they face.

In an open economy, then, policy-makers face a tradeoff between two competing sets of values. On the one hand, a fixed rate brings *stability and credibility*; on the other hand, it sacrifices *flexibility*. A fixed rate makes for more currency and monetary stability; a floating rate makes for more policy flexibility. Each set of values is desirable; obtaining each requires forgoing at least some of the other.

Level

HIGH OR LOW: CONSUMERS OR PRODUCERS? Policy-makers face another set of tradeoffs, and that is on the *level* of the exchange rate. The level of the real exchange rate affects the relative price of traded goods in both local and foreign markets. There is no clear economic-efficiency argument for or against any particular level. A strong (appreciated) currency gives residents greater purchasing power, but the fact that it makes foreign products relatively cheaper also subjects national producers of tradeable products to more foreign competition. When a real appreciation makes domestic goods more expensive relative to foreign, consumers of imports benefit while producers of goods that compete with imports (and exporters) lose. The result is a loss of competitiveness for tradeables producers.

A real depreciation has the opposite effects: it stimulates demand for locally produced tradeable products, which is good for their producers; but it makes consumers worse off by raising the prices they pay for foreign goods and services. In broader macroeconomic terms, a real depreciation can encourage exports, switch expenditures away from imports into domestic goods, invigorate the tradable sectors of the economy, and boost aggregate output. But a real depreciation can also be contractionary, because real money balances shrink as the result of the higher price level. And if a nation relies on imports for many vital items, such as oil, food, or capital goods, depreciation can reduce living standards, retard economic growth, and increase inflation.

Thus, the level of the exchange rate confronts policy-makers with two desirable but mutually exclusive goals—stimulating local tradeables producers, and raising local purchasing power. The benefit of increasing the competitiveness of national producers comes at the cost of reducing the real income of national consumers, and vice versa. To paraphrase Abraham Lincoln, you cannot please all of the people all of the time.

In some instances, especially in developing countries, the tradeoffs discussed above can be collapsed into one dimension. The strongest supporters of exchange rate flexibility and a depreciated currency are typically those producers concerned about their competitiveness in import and export markets. The strongest supporters of a fixed exchange rate are typically those concerned about currency stability and monetary credibility. So in many cases, the principal conflict can be expressed as one between *competitiveness* and *credibility*.

POLITICAL FACTORS IN THE DETERMINATION OF CURRENCY POLICY

Selecting an exchange rate regime is a highly political decision: governments must make tradeoffs among values that are given different importance by different sociopolitical actors. With regard to the regime (fixed or floating), the choice is monetary stability and credibility versus monetary flexibility. With regard to the level (depreciated or appreciated), the choice is between competitiveness and purchasing power. Governments must weigh the relative importance of the stability of nominal macroeconomic variables, the competitiveness of producers of tradable products, and the purchasing power of consumers.

The decisions they make have domestic distributional consequences—a fact that is not lost on interest groups or electorates at large. Governments face pressures:

- for reduced volatility, from those who are internationally exposed, including export producers and those with foreign exchange liabilities, such as firms with dollar debts (suggesting a desire for a fixed exchange rate);
- for favorable relative price effects, especially from tradeables producers (suggesting a desire for a depreciated currency, hence floating);
- for purchasing power, from consumers (suggesting a desire for an appreciated currency).

Below I discuss the pressures exacted by interest groups and by electorates with regard to currency policy, and offer some evidence from Latin America about how governments have responded.

Special Interest Groups

As regards the *exchange rate regime*, we can array groups along a continuum that measures the extent to which they are involved in international or domestic economic activity (Frieden 1991). Groups who are heavily involved in foreign trade and investment—typically including the commercial and financial sectors and foreign currency debtors—should favor exchange rate stability, since currency volatility is an everyday concern that makes their business riskier and more costly. By the same token, these groups care less about a loss of national monetary autonomy, since they typically do business in several countries, and can shift their business or assets abroad if domestic conditions become unfavorable.

By contrast, groups whose economic activity is confined to the domestic economy benefit from a floating regime. The nontradeables sector (for example, services, construction, transport) and import-competing producers of tradeable goods belong in this camp. They are not required to deal in foreign exchange and so are free of the risks and costs of currency volatility. They are highly sensitive to domestic macroeconomic conditions and thus favor the national autonomy made possible by floating.

Tradeables producers are also likely to oppose a fixed rate, for two reasons. First, the adoption of a fixed rate in inflationary conditions—such as have characterized much of Latin America—usually leads to a transitional real appreciation, with detrimental effects on tradeables producers. This has been the experience of most exchange-rate-based stabilization programs. Second, a fixed rate eliminates the possibility of a depreciation to maintain or restore the competitiveness of tradeables producers.

The domestic interest group politics of the *level of the exchange rate* can also be represented simply, separating exporting and import-competing industries that lose, on the one hand, from domestically oriented (nontradeable) industries that gain from a currency appreciation, on the other. Domestic consumers also gain from an appreciation as the domestic currency prices of imported goods fall, lowering the cost of living. Currency depreciations have the opposite effects, helping exporting and import-competing industries at the expense of domestic consumers and producers of nontraded goods and services.

Among tradeables producers, the degree of concern about currency movements depends upon how directly they are affected by changes in the exchange rate. If import-competing firms that face an appreciation of the home currency are able to keep their prices high—as will happen if foreign producers do not pass the expected price decline through to local consumers—they will be less concerned about the appreciation. Generally, tradeables industries with high pass-through are more sensitive to the relative price effects of currency movements than those with low pass-through, since their prices respond more directly to changes in exchange rates. And by extension, the level of the exchange rate is likely to be more politicized in developing than in developed countries, since the former tend to produce standardized goods and primary commodities, for which pass-through is high. Capturing an industry's sensitivity to exchange rate changes involves measuring the extent to which it sells products to foreign markets, uses foreign-made inputs, and, more directly, competes with foreign manufacturers on the basis of price.

The considerable variation of currency regimes in Latin America provides opportunities for at least a preliminary investigation of interest-group pressures. Given the characteristics described above, it seems likely that the manufacturing sector will prefer more flexible currency regimes in order to maintain the competitiveness of locally produced tradeables. In empirical work reported in Frieden, Ghezzi, and Stein (2001), we found that economies with larger manufacturing sectors were more prone to adopt either floating regimes or backward-looking crawling pegs, both of which tend to deliver more competitive exchange rates. . . . This can be seen in Table 1, which shows that countries with larger manufacturing sectors are less likely to have fixed exchange rates (a lower number in the table is associated with a more fixed rate).

Similarly, the larger the manufacturing sector is—indicating greater sensitivity to the competitive effects of currency movements—the less likely is a fixed rate. . . . In the closed economies of the import-substitution period, where manufacturers were mostly protected from foreign competition, this relationship was weaker or absent. . . .

It can also be seen that hyperinflationary episodes are associated with the use of a currency peg for credibility-enhancing purposes, whereas episodes of moderate inflation are not. . . . Having inflation greater than 1,000 percent increases the probability of adopting a fixed rate regime by nearly 21 percentage points.

TABLE 1 Exchange Rate Regimes Are Affected by the Size of the Manufacturing Sector, Latin America, 1972–1994

Smaller manufacturing sectors			Larger manufacturing sectors		
	Man/GDP	Scale of fixed/ floating		Man/GDP	Scale of fixed/ floating
Haiti	8.87	3.19	Dom Republic	17.33	.96
Panama	9.33	0.00	Venezuela	17.42	2.85
Barbados	10.12	0.00	Ecuador	19.37	2.35
Guyana	12.39	5.08	El Salvador	19.48	1.24
Trinidad and Tobago	12.61	2.73	Nicaragua	19.86	1.16
Suriname	13.82	2.08	Colombia	20.31	6.75
Guatemala	15.18	3.58	Chile	21.39	5.79
Honduras	15.24	2.86	Mexico	21.85	6.04
Paraguay	15.71	3.34	Costa Rica	22.83	4.29
Bolivia	16.03	4.80	Peru	23.47	5.79
Belize	16.65	0.00	Uruguay	23.66	6.09
Jamaica	17.22	4.50	Brazil	28.63	7.06
			Argentina	29.35	2.74
Average	13.60	2.68		22.30	4.35

Scale of Fixed/Floating is a 10 point scale with 0 = Fixed for every period, 10 = Floating for every period.

SOURCE: Frieden, Ghezzi, and Stein (2001).

Electoral Considerations

Elections are of recurrent importance in exchange rate policy-making. They may affect exchange rate policy for several reasons. As described in Frieden and Stein (2001), the income effect associated with depreciation reduces the purchasing power of the population; it can make depreciation unpopular and therefore politicians may want to avoid it at election time. Devaluations may also be unpopular because they generate inflation. On the other hand, a real appreciation can deliver an electorally popular reduction in inflation and an increase in purchasing power. In line with this, governments show a strong tendency to allow or engineer a real appreciation in the run-up to elections, which is then reversed after the government changes hands. An exchange rate electoral cycle boosts voters' incomes in the run-up to the election and imposes costs on voters only after the new government is in office. The delay results in a depreciation that is more costly than if it had occurred immediately, but newly elected governments appear to follow the rule of "Devalue immediately and blame it on your predecessors."

FIGURE 1 Exchange Rates in Argentina and Brazil (*pesos* and *reals* per US$)

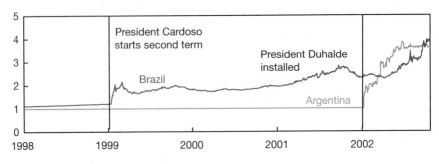

Evidence for Latin America, from individual country studies and a cross-country study, is generally consistent with these arguments (Frieden and Stein 2001). A cross-country study reported in Frieden, Ghezzi, and Stein (2001) examines the behavior of exchange rates before and after elections. Looking at 86 episodes of electoral changes in government, we found that the real exchange rate appreciated nearly 3.5 percent in the months leading to an election and depreciated on average 6 percent during the following four months.

. . . Latin America is a rich repository of experiences in which governments delayed devaluations until after elections: Mexico's ruling PRI party did so with some regularity between 1970 and 1994. More recent Argentine and Brazilian experiences are also expressive. As shown in Figure 1, each government held the exchange rate more or less constant until right after a new president (in the Brazilian case, a re-elected incumbent) took office. In pre-election months, both currencies appreciated substantially in real terms, with a powerful positive impact on the purchasing power of local residents. Immediately after taking office, each government let the currency float—more accurately, sink—to a substantially depreciated level.

The political economy of exchange rate policy is not only important for developing countries. For over thirty years the member states of the European Union have attempted, with varying degrees of success, to stabilize their currencies against one another. The eventual creation of the euro, and the continuing question of whether, when, and how other countries in and around Europe will join the euro zone, certainly respond to powerful domestic and international political pressures (see, for example, Eichengreen and Frieden 2001).

Exchange rates are critical in a wide variety of other settings in the context of an integrated world economy. Commercial and financial relations between the United States and East Asia, for example, have long implicated currency policies, sometimes sparking political conflict. In the early stages of their respective export drives, East Asian nations—first Japan, then South Korea and Taiwan, now China—have typically kept their exchange rates very weak to spur manufactured exports. The results often provoke protests from American manufacturers who press the US government to insist that East Asian governments allow or force their currencies to appreciate.

Conflict over the trade effects of currency values has most recently been played out between the United States and China. The issue has been complicated by the fact that—as was true in the early 1980s when the American target was Japan—the weakness of East Asian currencies is matched by the strength of the US dollar, which itself is in large part due to America's own fiscal policy and the resulting capital inflow. Whatever the ultimate resolution of these "global imbalances"—East Asian trade surpluses and American trade and fiscal deficits—there is little question that highly politicized currency policies played an important role in creating and propagating them. There is also little question that the unwinding of these imbalances will itself provoke political conflict over exchange rates and their effects.

CONCLUSION

Exchange rates are political. They affect the interests of powerful groups and of consumers. They affect elections, and are affected by them. International economic integration only heightens their impact and their political prominence. As the world economy has become more open—and especially as developing countries have become more open—exchange rates have become even more highly politicized, more controversial, and more subject to mass and special-interest political pressures.

Those who ignore the political economy of currency policy will make mistakes in developing feasible exchange rate policies. Both analysts and policymakers would be well advised to pay concentrated attention to political economy factors in exchange rate policy-making.

REFERENCES

Eichengreen, B., and J. Frieden, eds. 2001. *The Political Economy of European Monetary Unification*, 2nd ed. Boulder, CO: Westview Press.

Frieden, J. A. 1991. "Invested Interests: The Politics of National Economic Policy in a World of Global Finance," *International Organization*, 45: 425–51.

Frieden, J. A., P. Ghezzi, and E. Stein. 2001. "Politics and Exchange Rates: A Cross-Country Approach to Latin America." In *The Currency Game: Exchange Rate Politics in Latin America*, eds., J. A. Frieden and E. Stein. Baltimore, MD: Johns Hopkins University Press.

Frieden, J. A., and E. Stein. 2001. "The Political Economy of Exchange Rate Policy in Latin America: An Analytical Overview." In *The Currency Game: Exchange Rate Politics in Latin America*, eds., J. A. Frieden and E. Stein. Baltimore, MD: Johns Hopkins University Press.

Mundell, Robert A. 1963. "Capital Mobility and Stabilization Policy under Fixed and Flexible Exchange Rates," *Canadian Journal of Economic and Political Science* 29: 475–85.

15

Borrowing, Boom, and Bust: The Capital Flow Cycle

MENZIE D. CHINN AND JEFFRY A. FRIEDEN

The global financial crisis of 2008–2009 was the most striking example of the kinds of debt crises that have been common in the world economy for at least 200 years. In this reading, Menzie Chinn and Jeffry Frieden explain how the United States, along with many European countries, borrowed heavily from the rest of the world, used the money largely for consumption rather than productive investment, and eventually collapsed into crisis. Powerful interests gave governments incentives to encourage borrowing, even when it became clear that the borrowing boom was unsustainable. The American and European experience was strikingly similar to that of developing countries in the past: the capital flow cycle had become a nearly universal experience.

In the early 1990s, Thailand went through a tremendous construction boom. As tens of billions of dollars flooded into the country, lending to real estate firms soared. Builders doubled the amount of office space in Bangkok in just over three years. Cranes lined the skyline, and new suburban developments sprouted all over town. But by early 1997, the building boom was in trouble. In February, one banker reported bluntly on the state of the real estate market: "There are no transactions." One-fifth of all the housing units built in the previous five years was empty. One-fourth of all the office space in Bangkok was vacant. Stock prices of real estate companies were down nearly 95 percent. Thai banks found that nearly half of all the loans on their books were bad. Within a few months, Thailand crashed into the gravest financial crisis in its history.

And so it went in the United States. In 2004, the suburbs of Las Vegas and South Florida were booming with building activity. New developments were mapped out and built, prices were soaring, banks were eager to lend, people were impatient to buy. By 2010, a drive through these suburbs was surreal: neighborhood after neighborhood was empty. Either the new housing had never been occupied, or the formerly enthusiastic new owners had defaulted, been foreclosed on, and moved out. The boom had gone bust, and it dragged the rest of the American economy—and the world economy—with it.

How did America's foreign borrowing spree go so awry? What made our debt-financed boom turn out as badly as those of Thailand, Mexico, Russia, Argentina, and dozens of other countries in the past? What was it about the

$5 trillion Americans borrowed from foreigners between 2001 and 2007, or the way they borrowed it, or the way they spent it, that proved so unsound?

FEDERAL DEFICITS AND FED POLICY

America's latest bout of foreign borrowing began in 2001 with the federal government suddenly shifting from having a massive surplus to accumulating a massive deficit. As the government dipped into international financial markets, eventually borrowing a couple of trillion dollars, the deficit spending had three broad effects. First, in cutting taxes by hundreds of billions of dollars a year—an estimated $2 trillion over a decade—the government gave taxpayers that much more money to spend. Second, borrowing by the federal government sustained, even increased, government spending during the 2001 economic slowdown. This put money into Americans' hands to help stimulate the economy. Third, the deficit allowed the government to increase military spending in the aftermath of the September 11, 2001, attacks, especially after the invasions of Afghanistan and Iraq. Thus, federal foreign borrowing increased both public and private spending.

The Federal Reserve's policy of driving interest rates lower than they had been in decades was the next major spur to American borrowing. The Fed's principal tool of influence on the economy is its benchmark interest rate, the Federal Funds rate, which is what banks charge each other for money. Most people can't get the Federal Funds rate, but when banks pay less, or more, for their money, they adjust the interest rates they charge consumers and businesses accordingly. So the Fed's interest rate policy has a profound impact on the economy through its effect on borrowing and lending. If the economy is in the doldrums, the central bank can stimulate it by reducing interest rates and encouraging borrowing, which increases spending. If the economy is "overheating," risking inflation, the Fed can restrain it by raising interest rates and discouraging borrowing, which reduces spending.

The most widely accepted guideline for interest rate policy is one devised by John Taylor, a distinguished Stanford University macroeconomist. In 1993 Taylor proposed a relatively simple rule that central banks can follow to achieve price stability, low unemployment, and policy credibility. This "Taylor rule" adjusts the interest rate in line with changes in the inflation rate and the rate of economic growth, and is generally seen as defining an appropriate target for a reasonable monetary policy. A monetary policy that is too "tight"—with interest rates too high—could slow economic growth, while a monetary policy that is too "loose"—with interest rates too low—could lead to excessive borrowing and inflation. Over the course of the 1990s, monetary policy had generally been restrained and in line with the Taylor rule. For example, from 1995 to 2000, the Fed kept the Federal Funds rate at about 3 percent above the rate of inflation: inflation averaged 2.5 percent a year, while the Federal Funds rate averaged 5.5 percent. When George W. Bush was elected president, in November 2000, the rate was at 6.5 percent with inflation at about 3.4 percent.

Alan Greenspan was in charge of the nation's monetary policy at the time. After his initial appointment as chairman of the Federal Reserve by Ronald Reagan in 1987, he was reappointed by George H. W. Bush in 1991, reappointed again by Bill Clinton in 1996, and again in 2000. Greenspan, a lifelong Republican, had close ties . . . to Ayn Rand's "Objectivist" movement, which champions a radical individualist view of society. . . . Nonetheless, Greenspan served under President Clinton and seemed committed to monetary moderation and fiscal prudence. It came as a surprise to many when, despite his traditional fiscal conservatism, Greenspan supported George W. Bush's 2001 tax cuts and the large deficits they caused.

Soon after the 2001 Bush tax cuts went into effect, Greenspan's Fed began bringing interest rates down precipitously. By September 2001 the benchmark rate was about 3 percent; in December it went below 2 percent and kept falling. The central bank justified the policy because growth was slow in the aftermath of problems in the high-technology sector and after the terrorist attacks of September 11, 2001. This seemed reasonable. But the Fed kept pushing interest rates down.

Long after the economy began growing again, through most of 2003 and 2004, the Federal Funds rate stayed around 1 percent—the lowest rate in more than forty years. Greenspan raised the rate above 2 percent only in December 2004. Meanwhile, inflation was substantially higher than the prevailing interest rate. From 2002 through 2004, while the Federal Funds rate averaged 1.4 percent, the Consumer Price Index averaged 2.5 percent growth, so that the central bank's main interest rate was well *below* the rate of inflation. When an economy has "negative real interest rates"—that is, interest rates less than the inflation rate—lenders are effectively giving money away, and people have tremendous incentives to borrow.

The Federal Reserve was breaking the Taylor rule: a Taylor-rule Federal Funds rate would have averaged almost 3 to 4 percent between 2002 and 2004, rather than the barely 1.4 percent that was in place. This was an extraordinary episode in American monetary policy, during which the central bank purposely held interest rates below the rate of inflation for several years. Although it is always hard to know what goes on at the Fed, some cynics felt that Greenspan was trying to make sure that President George W. Bush would reappoint him when Greenspan's term ended in 2004. Certainly Greenspan's unexpected support for large-scale deficit spending, coupled with the uncharacteristically lax monetary policy, suggested an attempt to curry favor with the administration. In the event, Bush renominated Greenspan for an unprecedented fifth term as Fed chair in May 2004. And the low interest rates of 2002–2004 certainly helped secure the reelection of President Bush, who, after all, had lost the popular vote in 2000. As if to confirm the suspicions of the cynics, interest rates began rising again after the 2004 presidential election.

With interest rates at historic lows, and foreigners still eager to lend, Americans themselves borrowed in ever larger amounts. The total indebtedness of Americans—to each other and to foreigners—had been generally stable or slowly rising during the 1990s, equaling about 2.6 times the country's GDP by 2000. Between then and 2007, the country's total debt soared by $22 trillion, rising to over 3.4 times output. In those seven years, the debt of the average American rocketed from $93,000 to $158,000. While this was spurred by the burgeoning gross debt of the federal government—which went from $5.6 trillion to $9 trillion in those years, from about $20,000 per person to about $30,000 per person—private borrowing was galloping ahead as well. And while much of the financial action involved Americans lending to Americans, the scale of the borrowing was only made possible by the inflow from abroad.

Foreigners supplied much of the money that was allowing Americans to live beyond their means. Lending to the U.S. government was direct: foreigners simply bought Treasury securities. But foreign lending to individual Americans was largely indirect, intermediated through a complex financial system and a dizzying array of complicated financial instruments. In some cases, American banks borrowed from foreign banks or investors, using the additional funds to relend to American households. In other cases, American loans were packaged into bonds and other securities that were then sold to investors. In this latter process, called "securitization," an American investment bank might bundle together thousands of mortgages or credit card debts to underwrite a bond issue to be sold to investors, including those abroad. The bonds in question would compensate the investors out of the interest payments these thousands of homeowners and credit card holders made on their debts. The bond was a good deal for the foreign lenders, as it allowed them to diversify their holdings among many mortgages and credit cards, and gave them access to loans they regarded as high earning and safe. The ultimate borrowers, the homeowners and credit card holders, had no idea that much of the money they were borrowing eventually came from Germany, Kuwait, and China, but that was the reality.

Who was doing all this borrowing? The United States had been running a current account deficit—that is, borrowing from abroad—before 2000, but the proportions were smaller and the purposes to which the money was put were quite different. In the several years before 2000, the principal foreign debtors in the United States were private corporations and households, each of which was borrowing from abroad an amount equivalent to about 1 percent of GDP—the government was in surplus, and so it was not borrowing. But after 2000 there were two crucial changes. First, the total amounts borrowed skyrocketed, so that by 2003–2007 they were triple and quadruple what they had been ten years earlier. Second, the borrowers changed dramatically. Now the government was the largest single user of borrowed money. And as interest rates plummeted and private individuals were drawn into the financial frenzy, households doubled and tripled their foreign borrowing. Meanwhile, corporations actually went into surplus, financing their activities out of profits.

The fact that America's foreign borrowing was going exclusively to the government and to private households was a warning signal. International financial institutions, such as the International Monetary Fund, typically advise developing countries that borrowed funds should go into investments that raise the nation's capacity to produce, and so to pay off its debts. Government budget deficits and residential housing are unlikely to be productive; if the IMF saw a developing country using foreign debt to fund budget deficits and housing construction, it would raise red flags. And in fact the head of the Bank for International Settlements, the central bankers' central bank, did voice his concern early in 2006. . . . But almost nobody was listening. Living on borrowed time was too appealing.

ON BORROWED FUNDS

American households borrowed ever more, even surpassing the government in foreign borrowing in 2005. Americans borrowed to buy cars and computers, racking up credit card debt to go on vacation and go out to dinner. Between 2000 and 2007, consumer credit rose by a trillion dollars, from $1.5 to $2.5 trillion. And Americans borrowed to buy houses—especially to buy houses. As interest rates declined, tens of millions of Americans took advantage to refinance their mortgages or to buy new homes.

Household borrowing drove a remarkable growth in the housing market and a striking rise in housing prices. The average price of American homes, as measured by the widely used Case-Shiller index, was generally stable over the 1990s, but it skyrocketed after 2000. . . . Mortgage lending soared from about $750 billion in 2000 to over $2 trillion a year between 2002 and 2006. As more loans were written, average housing prices doubled in the country's major cities between 2001 and 2006—and rose by much more in some places. . . .

The housing boom was particularly pronounced in the South and Southwest. The population there was growing three times as fast as in the rest of the country, by two million people a year. In South Florida, people camped out overnight to be at the head of a line of thousands to buy into a new development in Wellington, near Palm Beach. Over three thousand people showed up for the development's grand opening, and the developers sold $35 million worth of homes in one weekend. A few miles south, in Weston, Florida, more than eight hundred hopeful buyers paid a thousand dollars apiece just to enter a lottery for a chance to buy one of 222 new townhouses; every last one sold within seven hours. Scenes like these were repeated in Phoenix and San Diego, Tampa and San Antonio. And home prices skyrocketed accordingly: between 2000 and 2006, the median price of a home in Miami went from $150,000 to over $400,000; in Las Vegas, from $135,000 to $310,000.

Despite the soaring prices, more Americans than ever found it easy, and cheap, to borrow to buy a home. The expansion of home ownership swelled the ranks of the homeowners, and the gain in housing wealth made existing homeowners better off. Making it easier for American families to buy their own home—or at least to live in a home whose mortgage was in their name— has been the goal of many American politicians. . . .

While there had been a push to expand home ownership under the Clinton administration, particularly in historically disadvantaged neighborhoods, the Bush administration's new efforts were much broader. It championed private ownership in general and home ownership in particular. . . .

Rising home prices and easy money drove a broader increase in other consumer spending. Those who already owned their own homes could take advantage of ready credit and the higher value of their homes to refinance their mortgages at lower payments and take cash out. The more housing prices rose and the lower interest rates got, the more existing homeowners could borrow against their homes. This in turn would allow them to spend more— transforming a home, as the saying went, into an ATM. By one estimate, for every thousand-dollar increase in a home's value, a family who would otherwise have had trouble borrowing could increase consumption spending by $110. As the national median house price shot from under $140,000 in 2000 to nearly $250,000 in 2006, the borrowing and housing booms allowed a median cash-strapped family to spend $12,000 more than otherwise—enough to buy a car, or take several vacations, or to remodel that now more valuable home.

Banks and other financial institutions profited handsomely from the borrowing boom. Whether they brought foreign lenders together with domestic borrowers, or originated mortgages and consumer loans, or innovated intricate financial instruments, there was much more work to be done and much more money to be made. Increased financial activity inflated the size of the financial sector, which added over a million jobs and increased its share of the country's GDP from 7.0 to 8.3 percent in the ten years leading up to 2007. The earnings of people in finance—especially at and near the top—soared along with housing and stock prices. Whereas the salaries of engineers and financiers with postgraduate degrees were roughly equivalent until the middle 1990s, by 2006 financiers were making one-third more than engineers. By then, one careful study estimated, financiers were overpaid by about 40 percent. The financial services sector was much bigger than it needed to be; every year, people in finance were earning at least $100 billion more than was economically justified.

Foreign debt–fed spending by Americans sucked in imports, more than doubling the country's trade deficit from 2001 to 2006. By then, Americans were buying abroad over $750 billion more than they were selling abroad. The big story here was a surge in imports, from $1.4 trillion in 2001 to $2.4 trillion in 2007.

Swelling imports were great for consumers, who found stores filled with inexpensive goods from abroad, but they devastated American manufacturing, especially producers of labor-intensive goods who competed most directly with imports. Between 2000 and 2007, the country lost almost three and a half million manufacturing jobs, nearly one-sixth of the total. Computer and electronics manufacturers shed a quarter of a million jobs. Garment and textile producers were particularly hard hit, losing over 300,000 jobs, more than one-third of the total. Burlington Industries of North Carolina, once the world's largest textile producer with over forty plants around the world, went bankrupt, and by early 2005, the sector was losing a factory a week, along with 1500 jobs.

A PREDICTABLE BUBBLE

The massive inflow of funds, the bloated financial sector, the surging imports, the orgy of consumption, the bubble in the housing market: all this was eerily familiar to anyone who had lived through, or observed, earlier debt crises. America was looking like any one of dozens of developing countries that had borrowed themselves into the poorhouse over the previous forty years.

Latin Americans might recall their borrowing in the 1970s and early 1980s, before their debt crisis began in 1982. Governments spent far more than they took in, and used foreign funds to fill the gap between spending and taxes; the Argentine and Mexican governments borrowed about half of what they needed from foreigners. The banking systems, which handled much of the capital inflow, swelled; those of Chile and Argentina doubled and tripled their share of the economy in a few short years. Housing prices soared; they increased by nearly tenfold in Chile over a little more than a decade. Stock markets boomed. And then it all came crashing down after August 1982, driving Latin America into a lost decade of depression, hyperinflation, and slow growth.

The same pattern was repeated fifteen years later in East Asia. Hundreds of billions of dollars flooded into the region's rapidly growing economies. By 1995, countries like Thailand and Malaysia were borrowing amounts equal to more than 8 percent of GDP every year, using foreign money to finance one-fifth and more of their total investment. Thai banks tripled their real estate lending between 1990 and 1995, as the property market boomed. All over the region there were spectacular increases in housing prices, in stock market indices, and in the size of banking sectors. But in 1997 it all collapsed. By the time it stopped falling, the Thai stock market was down almost 80 percent from its pre-1997 peak. This roller coaster ride was repeated in the middle and late 1990s in Russia. And at roughly the same time in Turkey. And in Mexico again in the early 1990s. And with an extraordinary vengeance in Argentina in the 1990s, leading up to a spectacular implosion in 2001.

America's housing and financial booms, and its gaping trade deficit, followed a well-worn script, one acted out by dozens of countries sliding down the slippery slope of this capital flow cycle. Large-scale foreign borrowing caused all of these domestic pathologies.

ANATOMY OF A BOOM

When a country's government, people, and firms borrow abroad, capital flows into the country, which increases the ability of local residents to buy goods and services. Some of what they buy are hard goods, such as cars and consumer electronics. In the American borrowing boom, the connection was often direct, as easy money helped consumers finance purchases of these big-ticket items.

More spending on computers, clothing, furniture, and other things that can be traded easily across borders increased imports by 50 percent between 2001 and 2005. Meanwhile, exports grew very slowly, so that by 2005 the trade deficit was well over $700 billion. The average American family of four was buying $30,000 worth of goods and services from abroad every year, while the country was only selling $20,000 worth abroad per family. The difference was paid with borrowed money.

Borrowers also spend borrowed money on things that can't easily be traded internationally: housing, financial services, medical care, education, personal services. Increased demand for these goods and services simply drives up their prices. Their supply also increases, but not quickly enough to meet all of the increased demand—it takes a long time for the supply of single-family homes or doctors to grow. Just as foreign borrowing causes a surge in imports, it causes a surge in the relative prices of housing, restaurant food, medical care, and other services.

Those living through a borrowing boom see these developments in a number of ways. People have more money to spend, and things from abroad seem cheaper, for example, imports and vacations. At the same time, goods and services that do not enter world trade get more expensive. This can be a boon to some, such as homeowners whose properties rise in value. But it can also lead to soaring prices for health care, education, and transportation. Higher prices for these services also drive up the price of manufacturing at home, again making it hard for local producers to compete with foreigners.

Economists capture this process by dividing everything in an economy into two types of goods and services. One type of good can easily be traded across borders: clothing, steel, wheat, cars. Because these goods are traded, their prices cannot vary much from country to country (leaving aside trade barriers and transportation costs). The value of these "tradables" tends toward an international price, times the exchange rate. The Mexican price of steel is simply its world price times whatever the peso is worth today.

A second kind of good or service has to be consumed where it is produced; it cannot be traded at all or easily. These "nontradables" are mostly services, such as haircuts and taxi rides. The prices of nontradable services can vary widely, since there is little international competition, for instance, in haircuts.

Travelers know this intuitively: cars cost pretty much the same everywhere, while haircuts and taxi rides can be much cheaper in some (especially poor) countries than in others. The main nontradable is housing, and shelter is a crucial part of every household's budget—in America, it accounts for about a third of consumer spending.

A borrowing boom raises the prices of nontradables, such as financial services, insurance, and real estate. This is good for those who work in these industries, and for people who own nontradables, such as housing. But the surge in imports, and the rise in other prices, is bad for producers of tradables, such as manufactured goods and agricultural products.

This is precisely what was happening to the United States after 2001. Nontradables sectors boomed, while tradables sectors lagged. Between 2000 and 2007, prices of services rose by 25 percent, while prices of durable consumer products declined by 13 percent. The import surge and the rise in nontradables prices savaged the manufacturing and agriculture sectors, which together lost nearly four million jobs. But finance, insurance, and real estate were growing at more than three times the pace of manufacturing, adding over a million jobs in five years.

Sometimes foreign borrowing drives the country's currency up directly. Foreigners lend to Americans by buying American bonds, mortgages, and other securities. To do so they also have to buy dollars, so the dollar's value rises. The stronger currency makes imports cheaper in domestic currency, and locally produced goods more expensive to foreigners. Local residents buy more imported goods, local producers sell less of what they make, the trade deficit grows, and national producers of traded goods complain. Back in the early and middle 1980s, when the Reagan administration's budget and current account deficits led to a rise in the dollar's value by more than 50 percent, imports soared and exports collapsed, millions of manufacturing jobs were lost, and demands for protection from foreign goods skyrocketed.

Economists capture both of these effects—on the currency, and on the relative prices of tradables and nontradables—with the concept of the "real exchange rate." This takes into account both the "nominal" exchange rate—a currency's stated value in terms of another currency—and the relationship between prices at home and abroad. A currency's real exchange rate can rise, or appreciate, in one of two ways. First, prices can stay the same while the currency rises in nominal value. If the dollar goes up from 1.0 to 1.2 euro while American and European prices stay the same, Americans can buy 20 percent more with their dollars in Europe. The second way is for the currency to stay the same while American prices and wages rise by 20 percent. Then, again, Americans can buy 20 percent more in Europe with their dollars because European prices are now that much lower than American prices.

The American trajectory after 2001 was in line with the typical experience of a country embarked on a major foreign borrowing binge, with some variations. In developing countries, borrowing booms are often accompanied by a spike in the ostentatious consumption of luxury cars, foreign liquor and per-fume, and expensive electronics by affluent consumers who take advantage of the easy money to buy imports they couldn't normally afford—or to travel abroad. When Latin America is in the expansion phase of one of its debt cycles, the airplanes to Miami and Los Angeles are crowded with Latin American tourists. On the way back to Buenos Aires or São Paulo, the Argentines and Brazilians cram the baggage holds and overheads full of American televisions and computers that now seem ridiculously cheap to them. Americans didn't need to travel any farther than the nearest Wal-Mart to fill their homes with foreign goods. Meanwhile, as borrowing increases the amount of money people have to spend, they use some of this increased purchasing power to buy financial assets and real estate. So stock prices and housing prices rise dramatically.

The United States was right on track.

THE BUSH BOOM BUBBLES

By 2005, the joint effects of America's foreign borrowing and loose monetary policy were everywhere. The capital inflow swelled imports and pumped up demand for nontraded goods and services. Nontradables sectors, especially financial services, insurance, and real estate, expanded rapidly. Low interest rates allowed consumers to buy more goods on credit, and more households to buy a home. Those who already owned their home found that rising housing prices and low interest rates made it irresistible to borrow and consume even more. The same was true about the spectacular rise in the stock market and in financial investments more generally: as households saw their retirement and other savings rise, they had every reason to consume more and save less.

Rising home prices, falling interest rates, and soaring consumption fed on each other. Families whose homes were more valuable saw themselves as wealthier, and greater wealth justified more spending. There was nothing ficti-tious about this new-found wealth, for the family could use it to borrow and spend even more. Millions of Americans found that they could make use of a financial arrangement that was becoming commonplace, a home equity line of credit, to borrow against their now more valuable home. The new money could then be spent on home improvements, new appliances, or a vacation. . . .

But by 2005 the housing boom seemed clearly to have turned into a bubble. Housing prices were rising virtually everywhere, and in some areas they had reached levels that were almost certainly unsustainable. For example, by early 2006 the median home price in San Diego was $500,000. But a standard index of affordability, which calculates how many households could afford the basic cost of living in their homes, reveals that barely one San Diego household in twenty could afford to live in the region's median home. . . .

It seemed clear to many that the United States was waltzing down a path well worn by other countries that had ended up in serious crises. The economic expansion had become a boom, and the boom had created a bubble in the housing and financial markets. And, in fact, many economists and other observers started sounding alarm bells about the panoply of potential problems, of which the housing bubble was just one. At least as worrying were the fiscal deficit, the current account deficit, the burgeoning foreign debt, the consumption boom, and the swollen financial markets.

Many of the cautionary notes came from impeccable sources. Raghuram Rajan took leave from teaching finance at the University of Chicago's business school to serve as chief economist of the IMF for much of the boom period, from 2003 until 2007. In August 2005, at an annual gathering at Jackson Hole, Wyoming, he was explicit about the risks inherent in financial globalization. While the rise of finance had brought undoubted benefits, he argued, "the financial risks that are being created by the system are indeed greater" than in the past. He pointed out that while free-wheeling and internationally linked financial markets can draw economies up together, they can also pull them down together, which could conceivably cause "a catastrophic meltdown."[1]

New York University economist Nouriel Roubini warned so often, and so alarmingly, of trouble to come that journalists dubbed him "Dr. Doom." Late in 2006, he told an audience that the United States faced "a once-in-a-lifetime housing bust, an oil shock, sharply declining consumer confidence and, ultimately, a deep recession . . . homeowners defaulting on mortgages, trillions of dollars of mortgage-backed securities unraveling worldwide and the global financial system shuddering to a halt." Dr. Doom went on to point out that "these developments . . . could cripple or destroy hedge funds, investment banks and other major financial institutions like Fannie Mae and Freddie Mac."[2]

As housing prices began to decline late in 2006, warnings of impending doom proliferated. . . .

But for every Cassandra warning of impending trouble, there was an Apollo to neutralize the dire predictions. Some were blinded by their own economic or political interests, others by partisanship or ideology.

SPECIAL INTERESTS AND SPECIAL PLEADING

Why did the Bush administration ignore all the warnings, and all the signs that the economy was in an unsustainable bubble? To be sure, no government likes to put the brakes on a hard-driving economy. One of the most famous phrases in all of economic policymaking is that of William McChesney Martin Jr., chairman of the Fed from 1951 to 1970, who described the job of a central banker as being "to take away the punch bowl just as the party gets going."

In the case of the roaring Bush boom and bubble, some powerful interests had a major stake in keeping financial and housing markets rising. The lending boom and deregulation swelled the financial system like never before, in ways closely linked to housing markets. American bankers had written millions of mortgages whose viability was predicated on continually rising housing prices. If housing prices leveled off, or even fell, many of these mortgages would go bad and drag the creditors with them.

The political economy of housing itself was closely related: much of the increased lending and spending went into housing, so that home builders and related industries made spectacular profits, as did those in the real estate business. The construction industry, including home builders, is well organized and well represented in Washington. . . .

Realtors, too, are highly political—the National Association of Realtors is typically the largest single PAC contributor to national candidates—and leans strongly toward Republicans. Even Freddie Mac and Fannie Mae—two government-sponsored agencies that support the housing market by buying up mortgages from banks that originate them—made massive political contributions, some $170 million during the boom decade. Academic studies have confirmed the general impression that mortgage lending became increasingly politicized as the boom progressed. One such analysis found that campaign contributions and lobbying by the mortgage industry, along with the importance of real or potential subprime mortgage borrowers in a congressman's district, had a powerful impact on congressional voting behavior toward the housing boom, and that this impact gained strength as the boom went on.

The administration had to take electoral considerations into account too. Many of the states benefiting most directly from the building boom were politically important, either because of their size or because they were hotly contested between the parties: Florida, Colorado, Arizona, Nevada.

And as the boom continued, it was not just that influential interest groups had come to rely on the formula established after 2001; it was that any interruption in the process was a threat. Many of the newly written mortgages had been made to borrowers who were barely able—if able at all—to service their debts, in the expectation that rising housing prices would make the properties worth more, hence more creditworthy. This bet would pay off, however, only if housing prices continued to rise. And much of the growth of the financial system had been built on the edifice of new housing-finance instruments that depended on the underlying value of the mortgage loans. If the mortgages that served as foundation to the financial edifice went bad, the entire building risked collapsing, floor by floor. So the housing boom had not only been lucrative; it had made the profitability, perhaps even the very survival, of major industries reliant on its continuation. A substantial slowdown risked bringing down the entire house of cards. Any government would contemplate this possibility anxiously, especially one that was reliant on political support from the regions where the housing boom was strongest, and from industries most dependent on a continuation of the boom.

And so defenders of faith in the Bush boom abounded, typically in and around the Bush administration. Early in 2005 in the *Washington Times*, James

Miller III, who had served as Ronald Reagan's budget director, lauded "the efficient U.S. arrangements for housing finance" as "the envy of every other country." The trillions going into home loans reflected the accumulated wisdom of a competitive financial system: "Gone are the days of mortgage credit crunches and exorbitant mortgage rates spreads. American homeowners . . . are assured of a steady, liquid, and generally affordable supply of mortgage credit. And investors, both domestic and foreign, are provided a flow of debt- and mortgage-related securities that are highly liquid, transparent, and secure."[3]

Also in 2005, Alan Reynolds of the Cato Institute disparaged the "economic pessimists, who try to persuade us terrible things are about to happen. A perennial favorite is the 'housing bubble' about to burst, with a supposedly devastating impact on household wealth. . . . In short, we are asked to worry about something that has never happened for reasons still to be coherently explained. 'Housing bubble' worrywarts have long been hopelessly confused. It would have been financially foolhardy to listen to them in 2002. It still is."[4]

A few months later Larry Kudlow, the *National Review*'s economics editor, wrote a column titled "The Housing Bears Are Wrong Again," whose subtitle claimed that the housing sector was "writing [a] how-to guide on wealth creation." In it, Kudlow dismissed "all the bubbleheads who expect housing-price crashes in Las Vegas or Naples, Florida, to bring down the consumer, the rest of the economy, and the entire stock market."[5] In the subsequent three years, the housing sector oversaw the destruction of trillions of dollars in household wealth; and housing prices in Las Vegas and Naples, Florida, declined by over 50 percent, bringing down the consumer, the rest of the economy, and the entire stock market. And despite Miller's faith in the mortgage market, the lack of transparency and liquidity in the securities being snapped up by investors, domestic and foreign, very nearly brought down the entire international financial order.

The fact that many of the optimists worked for the housing industry might have been a tip-off. One, David Lereah, then the chief economist of the National Association of Realtors, published a book in 2005 called *Are You Missing the Real Estate Boom?* and re-released it in February 2006 with an even less subtle new title: *Why the Real Estate Boom Will Not Bust*. Of course, Lereah's advice devastated those who followed it. Nonetheless, as he told *BusinessWeek* several years later, after leaving his position with the housing lobby, "I worked for an association promoting housing, and it was my job to represent their interests."[6]

Nonetheless, most Americans found it more appealing to sit back and enjoy the rapid growth, rising housing prices, and supremely bullish stock market. Certainly the government had little reason to rein in the celebratory consumption binge—especially as a controversial war in Iraq threatened the administration's popularity. In any case, the United States was hardly alone in living in a financial and housing bubble.

AMERICA HAS COMPANY

People in other parts of the world had also discovered the attractions of debt-financed consumption. Local regulators also encouraged new financial opportunities and new financial instruments. And they all went through the same sorts of experiences as the United States.

The government and people of the United Kingdom, like their American brethren, borrowed heavily from abroad to increase consumption—as in the United States, British investment as a share of GDP actually went down between 2000 and 2007. The country's imports skyrocketed while exports stagnated, so the trade deficit shot from $50 billion in 2000 to $180 billion in 2007. . . .

Meanwhile, the housing market in the United Kingdom was going through a boom even greater than the American one: the average price of a house sold in the United Kingdom skyrocketed from £80,000 in 2000 to £180,000 in 2007, an increase of 125 percent. In dollar terms, at market exchange rates, the increase was even more staggering, from $130,000 to $350,000. The average house in London cost nearly £500,000 by 2007, nearly $1 million; housing prices over the decade rose more than four times faster than people's incomes. In two-thirds of the country's towns, housing was priced beyond the financial reach of average government workers.

The financial markets in the United Kingdom bubbled upward with its home prices. The City, London's financial center, had become the engine of growth for the entire economy. The City alone employed nearly 350,000 people and was adding workers at the rate of nearly 100 a week. By 2004 the country's financial sector already accounted for nearly one-third of the nation's economy, its economic output double that of British manufacturing.

Ireland was, if anything, embarked on an even more remarkable debt-financed consumption boom. As tens of billions of dollars poured into the Irish banking system from Asia and the rest of Europe, and thence into the Irish economy, familiar patterns emerged. The financial services and construction sectors grew ever more outsized. By 2007, nearly one-third of Irish workers were in construction or finance—about double the proportion prevailing in the recent past. In 1997 there were 245,000 people employed in the construction and financial services sectors, about 15 percent less than in industry; by 2007, this was up to 568,000 workers, just about double the number of those employed in manufacturing.

Irish borrowing turned the country into a major financial center and created a housing bubble that put all others to shame. Between 1997 and 2007 the *average* house price in Dublin shot up from $115,000 to $550,000. This was remarkable for a medium-size city in a small country with an ample supply of buildable land. By 2007, the average house in Dublin cost two and a half times as much as the median house in America's metropolitan areas, and substantially more than the median house in the New York metropolitan area. Most of this housing bubble was financed abroad—the net indebtedness of Irish banks to the rest of the world went from 10 percent of GDP in 2003 to 60 percent in early 2008. And it was accomplished without any unusual financial developments—no subprime mortgages, no novel approach to securitization. It was just an old-fashioned housing bubble, fueled by old-fashioned foreign borrowing.

Spain, too, built its housing and financial bubble much the old-fashioned way, borrowing a trillion dollars and more abroad. And as with the other deficit nations, the lion's share of the borrowing went into a housing boom and bubble. The cost of housing rose so rapidly in Spain that there was serious concern about pricing much of the population out of the market. This led to the proliferation of "mini-flats," apartments of 30 square meters (about 320 square feet), and their aggressive promotion by the country's housing minister. Even this was no guarantee of affordability; in a distant suburb of Madrid, mini-flats were going for nearly $200,000.

It was not just membership in the euro zone that made foreigners eager to lend to Spain and Ireland; the monetary policy of the European Central Bank in Frankfurt encouraged Spanish and Irish households and firms to borrow. Both Spain and Ireland had relatively high interest rates before the euro was created in 1999; afterward interest rates in the two countries moved quickly down toward euro-zone levels. On top of this, after 1999 euro monetary policy was set, for the euro zone as a whole, by the European Central Bank in Frankfurt. Between 2002 and 2005 the Central Bank, like the Fed, kept interest rates very low—2 or 3 percent when inflation was about 2 percent. This meant that real interest rates—taking inflation into account—were around zero for the average euro-zone country. But Spain and Ireland were growing faster than the rest of the new euro bloc, and their prices were rising faster than elsewhere. This meant that in Ireland and Spain, where inflation was 3 or 4 percent, real interest rates were negative. In Spain, for example, while mortgage interest rates had been around 11 percent in the late 1990s, by 2005 they were down to 3 or 4 percent—roughly the same as inflation. As in the United States, this gave people a powerful incentive to borrow as much cheap money as they could, to buy houses that were rising in value 10 percent or more every year.

At the height of the building boom, as in Ireland, one Spanish worker of every seven was employed in housing construction. Half a million new homes were being built every year—roughly equal to all the new homes in Italy, France, and Germany *combined*—in a country with about 16 million households. The amount of housing loans outstanding skyrocketed from $180 billion in 2000 to $860 billion in 2007. Over the ten years to 2007, housing prices tripled, second only to Ireland among developed countries; by then, the average house in Madrid cost an unheard-of $400,000.

Plenty of people sounded alarms, abroad and in the United States, that these bubbling economies were headed for trouble. But it was hard for national governments basking in the light of booming economies to take the alarms seriously. Between the economic and political influence of bankers and home builders, the electoral importance of those who were benefiting from the expansion, and the political requirements of incumbency, it was easy to keep the machine going, even if the best mechanics were warning about its weaknesses. After all, there had been warnings before, and sometimes they hadn't come true. Perhaps this capital flow cycle, this borrowing boom, was not like the ones that had come before it; perhaps it would keep going without crashing and burning.

"WE ARE DIFFERENT"

People in the United States, United Kingdom, Spain, Ireland, and the other big borrowing nations were not the first to believe—or to want to believe—that they would escape calamity, that they were different.[7] Generations of politicians, in scores of countries, have convinced themselves that warnings of economic dangers are overblown. Capital flow cycles of the sort the United States was experiencing are enormously enjoyable to almost everyone, especially governments that can take the credit for the upswing. Forewarnings of impending problems are never welcome, even though in retrospect it would probably have been wise—and even self-interested—for governments to take them seriously. Public opinion, and voters, are rarely kind to governments that oversee earth-shaking crises. So why do politicians ignore intimations of impending doom?

Good times often reinforce themselves, not least in the minds of politicians. When the economy is growing, they tend to credit their own talents; when the economy hits the skids, politicians tend to blame outside forces. And when an economy is growing particularly strongly, and attracting trillions of dollars from investors around the world—whom, one assumes, are putting their money where their beliefs in quality are—and history's most sophisticated financial system is trumpeting the wonders of advanced risk management, then it is easy to convince oneself that previous cycles that ended badly are no guide to current developments. Our economy is sound. Our people are unusually productive. Our economic management is extraordinarily competent. Our institutions are uniquely secure.

Such beliefs are common, however, to almost all such capital flow cycles, including those that ended unambiguously badly. The tendency to ignore warning signals is nearly universal and goes back hundreds of years. Denial often lasts long after the fact, when in retrospect it seems obvious to everyone that they had experienced an unsustainable boom. After most recent debt or currency crises, at least some of the policymakers in office at the time of the crisis continued to insist that the problem was with irrational speculators, or politically motivated opponents, or misinformed foreigners. . . .

Policymakers may hope that their luck will carry them through, or they might engage in what could be called "rational procrastination." A collapse could happen, which would be a bad thing, but it might come well into the future—and far into the future for a politician usually means after the next election. Facing a trade-off between recession now versus recession later makes the choice easy: you're in office now, somebody else will be in office later. Or the forecasts might be wrong, and a wonderful surprise—a drop in the price of oil, a rise in the price of an export commodity—might solve the problem. So you roll the dice: don't adjust, keep the boom alive, hope that the experts are wrong and the economy either stays healthy long enough for you to win the election or it gets bailed out by some happy coincidence. It's a long shot, but if the alternative is the end of your political career, it might be a gamble worth taking to try to resurrect your political fortunes.

And so perhaps the Republicans weren't simply ignoring the economic advice. Perhaps they were hoping that the decline would come late enough to allow them to win the 2008 election. Or perhaps they were hoping that something unexpected, and wonderful, would come along to salvage the economy. In the event, they were wrong on both counts, but maybe it was politically worth the risk. Anyway, it is not as though there were massive political pressures to rein in the expansion and impose economic restraint. But why weren't there? Certainly somebody other than academic observers had an interest in keeping the American economy from collapsing.

WHO MIGHT HAVE BELLED THE CAT?

The forces for American economic restraint were weak. They often are in boom times—but not always. There have been instances in which a bubbling economy that experts tag as unsustainable is brought down gradually. It doesn't happen that often, and it doesn't happen without cost. Nonetheless, if policymakers can decompress a booming economy before it turns into an irreversible bubble, they may be able to avoid a terrible crash.

This was, for example, the case of Brazil in the mid and late 1990s. Like Argentina a few years before, Brazil in 1994 fixed its currency to the dollar to bring inflation down. This worked, and by 1997 the economy was booming. But signs of stress were everywhere. Because inflation had come down gradually, the real exchange rate had been going up (appreciating): prices of non-tradables had risen about 50 percent relative to tradables. As a result, millions of jobs were lost in the tradables sectors, especially manufacturing and agriculture, and the job growth in service sectors did not keep up with losses elsewhere. Soon economists began insisting that the government needed to delink the currency (called the "real") from the dollar and devalue. The Brazilian government delayed a bit, until the 1998 election was over and won. But in January 1999 the government did in fact devalue the real. The shock pushed the country into a very mild recession, from which the economy recovered quickly. Meanwhile, it was increasingly clear that Argentina needed to do the same, devaluing its currency to avoid a crisis. Yet successive Argentine governments refused to act. By 2001, the long-delayed adjustment was forced on the country—leading to history's biggest default and Argentina's most severe economic collapse. But Brazil had avoided the worst, demonstrating that government action to avoid a collapse is not impossible. When does it happen?

Some things delay a constructive government response to an impending crisis, while others seem to permit or accelerate one. It is no surprise that an impending election makes a government very reluctant to hit the economic brakes. So too does political weakness, as a fragile government is unlikely to be able to get support for harsh policies. By this standard, if the Argentine elections had been earlier, and the Argentine government had been more secure in office—like its Brazilian counterpart—it too might have engineered a more gradual decompression.

Another force for delay is debt. If governments, firms, and households in a booming economy have taken on large debts, slowing the economy is likely to increase the real burden of debt. In a boom, prices of assets like housing and stocks rise, so that loans taken out against them are lucrative. But if prices stop rising, or fall, the real debt burden grows. Again, this was the case in most of the financial and currency crises of the 1980s and 1990s: heavily indebted companies and governments needed the merry-go-round to continue.

Some economic and political forces—in particular, the influence of manufacturers and farmers—tend to rein in borrowing booms. The reason goes back to the impact of foreign borrowing on tradables and nontradables. Binges such as those experienced by borrowing countries raise domestic prices and wages. Local manufacturers and farmers eventually find themselves priced out of world markets. Since borrowing also leads to a surge of imports, often imports that compete with local products, the results can be disastrous for domestic industry and agriculture. One of the strongest predictors of government action to pop a currency or financial bubble before it becomes unmanageable is the size of the manufacturing and farming sectors: the bigger they are, the more political power they have, and the sooner the government acts.

In the American borrowing boom of the early and middle 1980s, in fact, American farmers and manufacturers were vocal in their concern. Between 1980 and 1985, that era's capital inflow led the prices of services to rise twice as fast as those of manufactured goods, while farm prices actually dropped. In this instance, the problem was reflected in a very strong appreciation of the dollar, which farmers and manufacturers were desperate to limit or reverse. . . . Sympathetic members of Congress introduced a flurry of protectionist trade bills, and manufacturers tripled the number of protectionist complaints they filed with the International Trade Commission. This pressure was important in encouraging the Reagan administration to work to restrain the dollar's value, eventually moderating and reversing the harm it was doing to America's farmers and manufacturers.

But after 2001, there were few such expressions of concern. The economy had changed fundamentally in less than twenty years, and many of the manufacturing industries that had complained so bitterly in the 1980s had long since left the country. Where there had been nearly 20 million manufacturing workers in America in 1980, by 2006 there were barely 14 million; manufacturing had plummeted from employing more than one in five American workers to just one in ten. Globalization had led many American industries to outsource production to lower-wage locations, mainly in East Asia and Latin America. Many of the industries that had not shifted production simply shrank or went out of business. Meanwhile, American farmers had become so reliant on government supports that their market position was less relevant than their political backing. And a worldwide increase in farm prices in 2007 stanched whatever agricultural concerns there might have been. So while the Bush boom had effects of special concern to American manufacturers and farmers engaged in international competition—it led to a huge upsurge in imports and raised the price of doing business in America—there were now very few such manufacturers and farmers around. The potential complainants had taken their factories elsewhere, gone out of business, or resigned themselves to relying on government hand-outs. There was almost nobody left to complain.

STAYING OUT OF TROUBLE

Those who thought that the Bush boom between 2001 and 2007 was unique were wrong. The main features of the American trajectory were common to the United States, Spain, Ireland, and the United Kingdom—and to Iceland, Greece, to the Baltic states of Lithuania, Estonia, and Latvia, and to many other countries that became major debtors over the course of the decade. In these countries, as in dozens of others over hundreds of years, foreign borrowing fostered financial and housing booms, and trade deficits. The United States after 2001 could not escape the macroeconomic realities of a borrowing nation.

But there is nothing inevitable about borrowers running into crises. Nor is it inevitable that the problems of borrowing countries will lead to crisis. This is true even if the problems are homemade, as they were in the United States, whose fiscal and monetary policies were central to the borrowing boom and eventual bubble.

The man who took over from Alan Greenspan at the helm of the Federal Reserve in 2006, Ben Bernanke, was intellectually well equipped to evaluate financial threats. Bernanke is an MIT-trained economist who was chair of the Princeton University Department of Economics until he joined the Fed's Board of Governors in 2002. Three years later, Bernanke took over the chairmanship of the Bush administration's Council of Economic Advisers, and after only a few months in that position he was appointed to succeed Greenspan at the Fed.

Bernanke was only the second Fed chair to have an academic background in economics (the first was Arthur Burns, who served in the 1970s). Bernanke was indeed a prominent and respected academic economist long before assuming his post. Much of his scholarship, with titles such as "Permanent Income, Liquidity, and Expenditure on Automobiles," was of interest only to other scholars. But Bernanke also had a major interest in financial crises, and his most famous scholarship looked at what happened to countries during the Great Depression. On the basis of detailed studies of the Depression experience, in the United States and elsewhere, Bernanke concluded that the scale of a country's collapse did not just depend on its macroeconomic conditions, or on its debt burden, or on how serious the shocks it faced were. What really pushed a country over the brink, from a recession to a full-fledged catastrophe, was a financial system prone to panics, one that could not withstand the series of monetary and other shocks to which it was subjected.

Bernanke's conclusion, that financial strength could help protect against crisis, should have reassured Americans. Certainly it reassured Bernanke, who early in 2007 attempted to set minds at rest about the possibility that the growing difficulties in one segment of the mortgage market might portend more extensive problems: "the effect of the troubles in the subprime sector on the broader housing market will likely be limited, and we do not expect significant spill-overs from the subprime market to the rest of the economy or to the financial system."[8]

So calm continued to reign among policymakers and the general public, even as the housing market began to slow in 2006 and 2007 and as problems developed in one segment of the mortgage market, that for subprime mortgages. For the American financial system was, by common agreement, one of the world's most stable. There had not been bank panics in the United States since the 1930s. There were dozens of state and federal regulatory agencies watching over the financial system. Macroeconomic imbalances might be the unavoidable result of the country's foreign borrowing, but strong banks and sober regulators were a guarantee against serious crisis.

Or so it seemed.

NOTES

1. Raghuram Rajan, "Has financial development made the world riskier?" *European Financial Management* 12 (2006): 499–533 (quote on 502).

2. Stephen Mihm, "Dr. Doom," *New York Times Magazine*, August 17, 2008, 26.

3. James Miller III, "Should homeowners worry?" *Washington Times*, January 7, 2005, A17.

4. Alan Reynolds, "No housing bubble trouble," *Washington Times*, January 8, 2005, http://www.washingtontimes.com/news/2005/jan/08/20050108-105440-9091r/?page=1.

5. Larry Kudlow, "The housing bears are wrong again: this tax-advantaged sector is writing how-to guide on wealth creation," *National Review* online, June 20, 2005, http://old.nationalreview.com/kudlow/kudlow200506201040.asp.

6. Prashant Gopal, "Former housing industry economist who famously said there was no housing bubble now admits he was wrong," *BusinessWeek*, January 5, 2009, http://www.businessweek.com/the_thread/hotproperty/archives/2009/01/former_housing.html.

7. With apologies to Carmen Reinhart and Kenneth Rogoff, *This Time Is Different* (Princeton: Princeton University Press, 2009).

8. Benjamin Bernanke, "The economic outlook," Testimony before the Joint Economic Committee, U.S. Congress, Washington, DC, March 28, 2007.

16

The Political Economy of the Euro Crisis

MARK COPELOVITCH, JEFFRY A. FRIEDEN, AND STEFANIE WALTER

Like the rest of the world, the member states of the European Union (EU) were affected by the global financial crisis of 2008–2009. However, in the EU, and in particular in the Eurozone—the countries that have adopted the euro as a common currency—the crisis persisted for many more years. This reading describes the course of the most serious crisis in the history of the EU. It shows how the interactions among the member states of the Eurozone, and the operation of the institutions of the European Union, created the conditions for the crisis. These interactions, and these institutions, went on to make the resolution of the crisis politically controversial and extremely difficult. The conflicts of interest among the members of the Eurozone, which persist, have presented European institutions with great challenges, which have only been increased by the British decision to exit the Union.

The Euro crisis has developed into the most serious economic and political crisis in the history of the European Union (EU). By 2016, 9 years after the outbreak of the global financial crisis in 2007, economic activity in the EU and the Eurozone was still below its pre-crisis level. At this point, the joint effects of the global financial crisis and the Euro crisis have caused more lasting economic damage in Europe than the Great Depression of the 1930s. The political consequences have also been severe. Conflict among EU member states has threatened the progress of European integration, whereas polarization and unrest have unsettled domestic politics in a host of European countries. The crisis has indeed brought into question the very nature and future of European integration generally, and of monetary integration specifically. . . .

. . . We focus specifically on analyzing the politics of the Euro crisis using the tools of political economy and applying the insights generated by past research on the politics of international money and finance to provide a richer understanding of the political and economic constraints created by the crisis and encountered by Eurozone governments as they attempt to resolve it. The aim . . . is to improve our understanding of the causes, consequences, and implications of the highly unusual nature of the Euro crisis: a financial crisis among developed countries within a supranational monetary union.

The remainder of this . . . essay proceeds as follows. First, we begin with a summary of the course of the crisis and of its underlying causes, to set the stage for the analyses that follow. We then review the ways in which comparative and international political economy can help us understand the crisis. . . .

THE CRISIS: A BRIEF CHRONOLOGY

In January 2009, European policymakers celebrated the 10th anniversary of the Euro's introduction. EMU had become a reality in January 1999, when a group of 11 EU member states adopted the Euro for financial transactions and later replaced their national currencies with the new common currency. Although there had been considerable skepticism about the viability of this project in the years preceding the Euro's introduction . . . , the general perception among policymakers at the end of the Euro's first decade was that it had been an "unquestionable success" and a "rock of macroeconomic stability" that had helped Europe to weather the 2007–2008 global financial crisis.

Unfortunately, this optimism proved premature. In late 2009, the newly elected Greek government disclosed that the country's budget deficit was significantly higher than previously estimated and far higher than the Eurozone rules established in the Stability and Growth Pact (SGP) allowed. When the major rating agencies subsequently downgraded Greece's credit ratings in December 2009, and spreads on Greek bonds soared to pre-EMU levels, the Euro crisis had begun. Despite implementing austerity measures in the first months of 2010, the Greek government soon had to ask for outside help. Such help, however, did not materialize quickly, as European leaders engaged in long and intense debates about whether and how to support the country. In early May 2010, they finally approved a financial assistance program, in which Eurozone member states together with the International Monetary Fund (IMF) would provide Greece with financial assistance in return for fiscal austerity and structural reforms. The implementation of these measures proved politically difficult, however, as Greek policymakers faced widespread domestic protests against the policies in question.

In addition to the Greek assistance package, European policymakers tried to combat the crisis with additional policy measures. They created the European Financial Stability Facility (EFSF), with a mandate to provide assistance to Euro area Member States in financial distress and a lending capacity of €440 billion. Negotiations also began to strengthen the SGP and to introduce greater macroeconomic surveillance, including attention to the emergence of macroeconomic imbalances—a process that would eventually lead to the adoption of the "Six-Pack" of reforms in December 2011. The European Central Bank (ECB) announced exceptional measures that included sovereign debt purchases on secondary markets. In December 2010, the European Council agreed to establish a permanent crisis resolution mechanism for the countries of the Euro area, the European Stability Mechanism (ESM), which began operating in September 2012, and replaced temporary EU funding programs such as the EFSF.

In spite of these efforts, the crisis deepened in the following months. Borrowing costs soared in the Eurozone periphery, especially for Ireland and Portugal—where huge credit booms had turned into busts during the global financial crisis—against the backdrop of worsening outlooks in several Eurozone countries and speculation that private creditors might have to share the cost of future defaults with taxpayers. Both countries received EU-IMF bailouts—€85 billion for Ireland in November 2010, and €78 billion for Portugal in May 2011—under the auspices of the Troika, a tripartite committee formed by the European Commission, ECB, and IMF. With bond spreads on Spanish and Italian government bonds the next to rise, the ECB announced that it would resume its sovereign bond purchases to lower crisis countries' borrowing costs.

In the meantime, tensions mounted in Greece about new austerity measures, and for the first time, the possibility of a "Grexit"—a Greek exit from the Eurozone—was openly discussed. After difficult and protracted negotiations, Greece finally received a second financial assistance package totaling €130 billion in March 2012, which for the first time included a significant haircut for private creditors. In June 2012, Spain requested and received financial assistance of up to €100 billion to recapitalize its banking sector. In the same month, Cyprus requested a financial assistance package, which it received after long negotiations in March 2013 and in the context of which heavy losses were forced on wealthy bank depositors. With Europe in recession, pervasive downgrading of European countries' credit ratings, widespread anti-austerity protests, and the more general sense that policymakers were doing too little, too late to address the underlying problems, the Eurozone crisis continued to accelerate.

The Euro crisis also generated large political costs for member-state governments. Domestically, the implementation of austerity measures and structural reforms proved difficult and politically costly. One government after the other fell, radical populist parties were strengthened, and general satisfaction among citizens with the EU reached unprecedented lows. At the European level, policymakers struggled to reform the architecture of EMU. Issues such as banking and fiscal union and other measures were hotly debated and highly controversial. Not surprisingly, the outcomes of the political bargains were compromises. In March 2012, all European leaders, except those from the United Kingdom and the Czech Republic, signed the "fiscal compact," a treaty designed to force member-state governments to balance their budgets over the business cycle. In June 2012, Eurozone leaders endorsed the idea of a banking union, in which Eurozone banks would operate under a set of common rules, with a single supervisory authority and a single resolution mechanism for bank failures. They also proposed a "growth compact," following increasing calls for an agenda focused on growth, rather than austerity. Marking a turning point of the crisis, the ECB also stepped up its interventions, with Mario Draghi famously stating in July 2012, that the ECB stood ready to do "whatever it takes to preserve the euro" und unveiling a new bond purchasing program, called "Outright Monetary Transactions" (OMT).

After these events, a semblance of calm and stability returned to the Eurozone. Severe market stress subsided, adjustment in the crisis countries progressed, and the first countries began to exit the Eurozone assistance programs (Ireland in December 2013, Spain in January 2014, Portugal in May 2014). However, despite these encouraging developments, the crisis took center stage again in January 2015, when Alexis Tsipras and the left-wing Syriza party were voted into office in Greece, on the promise to simultaneously end austerity and keep the country in the Eurozone. In the ensuing months, protracted and difficult negotiations between Greece and the Troika ultimately ended in deadlock. With the expiration deadline for Greece's existing program approaching, liquidity problems mounting, and a take-it-or-leave-it offer from the creditors on the table, Tsipras broke off the negotiations and called a referendum on the proposal—recommending that voters reject the proposal to improve Greece's bargaining position. What followed was an intense week, during which Greece had to close its banks and impose capital controls and became the first industrialized country to default on an IMF loan. Although European and Greek policymakers warned that a rejection of the creditor proposal would lead to "Grexit," and polls showed that a large majority of Greeks wanted to remain in the Eurozone, 61% of voters rejected the creditor proposal in the referendum. This vote tested the Eurozone's pledge to be an irrevocable and irreversible monetary union in unprecedented ways. Several European governments openly called for Greece's permanent or temporary exit from the monetary union. After a Euro-summit that lasted more than 17 hours Greece ultimately accepted a third bailout package whose terms were harsher than those rejected by the Greek people in the referendum.

Meanwhile, developments in the other crisis countries were somewhat more encouraging. Growth picked up and turned positive in Ireland, Portugal, and Spain in 2014, and the ongoing crisis in Greece hardly affected the bond spreads in these countries. Overall, the European economy entered a phase of recovery, boosted also by the ECB's decision to adopt and implement quantitative easing (QE) in January 2015 to combat deflationary pressures. Nevertheless, huge challenges remain for the crisis countries and the Eurozone as a whole. At the time of writing, growth remains sluggish throughout most of the region, unemployment rates have reached record highs, especially among the young, and public debt remains substantial. The crisis has exposed the difficulties of crisis management in a confederation of states bound together by economic, but not political union. And the rise of anti-European parties in the European elections of June 2014, the political stalemates that have followed the 2015 elections in both Portugal and Spain (which brought large wins for political parties opposed to austerity and/or the political establishment), and mounting social and political tensions attest to the serious and enduring domestic political consequences of the Euro crisis.

Ultimately, the underlying causes of the crisis have not been resolved, and the narrative that the crisis has ended is misguided. Thus, although the short-term panic has subsided once again, serious questions remain about both the management and resolution of the ongoing crisis and the future of the monetary union itself.

ANALYZING THE CAUSES AND DYNAMICS OF THE EURO CRISIS

A good political economy analysis of the Euro crisis requires a clear understanding of why the crisis occurred in the first place. Fortunately, there is a growing consensus among economists about the causes of the Euro crisis: the crisis was a classic balance-of-payments crisis, triggered by a "sudden stop" of capital inflows into those Eurozone countries with large current account deficits, which had become dependent on foreign lending. The crisis was amplified by the lack of a lender of last resort, the fact that the classic crisis response—devaluation—was no longer among the menu of options, the close links between banks and governments as well as the predominance of bank financing in the Eurozone, and rigid factor and product markets. As such, the Euro crisis has its roots in features of the construction of the EMU itself—features that in turn are due to the difficult political economy of the creation of the single currency. . . . At the time of the introduction of the Euro, there were at least four important issues that had not yet been resolved. Ultimately, all four contributed to the crisis as it unfolded.

a. Macroeconomic Divergence

It is challenging to adopt a single monetary policy for a highly differentiated set of member countries that do not qualify as an optimum currency area. Therefore, the first problem that EMU, like any currency union, faced was the underlying differences in macroeconomic conditions among the member states. In 1999, at the outset of EMU, there were, in fact, substantial macroeconomic divergences among the member states. Most importantly, there was a clear difference between the Northern European countries and the peripheral European economies. Northern European countries were growing slowly or not at all, whereas the peripheral European countries—not just in the South, but also including Ireland and, outside the Eurozone, some countries in Central and Eastern Europe—were instead growing rapidly, with wages and prices rising.

Germany and Spain are important and representative examples. In the simplest terms, the German economy was stagnant in the years following the Euro's introduction, while Spain's was growing quite rapidly. However, a decade of wage restraint and austerity following German unification made the country's manufacturing sector increasingly competitive, as Germany returned to its traditional export-oriented position. In Spain, however, wages were rising quickly as the economy boomed. Consequently, inflation was at or near zero in Germany, while prices were rising more rapidly in Spain. Between 1998 and 2007, German inflation averaged just 1.5% a year, while in Spain, it averaged 3.2%. Compounded over nearly a decade, these differentials in growth and inflation led to a substantial divergence in labor costs within the Eurozone: between 1998 and 2007, unit labor costs in Germany actually fell by 3.9%, while in Spain, they rose by 30.4%.

Despite these divergences, the ECB could only implement a single monetary policy for the Eurozone, and it chose one that attempted to find a middle ground between the needs of Northern and Southern Eurozone member states. For most of this period, the ECB's main interest rate was around 3%. This meant, most importantly, that interest rates in the peripheral countries were very low compared with national inflation: real interest rates in Germany were about 2%, while they were slightly negative in Spain. These low, even negative, real interest rates, gave households and other economic agents in peripheral countries such as Spain strong incentives to borrow, whereas stagnation in the North gave investors strong incentives to lend. In Germany, moreover, the traditionally high savings rate rose further as its population aged and trade surpluses accumulated. The result was a massive flow of funds from the surplus countries of Northern Europe to the deficit countries of the Eurozone periphery.

These capital flows from North to South reinforced the macroeconomic divergences within the monetary union. In the periphery, the debt-financed consumption boom raised wages and prices, which further increased the difference between the two regions. Trends in the various countries' real effective exchange rates indicated the growing divergence: between 1999 and 2008, Germany's intra-Eurozone real exchange rate declined by nearly 20%, while the Spanish real exchange rate appreciated by more than 25%. In sum, the ECB's single monetary policy led to a very unbalanced pattern of capital flows and growth in the Eurozone's first decade.

These imbalances were reflected almost immediately in the balance of payments of the Northern and peripheral European countries. In 1998, both Spain and Germany had small current account deficits of about 1% of gross domestic product (GDP), while Italy and Ireland were running surpluses. By 2008, however, Germany's current account surplus had surged to 6% of GDP, while Spain, Ireland, and Italy had deficits of 10%, 6%, and 3% respectively. Simply put, Northern European surpluses—above all, those of Germany—were financing the Eurozone periphery's deficits. Contrary to popular impressions, the vast majority of these loans went to private borrowers. Greece and, to a lesser extent, Portugal were the only peripheral countries whose governments ran major budget deficits in this period. Capital inflows to Spain, for example, went almost entirely to the private financial sector and were channeled primarily into the country's booming housing market.

These North–South capital flows accelerated the divergences among Eurozone economies, further speeding growth and price increases in the periphery, especially in such non-tradable sectors as housing. As housing prices rose, incentives to borrow (and lend) rose further, and Northern current account surpluses and Southern deficits grew apace. Political leaders in the North had little reason to discourage their investors from taking advantage of profit opportunities in the periphery, whereas political leaders in the periphery had little reason to discourage their people from participating in the debt-financed expansion. Eventually, this boom turned into a huge problem once the bubble burst. Not surprisingly, the larger a country's current account deficit, the more severely the country got hit by the Euro crisis.

b. Lack of Fiscal Policy Coordination

The regional imbalances that resulted from these macroeconomic divergences, and which were exaggerated by the large-scale capital flows, might have been reduced if national governments had collaborated to counteract some of these trends with their fiscal policies. By imposing more restrictive fiscal policies, booming peripheral countries such as Spain could have restrained demand, which would have limited the size of the current account deficit and the inflow of foreign capital. Likewise, surplus countries such as Germany could have adopted more expansionary fiscal policies to stimulate domestic demand and restrain capital outflows to the South.

Several reasons explain why European policymakers did not coordinate their fiscal policies to address the growing imbalances across the Eurozone. First, countries give up their monetary policy autonomy when joining a monetary union. At the same time, the effectiveness of fiscal policy is enhanced. As a result, national political leaders were loath to give up their one remaining tool of national macroeconomic policy, especially one that had just become more effective. Second, taking away the (fiscal) punch bowl when the party is rolling has always been difficult for policymakers, and this was true for policymakers in the peripheral countries as well. The fact that markets priced government borrowing at much lower interest rates than before the start of EMU further created incentives to borrow on financial markets. . . . Although all members of the Eurozone share a common central bank, they have complete autonomy on fiscal policy as well as on most other economic and regulatory policies.

The architects of EMU recognized these problems and constructed the SGP to ensure fiscal discipline across the Eurozone. However, these provisions proved inadequate, providing a third reason why fiscal policies were not coordinated. These rules were never truly enforced, especially once the two largest member states, France and Germany, violated them with impunity in the first 5 years of the monetary union and as influential states tweaked them in their favor. . . . In addition, in many peripheral countries, the fiscal risks associated with the large capital inflows did not show up in their public debt and deficit figures. Because these capital inflows largely poured into the private sector, which boomed and generated fiscal revenues, the countries' fiscal policies did not appear overly pro-cyclical in the years preceding the crisis. For example, both Ireland and Spain, two of the countries most strongly hit by the crisis, recorded fiscal surpluses in the years preceding the crisis. The Eurozone problems only turned into a sovereign debt crisis after the Irish and Spanish governments had to support domestic banks badly hurt by the global financial crisis, turning private debt into public debt.

c. Fragmented Financial Regulation

Although the Eurozone quickly became a largely integrated single financial market, financial regulation remained very decentralized in the hands of national central banks and regulatory agencies. This created the possibility for regulatory arbitrage, as financial institutions exploited gaps in the regulatory environment to seek out higher yield, and higher risk, loans. The fragmented regulatory environment also created great uncertainty as to who would ultimately be responsible for banking problems that might arise within the Eurozone. It also meant that national regulators did not internalize the potential systemic effects of the financial flows taking place.

Nonetheless, national policymakers, regulators, and financial institutions resisted attempts to further harmonize or centralize financial regulation, fearing that this would put their own domestic firms at a competitive disadvantage. As a result, financial institutions took on risks that were probably greater than national regulators realized, and certainly created systemic risks that nobody was monitoring. Once the global financial crisis put banking sectors under stress, these risks became readily apparent. The global crisis also exposed the high level of interconnectedness of European financial markets, which created substantial contagion risks and turned even small economies such as Greece into systemically important actors. Thus, the Eurozone crisis hit an economic unit that had an established, respected central bank to make monetary policy but no analogous fiscal or regulatory policymaking body—and hence, no other unitary economic policy instruments.

d. Lack of a Credible No-Bailout Commitment

A fourth problem was that many market participants anticipated that if and when financial difficulties arose in one of the Eurozone member states, the other member states would be forced to bail it out. This expectation was widespread, despite attempts by Eurozone and national authorities to insist that there would be no such bailouts. International and regional experience told market operators otherwise: because a major financial meltdown in one country could threaten the stability of the entire Eurozone, it would force other countries to respond. Inasmuch as there were expectations of a bail-out, market participants did not have to worry unduly about the risks associated with weaknesses in an individual Eurozone country's financial system. Consequently, spreads on borrowing by households and governments in all Eurozone countries declined precipitously when the Euro was introduced, and remained extremely small until the crisis. For almost 10 years, governments and private borrowers in the Eurozone could borrow at interest rates roughly equal to those charged to borrowers in Germany.

For Southern Eurozone countries, the costs of international borrowing consequently fell to historically low levels, which further encouraged borrowing by these economies. This was true both in the case of loans to private industry—such as those made to Spanish and Irish banks and the real estate sector—and in the case of public-sector loans—such as those to the Greek government. If markets had fully accounted for the riskiness of the loans being made, the size of international capital flows would have been smaller and the imbalances among Eurozone countries would have been reduced. However, the markets believed—more or less correctly, as it turned out—that the integrated nature of the single market and single currency made it inevitable that, if a member of the Eurozone fell into crisis, other members would be forced to bail it out. Although policymakers protested to the contrary, they could not agree on plausible preparations for such a crisis, and so their commitments were not credible. As a result, public and private borrowers in the periphery accumulated significant foreign debt, and banks and other creditors in the surplus countries accumulated significant exposure to widespread default in the periphery.

Ultimately, these four problems came together to bring the Eurozone close to collapse. The massive capital flows from the North to the periphery led to a boom, and then a bubble, in the periphery. As the 2007–2008 crisis accelerated, this bubble burst. Financial institutions throughout the Eurozone turned out to be holding trillions of Euros worth of questionable assets. This was true of investors in the creditor (Northern) countries, and of financial institutions in the debtor (peripheral) countries, as much of the lending was intermediated through local banks. Peripheral governments found themselves compelled to bail out their illiquid or insolvent banks, at extraordinary expense. The result was a Eurozone debt crisis, in which peripheral countries owed debts they could not service to Northern European creditors.

Once the crisis hit, it immediately dissolved—as do all balance of payments crises—into bitter conflicts over how the burden of adjusting to the accumulated debts and current account imbalances would be distributed. . . . The pure economics of such circumstances is clear: the "asymmetry of the adjustment burden" means that in crisis, deficit countries have no choice but to adjust, whereas surplus countries are under no such pressure. Surplus countries therefore often succeed in shifting a disproportionate part of the adjustment burden onto deficit states. However, the response to the crisis was highly politicized. Surplus countries, home to most of the creditors, insisted that deficit countries impose severe austerity measures to service the debts as contracted, or as close to the original contract as possible. Deficit countries insisted instead on less stringent austerity policies and more extensive relief and debt restructuring.

Debt and balance-of-payments crises give rise to political conflict over the distribution of the adjustment burden not only *among* countries but also *within* countries. Within debtor nations, citizens clashed over who would be asked to sacrifice to maintain or restore debt service and to rebalance the current account: taxpayers, financial institutions, public employees, beneficiaries of public programs, or others. There are many ways to allocate the costs of servicing accumulated debts and implementing structural reforms, and politics in deficit and debtor nations revolved around determining who would shoulder these costs. Likewise, surplus and creditor nations faced debates about whether and how the country should shoulder some of the adjustment burden, and whether and how it should support struggling financial institutions exposed to default risk in the periphery. As a result, more or less open distributive conflicts have characterized and powerfully affected government policies toward the Euro crisis.

These conflicts have been exacerbated by the inability of individual Eurozone governments to control their exchange rate. If, as had happened in the European Monetary System (EMS) crisis in 1992–1993, peripheral governments had been able to devalue, recovery from the crisis would almost certainly have been more rapid—to the benefit of both debtors and creditors. In the absence of this option, however, the crisis has persisted and deepened. All of the Eurozone debtor nations have undertaken serious austerity measures whose costs have fallen primarily on public employees, beneficiaries of public spending, and workers in the private sector. Many countries, especially those under the auspices of the Troika, have implemented far-reaching structural reforms as well, although structural reforms have progressed much more slowly in other countries, such as Italy or France. Taxpayers in the creditor nations in the Eurozone have shouldered financial rescue packages of hitherto unimaginable proportions, whereas investors and the financial sector have benefited from low interest rates and the indirect public support for their investments in the Eurozone periphery.

In light of these large distributive consequences of the crisis, it is perhaps even more striking that the political consequences of these developments have so far been comparatively small. Although there have been some protests, none of the debtor nations, with the possible exception of Greece, has experienced the kinds of political upheavals we have seen in previous debt and balance-of-payments crises. . . . And although many governments have fallen and although Eurosceptic parties have recently gained in the polls, the basic institutional set-up, including EMU, remains essentially unchallenged.

THE POLITICAL ECONOMY OF THE EURO CRISIS

. . . In recent years, scholars of comparative political economy (CPE) and international political economy (IPE) have developed a keen understanding of the significant trade-offs confronting policymakers in the realms of fiscal, monetary, financial, and exchange-rate policy, and the implications these trade-offs have for economic policymaking. Policymakers in the Eurozone confront a number of these trade-offs, which strongly affect the incentives they face as they weigh their options. For one, many policy options are constrained by the well-known open-economy trilemma, which follows from the Mundell–Fleming model: when capital markets are open, as is the case in the EU, policymakers must choose between exchange-rate stability and domestic policy autonomy. IPE research has shown that the costs of sacrificing domestic economic goals to achieve exchange rate stability are particularly high for democratically elected policymakers, but that these costs also vary substantially across different political settings. For example, veto player configurations, legislative and electoral institutions, and the influence of special interests all affect the degree to which foregoing monetary policy autonomy is costly to political leaders. Another implication of the Mundell–Fleming model is that, although monetary policy autonomy is sacrificed in a fixed exchange rate regime like the Eurozone, fiscal policy becomes more effective, at least in the short run. This can create powerful incentives to use fiscal measures for political reasons, which help explain why there were strong incentives for European governments not to adhere to the fiscal rules set forth in the Maastricht Treaty.

The trade-off between exchange-rate stability and domestic monetary policy autonomy becomes particularly acute in times of crisis, where governments operating under the constraint of fixed exchange rates have to implement painful domestic adjustments to address balance-of-payments imbalances. Much research has shown, however, that the resolution of such imbalances through "internal adjustment" is a politically contentious issue. It typically involves high unemployment and falling asset prices in deficit countries and higher rates of inflation in surplus countries, and bars the option to let the exchange rate carry at least part of the necessary adjustment. It is quite obvious that, in both surplus and deficit countries, internal adjustment is not politically attractive.

Not surprisingly, the alternative to substantial internal adjustments in a currency union—namely, a financing of the current account deficits through public funds—has enjoyed broad support during the Euro crisis. Bailout funds administered through the Troika or the TARGET2 balances within the ECB system have played an important role in European crisis management. However, this policy option also entails a number of trade-offs. For example, research on the politics of the IMF and its lending behavior has highlighted the trade-offs involved in granting and receiving bailouts in previous crises. This research has shown that answers to the question of who gets how much money under what conditions (and under what circumstances surplus countries are willing to pay) can vary significantly. Not all countries experiencing crisis are treated equally, and political factors—notably, the interests of the Fund's large shareholders and the incentives of the IMF's professional bureaucrats—play an important role in this context.

Although much of this research assumes that such bailouts are limited, this may in fact not be true for the Euro crisis. The increasing integration of financial markets has created new trade-offs for the Eurozone and has put the question of fiscal and banking union and possibly a long-run transfer union on the table. This issue points to an additional complication: the potential contradiction between short- and long-term policy goals. If the costs and benefits involved in the different choices were realized at the same time, many of the trade-offs invoked by the open economy trilemma and other economic constraints would be politically clearer. However, this is rarely the case. In terms of bailouts, this timing issue raises the possibility that the bailout facilities that were created to manage short-term pressures on national economies are transformed into a more permanent transfer union, which in turn raises the question as to whether member states would be willing to go along with this model. It also confronts European policymakers with an additional political trade-off between national autonomy and democratic accountability over fiscal policy, on one hand, and financial and economic stability, on the other. In the long run, the fundamental problem facing European policymakers is likely to involve a choice between a closer union—involving more permanent transfers of funds among member states and the delegation of some fiscal autonomy to Brussels—or a break-up of the Euro project in its current form.

In sum, the extensive literature on the political economy of money and finance highlights the difficult trade-offs confronting policymakers as they wrestle with responses to the Euro crisis. At the same time, the politics of the Euro crisis are affected by the novel aspects of having a financial crisis occur within the economic and institutional context of a monetary union of advanced economies. It is therefore not surprising that the course of the Euro crisis has been striking on many dimensions: the depth and long duration of the crisis, the extent of IMF involvement, the return of the specter of sovereign default in industrialized countries, the sudden stop in capital flows in developed countries, the prolonged deadlock among European governments and institutions about crisis resolution, and the threat that the crisis has posed to European integration itself.

Apart from the inability of Eurozone countries to devalue their currencies, two key differences from previous debt and financial crises are particularly salient. First, prior to the Euro crisis, nearly all modern experience with this international bargaining about crisis resolution involved developing countries and emerging markets, typically under the auspices of the IMF. The international politics of the Euro crisis has unfolded quite differently. Although the IMF has been extensively involved as part of the Troika, most of the bargaining has taken place directly among member states of the EU, along with the institutions of the EU more generally. In addition, with the notable exception of Greek debt—and in marked contrast to previous financial crises—there has been little meaningful debt relief granted to the debtor nations. In other words, with the exception of Greece, most of the costs associated with the foreign debts accumulated between 1999 and 2008 have been borne by the debtors, whereas creditors have largely been rescued by a series of European and national packages to limit the impact of the debt crisis on national financial systems. Likewise, most of the cost of adjusting to the large current account balances has been borne by the deficit countries, which have seen large reductions in growth, jobs, and spending, whereas surplus countries have barely seen any increases in domestic consumption and inflation.

Second, perhaps the most salient distinguishing feature of the Euro crisis is that it has unfolded within the context of a long and ongoing historical process of regional economic integration, of which monetary union is now a central element. Both debtor and creditor nations within the Eurozone are also part of the broader single market of the EU, within which goods, capital, and (most) people can move more or less as freely as they do within single nations. Nonetheless, although the single market was quite complete and there were many EU-wide political and regulatory institutions in place by 1999, substantial economic policy authority still remained vested in national states at the outset of the crisis. This includes, most importantly, fiscal policy and financial regulatory authority. Thus, the crisis has taken place—as no previous sovereign debt crisis had—within the unique economic and political context of an extensive yet incomplete regional integration scheme, where monetary and fiscal policy authority is divided between actors and institutions at both the supranational and national levels. While complicating the resolution of the crisis, these unique features make the Euro crisis a useful and fascinating case for clarifying the scope conditions of existing theories in comparative and international economy. . . .

CONCLUSION

. . . Although exchange-rate and monetary policy have long been thought to be a complex and technocratic field in which ordinary citizens have no well-informed interests, this has changed in the setting of EMU and the Euro crisis, where the consequences of these decisions have become much more visible and politicized. Most prominently, the Greek referendum on the proposed bailout package from July 2015 has turned the Greek people into a key actor in the crisis. However, crisis politics have been politicized in surplus countries as well. For example, an unprecedented number of 37,000 German citizens called on the German constitutional court in 2012 to rule over whether the European Stability Mechanism was in line with the German constitution.

This demonstrates that it will become more difficult to make important decisions in crisis-related policy fields without consideration of the public's reactions. Mass publics are also increasingly important because of the broad macroeconomic consequences of EMU. For example, high unemployment rates in peripheral countries and increasing shares of non-performing loans on bank balance sheets leave households directly exposed to the effects of the crisis. In addition, the growing importance of mass public opinion is visible in the growing concern among ordinary citizens about the future direction of the European project more generally and the increasing success of euroskeptic parties across Europe.

Second, . . . as is now abundantly clear, the currency union affects not only monetary and exchange rate policy (and fiscal policy), but also the relationship between monetary policy and such other arenas as labor market policies and financial regulation. EMU has had far more intrusive and far-reaching consequences on national economies than many Europeans realized at the time of its founding. This has been evident in the conditions imposed on debtor countries by the Troika, which span a large variety of policies, but which also have varied substantially across cases and over time during the Euro crisis. Moreover, the domestic reach of the crisis extends to all member states, as European-level decisions—such as bailout programs, banking union, or banking supervision—have important effects at the national level. As a result, negotiations about such decisions within supranational institutions such as the European Commission and the Troika have been very difficult and contentious, and have been strongly influenced by the national interests affected by these decisions.

Third, as we have noted earlier, . . . the underlying economic problems of the Eurozone have persisted since its inception and continue to have enormous economic and political implications today. Increasingly, then, the appropriate analogy for the Eurozone is not the Great Depression, but rather Japan, which has been mired in an era of stagnation since the 1990s, and whose persistent problems (debt-laden banks, unfavorable demographics, persistent deflationary pressures) appear disturbingly similar to those of the Eurozone today. Faced with the possibility of long-term "secular stagnation," Europe's debt problems look even more serious and threatening to the long-term success of EMU. Unless economic growth returns to the Euro area, Greece and other member states face the possibility of decades of grinding deflation, long-term unemployment, and stagnation. Given the persistent and massive unemployment in the debtor countries, as well as the major electoral shakeups seen to date within Eurozone member states, this scenario does not bode well for the future of European monetary integration. . . .

Ultimately, the key debates about the structure of Eurozone governance have changed little since the 1990s. In the years between the signing of the Maastricht Treaty and the launch of the Euro, it became very clear that, although policy-makers were unified in their goal of creating a stable Euro and Eurozone, domestic politics within EMU member states were such that no country was able to agree to the sorts of policies and institutions that would have enabled the Eurozone to avoid the problems that have plagued it since 2010. In this sense, there is a *plus ça change* quality about the political and economic debates within the Eurozone today. Faced with the same set of persistent macroeconomic imbalances and similar implacable domestic political barriers to further integration, European policymakers and national-level politicians in EMU member states continue to face serious questions about the future stability and prospects of the single currency, and these are further tested as the EU faces additional challenges in other policy fields such as the refugee crisis or the conflict between Russia and Ukraine. Ensuring the long-term viability of the monetary union will require policymakers to adopt some combination of the policies and institutions—a true Eurozone lender of last resort, a growth and stability pact with strict monitoring and enforcement mechanisms, increased labor mobility between Eurozone member states, and/or a more extensive fiscal and political union—necessary to maintain a monetary union among disparate national economies with large and persistent macroeconomic imbalances.

Whether or not European policymakers are able to overcome the domestic and international obstacles to such cooperation is, as always, a political rather than an economic question. Indeed, it is important to note that there are no technical obstacles to the adoption of any of the policy or institutional solutions to resolving the Euro crisis and addressing the imbalances within the monetary union. The ultimate problem is that adoption of any of them remains, now and for the foreseeable future, politically infeasible. . . .

17

Political System Transparency and Monetary Commitment Regimes

J. LAWRENCE BROZ

Governments interested in providing monetary stability have typically followed one of two strategies. The first is to establish an independent central bank, committed to low and stable inflation. The second is to adopt a fixed exchange rate, which commits the government to maintaining stable prices. In this reading, J. Lawrence Broz argues that institutional differences among countries help explain this choice. Democracies can credibly create independent central banks, because attempts to manipulate them will be seen by the voters and the free press. Dictatorships, on the other hand, will find it hard to convince people that the central bank is truly independent. Therefore, he expects democracies to tend to use central bank independence more frequently, and dictatorships to be more likely to adopt fixed exchange rates.

INTRODUCTION

Central bank independence and fixed exchange rates are commitment mechanisms that can assist governments in maintaining credibility for low-inflation monetary policy objectives. In this article, I explore the political factors that shape the choice and effectiveness (in controlling inflation) of these alternatives.

My argument is that the degree of transparency of the monetary commitment mechanism is inversely related to the degree of transparency in the political system. Transparency is the ease with which the public can monitor the government with respect to its commitments. Central bank independence (CBI) and fixed exchange rates (pegs) differ in terms of transparency. While legal CBI is an opaque commitment technology that is difficult to monitor, a commitment to an exchange-rate peg is more easily observed; in the extreme, either the peg is sustained or it collapses. In nations where public decision making is opaque and unconstrained (that is, in autocracies), governments must look to a commitment technology that is more transparent and constrained (that is, fixed exchange rates) than the government itself. The transparency of the peg *substitutes* for political system transparency to assist in engendering low inflation expectations. However, in nations where political decision making is transparent (that is, in democracies), legal CBI can help resolve the time-inconsistency problem and produce low inflation. The openness of the political system allows the attentive public or the political opposition to observe government pressures on the central bank, making it costly for the government to conceal or misrepresent its actions. Informal transgressions of CBI are likely to be detected by interested private agents and exploited by the political opposition when the political process is transparent.

This analysis extends the logic of time-inconsistency to the problem of explaining the choice of monetary institutions. If governments sincerely seek to lower inflation by way of an institutional commitment, why do some adopt CBI while others commit to an exchange-rate peg for credibility purposes? My substitution hypothesis hinges on the disparate transparency characteristics of monetary commitments on the one hand and of political institutions on the other. A credible commitment to low inflation requires transparency to detect and punish government opportunism. Transparency, however, can be supplied directly, by way of transparent monetary institutions, or indirectly, via general political institutions. The former are obviously easier to change.

I provide two tests of the argument that the transparency of the monetary commitment and the transparency of the political system are substitutes. First, I estimate the determinants of exchange-rate-regime choice for a panel of more than 100 countries during the period from 1973 to 1995. The expectation is that, all else equal, countries with opaque domestic political systems (autocracies) will have a higher probability of adopting pegged exchange rates than countries with transparent political systems (democracies). For autocracies, a formally independent central bank is not a credible commitment because the opacity of the political system makes it difficult to detect and punish governmental efforts to subvert the autonomy of the central bank. Opaque domestic political institutions should thus be positively associated with fixed exchange rates. The findings indicate that, controlling for other factors, opaque political systems are indeed significantly more likely to peg than transparent systems.

Second, I estimate the institutional determinants of inflation in a cross-section of sixty-nine developed and developing countries. A testable implication of the substitution hypothesis is that a formally independent central bank will be effective in lowering inflation only when the political system is transparent. . . . I find that the opaque commitment technology (CBI) is modestly effective in limiting inflation in countries with more-transparent political systems. Neither CBI nor political-system transparency is associated with lower inflation independently; a negative relationship between CBI and inflation is found only when political openness imparts the necessary transparency to this opaque monetary commitment. On the other hand, the transparent commitment technology (pegging) constrains inflation even in the absence of democratic institutions or extensive civil freedoms.

The article is organized as follows. I first describe briefly the time-inconsistency problem in monetary policy and the transparency characteristics of alternative institutional solutions to it. I then examine the transparency aspects of political systems and develop the hypotheses regarding the substitution of commitment mechanism transparency for political system transparency. In the next section, I test the substitution hypothesis with respect to the choice of exchange-rate regimes. Finally, I test the implication that CBI lowers inflation in the context of transparent political systems. I conclude with a discussion of additional implications and future research.

TIME-INCONSISTENCY IN MONETARY POLICY

There is broad consensus among economists that inflation is detrimental to growth and that successful monetary policy—that is, a policy that generates low inflation without incurring large output losses—requires "credibility." The credibility problem relates to the fact that the money supply can be expanded to whatever level by fiat. . . . Credibility involves persuading private agents that the monetary policymaker will not exploit the flexibility inherent in a fiat standard to achieve short-run output gains.

Although explicit political pressures are absent in the original models of time-inconsistency, the problem generalizes to the introduction of democratic political processes (elections) and rational political actors (politicians, parties, and interest groups). . . . Yet it is important to note that the classic time-inconsistency problem is not exclusive to democracies. It befalls dictators (benevolent or otherwise) and elected politicians alike because *ex post* economic incentives are sufficient to generate counterproductive policies and inefficiently high inflation. I thus assume that countries with political systems of every stripe must find a resolution to the time-inconsistency problem. While the problem itself extends to all countries, a host of political and economic factors can affect the degree to which politicians behave inconsistently over time. For example, high levels of political instability may shorten the time horizon of leaders and thus weaken their ability to precommit. . . .

TRANSPARENCY IN MONETARY COMMITMENTS

Several solutions have been suggested to enhance the credibility of the monetary policymaker. While these solutions take varied forms—CBI, exchange-rate pegs, and other nominal anchors such as money growth rules or inflation targeting—they each involve changing the rules or institutional structure of policymaking to limit the scope for discretionary opportunism. Two of the most prominent forms of delegated decision making are CBI and fixed exchange-rate regimes. In theory, CBI and pegs can both have a positive influence on credibility and thereby on inflation performance. They are not, however, perfect substitutes. One difference involves the degree to which the institutions actually invoke a trade-off between *credibility* and *flexibility*. Another attribute on which they differ is *transparency*—the ease with which the public can monitor government behavior with respect to the commitment.

Ideally, a monetary commitment should impose the constraint necessary to resolve the credibility problem but leave policymakers with enough flexibility to respond optimally to shocks. This is the classic case for discretion in the "rules versus discretion" debate. CBI has apparent welfare advantages over pegging on this account. Empirical evidence suggests that the low-inflation credibility generated by CBI does *not* come at the cost of higher output variability, that is, at the cost of forgone flexibility. In contrast, pegs leave little or no room for policy to perform a stabilizing role, which helps account for the finding that output is more variable in countries with fixed rates. . . . But a peg may improve credibility precisely because it comes at the cost of flexibility. The knowledge that this costly trade-off exists lends credibility to the commitment since it will not be optimal to incur the cost except under the most unusual circumstances. In the spirit of signaling games, the greater the credibility problem, the more likely it is that a country will choose (costly) fixed exchange rates.

While CBI would seem to have efficiency advantages over pegs in terms of the credibility-flexibility trade-off, the two institutions differ on another dimension—*transparency*. This difference is potentially important, because a commitment is only effective in producing desired goals insofar as it is verifiable. Transparency is the ease with which the public can verify and punish government misbehavior with respect to an institutional commitment. A peg has a clear advantage over CBI in this respect because an exchange-rate target is a simple and clear promise to which the government can be held accountable. When a government adopts policies that are inconsistent with maintaining an exchange-rate target, the eventual result is a currency collapse. If the government does not put its financial house in order, wage and price inflation will not be checked. The exchange rate will become steadily overvalued, and intervention in support of the currency will drain international reserves. Anticipating the exhaustion of the country's reserves, speculators will run the central bank, thus forcing abandonment of the peg—a highly visible event. Doubts about the timing of a market attack on a currency are less important than the fact that it is bound to happen if a government's policies are inconsistent with the peg.

The simplicity and clarity of an exchange-rate target make it a transparent commitment because the interested public can directly monitor broken promises by the government. This transparency, in turn, enables the public to hold the government directly accountable if it abandons the peg. . . . When governments shoulder direct responsibility for a transparent exchange-rate commitment, they pay political costs when the commitment is broken.

CBI, by contrast, is an opaque commitment mechanism in the sense that it is quite difficult for the public to monitor what the government does in relation to a central bank. Even specialists find it tremendously hard to measure the *actual* autonomy of central banks, which is essential for credibility. . . .

The opaque nature of the CBI commitment suggests that the credibility of CBI is not established by the ability of the public to directly observe broken promises, as with fixed exchange rates. Actual CBI depends on the government's commitment to it: delegating monetary policy to an independent central bank does not solve the credibility problem, "it merely relocates" it to the government that makes the delegation decision. Something must make the government's CBI commitment credible, and the transparency of the political system is a likely candidate.

TRANSPARENCY IN POLITICAL SYSTEMS

Governments create the institutions that constrain their own discretion. If there are no political costs to governments of revising or overturning the constraining institution, the commitment arrangement provides no credibility gains. When a government can renege without cost on a commitment arrangement, the arrangement will have no more effect on inflation expectations than when the government conducts monetary policy on its own. Before costs can be imposed, however, opportunism must be detected. If a government violates its promise and the public cannot detect the violation, or cannot distinguish meddling from an unanticipated disturbance, the government will bear few, if any, costs from acting opportunistically. In the absence of transparency and costs, the commitment will not be credible.

In the case of a peg, transparency and political costs are built into the commitment mechanism. By pegging, the government makes an easily verifiable commitment and bears political costs when it breaks that commitment. CBI, in contrast, is not directly observable and therefore cannot, on its own, generate the political costs required to adequately guarantee a commitment to low inflation. How then can it be made credible? I argue that transparency in political systems can provide the necessary monitoring and enforcement functions. Transparency in the political system means that public decisions are made openly, in the context of competing interests and demands, political competition, and sources of independent information. Governments will have greater difficulty hiding their actions and avoiding the costs of opportunism when the political system is transparent. When government discretion is constrained by transparent political institutions, even an opaque monetary technology such as CBI may be credible.

The argument borrows from James Fearon and Donald Wittman, who reason that institutions of political accountability—democratic institutions—facilitate information revelation and thereby improve a government's ability to send credible signals.[1] According to Fearon, governments incur "audience costs" if they make a threat or promise that they later fail to carry out. This suggests a role for political institutions, because the magnitude of these costs should depend on how easily domestic audiences can punish leaders. Fearon hypothesizes that democratic institutions generate higher audience costs, and hence democratic states can send more-credible signals of resolve. . . .

1. See Fearon 1994; and Wittman 1989.

Audience costs are the domestic political costs the government would bear if it failed to make good on a promise. In the case of a promise to respect the independence of the central bank, the *attentive* audiences include social actors with a stake in low inflation and the political opposition. Among the constellation of private interests that most strongly support CBI is the financial services sector. As creditors, banks are natural allies of the central bank and make up a powerful low-inflation constituency. In the United States, for example, the Federal Reserve relies on the support of the banking industry when its independence is threatened. Other allies of CBI include pensioners and institutional investors in fixed-rate corporate and government debt. These pro-CBI audiences, not individual voters, have special incentives to monitor government–central bank relations and report government misdeeds.

Where political institutions allow for the expression and representation of societal preferences, pro-CBI audiences will find politicians willing to defend the central bank. With support from their inflation-averse principals, these politicians may gravitate toward legislative committees or cabinet ministries that control monetary legislation. When inflation-averse politicians sit on committees or ministries with agenda power and oversight responsibilities for monetary policy, informal pressures on the central bank are very likely to come to light. More generally, electoral competition provides opposition politicians with incentives to guard the central bank from government interference. The incentives to reveal information will be greater when the low-inflation political party is in the minority or is a member of the governing coalition. When the opposition has a strong preference for low inflation, the government will tread on CBI only at its own peril.

Civil liberties, particularly the freedom of expression, increase the transparency of the political process and make it easier for the public to obtain information on government reneging. Where media sources are independent of the government, the public can better monitor the government's behavior with respect to the central bank, even to the point of differentiating monetary expansions due to political pressure from expansions that result from changes in velocity or other "uncontrollable" forces. In the United States and other open societies, the financial press closely monitors relations between the government and the central bank and provides analyses of policy changes. Back-channel political pressures on Federal Reserve officials are not secret for long, and media coverage has proven to be costly to the offending administrations.

The monitoring role of interested domestic audiences and the magnitude of the costs these audiences can impose depend on the basic characteristics of the political system. In a transparent polity, civil liberties are afforded to a heterogeneous population, political parties compete openly for votes in regular and free elections, and the media is free to monitor the government. Political process transparency lowers the costs to the attentive public of detecting government manipulation of monetary policy and raises the costs to the government of interfering with the central bank. Inflation hawks in society and

FIGURE 1 Substitute Sources of Transparency

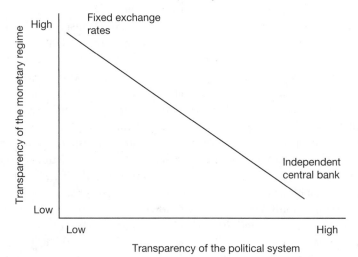

political challengers have interests in exposing violations of the CBI commitment; this puts constraints on the government's ability to conceal or misrepresent its actions. Political competition ensures that opposition politicians and perhaps even the mass public will capitalize on the information and impose costs on the government.

In opaque political systems, where there are severe restrictions on political expression, electoral and partisan competition, and the media, the audience costs of subverting CBI are low. Domestic anti-inflation groups and the political opposition cannot perform their monitoring and sanctioning roles. Without political transparency, an opaque monetary commitment like CBI is not likely to be credible. Autocrats may find that legal CBI is not effective in lowering inflation. Credibility-seeking autocratic governments must look to a more transparent monetary commitment, like pegging.

In sum, a monetary commitment need not be *directly* transparent to impose costs on a government. CBI is not directly transparent. However, the costs needed to render an opaque commitment credible can be obtained *indirectly* by way of a political system that is itself highly transparent. In the following section, I lay out some testable implications.

POLITICAL INSTITUTIONS AND MONETARY COMMITMENTS AS SUBSTITUTES

Transparency is a necessary characteristic of any credible government commitment. The public must be able to know when the government violates a commitment to impose audience costs. Transparency can be purchased by way of an easily observed commitment technology or generated indirectly via transparent political institutions. Commitment mechanisms and political institutions are *substitute* sources of transparency.

Figure 1 depicts this negative relationship: the more transparent the political system, the less transparent the monetary commitment. CBI is the less transparent but more flexible commitment technology. It is associated with transparent political systems. A fixed exchange rate is the more transparent but less flexible technology. It is found more often in opaque political systems. When the political process is very open, CBI is rendered transparent indirectly through active monitoring by interested private and political agents. When political decision making is opaque, the government can import transparency by way of a peg—a commitment that is more transparent and constrained than the government. The transparency of the monetary commitment *substitutes* for the transparency of the political system to engender low inflation expectations.

The foregoing analysis suggests the following hypotheses. (1) *Countries with opaque political systems will have a higher probability of adopting a peg than countries with transparent political institutions.* This tests the argument that the choice of exchange-rate regime is shaped by political system transparency. The propensity to choose a pegged regime should be negatively associated with the transparency of the political system. (2) *Legal CBI has a negative effect on inflation in politically transparent nations.* Since only legal CBI is directly observable, I test the implication that the effectiveness of statutory CBI in limiting inflation is conditional upon the transparency characteristics of the domestic political system. . . .

EVIDENCE, PART I

The first test is to examine whether the transparency of the domestic political system affects the choice of exchange-rate regime. My substitution hypothesis predicts that countries with opaque domestic political institutions (autocracies) will have a higher probability of fixing the exchange rate than countries with transparent political institutions. CBI is not a credible option for autocracies because the closed nature of public decision making renders it difficult to detect and sanction governmental interference with the central bank. Sincere governments that want to establish low-inflation credentials must look to a commitment mechanism that is more transparent than the political system. The propensity to peg should thus be negatively associated with the transparency of domestic political institutions.

I use cross-country, time-series data to test the prediction. The panel has yearly observations on as many as 152 countries during the 1973–1995 period. Data availability constraints on some covariates reduce the sample size to around 2,300 observations (109 countries). The dependent variable is the exchange-rate regime. . . . Thus, a 4 = Fixed (pegged to the dollar, some other currency, the SDR, or a basket of currencies); 3 = Limited Flexibility (for cases such as the European Monetary System [EMS]); 2 = Managed Floating; and

1 = Free Floating. The variable of interest is POLITY, an aggregate index of the "general openness of political institutions" from Polity III. . . . POLITY ranges from –10 (most autocratic) to 10 (most democratic) and provides a fairly good stand-in for the openness of public decision-making. . . .

. . . Table [1] presents the results.

The strongest and most consistent result is that exchange-rate regimes are slow to change: the lagged dependent variable is highly significant and has a large value. Although regime choice is path-dependent, it is influenced by other factors. Model 1 considers the relationship between political system characteristics and exchange-rate-regime choice, controlling for level of economic development. The estimated coefficient of POLITY, my proxy for political transparency, is negative and highly significant ($z = -4.41$), which suggests

TABLE 1   Political Transparency and Exchange-Rate Regime Choice, 1973–1995

Dependent variable: exchange-rate regime (Float=1 to Fixed=4)	(1) Baseline	(2) Optimal currency area controls	(3) Other controls
Lagged dependent variable	1.36**	1.29**	1.24**
	(.061)	(.067)	(.072)
POLITY (from low = –10 to high = 10)	–.020**	–.015**	–.016**
	(.005)	(.005)	(.005)
Wealth (per capita GDP)	–.011*	.023**	.024**
	(.005)	(.008)	(.009)
SIZE (Log of GDP)		–.239**	–.257**
		(.057)	(.063)
TRADE OPENNESS (X + M/GDP)		.169*	.121
		(.088)	(.097)
INFLATION DIFFERENTIAL (Country—World, logged and lagged)		–.306	–.212
		(.262)	(.261)
FINANCIAL OPENNESS (from low = 0 to high = 14)		–.068**	–.054*
		(.024)	(.026)
INT'L RESERVES (in months of imports)			.041**
			(.014)
FEASIBILITY (% of sample pegging)			1.211**
			(.427)
GOVERNMENT CRISES (Count)			.032
			(.093)
Pseudo R^2	.48	.47	.47
Prob > chi^2	0.00	0.00	0.00
Observations	2300	1983	1531

*$p < .05$, **$p < .01$.

NOTE: Ordered probit specification with robust (White's heteroskedastic-consistent) standard errors in parentheses.

that the propensity to peg is inversely related to the level of political system transparency. It is also quantitatively large: when POLITY is set at its highest level (10) and all other variables are held at their means, the predicted probability of choosing a fixed exchange rate (Category 4) is 0.68, with a 5 percent margin of error. In contrast, when POLITY is set at its lowest level (–10), the predicted probability of pegging is 0.53. Being autocratic increases the probability of pegging by a statistically significant 15 percent.

Of course, other factors influence the choice of exchange-rate system, and some may be correlated with political regime type. The OCA literature points to several considerations. Economic size, openness to trade, inflation performance relative to trading partners, and degree of financial openness are perhaps the most important considerations. The typical finding is that a peg (or a greater degree of fixity) is generally superior for small, open economies that have low inflation differentials with their trading partners and a lower degree of international financial integration. I include controls for these economic determinants in Model 2. Economic SIZE is measured as the log of GDP in constant U.S. dollars. TRADE OPENNESS is exports plus imports as a share of GDP. INFLATION DIFFERENTIAL is the absolute difference between the inflation rate of the country and the world inflation rate, logged. This term is lagged one period to avoid potential endogeneity problems. FINANCIAL OPENNESS is a fourteen-point scale derived from the IMF's *Exchange Arrangements and Exchange Restrictions*. . . .

The most important result in Model 2 is that the POLITY coefficient estimate remains significant and negative—the controls do not undermine this key finding. However, including SIZE does lead to a sign reversal in the WEALTH coefficient, the control for economic development. While collinearity between these terms is high ($r = 0.54$), the results suggest that, controlling for size, richer countries tend to prefer more fixity in their exchange rates. One interpretation, often heard in the context of the EMS, is that wealthy countries desire stable exchange rates as a means of lowering the transaction costs of international trade and investment. . . .

As for SIZE, the result confirms the implications of the OCA approach: the larger the economy, the stronger the case for flexible rates.

The other controls have the expected signs. The negative sign on the inflation differential indicates that the more divergent a country's inflation from the world rate, the greater the need for frequent exchange-rate changes. Divergent inflation rates make it difficult to sustain a fixed rate. A high degree of international financial integration also mitigates fixed exchange rates: FINANCIAL OPENNESS is negative and significantly related to pegging, presumably because a high degree of capital mobility makes it difficult to maintain a peg.

Other influences are examined in Model 3. First, I include the size of a country's foreign currency reserves, INT'L RESERVES, measured in months of imports. Larger reserves should make it easier to sustain a peg. The coefficient estimate is positive and significant—but very likely endogenous. Peggers would certainly try to maintain larger reserves than countries on more flexible regimes.

More important as a control is the general "feasibility" of fixed exchange rates over time, given structural changes in the international environment, global shocks, and changes in expert opinion. There has been a steady decline in the number of pegging countries over time. In 1973, 87 percent of the world's nations pegged; by 1995, the figure had dropped to 36 percent. The oil shocks of the 1970s, the debt crisis of the 1980s, large fluctuations in the value of the major currencies, increasing international capital mobility, and a number of dramatic speculative currency attacks surely influenced this shift away from currency pegs. Rather than include a time trend, I . . . use a variable— FEASIBILITY—that measures the percentage of countries of the world with pegs. I expect the sign to be positive, as it is. The choice of a fixed exchange rate is positively and significantly related to the general climate of opinion regarding pegging. Note that, even though this is a large effect, the POLITY result hardly changes from the previous specification. . . .

. . . Figure [2] demonstrates what happens to the predicted probability of adopting a fixed exchange rate as POLITY is allowed to vary over its entire observable range and all other covariates are held at their means. The figure shows that authoritarian polities are significantly more likely than democratic polities to adopt fixed exchange rates. The probability of adopting a peg is around 58 percent if a country is completely authoritarian and about 44 percent if it is fully democratic. While the prediction is relatively tight for democratic regimes, the confidence intervals widen once the Polity score falls below negative seven. In fact, the probability of pegging for the most authoritarian polities varies by so much that, at the lower bound on the interval (0.51), it approaches, but does not overlap, the upper bound for fully democratic regimes (0.48). Although authoritarian countries can sporadically exhibit probabilities

FIGURE 2 Predicted Probability of Fixing the Exchange Rate by POLITY Score

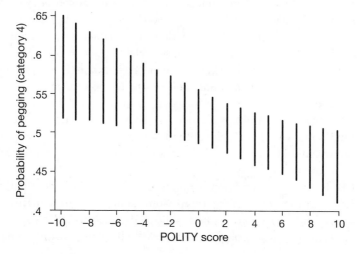

close to those of some weakly democratic nations, the probability of pegging remains significantly more likely for these nations.

Overall, these findings indicate support for the transparency hypothesis. Autocratic systems lack the transparency to make an internal monetary commitment (for example, CBI) credible. Autocracies thus substitute the transparency of a visible commitment to a foreign currency peg for the transparency they lack internally. . . .

EVIDENCE, PART II

In this section, I use cross-country data to test the implication that formal/legal CBI will have a negative impact on inflation only in countries with transparent political systems. A more direct test of the relationship between political transparency and CBI is not possible because the credibility of CBI, or *actual* CBI, is unobservable. However, since we can observe the kind of CBI obtained through legislation, it is possible to examine the implication that formal/legal CBI is rendered credible by an open political system. The sample consists of sixty-nine developed and developing countries during the 1973–1989 period. Each observation pertains to a single country, with all values in period averages. . . . Legal CBI is an appropriate indicator because my argument predicts when formal/legal independence will have an impact on inflation performance. Specifically, I expect a high value of CBI to have a negative impact on inflation only when the domestic political system is transparent. . . .

The dependent variable is the inflation rate, measured as the log of the average annual change in the consumer price index. I use two alternative proxy indicators for the transparency of political systems: POLITY and CIVIL LIBERTIES. POLITY is from Polity III, as described previously. A high value corresponds to a political system in which leaders are freely chosen from among competing groups and individuals who were not designated by the government. This maps loosely to one conception of political transparency inasmuch as it captures the ability of the *political opposition* to openly scrutinize the government and compete freely in elections. CIVIL LIBERTIES is an alternative indicator, from the Gastil/Freedom House series. Although there is extensive overlap in the two series ($r=0.90$), CIVIL LIBERTIES is explicitly designed to pick up the ability of *private individuals and groups* to monitor and criticize the government and to freely engage in social, political, and economic activity. Freedom of expression and the media weigh heavily in this index. Overall, the civil liberties index is slightly closer than polity to my conception of political transparency, in that it captures the ability of social actors to monitor government opportunism. . . .

. . . CBI is associated with lower inflation when a nation's political system is more democratic (more transparent). Some simple algebraic manipulation of the coefficients reveals that the conditional effect of CBI on inflation is negative for nations with polity scores above eight. Thus, CBI has a negative influence on inflation only in the most democratic states. The reason may be that it takes strongly democratic institutions to enable society's inflation hawks to monitor the many ways that governments tamper with the policy independence of the central bank.

Another part of my argument is that countries that peg will enjoy lower inflation irrespective of the transparency of their political systems. Pegging is a very transparent and therefore credible commitment in its own right. . . . The coefficient estimate for peg is correctly signed and significant. This suggests that a transparent commitment to a peg reduces inflation regardless of regime type. . . .

. . . [I] replicate the analysis using CIVIL LIBERTIES as the proxy for political system transparency. Not surprisingly, the results are very similar. However, the size and the significance level of the interaction variable of interest, CIVIL LIBERTIES×CBI, improve over prior estimates using the polity measure (see Figure 3). This may be due to the fact that civil freedoms are closer to my concept of political transparency than the democracy indicator. Freedom of expression, organization, and dissent is a precondition for effective monitoring of government commitments. The ability to openly denounce the government when it meddles in central bank affairs is a crucial first step in applying audience costs. Once the transgression is exposed (by the media, for example), democratic institutions allow for sanctioning by way of electoral competition.

To illustrate the substantive effect of CBI conditioned on the level of civil liberties, I estimated expected values of inflation . . . by holding CIVIL LIBERTIES at a high level (75th percentile), setting WEALTH to its mean, and then increasing CBI incrementally from its lowest to its highest value. I generated expected values and 95 percent confidence intervals. . . . As part of the simulation, I

FIGURE 3 Effect of CBI Conditioned on CIVIL LIBERTIES: High CIVIL LIBERTIES (75th percentile)

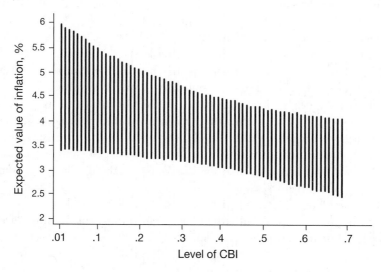

FIGURE 4 Effect of CBI Conditioned on CIVIL LIBERTIES: Low CIVIL LIBERTIES (25th percentile)

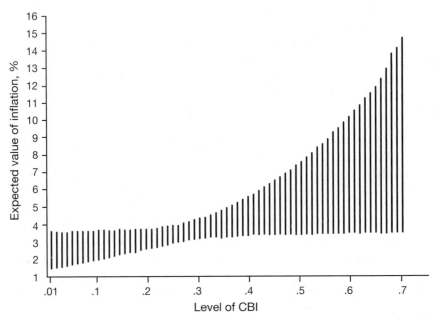

exponentiated the expected values to yield more meaningful results—inflation rates rather than logged inflation. Figure 3 shows that there is a slightly *negative* relationship between CBI and inflation in democratic settings. These results provide modest support for the argument that CBI generates lower inflation in the context of transparent political institutions. In democracies, CBI constrains government opportunism and thus provides meaningful information about the commitment to low inflation.

As for autocracies, the effect of CBI is very perverse. Figure 4 replicates the simulation but with CIVIL LIBERTIES set at a low level (25th percentile). There is a *positive* relationship between CBI and inflation in nondemocratic settings. Why a formally independent central bank might raise inflation in the absence of democracy or civil liberties is a legitimate puzzle. It could be that those states that are the least likely to be credible would go to great pains to profess the supposed independence of the central bank. Legal CBI might thus send a preserve signal to wage and price setters, creating an even greater time-inconsistency problem.

Note also that the level of uncertainty surrounding these estimates increases dramatically as CBI increases. This suggests that, when the political system is not transparent, the effect on inflation of a statutorily independent central bank is highly varied. Overall, legal CBI signals little about the commitment to low inflation in autocratic settings.

CONCLUSION

The underlying presumption of this paper is that governments choose monetary institutions at least in part according to their usefulness in resolving the time-inconsistency problem. Credible monetary commitments must be transparent for governmental opportunism to be detected and punished. Transparency, however, need not be a characteristic of the commitment technology itself. In the case of CBI—an opaque technology—a transparent political system can be a workable substitute. When the political process is open, as in democracies, CBI is rendered transparent indirectly through active monitoring and sanctioning by interested private and political agents. When political decision making is not transparent, as in autocracies, the government can import transparency by way of a commitment technology that is more transparent than the political system. For autocratic governments, a highly transparent monetary commitment such as a peg can substitute for the transparency of the political system to engender low inflation expectations.

REFERENCES

Fearon, James D. 1994. Domestic Political Audiences and the Escalation of International Disputes. *American Political Science Review* 88 (3): 577–92.

Wittman, Donald. 1989. Why Democracies Produce Efficient Results. *Journal of Political Economy* 97 (6): 1395–434.

V

TRADE

The international trade regime constructed under American leadership after World War II and now embodied in the World Trade Organization (WTO) has facilitated the emergence of the most open international economy in modern history. After World War II, political leaders in the United States and many other advanced industrialized countries believed, on the basis of their experience during the Great Depression of the 1930s, that protectionism contributes to depressions, depressions magnify political instability, and protectionism therefore leads to war. Drawing on these beliefs, the United States led the postwar fight for a new trade regime to be based on the economic principle of comparative advantage. Tariffs were to be lowered, and each country would specialize in those goods that it produced best and trade for the products of other countries, as appropriate. To the extent this goal was achieved, American decision makers and others believed that all countries would be better off and prosperity would be reinforced.

The American vision for the postwar trade regime was originally outlined in a plan for an International Trade Organization (ITO), which was intended to complement the International Monetary Fund. As presented in 1945, the American plan offered rules for all aspects of international trade relations. The Havana Charter, which created the ITO, was finally completed in 1947. A product of many international compromises, the Havana Charter was the subject of considerable opposition within the United States. Republican protectionists opposed the treaty because they felt it went too far in the direction of free trade, while free-trade groups failed to support it because it did not go far enough. President Harry Truman, knowing that the treaty faced almost certain defeat, never submitted the Havana Charter to Congress for ratification. In the absence of American support, the nascent ITO died a quick and quiet death. The General Agreement on Tariffs and Trade (GATT) was drawn up in 1947 to provide a basis for the trade negotiations then under way in Geneva. Intended merely as a temporary agreement to last only until the Havana Charter was fully implemented, the GATT became, by default, the principal basis for the international trade regime. The GATT was finally replaced by the WTO in 1995.[1]

Despite its supposedly temporary origins, the GATT was, for decades, the most important international institution in the trade area. Trade negotiations within the GATT—and now, the WTO—proceed in "rounds," typically initiated by new grants of negotiating authority delegated from the U.S. Congress to the president. Since 1947, there have been eight rounds of negotiations, each resulting in a new treaty, which was subsequently ratified by member states under their individual constitutional provisions.

The WTO is based on three primary norms. First, all members agree to extend unconditional most-favored-nation (MFN) status to one another. Under this agreement, no country receives any preferential treatment not accorded to all other MFN countries. Additionally, any benefits acquired by one country are automatically extended to all MFN partners. The only exceptions to this rule are customs unions, such as the European Union.

Second, the WTO is based on the norm of reciprocity—the concept that any country that benefits from another's tariff reduction should reciprocate to an equivalent extent. This norm ensures fair and equitable tariff reductions by all countries. In conjunction with the MFN (or nondiscrimination) norm, it also serves to reinforce the downward spiral of tariffs initiated by the actions of any one country.

Third, "safeguards," or loopholes and exceptions to other norms, are recognized as acceptable if they are temporary and imposed for short-term balance-of-payments reasons. Exceptions are also allowed for countries experiencing severe market disruptions from increased imports.

The GATT and WTO have been extremely successful in obtaining the declared goal of freer trade and lower tariffs. By the end of the Kennedy Round of the GATT in 1967 (initiated by President John F. Kennedy in 1962), tariffs on dutiable nonagricultural items had declined to approximately 10 percent in the advanced industrialized countries. In the Tokyo Round, concluded in 1979, tariffs in these same countries were reduced to approximately 5 percent, and member countries pledged to reduce their remaining tariffs by a further 40 percent in the Uruguay Round, concluded in late 1993. These significant reductions initiated an era of unprecedented growth in international trade.

The GATT and WTO continued to be an active force for liberalization in the late 1980s and early 1990s, as the Uruguay Round produced new agreements on the thorny issues of services and agricultural trade—two areas that had been excluded from earlier negotiations. Governments have long regulated many of their domestic service industries, such as insurance, banking, and financial services. Often differing dramatically from country to country, these regulations operate like politically contentious barriers to trade. Likewise, governments in most developed countries subsidize their agricultural sectors, leading to reduced imports and increasing surpluses that can only be managed through substantial sales abroad. Nearly all analysts agree that national and global welfare could be enhanced by reducing agricultural subsidies and returning to trade based on the principle of comparative advantage; yet as the prolonged negotiations of the Uruguay Round demonstrated, politicians found it difficult to resist demands from farmers for continued government intervention. Here, as in other areas, the tension between national wealth and the demands of domestic interest groups has created a difficult diplomatic issue—but one that, after years of comparative neglect, finally made it onto the trade liberalization agenda. The Uruguay Round made substantial progress on many fronts, including services and agricultural trade; the primary exception, from the American point of view, was entertainment products such as films, which were excluded from the final agreement at the insistence of the European Union.

In the aftermath of the Uruguay Round, farm subsidies have once again been a major sticking point in progress toward further trade liberalization. Bargaining in the "Doha Round" of WTO trade negotiations, which began at a WTO ministerial meeting in 2001 in Doha, Qatar, has stalled repeatedly over agricultural policies. The most significant differences are between developed nations with extensive farm subsidy programs (e.g., the European Union, the United States, and Japan) and developing countries that want greater access to rich-country agricultural and industrial markets (e.g., Brazil, India, China, and South Africa). As the most heavily protected sector in world trade, agricultural reform stands to deliver the greatest economic benefits. Ironically, agriculture appears to be the sector most resistant to change.

Outside of agriculture, tariffs have been declining and trade increasing, but new threats have emerged to the international trade regime. Especially in times of economic difficulty, industry demands for some form of protection persist in nearly all countries. Increasingly, governments have sought to satisfy these demands for protection through nontariff barriers to trade (NTBs). The most important of these NTBs are voluntary export restraints, in which exporters agree to restrain or limit their sales in the importer's market. Estimates suggest that almost 20 percent of all goods imported into the European Union, for instance, enter under some type of NTB.[2] Although the Uruguay Round agreement helped to limit their growth, NTBs remain an important impediment to trade.

The readings in this section address the causes and implications of trade policy. In Reading 18, Barry Eichengreen focuses on the domestic interests in play in the United States in the late 1920s to account for the Smoot-Hawley Tariff, which contained some of the highest duties in history. In Reading 19 Raymond Hicks, Helen Milner, and Dustin Tingley analyze a Costa Rican referendum on a trade agreement, showing the role of economic interests and political parties in shaping opinions on the country's trade relations. Andy Baker, in Reading 20, focuses on the interests of consumers who stand to benefit from greater trade openness, which provides them with access to less expensive and more varied goods from which to choose. In Reading 21, Paola

Conconi, Giovanni Facchini, and Maurizio Zanardi shift our attention to examine how electoral institutions affect the making of trade policy, arguing that the approach of elections leads members of Congress to be more favorably inclined to trade protection. Finally, in Reading 22 Richard Baldwin addresses the dramatic increase in preferential trade agreements that some see as an institutional alternative, perhaps even a threat, to the WTO regime. He explores the origins of the GATT and WTO, and considers the implications of the rise of these preferential agreements for the future of the WTO.

NOTES

1. The GATT continues to exist as a legal entity related to the WTO. Nonetheless, the GATT secretariat and director general were transferred to the WTO, and the latter organization is expected to subsume, and fully replace, its predecessor over time. Except where specifically referring to the GATT, we refer to the international trade regime as the WTO.

2. Based on the import coverage ratio from the Organization for Economic Co-operation and Development (OECD), *Indicators of Tariff and Non-Tariff Trade Barriers* (Paris: OECD, 1997), p. 53.

18

The Political Economy of the Smoot-Hawley Tariff
BARRY EICHENGREEN

Barry Eichengreen explains the passage of the Smoot-Hawley Tariff Act of 1930, which set historically high tariffs on thousands of items in the United States and likely contributed to the problems of the Great Depression. Eichengreen argues that economic interest groups were the key actors underlying the passage of the act. He asserts that certain sectors of agriculture and industry interacted so as to support each other's desire for protection; together, this coalition pressured the U.S. government to pass the highly restrictive Smoot-Hawley Tariff. He shows both how the actions of self-interested groups in national societies affect the making of foreign economic policy and how international political and market forces can influence the interests of societal actors.

The intimate connection between the Great Depression and the Smoot-Hawley Tariff of 1930 was recognized by contemporaries and continues to be emphasized by historical scholars. But just as contemporaries, while agreeing on its importance, nonetheless viewed the tariff in a variety of different ways, historians of the era have achieved no consensus on the tariff's origins and effects. The definitive study of the Smoot-Hawley's origins, by Schattschneider [1935], portrays the tariff as a classic example of pork-barrel politics, with each member of Congress after his particular piece of pork. Revisionist treatments characterize it instead as a classic instance of party politics; protectionism being the household remedy of the Republican Party, the tariff's adoption is ascribed to the outcome of the 1928 election. Yet proponents of neither interpretation provide an adequate analysis of the relationship of Smoot-Hawley to the Depression. . . .

POLITICS, PRESSURES AND THE TARIFF

The debate surrounding the passage of the Tariff Act of 1930 remains a classic study in the political economy of protection. A number of theories have been developed to explain Smoot-Hawley's adoption, starting with that advanced in Schattschneider's [1935] classic monograph whose title this section bears.

Schattschneider's influential study "set the tone for a whole generation of political writing on pressure groups. . . ." and "cut the lens through which

Americans have since visualized the making of U.S. foreign trade policy. . . ."[1] Schattschneider focused on the influence of special interest groups. In his account, the actions of lobbyists and special interests were responsible for both the tariff's adoption and its form.

Schattschneider dubbed the principal around which the tariff coalition organized "reciprocal noninterference." The coalition was assembled by offering limited protection to everyone involved. Since only moderate protection was provided and no single import-competing sector reaped extraordinary benefits at the expense of others, they could combine in support of tariff legislation. In addition, under provisions of the original House and Senate bills, credits (or "debentures") were to be made available to exporters, extending the coalition beyond the import-competing to the export-producing sector. Not just the number of duties raised but the very process by which the bill was passed is invoked in support of the log-rolling interpretation. Passage required 14 months from when Hoover called a special session of Congress to when the final bill was signed. The record of public hearings in which the bill was discussed ran to 20,000 pages, while the final bill provided tariff schedules for more than 20,000 items. Since insurgency was easier under Senate than House rules, log-rolling was more conspicuous there: the Senate amended the House bill over 1,200 times, most of them on the Senate floor. Still other changes were engineered in conference committee.

If the distinguishing feature of the Tariff Act of 1930 was the dominance of special interests, one must ask why they had grown so much more powerful. Schattschneider provides no explicit answer, although he indicts Hoover for failing to guide the legislation through Congress. But the systematic explanation implicit in his analysis is the rise of the "new lobby." Although fraternal, religious, social, and economic groups had always been part of the American scene, they had never been so well organized or visible in the Capitol as in the 1920s. . . .

A number of influences prompted the rise of the new lobby. First, the activities of the "muckrakers" in the first decade of the twentieth century had intensified public scrutiny of political affairs. Second, whereas businessmen had traditionally dealt with government in "a spasmodic and haphazard fashion," the panic of 1907 spurred them to cultivate more systematic representation. Simultaneously, the U.S. Chamber of Commerce took a more prominent role in representing the interests of business. . . . Finally, much as the Chamber of Commerce represented business's general interests, trade associations filled this role for more specialized groups. A Department of Commerce publication listed some 1,500 organizations classified as trade associations, nearly double the number known to exist in 1914. Some were organized by products produced, others by materials used, still others by markets in which sales took place. Like the other three influences, the growth of trade associations was a distinctively twentieth-century development, but in contrast to other trends, which had been under way in the early years of the century, the sudden rise to prominence of trade associations was attributable to World War I. The war effort required closer ties between government and industry, but upon attempting to establish them the authorities found it difficult to deal with individual enterprises and requested that associations be formed. If the war occasioned the formation and growth of trade associations, the armistice by no means signalled their demise. Once formed into an association the process of marshalling a constituency was no longer so difficult. Improvements in communication, notably the telephone, reinforced these advantages, and associations quickly learned to use pamphlets and other media to publicize their case. The adoption of new Congressional rules made it more difficult for powerful individuals to dictate policy, opening the legislative process to competing interests.

The same forces tending to promote effective representation of industrial interests in Washington encouraged the formation of effective organizations representing farmers and labor. The American farm movement had long been distinguished by its inability to organize effectively and represent its interests before Congress. The ad hoc methods of agricultural organizations, such as sending a representative to Washington in response to specific developments, had proven ineffectual. For agriculture as for industry, World War I and the impetus it provided for the formation of the War Trade Board and the Food Administration permitted farmers' organizations to assume new importance. In 1918 the National Grange opened a permanent legislative office in Washington, and the militant American Farm Bureau Federation, founded in 1919, lobbied actively for farm legislation. In 1921 a bipartisan Farm Bloc of senators and congressmen from the South and West was formed, and it acquired a pivotal position in the balance of power in the 66th and 67th Congresses. Although it had at best mixed success in passing farm legislation before falling into disarray, the prominence of the Farm Bloc did much to alert agricultural interests to the advantages of effective congressional representation.

By encouraging the development of direct government-labor relations, the war had a similar impact on the American Federation of Labor. While maintaining its distance from party politics, by the 1920s the AFL was commonly acknowledged as the most formidable group in the United States other than the political parties. Thus, in the 1920s the three principal American interest groups—business, agriculture, and labor—were for the first time ably represented in Washington.

The rise of the new lobby is consistent with Schattschneider's characterization of Smoot-Hawley as an instance of pork-barrel politics. But his theory of reciprocal noninterference—that the Smoot-Hawley bill by offering something for everyone garnered widespread support—fails to confront the question of why the vote on the final bill so closely followed party lines, with only 5 Democratic Senators voting in favor and 11 Republicans against. Neither does it explain why tariff-rate increases differed so widely by schedule.

An alternative explanation, recently advanced by Pastor [1980], is that Smoot-Hawley is simply an instance of party politics. Protection in general and for industry in particular was regularly advocated by the Republican Party. With the White House occupied by a Republican President and the Senate in Republican hands, there were few obstacles to revising upward existing tariff schedules. It is curious that this straightforward explanation has attracted so little attention. It may be that partisan aspects of the debate were disguised by the absence of a change in party in 1928 like that following the 1920 election which preceded the 1922 Fordney-McCumber Tariff Act. Moreover, the issue of protection had not been hotly disputed in the 1928 campaign. Although the Democrats had traditionally campaigned on the basis of staunch opposition to protectionist measures, in 1928 they moderated their position and joined the Republicans in endorsing protection, albeit in vague and reserved terms. . . . Given the extent of consensus, there was little debate in the subsequent Congress over principles of free trade and protection. Hence even Free Traders among the Democrats were ill positioned to mount effective opposition to tariff increases.

The problem with this partisan interpretation is that it provides no explanation for Smoot-Hawley's timing or its form. It is suggested that Congress was simply accustomed to engaging in tariff revision every seven years (the average life of a tariff law between the Acts of 1883 and 1930), and that by 1929 Congress and the public had recovered from the exhausting Fordney-McCumber deliberations of 1920–1922. But this mechanical explanation neither recognizes links between protectionist pressure and economic events nor provides an explanation for the observed variation in import duty levels.

The explanation coming closest to satisfying these requirements is the view of Smoot-Hawley as a response to the problems of American agriculture. The explanation runs as follows. While the 1920s were boom years for the country as a whole, prosperity was unevenly distributed. After benefiting from high prices from 1917 to 1920, American agriculture failed to recover from the recession of 1920–1921. For much of the decade, farm gate prices declined relative to the prices of nonagricultural goods. . . . In 1926, a relatively favorable year for farmers when average wholesale prices were 51 percent above their 1913 levels, the prices of farm products were only 42 percent above those levels. The explanation for lagging prices was that World War I had prompted the expansion of agricultural production outside Europe. While European sugar production, for example, fell by 50 percent during the war, the shortfall was offset by expanding output in Cuba, Java, and South America. Once European production recovered, often under cover of import duties or production subsidies, world prices were depressed. Similarly, wartime disruptions of the global wheat market greatly stimulated production in Argentina, Australia, Canada, and the United States. The consequent decline in prices was magnified in the second half of the 1920s by the imposition of import duties on wheat by Germany, Italy, and France.

Agrarian distress in the United States took various forms, notably farm foreclosures which, after averaging 3.2 per thousand farms between 1913 and

1920, rose to 10.7 per thousand in 1921–25 and 17.0 per thousand in 1926–1929. Foreclosure reflected not just the declining relative price of agricultural products but overall price level trends; since much agricultural land had turned over between 1917 and 1920 when prices were high, the subsequent deflation greatly augmented the burden of mortgage debt. The value of total farm mortgage debt rose by 45 percent between 1917 and 1920 and by a further 28 percent between 1920 and 1923 despite the deflation that set in after the beginning of the decade. The foreclosures of the second half of the 1920s were most heavily concentrated in Idaho, Montana, North and South Dakota, Colorado, and Arizona, the sources of strongest pressure for agrarian relief.

In the 1928 presidential campaign Hoover laid stress on tariff protection for agriculture. Previously, agriculture had been the recipient of only modest tariffs, in part because duties on farm imports would have been ineffective given U.S. status as a net exporter of most agricultural goods (sugar, wool, and hides being the principal exceptions). In 1922, for reasons detailed above, the U.S. balance of trade in farm products turned negative, where it remained except in 1925 for the duration of the decade. Hence an expanding segment of American agriculture grew to appreciate the relevance of tariff protection.

By this interpretation, Smoot-Hawley was predominantly a form of agricultural relief. . . . Farm interests were well positioned to press their case. Although the United States had grown increasingly urbanized over preceding decades, Congress had not been reapportioned following the 1920 Census. Consequently, farm interests were overrepresented in the House, just as, on the two senator per state rule, they were overrepresented in the Senate.

This characterization of Smoot-Hawley as an agricultural measure won by the West over the opposition of the East is consistent not only with the partisan interpretation, given the regional concentration of Democratic and Republican voters, but it explains a number of defections from party ranks. To the extent that agricultural distress intensified with the onset of the Depression, it links the tariff to macroeconomic conditions. Where it falls short is in explaining why tariffs on manufactured imports were raised as part of an agrarian relief measure, or why the tariff was supported not only by representatives of agricultural districts but by those of industrial regions as well. Many accounts emphasize the extent of discord between agriculture and industry. . . . What explains the pattern of voting and the tariff schedule that emerged from Congressional debate?

A MODEL OF THE TARIFF-MAKING PROCESS

The framework I use to analyze the adoption of Smoot-Hawley is a variant of Gerschenkron's [1943] model of the political economy of protection. This is a member of the class of "interest-group models" of tariff formation. . . . I first review Gerschenkron's application of his model to Bismarckian Germany before adapting it to analysis of the Smoot-Hawley Tariff.

In Gerschenkron's model, a tariff is adopted when narrow yet well-placed interest groups combine in its support. Gerschenkron divides German society not merely along sectoral lines but into heavy industry (producers of basic products such as coal, iron, and steel), light industry (manufacturers of consumer goods, along with whom might be included artisans and shopkeepers), large agriculture (the Junkers, or estate owners of the east), and small agriculture (commercial producers located primarily west of the Elbe). He explains the Bismarckian tariff as a coalition of iron and rye, allying large agriculture and heavy industry.

In the 1870s as in the 1920s, the impetus for agrarian protection was the fall in grain prices. The position of traditional German agriculture, which specialized in grain, was seriously undermined. The alternative to continued grain production behind tariff walls was to shift into the production of high quality foodstuffs such as dairy products and meat for rapidly expanding urban markets. Cheap imported grain could serve as an input into such production. But, crucially, large and small agriculture differed in their capacity to adjust. Variations in soil quality and proximity to urban markets provided greater scope for the production of dairy products and meat west of the Elbe. In addition, dairy products, meats, and vegetables were most efficiently produced on small owner-managed farms. Hence costs of adjustment were lowest where long-term leaseholders and small owner-managed farms predominated—west of the Elbe—and highest where landless laborers worked large estates. The model predicts that small agriculture should have opposed agricultural protection due to its impact on costs, while large agriculture should have favored it.

Neither light nor heavy industry, with the possible exception of yarn spinning, desperately required protection from import competition. Under competitive conditions, Germany probably would have imported grain and exported both light manufactures and the products of the basic industries. While it is not clear that import duties on industrial goods would have succeeded in raising the prices of domestically produced goods, given competition at home but the net export position of German manufacturers, heavy industry in fact supported the imposition of a tariff on manufactured goods. One interpretation is that, with high levels of fixed capital, heavy industry was exceptionally susceptible to cyclical fluctuations. Tariffs may have reduced the risk of falling prices, thereby encouraging the fixed investments which permitted scale economies to be reaped. A more compelling interpretation is that barriers to cheap imports were a necessary condition for firms producing basic goods to combine and extract monopoly profits from domestic users. Consistent with this interpretation, producers of final goods like stoves, pots and pans, shovels, and rakes opposed tariffs on the products of basic industries because of their impact on production costs.

What is relevant for our purposes is that no group favored the final outcome: high tariffs on both agricultural and industrial goods. But because of the dispersion of interests, action required compromise. The two likely outcomes were a coalition of large industrialists and landowners obtaining general protection, and a coalition of small manufacturers and farmers successfully defending free trade. Gerschenkron ascribes the victory of the protectionist coalition to institutional factors. The Junkers, as members of the squirearchy, occupied a privileged position in the political system. Not only did they staff the bureaucracy and judiciary but, like the wealthy industrialists, they benefitted from the structure of the electoral system. Heavy industry, aided by smaller numbers, organized more effectively than small manufacturing. Managers of large enterprises formed new associations and worked to convert existing ones to protectionism. Their cause was not hurt by the fact that the Chancellor found protection a useful tool for achieving his political goals and played an active role in forging the alliance of iron and rye.

Gerschenkron's model can be applied to the case of the Smoot-Hawley Tariff by again distinguishing industry by size and agriculture by region. Naturally, the interests of the groups and the coalitions are entirely different from those observed in Bismarckian Germany. So is the role of national leadership. Nonetheless, distinctions of region and scale shed considerable light on the American case.

In the case of Smoot-Hawley, it is useful to distinguish sheltered from unsheltered agriculture and, as in Germany, light from heavy industry, where it is light industry and unsheltered agriculture that combined to support protection. As noted previously, critics of the Smoot-Hawley Tariff argued that duties on agricultural products would not be "effective" in raising prices because the United States was a net exporter of these goods. . . . The problem with this contention is that net trade may not be the appropriate indicator of the effectiveness of a tariff. It may mislead either if there existed segmented regional markets or if products were heterogeneous. For goods such as wheat with a high ratio of value to volume, there existed not merely a national but an international market. But wheat was not a homogenous product, and the United States both imported and exported different grades of what was often regarded in policy debate as a single commodity. Since, for example, little if any exportable surplus of high grade milling wheat was produced in the United States, it was argued that a tariff would therefore be effective in raising the Minneapolis price relative to that prevailing in Winnipeg. Even if the product was homogenous, for perishable products the United States was sufficiently large geographically that transport costs might impede the equalization of prices across regions. . . . Northern states like Minnesota and Eastern Seaboard states like Massachusetts might find their markets flooded by cheap Canadian potatoes, milk, cream, butter, and eggs. Since these goods could not penetrate further into the interior because of their high ratio of volume to value or due to the danger of spoilage, inland producers remained insulated from imports. Moreover, Southern farmers who engaged in the production of cotton (other than the long staple variety, which was imported and received a generous increase in tariff protection under the 1930 Act) were oriented toward the export market. Northern farmers close to the Canadian border had reason to favor protection to a much greater extent than their counterparts in the Interior or the South.

There existed equally sharp divisions within manufacturing. The pressure for protection was greatest in light industry concentrating in the batch production of goods tailored to market. Heavy industry and manufacturers of standardized products had mechanized their operations and largely held their own against foreign competition. But labor-intensive industries dominated by small-scale firms experienced growing competition from abroad. In the bottle-making industry, producers of "fancy ware" such as perfume and toilet water bottles suffered from an increasing volume of French imports. Manufacturers of watches faced Swiss competition and producers of jewelry complained of German imports. Eastern glove manufacturers experienced difficulty in matching the prices of foreign goods. The New England shoe industry experienced competition from Czechoslovak producers. Some producers were sheltered by relatively generous Fordney-McCumber duties. But, for most, foreign trends such as the desperate attempts of English mills to hold onto market share exacerbated their woes. Still, only a minority of American industries were seriously injured by competition from foreign goods.

In opposition stood heavy industries producing standardized products, particularly segments which relied on the assembly line, mass production, the latest technology and the multi-divisional form. By the turn of the century, the United States had gained a competitive advantage in many of the industries of the Second Industrial Revolution, automobiles being a prime example. In 1929 motor cars and parts comprised 10 percent of total U.S. merchandise exports, while imports were negligible due only partially to a modicum of tariff protection. Given the importance of export sales and the anticipated impact of a tariff on production costs, the automobile producers, led by Henry Ford, made clear their opposition to the tariff bill. The same was true of producers of farm machinery, iron and steel bars, sheet, rails, and metal manufactures.

The banking community had traditionally supported the protectionist system. Bankers doing business in industrial regions where firms depended on the tariff favored the maintenance of protection. But in the 1920s their support was tempered by events. World War I had transformed the United States from a debtor to a creditor nation and reoriented America's banking business abroad. Already in 1923 spokesmen for the financial community acknowledged that Europe's continued ability to service its dollar debt hinged upon foreign industries' access to American markets.

The opposite shift was evident in the attitudes of organized labor. Traditionally, labor had opposed protection for its impact on the cost of living. Those groups of workers injured by import competition were incapable of changing this policy. For half a century the AFL's position on the tariff had been one of carefully cultivated neutrality. Although individual unions might lobby for protection against imported goods or for lower duties on raw materials, the Federation's policy was to take no position on the issue. In 1930 it went only so far as to accede to individual unions' requests for legislative assistance. However, at the November 1928 AFL convention the first official caucus of pro-tariff unions was formed. This "Wage Earners Protective Conference" represented 8 or 9 percent of the Federation's membership, the leading participants including the photo-engravers, wallpaper craftsmen, glass bottle blowers, and potters. Clearly, labor's traditional opposition to protection was attenuated by the success of pro-tariff unions in organizing to lobby for a change in policy.

In sum, the situation in 1930 appeared as follows. Farmers along the Canadian border and Eastern seaboard desired higher protection but, comprising only a minority of American agriculture, found it difficult to obtain alone. Light industries producing goods tailored to market also desired protection but similarly comprised only a portion of American manufacturing. In principle, neither group favored protection for the other, but each was willing to support the claims of its counterpart in return for participation in the coalition. While agriculture received generous protection under the final Smoot-Hawley bill, so did light industry producing goods tailored to market. . . .

This interpretation has advantages over the view of Smoot-Hawley that divides the American economy into monolithic agricultural and industrial blocs. It explains why sections of the industrial Midwest and East should have complained about the height of agricultural tariffs, and why certain agrarian interests, notably in the South, should have complained of industrial protection. It is consistent also with the observed alliance of industrial and agricultural protectionists and explains why the Smoot-Hawley Tariff, originally conceived as agricultural relief, evolved into a bill extending protection to portions of both industry and agriculture. It is consistent with Schattschneider's emphasis on log-rolling aspects of the legislative process, but rather than characterizing log-rolling as entirely general suggests that "reciprocal noninterference" should have favored border agriculture and light industry. It is consistent with the notion that Hoover lost control of the legislative process by permitting the debate to extend beyond the question of agricultural relief and with the inference that Hoover failed to take forceful action on the grounds that he saw the small businesses which dominated light industry as his constituency, but not necessarily with the opinion of Senator Borah that a narrowly agricultural tariff could have passed in 1929 had Hoover taken the bit in his teeth. National leadership, while important in both Gerschenkron's and this paper's application of the model, plays opposite roles in the two instances, since Bismarck favored widespread protection and played a prominent role in obtaining it, while Hoover personally opposed blanket protection but failed to effectively guide the legislative process. Finally, by invoking the rise of the trade association, the model can be used to explain how diverse agricultural and industrial interests succeeded in influencing the legislative process.

The model can be elaborated in various directions. One extension would introduce the long history of protectionism in the United States and the country's habit of neglecting the impact of its economic policies on the rest of the world. Another would build on the tendency of the Depression to undermine confidence in the self-equilibrating nature of the market. In many countries, the depth of the Depression provided a rationale for the extension of economic planning. In Britain, for example, Keynes went so far for a time as to argue for central planning along Soviet lines. In the United States this desire for intervention and control was most clearly manifest in the New Deal, but the same tendencies contributed to the pressure for tariff protection in 1930. . . .

CONCLUSION

. . . Economic histories view the Great Depression and the Smoot-Hawley Tariff as inextricably bound up with one another. They assign a central role to the Depression in explaining the passage of the 1930 Tariff Act and at the same time emphasize the role of the tariff in the singular depth and long duration of the slump. This paper has reexamined the historical evidence on both points. It is not hard to identify relationships linking the tariff to the Depression and vice versa. But the evidence examined here suggests that previous accounts have conveyed what is at best an incomplete and at worst a misleading impression of the mechanisms at work. It is clear that the severity of the initial business cycle downturn lent additional impetus to the campaign for protection. But it is equally clear that the impact of the downturn on the movement for protection worked through different channels than typically posited. Rather than simply strengthening the hand of a Republican Executive predisposed toward protection, or increasing the burden borne by a depressed agricultural sector which had long been agitating for tariff protection, the uneven impact of the Depression occasioned the birth of a protectionist coalition comprised of producers particularly hard hit by import competition: border agriculture and small-scale industry engaged in the production of specialty goods. That coalition was able to obtain for its members substantial increases in levels of tariff protection because of an unusual conjuncture of distinct if related developments including reforms of Congressional procedure, the rise of trade associations and the growth of interventionist sentiment. The experience of Smoot-Hawley documents how macroeconomic distress accompanied by import penetration gives rise to protectionist pressure, but does so only once the analysis transcends the model of monolithic agricultural and industrial blocs. . . .

NOTE

1. The first quote is from Bauer et al. [1972: 25], the second from Pastor [1980: 70].

REFERENCES

Bauer, Raymond, Ithiel de Sola Pool, and L.A. Dexter. 1972. *American Business and Public Policy.* Chicago: Aldine-Atherton.

Gerschenkron, Alexander. 1943. *Bread and Democracy in Germany.* University of California Press.

Pastor, Robert A. 1980. *Congress and the Politics of U.S. Foreign Economic Policy, 1929–1976.* University of California Press.

Schattschneider, E.E. 1935. *Politics, Pressures and the Tariff.* Prentice-Hall.

19

Trade Policy, Economic Interests, and Party Politics in a Developing Country: The Political Economy of CAFTA-DR

RAYMOND HICKS, HELEN V. MILNER, AND DUSTIN TINGLEY

In 2004, the United States, five Central American nations, and the Dominican Republic signed a preferential trade agreement, usually known as CAFTA-DR (Central American–Dominican Republic Free Trade Agreement). In Costa Rica, the country's accession to the agreement was put to a national referendum. Raymond Hicks, Helen V. Milner, and Dustin Tingley examine voting patterns on the referendum in order to understand the sources of support for, and opposition to, trade liberalization in this context. They find that specific economic interests have a powerful impact, but they also find that partisan political institutions play a major role as well.

In October 2007, Costa Rica held the first public referendum on a trade agreement in a developing country to decide the fate of the Central American-Dominican Republic Free Trade Agreement (CAFTA-DR), the agreement signed in 2004 between the five Central American Common Market countries (Costa Rica, El Salvador, Guatemala, Honduras, and Nicaragua), the Dominican Republic, and the United States. The referendum passed by a razor-thin margin, 51.56–48.44%, with a turnout of 59.2% of the eligible population. Unlike portrayals of the legislative vote on CAFTA-DR in the United States, the issue was highly salient and politicized in Costa Rica.

Existing arguments about individual trade policy preferences focus largely on public opinion surveys, elections with trade as one key issue, or legislative voting, all of which are indirect measures of public preferences. In none of these cases does the public directly control the outcome of a trade policy initiative. In this referendum, voters decided whether Costa Rica would accept or reject the trade agreement. The referendum provides a unique opportunity to consider the role of domestic politics in shaping how voters form preferences over trade policy.

There exist three contrasting models of trade policy preference formation. Bottom-up models assume that individuals form preferences based on their particular circumstances. A common type of bottom-up model in international and comparative political economy assumes that voters calculate the economic consequences of policy and vote based on the personal economic consequences of a policy change. In contrast, more recent research on individual preferences suggests that voters respond to issues like CAFTA-DR based upon their views on non-economic factors, like socialization, ethnocentrism, or nationalism. These bottom-up models leave little room for political actors to effect policy changes, and the more recent work argues that economic factors do not play an important role in shaping individual preferences. Top-down approaches, however, suggest that voters are often uncertain about their preferences or can be swayed by political elites who, because of their public position, resources, and information, have the capacity to influence public opinion. Of course, both processes may occur simultaneously, which may be why disentangling elite and public influence is so difficult.

We utilize new data and a variety of methods to investigate who supported and opposed CAFTA-DR. We contrast predictions made by the two main economic models of trade policy preferences and show that specific factor models provide a much better fit than do Stolper-Samuelson ones. Controlling for a variety of different economic preferences, we argue that politics, especially party politics, played a substantial role in affecting how the public voted in the referendum. We show that parties use knowledge about the distributive consequences of policy to frame the debate for different audiences. We thus combine an explanation focusing on the trade policy preferences of the public (so-called bottom-up approaches) with a top-down model that elites (here, government leaders and parties) can shape public preferences. While voters are likely to act on their economic self-interest, there is room for politicians to influence how voters see agreements affecting their economic interests. Economic agreements such as CAFTA-DR are complex and have varying distributional consequences. Politicians can emphasize different consequences of policy to different audiences to build, or erode, support for the agreement. Thus, we argue that both bottom-up and top-down forces shape policy preferences.

Our paper first provides background on the CAFTA-DR agreement. Second, we discuss bottom-up and top-down arguments in detail. We examine the two central models of trade policy preferences derived from economic theory, contrasting predictions made by the Heckscher-Ohlin (HO) and Stolper-Samuelson (SS) models of trade to those made by the specific factor model of Ricardo-Viner (RV). The specific factor model predicts that export-oriented industries are more likely to support CAFTA-DR. We then formulate hypotheses about voter preferences for CAFTA-DR and the role of political elites, using theories about the ways parties use cues and frames. Many political actors can cue and frame messages for voters, but they may only be successful if they are well organized enough to present their message effectively and broadly. Finally, we combine the top-down and bottom-up approaches to focus on *how* political elites will frame their message.

We examine our hypotheses using three different sources of data. Initially, we quantitatively test our hypotheses about support and opposition to CAFTA-DR in Costa Rica using district-level referendum vote returns. Controlling for economic characteristics at the lowest level of geographic aggregation possible, we show how well-organized parties are better able to use cueing and framing to influence voters than less-organized parties. The differential impact of the main parties on the referendum results, given their different organizational capacities for influence, is a key factor in identifying their effects. Next, we present individual-level survey analyses, which are less susceptible to the ecological inference problem. Finally, qualitative evidence about how political parties and other social actors framed their message suggests support for the causal mechanisms we hypothesize. Identifying the causal effects of political parties is difficult, and thus, we draw on a variety of evidence including fixed-effects models to control for omitted variables and survey evidence. We provide the most systematic analysis to date of this unique window into mass politics around trade policy. Our inferences extend beyond Costa Rica, especially since a wave of developing nations has undergone both democratization and trade liberalization since the 1980s.

CAFTA-DR BACKGROUND

In 2002, President Bush received Congressional approval to begin trade negotiations with five Central American countries (Costa Rica, El Salvador, Guatemala, Honduras, and Nicaragua; the Dominican Republic joined the negotiations in 2004). Of the countries involved in CAFTA-DR, the United States is by far Costa Rica's largest trading partner, as 45% of Costa Rican exports go to the United States and 45% of imports are from the United States. In contrast, about 16% of Costa Rican exports go to, and less than 5% of imports are from, Central America. Also, the investment, labor, intellectual property rights, and telecommunications provisions of the agreement—to which its critics were most vociferously opposed—were included at the insistence of the United States. Thus, in Costa Rican eyes, CAFTA-DR was largely an agreement with the capital-abundant United States (the supplementary materials have more detail on CAFTA-DR's effect on trade restrictions between Costa Rica and the United States).

Negotiations began in 2003 under President Abel Pacheco of the Social Christian Unity Party (PUSC), but involved representatives from the major political parties and various business and civil society interests in Costa Rica. This followed the 2002 elections, which did not feature debates about the trade agreement. The agreement was signed in August 2004. By the end of 2005, Costa Rica was the only country that had not ratified it. By 2006, new presidential elections were in full swing, and CAFTA-DR became an issue in the presidential campaign. Oscar Arias of the left-leaning National Liberation Party (PLN), with traditional mass support from poorer sections of Costa Rican society, vigorously supported the agreement, arguing that CAFTA-DR was necessary for Costa Rica's future economic development, while Otton Solís of the relatively new Citizens' Action Party (PAC) opposed it, calling for a complete renegotiation of the agreement. Thus, even prior to the 2007 CAFTA-DR referendum, parties competed for voters by taking different positions on

CAFTA-DR. But the 2006 election was about more than just CAFTA-DR. The personalities and histories of the two presidential contenders were important. Arias of the PLN had been president before and had to have the constitution changed so that he could run again. This change was highly contested. It appears to help explain why the 2006 presidential election turned out so close (only 18,000 votes difference). And it also is related to the fact that wide differences existed in the PLN and PAC's presidential vote share versus their legislative vote shares. Solis of the newly formed PAC got 14.5% more of the vote than did his legislative party. Voters were focused on more than just CAFTA-DR in this election.

Arias barely won the 2006 presidential election; and his party alone did not have enough votes to control the legislative assembly. Opponents of CAFTA-DR delayed the vote on the agreement. Because there was a deadline for its ratification, the opponents hoped to kill the agreement this way. But amid this contestation, the Costa Rican Supreme Court announced that a public referendum might be possible. The PLN government chose this route to avoid the delaying tactics and began an intense campaign for public support. The PAC maintained its opposition. The PAC collected many different groups under its umbrella, those opposing Arias' second term, those opposed to CAFTA-DR, those opposed to privatization of major government-run industries (such as electricity and telecommunications), and those opposed to general neoliberal policies such as fiscal austerity. The PAC then had a hard time mobilizing a united front against CAFTA-DR. Because "significant CAFTA-DR opponents did not necessarily share a common agenda, their demands were seldom expressed in a unitary action platform." Nevertheless, the nationwide referendum was held on October 7, 2007 and passed with just 51.56% of the vote. Combining the 2007 referendum results with election data and surveys about the agreement *before* the referendum provides the most direct data for determining how voters form preferences over trade policy.

THEORIES ABOUT TRADE PREFERENCES: BOTTOM-UP AND TOP-DOWN

Bottom-Up Preferences: Stolper-Samuelson versus Ricardo-Viner

Bottom-up preference models assume that there are distributive consequences of trade policy and the public votes based on their perception of how it will affect them, their family, or, more broadly, their country. Standard arguments about the role of economic interests in determining trade policy preferences tend to draw on the Heckscher-Ohlin (HO) theorem and its related Stolper-Samuelson (SS) one. The theorems suggest that owners of relatively scarce factors lose from trade liberalization, whereas owners of abundant factors gain. The United States is the primary trade partner of Costa Rica, and compared to the United States, Costa Rica is labor-abundant and capital-scarce. Costa Rica's GDP per capita in constant dollars was only 12% that of the United

States in 2005 ($37,084 for the United States compared to $4,504 for Costa Rica), and while 87% of the US population aged 25–34 have a high school diploma, in Costa Rica, only 57% of the Costa Rican population aged 20–29 had at least a 9th grade education (as of 2000). Given these relative endowments, the Stolper-Samuelson theorem predicts that trade liberalization will lead to increasing returns to unskilled labor and decreasing returns to capital (especially high-skilled, human capital) in Costa Rica. Thus, the SS model predicts high-skilled labor will oppose the agreement and low-skilled workers will support it.

Recent models and data suggest that the SS view of trade and its distributional consequences may not be applicable in developing countries. Many developing countries that have liberalized their trade have experienced gains for higher-skilled workers and losses for lower-skilled ones. . . . The main alternative specification of bottom-up trade preferences comes from the so-called Ricardo-Viner (RV) model. This model assumes that factors of production may not be mobile, hence its name as the specific factor model. One factor of production at least is usually assumed to be tied to an industry, implying that its returns depend on that industry's fortunes. For factors that are specific to the export-oriented sector(s), trade liberalization produces gains and thus they should favor it. For factors that are specific to the import-competing industries, they should face losses from trade liberalization and hence oppose it. The preferences of more mobile factors will depend on their consumption patterns, which in developing countries are often weighted more toward import-competing ones. Based on the RV model, we expect export-oriented sectors to benefit most from CAFTA-DR and thus be strong supporters. These industries tend to also employ the most high-skilled workers.

Indeed, scholars have claimed that exports in Costa Rica benefit higher-skill sectors. Costa Rica's exports to the United States have shifted in recent years so that technology-intensive products are more important than either labor-intensive or primary goods. This has increased the demand for high-skill jobs and their wages. With CAFTA-DR securing the access of these exports to the United States, its impact is likely to be further export growth and increasing high-skill wages. If RV models are correct, one would expect export-oriented sectors to benefit most from CAFTA-DR and thus be strong supporters. These industries tend to also employ the most high-skilled workers. Hence, the RV model leads to contrary predictions from the SS model. In the next section, we discuss top-down models and then describe how the two can be combined.

Top-Down Influences: Political Actors and Social Elites

Even if Costa Rican voters based their decisions on economic self-interest, there is still room for political elites to influence voters. Like most trade agreements, CAFTA-DR, which was over 340 pages not including the tariff schedules, was complex and could have many different effects. Uncertainty about these effects opens up opportunities for elite influence.

We focus on political elites, namely parties and the government, as the actors most able to cue and frame debates. This is not to say that social actors were unimportant. As others have stressed, social actors (e.g., labor unions, student and academic groups, religious organizations) played a very active role in the debate. The anti-CAFTA-DR, or "No," campaign depended largely on social actors to deliver its message. The political party opposed to the agreement, the PAC, let this grassroots social movement play the primary role against it. While some claim that the behind-the-scenes approach of the PAC and divisions within the PLN meant that parties played little role in the referendum campaign, our conclusions differ. The PAC played a lesser role because it was a new party with limited organizational capacity and embraced many groups with different concerns. The well-established PLN and its governmental elites played a more significant role. In our empirical analysis, we estimate the effects of parties controlling for economic variables that could influence preferences. Our qualitative section analyzes mechanisms of cueing, framing, and organizational differences.

The literature on party influence identifies a number of mechanisms that parties and other elites use to shape voters' preferences. Key concepts are cueing and framing. With *cueing*, parties provide shortcuts to party members as to how to vote. Cues serve a heuristic role, giving voters information about how to vote on a complex policy choice, such as a referendum. Such cueing is likely to be important because of the complexity of the CAFTA-DR agreement, where the economic "winners" and "losers" might not be clearly defined.

Framing refers to the way in which a message is presented, with certain features emphasized over others, which causes voters to evaluate the merits of the choice in specific ways. For the CAFTA-DR referendum, framing implies that political elites should emphasize particular aspects of the lengthy agreement in order to induce public support or opposition, given what they knew about their constituents' values. Parties should also cast a policy proposal as being close to the position of the median voter, while casting the reversion point (i.e., a rejection of the referendum) as representing an extreme position. To employ both cueing and framing, parties should (i) publicize their position on the policy; (ii) frame the policy as being efficiency enhancing (better for the country as a whole) and its rejection as costly for the country, and (iii) frame the policy in particular ways tailored to appeal to particular groups of people. Opposing parties are expected to argue the opposite of ii, while still tailoring their messages. Of course, there are other goals that cueing and framing might be used for, such as appeals for equality or stability. Both cueing and framing emphasize an information-based model of trade preference formation. Specifically, we argue that politicians understand the economic distributive consequences of policy and tailor their messages accordingly. When speaking to audiences from export-oriented regions, pro-CAFTA-DR elites will emphasize the job benefits of voting for CAFTA-DR and the job costs of voting against CAFTA-DR. When speaking to audiences from import-competing areas, whose jobs may be lost because of CAFTA-DR, pro-CAFTA-DR elites will emphasize the overall benefits to the country rather than job-related benefits.

In addition, the organizational strength of political parties may influence how well they can affect voters. First, better organized groups might be more effective in cueing and framing since they can present such messages more broadly and professionally. Second, national parties with extensive geographic coverage can pressure local party officials who can then directly cue and frame the issues to their constituents. Third, parties with extensive national organizations may be able to reach and mobilize undecided voters, who are often the least informed. The effectiveness of cueing and framing should be a function of the organizational strengths of parties. Our discussion of bottom-up and top-down sources of preferences leads to four main hypotheses.

Bottom-Up Economic Theories

> **Hypothesis 1 (SS model):** *Voters with lower-skill levels should be more likely to support CAFTA-DR than high-skill voters.*
>
> **Hypothesis 1b (RV model):** *Voters in export-oriented industries should be most likely to support CAFTA-DR.*

Top-Down Political Theories

> **Hypothesis 2 (party differences):** *Controlling for economic factors, the more a party supports (opposes) CAFTA-DR, the more likely voters for that party will be to support (oppose) CAFTA-DR.*
>
> **Hypothesis 3 (organizational power of parties):** *Controlling for economic factors, the more organized PLN will be better able to get their message out and will therefore have a larger influence on voter preferences than less well-organized parties like the PAC.*

EMPIRICAL EVIDENCE

We use several new data sets and qualitative information to test our hypotheses. These data are unique in that the referendum involved citizens making choices directly on trade policy. Numerous problems remain with establishing the causal influence of economic and political variables on the public, including measurement error and omitted variable bias that can result in endogeneity. We employ a number of strategies to deal with these problems, including using fixed effects to deal with endogeneity and omitted variables, survey analysis of individuals, and qualitative evidence on the role of parties. None of these methods alone is perfect, but together they suggest that political elites and parties had an important influence on public preferences for CAFTA-DR. We first present results based on district-level referendum returns, then discuss evidence from public opinion surveys in order to address concerns about ecological inference problems, and finally discuss qualitative information that explores the causal story in our hypotheses.

District-Level Referendum Results

What impact did economically derived and politically motivated preferences have on voting for the CAFTA-DR referendum? Using referendum results for 473 Costa Rican administrative districts in 2007, we calculated the percentage of votes cast in favor of CAFTA-DR (*pero_yes*) for each district, which forms our dependent variable for this section. Costa Rica has 7 provinces divided into 81 cantons and 473 administrative districts, which are further subdivided into 1955 electoral districts, or polling places for voters. We attempted to collect all data at the most disaggregated level possible, and we conduct analyses at the administrative and electoral district levels in order to reduce any ecological inference problems. To examine our hypotheses, we link these referendum results to data collected from the 2000 Costa Rican census and electoral data from the 2006 legislative elections to see whether district-level referendum vote returns in 2007 correlate with district-level political and demographic characteristics. We examine how voting in the 2007 referendum was affected by a party's vote share in earlier elections to explore the role of top-down political pressures.

Our approach to explaining referendum voting as a function of previous party voting and economic variables is very similar to research on referendums in other contexts. Research on referendums within Europe, for example, used party returns in the last election as well as measures of cleavages, which include economic characteristics such as percentage of primary sector workers, occupational skill level, and education level.

ECONOMIC VARIABLES. Our first two hypotheses predict that individuals form preferences about trade policy based on their economic interests. For SS models, we expect that low-skill voters should favor, and high-skill ones oppose, CAFTA-DR. We map district-level census occupational data onto a proxy measure for skill levels. Existing work classifies particular industries onto an "International Social Economic Index" (ISEI), which measures "the attributes of occupations that convert a person's education into income" (Ganzeboom, de Graaf and Treiman 1992: 212). We scored each occupational category according to the ISEI, with higher scores having higher-skill levels. Next, we calculated the *percentage* of workers in each district that fell into a "low" ISEI occupation, defined as occupations below the national mean minus one standard deviation. This ISEI-based measure (*LowSocEcon%*) is our main economic independent variable; it measures the skill level of each district.

To test alternative theoretical expectations derived from the RV model, we constructed a variable that identifies the most export-oriented sectors; these industries are the largest Costa Rican exporters and correspond to relatively high-skill manufacturing industries. Then using our census employment data, we calculated district-level employment in these export-oriented manufacturing industries as a percentage of total employment, *Export %*, Because there is no trade data at the district level for constructing a district-level measure of exports, this measure is the best one available. This variable should positively influence support for CAFTA-DR since groups in export-oriented industries should be most supportive of trade.

To get closer to a district-level measure, we also identified the location of every district that had a free trade zone business designation, using data from resources provided by Costa Rica's investment promotion agency (CIN-DE). This variable (*FTZ*) also measures the presence of export-oriented industries and should positively influence CAFTA-DR voting in an RV model. But these zones are not the only places that contain industries that export in Costa Rica, so this measure is also partial; using both measures of export orientation should provide more confidence in our results.

We thus try to control for the most important bottom-up influences on trade preferences at the district level, which is critical for our identification of top-down political effects. Our data enable the most systematic accounting for economic effects to date in a developing country analysis of trade preferences. These controls are all at the district level and hence face ecological inference problems. Our analysis assumes that these variables tap sociotropic concerns, but also reflect on average individual-level considerations. For example, an individual living in a district with an FTZ is more likely affected by the FTZ than an individual living in a district without an FTZ. Controlling for the most prominent factors that might generate bottom-up support for CAFTA-DR means that our analysis of the role of parties is much less likely to suffer from omitted economic variables.

We include as control variables a canton-level measure of the percent of the workforce that was unemployed, *% Unempl*, a district-level measure of employment in the public sector, *PubEmpl%*, as interviews with several country experts suggested public versus private sector divisions, and an additional measure of development as the percentage of households with a television, *TV%*.

Table 1 presents models regressing the percentage of pro-CAFTA-DR votes (*perc_yes*) in the 2007 referendum on economic and political variables. Models 1 and 3 do not include canton-level fixed effects, whereas the remaining models include fixed effects in order to deal with potential omitted variables. Models 1–4 use the larger administrative district unit of analysis; models 5, 6, and 7 show that at the more disaggregated level of the electoral district, we find similar results. We estimate models using a complete battery of economic models. Because unemployment data are only available at the canton level, it cannot be included in the fixed-effects models. Model 7 uses district-level fixed effects and so none of our controls can be used.

The use of canton-level fixed effects is important. There are roughly 5–6 districts per canton. Using fixed effects helps us deal with any endogeneity caused by potential omitted variables. If individual preferences about trade, rather than a party's cueing and framing, lead voters to choose a party that

TABLE 1 Percent of Referendum Votes Pro-CAFTA-DR

	Model 1	Model 2	Model 3	Model 4	Model 5	Model 6	Model 7
%PLN06	0.38 (0.11)**	0.28 (0.08)**			0.33 (0.05)**		0.33 (0.05)**
%PAC06	−0.04 (0.15)	−0.25 (0.09)**			−0.21 (0.05)**		−0.15 (0.06)**
%PUSC06	0.48 (0.17)**	0.33 (0.14)*			0.13 (0.10)*		0.00 (0.08)**
%Libert06	0.30 (0.17)*	0.20 (0.23)			0.32 (0.07)**		0.37 (0.08)**
PLN-%Change			0.11 (0.02)**	0.08 (0.03)**		0.02 (0.01)	
PAC% Change			0.00 (0.01)	−0.01 (0.01)		−0.01 (0.00)*	
PUSC-% Change			0.18 (0.05)**	0.16 (0.04)**		−0.01 (0.02)	
LIB-% Change			0.01 (0.00)**	0.01 (0.00)*		0.00 (0.00)*	
Export%	3.38 (1.21)**	1.99 (0.91)*	3.24 (1.16)**	2.37 (1.00)*	1.73 (1.22)	2.50 (1.60)	
FTZ	0.03 (0.01)*	0.02 (0.01)*	0.02 (0.01)	0.02 (0.01)*	0.02 (0.01)*	0.04 (0.01)**	
LowSocEcon%	−0.23 (0.05)**	−0.18 (0.05)**	−0.22 (0.05)**	−0.18 (0.04)**	−0.19 (0.04)**	−0.21 (0.04)**	
%Unempl	0.01 (0.00)*		0.01 (0.00)**				
%PubEmpl	−0.60 (0.11)**	−0.32 (0.10)**	−0.61 (0.12)**	−0.45 (0.10)**	−0.50 (0.11)**	−0.59 (0.13)**	
TV%	0.28 (0.05)**	0.17 (0.07)*	0.22 (0.05)**	0.12 (0.06)	0.13 (0.05)**	0.05 (0.07)	
Constant	0.13 (0.10)	0.33 (0.09)**	0.46 (0.07)**	0.58 (0.06)**	0.35 (0.05)**	0.56 (0.06)**	0.35 (0.03)**
Observations	459	459	458	458	1761	1563	1787
Level	District	District	District	District	Electoral district	Electoral district	Electoral district
Fixed effects	None	Canton	None	Canton	Canton	Canton	District
BIC	−908.97	−1254.37	−904.22	−1217.80	−2674.47	−2295.86	−3358.76
R^2	0.50	0.13	0.49	0.26	0.19	0.09	0.13
Between R^2		0.58		0.55	0.58	0.47	0.09

$p < .1$, *$p < .05$, **$p < .01$; Standard errors, clustered at canton level, in parentheses. The number of observations in the change models varies because not all parties received votes in all administrative or electoral districts. Redistricting between the 2000 census and the 2006 elections also means a few observations of districts were lost.

supports CAFTA-DR—that is, if endogeneity is present—then the problem involves a failure to include a variable that captures what creates these preferences about trade in the first place. Since we include all of the most important economic variables at the district level that might lead to this preference, there must be some other omitted variable. Since observations are at the district level, we include canton-level fixed effects to address this. These identify the influence of the explanatory variables as the district's deviations from the canton means (or district means in model 7). This controls for any variables constant at the canton level. There is no evidence that major political or economic factors vary across districts; rather provinces or cantons are the site of the most important cleavages. If there is a canton-level (or province-level) omitted variable, such as differences in "political culture" that we cannot measure, these fixed effects will capture the influence of these omitted variables. They also deal with the problem of unobserved economic variables that are constant within a canton (or province) but might be correlated with our partisan or other economic variables.

The results consistently show that the SS theorem does not fit this data, while the RV model does. The coefficient on the *LowSocEcon %* variable is consistently negative and significant. Districts with a high percentage of low-skill workers are significantly less likely to vote in favor of CAFTA-DR. Similarly, districts with a higher percentage of university-educated individuals were more supportive of CAFTA-DR (*LowSocEcon %* has a negative effect whether or not we also control for education). In contrast, the RV theory better fits the economic preferences we observe. The measures of a district's export orientation that we use are positively related to support for CAFTA-DR. Districts containing the most export-oriented industries, *Export%*, are strongly favorable to CAFTA-DR in all of our regressions. Increasing this variable by one standard deviation increases Yes votes in a district by 1–2%, an important amount given the referendum passed by only 1.5%. Districts with a free trade zone, *FTZ*, also are more supportive of CAFTA-DR. In model 2, an FTZ increases Yes votes in a district by 2%. These results support hypothesis 1b, and not 1a.

POLITICAL VARIABLES.   Do political variables explain additional variation in the referendum returns once we control for economic preferences? For our main political variables, we use electoral returns of the four main Costa Rican parties from the 2006 legislative assembly elections and presidential elections, operationalized as the percentage of the vote received by each party in each district. We also present results using the percentage change in vote share from the respective 2002 election ((2006 vote share–2002 vote share) / 2002 vote share). In the 2006 presidential elections, the two main parties were competing for voters by differentiating their stances in part on CAFTA-DR and in part on other issues such as Arias' reelection. Political elites in the PLN supported CAFTA-DR, while the PAC largely opposed it for a wide variety of reasons. Thus, it is important to include the economic control variables. Controlling for the economic reasons voters might support a party or the referendum, were political elites able to induce voters who supported them in 2006 to vote the party line on CAFTA-DR in 2007? Remember that the referendum barely passed; despite being tied or behind in the polls in late 2007, the Yes vote eked out a victory by 1.6%. Could the PLN have helped swing the vote?

If hypothesis 2 is correct, then voters supporting pro-CAFTA-DR (anti-CAFTA-DR) parties in 2006, like the PLN (the PAC), should be more likely to support (oppose) the referendum in 2007. Thus, *%PAC06* should be negatively related to the referendum, and *%PLN06* should be positively related. Also, the PLN was a well-established party that had alternated in power since democratization, while the PAC was founded only in 2001, included many disparate groups with different objections to CAFTA-DR, and was consequently not as well organized. If hypothesis 3 is correct, then voters supporting the PLN should be more likely to support the referendum. Parties—whether pro- or anti-CAFTA-DR—lacking organizational strength should have less influence on voters in 2007. Hence, the PAC vote share, *%PAC06*, should be negative but less significant and smaller in magnitude than the PLN.

The results largely support our predications. We find a positive and significant coefficient for the PLN in every model. The coefficient for the PAC was negative but insignificant in all but models 2, 5, 6, and 7 where it was negative and significant. This evidence is partially supportive of hypotheses 2 and 3: these parties should have opposite influences on voters, but the PLN should have a greater influence due to its stronger organizational ability. In models 5 and 7, the PAC coefficient is half the size of the PLN. In model 2, the marginal effects of the PAC are similar in size to the PLN, and their effects overall are quite different since the mean and variance of the PAC and PLN variables are so different. The PLN has a much greater effect with a coefficient of the same size since its mean is much larger. . . . The distribution of the PAC and PLN variables amplifies the differences between the effect of the PLN and the PAC. At the mean value of PLN vote share, the Yes vote would increase by 11%, while at the mean vote share of the PAC, the Yes vote would decline by about 6%. Since the difference between the Yes and No share in the referendum was only 3%, the difference between the PLN and the PAC effect represents the difference between the referendum succeeding or failing. . . .

Models that use changes in vote share between 2002 and 2006 show similar results. Models 3, 4, and 6 display these results using vote changes as a percentage of the 2002 vote for each party. These models in effect explore the changes in party vote share before the treatment (i.e., CAFTA-DR is introduced) and after it has been introduced (i.e., by 2006). Conditional on the controls and fixed effects, these models of vote changes show a strong influence of the PLN but not the PAC. We also collected election return data at a level lower than available for economic data: the electoral district. These electoral districts are within the 473 administrative districts and hence are less aggregated. We present these results in models 5, 6, and 7 and include either the economic variables and canton fixed effects or administrative district fixed effects. Our results show an important influence of the PLN, but not the PAC. . . .

The potential for omitted variable bias is important. Our fixed-effects strategy gives us more confidence in our results. In particular, the relationship between economic or social characteristics and party affiliation could bias our estimate of partisan effects if there is an omitted variable that is also correlated with partisanship and voting. For example, if we do not control for our skill variable, the effects of the PAC become much larger. With canton fixed effects if this variable is constant within a canton, then such omitted variables are controlled for, as well as variables that vary at higher geographic levels like provinces, which capture different government administrative regions. While there could always be omitted variables that vary at the district level, our comprehensive collection of variables at the district level—suggested by theory to be important—helps to guard against this possibility within our fixed-effects specifications. Concerns about our results should be predicated on claims about specific omitted variables that vary at the district level and not the canton level. The fixed effects are also likely to pick up any cultural variation that others suggest might influence trade policy preferences (such as ethnocentrism). The fact that our economic variables remain substantively important and significant suggests, as others have, that economic explanations should not be dismissed.

A final concern is that we make inferences about individuals through aggregated data, known as an *ecological inference* problem. To increase confidence in our results, we do two things. First, . . . we estimate the percentage of PLN voters in the 2006 election who voted Yes on the referendum We find that about 75% of PLN voters voted Yes compared to only 34% of non-PLN voters.

Second, we analyzed individual-level survey data from the Universidad de Costa Rica. . . . Individual-level survey data does not face an ecological inference problem. Several results stand out. Results using income or education as skill proxies were not supportive of SS predictions. The poor fit of the education measure suggests some pause in accepting socialization based accounts of preference formation. Unfortunately the surveys did not contain industry-level affiliations or other cultural variables, which are uncommon even in many U.S. surveys.

Lacking detailed industry membership, we test the RV predictions by comparing support by individuals in districts with free trade zones and those without. Using data from the 2008 Latin American Public Opinion Project (LAPOP) surveys, which included district-level indicators (the UCR data had no geographic information on respondents), we merged in the FTZ data. Individuals in districts with an FTZ were significantly more likely to be CAFTA-DR supporters. For example, in the 2008 survey, individuals were asked how they voted on CAFTA-DR. In districts with an FTZ, 73% said they had compared to 61% in districts without an FTZ ($t = 1.8$). We also find a strong influence of parties across the surveys. . . . In sum, individual-level data support our claims that economic motivations described by RV and party politics were important explanatory factors in the CAFTA-DR referendum vote. . . .

Qualitative Evidence

Qualitative evidence shows that political parties and elites, especially from the PLN, had substantial organizational power, enabling them to mobilize voters and frame their message to different audiences. This organizational ability was a key difference between the PLN and PAC. The PLN had been one of two major parties since the 1950s, while the PAC was a new party. These features of parties help explain the effects captured in our quantitative section. We first discuss the organizational capacity of the PLN and its ability to engage in targeted framing strategies and then contrast it with the PAC. We also discuss the salience of economic arguments, showing their importance. Appeals to cultural factors, like ethnocentrism, were present but played only a small role.

PARTY ORGANIZATION.   Well-organized parties can reach and mobilize voters, as well as help frame the considerations voters use in evaluating policies. Key planks of the Yes campaign's strategy were the formalized involvement of the PLN and a mass media campaign. This reflected an appreciation of the importance that an organized political party can play. The importance of organizational abilities could be most salient in rural areas where voters are least informed, dispersed, and harder to reach. While both the pro- and anti-CAFTA-DR campaigns were active in urban areas, the pro-CAFTA-DR campaign was more active in rural areas. Indeed, scholars have remarked on the extensive and developed organization of the PLN throughout the country. The pro-campaign led by the PLN set up 50 "casas del sí" to serve as informational centers in rural areas. The PLN organized a massive operation to bus voters to polling places, using over 20,000 vehicles, especially in rural areas. Turning to local party officials, those most likely to have a local impact, during legislative recesses in May and September 2007, 25 PLN deputies promised to return to their regions to campaign for a Yes vote on CAFTA-DR and to designate local leaders who would act as "multipliers" to get out Yes votes. Even direct pressure on canton-level mayors was suggested. The PLN's organizational abilities allowed them to reach voters, which as we discuss next allowed them to deploy cueing and framing strategies to a greater variety of potential voters.

PARTY CUEING/FRAMING.   With greater organizational abilities, the PLN was able to target appeals tailored to different economic groups through cueing and framing. The PLN government, led by Arias, provided clear cues to supporters by encouraging CAFTA-DR's adoption and tailoring their message of support to different audiences. The Alianza Ciudadana por el Sí, an umbrella campaign whose executive committee included PLN, PUSC, and Partido Unión Nacional members, produced different materials for different audiences. In sum, the Yes side was aware of voter differences and tailored information accordingly.

Examples of these tailored appeals drew on the type of RV preferences we observed in the quantitative section. Pro-CAFTA-DR rallies were held at particular industrial parks, and messages were tailored to these populations, often stressing the role of DFI in providing their job. At the opening of the Cartago Industrial Park, Arias stressed the wealth-generating effects of CAFTA-DR, famously stating "que vienen en bicicleta, con el TLC vendrán en motocicleta BMW, y los que vienen en un Hyundai, vendrán en un Mercedes Benz".[1] At the same time, Arias stressed the potential negative consequences of not passing the referendum, arguing that people would have more difficulty finding a job if CAFTA-DR failed to pass.

When Arias campaigned in rural areas, which some observers argue was key in deciding CAFTA-DR, Arias tried to reassure agricultural workers about their jobs. He stressed that the exporting industries would benefit from the agreement, supporting not only the Ricardo-Viner model, but our own attempt to combine top-down and bottom-up preferences, given the substantial uncertainty faced by agricultural sectors. Arias also underlined during his rural tour the job creation CAFTA-DR would provide to the country as a whole and the beneficial effect the trade agreement would have on consumer prices. Appealing directly to consumers, Arias said that CAFTA-DR would lower prices and expand selection of consumer goods. The PLN also emphasized that CAFTA-DR would not reduce social spending.

More broadly, the activities of the PLN were consistent with previous work suggesting that influential parties will also cue and frame referenda efforts as in the interests of the median voter, while emphasizing the negative effects of rejecting the agreement and portraying opponents as extreme. The Arias government and many in the PLN repeatedly argued that rejecting CAFTA-DR would lead to negative consequences for the country because of its deleterious effects on exports and DFI in Costa Rica. In a television interview in late September, President Arias rejected the demands of some actors on the No side for a renegotiation of the agreement, stating that it would be impossible, "an opium dream," thus framing the referendum as a take-it-or-leave-it opportunity for a trade agreement with the United States and hence the high costs of rejecting the agreement. Pro-CAFTA-DR politicians reinforced the image of an extreme opposition by suggesting the No campaign was under the control of Hugo Chavez and Fidel Castro. These efforts were designed to counter the emotional appeals of activist groups opposed to CAFTA-DR, by framing the severe economic consequences of rejection.

In contrast, the PAC had very little organization, especially in the country's rural areas. Solon, head of the PAC in March 2006, recognized the important role of organization and territorial reach, saying, "We did not see with crystal

---

1. Translated as "Those that come to work by bicycle will come on a BMW motorcycle under CAFTA and those that arrive in a Hyundai will drive a Mercedes Benz" (http://laverdaddeoscararias .blogspot.com/2007/05/arias-enfatiza-campana-del-si-al-tlc-en.html).

clarity that our great weakness was in the outlying areas. . . . We lacked an organizational force and this is decisive. . . . We need to greatly improve in territorial structure" (Murillo 2006). In contrast to the PLN's transportation ability, the PAC contribution paled in comparison. Outside of urban areas, anti-CAFTA-DR flags on cars and houses, graffiti, and bumper stickers were "few and far between." Neither the PAC nor the social groups dedicated to stopping CAFTA-DR had a strong presence in rural areas. Instead, the No campaign was concentrated in urban areas and with a smaller partisan role.

In contrast to the PLN, the PAC largely relied on social groups to spread its message. These social groups were active, drew on a broad cross-section of groups, and relied on messages related to national sovereignty and Costa Rican national welfare. The role of political parties was less salient for the No side. While these social groups had an important impact on the vote, the PAC took a less active role compared to the PLN. One way to see this difference is from the survey evidence discussed previously, showing that a greater percentage of Yes voters cited political sources as influencing their votes than did No voters. An explanation of this consistent with our theory focuses on the greater organizational ability, and hence greater ability to mobilize voters and frame issues, of the PLN.

Both qualitative and quantitative evidence show that while economic self-interest influences trade policy preferences, top-down, political pressures can also shape trade policy preferences. The PLN engaged in an organized informational campaign, while the PAC played a smaller role, as it was less organized and gave voters more ambiguous cues about where they stood on trade liberalization. Overall, the PLN was a more organized party, issued a clearer cue, and framed CAFTA-DR in many of the ways scholars of political influence have suggested.

Discourse on the agreement included a heavy economic component, with appeals to both sectoral interests (as predicted by hypotheses 1a, b), but also to broader benefits such as consumer prices. Political parties tried to influence trade policy outcomes by framing the messages so they complemented the economic consequences of the policy. While social groups in the No campaign emphasized anti-Americanism or anti-capitalist sentiments, less evidence exists that voters on the Yes side (i.e., the majority of voters that passed the referendum) were compelled by cultural motivations like non-ethnocentrism "learned" preferences via an economics education or equity considerations in determinants of trade preferences. The extent to which these non-economic rationales appeal to voters in developing countries may be more limited.

CONCLUSION

The CAFTA-DR referendum in Costa Rica was the first direct public vote on a trade agreement in the developing world. It barely passed, and we think that one factor that aided passage at the end was the political cueing and framing done by the leading party, the PLN. Our micro-level study of trade policy in a developing country produces two new results. First, the economic bases of support for trade liberalization may be different than many scholars have assumed. We find little support for the standard Stolper–Samuelson model (H1a), which suggests that in developing countries, unskilled labor, which is most abundant will be more favorable toward trade. Individuals with lower levels of human capital, and districts with high concentrations of low-skilled workers, were not more likely to support CAFTA-DR. Instead, we find the economic bases of support for CAFTA-DR fit the Ricardo-Viner specific factor model of trade better. Industries with a strong orientation toward exports were more supportive of CAFTA-DR. This result may arise because globalization of the international economy means that foreign investment is now tightly linked to export industries and high-skilled workers in firms' global production chains.

Second, because of the uncertainty surrounding trade policy and the complexity of trade agreements, political elites can have an important impact on public attitudes toward trade. Political elites can use various strategies involving both communication and organizational resources to reinforce the link between voters' positions and their economic interests or to persuade voters to adopt positions that might be at odds with their economic interests. Such elite, or top-down, preference formation processes have been little studied in the political economy of trade. The role of elites might help resolve debates in the literature on the primacy of cultural or economic factors. The relative role of each depends on how elites frame the debate.

We used a variety of quantitative and qualitative data and empirical methods to bolster confidence in our results. Controlling for the most well-known economic variables, the association between previous voting for the PLN and the vote for CAFTA-DR in 2007 strongly suggests that well-organized parties can use their rhetorical and political resources to shape individuals' policy preferences. But parties are less able to convert voters to their positions when they are not well organized, as evidence about the PAC shows. An important concern is that omitted economic or cultural variables are correlated with political variables, inducing endogeneity. We have presented a wide variety of analyses to mitigate these problems, including the use of canton-level fixed effects. Unless there are specific omitted variables at the district level that can be adduced to explain both trade preferences and party identification, then these strategies should reassure readers about our claims. We have found no discussion of major political or economic factors that vary at the district level in Costa Rica, and hence, we feel that canton-level fixed effects are strong measures to rule out endogeneity. Individual survey analysis, which resolves ecological inference problems, and qualitative evidence also support our claims. Finally, while others have stressed the importance of different characteristics of individuals for their receptiveness to elite communication, we focus on the internal characteristics of parties to explain their differential success. Our work extends the identification of the conditions under which we expect political elites to be able to influence voters.

Our findings about Costa Rica have more general implications. Baker's research (2008) on Latin American countries underscores our results; he does not find much support for Stolper-Samuelson models of individual preferences, instead finding evidence of top-down political pressures on trade preferences. Our results suggest that top-down political pressures, especially from parties and their messages, have been overlooked in studies of trade policy since little data, especially cross-national, exists to analyze their effects. Finally, the politics of trade policy in developing countries are not the mirror image of those in developed countries, as models like Stolper-Samuelson would predict. Instead, the economic cleavages look similar to those in developed countries, with high-skill individuals in export-oriented sectors supporting trade and low-skill in import-competing ones opposing it. Other variables, such as cultural attitudes, appear less salient in this case where citizens were asked to vote directly on a trade policy. Political cleavages around trade and globalization generally may follow more of a specific factors (RV) logic than a Stolper-Samuelson one in the developing world.

The role of parties and political elites may be of great importance in shaping the policies of developing countries toward the world economy. In the CAFTA-DR case, the PLN's support was essential for the referendum's success. By providing clear cues and frames for voters, especially in the closing days of the referendum, the Arias government and its long-standing, well-organized party, the PLN, counterbalanced the emotional appeals of the No campaign led by social groups. Political elites in developing countries may have greater ability to shape debates and policies toward trade than previously acknowledged.

REFERENCES

Baker, Andy. 2008. *The Market and the Masses in Latin America: Policy Reform and Consumption in Liberalizing Economies.* New York: Cambridge University Press.

Ganzeboom, Harry, Paul de Graaf, and Daniel Treiman. 1992. A Standard International Socio-Economic Index of Occupational Status. *Social Science Research* 21: 1–56.

Murillo, Alvaro. 2006. PLN Pecó De Triunfalista Y El PAC Fue Muy Urbano. *La Nación,* March 13.

20

Who Wants to Globalize? Consumer Tastes and Labor Markets in a Theory of Trade Policy Beliefs

ANDY BAKER

Most analyses of the politics of trade policy focus either on particularistic spe-cial interests or on interactions among countries. Without denying the impor-tance of these factors, Andy Baker emphasizes that trade and trade policy can have powerful effects on consumers. There are a variety of such effects; one of the more interesting is that freer trade can provide lower prices to consumers, especially in poor countries. This can give consumers an interest in pressing for trade liberalization, even where producers push for protection. Baker provides a rounded account of the wide variety of interests in contention in the domestic politics of trade policy.

The "Battle of Seattle," the Cancún walkout, stubborn agricultural subsidies, violence at the Genoa G8 and the S26 Prague meetings, outrage over outsourc-ing, the annual World Social Forums: all are among the events that observers cite as evidence of a worldwide backlash against globalization. With everyone from violent anarchists to armchair protectionists voicing concerns over unemployment, wages, sweatshops, the environment, national identity, and democratic sovereignty, many consider the continued opening of global mar-kets to be imperiled. While these events and arguments receive much atten-tion, however, the largely unmentioned engine of globalization is the allure of consumption. The U.S. trade deficit with China is driven by Americans' addic-tion to cheap imports. Despite boycotts and protests over its continued expan-sion, 100 million people visit a Wal-Mart store every week. Months after French farmer José Bové tractored over a McDonald's restaurant, declaring that "the French people . . . are with us in this fight against junk food and globalization," the corporation opened its one-thousandth franchise in that country. In short, while citizens as producers and nation-state residents may complain about globalization, citizens as consumers often find it hard to resist.

Does such consumption behavior resonate in citizens' beliefs about inter-national trade? Despite the huge influence of trade on consumer options and prices, scholars of mass attitudes have largely ignored consumer tastes and demand patterns as sources of beliefs and domestic cleavages over globaliza-tion. This article develops and tests a theory of mass trade policy preferences that incorporates the heterogeneous welfare effects of labor-market outcomes, which have been the exclusive focus of scholars to date, *and* consumption behavior. I draw from the classic Heckscher-Ohlin trade theory to explain variation in mass commitments to protectionism across individuals and countries. . . .

THE HECKSCHER-OHLIN MODEL

The Heckscher-Ohlin (H-O) trade theory has dominated the literature on trade policy attitudes. These applications of the theory have used a version of the model that categorizes workers into two factors of production: skilled and unskilled labor. Countries are thus classified as skill-abundant or skill-scarce based on their supply of skill relative to other countries. Goods are skilled labor-intensive or unskilled labor-intensive based on the relative weight of factors used in their production. H-O holds that upon liberalizing trade, a country will tend to export goods whose production is intensive in its abundant factor while importing goods that are intensive in its scarce factor. Global demand for a country's abundant-factor-intensive goods increases and, as a result, so does their domestic price. In contrast, trade increases the domestic supply and thus lowers the domestic price of goods intensive in a country's scarce factor. Real wages for the abundant factor increase while those for the scarce factor decrease, so trade liberalization has important domestic income distribution consequences: it raises the relative wages of skilled workers in skill-abundant countries while lowering the relative wages of skilled workers in skill-scarce countries.

When applied to public opinion, the H-O-inspired hypothesis posits that the correlation between worker skill and support for free trade should be positive in skill-abundant countries and negative in skill-scarce countries. Extant findings on mass opinions toward trade policy partially reflect these expectations. . . . At the same time, [studies] fail to reveal the expected negative correlation between skill and pro-trade sentiment in most developing countries. They also have roundly ignored other factors of production, namely land and capital. Most importantly, this literature has tended to overlook varying demand and consumption patterns as a possible source of trade policy preferences.

NONHOMOTHETIC TASTES: CONSUMER PREFERENCES IN THE H-O FRAMEWORK

The standard H-O model and its public opinion applications assume homothetic tastes: the ratio of skilled labor-intensive goods to unskilled labor-intensive goods within the set of goods consumed is equivalent for every worker in every country. Stated differently, the share of each worker's consumption bundle that is devoted to skill-intensive goods is identical. This assumption makes the H-O results more tractable. The distributional impact of changing trade flows is assumed to occur solely through labor market shifts: changes in the supply of and demand for workers' employable assets. However, if, as is the case empirically, consumption budgets are allowed to vary—i.e., tastes are "nonhomothetic"—trade-induced price changes also produce differential welfare impacts because of varying consumer tastes.

Recall that trade liberalization raises the prices of a country's exportable goods while lowering those of its imported goods. As a result, *workers that heavily consume their country's exportable goods experience price increases for their consumption bundles relative to workers that more heavily consume imported and import-competing goods.* Stated generally, holding skill level constant, heavy consumers of goods that are intensive in their country's abundant factor undergo relative *real* wage (i.e., purchasing power) losses from trade liberalization compared to heavy consumers of the scarce-factor-intensive good. Therefore, the propensity to consume skill-intensive goods should be negatively correlated with support for free trade in skill-abundant countries and positively associated with pro-trade inclinations in skill-scarce countries.

In the empirical literature on international trade, economists have been of two minds with respect to consumer tastes. While homothetic tastes [are] a rarely relaxed assumption, studies in which demand patterns are allowed to be nonhomothetic indicate that their empirical implications can be vast. For starters, the classic and influential study of Prebisch (1950), which provided the intellectual justification for decades of import substitution in Latin America, claimed that the South's terms of trade would slowly decline with global economic growth because the South specialized in goods with lower income elasticities of demand (worldwide) than the North. A series of subsequent studies has been largely motivated by Linder's (1961) finding that high-income individuals and countries tend to consume manufactured goods at a higher rate than low-income individuals and countries. These studies have found that shared demand patterns encourage North-North (or intra-industry) trade, increasing flows by as much as 25%, while divergent consumer tastes discourage North-South (or inter-industry) trade. Most recently, the rising gap between skilled labor's and unskilled labor's wages around the world has been attributed to the fact that economic growth increases the relative demand for skill-intensive goods because wealthier citizens have consumption baskets with more skill-intensive goods.

Moreover, even beyond these pure economic results, cognitive and psychological reasons exist for why political scientists, in particular, should suspect that consumer tastes and habits are an important source of mass trade policy preferences. Citizens are well-known for being "cognitive-misers" when it comes to politics, so they often learn about policy issues when relevant information comes available as a "by-product" of normal activities. Consumption, in one form or another, is an activity that most human beings engage in nearly every day, while in even the most advanced economies only 70% of the population is actually in the labor market and far fewer work in a tradable goods sector. In short, many citizens may be more prone to consider trade as consumers than as producers. Overall, however, despite this long list of theoretical and empirical findings, scholars of trade policy coalitions and mass beliefs about globalization have almost completely ignored variation in consumer tastes as a potential source of preferences, exclusively focusing instead on employable assets.

THEORETICAL ALTERNATIVES

The trade policy attitudes literature has applied several other economic theories besides H-O. Although under different theoretical guises, one set of alternatives claims that individual skill and protectionist sentiment should be negatively correlated in *all* countries, regardless of factor endowments. Beaulieu, Benarroch, and Gaisford (2004) develop an intra-industry trade model that suggests that trade liberalization measures in recent years have been asymmetrically concentrated in skill-intensive goods; unskilled workers still face protectionist barriers to the goods they tend to produce. Gabel (1998) posits the human capital thesis, claiming that a higher stock of formal skills makes individuals more adaptable to changing labor markets. While both sets of authors do find evidence indicating a cross-national positive association between individual skill and pro-trade attitudes, their survey data come almost exclusively from developed countries, where the H-O-inspired theory has identical empirical implications.

That said, scholars using public opinion data from the developing world have reported rather limited evidence for the H-O-inspired expectation of a negative correlation between skill and pro-trade sentiment. Indeed, this parallels the surprise of many economists at the failure of Latin American and other lower-middle income countries to reduce wage inequality through trade liberalization. Economists have proposed a slew of explanations for this trend, but I consider just two in this article. First, illiterate and other poorly trained workers in developing countries, designated as *"NO-EDs,"* do not have even the minimal skills to benefit from unskilled labor-intensive exports. *NO-EDs* therefore may not have experienced the wage pull that more educated but still unskilled compatriots might have enjoyed. Second, the comparative advantage of many developing countries may no longer lie in unskilled labor at all. Half of the world's unskilled labor force resides in just five Asian nations (Bangladesh, China, India, Indonesia, and Pakistan) that have recently entered global markets, so many lower-middle and middle-income countries have seen their comparative advantages shift away from unskilled workers.

A final theoretical alternative is "new trade theory," which has rather divergent expectations from traditional trade models like H-O. In new trade theory, countries trade because they have different specializations that may not necessarily be based on variation in resource endowments. New trade theory drops H-O's assumption of constant returns to scale. Instead, the specializations a country achieves through economies of scale provide a basis from which to export, while the lack of specialization in certain areas creates a need to import. New trade theory also relaxes H-O's assumption of no transport costs, noting that international trade volumes have increased as transport costs have declined. Indeed, low transport cost, in the form of geographical proximity to the world's epicenters of production and consumption, can itself be a source of comparative advantage. . . .

DATA, MODEL, MEASUREMENT, AND HYPOTHESES

A proper test of whether any of these economic theories helps predict trade attitudes requires survey data from both high-skill and low-skill countries. This is largely because H-O and the other skill-based theories have identical observable implications in the developed world: formal skill level and protectionist sentiment should be negatively correlated. To date, however, almost all research on mass attitudes toward trade policy has been conducted with data from a single country or multiple countries in the developed world. Studies explaining trade attitudes in the developing world have also been conducted on samples of homogenous countries. . . .

To avoid the pitfalls of most previous work, I analyze the 1995–1997 *World Values Survey* (WVS), which measured trade attitudes in over 40 countries ranging in per capita income (at PPP) from US$832 in Nigeria to US$27,395 in the United States. The 41 countries in my analysis . . . include 16 that were below the worldwide median per capita income (US$4,000). The survey contains the following binary measure of trade preferences: "Do you think it is better if (1) goods made in other countries can be imported and sold here if people want to buy them, or that (0) there should be stricter limits on selling foreign goods here to protect the jobs of people in this country?" This variable, dropping "don't know" and other nonresponses, is the dependent variable in the model described and reported in this and the following section. A score of one on this *Supports Free Trade?* variable indicates backing for free trade while a score of zero indicates protectionist sentiment.

MULTILEVEL MODEL SPECIFICATION

The causal heterogeneity hypothesized above as well as the multinational nature of the dataset require a multilevel statistical model. This subsection describes the independent variables included in a series of hierarchical binary logit models of trade attitudes in 41 countries.

SKILL: MEASUREMENT AND HYPOTHESES. A central variable in the H-O model is skill at both the individual and national level, yet skill is a difficult trait to measure. Years of formal education level is often used, but education alone ignores (1) experience-based or post-schooling acquisition of skill, (2) massive domestic and international variation in schooling quality, (3) differences in achievement within equivalent education levels, and (4) the fact that not all skills acquired through formal education are market-relevant. More-over, education has also been used by political scientists to measure other concepts related to trade preferences like "cognitive mobilization" and resis-tance to nationalism, susceptibility to protectionist framing effects, exposure to teaching from a free-market perspective, and awareness of elite messages. As such, I use only the economically relevant aspects of formal education to measure skill in this article.

To do so at the individual level, I conducted for each country a factor analy-sis of formal education level, income, and occupation. . . . In every country these three variables were highly correlated and loaded on only one signifi-cant dimension. The factor scores from this dimension are the measures of *Individual Skill*, or $skill_i$, and they capture only the income- and occupation-relevant aspects of formal education.

Testing the H-O-inspired theory also requires a measure of each country's skill endowments, $skill_j$. Again, education-based measures are precarious: they require making a common and arbitrary cut-off in every country dividing skilled and unskilled labor (often at "some post-secondary education"). Exist-ing datasets of cross-national formal education are rife with extrapolation, unintuitive findings, missing data, and outliers. As such, I use 1995 per-capita GDP at PPP (logged), a variable that is much more available and more mean-ingfully captures the economically relevant aspect of skill endowments. Because the meaning of a zero value on this variable is important in an inter-active model, I center it at its 1995 international median.

To test the H-O-inspired theory, the coefficient on individual skill ($skill_i$) is allowed to vary by country and is estimated as a function of country skill ($skill_j$). That is,

$$\beta(skill_i)_j = \gamma_{(skill_i)0} + \gamma_{(skill_i)1} \bullet skill_j + u_{(skill_i)j} \tag{1}$$

The two γ coefficients can be interpreted similarly to those in an interaction model: $\gamma_{(skill_i)0}$ is the slope on individual skill when country skill equals zero (its international median), and $\gamma_{(skill_i)1}$ is akin to the interaction coefficient for individual skill × country skill. The H-O-inspired hypotheses are that $\gamma_{(skill_i)1} > 0$ and $\gamma_{(skill_i)0} = 0$. The former would indicate that individual skill is more posi-tively related to free trade support in skill-abundant countries than in skill-scarce countries. The latter would indicate that the relationship is zero in countries with the median skill level. A combination of $\gamma_{(skill_i)0} > 0$ and $\gamma_{(skill_i)1} = 0$ would be in line with the human capital and intra-industry trade theories, since it would indicate that skill is positively and equally correlated with free trade support in every country.

I control for individuals that do not cross a minimum skill threshold (respon-dents without a completed primary education) with a dummy variable for *NO-EDs*. The parameter $\gamma_{(NO=ED)}$ therefore indicates how much *NO-EDs* deviate from the level of support for free trade that their raw skill level would dictate.

If Wood is right, such that *NO-EDs* really do not benefit from any skill-related comparative advantage, this coefficient should be negative.

MEASURING CONSUMER TASTES, LAND, AND CAPITAL.   Precise measures of consumption patterns are expensive and time-consuming to collect. Because they require a sample of families to record expenditure patterns for at least a week (and often longer), household budget surveys are scant. The World Values Survey, obviously, does not contain one; indeed, no existing study of family consumption patterns is coupled with a set of attitudinal questions that queries trade policy beliefs. However, a rich research tradition . . . links consumption patterns to income, which I use as a proxy for consumer tastes.

For the purposes of this article, then, linking income with the propensity to consume skill-intensive goods is crucial yet straightforward. Within a given country, skill-intensive goods comprise a higher share of high-income consumption bundles than of low-income bundles . . . Indeed, it is a well-established, cross-national fact that wealthy individuals consume skill-intensive goods and (especially) services—like motor vehicles, computers, fashionable clothing, education, health care, insurance, entertainment—at a higher rate than poor consumers. The poor, on the other hand, consume low skill-intensive, necessity items—like food, home energy, and inexpensive clothing—at higher rates. Studies in international economics of nonhomothetic tastes invariably find income to be the primary correlate of various aspects of demand patterns. $Income_i$, then, measures differences in consumer tastes. The slope on income should also depend on country skill endowment, so the income coefficient is also estimated as a function of country skill, similar to equation 1:

$$\beta_{(income_i)j} = \gamma_{(income_i)0} + \gamma_{(income_i)1} \cdot skill_j$$
$$+ u_{(income_i)j} \qquad (2)$$

The nonhomothetic tastes hypothesis is $\gamma_{(income_i)1} < 0$, which would indicate that income is more negatively correlated with free trade support in high-skill countries than in low-skill countries.

Unlike previous scholars of trade policy attitudes, I test the impact of land and capital as factors of production. At the country level, land is the number of square kilometers of arable land while capital stock is the absolute amount of investment in U.S. dollars in 1996. The ratio of these two factor quantities (multiplied by a scale factor of 1,000,000 to ease estimation and interpretation) is the *Land Abundance$_j$* variable used in the analysis. It is also centered at its international median. Although direct ownership of land and capital is also difficult to ascertain in standard public opinion surveys, the size of one's town or city of residence serves as a viable proxy. Land is by definition abundant in rural areas, while capital (factories, machinery, roads, etc.) is abundant in urban areas. As such, *Town Size$_i$* of residence is a good measure of the degree to which a respondent's livelihood depends on land relative to capital. The coefficients for these variables are as follows:

$$
\begin{aligned}
\beta_{(Town\ Size_i)j} = {} & \gamma_{(Town\ Size_i)0} \\
& + \gamma_{(Town\ Size_i)1} \cdot Land\ Abundance_j \\
& + u_{(Town\ Size_i)j}.
\end{aligned}
\tag{3}
$$

According to the H-O-inspired model, $\gamma_{(Town\ Size_i)0} = 0$ and $\gamma_{(Town\ Size_i)1} < 0$.

OTHER INDEPENDENT VARIABLES. The models contain other variables to control for confounding factors. Because the total returns are lower, older workers may be more reluctant to adjust their lifestyle (job change, retraining, relocation) in the face of shifting labor markets. I expect respondent's Age_i to be negatively correlated with free-trade sentiment. Because of childbirth, child-rearing, and discrimination, women also face a more precarious labor market worldwide than men. $Women_i$ may, like the elderly, prefer protection from the vicissitudes of the global market. I also control for *Nationalist Sentiment_i*, which is positively correlated with skill in most countries and is probably negatively associated with support for international trade. Omitting this variable could result in an upwardly biased $\gamma_{(skill_i)0}$, although I also consider models without nationalism because it is potentially endogenous to trade attitudes.

Finally, a surprising amount of evidence from a wide variety of countries indicates that a high degree of political awareness leads to more support for trade liberalization and other market policies. This may be because highly aware citizens are more exposed to discourse from international elites comprising the pro-market "Davos Culture" and "Washington Consensus". Alternatively, they may be more exposed to relevant messages from domestic elites, which in recent years seem to have been, on balance, more favorable toward economic liberalization and integration. Regardless, *Political Interest_i* is positively correlated with skill and town size in nearly every country, so it is an important control variable. However, the nature of this relationship may vary with country characteristics, for example, if domestic elites are more pro-trade in skill-abundant countries than in skill-scarce ones. To allow for this potentially confounding interaction effect, the coefficient on political interest is estimated as a function of country skill endowments.

REMAINING SPECIFICATION DECISIONS. All individual-level variables (except age and women) are centered around their country means and divided by their country-level standard deviations, so each is expressed as the respondent's distance in standard deviations from her or his country mean (i.e., z-scores). This means that results reflect merely common tendencies in *domestic* cleavages over trade policy. Slopes for individual skill, income, town size, and political interest vary systematically with country traits; the remaining variance in cross-country slopes $(Var[u_{xj}])$ is assumed to be random and normally distributed. Slopes for variables that are not modeled as functions of level-two variables (age, gender, and nationalism) are estimated as normally distributed random coefficients, varying unsystematically across countries.

Missing data was a concern because of item nonresponse (e.g., refusal to report income) and unasked questions in some countries (e.g., interest was not asked in Pakistan). To avoid a severe loss of cases, I used multiple imputation. Finally, I used the individual-level probability weights reported with the WVS data (to correct for under- and overrepresentation of groups) as well as country-level probability weights corresponding to the inverse of each country's share of the world population. These weights make the results pertain to a cluster sample of the world population, although I also consider the robustness of findings to exclusion of these weights.

RESULTS

The hierarchical binary logit results are reported in Table 1, although the estimated variance components of the random coefficients are not shown to reduce clutter. The variables that are the primary tests of the H-O-inspired model and its extension to consumer tastes are coupled with their corresponding coefficient symbols from equations 1, 2, and 3. . . .

First, the attitudinal relevance of consumer tastes is demonstrated by the robust finding that the association between income (tendency to consume skill-intensive goods and services) and pro-trade attitudes grows increasingly negative as a country's skill endowment grows ($\gamma_{(income_j)1} < 0$). This finding is statistically significant. . . . Figure 1 demonstrates its substantive impact by plotting the predicted slopes for some exemplary countries. Interestingly, this variation is around a positive median (because $\gamma_{(income_j)0} > 0$): only in moderately high-skilled countries (like South Korea) and upward are the poor *not* more protectionist than the rich. On the whole, however, observed patterns strongly support the importance of nonhomothetic tastes to trade policy beliefs.

Second, . . . the correlation between individual skill and support for free trade grows increasingly positive as country skill endowment grows ($\gamma_{(skill_j)1} > 0$). Despite the use of different data, measures, and methods, this result, which lends strong support to the H-O-inspired model, replicates that of several other scholars and is thus one of the most important and robust findings in the trade policy attitudes literature.

At the same time, however, the correlation between individual skill and support for free trade is strongly positive even in countries with the international median level of skill ($\gamma_{(skill_j)0} > 0$). Indeed, this correlation is statistically *below* zero . . . only for the least skill-endowed country in the sample, Nigeria. Among unskilled-labor powerhouses Bangladesh, Pakistan, India, and China, the slope between skill and support for free trade is essentially flat. In short, these results seem to correspond to a necessarily modified version of H-O: while the correlation between skill and pro-trade attitudes *does* decline with decreasing country skill endowments, the variation in this correlation is around an already positive median value.

TABLE 1 Determinants of Individual-Level Trade Policy Attitudes in 41 Countries: Hierarchical Binary Logit Estimates

Independent Variables	
Cross-Level Multiplicative Terms	
Income$_i$ × Skill Abundance$_j$ ($\gamma_{(incomei)1}$)	−.0642**
	(.0241)
Skill$_i$ × Skill Abundance$_j$ ($\gamma_{(skilli)1}$)	.2509**
	(.0402)
Town Size$_i$ × Land Abundance$_j$ ($\gamma_{(Town\,Sizei)1}$)	−.0444*
	(.0257)
Political Interest$_i$ × Skill Abundance$_j$	.0056
	(.0275)
Individual-Level Variables	
Income$_i$ ($\gamma_{(incomei)0}$)	.1365**
	(.0326)
Skill$_i$ ($\gamma_{(skilli)0}$)	.1978**
	(.0451)
NO-EDs$_i$	.2222*
	(.0962)
Town Size$_i$ ($\gamma_{(Town\,Sizei)0}$)	.0591
	(.0400)
Age$_i$	−.0154**
	(.0023)
Woman$_i$	−.1945**
	(.0513)
Political Interest$_i$	−.0207
	(.0148)
Nationalist Sentiment$_i$	−.1701**
	(.0265)
Intercept	.4020
	(.2700)

NOTE: N = 53,961, J = 41. Entries are restricted maximum-likelihood estimates with robust standard errors in parentheses. The dependent variable is a binary indicator of (0) protectionist or (1) pro-trade sentiment. Variance components (τ_{xx}, or Var[u_{xj}]) for each individual-level coefficient are available from the author upon request. *p < .05 and **p < .01.

The existence of both tendencies no doubt explains the apparently contradictory findings of scholars who have limited their analyses to middle- and upper-income countries. . . . An exploration of the sources of this pattern lies well beyond the scope of this article, as economists themselves disagree on why trade has not reduced inequality in lower- and lower-middle-income countries in recent years. It is clear, however, that *NO-EDs* are not responsible for

FIGURE 1 Impact of Individual Income as a Function of Country Skill Endowment: Estimates and 95% Confidence Intervals for $E(\beta_{(Income)_j})$

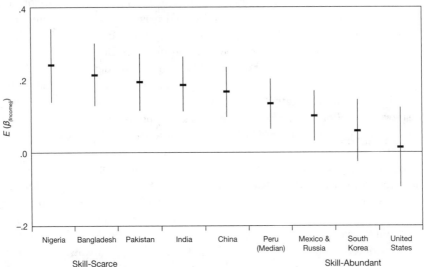

this tendency, as the inclusion of this dummy variable does not eliminate the positive correlation between skill and support for free trade in most countries. In fact, *NO-EDs* are actually slightly *more* favorable toward free trade than their skill level would dictate.

Third, support for the relevance of land and capital endowments as determinants of trade attitudes is more mixed. In the preferred model factor endowments matter in the hypothesized direction: rural dwellers are more pro-trade relative to urban dwellers in land-abundant countries than in capital-abundant ones ($\gamma_{(Town\ Size_j)1} < 0$). But this finding is not very robust, and as in the case of skill endowments, this variation in slope tends to be around a positive median ($\gamma_{(Town\ Size_j)0} > 0$): urban residents tend to be less protectionist than rural residents in countries with median degrees of land abundance (e.g., China). The weaker predictive power of these factors is perhaps due to the fact that capital is more internationally mobile than labor.

Finally, a few interesting patterns emerge among the control variables. The most robust findings are that women, the elderly, and nationalists are on average far more protectionist than other compatriots. The impact of exposure to elite discourse, by contrast, is unclear. Political interest may increase support for trade in skill-abundant countries while reducing it in skill-scarce countries (a potential sign that elites in the former are more pro-trade than in the latter), but this finding is neither robust nor does it hold in the preferred model. . . .

DISCUSSION AND CONCLUSION

Consumer tastes matter, then, for explaining trade attitudes. The allure of globalization's benefits for consumer options and prices varies across individuals and countries, a fact that is reflected in overall beliefs about trade policy. The more conventional notions about the sources of trade policy beliefs also hold: employable assets and labor markets are important determinants of citizens' reactions to globalization. . . . Heavy consumers of exportables (the poor in skill-scarce countries and the wealthy in skill-abundant ones) tend to be more protectionist than heavy consumers of imports and import-competing goods (the poor in skill-abundant countries and the wealthy in skill-scarce countries). . . .

The findings on consumer tastes echo various elements of conventional wisdom regarding trade and consumption patterns. Bhagwati argues the following regarding the costs of protection: "Current protection in the United States seems particularly aimed at lower-end consumer goods . . . that have virtually gone out of production in the United States by now and where the net effect on our workers' well-being comes not from the effect on their wages in employment, but overwhelmingly from their role as consumers" (Bhagwati 2004, 127). It is for similar reasons that, because it sells so many inexpensive Chinese imports, Michael Cox has said that "Wal-Mart is the greatest thing that ever happened to low-income Americans" (Lohr 2003). On the flip side, middle- and upper-class consumers in less developed countries tend to appreciate the influx of luxury goods and services (electronic appliances, vehicles, foreign entertainment) that arrive on the heels of trade liberalization.

Combined with the standard H-O effects regarding individual skill, these results suggest that the consumption and labor-market channels produce cross-cutting welfare effects. Consider that "poor countries produce necessities, and rich countries produce luxuries" (Dalgin, Mitra, and Trindade 2004, 19), a pattern that is bolstered by the fact that poor countries tend to produce low quality goods while rich countries produce high quality goods. Therefore, a poor country's exports (the products that increase in price under trade liberalization) tend to be goods that its poor citizens consume at a higher rate than its wealthy citizens. Conversely, a rich country's exports tend to be products that its rich citizens consume at a higher rate than its poor citizens. Because skill and income are correlated in all societies, consumption tastes may offset somewhat the labor-market impact of trade.

Despite these cross-cutting effects, it is hard to ignore the unequivocal finding that this cross-national causal heterogeneity varies around substantively important and revealing medians that do not conform to H-O expectations. In nearly every country, the poor and the unskilled tend to be more protectionist than the wealthy and the skilled. Globalization's critics thus seem to have fodder for their complaints about trade's detrimental impact on the poor. The picture, however, is not so one-sided. Many citizens, including those that live in the South, see trade as a remedy to high consumer prices. Moreover, once controlling for nationalism and certain economic interests, citizens in less developed countries are actually more enthusiastic about free trade than those in the North. Global patterns of support for free trade thus defy simplistic descriptions because citizens consider the issue from a diversity of perspectives.

REFERENCES

Beaulieu, Eugene, Michael Benarroch, and James Gaisford. 2004. "Intra-Industry Trade Liberalization, Wage Inequality and Trade Policy Preferences." *University of Calgary Discussion Paper*, 06.

Bhagwati, Jagdish. 2004. *In Defense of Globalization*. Oxford: Oxford University Press.

Dalgin, Muhammed, Devashish Mitra, and Vitor Trindade. 2004. "Inequality, Nonhomothetic Preferences, and Trade: A Gravity Approach." NBER Working Paper, W10800.

Gabel, Matthew. 1998. *Interests and Integration: Market Liberalization, Public Opinion, and the European Union*. Ann Arbor: University of Michigan Press.

Linder, Staffan. 1961. *An Essay on Trade and Transformation*. Almqvist and Wicksell: Stockholm.

Lohr, Steve. 2003. "Discount Nation: Is Wal-Mart Good for America?" *The New York Times*. On-line edition. 12/7/03.

Prebisch, Raúl. 1950. *The Economic Development of Latin America and Its Principal Problems*. New York: United Nations.

21

Policymakers' Horizon and Trade Reforms: The Protectionist Effect of Elections

PAOLA CONCONI, GIOVANNI FACCHINI, AND MAURIZIO ZANARDI

Trade policy is made, or heavily influenced, by elected politicians. In this reading, Paola Conconi, Giovanni Facchini, and Maurizio Zanardi analyze the impact of American electoral institutions on American trade policy. They argue that members of Congress facing imminent elections are significantly more protectionist than those who are not facing electoral pressures. This is true even of the same politicians as elections approach: senators, for example, become more protectionist when they are up for reelection than when they are not. The clear implication is that electoral institutions must be taken into account in trying to explain how and why trade policy is made.

1. INTRODUCTION

As pointed out by Rodrik (1995), "no other area of economics displays such a gap between what policymakers practice and what economists preach as does international trade." Why do policymakers often fail to support trade liberalization, favoring instead protectionist policies?

Anecdotal evidence suggests that electoral incentives play a key role in answering this question. . . .

In this paper, we provide systematic evidence that electoral incentives lead politicians to take a protectionist stance. In particular, we show that the political horizon of U.S. congressmen—the length of their terms in office and how close they are to facing elections—crucially affects their support for trade liberalization reforms. The focus on the United States is not only due to the availability of roll-call votes, but also to the specific institutional features of the U.S. Congress, in which House and Senate representatives serve respectively two- and six-year terms, and one-third of the Senate is up for re-election every two years. Inter-cameral differences in term length and the staggered structure of the Senate make the U.S. Congress an ideal setting to understand how policymakers' horizon shapes their trade policy decisions: at any point in time, it is possible to compare the voting behavior of legislators with mandates of different lengths, as well as the behavior of senators belonging to different "generations," i.e., facing elections at different times. Exploiting the fact that many senators cast multiple votes on trade reforms, we can also study whether election proximity affects the stance of individual legislators during their terms in office.

To carry out our analysis, we collect data on individual roll-call votes on trade liberalization bills introduced in the U.S. Congress since the early 1970s. These include the ratification and implementation of multilateral trade agreements (Tokyo and Uruguay Round of the GATT) and preferential trade agreements (e.g., the Canada–United States Free Trade Agreement, NAFTA) negotiated during this period, as well as the conferral and extension of fast track trade negotiating authority to the president. We have complemented this data with information on many characteristics of the legislators and their constituencies, covering both economic and non-economic drivers of individual voting decisions on trade reforms.

We compare first the voting behavior of House and Senate members. In line with previous studies, we show that senators are more likely to support trade liberalization than House representatives. Crucially, however, we find no significant difference between House members and the last generation of senators, two groups of legislators who are up for reelection at the same time. This result provides an explanation for the observed inter-cameral differences in trade policy votes. Some scholars have argued that senators are less protectionist than House members because they represent larger constituencies; however, . . . constituency size is actually unrelated to congressmen's votes on trade and cannot explain inter-cameral differences. Our analysis suggests that these are instead driven by differences in term length: senators are generally more supportive of trade liberalization because they serve longer mandates; as they approach the end of their terms, they become as protectionist as House members.

We then focus on the role of election proximity, comparing the voting behavior of different generations of senators. We find that the last generation is significantly more protectionist than the previous two. The effect is sizable: members of the Senate who are in the last two years of their mandates are around 10 percentage points less likely to support trade liberalization than senators in the first four years. The results continue to hold when—rather than comparing different individuals voting on the same bill—we study the behavior of the same individual over time. Inter-generational differences are also robust to including a wealth of controls for legislators (e.g., party affiliation and whether it is the same as the executive's, age, gender, campaign contributions received from labor and corporate groups) and their constituencies (e.g., employment in export/import-competing industries, percentage of high skilled workers, size), focusing on different subsets of trade reforms, and using alternative econometric methodologies. The protectionist effect of election proximity is pervasive: even senators representing export constituencies, in which a majority of the electorate should gain from trade liberalization, become significantly more protectionist at the end of their terms.

To verify whether inter-generational differences are driven by electoral incentives, we carry out two falsification exercises, focusing on senators who are retiring (i.e., have announced that they will not stand for re-election) or hold safe seats (i.e., have been elected with a large margin of victory). We find that election proximity has no impact on the voting behavior of these legislators, suggesting that re-election motives are the key reason behind the cyclical behavior observed among U.S. senators at large.

The observed patterns in the voting behavior of Congress members cannot be readily explained by existing models in the literature on the political economy of trade policy, which do not consider the role of term length and electoral calendars. Our findings suggest that re-election motives deter politicians from supporting trade liberalization reforms and that this effect is stronger at the end of their terms, when their policy decisions have a bigger impact on their chances to retain office.

The remainder of the paper is organized as follows. Section 2 briefly reviews the related literature. Section 3 describes the dataset and variables used in our analysis. Section 4 examines the role of term length, comparing the voting behavior of House and Senate members. Section 5 focuses on the effect of election proximity, comparing the voting behavior of different generations of senators. Section 6 discusses possible mechanisms behind our empirical findings. Section 7 concludes, pointing to avenues for future research.

2. RELATED LITERATURE

Our paper is related to several strands of the literature. First, it contributes to the analysis of the political economy of trade policy. Several studies have focused on voting and elections. Much attention has also been devoted to the role of lobby groups. Other studies have focused on different political factors, such as governments' inability to commit to policy choices or ratification rules. This is the first paper to emphasize the importance of term length and election proximity.

Our analysis builds also on a large body of work that has studied the political economy obstacles to the adoption of economic reforms, i.e., major policy changes that go beyond regular government decisions, including structural reforms (e.g., trade or labor market liberalization) and stabilization reforms (e.g., important fiscal adjustments to drastically reduce budget deficits and/or inflation). . . .

Our work is also related to the literature on political business cycles, which emphasizes the importance of electoral calendars when politicians are office motivated. Close to election, incumbent politicians manipulate regular government decisions on fiscal and monetary policies to signal their competence. Our paper shows that electoral calendars crucially affect legislators' choices on trade liberalization reforms. . . .

3. DATA

To carry out our analysis, we have assembled a novel dataset that allows us to link congressmen's voting behavior on a trade liberalization bill to a wealth of characteristics of the legislators and their constituencies. This enables us to investigate the role played by both economic and non-economic drivers of individual decisions. In this section, we describe our data, starting from our dependent variable. We discuss next the individual-level characteristics, and finally turn to the procedure we have followed to construct our constituency-level controls.

3.1. Votes on Trade Reforms

Our analysis focuses on recorded (roll-call) final passage votes on all major trade liberalization bills introduced in the U.S. Congress between 1973 and 2005. By looking at final passage votes, we exclude votes on amendments and other intermediate procedural steps from our analysis. We have decided to follow this strategy because the expectations on the effects of floor amendments are less clear cut than for final passage votes. Voting on amendments is often strategic and is therefore less likely to distinctly reflect the interests of the legislator's constituency.

. . . The bills included in our analysis, cover the implementation of multilateral trade agreements (Tokyo and Uruguay Round rounds of the GATT) and preferential trade agreements negotiated in this period, as well as the initiatives to confer or extend fast track trade negotiating authority to the President.

We distinguish between the 50 U.S. states—electing each two representatives for the Senate—and the 435 congressional districts—each electing one member of the House of Representatives. Overall, we consider 29 votes. For each of them, we collect the identity of the congressmen, their state or district, and their decision (in favor or against) from roll-call records. . . .

3.2. Characteristics of Legislators

. . . As already discussed, one-third of the Senate is elected every two years, together with the entire House. We classify senators as belonging to the first (second) generation if they are in the first (middle) two years of their terms. The third generation denotes senators who are in the last two years of their terms and are thus closest to facing re-election.

Party affiliation is known to be a strong predictor of a politician's support for trade liberalization, with Democrats being systematically more protectionist than Republicans for the period under consideration in our study. . . .

Since trade liberalization bills are usually supported by the administration, legislators' voting behavior may also depend on the congruence (or lack thereof) between their party affiliation and that of the executive. . . .

Since age and gender have been shown to be important drivers of individual-level preferences for trade policy, control for the role of demographic characteristics of a congressman. . . .

Another set of variables have only been collected for senators, since they are used to verify the robustness of the effects of election proximity. In particular, we have constructed two controls to capture the extent to which legislators are exposed to competition for their seats, in order to assess the role played by re-election incentives in explaining inter-generational differences in senators' voting behavior. . . .

A long tradition has emphasized the importance of lobbies' contributions in shaping international trade policy and the voting behavior of U.S. congressmen on trade liberalization bills. . . .

3.3. Characteristics of Constituencies

In order to capture the trade policy interests of each constituency, we control for the time-varying share of import-competing workers in a given state or congressional district. To do so, we first define an industry (i.e., at 2-digit SIC level or 3-digit NAICS level) as being import-competing (export), if the U.S. as a whole is a net importer (exporter) in that industry in a given year. We then collect information on employment in import-competing and export industries for all constituencies. . . .

As an alternative, more long-term measure of the trade interests of a congressman's constituency, we have also constructed a proxy for the relative abundance of skilled labor. . . .

4. INTER-CAMERAL DIFFERENCES IN VOTING BEHAVIOR

In this section, we start by examining the voting behavior of all congressmen, to verify whether House members are more protectionist than Senate members. . . . We then contrast House members with different generations of senators to establish whether inter-cameral differences are driven by term length.

4.1. House vs. Senate

We first compare the behavior of Senate and House members. . . .

. . . inter-cameral differences in congressmen's voting behavior on trade reforms are sizable: senate membership increases the probability of supporting trade liberalization by 11.6 percentage points. Concerning the other legislators' controls, we find that support for trade reforms is significantly lower for members of the Democratic party. Legislators who belong to the same party as the executive are more likely to vote in favor of trade liberalization bills, while older legislators tend to be more protectionist. In terms of state characteristics, . . . the larger the share of export workers in a constituency, the more likely its representative is to favor a reduction in trade barriers. . . .

. . . We find that congressmen representing more highly skilled districts are more likely to support trade liberalization measures, a result consistent with a Heckscher–Ohlin model in which U.S. imports are relatively unskilled-labor intensive. . . .

Next, we exploit the staggered nature of senators' mandates. This specific institutional feature of the U.S. Congress implies that, at any point in time, one-third of the senators have the same "political horizon" as House members (i.e., they face elections in less than two years).

. . . Since electoral calendars are exogenously assigned to each Senate seat, we can compare the voting of legislators with different remaining time in office. . . .

. . . Senators from the first generation are between 13.2 and 17.7% more likely to support trade liberalization bills (over the average predicted probability) than members of the House. . . .

5. DIFFERENT GENERATIONS OF SENATORS

We now move to the core of our analysis, in which we examine the role of election proximity on legislators' voting behavior. To do so, we focus on votes cast in the U.S. Senate alone, exploiting its staggered structure and the fact that many of its members have voted on several trade bills during their careers.

We follow two complementary strategies to identify the effect of election proximity. First, we compare the voting behavior of senators who belong to different generations. . . .

Second, since our sample spans four decades, we can observe the votes that the same senator has cast on different trade bills. We can thus exploit the time variation in the voting behavior of individual senators. . . .

. . . Senators who are in the last two years of their terms are less likely to support trade liberalization reforms than . . . senators in the first two years of their terms.

In terms of magnitude . . . third-generation senators are around 10 percentage point less likely to support trade liberalization. This can also be seen in Fig. 1 where we plot predicted probabilities for senators belonging to different generations. . . .

Much of the existing literature on the political economy of trade policy has emphasized the role of lobbying. . . . We investigate whether our results on inter-generational differences in senators' voting behavior are robust to controlling for the influence of organized pressure groups. In particular, we supplement our benchmark specification . . . by accounting separately for the amount of corporate and labor contributions received by a given senator during

FIGURE 1 Predicted Probabilities, Different Generations of Senators

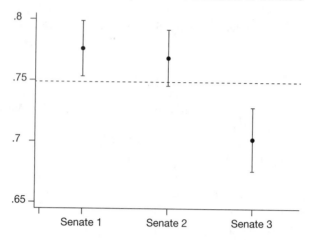

each congressional cycle, i.e., when belonging to different generations. In line with what [was] found in previous studies, we find that labor (corporate) contributions have a significant negative (positive) impact on legislators' support for trade liberalization bills. . . .

We now turn to the analysis of the impact of election proximity on the voting behavior of individual senators. This alternative strategy allows us to account for time-invariant unobservable characteristics of legislators that can affect their stance on trade policy. . . .

. . . A senator in the last two years of his mandate is systematically less likely to support trade liberalization than the same individual in the first four years of his mandate. In fact, various senators *never* supported trade liberalization bills in the last two years before re-election, but did vote in favor at least once earlier in their terms. . . .

The results . . . show that individual senators "flip flop" on trade policy, supporting trade liberalization reforms earlier in their terms, but opposing them when they approach re-election.

The results presented above show that senators are significantly less likely to support trade liberalization reforms when they are close to facing elections. Is this finding driven solely by the voting behavior of "anti-trade" legislators, i.e., representatives of import-competing constituencies and members of the Democratic party? To address this question, we examine whether intergenerational differences in senators' voting behavior are affected by the trade exposure of their constituencies and their party affiliation. . . .

We find that, earlier in their mandate, representatives of export constituencies are more willing to support trade liberalization reforms than representatives of import-competing ones. . . . However, this difference disappears at the end of their mandate. . . . Interestingly, our results show that election proximity reduces support for trade liberalization among representatives of both import-competing constituencies . . . and export constituencies. . . .

. . . The results confirm that members of the Democratic party are less supportive of trade liberalization than those of the Republican party. However, senators from both parties become more protectionist in the last two years of their mandate: inter-generational differences are observed among Republicans . . . as well as Democrats. . . .

. . . Election proximity has a pervasive effect, i.e., it deters legislators from supporting trade liberalization reforms, even if they represent constituencies in which most workers are employed in export industries or they belong to the Republican party.

. . . Election proximity leads legislators to become more protectionist. What drives this result? A natural explanation is represented by electoral incentives. To assess their role . . . we carry out two falsification exercises; first, we examine the voting behavior of senators who have announced their retirement, and thus do not care about their re-election chances; second, we focus on senators holding safe seats, who have little chance of losing office. If re-election motives are the reason behind the inter-generational differences in voting behavior documented above, we would expect the protectionist effect of election proximity to disappear for senators who are not seeking re-election or hold safe seats.

. . . Retiring senators are more likely to vote in favor of trade reforms. Crucially, election proximity does not affect their support for trade liberalization; . . . retiring senators do not change their voting behavior over their mandates.

The results . . . suggest that the protectionist effect of election proximity is driven by politicians' desire to retain office. Interestingly, two of the trade liberalization votes in our sample (the first approval of fast track in December 1974 and the ratification of the Uruguay Round Agreement in December 1994) occurred in a "lame duck" session (after the November general elections, but before the newly elected senators had taken their seats). In line with the results on retiring senators, none of the defeated senators voted against these bills.

. . . Holding a safe seat increases the likelihood that a senator votes in favor of trade liberalization. . . . Senators who are not concerned about losing office do not change their voting behavior on trade reforms when they approach re-election. By contrast . . . election proximity has a protectionist effect on the voting behavior of senators who do not hold safe seats.

The results . . . strongly suggest that the protectionist effect of election proximity is driven by re-election motives: the estimates . . . indicate that, for senators who are running for re-election or whose seats are contested, the probability of supporting trade liberalization is between 10 and 11 percentage points lower in the last two years of their mandate; . . . this cyclical behavior disappears for senators who are not afraid of losing office, either because they are retiring or because they hold safe seats.

6. DISCUSSION

The findings presented in the previous two sections show that the political horizon of legislators crucially affects their voting behavior on trade liberalization reforms. In particular, i) House Representatives are generally more protectionist than Senate members, but inter-cameral differences disappear for the last generation of senators, who are up for re-election at the same time as House members; ii) election proximity reduces senators' support for trade liberalization, a result that holds both when comparing different legislators voting on the same bill and individual legislators voting on different bills; iii) the protectionist effect of election proximity is pervasive; it applies not only to senators who generally oppose trade liberalization (members of the Democratic party and representatives of import-competing constituencies), but also to more pro-trade senators (members of the Republican party and representatives of export-oriented constituencies); and iv) inter-generational differences disappear only for senators who are not concerned about losing office, either because they have decided to step down or because they hold very safe seats.

Existing theories on the political economy of trade policy cannot readily explain these findings, since they do not consider the role of term length and election proximity. In this section, we discuss possible mechanisms that could explain the observed patterns in congressmen's voting behavior on trade reforms.

The fact that politicians are less supportive of trade liberalization reforms when they are close to re-election suggests the existence of a *protectionist bias* in trade policy. The existence of such a bias is a well known stylized fact and several explanations have been proposed for it. In models of majoritarian electoral politics, protectionist policies may simply arise if the median voter is an unskilled worker and there is no way to compensate the losers from trade liberalization. In this case, the protectionist stance of politicians may simply reflect the interests of the majority of the electorate. A protectionist bias can also arise if preferences exhibit loss aversion, implying that individuals place a larger welfare weight on the losses than on the gains from trade liberalization. Asymmetries in information can also play a role: voters may prefer protection over free trade because they are better informed about the trade barriers that help them as producers than those that hurt them as consumers. As it turns out, opinion polls show that most Americans oppose trade liberalization. Interestingly, however, they also reveal that only a minority of respondents consider trade policy as a salient issue, which affects their voting decisions. As a result, rather than responding to the interests of the median voter, politicians may be accountable to a minority of voters who care intensely about trade policy.

A protectionist bias in trade policy can explain why politicians are often reluctant to support trade liberalization. By itself, however, this does not provide a rationale for the protectionist effect of election proximity. A *recency bias* in voters' behavior can instead explain why politicians are more likely to oppose trade reforms when they are close to re-election. If voters attach more weight to recent rather than earlier performance of their representatives, the policy choices of incumbent politicians at the end of their terms will have a bigger impact on their ability to retain office.

Note that, if politicians were only office motivated, they would not alter their voting behavior throughout their mandates, even if voters are protectionist and suffer from a recency bias. To explain our findings, a third element is needed: politicians must face a *trade-off* between their *policy preferences* and their *re-election motives*. This could be the case, for example, if they are more supportive than citizens of trade liberalization reforms because they are better informed about their long-run benefits. Combining this trade-off with the protectionist and recency biases can explain why politicians "flip flop" on trade policy, supporting trade liberalization reforms earlier in their terms, but opposing them when they approach re-election.

7. CONCLUSIONS

This paper shows that electoral incentives play an important role in shaping legislators' support for trade liberalization reforms. Our analysis exploits the institutional features of the U.S. Congress—in which House and Senate members serve respectively two- and six-year terms, and one-third of senators face elections every two years—to examine the impact of term length and election proximity on congressmen's voting behavior on trade liberalization reforms.

We show that House representatives are more protectionist than members of the Senate. However, this difference disappears for the last generation of senators, who face elections at the same time as House members. This finding provides an explanation for the observed inter-cameral differences in votes on trade policy: these are not driven by differences in constituency size or by unobserved characteristics of legislators correlated with their trade stance; rather, senators are generally more supportive of trade liberalization reforms because they serve longer mandates and are thus less responsive to short-term electoral pressure.

When restricting our attention to the upper house, we find that the last generation is more protectionist than the previous two: senators who are in the last two years of their terms are less likely to support trade liberalization than senators who are further away from re-election. This result holds both when comparing the behavior of different legislators voting on the same bill, and the behavior of the same legislator over time. It is also robust to the inclusion of a large set of controls for congressmen and their constituencies, and the use of different econometric methodologies. We also show that calendar effects are pervasive: all senators, even those representing export-oriented constituencies, in which a majority of voters should benefit from trade liberalization, take a more protectionist stance as they approach re-election. Inter-generational differences disappear only for senators who hold very safe seats or are retiring, suggesting that the protectionist effect of election proximity is driven by the fear of losing office.

Our analysis calls for new theoretical models to shed light on the mechanisms through which electoral incentives affect policymakers' voting behavior. In particular, existing models in the political economy of trade cannot readily explain our empirical findings, since they do not examine the role of term length and election proximity. . . .

REFERENCES

Rodrik, Dani. 1995. The Political Economy of Trade Policy. In *Handbook of International Economics*, G. Grossman and K. Rogoff, eds., vol. 3. Amsterdam: North-Holland.

22

The World Trade Organization and the Future of Multilateralism

RICHARD BALDWIN

Since the 1940s international trade has largely been governed by interactions among governments under the institutional auspices of the GATT and now the WTO. In recent years, however, this inclusive multilateral institution has been supplemented—some might say challenged—by a large and growing number of bilateral or regional trade agreements. Some regard this as an institutional challenge to the WTO system; others see it as complementary. In this reading, Richard Baldwin explains the development of the GATT-WTO system, why these regional agreements have proliferated, and what this might mean for future interactions among countries in the international trading system.

When the General Agreement on Tariffs and Trade was signed by 23 nations in 1947, the goal was to establish a rules-based world trading system and to facilitate mutually advantageous trade liberalization. As the GATT evolved over time and morphed into the World Trade Organization in 1993, both goals have largely been achieved. The WTO presides over a rule-based trading system based on norms that are almost universally accepted and respected by its 163 members. Tariffs today are below 5 percent on most trade, and zero for a very large share of imports.

Despite its manifest success, the WTO is widely regarded as suffering from a deep malaise. The main reason is that the latest WTO negotiation, the Doha Round, has staggered between failures, flops, and false dawns since it was launched in 2001. But the Doha logjam has not inhibited tariff liberalization—far from it. During the last 15 years, most WTO members have massively lowered barriers to trade, investment, and services bilaterally, regionally, and unilaterally—indeed, everywhere except through the WTO. The massive tariff cutting that has taken place around the world . . . has been at least as great as in the previous successful WTO rounds. Moreover, the Doha gridlock has also not dampened nations' interest in the WTO; 20 nations, including China and Russia, have joined since 2001.

This paper begins by sketching the historical context of the original GATT agreement. It then discusses how the rules and principles behind the GATT rounds combined to create a juggernaut of political economy momentum in which nations kept joining the GATT and tariffs kept falling.

The paper then turns to the current woes of the WTO and why its magic seems to have failed in the Doha Round. Two major sets of reasons emerge in this discussion. First, the last round of GATT negotiations, the Uruguay Round, sought to generate additional momentum for free trade through broadening its focus, both in terms of more countries joining and in terms of additional areas that would be covered by the agreement. However, these steps toward broadening also required altering some of the historical rules and principles that had generated momentum toward free trade. The changes altered and may even have ended the political economy momentum of the WTO. Second, the rules and procedures of the WTO were designed for a global economy in which made-here–sold-there goods moved across national borders. But the rapid rising of offshoring from high-technology nations to low-wage nations has created a new type of international commerce. In essence, the flows of goods, services, investment, training, and know-how that used to move inside or between advanced-nation factories have now become part of international commerce. For this sort of offshoring-linked international commerce, the trade rules that matter are less about tariffs and more about protection of investments and intellectual property, along with legal and regulatory steps to assure that the two-way flows of goods, services, investment, and people will not be impeded.

It's possible to imagine a hypothetical WTO that would incorporate these rules. But in practice, the rules are being written in a series of regional and megaregional agreements like the Trans-Pacific Partnership (TPP) and Transatlantic Trade and Investment Partnership (TTIP) between the United States and the European Union. The most likely outcome for the future governance of international trade is a two-pillar structure in which the WTO continues to govern with its 1994-era rules while the new rules for international production networks, or "global value chains," are set by a decentralized process of sometimes overlapping and inconsistent megaregional agreements.

THE HISTORICAL CONTEXT FOR THE PRINCIPLES OF GATT

The GATT was launched in unusual times. The demand for trade liberalization was great, because tariffs were still high from the Smoot-Hawley tariff and retaliations in the 1930s. The supply of trade liberalization was, in general terms, also great as leaders of the largest trading nations wanted to avoid the protectionist mistakes of the 1920s and 1930s. The demand for and supply of trade liberalization were also powerfully driven by the political climate in the aftermath of World War I and the outbreak of the Cold War, a setting in which world trade integration became a geostrategic issue as well as a commercial issue.

The GATT's design was heavily influenced by lessons drawn from historical trade liberalization efforts. Pre–World War I globalization had few international organizations, supported instead by Pax Britannica. During World War II, the United States effectively became the global leader, and it wanted postwar globalization to be based on international institutions. The US Congress, however, which controls US trade policy, was refusing to bind its hands with a new international organization. Instead, trade liberalization would be buttressed by a "general agreement" but no formal organization like the International Monetary Fund. The GATT was based on several principles.

ONE GENERAL AND FIVE SPECIFIC PRINCIPLES

There is no definitive list of principles in the GATT and WTO, and authors differ on exactly what such a list might include. . . . However, it is useful to think of one general and five specific principles. The general principle—what might be called the constitutional principle—is that the world trade system should be rules-based, not results-based. The GATT, and now the WTO, focuses on the design, implementation, updating, and enforcement of procedures, rules, and guidelines rather than on seeking to agree upon the volume of exports or market shares. This overreaching constitutional principle is implemented with five specific principles.

1) *Nondiscrimination.* This rule has two aspects: nondiscrimination at the border and nondiscrimination behind the border. Nondiscrimination at the border, called "most favored nation treatment" in the WTO's circumlocutive parlance (since WTO members should treat no nation better than it treats its most favored trading partner), means that any tariff which is applied should be applied equally to all WTO members. Many exceptions are allowed (for example, free trade agreements), but these are controlled by explicit conditions. The other aspect of nondiscrimination is called "national treatment," which is the rule that within each country, taxes and regulations should be applied evenly to domestic and imported goods.
2) *Transparency.* Liberalizing trade and reducing conflicts over trade is easier when the actual policies are transparent to all by having been made public.
3) *Reciprocity.* Nations that remove barriers to imports can expect other nations to reciprocate. Again, exceptions are made, with the most notable example being that, during the GATT era, developing nations benefited from the market opening of other nations due to the most-favored-nation provisions, but they were allowed not to reduce their own tariffs. Reciprocity also applies to retaliation. When a nation engages in a practice or policy that undoes the gain another member had from a previous agreement, the aggrieved nation has the right to reciprocate—that is, to retaliate.

4) *Flexibility, or "safety valves."* The founders of the GATT knew that members would occasionally be subject to irresistible domestic pressure to impose trade barriers. Rather than threatening implausibly dire consequences for such actions, the GATT allows some exceptions in which nations can at times impose trade barriers, but seeks to discipline them with various strictures and requirements for compensation.

5) *Consensus decision-making*: Like the other principles, this one has exceptions, but most WTO decisions are by consensus.

As the next section explains, interactions among these principles generated a political economy momentum that drove trade liberalization. As the following section explains, changes made in the 1990s help to explain why the momentum has ground to a halt.

A TARIFF-CUTTING JUGGERNAUT

GATT is widely viewed as having facilitated the reduction of tariffs—at least in the developed nations. Systematic data on tariffs for a broad range of nations is available only from the 1980s, but a cruder measure called the "effective tariff rate"—that is, tariff revenue divided by the value of imports—has been collected back to the beginning of GATT. . . . An obvious problem with the effective tariff rate measure is that really high tariffs result in very low imports and so tend to get little weight in the average. In addition, the effective tariff rates for individual nations can be very noisy over periods of only a few years because they reflect both changes in tariff rates and changes in patterns of imports. Despite these well-known problems, effective rates give a reasonable general idea of tariff-cutting patterns under the GATT.

Two salient facts that emerge . . . are that low-income nations have always had higher tariffs and developed nations reduced their tariffs steadily while poor nations only started doing so in the 1980s. . . .

Four Phases of Trade Liberalization under the GATT: 1950–1994

. . . The first phase of GATT rounds, up until 1960, began with a substantial wave of tariff cutting in the 1947 inaugural Geneva Round. . . . However, the other early rounds were not focused on tariff cutting. Instead, they considered details of rules and accessions such as those of Germany (1951) and Japan (1955). Moreover, tariffs were not the main trade hindrance to international trade in the 1950s. Instead, restrictions remaining from wartime, along with state trading and inconvertible currencies, were the binding constraints.

The second phase from 1960 up to 1972 was triggered by European regional trade liberalization. For example, the Dillon Round (1960–1961) dealt with the tariff concessions European members had to make to other GATT members in compensation for the formation of their customs union. The Kennedy Round (1963–1967) was, in part, an effort by the United States, Japan, and other large exporters to redress the trade diversion arising from this customs union. The decline in tariff rates in developed countries after about 1967 was in part due to GATT, but also to non-GATT steps like elimination of tariffs across much of Europe, and the US–Canada Auto Pact of 1965 which eliminated tariffs on bilateral auto trade. In this phase, regionalism and multilateralism advanced hand-in-hand. By contrast, tariffs in low-income nations did not fall since GATT rules excused them from reciprocally cutting their tariff in GATT talks. This is an exception to the nondiscrimination principle called "Special and Differential Treatment" for developing-nation members.

The third phase of trade liberalization started around 1973, and again multilateralism and regionalism advanced together. The GATT's Tokyo Round talks were launched the same year that the European Union enlarged (Britain, Ireland, and Denmark joined) and signed bilateral free trade agreements with most other West European nations. The 1970s are a period when the "effective tariff" measure can be deceiving. It looks as if substantial tariff cutting happened in developed nations although no GATT-required cuts were implemented until the round finished in 1979. The illusion arises from the 1970s price hikes that raised the import shares for oil; as developed nations had low or zero tariffs on imported oil, the relative price change looks like a cut in the average tariff. . . .

The fourth wave of multilateral and regional trade talks arose in the mid-1980s. In 1986, GATT members launched the Uruguay Round, the United States and Canada started talks about a bilateral free-trade agreement, and the European Union enlarged to include Spain and Portugal while launching its Single Market Program, which eliminated a vast range of nontariff barriers to cross-border movements of goods, services, and workers. Effective tariffs fell gently in developed nations, probably mostly due to regional rather than multilateral liberalization. For example, at the time the Uruguay Round was launched in 1986, about 40 percent of global trade took place inside free-trade areas, with about half of that within the European Union. The really original element in this fourth phase was the rapid tariff cutting by developing nations—but they did this outside the GATT and for reasons driven by changes in their attitudes towards high tariffs on industrial goods (more on this change below). Developing nations also signed many regional trade agreements, like Mercosur in South America and the South African Customs Union. These had some effect on tariffs, but many developing nations lowered their multilateral tariffs at the same time as they cut tariffs with their partners in free-trade agreements.

As this sketch of the four phases reveals, the momentum toward cutting tariffs includes both multilateral and regional trade agreements. Thus, the underlying question is what generates this kind of political economy momentum.

THE JUGGERNAUT DYNAMICS OF TARIFF CUTTING

Tariffs, like most economic policies, are the outcome of a political economy process. To explain why governments lower tariffs they previously found politically optimal to impose, the literature points to the role of trade agreements. The basic approach models the process as a one-time switch from a noncooperative outcome to a cooperative outcome facilitated by a trade agreement. This helps explain the initial drop in American tariffs at the start of the GATT . . . , but a switch from one form of equilibrium to another leaves out most of the richness of how the GATT fostered multiple forms of tariff cutting over successive rounds. In addition, it does not explain why developing nations acted outside the GATT to cut their tariffs starting in the mid-1980s.

More elaborate approaches to the political economy of tariff cutting draw on the intuitive, if informal, two-level game approach of Putnam (1988) as formalized by Grossman and Helpman (1995). This approach argues that governments negotiate both with special interest groups within their nation and other governments internationally. The discussion here is organized around a version of the two-level-game approach that I introduced in 1994, which I called the "juggernaut effect." It is easiest to explain in the historical context.

Before the GATT, exporters had only a very indirect interest in their nation's import tariffs. But under the GATT reciprocity principle, foreign tariff levels became linked to domestic tariff levels. Of course, this connection only held for developed nations who followed the reciprocity principle. In a way, the GATT's success was not due to the international deal itself. It was due to the way the principles behind the international deal altered domestic political realities in developed-nation members. Also, remember that developing-nation governments were excused from reciprocity by the Special and Differential Treatment rule, and thus faced the same array of domestic pro- and anti-tariff special interests before, during, and after each GATT round. In theory and practice, this meant that they did not lower tariffs that they previously found optimal to impose.

In the juggernaut story, the first round of tariff cuts creates political economy momentum. As tariffs drop, pro-tariff import-competing firms face additional international competition. Many of them shrink, become less profitable, and even go out of business. Conversely, foreign tariff cutting boosts exporters. They expand and become more profitable. In this way, a one-off tariff cut weakens protectionist forces and strengthens liberalization forces from a political economy perspective. A few years down the road, when another multilateral GATT round is launched, the altered political economy power of importers and exporters comes into play. As before, exporters have an incentive to fight for domestic tariff cuts due to the reciprocity principle, and import-competing firms have an incentive to fight against them. But since the anti-liberalization camp is systematically weaker and the pro-liberalization camp is systematically stronger than during the last round, all the governments playing reciprocally find it politically optimal to cut tariffs again. As these fresh tariff cuts are phased in, the exit of import-competing firms and entry of exporters again reshapes the political landscape inside each participating nation, and the cycle restarts. The juggernaut rolls forward.

This dynamic also suggests an explanation for why multilateral and regional tariff-cutting progressed in tandem. Once the original tariff cuts weaken protectionists and strengthen liberalizers, governments find it optimal to lower tariffs both multilaterally and regionally.

A related political economy dynamic is that regional trade agreements can kick-start multilateral trade liberalization. For example, . . . US effective tariff rates suggest that the juggernaut had run low on momentum by the end of the 1950s. However, when the countries of Western Europe began cutting their intra-European tariffs from 1959, the resulting tariff discrimination aroused the concerns of exporters in the United States, Japan, and Canada. At that time, North America and Japan both sent roughly one-third of their exports to Europe, and their firms feared losing these markets to European firms who enjoyed zero tariffs inside the customs union. As the impact of the discrimination would be reduced by lower EU most-favored-nation tariffs, North American and Japanese exporters lobbied for a GATT Round as a way of countermanding the discrimination. A similar thing may have happened when the European customs union was enlarged in 1973—the same year that the Tokyo Round talks started.

Avoiding Backsliding: Binding Plus Allowing Retaliation

The GATT had other mechanisms to keep this gradual, mutually advantageous tariff cutting on track. After all, the "juggernaut" process of political economy momentum can work in reverse—as it had in the 1930s. Thus, the GATT process included a set of rules designed to make political reversals difficult for individual members. One rule was the principle that a nation's past tariff cuts were "bound" in the sense that previously agreed tariff levels were not open to further negotiation. Moreover, a nation's partners could retaliate against any violation of such tariff "bindings" by raising their own tariffs against the violating nation's exports. The effect was to ensure that each nation's exporters would be punished for any backsliding by its own government. This gave exporters an incentive to push their government to respect the bindings. Notice that this design element did not depend on the nation's own government; instead, it was enforced by the risk that foreign governments would retaliate by raising tariffs.

Three Escape Hatches

How could the many countries of the GATT reach agreements while working on a consensus principle? One answer is that some escape hatches were historically allowed, which made it easier for members to agree to the tariff cuts in the first place.

As one example of an escape hatch, a variety of GATT practices on "Special and Differential Treatment" meant that developing nations were not subject to GATT disciplines. They were exempted from an expectation of reciprocally cutting their tariffs, and they could mostly ignore any GATT rules with which they didn't agree. In short, the low-income nations that were part of GATT could typically follow a policy of "don't obey, don't object." However, being excused from reciprocity did not mean the developing nations were indifferent to the GATT's success. The GATT's most-favored-nation principle meant that the tariff cuts agreed among the developed nations were automatically extended to developing-nation exporters. They were free riders who liked the ride. The developed countries were mostly happy to allow this free riding because developing-nation markets were, at the time, rather insignificant.

A second kind of escape hatch emerged in the 1960s and 1970s during the Tokyo Rounds, in which negotiations on trade rules were undertaken by the so-called "codes" approach. In this approach, each set of rules agreed upon was adopted in the form of a code that would be binding only for those members that voluntarily signed them—which in practice typically meant the developed nations. For example, during the Tokyo Round a number of issues beyond tariffs (such as restraints on production subsidies) were put on the agenda using the "codes" approach; many of these issues involved new forms of protection that had arisen in the 1960s and 1970s to offset competitive effects of earlier tariff cuts. However, the principle of nondiscrimination meant that countries that did agree to these codes were (mostly) obliged to extend the rules to all GATT members, even those that did not sign the codes.

A third escape hatch arose because the GATT dispute settlement system wasn't strong enough to enforce compliance. Disputes were brought before a panel whose rulings were reviewed by a group of members that included the disputing parties. According to the consensus principle, the Panel ruling was only accepted if all parties agreed. For example, in 1959 the European Free Trade Association (EFTA) nations wanted free trade among themselves, but only on industrial goods. In 1965, the United States and Canada wanted to liberalize bilateral trade in the auto sector. When GATT panels were formed to investigate the "GATT-legality" of these limited free trade agreements, the EFTA nations and the United States blocked the panel from reaching a conclusion.

Of course, if GATT members had extremely diverse preferences, escape hatches like blocking the dispute resolution process could have become a main exit, thus rendering the rules useless. But instead, the combination of a dispute procedure with an escape hatch facilitated agreements by allowing GATT members to be satisfied with wording that could be described as "constructively ambiguous." The GATT's quasi-legal dispute mechanism with escape hatch could be relied upon to settle disputes, or at least to help frame future negotiations aimed at clarifying ambiguities if and when such clarification proved important.

Causality

The story as told hereto has been of the GATT causing tariff cuts, but how do we know that it was not a third effect causing both GATT membership and tariff cutting? The prima facie evidence is clear, even if the econometrics has not been done due to the lack of high-quality historical tariff data. Two types of tariffs were not subject to the juggernaut "treatment"—all developing-nation tariffs, and agricultural tariffs of all GATT members. Neither set of tariffs fell during the GATT days: agricultural tariffs because they were not on the negotiating table, and developing-nation tariffs because they were excused from reciprocal cuts. This suggests that no third factor was causing tariff-cutting pressures across the board; instead, the juggernaut treatment only worked on the tariffs to which it was applied.

Refueling the Juggernaut, But Closing the Escape Hatches

By the 1970s, tariffs in the developed nations were already fairly low—at least on the products on which they had been willing to negotiate. Agriculture and labor-intensive industrial goods like clothing had been explicitly taken off the bargaining table when the agendas were set for the earlier GATT rounds. In this way, the GATT liberalization resulted mostly in tariff cutting in areas that were of most interest to developed nation exporters, basically industrial goods. Developing-nation exporters, who didn't have any "skin in the game" due to Special and Differential Treatment, were often disappointed in the lack of liberalization of agriculture and labor-intensive manufactures.

To refuel the trade liberalization juggernaut, the developed nations that had mostly driven the GATT process decided to broaden the agenda. The process started during the Tokyo Round with the "codes" approach to including non-tariff issues in the negotiations. Then with the Uruguay Round starting in 1986, new areas of interest to exporters in developed nations were put on the negotiating table, notably intellectual property issues, restrictions on foreign investment, and exported services issues. These areas came to be known as TRIPs (Trade-Related Intellectual Property), TRIMs (Trade-Related Investment Measures), and services, respectively. Additionally, two sectors still marked by high tariffs—agriculture and clothing—were put on the table to fuel the interest of agriculture exporters and low-wage exporters. It was hoped this constellation of new issues would refuel the juggernaut by rebalancing interests along North and South lines. Northern exporters were to gain from new rules and new market access in TRIPs, TRIMs, and services, while Southern exporters were to gain from freer trade in food and clothing. However, the dynamics of the negotiations and the increasing importance of emerging market economies meant that as the agenda was broadened, some of the earlier escape hatches were closed up.

For example, industrial nations' domestic laws already assured intellectual property protection for foreigners, so the expected gains for intellectual-property exporters from developed countries would come primarily from getting developing nations to adopt the standards of developed countries on patents, copyrights, and the like. During the Uruguay Round, developed countries feared that their opening of agriculture and textile markets would be pocketed by developing nations, while new disciplines on TRIPs, TRIMs, and services would be picked apart. A voluntary codes approach just would not do for a deal balanced in this way. The developing nations most likely to be affected would be those most likely to opt out. As a result, the Uruguay Round ended up including a feature called the Single Undertaking. All members, developed, and developing alike—even those that had not participated actively in the negotiations—were obliged to accept all the Uruguay Round agreements as one package. The basic outlines of the package-deal approach had been discussed in December 1991. Nevertheless, it clearly came as a surprise to many developing country members, especially those that did not follow the Uruguay Round through its eight years of twists and turns.

In addition, because the new areas involved considerable ambiguity and newness, members participating in the Uruguay Round negotiations decided it was necessary to greatly reduce the wiggle room in the dispute procedure. Both North and South feared that exporters' gains in the new areas might be offset by murky forms of protection or slippery national interpretations of the rules. For example, many governments in emerging economies were concerned that the United States was prone to taking unilateral action against whatever the US government considered to be an unfair trade practice under Section 301 of the Trade Act of 1974. The Uruguay agreement eliminated the possibility of blocking the initiation of a dispute resolution or adoption of a panel ruling, and applied this to all the areas in the Single Undertaking. The new adjudication procedure welded shut the earlier escape hatch.

Win-Win Multilateral Cooperation

From its start in 1946 until it was superseded by the World Trade Organization in 1995, the GATT promoted win-win multilateral cooperation by setting up what Douglass North would call an "institution"—constraints that guide political and economic interactions consisting of formal rules and informal restraints. The principles of the GATT fostered a self-enforcing pattern of cooperation and success. As the GATT's liberalization process started working its magic, exports of manufactured goods boomed—growing twice as fast as the production of manufactured goods from the late 1960s until just before the collapse of trade in 2009. Booming trade and incomes strengthened the belief of GATT members that following the code of conduct was good policy. As nations and interest groups came to expect that the rules would be respected, they adopted behaviors that conformed to the rules, thus making compliance almost automatic.

THE WOES OF THE WTO

A performance review of the WTO would produce an unbalanced report card. Little progress has been made on the trade liberalization front for almost two decades, since a handful of agreements in 1997. The Doha Round that started in 2001 is stalled. Of the WTO's functions, only the dispute settlement mechanism would receive a high performance score. Why did the GATT trade liberalization magic stop working for the WTO? I consider both external and internal reasons, and then consider the implications for multilateral and regional trade talks.

External Sources

The most commonly cited causes of the WTO's difficulties involve the lost dominance of the advanced economies. This occurred in two ways. First, as discussed above, the GATT was all about exchanges of market access, so market-size was the coinage of the realm. In the GATT period, the United States, European Union, Japan, and Canada—known as the Quad—dominated on this metric, accounting for two-thirds of world imports. The rapid growth of emerging economies changed this. Today, the Quad accounts for only half of world imports. Second, the sheer number of developing country members has shifted power in the organization and made talks more difficult. Since the last successful GATT/WTO negotiation was launched in 1986, over 70 developing nations have joined, about half of them since the WTO was created. Importantly, this includes China who rejoined in 2001 (having quit two years after joining in 1948).

In theory, more member nations does not necessarily hinder tariff cutting: after all, more nations could mean more demand and more supply for better market access. In practice, however, developing countries became active in more new defensive coalitions (that is, groups interested in preventing better access to their own markets) than in new offensive coalitions (groups interested in getting better access to foreign markets) (Patel 2007). The reason is straightforward. The reciprocity principle and small size of most developing markets limited their ability to ask foreigners to open up their markets. Hence, such countries had little to gain from new offensive coalitions. The consensus principle, by contrast, gave developing-nation coalitions a good deal of blocking power, which they used to block efforts to open their most politically sensitive markets.

Regionalism also created challenges. Regional trade agreements have always been part of the trade governance landscape. From around 1990, however, they played a very different role as the number of agreements skyrocketed. As all of these involved tariff cutting that would otherwise have had to be funneled through the WTO, and as all of these took up political economic "capital," the rise of regionalism probably made it harder to conclude the Uruguay Round. Concluding the Doha Round would probably be easier if, when it comes to trade liberalization, the WTO was the "only game in town."

Many of these new regional trade agreements were "deep" in the sense [that] . . . they went beyond tariff-cutting and included legally binding assurances aimed at making signatories more business-friendly to trade and investment flows from other signatories (recall that the GATT agreements are not legally binding). . . . At about the same time, an old form of economic integration agreement became very popular, the bilateral investment treaty. . . . Basically, these are concessions of sovereignty undertaken to encourage inward investment. For example, signatories usually commit to resolve investor–state disputes in a forum based in Washington, DC, rather than in national courts. In their heyday, scores of bilateral investment treaties were signed annually. By the late 1990s, most developing nations had already signed them with their major investment partners, so the number fell off sharply. There are now over 3,000 such agreements in existence.

The boom in the investment treaties and deep provisions did not create a direct competitor to the WTO. But they provide revealed-preference evidence that many WTO members were looking for disciplines that went far beyond the "shallow" disciplines included in WTO talks. In other words, the demand for policy reforms shifted away from the sort of disciplines that the WTO was set up to negotiate.

A different challenge came from unilateral tariff-cutting by developing nations. The rise of offshoring opened a new pathway to industrialization. The old, import-substitution path meant building a supply chain at home in order to become competitive abroad. High tariffs were often viewed as part of this process. The new offshoring-led path involved joining an international production network to become competitive, and then industrializing by expanding the quantity and range of tasks performed. In this new development model, tariffs hinder rather than help industrialization, so developing-nation tariffs started to fall rapidly independently of WTO talks. . . . To maintain flexibility, the developed nations did not "bind" the tariffs in the WTO even when they lowered them on a nondiscriminatory basis.

Because two-way tariff cutting had been the main fuel for the political economy juggernaut of trade liberalization, this unilateralism made multilateral talks less attractive to many developed members whose exporters saw their sales to developed nations boom even as Doha Round staggered from failure to failure. Why fight domestic protectionists at home when foreigners were lowering their tariffs unilaterally?

Internal Sources

These external challenges were magnified by big changes in the way WTO talks were organized, as opposed to those under the GATT. To put it bluntly, GATT multilateral negotiations involved the Quad (the United States, European Union, Japan, and Canada) bargaining among themselves over tariff cuts that they allowed the developing-nation members to free ride upon. WTO negotiations, by contrast, require binding tariff cuts and other policy commitments from all but the poorest members. In a political economy sense, the WTO and GATT are quite different international organizations. Specifically, as the Doha Round results would be binding equally on every member unless explicit exceptions were made, the "don't obey don't object" option that developing nations had under the GATT was cancelled under the WTO. Not surprisingly, they have been far more vocal in the Doha Round than they were in GATT rounds, objecting to provisions that threatened their domestic interests.

Implications for Multilateral Trade Talks

The impact of these challenges was not immediately apparent. In the years following the 1994 agreement that set up the WTO, multilateral talks worked much as before. A few bits of leftover business, like the 1997 Financial Services Agreement and Information Technology Agreement, were handled in the usual fashion in negotiations led by developed economies. But as the Doha Round got underway, the world discovered that the GATT's juggernaut magic would not work in the WTO. Specifically, the external and internal challenges had three momentous implications for the WTO multilateral negotiations.

First, multilateral negotiations under the WTO are more difficult. As explained above, the Single Undertaking principle meant that instead of four veto-players (the Quad nations of the United States, European Union, Japan, and Canada) and dozens of free riders as under the GATT, the Doha Round has more than 100 potential veto-players. Second, business interest in the Doha Round is much less forceful. The agenda for the talks, set in 2001, focused on tariff cutting in industrial goods and trade distortions in agricultural and service sectors. Industrial trade accounts for 80 percent of all trade, but business interest was dampened by the fact that tariffs in the Quad nations were already low, and those in the major developing nations had been lowered unilaterally. From a WTO perspective, the exporters of developed nations were now the free riders on unilateral tariff cutting by emerging markets. This greatly reduced their interest in lobbying their own governments for a Doha deal.

Second, a particular detail of WTO procedures has made unilateral tariff-cutting a major problem for the Doha Round. Following long-standing practice, WTO tariff-cutting talks focus on "bound" tariff rates, not applied rates. For many WTO members, actual applied rates are so much lower than the bound rates that the proposed Doha cuts would only reduce the distance between bound and applied tariffs, without actually lowering the applied rates. . . . Five decades of GATT talks had already lowered bound rates in the developed economies to less than 3 percent on average. In most of the large developing nations, bound rates are quite high, but applied rates are lower. Even in China, the third-largest global market for exports, the applied rate is about 8 percent. If the developing nations had not lowered their applied rates so much below their bound rates, developed nation exporters would have had something to fight for.

Similarly in agriculture, the biggest protectionists—the European Union and Japan—unilaterally lowered distortions for purely domestic reasons. The political power of rich-nation farm lobbies has dropped as farm populations have fallen and awareness has risen about the fact that most farm support goes to wealthy landowners and agri-corporations. The European Union broadly switched its agriculture support policies to non-trade-distorting forms and basically eliminated export subsidies in major reforms that took place in 2003, 2008, and 2013. Japan still has astronomical tariffs on a handful of products like rice, but it too is shifting unilaterally towards non-trade-distorting policies with major reforms in 2003 and 2007. While agriculture trade is hardly free and fair (and the United States increased trade distortions with its 2014 US Farm Bill), the mercantilist gain from a conclusion of the Doha Round is clearly lower in 2016 than it would have been in 2001. Moreover, a number of emerging markets have deployed some of their new-found wealth in the form of new trade-distorting agriculture policies of their own. They are, in essence, reacting to exactly the same rural–urban domestic politics that produced agriculture protection in the United States, European Union, and Japan. This has created new opponents to agricultural trade opening.

Third, the rise of offshoring has created a political economy demand and supply for disciplines that underpin international production networks. As these disciplines were not included in the Doha Round's 2001 agenda, and dozens of WTO members have vetoed all moves to expand the agenda, the supply and demand are meeting outside the WTO—mainly in the deep regional trade agreements and bilateral investment treaties. The rapid rise in production unbundling—sometimes called "global value chains"—has meant that the world's most dynamic trade involves a nexus of trade in goods, services, know-how, physical investment, key personnel, and financial capital. Many developing nations sought and are still seeking to attract this offshoring activity. Firms in the high-income nations are interested in providing it—as long as they have assurances that host nations will respect their tangible and intangible property rights, and ensure that the necessary flows of goods, services, investment, capital, and people will be unimpeded.

These assurances have been provided in dozens of deep bilateral and regional trade agreements and in the bilateral investment treaties. This "spaghetti bowl" (as it is sometimes called) of intertwined agreements is clearly not optimal for international production sharing. As a result, a number of so-called megaregionals like the Trans-Pacific Partnership and Trans-Atlantic Trade and Investment Partnership have emerged to multilateralize some of the disciplines at a regional level. . . . In short, the political economy switched from "my market for yours" to "my factories for your reform"—that is, developing-nation trade liberalization and pro-business reforms in exchange for production facilities from developed nations.

THE FUTURE OF MULTILATERALISM, REGIONALISM, AND THE WTO

The WTO is a pillar of multilateral economic governance, as was the GATT before it. Its prime mission is to establish rules of the road and facilitate negotiation of mutually advantageous trade liberalization. In the main, the WTO can claim "mission accomplished." It oversees a set of near-universal norms for rule-based trade, and it runs a dispute settlement mechanism that routinely arbitrates disputes and issues rulings that are universally followed even though it has no direct enforcement power. Most telling of all, nations vote with their feet by joining the WTO, even though the requisite reforms typically involve high domestic political costs.

However, the WTO seems frozen in time. The last updating of its rulebook and its last major trade liberalization came in 1994, when Bill Clinton, Gerhard Schroeder, Hashimoto Ryutaro, and Li Peng were in power and the Internet barely existed. The current WTO talks, the Doha Round, are focused entirely on 20th-century issues such as tariffs on industrial and agricultural goods, along with trade-distorting policies in agriculture and services.

While a couple of small agreements have been completed, the Doha Round is in its 15th year and nowhere near done. This 15-year fail trail, however, has not stalled global trade opening and rule-writing. For 20 years, new rule-writing and trade liberalization has proceeded apace along three axes—all of them outside the ambit of the WTO. First, a great deal of tariff cutting has been done unilaterally by WTO members, especially developing-nation members. Second, new disciplines on international investment—flows that are now intimately entwined with trade in goods and services—have been established by a network of over 3,000 bilateral investment treaties. Third, the new rules and deep disciplines that have underpinned the rapid expansion of offshoring and the internationalization of production have been written into deep regional trade agreements, especially those between advanced and emerging economies.

These observations invite two questions: Is the lack of multilaterialism worrisome? What is the future of the WTO and multilateralism?

Is the Lack of Multilateralism Worrisome?

Two decades ago, the explosion of bilateral deals . . . sparked a debate on multilateralism versus regionalism. Authors such as Bhagwati (1993) decried regionalism as dangerous. He pointed to a "small-think" danger—that the inefficiencies of trade diversion would diminish welfare—and a "big-think" dangers—that regionalism would block the path to global free trade.

As it turned out, global tariff-cutting since the rise of regionalism has proceeded as quickly as ever, but outside the WTO. . . . As a result, the specter that regional trading agreements would inefficiently divert trade never really appeared. Measures based on detailed tariff data show that little of world trade is affected by tariff preference margins of 5 percent or more. After all, the most-favored-nation tariffs are zero or very low on most of the world's large trade flows, and so bilateral and regional trade agreements provide a relatively small incentive to divert trade. Where tariffs remain high, bilateral and regional trade deals tend to exclude such "sensitive" items, so no preference is created either. Overall, the econometric evidence suggests that trade diversion due to bilateral and regional agreements is not a first-order concern in the world economy.

As for the systemic, big-think danger, it is hard to know what would have happened if somehow nations had not signed the hundreds of bilateral agreements that they did. But one thing is clear. The rise of preferential tariffs within bilateral and regional agreements has not blocked the path to overall global tariff-cutting. Virtually all of the developing-nation WTO members who engaged in bilateral, discriminatory liberalization have simultaneously been engaged in unilateral, nondiscriminatory liberalization.

Importantly, the trade creation/diversion concern only applies to bilateral and multilateral liberalization that is truly discriminatory against trade from countries not included in the agreement. However, many of the deep regional trade agreement provisions concern matters where discrimination is impractical. Such disciplines impinge upon corporations, services, capital, and intellectual property, and in these areas it is difficult to write rules that identify the nationality of such things in a way that clever lawyers cannot get around. For example, the Japan–Thailand regional trade agreement allows Japanese banks to sell certain financial services in Thailand. But since it is difficult to determine which banks are Japanese, the agreement grants the privilege to any bank registered and regulated in Japan—which makes most large U.S. and EU banks "Japanese" for the purposes of the agreement. This phenomenon of "soft preferences" also arose from the EU's Single Market program (which is the biggest and deepest of all regional trade agreements). As it turned out, many EU reforms were helpful to non-EU firms even though their nations were not signatories.

Future of Multilateralism

The WTO's paralysis in the face of frenetic tariff cutting and rule writing outside the organization can be attributed to two factors. First, the Doha Agenda was set for a world economy that is no longer with us. If Doha had been concluded in a few years as planned, the juggernaut effect might have worked. But with the rise of China, the rise of offshoring, and the rise of unilateralism, the negotiating items on the Doha agenda no longer provide a win–win bargain for all. Second, the natural step of expanding the WTO agenda to include some of the disciplines routinely agreed in deep regional trade agreements is blocked by nations who have been largely left aside by the rise of offshoring. They feel that they were promised, in 2001, a "rebalancing" that would involve reduced barriers to exports of agricultural and labor-intensive goods. Until they get their rebalancing, they have been willing to veto an expansion of the agenda.

Since important network externalities can be won by moving away from bilateralism and towards multilateralism when it comes to some deep provisions that are commonly found in regional trade agreements, the WTO's paralysis has led to plurilateral deals being done elsewhere. The thousands of bilateral investment treaties, for instance, are not all that different, and so network externalities could be realized by melding them together. The emergence of so-called megaregionals like the Trans-Pacific Partnership and Trans-Atlantic Trade and Investment Partnership should be thought of as partial multilateralization of existing deep disciplines by sub-groups of WTO members who are deeply involved in offshoring and global value chains.

The megaregionals like the Trans-Pacific Partnership and Trans-Atlantic Trade and Investment Partnership, however, are not a good substitute for multilateralization inside the WTO. They will create an international trading system marked by fragmentation (because they are not harmonized among themselves) and exclusion (because emerging trade giants like China and India are not members now and may never be). Whatever the conceptual merits of moving the megaregionals into the WTO, I have argued elsewhere that the actual WTO does not seem well-suited to the task. First, as mentioned, the WTO seems incapable of getting beyond the Doha Round and incapable of addressing deep disciplines until it does. Second, a situation where China, India, and other large emerging markets stay outside the megaregionals may prove to be stable. The "soft preferences" arising from the megaregionals may not prove very damaging to large outsiders who can use their market size and unilateral harmonization to offset the negative effects. For example, those European outsiders who decided to stay out of the EU could still make adjustments and live with the soft preferences. A domino effect, however, is likely to draw in smaller outsiders wishing to participate in the international production networks inside the megaregionals.

What all this suggests is that world trade governance is heading towards a two-pillar system. The first pillar, the WTO, continues to govern traditional trade as it has done since it was founded in 1995. The second pillar is a system where disciplines on trade in intermediate goods and services, investment and intellectual property protection, capital flows, and the movement of key personnel are multi-lateralised in megaregionals. China and certain other large emerging markets may have enough economic clout to counter their exclusion from the current megaregionals. Live and let live within this two-pillar system is a very likely outcome.

REFERENCES

Bhagwati, Jagdish N. 1993. "The Diminished Giant Syndrome." *Foreign Affairs*, Spring, pp. 22–26.

Grossman, Gene, and Elhanan Helpman. 1995. "Trade Wars and Trade Talks." *Journal of Political Economy* 103 (4): 675–708.

Patel, Mayur. 2007. "New Faces it the Green Room: Developing Country Coalitions and Decision-Making in the WTO." GEG Working Paper 2007/33, Global Trade Governance Project.

Putnam, Robert D. 1988. "Diplomacy and Domestic Politics: The Logic of Two-Level Games." *International Organization* 42 (3): 427–60.

VI

MIGRATION

International migration—the movement of people across national borders—is at the center of controversies about globalization. Opponents claim that immigrants suppress the wages of native workers, threaten national identity, create security risks and crime problems, impose welfare burdens, undermine social capital, and provoke a host of other ills. Immigration is unpopular, particularly among people with less education and in places with welfare programs available to migrants. Immigration policy has not been liberalized since World War II, in stark contrast to the gradual removal of trade barriers and the reduction of controls on capital flows. Governments today allow foreign goods and foreign capital to enter their borders with few limitations, but they impose tough restrictions on people trying do the same thing. World migration is anything but "mass" migration.

It wasn't always this way. In the second half of the nineteenth century, countries had open immigration policies but were relatively closed to trade—exactly the opposite of today. Encouraged by high wages and falling transportation costs, over 60 million poorer Europeans took advantage of open immigration policies and emigrated to the vast lands of North and South America and Australasia. Three-fifths went to the United States, but there were large flows to South America, particularly Argentina and Brazil. A steady stream of people also flowed from England to Australia, New Zealand, and South Africa. By 1914, there was hardly a town or city anywhere in the New World whose labor markets had not been influenced by the presence of strangers who had immigrated from the Old World.

How do we account for the reversal in immigration policies between the late nineteenth century and now? More generally, which interests, interactions, and institutional forces shape immigration policy? The readings in this section provide a sample of how researchers have addressed these questions.

As Gary P. Freeman and Alan K. Kessler (Reading 23) emphasize, scholars usually begin by trying to understand the factors that shape individual attitudes toward immigration. This focus on attitudes is based on the assumption that public opinion drives immigration policy. Research on public opinion has found evidence that both material economic interests and factors related to cultural identity shape immigration attitudes. When natives perceive a job market threat from immigrants, or when they expect to pay higher taxes to support immigrants' use of welfare programs, they are more likely to oppose immigration out of personal self-interest. But opposition to immigration is also related to noneconomic factors, such as the cultural and ethnic distance between natives and the immigrant population, a fear of loss of national characteristics and identity, and a taste for cultural homogeneity.

The impact of such noneconomic factors on mass attitudes may not be all that surprising, given that migration is the most "intimate" form of globalization, putting nationals in day-to-day contact with foreign-born peoples and cultures. But public opinion may not be the only factor that drives immigration policy, or even the most important factor. For example, it is unlikely that public opinion can explain why immigration policy was so open in the late nineteenth century, an era noted for populism and strong nativist sentiment. Institutional factors may have been at play in this period since most New World countries limited the franchise to the property-owning upper and middle classes, who benefit from immigration. Freeman and Kessler move beyond the discussion of mass attitudes to incorporate political science treatments that emphasize institutions—most notably, the executive and legislative branches of government and the role of organized interest groups within this institutional structure. From an institutional perspective, organized groups may have more impact on policy than unorganized mass opinion because vote-maximizing politicians find it in their electoral interest to cater to these groups.

A similar approach underlies Margaret E. Peters' (Reading 24) analysis of how trade policy has shaped immigration policy over the past two centuries. She focuses on the interests of business firms, who lobby for open immigration when trade policy is closed, so as to lower their labor costs. When trade policy is open, by contrast, business interests must adapt to import competition by increasing their productivity or go out of business. Either way, the business community has less need of cheap labor when trade policy is open and therefore reduces its pressure for open immigration.

The final reading in this section gets into the nitty-gritty of immigration policymaking in the United States, exploring how the interaction of pro-immigration and anti-immigration interest groups shapes U.S. immigration policy at the sector level. Giovanni Facchini, Anna Maria Mayda, and Prachi Mishra (Reading 25) find that restrictions on immigration are lower in sectors in which business interest groups incur larger lobbying expenditures and higher in sectors where labor unions are more important.

23

Political Economy and Migration Policy

GARY P. FREEMAN AND ALAN K. KESSLER

Economists and political scientists have much to offer each other in the study of migration policy, but economists have mostly ignored the ways in which politics and political institutions constrain migration markets, and political scientists have not always given enough attention to the economic aspects of migration. In this reading, Gary P. Freeman and Alan K. Kessler first consider the economic effects of migration, as drawn from theories of labor markets, international trade, and public finance, and then link them to political analyses that stress the role of states, institutions, and interest groups. They conclude that a combined political economy approach holds great promise in terms of understanding the sources of migration policy.

INTRODUCTION

Economists studying migration have slighted the investigation of migration policies, the role of states in formulating those policies, and that of politics in shaping policy outcomes. Political science, for its part, has deployed an eclectic assortment of theoretical and analytical tools, as many drawn from cognate disciplines as from political science itself. . . . Nevertheless, political science has not systematically integrated economic and political concepts concerning immigration.

We argue that both economics and political science would be well-served to join forces more self-consciously in the study of migration politics. The strengths of each discipline complement those of the other and make good some of their deficiencies. The discipline of economics provides some of the most promising and sophisticated theories, concepts, and empirical methods for analyzing migration politics. Although neoclassical economics is criticized for taking preferences as given (especially as applied in rational choice perspectives), economic theory and analysis may be employed to give useful, if partial, answers to the question as to where preferences come from. We do not believe that immigration preferences always reflect underlying material interests, but we argue that the material stakes of migration are critical inputs into the migration policy process that must be taken into account, and that economic models produce testable hypotheses as to their identity. Political science, on the other hand, specializes in analyzing the institutions and processes that frame, shape, transform, distort, and channel economic and non-economic preferences into policy agendas and outcomes, but has more difficulty explaining the origins of the preferences of actors. Economic models of migration devoid of political dimensions and political models that fail to credit the economic underpinnings of the migration process risk being naïve and incomplete.

Economics and political science can be usefully combined to create political economy approaches well-suited to address particular questions about migration policy. We discuss three leading approaches from political science in the migration policy literature: statist, institutionalist, and interest-group. We divide economic perspectives on migration into two broad categories: the study of wage and income effects of migration carried out by labor market and trade economists, and the study of the fiscal or transfer effects of migration derived from the field of public finance. These five perspectives from the two disciplines, when combined, yield six analytical perspectives, as depicted in Table 1.

Part 1 of this paper reviews political science perspectives on migration policy, focusing on states, institutions, and interest groups. Part 2 looks at the economics of migration policy, laying out theoretical models that investigate the wage, income, and fiscal effects of migration. Part 3 seeks to demonstrate the promise of combining ideas drawn from the two disciplines by exploring insights to be gained from statist, institutionalist, and interest-group approaches that investigate hypotheses derived from economic models of wage, income, and fiscal effects of migration.

POLITICAL SCIENCE AND MIGRATION POLICY: STATES, INSTITUTIONS, AND INTEREST GROUPS

The contemporary literature on the politics of migration policy is scarcely 30 years old, but it has produced a broad array of interpretive schemes. A number of reviews have tried to make sense of the field by categorizing research according to its (often unselfconscious) analytical or theoretical points of view. A partial accounting of recent reviews yields interests, the liberal state, and globalization; Marxism, realism, liberalism, national identity, domestic politics, and institutionalism; interests, rights, and states; post-industrial change,

TABLE 1 Political Economy Approaches to Migration Policy

	Political science		
	Statist	Institutionalist	Interest group
Economics			
Wage and income effects	1	2	3
Fiscal effects	4	5	6

spatial (territorial) models, and trade theory; globalization, embedded realism, and path dependence; domestic interest groups, political institutions, and international factors; and power resources and constellation theories, state-centric and institutional theories, cost-benefit or economic theories, and cultural and racial/racialization theories. Making a necessarily arbitrary choice, we treat the political science literature here under the three headings of states, institutions, and interest groups.

The state was a central concept of traditional political science, but it nearly disappeared from view in the wake of the postwar behavioral revolution. The concept enjoyed something of a comeback in the 1970s with the relatively brief popularity of neo-Marxist theories and the more lasting resurgence of interest in institutions. States have always been a major component of realist international relations theory, where they are typically treated as unitary actors seeking to maximize the "national interest." In some models, the state is thought to arbitrate among competing domestic interests to determine policy. Debates on how and why this arbitration takes place reflected instrumentalist versus structural theories of the state and its relation to capital. American political scientists, perhaps reflecting their experience with a weak and fragmented liberal state, were less drawn to state theory than their counterparts in other regions of the world.

The combination of neglect of migration by political scientists with the fascination of economists for some version of push/pull theory in which individual migration decisions were a result of calculations of utility focused largely on employment markets and relative wages meant that the fundamental role of states in stimulating and organizing migration flows was slow to be recognized. Indeed, no one has yet produced a full-scale effort to apply a theory of the state to migration politics and policy. . . . Zolberg (1999) produced an articulate case for treating state regulations and policies as central to the character of migrations worldwide. Still, the motives that might underlie state actions remain poorly specified. . . .

Institutionalist accounts disaggregate the state, focusing on the distinct roles played by bureaucracies, political parties, electoral arrangements, executive/legislative relationships, etc. in the policy-making process. Institutions have been variously defined in straightforwardly empirical terms—parliament, president, party, electoral system—or more loosely to include rules and norms that are not necessarily or primarily embodied in formal organizations. Institutionalists have been the chief advocates of the notion of path dependence and the fuzzy and, therefore, indisputable claim that "history matters." The gist of their interpretation is that the determinants of policy are complex, difficult to pin down, and certainly not reducible to preferences of individual actors or group-level demands. Institutional inertia, policy legacies, and "contingency" must be taken into account.

Examples of institutionalist accounts of immigration policy abound. Inter-agency conflict "inside the state" is at the heart of some accounts. Political parties have been central to many immigration studies. Scholars have investigated the immigration preferences of mainstream parties, the sources of support for right-wing populist parties, and the effect of electoral arrangements on the success of anti-immigration parties. . . . Efforts to explain the variation across states in the shape and temperature of migration politics often focus on political opportunity structures that affect the capacities and incentives of various groups to organize and give voice to their preferences.

Interest-group . . . models of politics contest the idea that the individual can be the principal unit of analysis and instead search for propositions about how and when individuals coordinate their activities and engage in collective behavior. Work in this vein commonly attempts to link policy demands to concrete (or expected) gains and losses of identifiable sub-groups of the electorate and to the bargains and compromises they produce in pluralistic political systems. Interest-group approaches have focused on a broad array of groups positioned for or against immigration (Freeman 1995).

For all the insights research in political science yields, a singular failing is that it is unable to provide a convincing theoretical account of the origins of individual preferences on immigration or the motivations of institutions with respect to the issue. Statist analysis, for example, presumes that policy is designed to achieve the national interest, but provides few sure guidelines for determining what the national interest is in immigration policy. Should it be directed at defending national sovereignty and the sanctity of borders? In order to achieve these ends should states pursue open or restrictive, selective or permissive immigration policies? Should they mount policies designed to reap maximum economic benefit or trim policies in accord with popular prejudices or with an eye to social order? Hypotheses about state motivations require heroic assumptions that lack firm theoretical footing. Moreover, a statist model confronts the problem of explaining why liberal democratic receiving states adopt widely disparate immigration and citizenship policies. Recognizing this dilemma, scholars tend to differentiate across state structures, but this simply drives the analytical challenge back a step since it is then necessary to account for the erection of different types of state institutions, an accounting that requires, in order to avoid tautology, resort to non-statist theoretical approaches.

Similar problems plague institutionalist accounts. A plausible story can be woven, for example, that immigration policy emerges out of conflicts between central executives concerned about diplomatic and security issues and specific ministries responsible for labor markets, industry, or immigration and citizenship. These stories are, however, rooted in inferences about what institutions want based on empirical observations of their behavior rather than theoretically derived propositions. A recent review demonstrates the absence of systematic knowledge about the institutional arrangements developed in various receiving states to manage immigration and integration programs. There is little empirical evidence to support generalizations about the motivations of different bureaucratic bodies and no consensus as to whether diverse institutional configurations yield diverse policy outcomes.

Interest-group accounts appear on the surface to surmount this problem, but are in fact seriously challenged by it. Interest groups usually come with handy labels identifying them as labor unions, employer federations, and the like, that appear to provide a direct indicator of the "interest" being pursued. In practice, such studies are incomplete until they generate theoretical explanations for the particular issue positions taken by these groups and the motivations that impel them to organize.

ECONOMICS AND MIGRATION POLICY: WAGE, INCOME, AND FISCAL EFFECTS

The literature on the economics of migration is situated in the practice of a more theoretically and methodologically integrated social science discipline than political science. By far the majority of work on migration coming out of economics addresses its role in labor markets. We refer to these efforts as production function or aggregate output models. Most migration is thought to be undertaken for purposes of work. Migrants are therefore conceived as labor power, or embodied human capital, and their introduction into national or local labor markets is presumed to increase an economy's productive resources and capabilities. In the abstract, nations in a position to attract migrants should encourage immigration and sending states should discourage it. The logic of efficiency drives the unwavering conviction of most economists that immigration produces net gains up until the point at which the marginal productivity of labor is equalized globally.

The standard caveat is, of course, that aggregate gains for receiving states involve distributional trade-offs. . . . An influx of immigrants increases the economy's labor supply and productive resources, contributing to a rise in national income, or an "immigration surplus." At the same time, however, immigration entails a redistribution of income away from domestic laborers to migrants and capital owners, yielding potential avenues for political conflict among diverse economic (and non-economic) interests. A question that arises from the point of view of designing immigration policy, however, is whether those who gain from immigration (business, consumers, migrants, and the like) can (and are willing to) compensate those who lose in order to produce a net social gain. Another issue is the non-economic consequences of migration (ethnic conflict, political discontent, etc.). Both of these questions require the introduction of political variables into the analysis that potentially constrain the ability of decision-makers to direct policy toward any particular outcome.

A similar tension between efficiency and distribution characterizes work on immigration in international economics. The two most widely employed models of international trade, the Heckscher-Ohlin (H-O) and specific-factors models, give competing insights into the economic impact of immigration. Moving beyond a simple characterization of a closed, national labor market, trade economists assess how immigration affects returns to capital owners and laborers in an economy open to international goods and/or factor mobility. In the standard two-factor, two-good H-O model, in which countries endowed with different levels of resources exchange goods but factors are immobile, trade substitutes for migration. When countries trade, the relative prices of goods converge causing, in turn, a tendency toward factor price equalization (as countries exchange factors of production, typically capital or labor, indirectly via trade). Countries rich in labor thus export labor-intensive goods while countries rich in capital export goods embodying more capital than labor, and the convergence in relative prices of labor and capital erodes incentives for international migration in equilibrium. Where labor migration does occur, in the context of the Heckscher-Ohlin model, analysts expect immigration to exercise little long-run impact on national labor markets as new workers are instead absorbed into the production process. In this model, immigration does not affect the economic welfare of natives or immigrants and the immigration surplus is zero.

In other trade models, immigration contributes to aggregate national income but exercises downward pressure on wages. In two-factor models, where homogeneous capital and labor are inputs in production, an increase in the labor supply reduces wages as immigrants compete with, or substitute for, domestic workers in the labor market. With the introduction of additional factors, however, immigration may raise the marginal productivity of labor and increase incomes of non-competing workers. The specific-factors model offers the most straightforward context for illustrating potential gains to complementary domestic workers. In the model, three factors of production, typically land, labor, and capital, are combined to produce two goods, food and manufactures. Land and capital are tied to, or are specific to, the production of one good—food and manufactures respectively. Labor, on the other hand, can be used in the production of either good and is therefore considered mobile. If immigrants are concentrated primarily in agriculture, capital is specific to manufacturing, and domestic workers are free to move between sectors, then an influx of immigrants tends to lower wages in agriculture but raise returns to mobile labor. If capital is mobile and land and labor are tied to specific sectors, however, an influx of immigration is likely to benefit owners of capital at the expense of holders of land and labor. . . .

In both production function and trade-based models, the impact of immigration on wages drives political-economic responses in a predictable way. Yet the economic determinants of national policy are also influenced by the fiscal costs and benefits of immigration. Questions of public finance, or the net contribution of immigration to government revenue, point to an additional economic basis for support for and opposition to migration. If immigrants pay less in taxes than they receive in government benefits, opposition to immigration may stem from concern over fiscal rather than (or in addition to) wage effects. In this case, the range of political and economic interests engaged in immigration policy is broader than models from labor or trade economics suggest, and politics necessarily more complex. Taxpayers, for example, may resent costs attributed to immigrants—real or perceived—for their use of local public goods such as education, health-care, or income support, regardless of the impact of immigration on wages. Furthermore, because immigration is typically geographically concentrated, residents and elected officials in localities that bear a disproportionate share of such costs have greater incentives to oppose immigration, while those in other localities clearly have less. State and local representatives, as well as local interest groups, thus have fiscal incentives to court or curb immigration that may conflict with those of the national government, as tension between high immigrant states and the federal government in the United States attests.

Economic approaches to immigration thus offer diverse accounts of the costs and benefits of immigration, leaving analysts to select the model best suited to the political context in question. Because low-skilled workers or those with low education are likely to bear the brunt of labor market competition, redistribution of income is the key mechanism underlying potential political conflict. Where the impact of immigration on local labor markets appears "large," an increase in the labor supply accompanying an influx of immigrants is likely to exercise downward pressure on wages. In such a case, class conflict, or political cleavages pitting businesses and immigrants against labor, is likely to result. If the labor market impact of immigration is "small" or social programs mitigate adverse effects of competition, on the other hand, non-economic concerns are likely to dominate the political debate. How one defines large and small is, of course, crucial to characterizing politics and is subject to manipulation by organized political constituencies (lobby groups, media outlets, issue entrepreneurs, etc.). This is critical for understanding the interaction between economic and political approaches to immigration. We take up this argument again below.

If the labor market effects of immigration are of less immediate concern and the political debate instead is cast in terms of costs and benefits to taxpayers, the cast of characters engaged in policy debate is likely to change. Fiscal costs and benefits from immigration cut across class or sector-based lines, pitting taxpayers, localities, and diverse lobby and special interest groups against one another in the struggle over policy. Low-skilled workers adversely affected by immigration are, as in the previous case, likely to push for local or national redress, particularly in high-immigration localities. Where low-skilled workers are of similar ethnic or cultural background to immigrants, one may expect that solidarity rather than economic self-interest dampens incentives to oppose immigration, though ultimately the question remains an empirical one. Federalism, as in the US and German cases, adds additional complexity to this discussion, with sub-national governments looking to the central government for assistance in dealing with the consequences of policies that are a "national" responsibility.

Many of the observations and hypotheses discussed in this section are summarized in Table 2. In terms of standard production function or aggregate output accounts summarized across the first row of the table, the expected economic effects of immigration yield a familiar class-oriented account of potential political cleavages. Businesses benefiting from an increase in the supply of labor gain, while laborers competing with new immigrants face a more competitive labor market. Trade models, depicted in the second and third rows, offer a distinct starting-point for political economic analysis. In the H-O context, immigrants enter into the production process in a manner consistent with their skill-set, exercising little impact on the labor market and, hence, occasioning little reason for political action. The specific-factors model better approximates potential economic incentives that might generate political tensions in the short run (during the process of economic adjustment). Immigration is expected to depress wages of citizens and residents of similar skill, but

TABLE 2 Economic Models of Migration Effects and Projected Political Consequences

Model	Relevant actors	Economic effect	Politics
Production/ output model	Capital, labor	Profits increase, wages decrease	Class cleavages Capital +, labor −
H-O model*	2 factors (capital, labor) or skilled, unskilled labor	No wage effect (in long run), change in production	Model predicts none but expect short-run opposition from workers bearing cost of adjustment
Specific-factors model	3 factors (capital, land, labor) or skilled labor, unskilled labor, capital	Wages decrease; profits increase contingent on assumptions . . .	Sectoral cleavages Mobile factor +, specific factors −
Fiscal models	Young, middle-aged, elderly; federal vs. state?	Greater participation in welfare programs. In US, state-level costs of education, health care; federal govt. benefits from tax revenues	Class cleavages (?) Low-skilled workers − Skilled workers +/− (?) In US high immigrant states −, federal government +

*Heckscher-Ohlin model.
+ = wins, − = loses.

augment incomes of other socio-economic actors. A rich set of coalitional possibilities thus arises, with patterns of support for and opposition to immigration attuned to the mobility and sectoral affiliation of organized groups.

Fiscal models, highlighted in the bottom row, identify an even broader array of potential economic effects and offer a richer but complex set of political patterns. One might expect class tensions in light of perceived competition for public goods but matters of geographic concentration or regional or local politics (particularly in federal systems) complicate straightforward hypotheses. With respect to the beneficiaries of tax-funded programs versus those who are essentially tax-payers, the model predicts that beneficiaries favor a status quo in which they gain but are likely to face high collective action costs—a status quo bias effect. Because the situation is symmetrical, generally, welfare effects are opposite.

Economic models produce powerful hypotheses about the economic effects of various types of migration and, therefore, the stakes involved for migrants and natives. If actors respond to the economic incentives produced by migration, the models should be predictive of the political conflicts and coalitions generated by migration. One obstacle to testing these economic hypotheses is that the models from which they are derived are highly abstract, general, and simplified. In the real world, migration flows are more numerous and complex than the models can accommodate. Efforts to test trade models with historical data drawn from specific countries find considerable support, but confront important instances when economic predictions are not confirmed. Addressing the interaction of economic and non-economic considerations is also critical. Identifying the relative contribution of material and non-material determinants of policy remains a necessary step, as does a clearer account of the conditions under which one set of considerations may matter more than another and why.

CROSS-DISCIPLINARY POLITICAL ECONOMY APPROACHES

We argue that political science must be more open to and systematic about testing the plausibility of hypotheses about immigration policy interests and preferences derived from economics. Correspondingly, work from a more purely economics perspective must contend with the various ways in which political institutions, conflicts, and negotiation modify and shape how preferences evolve and are expressed politically. We seek to illustrate the advantages of such a combined approach by discussing the contributions—actual and possible—from work that weds analytical tools from both disciplines. We will discuss these under the three categories of states, institutions, and interest groups.

States, Economic Effects, and Immigration Policy

The logic that considers the state as a unitary actor capable of pursuing national interests predicts that states will favor open immigration in order to maximize aggregate economic and net fiscal gains, with the proviso that these gains must be balanced against other relevant concerns of the state that might be threatened by immigration. To take aggregate economic gain first, economic theory suggests a clear and powerful set of state preferences growing out of wage and income effects, but they are in many respects the least interesting of those we discuss in this article. Some might see them as statements of the obvious, or too simplistic to be descriptive of actual state behaviors. The most compelling aspect of the ideas related to wage and income effects has to do with the necessity of compensating losers from migration and of efforts to balance the quest for aggregate gain against competing priorities. The fiscal effects of migration, on the other hand, can be captured by policies that seek to maximize the revenue contributions of migrants, minimize their consumption of public benefits, or minimize the consumption of public benefits by natives that is a response to the effects of immigration, all of which turn out to be problematic policy objectives from the point of view of states.

The validity of broad generalizations about the policies states should pursue with regard to immigration can be tested via comparative analysis of the immigration policies of receiving states. There is no space here to explore this question adequately, such studies constituting a major research agenda for immigration scholars, but provisional evidence is mixed. Although there are numerous instances of states adopting economically-oriented immigration policies (the ambitious postwar immigration plans of Australia, for example, and the postwar guestworker schemes in Western Europe), for every program of this type one can point to equally impressive restrictive measures that seem to belie economic needs. Labor-short Britain attempted to close Commonwealth immigration in the 1960s and accepted only limited numbers of European displaced persons after World War II. Japan and South Korea currently pursue restrictive policies that belie labor market conditions. If the expectation of open immigration policies is the starting point of economic models, then a major task is to account for the substantial deviation of policies from that expectation in particular countries and times.

Beyond that, there is a complex interpretive issue involved in classifying immigration policies as restrictive or open. What exactly do large-scale irregular immigration, unauthorized employment, and rolling amnesties indicate about the intentions of policy-makers? Are they policy failures or are they at least partially intentional "gaps" designed to achieve economic goals indirectly or covertly? Does a tolerance of illegal border crossings and unauthorized work in the informal sector indicate preferences for actual open migration policies without formally endorsing them?

Turning to the fiscal effects of immigration, support for economic hypotheses from comparative evidence is, again, mixed. Consider first the matter of maximizing revenues from migrants. The most effective means for achieving this goal are combating irregular immigration, suppressing immigrant participation in the informal economy, and discouraging remittances to countries of origin. Irregular workers are more likely than natives to participate in the informal economy and workers there tend to underpay or avoid taxation on income altogether. Monies dispatched back home are not spent in the country of immigration and, thus, bypass consumption taxes. Whether states are making good-faith efforts to suppress the informal economy is a topic too broad for serious consideration here, but estimates suggest that informalization is pervasive in the United States (with the number of illegal migrants as high as 12 million) and in many European countries. With regard to remittances, liberal states lack the legal authority or the means to restrict them and to do so would undermine major incentives for migration in the first place. Indeed, the promise of remittances is employed as an inducement for sending states to enter into migration agreements. What is perhaps even more striking is the failure of either sending or receiving states to tax remittances in order to redirect spending from consumption to investment in the homeland or to capture more of the economic gains of migration in the host society. In sum, states may well wish to maximize revenues coming from migrants, but they appear ill-equipped to achieve this end.

With respect to limiting migrant access to publicly funded benefits, the record is more complicated. Some immigration programs have endeavored to prevent immigrants from participating in public benefits programs. Guest-worker schemes in Europe did not specifically stipulate that immigrants could not benefit from health care or housing subsidies, or the like. Instead, their temporary character, and the fact that residence permits were often linked to time-limited work permits, created a system in which immigrants who lost their jobs (and might be expected to resort to public benefit schemes) would be impelled to return home. These plans did not work as designed, of course. Authorities representing components of national states (welfare bureaucracies, local governments, and the courts) foiled these schemes by upholding immigrant claims to a vested interest in social benefits. States have sometimes taken aggressive steps to cut off migrant access to public largesse, as in the case of the UK and the USA. In the US case, some of the most serious efforts to limit immigrant consumption of public benefits have come from grassroots movements in states and localities heavily impacted by migration, and have been targeted against central government policies seen as too generous or poorly enforced. Studies . . . that indicate that in the USA the central government enjoys a net fiscal gain from migration whereas some states and localities do not, suggest that central governments have an incentive to offload the costs of immigration onto local communities.

One important fiscal issue is the possible impact of immigration on the financial viability of unfunded public pension programs. Immigration enthusiasts sometimes argue that, because of their relative youth and high rates of labor force activity, immigrants make a positive contribution to the stability of pension systems and other welfare programs. Immigrants may also contribute to social security funds but often never claim their benefits in retirement, either because they go back to countries of origin, make contributions to fictional social security accounts, or die on average earlier than native workers. Most serious studies indicate that migration can play only a limited and temporary role in redressing demographic imbalances of populations.

A second reason the statist political economy model needs amplification is that not all states are alike. Liberal states may have different priorities and capacities than those of authoritarian systems. A comparison of the outcomes of the temporary worker schemes in Europe and the United States with those run by the Gulf states is evidence enough of that. If, furthermore, liberal states are instrumentally or structurally capitalist, as has been argued, then we would expect their overriding concern to be to provide ample, flexible labor for capitalist interests. On the other hand, liberal states should, in principle, be both more inclined and under greater pressure to compensate immigration losers. They might also devise immigration policies to diminish the costs to domestic labor: limiting admissions to skilled labor, for example, mounting highly selective policies that privilege migrants targeted to niches where labor markets are tight, or recruiting temporary labor without political rights.

The statist perspective also invites analysis of the interaction of states, especially strategies of competition over the recruitment of skilled migrants and the incentives of states to enter into free migration regimes. . . . From the aggregate gain perspective, the key question may be how the reciprocity these arrangements are meant to establish affects access to migrant labor and the nature of compensation available for "losers."

Institutions and the Political Economy of Migration Policy

Work from the perspective of institutional analysis begins with the aggregate economic and net fiscal gain premises, but relaxes the assumption of a unitary state and introduces sub-state institutions. The main question posed in this analysis is whether various sub-state institutions pursue the same or dissimilar goals with respect to immigration and how their interaction may affect policy outcomes. The range of institutional variables is large. We concentrate here on three: (1) intra-state negotiations and competition among the executive, legislative, and judicial components of states, (2) varieties of political economy across states, and (3) the roles of political parties and party systems in aggregating and expressing societal interests.

Do executive, legislative, or judicial branches, on average or in any generalizable sense, favor immigration for economic gain, or do they follow alternative logics? It would seem reasonable that central executives (presidents, prime ministers, and agencies responsible for overall economic and budgetary policies) would take the larger view of what sort of immigration policy is beneficial to long-term growth prospects, whereas bureaucratic agencies linked to more sectoral or partial interests (interior, labor, industry, social welfare) would exhibit more short-term and specific preferences. Labor ministries may support short-term migration or look the other way in the face of illegal entry or work, while interior ministries might plausibly pursue more restrictive policies out of concern for social stability. . . .

Welfare-state institutions are especially pertinent to the issue of fiscal effects of migration. The most common welfare-state typology differentiates social democratic, corporatist, and liberal varieties. Other things being equal, one would anticipate that the most comprehensive and inclusive models—the social democratic and corporatist—would be most vulnerable to fiscal pressures arising from migration. To address this issue adequately, we need to know the rates of migrant participation in welfare programs across democracies, public perceptions of and attitudes toward these rates, and the role of immigration in stimulating backlash against welfare programs. We have only limited information on these issues.

. . . Hanson (2005) shows for the United States that migrant welfare program participation varies modestly over time but tends to substantially outstrip native use (2005: 28). However, migrant welfare participation rates vary widely across the states. The imputed fiscal burden of immigration on states is a function of the size and characteristics of the state's migrant population (especially its average skill endowment) and the generosity of the state's welfare programs. Hanson shows that the immigrant states of New York and California than it is on the low welfare/high immigration states of New Jersey, Florida, Texas, and Arizona (2005: 37).

Comparative data on the link between public perceptions of immigrant use of public benefits and support for the welfare state are scarce and contradictory. Whether immigration is playing a role in eroding support for the welfare state among native voters is an important question that is inherently difficult to answer and that has been too little studied. . . . Hanson (2005) and Hanson et al. (2005) present evidence consistent with the interpretation that welfare reforms in the United States in the 1990s that sought to reduce immigrant access to benefits had the effect of reducing high-skilled natives' support for immigration restrictions.

Moving beyond the internal structure of state authority, we can examine variations in the structural relationships between states, capital, and labor. Advocates of "varieties of capitalism" identify two types of political economy: the coordinated market and liberal market. This typology focuses on the means by which firms in different countries resolve coordination problems with respect to their core competencies (industrial relations, corporate governance, inter-firm relations, and relations with their own employees). The approach offers micro-foundations to explanations of why national responses to globalization vary along predictable lines. Another common typology distinguishes between social democratic, corporatist, and liberal political economies or welfare states. Neither the "varieties of capitalism" literature nor welfare-state typologies have systematically considered the implications of their models for responses of firms or states to international migration. It seems plausible that states more closely linked institutionally to organized labor and business, and committed to national-level bargaining over economic and social policy, would develop distinctive migration policies. For example, coordinated market economies might be expected to pursue stricter enforcement of labor market regulations and more aggressive development of activist labor market policies. These should reduce the likelihood of the emergence of dual labor markets and large underground sectors dominated by immigrant workers. Liberal market economies, for their part, can be expected to tolerate higher levels of illegal immigration, more unauthorized labor, and more business activity of questionable legality.

Political parties are key institutions in the process by which immigration policy is formulated, but because they aggregate blocs of voters and organized groups they could as sensibly be discussed in the next section on interest groups as here. Economic models drawn from the labor market and trade literatures suggest that liberal migration programs produce wage and income effects that favor capital over labor. We predict, therefore, that left parties tied to organized labor tend to support restrictive immigration measures while conservative, business-oriented parties support open immigration. Although there is astonishingly little systematic study of the immigration policy positions of mainstream parties, as opposed to that of extreme-right parties, one can piece together evidence that appears to contradict these hypotheses. Left parties seem torn between fealty to the indigenous working-class component of their base and responding to their intellectual and professional supporters' concern to protect the interests of migrant workers. They have, on the whole, adopted more liberal positions on immigration than have parties on the right. The latter have been equally split over solicitousness of the interests of business and attentiveness to grassroots, anti-immigrant sentiment in their ranks. On the whole, it is probably fair to say that left parties have tended to resolve the tensions they confront in favor of more open policies, whereas conservative parties have tended to resolve the tensions they confront in favor of more open policies, whereas conservative parties have tended to resolve theirs in favor of more restriction. Money (1999) presents a provocative thesis linking the immigration positions of mainstream parties in Britain, France, and Australia to the emergence of ethnic tensions in local constituencies critical to the outcome of national elections. There is also a growing literature that systematically explores the linkages between electoral rules and the emergence or success of extreme-right parties. The success of extremist parties greatly limits the options of mainstream parties and, generally, pushes them to the right on immigration issues.

Whether or not anti-immigrant attitudes are linked to public discontent with the welfare state, there is evidence that one of the factors leading voters to support extreme-right political parties in Europe is the perception of immigrant abuse of the welfare system. Fiscal effects present interesting challenges to the mainstream political parties. We saw above that left and right parties have trouble navigating the contradictory pressures created by the economic effects of migration. A similar pattern emerges with respect to fiscal effects. Conservative parties are naturally inclined to try to limit immigrant use of welfare in order to contain fiscal costs, but both pro-business and free-market inclinations push them in the opposite direction. Left parties, on the other hand, are typically in the position of seeking to expand immigrant access to welfare programs while at the same time defending immigration policies on economic grounds.

Interest Groups in the Migration Policy Process

Work in this vein employs standard production function and trade analysis to predict who wins and who loses from immigration's impact on labor supply and demand. Economic models suggest that class cleavages, especially those between skilled and unskilled labor, on the one hand, and organized labor and organized employers, on the other, are at the heart of immigration policy contestation. Labor market and trade theories predict who should experience concentrated or dispersed gains and losses from migration. Work combining these theories with interest-group analysis goes on to ask how groups mobilize or fail to mobilize to defend their interests. The chief advance of this combined perspective over either of its components is recognition that wage and income effects predicted by economic theory are not automatically translated into political demands. Political analysis of interest groups is supplemented, on the other hand, by theoretically driven expectations of the likely benefit/cost consequences of migration of skilled or unskilled labor.

Pioneering work on the economic sources of individual attitudes toward immigration has been done by Scheve and Slaughter (2001) and O'Rourke (2003). Using public opinion polls conducted in the United States, Scheve and Slaughter find support for hypotheses derived from the Heckscher-Ohlin and the proportional factors trade models. Specifically, they find that there is a robust skills cleavage over immigration policy, with highly skilled workers being less likely to support restrictionist immigration policies and low-skilled counterparts more likely to do so. These findings follow from the two models' hypothesized effects of immigration on workers at different skill levels. Their findings suggest "the potential for immigration politics to be connected to the mainstream redistributive politics over which political parties often contest elections" (Scheve and Slaughter 2001: 144). O'Rourke (2003) points out that Scheve and Slaughter cannot adequately test the H-O model with data from a single country. The theory predicts that the impact on immigration attitudes of being skilled or unskilled should depend on a country's skill endowments, with the skilled being less anti-immigration in more skill-abundant countries than in more unskilled-labor-abundant countries. O'Rourke tests the model against data from 24 countries with varying skill endowments (proxied by GDP per capita). He finds strong support for the hypotheses as they relate to attitudes toward globalization, but less impressive support for his hypotheses on immigration attitudes. However, his data confirm the theory's prediction that, other things being equal, a person who is protectionist is also likely to be anti-immigrant, and vice-versa.

Missing from these intriguing studies, of course, are propositions about the likely political expression and impact of the preferences opinion polling uncovers. If immigration policy were set by referendum, then the median voter would decide policy. Except for Switzerland, however, immigration policy is made through legislative and executive bodies that are more or less constrained by electoral competition that is typically decided by issues unrelated to immigration. In the legislative, administrative, and electoral process the interests of organized groups are more important than the opinions of individuals. Economic theory has the most to say about the likely preferences of labor and capital; in contemporary democracies this means the trade unions and employer federations.

At their most basic, economic models predict that trade unions should resist immigration because it imposes downward pressure on wages. The introduction of the idea that skilled and unskilled workers may have contrasting interests over immigration, and that this might depend on the skill endowments of the countries involved, greatly complicates the matter. Research should, following this line of reasoning, concentrate on whether a country's trade unions are organized along skill lines, how densely organized the workforce is, and how cohesive trade federations are. Most research in the rich Western countries shows that trade unions have traditionally taken a protectionist stance toward immigration. This has at times involved tolerance of migrants where they are guaranteed national-level wages and conditions, or where their recruitment is carefully targeted toward sectors with demonstrable shortages. In terms of our models, trade unions have tolerated immigration that is complementary to national labor, and opposed immigration that substitutes for it. Recently, some scholars have argued that the unions have undergone a change of heart and have embraced a more liberal view of immigration. While these studies point to puzzling and important developments in immigration politics, they have not advanced convincing explanations for them. Perhaps the trade unions have become more enlightened, perhaps they have resigned themselves to the inevitability of migration and are making the best of a bad situation, or perhaps the skill mix of contemporary entrants has modified their economic costs and benefits as experienced by labor.

Freeman (1995) predicts four modes of politics reflecting patterns of cost/benefit consequences of migration and the incentives they produce for individuals and groups to mobilize politically. Concentrated benefits and diffuse costs produce client politics dominated by beneficiary groups; diffuse costs and benefits yield majoritarian politics with no clear winners or losers; concentrated costs and diffuse benefits produce entrepreneurial politics as adversely affected groups seek to escape bearing the burden of policies; and concentrated costs and benefits spawn interest-group competition between roughly evenly matched adversaries.

A major deficiency of the model was the absence of theoretically driven expectations as to whether immigration produces concentrated or dispersed costs and benefits. The introduction of wage and income effects is a promising avenue for clarifying these matters. Our previous discussion of the significance of the size of migration's wage and income effects is relevant to the issue of the concentration and dispersion of benefits and costs. What is required is the addition of characterizations of interest-group configurations, in particular political systems. The concentration or diffuseness of effects, in this analysis, depends on the concentration and diffuseness of the interest groups affected by them (that is, if the number and range of groups is small or large and if the groups are themselves strongly organized or not). Consider a 2×2 matrix with economic cost (benefits) and political mobilization on the axes. If economic costs (benefits) are large and political groups concentrated, we get client politics. If economic costs (benefits) are large and political groups diffused, we get interest-group politics. Where economic costs (benefits) are small and political groups concentrated, entrepreneurial politics should follow; and small-cost (-benefit) diffuse groups should yield majoritarian politics. We predict the same four modes of politics as in Freeman (1995), but with different characterizations of the independent variables (see Table 3).

It is a commonplace that immigration politics produces "strange bedfellow" coalitions. Zolberg (1999) conceives of these as involving a matrix that includes the putative economic effects of migration intersecting with their putative political/cultural effects. In the area of the matrix where both are positive, he predicts "immigrationist" coalitions composed of co-ethnics, cosmopolitans, employers, and transporters. In the area where both are negative, he predicts "restrictionist" coalitions made up of native workers, local authorities, and traditional nationalists. Tichenor (2002) suggests an alternative framework based on attitudes toward immigration admissions and immigrant rights. Those favoring open admissions and expansive rights for immigrants are labeled cosmopolitans; those favoring restrictive admissions and expansive rights are nationalist egalitarians; those favoring expansive admissions and restricted rights are free market expansionists; while those favoring both restrictive admissions and restricted rights are classic exclusionists. These groups yield what appear to be unnatural coalitions between liberal cosmopolitans and business, for example, or between trade unions and classic exclusionists. Both Zolberg and Tichenor tap into the interplay between economic and political/

TABLE 3 Wage and Income Effects, Political Mobilization, and Modes of Politics

		Political mobilization	
		Concentrated	Diffuse
Wage/income effects	Large	Client	Interest group
	Small	Entrepreneurial	Majoritarian

cultural concerns. Both frameworks might be improved by a consideration of the diverse political consequences of fiscal versus wage effects.

Introducing fiscal effects into the analytical equation increases the number and range of interests potentially drawn into the political arena. As noted above, the most important examples are tax-payers and the residents and governments of local areas sharply impacted by immigration. The central point to register in this respect is that fiscal issues cut across the class and sectoral lines established over wage and income effects. Perceptions that large-scale immigration is connected to rising costs of public services can stimulate middle-class tax revolts among voters who might normally be supportive of immigration. Working-class voters may join a cross-class coalition in demanding relief from the fiscal burden of large-scale migration in high-impact areas. Fiscal costs can pit service payers (tax-payers) against service providers (bureaucrats, teachers, etc.) who argue for expanded budgets to meet immigrant demand.

As is the case with economic effects, the public perception of the fiscal effects of immigration is not fixed, but can be deliberately shaped by interested lobbies, the media, think-tanks, and politicians. Following the logic laid out above with respect to wage and income effects and interest groups, we anticipate that, whether fiscal effects are perceived to be large or small, whether their costs and benefits are concentrated or diffuse, and whether they fall on concentrated or diffuse interest systems, will determine the dominant mode of politics that will ensue.

CONCLUSION

The political economy of migration policy is a fertile field not yet fully cultivated. Economists are increasingly asking political and policy questions and incorporating political variables into their models. Political scientists are moving in the same direction, but could benefit from more systematic testing of economic hypotheses wedded to political propositions. This will require a more careful and self-conscious elucidation of political models of migration politics as much as the borrowing of concepts from economics. Specifically, political scientists must address where individual preferences on migration policy come from and how these are aggregated and processed via interest groups, institutions, and states. Our partial and brief consideration of the analytical terrain in the field of migration politics reveals its relatively undeveloped state. The three perspectives we introduced often do little more than identify a basket of potential independent variables with modest effort to stipulate how and when they come into play.

Our review of attempts to interpret comparative immigration policy outcomes via trade, labor market, and fiscal theoretical premises has uncovered significant relationships and suggestive data. Nonetheless, in a number of cases it seems apparent that economic models can only partially account for outcomes, in some cases perhaps not at all. These findings point to the need to take the political dimensions of migration policy into fuller account. Given the ubiquitous discussion of the economic dimensions of immigration phenomena in the political science literature, we think it is imperative that the debate be put on a more rigorous and systematic footing, yielding a more robust political economy of migration.

REFERENCES

Freeman, G. 1995. "Modes of immigration politics in liberal democratic states," *International Migration Review*, 29 (4): 881–902.

Hanson, G. 2005. *Why Does Immigration Divide America? Public Finance and Political Opposition to Open Borders*. Washington, DC: Institute for International Economics.

Hanson, G., K. Scheve, and M. Slaughter, 2005. *Local Public Finance and Individual Preferences over Globalization Strategies*. Cambridge, MA: National Bureau of Economic Research, Working Paper 11028.

Money, J. 1999. *Fences and Neighbors: The Political Geography of Immigration Control*. Ithaca: Cornell University Press.

O'Rourke, K. 2003. *Heckscher-Ohlin Theory and Individual Attitudes Towards Globalization*. Cambridge: National Bureau of Economic Research.

Scheve, K., and M. Slaughter, 2001. "Labor market competition and individual preferences over immigration policy." *The Review of Economics and Statistics* 83 (1): 133–45.

Tichenor, D. 2002. *Dividing Lines: The Politics of Immigration Control in America*. Princeton: Princeton University Press.

Zolberg, A. 1999. "Matters of state: theorizing immigration policy." In C. Hirschman, P. Kasinitz, and J. DeWind, eds. *Handbook of International Migration*. New York: Russell Sage Foundation.

24

Open Trade, Closed Borders: Immigration in the Era of Globalization

MARGARET E. PETERS

If nativist prejudice against foreigners is the explanation for why nations close their borders to immigrants, how do we account for the late nineteenth-century era of mass migration, when governments throughout the New World welcomed millions of immigrants? Prejudice has remained fairly constant over time while immigration policies have changed dramatically. Margaret E. Peters addresses this puzzle with an argument that is grounded in the interests of business firms. She argues that the business community's position on immigration policy has always been dependent on trade policy. When trade policy was protectionist in the late nineteenth century, firms lobbied for open immigration as a way to lower their labor costs. But as trade policy was liberalized after World War II, firm owners adapted to import competition by increasing their productivity, which meant that they had less need of cheap immigrant labor. As they adjusted to free trade policies, business interests reduced their pressure for open immigration, allowing politicians to be more responsive to nativist, labor, and fiscal pressures for immigration restrictions.

INTRODUCTION

What explains variation in immigration policy, especially policy regulating low-skill workers? A common argument invokes prejudice against foreigners as an explanation for why nations close their economies to immigrants.[1] This prejudice has been ubiquitous throughout history even as immigration policies changed. Social theories of this sort may be descriptively true but are not helpful in predicting variation in policy. Other scholars have turned to the role that native labor plays in protecting its interests against immigration, but they have not explained why labor is able to restrict immigration when it has not been able to restrict trade, even though open trade has wreaked as much, if not more, havoc on labor.[2] A third group of scholars focuses on states' concerns about the fiscal costs of immigrants as an explanation for the changes in policy over time.[3] While fiscal costs are likely to play a role, this argument

---

1. For example, Zolberg 2006.
2. For example, Mayda 2008.
3. For example, Hatton and Williamson 2005.

cannot explain exclusion prior to the creation of the modern welfare state in the early twentieth century. Finally, a fourth group of scholars has examined the power of immigrants themselves.[4] While immigrants clearly affect immigration policy in democracies, they have never been a sufficiently large plurality of the polity to be able to change policy on their own, and they have less voice in autocracies where they can more easily be deported.

What is missing from these political theories is a discussion of trade policy's effect on the politics of immigration, especially on the preferences and political behavior of firms. According to the Stolper-Samuelson theorem, openness through the movement of people, goods, or capital affects prices and wages in the same way, benefiting the abundant factor of production in the country while hurting the scarce factor. As openness in all three of these policy areas has the same effect, economic theory tells us little about which policy or policies states should choose when they want to open their economies. By this logic, states' choices of policy should either be idiosyncratic, or all three should open or close in tandem, since opening any one flow would lead to the same distributional consequences as opening the others. Yet, empirically, trade and immigration policy are rarely opened together, and states do not seem to choose these policies idiosyncratically. Instead, states often choose the same set of policies at the same time. For example, in the nineteenth century, most labor-scarce states—the states most likely to face immigration pressures—chose to open immigration and restrict trade to a greater or lesser degree. In contrast, most of these same states have chosen open trade since the 1950s but have restricted immigration. What explains these patterns and why do we rarely see trade and immigration open at the same time?

I argue that the choice to open or close trade changes the domestic political context in which immigration policy is made. Trade policy affects the composition of firms in the economy and their need for low-skill labor. Trade restrictions in labor-scarce states—the states studied in this article—lead to an increase in production in labor-intensive industries. Without a concomitant increase in the labor supply, wages will rise throughout the economy. Business interests, especially those producing nontradable goods or hurt by trade restrictions, have an incentive to push for open immigration when trade is restricted. In contrast, when trade is opened there is a decrease in labor-intensive production as labor-intensive firms go out of business. In such times, these firms will no longer push for open immigration. Additionally, they will lay off their workers, depressing wages throughout the economy, which reduces other firms' need for immigrant labor and their incentives to push for open immigration. Policymakers are then likely to restrict immigration to appease other constituencies, such as nativists, labor, and taxpayers concerned about the fiscal costs of immigration.

4. For example, Tichenor 2002.

This article diverges from the majority of the literature on international political economy by arguing for an integrated view of foreign economic policy. Recently, scholars have begun to examine how capital and trade policies act as substitutes for each other, how migration flows affect capital flows, and how remittances affect exchange rate policy. I continue this trend by examining the interaction of immigration and trade policy, something that has yet to be considered.

After further explicating the argument, I test it on a new data set of de jure immigration policy for nineteen countries from 1783–2010. This is one of the few data sets to measure immigration policy, and it covers the nineteenth, twentieth, and twenty-first centuries. The data show that trade and immigration policy are profoundly interrelated. The nineteenth century was generally a period of open immigration but relatively closed trade. The interwar period was a time of general closure to goods and people, although the states that had more open trade policies also restricted their immigration policies to a greater degree. After World War II, most states opened trade but continued to restrict immigration. The data thus show that increasing trade openness has led to increasingly restrictive immigration policies.

HOW TRADE POLICY AFFECTS IMMIGRATION POLICY

In this section I examine how trade policy affects immigration policy toward low-skill immigrants in low-skill labor-scarce states (henceforth, "immigration policy"). I focus on labor-scarce states because those are the states to which immigrants want to move because of their high wages and, therefore, those are the states that must decide whether or not to restrict immigration.

I examine policy toward low-skill immigrants for three reasons. First, the vast majority of potential immigrants, those who would migrate if they were legally allowed to, are low skilled. Currently, 23.5 percent of immigrants in the world have a high level of education; nonetheless, this level of skilled migration is endogenous to the policies in this study, meaning that without immigration barriers, the share of low-skill immigrants would increase greatly. Second, survey data show that flows of low-skill immigrants are more politicized in immigrant-receiving states than are flows of high-skill immigrants. Most historic episodes of nativism, such as the backlash against Asians and people from Southern and Eastern Europe throughout the New World in the nineteenth and early twentieth centuries, targeted these groups in part because they were low-skill immigrants. Finally, if we care about economic development, we should determine why wealthy states are not more open to low-skill immigration, as it has the ability to greatly increase developing world income.

I begin by examining a highly stylized economy that is affected by exogenous shocks in trade policy. To simplify the argument, I abstract away from all the other factors that could affect immigration policy, such as regime type, history as a colonial power, and national culture and identity, among other things. I control for these variables in the empirical section.

Assume there is a low-skill labor-scarce economy that at time t has one-third of its firms in the high-skill intensive export sector, another third in the low-skill intensive import-competing sector, and the final third in the service or nontradable sector, which I assume uses mostly low-skill labor. At some point in the future, time $t+1$, trade is restricted, which increases prices and production in the import-competing sector. As the import-competing sector grows, it will attract labor from the service sector and from the small pool of low-skill labor that was working in the export sector. Profits will go down for all firms as wages for low-skill labor increase. By opening immigration, policymakers can appease those firms hurt by the increase in wages due to the trade restrictions and thus reduce their opposition to trade barriers. Even though export-oriented firms would like freer trade, the increase in immigration decreases their labor costs and increases returns to their capital. Therefore, I expect that when trade is closed, firms clamor for open immigration and policymakers respond to their demands.

Now assume that, instead of restricting trade at time $t+1$, trade is opened for exogenous reasons. Open trade reduces the price of the goods that low-skill intensive firms produce and, under our classic trade models, leads these firms to close. When these firms close, they can no longer pressure policymakers for open immigration. Further, when these firms lay off their low-skill labor, those workers can be employed in the service and export sectors. The service and export sectors are then less likely to pressure policymakers for open immigration as well. Firms have a limited amount of political capital to spend and they may want to spend it elsewhere when wages for low-skill labor are already low. In addition, it may not be possible to lower wages further despite increases in immigration due to a minimum wage. As such, policymakers are likely to restrict immigration to appease groups such as nativists, labor, and taxpayers. Thus, I expect that when trade is opened, policymakers restrict immigration.

I next move away from a highly stylized economy to a more realistic one. In the case of trade closure, firms could increase productivity in response to high labor costs. By increasing productivity, these firms decrease their need for labor and their support for open immigration. Similarly, in the case of trade openness, low-skill firms could increase productivity to decrease labor costs, which again would decrease their support for open immigration. I expect, then, immigration policy to become more restricted over time as labor-saving technology increases.

An assumption of trade models in the existing literature is that as soon as trade opens, firms close. We know, however, that firms often stay in business after trade opens either by running at a loss or otherwise scaling back production. These threatened firms are likely to lobby policymakers for support to stay in business, reducing labor costs for example through increased immigration or subsidized production. Policymakers may open immigration or offer tax subsidies if the costs of doing so outweigh the costs of allowing the firm to close. If the threatened firm closes, policymakers will lose the tax revenue, jobs, and any political capital the firm would have provided. If policymakers choose to help firms by opening immigration, they potentially increase the fiscal cost of immigrants to the state and the risk of nativist backlash. If they choose to subsidize firms by using tax subsidies, they have less money to spend on other constituencies. In addition, depending on the trade regime, they may not be able to subsidize the firm without facing retaliation from trading partners.

While policymakers might be inclined to increase immigration or subsidize firms at moderate levels of trade openness, those strategies become more difficult at high levels of trade openness. More trade openness either decreases the price of goods at a greater rate or decreases the price of a greater number of goods. As such, to keep threatened firms in business, policymakers would need to increase immigration or increase subsidies even more. Yet we know from current public opinion data and from historical examples, such as the backlashes mentioned above and those against Muslim and East European immigrants in Europe today, that large-scale movements of immigrants are politically unpopular. Policymakers have to balance their desire to keep firms in business and the potential for such backlash. At high enough levels of trade, policymakers will find it less costly to allow firms to close than to face the anti-immigrant backlash.

What happens if the change in trade policy is not exogenous? First, could trade affect immigration policy if the policymaker chooses both trade and immigration policies? Under Gene Grossman and Elhanan Helpman's endogenous trade theory model, policymakers' choice of trade policy is affected by contributions (or bribes in an authoritarian context) from firms and concerns over the aggregate welfare of their constituents.[5] To restrict trade, policymakers have to receive enough in contributions from import-competing firms to make up for lower contributions from the export sector, the deadweight loss of trade barriers, and the political costs of a more open immigration policy. Assuming that import-competing firms are powerful, we expect that they should be able to contribute enough to gain protection. In fact, this is what happened in many countries, especially the United States and Germany, in the late nineteenth century.

Alexander Hamilton provides us with an example of a policymaker who chose the closed trade/open immigration bundle to appease the export sector at the time, agriculture. Hamilton famously argued that a tariff would provide the U.S. government with revenue as well as protect infant industries. Yet he also understood that agricultural interests opposed the tariffs for several

---

5. Grossman and Helpman 1994.

reasons: tariffs increased the price of manufactured goods; they might lead to retaliation from Great Britain, which was the major consumer of U.S. agricultural products; and they would lead to labor shortages and higher wages. It was likely prohibitively difficult to appease farmers with subsidies at the time. Further, Hamilton could not prevent British retaliation. He could, however, offer a more open immigration policy, which would ensure an agricultural labor supply and low wages. Hamilton recognized the trade-off between tariffs and immigration policy.

When policymakers choose open trade—even if they, as benevolent social planners, choose it because it will increase national income—they are privileging the export sector and, perhaps, the service sector, over the import-competing sector. Under a lobbying model, policymakers will only open trade if export-oriented firms offer enough political capital to overcome the political capital of import-competing firms, any losses in welfare from the eventual loss of threatened firms, and the impact of a change in immigration policy. Assuming that the export-oriented sector is wealthy enough, it should be possible for it to pay for free trade. Further, one could imagine that cynical policymakers open trade specifically to lower business demand for immigration, which would make it easier for them to close immigration. Thus, under an endogenous trade model, policymakers could be induced to open trade, even knowing that some firms will be lost and immigration will be restricted.

Second, is it possible that immigration policy is driving trade policy? If it is, we would expect that trade and immigration should be complements or that there should be little relationship between the two policies, but that they should not be substitutes. Immigration restrictions lead to higher wage costs and make low-skill firms less competitive, which would increase their opposition to trade openness. This increased opposition should make it harder for policymakers to maintain or increase trade openness, likely leading to trade restrictions. However, openness to immigration increases the competitiveness of low-skill firms and leads to less opposition to trade openness. At extreme levels of openness to immigration, this complementarity between immigration and trade may break down. If immigration openness leads the wage to converge to the world wage, prices for both low-skill and high-skill goods will converge to the world price. As argued by Robert Mundell, at that point there would be no gains from trade, as prices are already equal.[6] Policymakers would be free to have an open trade policy, an autarkic policy, or something in between, and prices would stay the same. Therefore, if immigration is the first-mover policy, then trade and immigration should be complements or there should be little relationship between the two, but they should not be substitutes.

Third, is it possible that some omitted variable is driving both policies? There are many variables that may affect trade and immigration policy, including

6. Mundell 1957.

domestic variables, such as democracy, and systemic variables, such as the existence of a hegemon. Below, I test whether the relationship between trade and immigration policy holds when accounting for these variables.

CROSS-NATIONAL IMMIGRATION POLICY, 1783–2010

One of the major obstacles to research on immigration has been the lack of longitudinal cross-national data. In response to this lacuna, this article examines data on the de jure immigration policy of nineteen countries over the last 225 years. The resulting data set is one of the few on immigration policy and, importantly, it covers the nineteenth, twentieth, and twenty-first centuries. I focus on a de jure measure of policy rather than a de facto measure of flows in part because of data limitations. . . .

There are two overlapping universes of cases to which the argument of this article could apply. First are the relatively low-skill, labor-scarce states. These are states that have relatively high wages in comparison to the rest of the world or in comparison to their major trading partners. Second are the states to which immigrants want to move. If immigrants are not interested in moving to the state, the state could choose any immigration policy, since migrants would not move there regardless of the policy. Previous research on migration suggests that migrants choose locations where wages are high relative to the transactional costs of moving. States that are very wealthy are likely to attract migrants from all over the world, while states that are relatively wealthy in comparison to their neighbors are likely to attract migrants from their neighbors but not from countries far away. The states chosen for this study, therefore, are all wealthy, low-skill labor-scarce states in comparison to the rest of the world or to their neighbors.

From the universe of wealthy countries, nineteen states and state-like entities were selected (Table 1) that have a range of values on the important explanatory variables for this study and on the alternative explanations in the literature. For my argument, it was important to find states that have different levels of trade openness and states that have had both open and closed trade policies. I control for several major alternative explanations in the literature as well: interest-group explanations based on the power of labor, nativists, and immigrants, as well as the fiscal costs of immigrants; societal explanations based on whether or not a state was a colonial power; regime type; and participation in wars. The states chosen vary in these dimensions. . . .

. . . Every state was coded through 2010, but states enter the data set when they gain control over their immigration policy, that is, when they obtain responsible government, independence, or otherwise emerge in their modern-day form.

Similar to trade, there are many different ways to regulate immigration. This study includes data on all laws on immigration and immigrant rights. Immigration policy is an amalgam of several policies, including those that

TABLE 1 Countries Included in the Data Set and the Dates of Inclusion

Group	Country
Settler States	Argentina (1810–2010)
	Australia (1787–2010)
	Brazil (1808–2010)
	Canada (1783–2010)
	New Zealand (1840–2010)
	South Africa (1806–2010)
	U.S. (1790–2010)
European Liberal Democracies	France (1793–2010)
	Germany (1871–2010)
	Netherlands (1815–2010)
	Switzerland (1848–2010)
	UK (1792–2010)
Export-Oriented Industrializers	Hong Kong (1843–2010)
	Japan (1868–2010)
	Singapore (1955–2010)
	South Korea (1948–2010)
	Taiwan (1949–2010)
Rentier States	Kuwait (1961–2010)
	Saudi Arabia (1950–2010)

regulate who gains entry to the state (border regulations), what rights immigrants receive (immigrant rights), and how the border is enforced (enforcement). Within each of these three categories, states have used numerous policy substitutes. After an exhaustive reading of more than 350 primary and secondary sources on the immigration policies of countries in Europe, the Middle East, East Asia, and the New World, I determined that there are twelve dimensions of regulations that are important for testing the hypotheses of this paper. Eight of the dimensions regulate entrance to the state. Four of these—work prohibitions, family reunification, refugee policy, and asylee policy—could also be considered rights; two cover immigrant rights; and two cover enforcement. Table 2 lists the different dimensions in each category and gives a brief description. Each dimension was coded from 1 to 5, with greater restrictions taking lower values.

Border regulations are often considered the most important aspect of immigration policy because they determine who gains entry to a state. The preferred method for controlling immigration in the late nineteenth century was to use national origin, for example, the Chinese Exclusion Act in the US, and German laws against Polish immigration. After World War II, nationality as a basis for restriction was delegitimized and skill requirements often replaced it as a way to restrict the same categories of immigrants. Yet nationality

TABLE 2 Dimensions of Immigration Policy

Category	Dimension	Coding Criteria
Border Regulations	nationality	number of nationalities restricted
	skill	restrictions based on skill or wealth
	quotas	numerical limits on entry
	recruitment	policies aimed at recruiting immigrants
	work prohibitions	restrictions on industries or positions held
	family reunification	distance of relatives allowed special entry
	refugee policy	entrance policies for refugees outside the state
	asylum policy	entrance policies for those claiming refugee status at the border
Immigrant Rights	citizenship	who can be a member of the state
	other rights	other rights immigrants possess
Enforcement	deportation	who can be deported and how
	other enforcement	other enforcement measures in place

restrictions are still used today, though cast in a more positive light—as in the EU—as free migration areas (FMAs). Similar to free trade areas, FMAs can lead to "migration diversion," as states often open their borders to migrants from within the FMA while restricting immigration from outside the FMA. For example, as most EU members have opened their borders to migrants from within the EU, they have restricted access from outside of the EU. For this study, what matters is the overall openness to low-skill immigration; thus, joining an FMA or a bilateral labor migration treaty only leads to greater openness if it does not lead to migration diversion.

Another way states have regulated entry is through recruitment measures. At times states allow private firms to recruit workers or they recruit workers themselves, and at other times they prohibit recruitment. States also regulate entry by controlling access to their labor markets, thus limiting the availability of positions in certain industries. Further, states allow varying levels of family reunification, and some states use numerical quotas. In general, we see that while there has been some variation in border regulations over time, regulations have gotten more restrictive.

Additionally, states have varied in their openness to refugees and asylees. No state had a formal refugee policy prior to World War II and many states still do not. After World War II, however, most states created asylum policies that were fairly generous at first but have been curtailed in recent years. These policies are categorized as border regulations, rather than immigrant rights, because refugees and asylees are often thought of as economic migrants in disguise and they often enter the labor market once granted entry into a country. Because of this, firms are keenly interested in refugee and asylum policy. In the nineteenth century, for example, agricultural interests in Canada and Argentina lobbied to recruit persecuted minorities in Eastern Europe and Russia to work on their farms. After World War II, congressional lobbying reports show that the American Farm Bureau lobbied for the Displaced Persons Act in hopes of receiving agricultural labor. Similarly to the rest of the border regulations, when I include refugee and asylum policies, we see that these policies have generally become more restrictive over time. While some states that had not previously adopted refugee and asylum provisions—such as Argentina, Brazil, and Japan—began to adopt them in the late twentieth century, many other states—including most European states—began to restrict them.

States also vary the legal rights they grant to immigrants. While there is no definitive proof that rights affect immigrants' choice of where to move, there is evidence that states act strategically when granting them. For example, in the nineteenth century, Argentina, Brazil, and Canada granted land to attract immigrants. Recently, the United States and many European states have limited access to the welfare system to deter immigration. Further, the treatment of immigrants affects the sending countries' willingness to allow emigration. In the 1920s, India limited the recruitment of workers due to mistreatment abroad, and the Philippines has done so more recently. A strategic state thus may change the rights they give to immigrants as a way to forestall the laws of sending states. The most important right is citizenship; citizenship allows the immigrant to have the same rights as the native. Citizenship laws vary from very restrictive—Saudi Arabia, for example, only grants citizenship to foreign-born wives—to very liberal—several settler states offer citizenship after only a few years' residence. Other rights vary greatly too, including the right to own land or a business, the right to access the welfare system, and even, occasionally, the right to vote. The trends in citizenship and other rights are more varied than the trends in border regulations. New democracies tend to increase both citizenship and other rights; established democracies increase citizenship while decreasing other rights, established welfare access; and autocracies increase rights without increasing citizenship.

Finally, states have used a myriad of different enforcement policies, and most states have increased enforcement in recent years. It is important to measure enforcement, because a restrictive immigration policy that is not enforced is effectively similar to an open policy. Deportation is often used to enforce immigration laws, yet there has been great variation in who can be deported and the form that the deportation process takes. The dimension "other enforcement" captures the variety of other measures states use to enforce their laws, including employer and carrier sanctions, fences and border patrols, and amnesties for those in the country illegally. As can be seen from the graphs, almost all states have increased enforcement over the last half-century.

The goal of a state's immigration policy is to attract or repel a certain number of immigrants. While there is no consensus on how these different dimensions affect the flow of immigrants, it is clear that not all dimensions affect migration equally. To combine these different policies into a single measure, I use principal component analysis. The analysis reveals that these dimensions combine to create two different factors: immigration policy and rights of immigrants.

The first factor, immigration policy, places more weight on nationality, skill, recruitment, quotas, deportation, and enforcement policies than the second factor, rights of immigrants, which places more weight on family reunification, refugee, asylee, citizenship, and work prohibition policies, and rights. Thus, the names for the two factors. Henceforth I focus on the immigration policy factor. The immigration policy variable now takes values between 2 and –2, with higher values signaling a more open policy.

. . . The data . . . confirm the conventional wisdom on the restrictiveness of immigration policy; among the states that had control of their immigration policy in the nineteenth century, that policy is more restrictive today than it was back then. Moreover, most states have increasingly adopted restrictions, at least since the end of the Bretton Woods era in the early 1970s. . . .

In sum, the immigration policy data show that even though these groups of states have used different immigration policies, all states restrict immigration more today than previously. What accounts for these restrictions?

THE HISTORY OF IMMIGRATION AND TRADE POLICY

Using the immigration policy variable, I next examine how immigration and trade policy have been used over time. Trade policy is measured as the percent of imports that are not dutied.

The nineteenth century was generally an era of relatively closed trade but open immigration. For the most part, states chose to restrict trade for reasons orthogonal to immigration policy: they needed to generate revenue—most states lacked the administrative capacity to use other forms of taxation—and to provide a barrier behind which domestic industry could develop. Barriers to trade were exacerbated by the relatively high cost of shipping and lack of communications technology as well. These barriers increased the size of domestic industry. The increase in labor-intensive industries led to increased wages and calls from business for increased immigration. For example, in 1875, Otto von Bismarck increased tariffs as a way to undermine the free-trade National Liberals and increase the German government's revenue. The reasons for opening trade in this case were largely orthogonal to immigration;

Bismarck had pushed for a relatively restrictive immigration policy, including mass expulsions of Poles, a few years prior to this change. Not long after the change in tariff policy, Germany began to reopen its borders to Polish guest workers. The main exception to this pattern is the UK, which had more open trade policies but more restrictive immigration policies than most states and, in 1905, was one of the first states to greatly restrict immigration. France also had more open trade during the middle of the nineteenth century, and it too had a more restrictive immigration policy than most other states.

At the end of the nineteenth century and in the interwar period, states closed their doors to immigrants and, after the Great Depression, to trade as well. Immigration restrictions were driven by several factors. Labor-saving technology likely decreased the need for labor. Improvements in shipping and communications technology decreased natural trade barriers, and more open trade policies decreased labor-intensive production in some states. The Great Depression was the final blow, leading to autarkic trade and immigration policies. Even though the argument predicts that closed trade should lead to more open immigration, we have reason to believe that this would not happen during a recession or depression. Most firms were not planning to expand production and those that did could likely use native, unemployed workers. Once the unemployment rate returned to its natural level we would expect firms to lobby for more open immigration.

After World War II, most states increasingly adopted policies of open trade but restricted immigration. Again the changes to trade policy were largely orthogonal to immigration policy: many in the West, including Cordell Hull, the U.S. Secretary of State under President Franklin Roosevelt; Harry Dexter White, the lead U.S. representative at the Bretton Woods conference; and John Maynard Keynes, the lead British representative at Bretton Woods, believed that opening trade was a matter of national security for both the United States and Western Europe and would help rebuild Europe and bind together Western economies, especially the economies of France and Germany. Similarly, the EU was conceived to increase trade in hopes of avoiding yet another European conflict. In comparison, migration, beyond the resettlement of refugees, was not addressed as part of the postwar order—freedom of movement was similarly heavily restricted in the early days of the predecessor to the EU, the European Coal and Steel Community (ECSC)—in part because the United States was unwilling to lead on immigration due to opposition in Congress and in part because many other states were unwilling to reopen immigration due to fears of large flows of poor refugees. Thus, trade was opened and institutionalized largely to unite and develop the West in face of the communist threat, a fear orthogonal to immigration.

As the Western economies regained their footing in the 1950s, many settler and European states opened their economies to a small degree to immigration. This openness may have allowed their labor-intensive firms to remain competitive, and in turn allowed these countries to further open trade. But there was a backlash to immigration and it was again restricted with the recessions of the late 1960s and early 1970s. Immigration in the twentieth century, however, was never opened as far as it had been in the nineteenth century, and today is relatively restricted while trade is open.

The export-oriented economies also followed a pattern similar to that of the European liberal democracies, about twenty years later. In the 1950s and 1960s, these states opened their economies to some trade but kept their currencies undervalued, which acted as a trade barrier. As standards of living and wages rose and more states industrialized, the export-oriented states began to open immigration slightly in an attempt to maintain their competitive edge. Firms in these states continued to lose ground due to exogenous changes in the world economy, especially the rise of China. Japan's competitiveness was also affected by U.S. pressure to revalue the Japanese currency. In most of the export-oriented economies, the competitive pressures combined with a backlash against immigration led these states to restrict it. The rentier states, in contrast, kept trade relatively restricted and opened their borders to workers of all skill levels after World War II. Recently the rentier states have shifted to more restrictive immigration policies in order to develop high-skilled service economies while increasing their openness to trade.

Table 3 examines the relationship between trade and immigration policy more rigorously, by regressing immigration policy on trade policy using an ordinary least squares (OLS) model. Each model contains country and year fixed effects to capture unchanging country characteristics and yearly shocks. In addition, a linear time trend for each state is included to ensure that the relationship is not spurious. Also included are polity as a measure of regime type, GDP growth, and an indicator variable for war. Model 1 examines all years of the data, while the next six models examine each historical era from preglobalization through the post–Bretton Woods era.

Over all years, we see a negative and statistically significant relationship between trade and immigration. A change in trade openness from the 25th percentile to the 75th percentile, or from a 17 percent average tariff level to a 4 percent average tariff level, leads to a -0.39 (95 percent confidence interval -0.64 to -0.15) change—about half a standard deviation change—in immigration policy. We also see a negative and statically significant relationship between trade and immigration if we examine each era. Argentina is an outlier in the post–Bretton Woods period and is excluded from the regression in model 7. After the end of its military dictatorship in 1983, Argentina adopted neoliberal economic policies and opened immigration by repealing the draconian enforcement policies of the dictatorship. Most recently, Argentina has restricted immigration, in line with the argument of this article.

The statistical significance of trade in each of the eras should give us greater confidence that we are discovering a true relationship between trade and immigration, not one caused by an omitted variable. In terms of our major systemic variables, the eras were marked by multipolarity, bipolarity, and uni-

TABLE 3 Immigration Policy Regressed on Trade Policy by Era

	All Years	Pre-globalization	19th Cen. Globalization	Interwar	Bretton Woods	Post–Bretton Woods	Post–Bretton Woods, w/o Argentina
Trade Openness	-3.04**	-1.81*	-1.68*	-3.25+	-1.27*	-1.33	-3.60**
	(0.89)	(0.67)	(0.58)	(1.66)	(0.55)	(1.20)	(1.13)
Years since Inclusion	-0.02***	-0.00	-0.02***	-0.03**	0.02	-0.01***	-0.01**
	(0.00)	(0.01)	(0.00)	(0.01)	(0.01)	(0.00)	(0.00)
Polity	0.01	0.06*	0.15	0.02	0.02+	0.01+	0.01
	(0.01)	(0.02)	(0.09)	(0.02)	(0.01)	(0.00)	(0.01)
GDP Growth	0.17	0.18	0.19	-0.16	0.03	0.16	0.01
	(0.16)	(0.16)	(0.12)	(0.33)	(0.36)	(0.18)	(0.16)
War	0.17	0.96	0.00	0.2	-0.01	-0.03	-0.03
	(0.12)	(0.52)	(0.05)	(0.21)	(0.09)	(0.04)	(0.04)
Constant	4.32***	2.07*	2.79***	6.02*	-1.97	1.78	3.74***
	(0.89)	(0.81)	(0.52)	(1.95)	(1.45)	(1.21)	(0.92)
Country FE	yes	yes	yes	yes	yes	yes	yes
Year FE	yes	yes	yes	yes	yes	yes	yes
Observations	1577	77	297	298	325	580	548
R^2	0.77	0.64	0.53	0.55	0.30	0.36	0.48

Robust standard errors in parentheses; + $p<0.10$, * $p<0.05$, ** $p<0.01$, *** $p<0.001$

polarity, and periods of economic hegemony; had different exchange rate regimes; and had different systemic levels of capital openness. The relationship between trade and immigration also holds if we examine other major theories of immigration, and holds through different waves of emigration from Asia, Europe, and Latin America; through wars and peacetime; and through good economic times and bad.

We can have some confidence that the relationship is driven by trade affecting immigration rather than immigration affecting trade. First, as discussed above, if immigration is the driver of trade policy, we would expect immigration and trade policy to be complements or for there to be no relationship between the two; they should not be substitutes. Second, as discussed above, a country's trade policy is often driven by reasons orthogonal to immigration policy.

Table 3 also provides evidence for an auxiliary hypothesis from the argument and from the literature. There is a negative and statistically significant coefficient on the years since the inclusion variable, which may signal the effect of changes in labor-saving technology. We can also conclude that there is no statistically significant effect of regime type (as measured by the Polity IV Project). This is somewhat surprising. Scholars . . . have argued that the enfranchisement of the masses leads policymakers to choose policies that benefit the average citizen. Greater democratization should lead to more immigration restrictions according to this logic, as immigrants compete with natives for scarce jobs. That is not what we see, though this may be due to how Polity codes democracy. Further, there is no effect of GDP growth on immigration—states close their doors to immigrants in good times and bad—and there is no effect of engaging in a war. . . .

CONCLUSION

States' immigration policies do not conform to the patterns that political analysts expect—sometimes immigration policy responds to increases in democracy, sometimes it responds to economic conditions, sometimes to increased nativist sentiment, and so on—because these expectations rely on variation in domestic factors to explain immigration policy and ignore the international context in which policy is made. This article argues that other foreign economic policies cannot be ignored: immigration policy cannot be understood without considering the effects of trade policy on a nation's economy.

By examining data on immigration policy in all its forms, comparable across countries and time, I find that trade and immigration policy are substitutes both economically and politically. The increased use of technology has allowed firms to use less labor, leading to greater immigration restrictions as well. This article additionally examines existing theories of immigration policy. I find that unions affect immigration policy and high levels of immigration lead to a backlash, as predicted. Most of the other dominant theories of immigration policy, however, are not supported by the data.

Trade and immigration openness should be viewed as substitutes, as economists predict, because of their effects on the national economy and industry, which lead to changing political support for the different policies. Closure to trade leads to greater production of low-skill labor-intensive goods, driving up the demand for low-skill labor and wages and leading to pressure from firms for increased immigration. Openness to trade subjects those same labor-intensive firms to increased competition, leading them to close their doors or become more high-skill intensive. Either way, with more open trade policies, demand for labor is reduced and immigration can be restricted.

While economists argue that trade and immigration policy are substitutes, they make few predictions about how the choice of one policy affects the other policies. This article shows that the sequencing of policies matters because the choice of one policy profoundly affects the domestic political context in which the other policies are made. In the nineteenth century, the choice to restrict trade to generate tax revenue and protect infant industries increased the demand for open immigration. After World War II, the choice to open trade first reduced the demand for open immigration and then allowed policymakers to restrict immigration.

In sum, this article increases our understanding of policy formation by examining the role that international factors play in constructing domestic policy. Economists have long argued that policies that govern the movement of goods, people, and capital are substitutes, yet political scientists have frequently ignored this argument when studying these three policies. Instead, these scholars have mostly focused on domestic factors and have therefore missed the effect that other foreign economic policy choices have on any discrete policy. This article brings these international factors back into focus by arguing that the choice of a given policy can have a path-dependent effect on other policy choices; the sequencing of the policies matters. Immigration policy cannot be understood without examining trade policy. Similarly, trade and other foreign economic policies should be examined in light of immigration policy.

REFERENCES

Grossman, Gene M., and Elhanan Helpman. 1994. "Protection for Sale." *The American Economic Review* 84, no. 4: 833–50.

Hatton, Timothy J., and Jeffrey G. Williamson. 2005. *Global Migration and the World Economy*. Cambridge, Mass.: MIT Press.

Mayda, Anna Maria. 2008. "Why Are People More Pro-Trade than Pro-Migration?" *Economic Letters* 101, no. 3: 160–63.

Mundell, Robert A. 1957. "International Trade and Factor Mobility." *American Economic Review* 47, no. 3: 321–35.

Tichenor, Daniel J. 2002. *Dividing Lines: The Politics of Immigration Control in America*. Princeton, N.J.: Princeton University Press.

Zolberg, Aristide R. 2006. *A Nation by Design: Immigration Policy in the Fashioning of America*. Cambridge, Mass.: Harvard University Press.

25

Do Interest Groups Affect U.S. Immigration Policy?

GIOVANNI FACCHINI, ANNA MARIA MAYDA, AND PRACHI MISHRA

Immigration policy is often targeted to specific sectors of the economy, as when the U.S. Congress allocates a set number of temporary work visas for foreigners to work in the health care, agricultural, and educational industries. In this reading, Giovanni Facchini, Anna Maria Mayda, and Prachi Mishra explore the role that interest groups play in shaping such sector-specific immigration policies. They focus on lobbying by labor and business groups, which have opposing interests. Labor groups want to reduce the number of visas in a sector so as to maintain higher wages for native workers, while business groups want to increase the number of visas in their industry in order to lower labor costs. They find evidence that both pro- and anti-immigration interest groups play a role in shaping migration policy across sectors. Barriers to migration are lower in sectors in which business interest groups incur larger lobbying expenditures and higher in sectors where labor unions are more important.

"Immigration policy today is driven by businesses that need more workers—skilled and unskilled, legal and illegal." (Goldsborough, 2000)

1. INTRODUCTION

On May 1, 2006, over a million demonstrators filled U.S. TV screens. They were mainly Latinos, who marched peacefully through America's cities in the hope that Congress would finally introduce legislation to overhaul the country's immigration policy. A year later, a bipartisan legislation was proposed by Senators Kennedy and Kyl but, since it was unveiled, "it has been stoned from all sides" (*The Economist*, May 24, 2007). Even though many observers have deemed the status quo unacceptable, no measures have been voted yet.

What determines U.S. immigration policy today? In particular, are political-economy factors important in shaping immigration to the United States? What is the role played by industry-specific interest groups? In this paper, we address these issues by analyzing the impact of political organization by business lobbies and workers' associations on the structure of U.S. migration policy across sectors between 2001 and 2005. This paper represents, to the best of our knowledge, the first study to provide systematic *empirical* evidence on the political-economy determinants of today's immigration policy in the United States and, in particular, on the role played by interest groups.

Trade and migration represent two of the main facets of international economic integration. A vast theoretical and empirical literature considers the political-economy determinants of *trade* policy trying to understand the forces that work against free trade. In contrast, the literature on the political economy of migration policy is very thin and mainly theoretical. This is in spite of the fact that, as trade restrictions have been drastically reduced, the benefits from the elimination of existing trade barriers are much smaller than the gains that could be achieved by freeing international migration. This gap in the literature is very surprising and can be partly explained by unavailability of data. The purpose of this paper is to offer a contribution toward filling it.

There exists abundant anecdotal evidence which suggests that political-economy factors and, in particular, interest groups play a key role in shaping U.S. immigration policy. Starting from the very birth of organized labor and for most of their history, unions have been actively engaged in efforts to limit inflows of foreign workers. The enactment of the first legislative measure to systematically limit immigration from a specific country—the Chinese Exclusion Act of 1882—was the result of the efforts of the newly founded Federation of Organized Trade and Labor Unions. One hundred years later, the AFL-CIO supported measures to reduce illegal immigration, that culminated in the 1986 Immigration Reform and Control Act. Finally, during the recent debate on the shortage of nurses, the American Nurses Association has strongly opposed a measure to increase the number of H1C visas, pointing out that ". . . the provision would lead to a flood of nurse immigrants and would damage the domestic work force" (*New York Times,* May 24, 2006).

At the same time, complementarities among production factors are fundamental in understanding the behavior of pressure groups. For instance, in the aftermath of the 2006 midterm elections, the vice president of Technet, a lobbying group for technology companies, stressed that the main goal of the reforms proposed by her group is the relaxation of migration policy constraints.

In addition, new visa categories have been introduced as the result of lobbying activities. An interesting example is the case of H2R visas. In 2005, the quota for H2B visas was filled with none of them going to the seafood industry in Maryland.[1] This industry started heavy lobbying of the Maryland senator Barbara A. Mikulski, who was able to add a last-minute amendment to the Tsunami Relief Act. As a result, a new visa category was introduced—the H2R—whose requirements are the same as for H2B visas, but there is no quota. This has substantially expanded the number of temporary, non-agricultural workers allowed to enter the country.

---

1. H2B visas are for temporary workers in unskilled, seasonal, non-agricultural occupations (for example in the planting-pine-trees industry, the resort industry, the seafood industry, the gardening industry in the North of the United States, etc.).

To carry out our analysis, we use a new, U.S. industry–level dataset that we create by combining information on the number of temporary work visas across sectors with data on the political activities of organized groups, both in favor [of] and against migration. The data set covers the period between 2001 and 2005. To capture the role played by organized labor, we use data on workers' union membership rates across sectors, from the Current Population Survey. In addition, and most importantly, we take advantage of a novel dataset developed by the Center for Responsive Politics that allows us to identify firms' lobbying expenditures by targeted policy area. We are thus able to use information on expenditures that are specifically channeled toward shaping immigration policy. This represents a significant improvement in the quality of the data compared to the existing international economics literature which has used, instead, political action committee (PAC) contributions. In fact, the latter represent only a small fraction (10%) of targeted political activity, the remainder being made up by lobbying expenditures. Furthermore, PAC contributions cannot be disaggregated by issue and, thus, cannot be easily linked to a particular policy.

Our empirical findings suggest that interest groups play a statistically significant and economically relevant role in shaping migration across sectors. Barriers to migration are—*ceteris paribus*—higher in sectors where labor unions are more important and lower in those sectors in which business lobbies are more active. Our preferred estimates suggest that a 10% increase in the size of lobbying expenditures per native worker by business groups is associated with a 3.1% larger number of visas per native worker, while a one-percentage-point increase in union density—for example, moving from 10 to 11 percentage points, which amounts to a 10% increase in union membership rate—reduces it by 3.1%. The results are robust to endogeneity issues which we address by introducing a number of industry-level control variables (e.g., output, prices, origin country effects, etc.), [and] by performing a falsification exercise.

The effects we estimate are the result of the use of a variety of policy tools. First, "visible" restrictions—like quotas—clearly have a fundamental impact. In particular, the existence (or lack) of quantitative restrictions applied to sector-specific visas (such as H1A and H1C for nurses, H2A for temporary agriculture workers, etc.) affects the allocation of visas across sectors. Next, the government can use a number of other instruments, such as sector-specific regulations, to manage access to the labor market in an industry—what we call "invisible" barriers.[2]

The remainder of the paper is organized as follows. Section 2 describes migration policy in the United States and provides the motivation for focus-

---

2. An example of an "invisible" barrier that acts as a form of protectionism is the set of rules that regulate the entry of foreign medical doctors in the U.S. healthcare system.

ing on industry-specific aspects of U.S. migration policy. Section 3 presents the theoretical background and the empirical specification. Section 4 describes the data, while the results of our empirical analysis are reported in Section 5. Finally, Section 6 concludes the paper.

2. MIGRATION POLICY IN THE UNITED STATES

Two main channels are available for non-citizens to enter the United States legally: permanent (immigrant) and temporary (non-immigrant) admission. Individuals entering under the first category are classified as "lawful permanent residents" (LPR) and receive a "green card." They are allowed to work in the United States and may apply for citizenship. Foreigners entering the country as non-immigrants are instead not allowed to work, with an exception made for those admitted under specific categories. Non-immigrants cannot directly apply for naturalization as they first need to be granted LPR status.

Current policies identify an annual flexible quota of 416,000 to 675,000 "green cards" for individuals admitted through family-sponsored preferences, employment preferences, and the diversity program. More than 5.5 million non-immigrant visas were instead issued on average per year between 2001 and 2005, which can be broadly classified as "work and related visas" and "other admissions." The latter represent approximately 85% of the total, whereas 835,294 work and related visas were approved on average every year. Of these, 315,372 were issued to "Temporary workers," under well-known visa categories like the H1B (workers of distinguished merit and ability), H1A and H1C (registered nurses and nurses in shortage area), H2A (workers in agricultural services), H2B (workers in other services), H3 (trainees), and H4 (spouses and children of temporary workers). The other work and related visas were assigned to, for example, "workers with extraordinary ability in the sciences, arts, education, business, or athletics," "internationally recognized athletes or entertainers," "religious workers," and "exchange visitors."

Many work visa categories are subject to an explicit quota set by Congress, as in the case of H1A, H1B, and, up to 2005, H2B visas, and lobbying seems to play an important role in determining whether a program is covered or not by a quota. For instance, universities and government research laboratories were able to obtain a permanent exemption from the overall H1B quota starting in 2000. Analogously, the introduction in 2005 of the H2R visa category has in practice eliminated the quota for non-agricultural temporary workers (H2B).

In this paper we will focus on temporary non-immigrant visas and, in particular, on work visas. In other words, we will not use the number of employment-based green cards, because on the one hand they represent only a very small fraction of the overall number of LPR admitted every year—and on the other, the Department of Homeland Security does not make data available on employment-based green cards by *sector*, which is the level at which we carry out our analysis.

Looking at the wide variety of existing non-immigrant work visas, we can immediately notice that some categories are occupation/sector specific. For instance, H1A and H1C visas are for nurses, H2A visas are for temporary agricultural workers, R1 visas are for religious workers, P visas are for performing artists and outstanding sportsmen, etc. At the same time, other important categories cannot be immediately linked to a specific sector. This is true for instance for H1B, L1, and H2B visas. Anecdotal evidence suggests that the existence of a visa specific to a sector is often the result of the lobbying activities carried out by that particular sector. For example, H1C visas for nurses were introduced in 1999 as the result of fierce lobbying by hospitals and nursing homes. Similarly, the H-2 program was created in 1943 when the Florida sugar cane industry obtained permission to hire Caribbean workers to cut sugar cane.[3] On the other hand, many other sectors have been less successful in obtaining a program specifically targeted to their needs. Still, the intensive lobbying activity carried out by firms active in these sectors suggests that the policymaker's final allocation of visas issued under the H1B or H2B programs across sectors might be influenced by lobbying activities.

In addition, whether sector-specific quotas exist or not, the data suggest that lobbying on immigration takes place at the sectoral level, since the top contributors are often associations representing specific industries, such as the American Hospital Association, the American Nursery and Landscape Association, the National Association of Homebuilders, and National Association of Computer Consultant Businesses, etc. (see http://www.opensecrets.org).

3. EMPIRICAL FRAMEWORK

The abundant anecdotal evidence discussed in the previous section shows that lobbying efforts are likely to have an impact on policy outcomes. In particular, it suggests that greater lobbying by organized labor increases the level of protection in an industry, whereas increased lobbying efforts by organized business owners make migration policy in a sector less restrictive. However, the predictions of the existing theoretical models are less conclusive.

Two frameworks are particularly worth discussing. The first is the workhorse of the endogenous trade policy literature, i.e., the "protection for sale" model by Grossman and Helpman (1994). In this setting, organized sectors represented by a pressure group lobby the government for trade protection. The game takes the form of a menu auction a la Bernheim and Whinston (1986) and, importantly, what matters for the equilibrium policy is the *existence* of a lobby—in other words, the fact that the interests of some sectors are represented in the political process, whereas the interests of some others are not.

---

3. Recently Congressman Anthony Weiner (NY) has proposed a bill to create a new visa category especially for models interested in working in the United States to benefit the New York fashion industry. See *The Economist*, June 21, 2008, "Beauty and the Geek."

In this framework, there is instead no general, straightforward relationship between the level of contributions paid by the organized groups and the policy outcome, as this relationship depends on the bargaining power of the players and on their outside options.

The second model worth mentioning is the "protection formation function" framework, which has been proposed by Findlay and Wellisz (1982). . . . The goal of this model is to explain the trade policy formation process but, differently from the protection for sale setting, it postulates the existence of a direct link between a lobby's efforts and actual policy outcomes through a protection formation function. In each sector, two opposite interests compete: a protectionist lobby and a pro-trade lobby and both offer the politician contributions to sway policy in their favor. . . .

These two standard models—and many others in the literature—thus suggest that assessing the link between lobbying efforts and policy outcomes is essentially an empirical question. . . .

4. DATA

In this section we first provide background information on lobbying expenditures. Next, we describe the sources of the other data we use in the empirical analysis. Finally, we present summary statistics for the main variables used in the regressions.

4.1. Lobbying Expenditures

In the United States, special interest groups can legally influence the policy formation process by offering campaign finance contributions or by carrying out lobbying activities. Campaign finance contributions and, in particular, contributions by political action committees (PACs) have been the focus of the literature. Yet PAC contributions are not the only route by which interest groups can influence policy makers and, given the existing limits on the size of PAC contributions, it is likely that they are not the most important one. In particular, it has been pointed out that lobbying expenditures are of ". . . an order of magnitude greater than total PAC expenditure" (Milyo et al., 2000). Hence, it is surprising that so few empirical papers have looked at the effectiveness of lobbying activities in shaping policy outcomes. One important reason for this relative lack of interest is that, while PAC contributions data has been available for a long time, only with the introduction of the Lobbying Disclosure Act of 1995, individuals and organizations have been required to provide a substantial amount of information on their lobbying activities. Starting from 1996, all lobbyists must file semi-annual reports to the Secretary of the Senate's Office of Public Records (SOPR), listing the name of each client (firm) and the total income they have received from each of them. At the same time, all firms with in-house lobbying departments are required to file similar reports stating the *total* dollar amount they have spent.

Importantly, legislation requires the disclosure not only of the dollar amounts actually received/spent, but also of the issues for which lobbying is carried out. SOPR provides a list of 76 general issues at least one of which has to be entered by the filer. For example, a lobbying firm, Morrison Public Affairs Group, lobbying on behalf of O'Grady Peyton Intl (a subsidiary of AMN Health Care Services) for the period January–June 2004 lists only one issue, i.e., immigration. Another example is a report filed by a client, i.e., Microsoft corporation, for its lobbying expenditures between January–June 2005. Besides immigration, Microsoft lists six other issues in this report. Thus, the new legislation provides access to a wealth of information, and the purpose of this paper is to use it to assess how lobbying influences migration policy.

The data on lobbying expenditures is compiled by the Center for Responsive Politics (CRP) in Washington, DC, using the semi-annual lobbying disclosure reports, which are posted on its website. We focus on reports covering lobbying activity that took place from 1998 through 2005. Due to unavailability of data on other variables, in particular visas, we restrict the analysis in this paper to the period 2001–2005. Annual lobbying expenditures and incomes (of lobbying firms) are calculated by adding mid-year totals and year-end totals. CRP also matches each firm to an industry using its own classification, which is similar to the SIC classification. We define "overall" or "total" lobbying expenditures in an industry as the sum of lobbying expenditures by all firms in that industry *on any issue*. The lobbying expenditures for immigration in an industry are calculated instead using a three-step procedure. First, only those firms are considered which list "immigration" as an issue in their lobbying report. Second, the total expenditure of these firms is split *equally* between the issues they lobbied for. Finally, these firm-level expenditures on immigration are aggregated for all firms within a given industry.

. . . Interest groups have spent on average about 3.8 billion U.S. dollars per political cycle on targeted political activity, which includes PAC campaign contributions and lobbying expenditures. Lobbying expenditures represent by far the bulk of all interest groups' money (close to 90%). Therefore, there are two advantages in using lobbying expenditures rather than PAC contributions to capture the intensity of the activity of pressure groups. First, the latter represent only a small fraction of interest groups' targeted political activity (10%), and any analysis of the role of lobbies in shaping policy based on only these figures could be misleading. Second, linking campaign contributions to particular policy issues is very difficult and often requires some ad-hoc assumptions, as no direct information is available on the purpose of the PAC contribution.

The importance of doing so is shown in Fig. 1—which is based on averages over three election cycles—where in the left panel we have a scatter plot of overall lobbying expenditures and PAC contributions, while in the right panel we have a scatter plot of lobbying expenditures associated with immigration policy and PAC contributions. In the left panel, we find a very high correlation between total lobbying expenditures and PAC contributions across sectors. This result is consistent with the political science literature and may suggest that PAC contributions are integral to groups' lobbying efforts and that they allow them to gain access to policymakers. In contrast, the very low correlation between PAC contributions and lobbying expenditures for migration policy, in the right panel, is striking. It suggests that, if we were to use the data on PAC contributions, we could obtain misleading results. Hence the use of our new dataset is fundamental in order to study how lobbying affects migration policy.

4.2. Other Data

The information on lobbying expenditures is merged with data on visas and on a number of additional variables. Data on visas covers the following letter categories: H1A, H1B, H1C, H2A, J1, O1, O2, P1, P2, P3, R1. . . . The other two potentially relevant work visa categories are L1 (intracompany transferees) and H2B–H2R (non-agricultural temporary workers) but, unfortunately, data on these visas is not available *by sector*. We obtain information on the number of H1B visas approved by NAICS sector from the USCIS. Finally, the figures for the other types of work visas come from the yearly "Report of the Visa Office," available online at http://travel.state.gov.

We also use data from the March Annual Demographic File and Income Supplement to the Current Population Survey (CPS) for the years 2001–2005. We restrict the data to individuals aged 18–64 in the civilian labor force and use the variable *ind1950* in the CPS to obtain information on the industry in which the worker performs or performed—in his most recent job, if unemployed at the time of the survey—his or her primary occupation. This variable is coded according to the 1950 Census Bureau industrial classification system. We aggregate the individual-level information available in the CPS dataset to the industry level to construct the following variables: total number of natives, fraction of union members, fraction of unemployed, and mean weekly earnings. To construct the latter three variables, we restrict the sample to natives, who are defined as native-born respondents, regardless of whether their parents are native-born or foreign-born. The weekly earnings are deflated using the U.S. GDP deflator from the IMF. All the variables are constructed using sampling weights as recommended by the CPS.

While we have direct information on the lobbying expenditures by capital owners (i.e., firms), our measure for workers is only indirect as CRP provides information on lobbying expenditures by unions mostly at the aggregate level. Therefore, we use the fraction of *natives* who are union members in each industry as our measure of political organization of labor in that sector. The rationale for this choice is that, in sectors where the union membership rate is higher, the free-rider problem associated with lobbying is likely to be less pronounced. That is, in those sectors there exist fewer non-union members (free-riders) who benefit from policies brought about by the lobbying activity and, therefore, the contributions by unions tend to be higher. Although our measure is indirect, using data on lobbying expenditures by unions which can be clearly identified with a sector, we find that the correlation between union density rates and lobbying expenditures is positive and significant (see Fig. 2). Finally, our measure of lobbying activity of organized labor is relevant for all visa types, including the H1B category, since it covers both membership in unions and in professional workers associations.

We also gather data on other control variables at the industry level. The data on output, price, and (inward) foreign direct investment (FDI) is from the Bureau of Economic Analysis. The data on the stock of domestic capital (in millions of current dollars) is from the Annual Capital Expenditures Survey (ACES). Finally, we also obtain data on end-of-the-year stock prices at the firm level from Standard and Poor's Compustat North America and aggregate it to compute measures of stock returns at the industry level. In order to measure push factors for migrants in source countries, we develop a sector-specific measure of shocks. In particular, we use information on years in which there was a shock in a developing country as captured by a war, earthquake, wind storm, or drought. The data on wars is from a database compiled by the Heidelberg Institute for International Conflict Research and the World Bank. . . . The industry-specific measure of shocks is given by a weighted average of the shocks in each origin country, with weights equal to the share of immigrants in that industry from each origin country. . . .

. . . On average between 2001 and 2005 an industry spends about $100,000 per year on immigration-related lobbying activities (when we split equally among the various issues). If we consider instead the *total* expenditures by firms in a sector which lobbies for immigration, on average an industry spends about $1.1 million per year. These values hide substantial cross-sectoral heterogeneity. . . . Engineering and computer services, and Educational services are the top spenders on lobbying for immigration. In this group we also find Hospitals, Food and related products, office machines and computer manufacturing and Agriculture. . . .

Before proceeding to the regression analysis, it is instructive to document bivariate relationships between key variables using simple scatter plots. Fig. 3 suggests that there exists a positive correlation between lobbying expenditures for immigration and the number of visas across sectors (both variables are, in this graph, averaged over the years 2001–2005 and scaled by the number of natives in each sector). Thus, these basic scatter plots suggest that sectors with larger lobbying expenditures on immigration are characterized by a higher number of visas. The relationship between union membership rates and the number of visas (divided by the number of natives) is instead negative, that is sectors with higher union densities have fewer immigrants on average over the period (Fig. 4).

FIGURE 1 Scatter Plots between Lobbying Expenditures and Campaign Contributions from Political Action Committees (PACs), 2001–2005

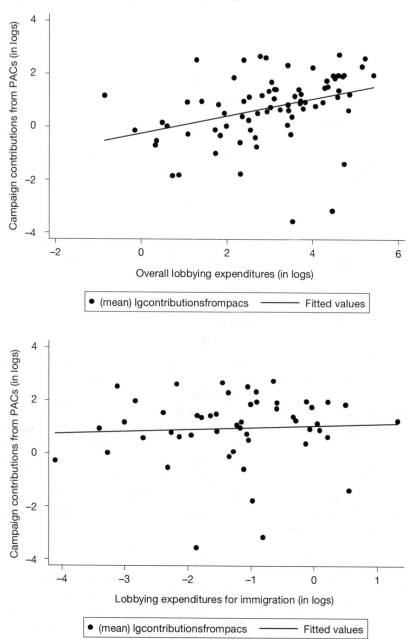

NOTES: The data on campaign contributions and lobbying expenditures are averaged over three election cycles—1999–2000, 2001–02, and 2003–04.

FIGURE 2 Scatter Plot between Lobbying Expenditures by Unions/Professional Assoc. and Union/Prof. Assoc. Membership Rates, 2001–2005

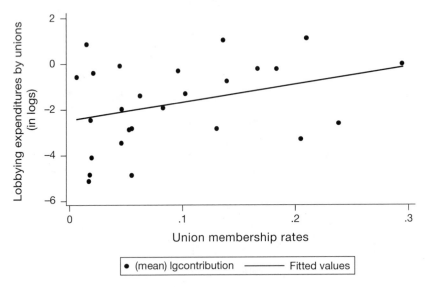

5. EMPIRICAL ANALYSIS

We focus in this paper on sector-specific aspects of U.S. migration policy and, as a result, we analyze the variation in the number of visas *across sectors*. We use data which is averaged over the five years between 2001 and 2005, that is, we only exploit the cross-sectional variation. Indeed, most of the variation in the data is across sectors, rather than over time. . . .

The dependent variable of the empirical analysis is the number of visas, divided by the number of native workers in the same sector (log (*visas/native workers*)). The two key explanatory variables are the log of the industry's lobbying expenditures on migration, divided by the number of native workers in the same sector (log (*lobbying exp/native workers*))—which measures the extent of political organization of capital—and the *union membership rate*, which equals (*native union members/native workers*) and measures the extent of political organization of labor.

Notice that our key variables are scaled by the number of native workers in the same sector. This is to control for differences in the sizes of industries, which could bias the estimated coefficients. For example, larger sectors which employ a higher number of native workers also tend to hire more immigrants and can spend larger sums on lobbying activity as well. Thus, without accounting for the size of the sector, the estimate of the impact of business lobbying expenditures would be biased upwards. The remainder of the section presents our results.

5.1. Main Results

Table 1 presents the main results of the empirical analysis using OLS estimation. In all tables, standard errors are *robust*, to account for heteroscedasticity. In regressions (1)–(2), we find a positive and significant (at the 1% level) coefficient on log(*lobbying exp/native workers*), and a negative and significant (at least at the 10% level) coefficient on native workers' *union membership rate*. These results suggest that barriers to migration are lower in those sectors in which business lobbies are more active, and higher in sectors where labor unions are more important. The two key variables of the empirical analysis explain 13% of the variation in the number of visas per native worker across sectors (regression (2)). In fact, log(*lobbying exp/native workers*) alone explains 11% of the variation. The magnitude of the coefficients (0.367 for log(*lobbying exp/native workers*) and –2.576 for *union membership rate*) in regression (2) implies that a 10% increase in the size of the industry's lobbying expenditures on migration per native worker raises the number of visas to that industry, per native worker, by 3.7%. In addition, a one-percentage-point increase in union density—for example, moving from 10 to 11 percentage points, which amounts to a 10% increase in the union membership rate—reduces it by 2.6%. We assess the robustness of these results in column (3) where we introduce a number of industry-level control variables.

Although our key variables are already scaled by the number of native workers, we are still concerned that our estimates might be driven by differences in the size of sectors. Therefore, in regression (3), we control for the value of output produced in each industry. Output is a more comprehensive measure of the size of a sector because it takes into account the impact of factors other than labor. In column (3), we also introduce the industry-specific unemployment rate, which is likely to be correlated with both the demand for foreign workers in that sector and the union membership rate. The sign of the correlation between union density and the industry-specific unemployment rate is a priori ambiguous. On the one hand, in sectors with higher unemployment rates, workers feel a bigger threat of being fired, which increases their incentive to join unions. On the other, in sectors with higher unemployment rates, the bargaining power of unions is lower, which implies that union densities are lower as well. Finally, the correlation between the unemployment rate and the number of visas is also a priori ambiguous.

Regression (3) also controls for the price of the good produced in a sector. To the extent that a positive price shock in an industry affects the marginal revenue product of labor differently for immigrant vs. native workers, there will be an effect on the labor demand for foreign workers relative to natives. We also control for the stock of capital (both domestic and foreign) used in each industry. To the extent that the degree of complementarity between capital and labor is higher (lower) for immigrant vs. native workers, sectors which

FIGURE 3 Lobbying Expenditures for Immigration and Visas

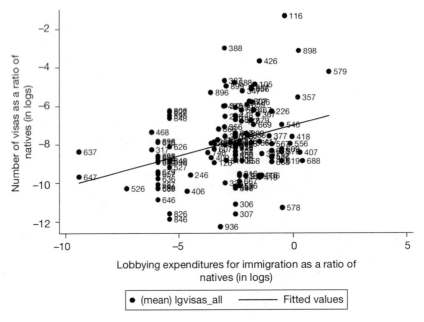

NOTE: All data are averaged over 2001–2005. The correlation between (log) lobbying expenditures for immigration and (log) number of visas (top panel) is 0.327 (robust standard error = 0.077; p-value = 0.000).

use more capital should also be characterized by higher (lower) demand for foreign workers. The results in regression (3) suggest that output, the unemployment rate, prices, and domestic and foreign capital all have an insignificant effect on the number of visas per native worker. Most importantly, our main findings on the key explanatory variables (log(*lobbying exp/native workers*) and *union membership rate*) survive the introduction of additional controls in column (3). The magnitude of the estimated coefficients on lobbying expenditure and union membership rates are only marginally affected by the introduction of the control variables: they remain of the same sign and the same (or higher) significance level.

As mentioned above, as a measure of migration restrictions, we use the number of visas *issued*. This is an *ex post* measure of quotas, which might be affected by the supply side of international migration flows. In other words, the number of visas issued is an equilibrium outcome that results from the interaction of migration policy and of those factors that affect the willingness of migrants to move. The rationale for using the *ex post* measure is that migration quotas are likely to be binding, for the most part, in the United States, which implies that changes in the number of visas coincide with policy changes.

FIGURE 4   Union/Prof. Membership Rates and Visas

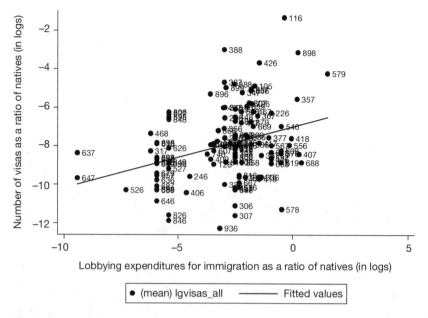

Notes Assoc. All data are averaged over 2001–2005. The correlation between union membership rates and (log) number of visas is –2.250 (robust standard error = 1.252; p-value = 0.074).

However, to address the possibility that the assumption of binding quotas does not hold, we assess the robustness of our results by including variables that affect the willingness of migrants to relocate and, therefore, the number of visas if migration quotas are not binding. In column (3), we control for negative shocks—such as wars, earthquakes, windstorms, or droughts—taking place in the origin countries of immigrants working in any given industry (*shocks*). The negative and significant coefficient on *shocks* can be interpreted as being driven by the ability of migrants to leave their origin countries. Although their willingness to migrate may increase following a shock, their ability is likely to decrease because credit constraints become more binding following the event. Another interpretation which is consistent with our political-economy framework is that immigrants from countries affected by a shock might be entitled to enter the United States as asylum seekers or political refugees and, in that case, the number of *work* visas in the sectors where those immigrants are employed will decrease. In column (3), we also account for pull factors by including the (log) U.S. lagged wages. As expected from a supply point of view, they have a positive and significant impact on the number of visas issued in a given sector. In other words, sectors with higher wages attract more immigrants. Alternatively, an interpretation related to policy is that

TABLE 1 Estimated Effect of Lobbying on Allocation of Visas, OLS

Dependent variable	Log (visas/native workers)			Log (visas)			Log (native workers)		
	[1]	[2]	[3]	[4]	[5]	[6]	[7]	[8]	[9]
Log (lobbying exp/native workers)	0.327***	0.367***	0.312***	0.301***	0.346***	0.315***	-0.033	-0.027	-0.058
	[0.077]	[0.081]	[0.087]	[0.084]	[0.091]	[0.087]	[0.069]	[0.073]	[0.046]
Union membership rate		-2.576*	-3.129**		-2.908*	-3.146**		-0.366	-0.448
		[1.477]	[1.546]		[1.688]	[1.529]		[1.336]	[0.787]
Log (output)			-0.047			-0.042			0.450***
			[0.226]			[0.225]			[0.114]
Unemployment rate			7.609			7.734			-0.56
			[5.856]			[5.667]			[3.084]
Log (price)			2.061			1.901			-2.722**
			[2.519]			[2.482]			[1.084]
Log (capital)			-0.232			-0.214			0.469***
			[0.229]			[0.224]			[0.104]
Log (FDI)			0.045			0.042			-0.019
			[0.096]			[0.093]			[0.044]
Shocks			-7.532**			-7.576***			3.554*
			[2.948]			[2.871]			[1.861]
Log (lag US wages)			10.186***			10.610***			-5.994***
			[3.423]			[3.329]			[2.248]
Log (number of native workers)			0.145			1.133***			
			[0.258]			[0.254]			
N	126	126	120	126	126	120	126	126	120
R-squared	0.11	0.13	0.26	0.07	0.09	0.52	0.00	0.00	0.76

All data are averaged over 2001–2005. Standard errors are corrected for heteroskedasticity, and denoted in parentheses.

*** Denotes significance at 1%.

** Denotes significance at 5%.

* Denotes significance at 10%.

authorities might be more willing and better able to accommodate the requests of pro-migration lobbyists that represent booming sectors. To conclude, as regression (3) shows, our results on the key variables are robust to the introduction of these additional regressors.

In the remainder of Table 1, we break down our dependent variable, log(*visas/ native workers*), and consider its numerator and denominator as separate dependent variables. First, in columns (4), (5), (6), we investigate whether our main results continue to hold if we do not scale the number of visas: we show that our estimates are unaffected. Second, and most importantly, we carry out a falsification exercise and consider the impact of the regressors on the number of *native* workers. If our two key explanatory variables had the same effect on the number of native workers as we find for the number of visas, our previous results could be driven by omitted variables that explain labor demand in general. Instead, columns (7), (8), (9) show that neither lobbying expenditures nor union membership rates are significant drivers of the number of native workers employed in an industry.

5.2. PAC vs. Lobbying Contributions

In Table 2, we use an alternative measure of lobbying expenditures on immigration, namely campaign contributions from Political Action Committees (PACs). Data on PAC campaign contributions has been used extensively in the international economics literature, but does not allow researchers to disentangle the different purposes for which a contribution is made. . . . When we use this proxy for the political organization of capital, we find the estimates of the coefficient on log(*campaign contributions/native workers*) to be not significant at conventional levels (see first two columns in Table 2). The data on PAC campaign contributions is compiled by two-year election cycles. In particular, we average PAC campaign contributions data over the 2001–02 and 2003–04 election cycles. In regressions (3)–(4), for comparison purposes, we look at the impact of log(*lobbying exp/native workers*) using data on lobbying expenditures which is averaged over the same years (2001–2004). The coefficient on log(*lobbying exp/native workers*) is very similar to what we found in Table 1. In addition, the last two columns in Table 2—where we introduce both measures of political organization of capital—clearly show that it is lobbying expenditures on migration, rather than PAC campaign contributions, that positively affect the number of visas. The results are striking and cast doubt on the use of PAC campaign contributions data as an appropriate indicator to examine the effect of lobbying on policy outcomes.

6. CONCLUSIONS

To the best of our knowledge, this paper represents the first study that attempts to provide systematic empirical evidence on the political-economy determinants of current U.S. immigration policy, focusing in particular on the role played

TABLE 2 Estimated Effect of Lobbying on Allocation of Visas, Campaign Contributions from PAC vs. Lobbying Expenditures

Dependent variable		Log (number of visas/native workers)				
	[1]	[2]	[3]	[4]	[5]	[6]
Log (PAC contribution / native workers)	0.191 [0.129]	-0.133 [0.164]			0.14 [0.139]	-0.322 [0.275]
Log (lobbying exp/native workers)			0.330*** [0.068]	0.252*** [0.083]	0.313*** [0.070]	0.247*** [0.083]
Union membership rate	-1.755 [1.102]	-3.000** [1.395]	-3.463** [1.478]	-3.887** [1.607]	-3.135** [1.403]	-3.964** [1.559]
Log (output)		-0.141 [0.190]		-0.092 [0.237]		-0.16 [0.236]
Unemployment rate		6.779 [5.277]		8.689 [5.603]		8.096 [5.681]
Log (price)		-0.902 [2.661]		1.163 [2.694]		0.025 [2.596]
Log (capital)		-0.087 [0.209]		-0.133 [0.216]		-0.113 [0.224]
Log (FDI)		0.180** [0.081]		0.08 [0.092]		0.154* [0.078]
shocks		-4.578** [2.155]		-6.010** [2.479]		-5.135** [2.458]
Log (lag US wages)		10.063*** [3.188]		8.966*** [3.332]		8.579*** [3.264]
Log (number of native workers)		-0.156 [0.236]		0.09 [0.264]		-0.237 [0.311]
N	133	127	119	113	118	112
R-squared	0.05	0.21	0.15	0.26	0.17	0.30

Standard errors are corrected for heteroskedasticity and denoted in parentheses. PACs stand for political action committees. The contributions by PACs are averaged over election cycles 2001–02 and 2003–04. For comparison, data on lobbying expenditures is averaged over the same period.

*** Denotes significance at 1%.

** Denotes significance at 5%.

by interest groups. To this end, we have constructed an industry-level dataset on lobbying expenditures by organized groups, combining it with information on the number of visas issued and on union membership rates. The analysis provides strong evidence that interest groups play a statistically significant and economically relevant role in shaping migration across sectors. Barriers to migration are higher in sectors where labor unions are more important and lower in those sectors in which business lobbies are more active. The main estimates suggest that a 10% increase in the size of lobbying expenditures per native worker by business groups is associated with a 3.1–5.0% larger number of visas per native worker, while a one-percentage point increase in the union membership rate (assumed to be a proxy for lobbying expenditures by labor groups) is associated with a 2.6–5.6% lower number of visas per native worker. The results are robust to introducing a number of industry-level control variables [and] to performing a falsification exercise . . . .

It is difficult to provide a precise account of all the channels through which U.S. immigration policy affects the allocation of visas across sectors. The effects we estimate can be the result of the use of a variety of policy tools. Besides the quantitative restrictions applied to sector-specific visas ("visible" restrictions such as quotas), several regulations substantially affect the number of visas issued across sectors (what we call "invisible" barriers). Interest groups can carry out their lobbying activity on both "visible" and "invisible" restrictions by approaching officials at different levels of policy making, depending on the nature of the measure they want to affect. For instance, for a "statutory change" like changing the cap on H1C visas for nurses, interest groups will lobby the Congress. For a "regulatory change" instead, like the H2A specific wage rate, interest groups lobby an agency in the executive branch such as the Department of Labor.

To conclude, the empirical results suggest that, independently from the channels through which these effects work, policymakers target a given allocation of immigrants across sectors. Moreover, political-economy forces play a quantitatively important role in determining the cross-sectoral allocation of immigrants. Further empirical work could explore other sources of data to analyze the variation in alternative measures of immigration policy—legal vs. illegal, temporary vs. permanent, etc. In addition, the paper could also be extended to examine the variation in immigration policy outcomes along occupation and geographical dimensions (for example, across U.S. districts). Finally, firm-level data on lobbying expenditures can be exploited to study the importance of political-economy forces in the determination of policies other than immigration—e.g., trade, environment, taxes, etc.

REFERENCES

Bernheim, B.D., and M.D. Whinston, 1986. Menu auctions, resource allocation, and economic influence. *Quarterly Journal of Economics* 101: 1–31.

Findlay, R., and S. Wellisz. 1982. Endogenous tariffs, the political economy of trade restrictions and welfare. In *Import Competition and Response*, J. Bhagwati, ed., 158–87. University of Chicago Press, Chicago.

Goldsborough, J. 2000. Out-of-control immigration. *Foreign Affairs* 79: 89–101.

Grossman, G.M., and E. Helpman. 1994. Protection for sale. *American Economic Review* 84: 833–850.

Milyo, J., D. Primo, and T. Groseclose. 2000. Corporate PAC campaign contributions in perspective. *Business and Politics* 2 (Art. 5).

VII

ECONOMIES IN DEVELOPMENT

The liberal international economy created after 1945 and the increase in international finance and trade (discussed in previous sections) have helped produce unprecedented levels of national and global growth. Within this broad pattern of economic success, however, there are important variations. While some countries and people enjoy the highest standards of living in human history, many more remain mired in poverty.

Indeed, the gap between the richest and the poorest people on earth not only is large but, by some measures, is growing wider. As of 2015, the richest 1 percent of the world's population accounts for half of the world's wealth, while the world's poorest two-thirds accounts for less than 3 percent.[1]

While economic growth has increased over the post-1945 period, raising the average standard of living around the globe, the gaps between some of the world's wealthiest and poorest societies have increased even faster. As Branko Milanovic explains in Reading 26, there are a variety of different ways of evaluating the status and evolution of global inequality. By any measure, the world is a very unequal place, but by some measures that inequality has been reduced over recent years. Milanovic clarifies the different concepts of global inequality and suggests their implications.

For decades, scholars and practitioners have debated the sources of economic growth and the best strategies for producing rapid increases in standards of living. Many analysts argue that development, at least in its initial stages, requires that the country insulate itself from more established economic powers and stimulate key industries at home through trade protection and government subsidies. Indeed, Alexander Hamilton, the first secretary of the treasury of the United States, argued for just such a policy in his famous *Report on Manufactures,* which he presented to the House of Representatives in 1791.

Starting in the 1930s with the collapse of the international economy in the Great Depression, many so-called developing countries began de facto strategies of import-substituting industrialization (ISI) in order to increase domestic production to fill the gap created by the decrease in foreign trade. After World War II, especially in Latin America but elsewhere as well, this de facto strategy was institutionalized de jure in high tariffs and explicit governmental policies of industrial promotion. Behind protective walls, countries sought to substitute domestic manufactures for foreign imports, first in light manufactures, such as textiles, apparel, and food processing, and later in intermediate and capital goods production.

Beginning in the 1960s, however, ISI started to come under increasing criticism. Government incentives for manufacturing benefited industry at the expense of agriculture—increasing rural-to-urban migration and often worsening income distribution—and produced many distortions and inefficiencies in the economy. The later stages of ISI, which focused on intermediate and capital goods production and were often more dependent on technology and economies of scale in production, also had the paradoxical effect of increasing national dependence on foreign firms and capital. Yet despite these criticisms, virtually all countries that have industrialized successfully have also adopted ISI for at least a brief period. While many economists argue that success occurs in spite of trade protection and government policies of industrial promotion, historical experience suggests that some degree of import substitution may be a necessary prerequisite for economic development.

In the 1980s, ISI generally gave way to policies of export-led growth. Many developing countries came to recognize the economic inefficiencies introduced by protectionist policies. The debt crisis of the early 1980s and the subsequent decline in new foreign lending increased the importance of exports as a means of earning foreign exchange. Rapid technological changes made "self-reliance" less attractive. There were also important political pressures to abandon ISI. The World Bank and International Monetary Fund (IMF), important sources of capital for developing countries, pressed vigorously for more liberal international economic policies. Proclaiming the "magic of the marketplace," the United States also pushed for more liberal economic policies in the developing world.

Particularly important in reorienting development policy was the success of the newly industrializing countries (NICs) of East Asia: South Korea, Taiwan, Hong Kong, and Singapore. All these states achieved impressive rates of economic growth and industrialization through strategies of aggressive export promotion. While they all adopted ISI during their initial stages of development, the NICs generally sought to work with, rather than against, international market forces. With well-educated labor forces but limited raw materials, the NICs exploited their comparative advantage in light manufactures and, over time, diversified into more capital-intensive production. Today, the NICs are among the most rapidly growing countries in the world, and they have achieved this result with relatively egalitarian income distributions.

The opening to the world economy of large developing countries, such as China and India, is further evidence that strategies of development now hinge on globalization. Prior to the 1980s, China and India had almost totally closed economies. Since then, they—and many other developing countries—have experienced high rates of growth while pursuing outward-oriented policies.

The sources of development are controversial, however. Some analysts give primacy to the outward-oriented strategies adopted by China, India, and other recent globalizers. Others focus on specific government policies or interactions with other nations. In Reading 27, Dani Rodrik surveys two centuries of economic growth and draws conclusions about both the policies and the politics that appear to be most likely to lead poor countries to catch up to richer nations.

In thinking about development, one underlying question has to do with the determinants of today's patterns of global wealth and poverty. In Reading 7, Daron Acemoglu placed at least some of the blame on the legacy of predatory colonialism. In Reading 28, Kenneth Sokoloff and Stanley Engerman also focus on the colonial experience. However, they argue that the economic structure of colonial societies created interests and institutions that had important, persistent effects on subsequent economic development. For them, the combination of economic interests and political institutions is a crucial component of any full explanation of why some countries are rich and others are poor.

An examination of the historical and contemporary international political economy can shed important light on these questions and produce essential insights into the future of the economies in development. Nonetheless, the final outcome of this process will not be known for many years and depends fundamentally on the weight of decades of past developments. As Karl Marx wrote in 1852, "Men make their own history, but they do not make it just as they please; they do not make it under circumstances chosen by themselves, but under circumstances directly encountered, given and transmitted from the past."[2]

NOTES

1. Credit Suisse Research Institute, *Global Wealth Report 2015* (October 2015), available at https://publications.credit-suisse.com/tasks/render/file/?fileID=F2425415-DCA7-80B8-EAD989AF9341D47E.

2. Karl Marx, *The Eighteenth Brumaire of Louis Napoleon* (1852; repr., New York: International Publishers, 1994).

26

Global Income Inequality in Numbers:
In History and Now

BRANKO MILANOVIC

The world is a very unequal place. However, in this reading, Branko Milanovic explores the complexities involved in understanding this inequality. The greatest inequalities are among countries rather than within countries. Still, whether the world is becoming more or less unequal depends on the sort of inequality in question. Milanovic explores three different concepts of inequality and provides a wealth of information to explain the various dimensions of global economic growth and its distribution.

When we think of income inequality, our first reaction is to think of it within the borders of a country. This is quite understandable in a world where the nation state is very important in determining one's income level and access to a number of benefits (from pensions to free health care), and where by far the dominant way in which political life is organized is at the level of a country. However, in the era of globalization another way to look at inequality between individuals is to go beyond the confines of a nation state and to look at inequality between all individuals in the world. Once we do so, many of the things about inequalities in general that we believe or think we know change; it is like going from a two-dimensional world to a three-dimensional one.

As the world becomes more integrated, the global dimension of inequality is likely to become increasingly relevant. This is for at least two reasons: the much-increased movement of factors of production across borders, and the greater influence of other people's (foreigners') standard of living and way of life on one's perceived income position and aspirations. Greater movement of capital, goods, technology, and ideas from one side of the globe to another implies greater connectivity with people who are not one's compatriots, and greater dependence on other nations for the generation of one's income. Movements of labor that illustrate this interdependence in a most obvious fashion are still less important than movements of capital, but they are increasing. The knowledge of how other people live and how much money they make influences strongly our perception of our own income and position in the income pyramid. An imaginary community of world citizens is thus built gradually. And once this is done, comparisons of actual incomes and welfare between different members of that imaginary community acquire importance. This is why global inequality will gain in importance, even if it is not as relevant or important for an average individual as inequality within his or her political community (nation state). Once we compare ourselves with people from other parts of the world, we are indeed interested in global income distribution. Global inequality begins to matter.

1. THREE CONCEPTS OF INEQUALITY AND HOW THEY HAVE EVOLVED OVER THE PAST 60 YEARS

When we talk about inequality that transcends national borders, often we have in mind not one but three different concepts—even when we are not fully aware of it. I am going to articulate these three concepts.

The first concept of inequality (let's call it *inequality 1*) is focused on inequality between nations of the world. It is an inequality statistic calculated across GDPs or mean incomes obtained from household surveys of all countries in the world, without population weighting. To show how this is done, consider the three individuals in the top row of Figure 1. The height of each person represents the GDP or mean income of his or her country. Somebody from a poor country would be represented as a short person, somebody from a middle-income country as a person of medium height, and somebody from a rich country as a very tall person. When we calculate this concept of inequality, we take all countries with their mean incomes—we have data for some 150 countries—and calculate the Gini coefficient. China and Luxembourg have the same importance, because we do not take population sizes into account. Every country counts the same, somewhat like in the UN General Assembly.

Consider now the second row of the figure, which would help us define concept 2 inequality or *inequality 2*. There, individuals from poor countries are all equally short as before and those from rich countries are all equally tall, but the difference lies in the fact that countries' population sizes are now taken into account. We do exactly the same thing as we did for inequality 1, but now China and Luxemburg (or any other country) enter the calculation with their populations. Introducing population is very important. As we shall see in the next section, during the past 25 years the movements in concept 1 and concept 2 inequalities were very different. Recall, however, that in both cases the calculation takes into account not the actual incomes of individuals but country averages.

Inequality 3 is the global inequality, which is the most important concept for those interested in the world as composed of individuals, not nations. Unlike the first two concepts, this one is individual-based: each person, regardless of his or her country, enters in the calculation with their actual income. In Figure 1, this is represented by the different heights of individuals who belong to the same country. Not all Americans earn the average income of the United States, nor do all Chinese earn the average income of China. Indeed in row 3, the poorest person is from the middle-income country, while his compatriot is the second richest (the second tallest) in our group of ten individuals.

FIGURE 1 Three Concepts of Inequality Defined

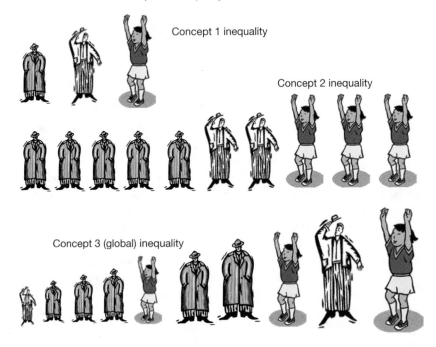

Concept 1 inequality

Concept 2 inequality

Concept 3 (global) inequality

But moving from concept 2 to concept 3 inequality is not easy. The chief difficulty comes from the fact that to calculate concept 3 inequality we need access to house-hold surveys with data on individual incomes or consumption. Income or consumption have to be measured using the same or similar methodology, and surveys need to be available from as many countries as possible. Perhaps at least 120–130 surveys are needed in order to cover more than 90 percent of the world population and account for 95 or more percent of world income. Ideally, of course, we would like to have surveys from every country in the world. This is a very hard requirement. There are still quite a few countries, mostly in Africa, where household surveys are not conducted regularly and where methodologies change (sometimes rather brusquely) from one survey to another, thus rendering comparisons difficult.

Because the calculation of global inequality relies on household surveys, we cannot calculate inequality 3 with much precision for the period before the mid- or late 1980s. There are simply no household surveys available for many parts of the world. The first available Chinese household surveys are from 1982, the first usable surveys from the former Soviet Union are from 1988, and for many sub-Saharan African countries, the earliest household surveys date from the mid-1980s. Thus, for the past, we have to rely on much more tentative data, where countries' income distributions are only approximated using various more or less reliable methods. This is particularly the case if we wish to study global inequality over the long term, covering the 19th century as well—a topic that I will discuss in Section 3.

Figure 2 displays the movements of the three types of inequalities after the Second World War. The Gini coefficient is on the vertical axis. Inequality 1 was stable from 1960 to 1980. This means that there was no systematically faster or slower growth of poor or rich countries. The gap between poor and rich countries was neither closing nor growing. Divergence started only at the beginning of globalization, around 1980, and went on until the turn of the century. These two decades were very bad as far as convergence (or catching up by poor countries) is concerned: rich countries grew, on average, faster than poor countries. However, China and India, which are the huge success stories of that period and the two most populous countries in the world, do not enter into the calculation of inequality 1 with greater weights than any other country.

Let us now consider further Figure 2. Why is it called "the mother of all inequality disputes"? To see what the dispute is about, consider the difference in the movements of inequality 1 and inequality 2. While the first, as we just saw, rose during the globalization era, the second declined—at times even dramatically. Measured by inequality 2, the world has certainly become a much better ("more convergent" or more equal) place precisely during the same period. Thus, those who desire to emphasize the unevenness of globalization tend to focus on growing inter-country gaps without taking into account sizes of population, and prefer inequality 1. Those who wish to focus on the positive aspects of globalization tend to favor concept 2, and to point to the indubitable successes of China and India. In effect, to grasp intuitively why and how concept 2 inequality declined, we need to recall that in these calculations, China counts for a lot because of its large population size. And China, which started from an extremely low level of income in the 1980s, has grown very quickly during the past three decades, converging on the rich world. Until recently, it was China alone that had been preventing a rise in global inequality as measured by concept 2. But now it has "support" from India, which is also recording high rates of growth and has also started from a very low baseline. The high rates of growth of these two countries are thus the major factor underlying the downward trend of inequality 2.

Inequality 3 can be calculated, as mentioned earlier, only from the mid-1980s because we do not have household surveys that go back further in time. Figure 2 shows that inequality 3 is higher than inequality 2. This is true by definition: in inequality 3 people enter the calculations with their actual incomes, not with country averages. A quick glance at Figure 1 shows that the variability of heights is greater in the third row than in the second. Averaging out reduces measured inequality.

To calculate "true" global inequality, we have to adjust people's incomes with the price levels they face; of course, these differ between countries. We are interested in the real welfare of people, and those living in "cheaper" countries will get a boost in their incomes compared to what they make in nominal dollar

FIGURE 2   International and Global Inequality, 1952–2011: "The Mother of All Inequality Disputes"

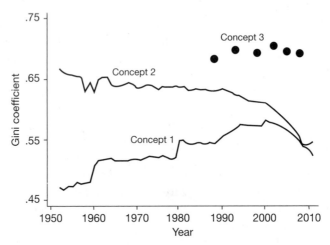

terms. The currency we use is the international (or purchasing power parity (PPP)) dollar with which, in principle, one can buy the same amount of goods and services in any country. Indeed, if we were not to adjust for the differences in price levels, and were to use nominal dollars, global inequality would have been even higher. This is because price levels tend to be lower in poorer countries, and the income of people living in poorer countries thus gets a significant "boost" when we use PPP dollars.

Often, a key issue of concern regarding global inequality is not only its level but its trend: has it been going up or down during the globalization era? Global Inequality is calculated at approximately five-year intervals, from 1988 (the first dot on the left in Figure 2) to 2008 (the last dot on the right). If we compare this last dot with a couple of dots for the earlier years, we see something that may be historically important: perhaps for the first time since the Industrial Revolution, there may have been a decline in global inequality. Between 2002 and 2008, global Gini decreased by 1.4 points. We must not rush to conclude that what we see in the most recent years represents a real or irreversible decline, or a new trend, because we do not know if the decline in global inequality will continue over the next decades. So far it is just a tiny drop, a kink in the trend, but it is indeed a hopeful sign. For the first time in almost 200 years—after a long period during which global inequality rose and then reached a very high plateau—it may be setting onto a downward path.

The main reason for this break in the previous trend is what also underlies the decrease in concept 2 inequality: the fast growth of relatively poor and very populous countries, most notably China and India. Their growth, reflected in the rising real incomes of their populations, has not only curbed the rise in global inequality but pushed it down slightly. China's and India's roles stand in marked contrast to the two other factors that influence global inequality and that have both been clearly pro-inequality. The first is the divergence of countries' mean incomes that lasted from around 1980 to 2000; the second is the rise in within-national inequalities in many countries. The catching up of poor and large countries has been the sole factor offsetting these upward pressures. But it has been such a strong factor that it has either kept global inequality from rising or (more recently, with the acceleration of Indian growth) reduced it.

What can we say about the level of global inequality? What does the Gini of about 70, which is the value of global inequality (see Figure 2), mean? One way to look at it is to take the whole income of the world and divide it into two halves: the richest 8 percent will take one half and the other 92 percent of the population will take another half. So, it is a 92–8 world. Applying the same type of division to the US income, the numbers are 78 and 22. Or using Germany, the numbers are 71 and 29. Another way to look at it is to compare what percentage of the world's population, ranked from the poorest to the richest, is needed to get to the cumulative one-fifth of global income. Three-quarters of the (poorer) world population are needed to get to the first fifth of total income, but only 1.7 percent of those at the top suffice to get to the last fifth.

Global inequality is much greater than inequality within any individual country. . . . Global inequality is substantially greater than inequality in Brazil, a country that is often held as an exemplar of excessive inequality (despite the recent improvements under the Lula presidency). And it is almost twice as great as inequality in the United States. . . .

2. FROM THE FALL OF THE BERLIN WALL TO THE GLOBAL FINANCIAL CRISIS: WHO WON AND WHO LOST

Generally two groups of people are thought to be the big winners of the past two decades of globalization: firstly the very rich, those at the top of national and global income distributions; secondly the middle classes of the emerging market economies, particularly China, India, Indonesia, and Brazil. Is this true? . . .

What parts of the global income distribution registered the largest gains between 1988 and 2008? . . . It is indeed among the very top of the global income distribution and among the "emerging global middle class," which includes more than a third of the world's population, that we find most significant increases in per-capita income. The top 1 percent has seen its real income rise by more than 60 percent over those two decades. However, the largest increases were registered around the median; 80 percent real increase at the median itself and some 70 percent around it. It is between the 50th and 60th percentiles of global income distribution that we find some 200 million Chinese, 90 million Indians, and about 30 million people each from Indonesia, Brazil, and Egypt. These two groups—the global top 1 percent and the middle classes of the emerging market economies—are indeed the main winners of globalization.

The surprise is that those in the bottom third of global income distribution have also made significant gains, with real incomes rising between over 40 percent and almost 70 percent. The only exception is the poorest 5 percent of the population, whose real incomes have remained the same. This income increase at the bottom of the global pyramid has allowed the proportion of what the World Bank calls the absolute poor (people whose per-capita income is less than 1.25 PPP dollars per day) to go down from 44 percent to 23 percent over approximately the same 20 years.

But the biggest losers (other than the very poorest 5 percent), or at least the "nonwinners," of globalization were those between the 75th and 90th percentiles of global income distribution, whose real income gains were essentially nil. These people, who may be called a global upper middle class, include many from former communist countries and Latin America, as well as those citizens of rich countries whose incomes stagnated.

Global income distribution has changed in a remarkable way. It was probably the most profound global reshuffle of people's economic positions since the Industrial Revolution. Broadly speaking the bottom third, with the exception of the very poorest, became significantly better off and many of the people there escaped absolute poverty. The middle third or more became much richer, seeing their real incomes rise by approximately 3 percent per capita annually.

However, the most interesting developments happened among the top quartile: the top 1 percent, and to a somewhat lesser extent the top 5 percent, gained significantly; the next 20 percent either gained very little or had stagnant real incomes. This created polarization among the richest quartile of world population, allowing the top 1 percent to pull ahead of the other rich and to reaffirm in fact—and even more so in public perception—its preponderant role as a winner of globalization.

Who are the people in the global top 1 percent? Despite its name, it is a less "exclusive" club than the U.S. top 1 percent: the global top 1 percent consists of more than 60 million people; the U.S. top 1 percent only 3 million. Thus, among the global top 1 percent, we find the richest 12 percent of Americans (more than 30 million people) and between 3 and 6 percent of the richest Britons, Japanese, Germans, and French. It is a "club" that is still overwhelmingly composed of the "old rich" world of Western Europe, Northern America, and Japan. The richest 1 percent of the embattled euro countries of Italy, Spain, Portugal, and Greece are all part of the global top 1 percentile. The richest 1 percent of Brazilians, Russians, and South Africans belong there too.

To which countries and income groups do the winners and losers belong? Consider the people in the median of their national income distributions in 1988 and 2008. In 1988, a person with a median income in China was richer than only 10 percent of the world's population. Twenty years later, a person at that same position within Chinese income distribution was richer than more than half of the world's population. Thus, he or she leapfrogged over more than 40 percent of people in the world.

For India the improvement was more modest, but still remarkable. A person with a median income went from being at the 10th percentile globally to the 27th. A person at the same income position in Indonesia went from the 25th to 39th global percentile. A person with the median income in Brazil gained as well. He or she went from being around the 40th percentile of the global income distribution to about the 66th percentile. Meanwhile, the position of large European countries and the United States remained about the same, with median income recipients there in the 80s and 90s of global percentiles. But if the economic crisis that currently affects these countries persists, we should not be surprised if we find the median individual in the "rich world" becoming globally somewhat poorer.

Who lost between 1988 and 2008? Mostly people in Africa, some in Latin America and post-communist countries. The average Kenyan went down from the 22nd to the 12th percentile globally, the average Nigerian from the 16th to 13th percentile. A different way to see this is to look at how far behind the global median was an average African in 1988 and 20 years later.

In 1988, an African with the median income of the continent had an income equal to two-thirds of the global median. In 2008, that proportion had declined to less than half. The position of a median-income person in post-communist countries slid from around the 75th global percentile to the 73rd. The relative declines of Africa, Eastern Europe, and the former Soviet Union confirm the failure of these parts of the world to adjust well to globalization, at least up to the early years of the 21st century. Their improved recent performance is still too fragile to have been reflected in the survey data. . . .

The bottom line is that these results show a remarkable change in underlying global income distribution. We now live in a world with a bulge around the median, with significantly rising incomes for the entire second third (or more) of the global income distribution. That is the new aspiring global middle class. We also see the growing wealth, and probably power, of those at the very top and, remarkably, stagnant incomes for both the people just below the "enchanted" richest 1 or 5 percent and the world's poorest.

3. GLOBAL INEQUALITY OVER THE LONG TERM: FROM PROLETARIANS TO MIGRANTS

I will now look at global inequality over the long sweep of history. It is here that we can establish an important finding, which, I think, goes into some core issues of political philosophy and economics.

Let us try to do for the entire period since the Industrial Revolution the same type of global inequality calculations that we have just shown for the last

20 years. We ask, "what was global inequality around the mid-19th century?" It is an impossible question to answer with any precision, because we do not have household surveys or any other reliable sources of income data for these times. Nonetheless, some important attempts to estimate it have been made before. . . .

The basic story that emerges from these calculations of income inequality in far-away times is that since the Industrial Revolution, which launched a score of European countries and their overseas offshoots onto a path of faster growth, global inequality kept on rising until the mid-20th century. There was a period of more than a century of steady increase in global inequality, followed by perhaps 50 years (between the end of the Second World War and the turn of the 21st century) when global inequality remained on a high plateau, changing very little. We can see this in Figure 2, where the six dots are all within several Gini points of each other; that is, within one standard error of the calculated Gini coefficients. It is only in the early 21st century that global inequality might have commenced its downward course. If indeed this comes to pass, global inequality would have charted a gigantic inverted U-shaped curve and perhaps in some 50 years—if the emerging market economies continue to grow faster than the rich world—we might be back to the state of affairs that existed around the time of the Industrial Revolution. . . .

. . . The shares of the two factors determining global inequality have changed in a remarkable fashion. Global inequality can be decomposed into two parts. The first part results from differences in incomes within nations, which means that that part of total inequality is caused by income differences between rich and poor Americans, rich and poor Chinese, rich and poor Egyptians, and so on for all the countries in the world. If one adds up all of these within-nation inequalities, one gets their aggregate contribution to global inequality. This is what I call the "class" component to global inequality because it accounts for (the sum of) income inequalities between different "income classes" within countries. The second component, which I call the "location" component, refers to the differences between the mean incomes of all the countries in the world. So there, one actually asks "how much are the gaps in average incomes between the UK and China, between The Netherlands and India, between the US and Mexico, and so on influencing global inequality?" It is the sum of inter-country differences in mean incomes. In technical terms, the first part ("class") is also called "within inequality", the second part ("location") is called "between inequality."

. . . Around 1870, class explained more than two-thirds of global inequality. And now? The proportions have exactly flipped: more than two-thirds of total inequality is due to location. The implication of this overwhelming importance of location, or citizenship (which is the same)—i.e., being a member of a rich or poor country—for our lifetime incomes can also be captured very well by another exercise. We divide the population of each country into 100 income percentiles, ranked from the poorest to the richest. Now, if we run a regression with income levels of these percentiles (for 120 countries, this gives 12,000 observations) as the dependent variable, and on the other side of the regression use the mean income of the country where each percentile comes from as the only explanatory variable, we explain more than half of the variability in individual incomes. This is a remarkable achievement for a single explanatory variable. Differently put, more than 50 percent of one's income depends on the average income of the country where a person lives or was born (the two things being the same for 97 percent of world population). This underlines the importance of the location element today. There are, of course, other factors that matter for one's income: from gender and parental education (which are, from an individual point of view, externally given circumstances) to factors like own education, effort, and luck (which are not). They all influence our income level. But the remarkable thing is that a very large chunk of our income will be determined by only one variable, which generally we acquire at birth: citizenship. It is almost the same as saying that if I know nothing about any given individual in the world I can, with a reasonable amount of confidence, predict his or her income just from the knowledge of his or her citizenship.

. . . We live today in a non-Marxian world. Karl Marx could write eloquently in 1867 in *Das Kapital*, or earlier in *The Manifesto*, about proletarians in different parts of the world—peasants in India, workers in England, France, or Germany—sharing the same political interests. They were invariably poor and, importantly, they were all about equally poor, eking out a barely-above-subsistence existence, regardless of the country in which they lived. There was not much of a difference in their material positions. One could imagine and promote proletarian solidarity, and consequently—because equally poor people of different nations faced equally rich people in their own nations—a generalized class conflict. . . . There were no national contradictions, just a worldwide class contradiction. This was a broadly accurate description of the situation at that time.

But if the world's actual situation is such that the greatest disparities are caused by the income gaps between nations, then proletarian solidarity does not make much sense. Indeed, the income levels of poor individuals in poor countries are much lower than those of poor people in rich countries. People who are considered nationally poor in the United States or the EU have incomes that are many times greater than incomes of the poor people in poor countries and, moreover, often greater than the incomes of the middle class in poor countries. And if that gap is so wide, then one cannot expect any kind of coalition between such income-heterogeneous groups of nationally poor people—or at least not any coalition based on the similarity of their material positions and near identity of their economic interests. Proletarian solidarity is dead because there is no longer such a thing as the global proletariat. This is why ours is a distinctly non-Marxian world. . . .

5. CONCLUDING REMARKS: PHILOSOPHICAL REFLECTIONS AND POLITICAL IMPLICATIONS

I want to conclude with two points that I think can be derived from what I have discussed so far.

The first one is an issue for political philosophy. If most of global inequality is due to differences in location, can we treat location, and thus citizenship, as a rent or a premium (or, conversely, as a penalty)? Is citizenship—belonging to a given country, most often through birth—something that gives us by itself the right to greater income? Is there a difference in our view of the matter if we take a global, as opposed to national, perspective? Is there a contradiction between the two?

Within a single country, society tries in principle to limit the advantages that accrue to people born in rich families. The advantages include access to better education and health care, to powerful friends and private information, and of course greater wealth. Society tries to limit these inherited advantages by either taxing wealth or by making education, health, etc. available to all, regardless of their income level. But what is the case in the "global world"? The situation is, at one level, very similar. There are rich countries that have accumulated lots of wealth and transmit that wealth, along with many other advantages, to the next generations of their citizens. This is why, for example, the poorest Americans are relatively well off by world standards. They are lucky to have been born in the country that is rich (or has become rich: the case was different for the poorest Americans in the 17th century). And there are also people from poor countries who do not have wealth or the advantages and opportunities it confers. In stark contrast to the within-country case, this is considered unobjectionable; or rather it is not questioned whether one may keep on benefiting from something that the previous generations have created and one has simply inherited by virtue of birth. In one case, we frown upon the transmission of family-acquired wealth to offsprings if two different individuals belong to the same nation. In the other case, we take it as normal that there is a transmission of collectively acquired wealth over generations within the same nation, and if two individuals belong to two different nations we do not even think about, much less question, such acquired differences in wealth, income, and global social position.

In political philosophy, there are good arguments to go on with that approach (as we do implicitly today) and there are also good arguments to disapprove of it. It is hard to decide which way is right. But what we can do is to put that argument on the table and open it for discussion.

The second implication concerns the issue of migration. If citizenship explains 50 percent or more of variability in global incomes, then there are three ways in which global inequality can be reduced. The first is by high growth rates of poor countries. This requires an acceleration of income growth in poor countries, and of course continued high rates of growth in India,

China, Indonesia, etc. The second way is to introduce global redistributive schemes. Yet it is very difficult to see how that could happen. Currently, development assistance is a little over $100 billion a year. This is just five times more than the bonus Goldman Sachs paid itself during one crisis year. Rich countries are not willing to spend very much money to help poor countries. The willingness to help poor countries is now, with the ongoing economic crisis in the west, probably reaching its nadir. The third way in which global inequality and poverty can be reduced is through migration. Migration is likely to become one of the key problems—or solutions, depending on one's viewpoint—of the 21st century. To give just one stark example: if you classify countries by their GDP per capita level into four "worlds," going from the rich world of advanced nations (with GDPs per capita of over $20,000 per year) to the poorest, fourth, world (with incomes under $1,000 per year), there are seven points in the world where rich and poor countries are geographically closest to each other—whether it is because they share a border, or because the sea distance between them is minimal. You would not be surprised to find out that all seven of these points have mines, boat patrols, walls, and fences to prevent free movement of people. The rich world is fencing itself in, or fencing others out. But the pressures of migration are remaining strong, despite the current crisis, simply because the differences in income levels are so huge.

I conclude with something that resembles a slogan: either poor countries will become richer, or poor people will move to rich countries. Actually, these two developments can be seen as equivalent. Development is about people: either poor people have ways to become richer where they are now, or they can become rich by moving somewhere else. Looked at from above, there is no real difference between the two options. But from the point of view of real politics, there is a whole world of difference.

27

The Past, Present, and Future of Economic Growth

DANI RODRIK

There are major disagreements about the sources of successful economic growth and development. In this reading, Dani Rodrik first surveys the experiences of economic growth over the past century or more, including in particular those countries that have been especially successful at raising living standards toward or to the level of the industrialized world. Rodrik goes on to summarize what he sees as the lessons of successful (and unsuccessful) development experiences. He regards appropriate political and policy institutions as essential, emphasizing that government involvement in the economy, especially to encourage industrialization, has typically been a major component of developmental success.

The past decade has been an extraordinarily good one for developing nations and their mostly poor citizens—so good, in fact, that it has become commonplace to look upon them as potential saviors of the world economy. Their economies have expanded at unprecedented rates, resulting in both a large reduction in extreme poverty and a significant expansion of the middle class. The differential between the growth rates of developing and advanced nations expanded to more than five percentage points, assisted in part by the decline in the economic performance of the rich countries. China, India, and a small number of other Asian countries were responsible for the bulk of this superlative performance. But Latin America and Africa resumed growth as well, catching up with (and often surpassing) the growth rates they had experienced during the 1950s and 1960s.

Economic growth is a precondition for the improvement of living standards and lifetime possibilities for the "average" citizen of the developing world. Can this recent performance be sustained into the future, decisively reversing the "great divergence" that has split the world into rich and poor countries since the nineteenth century?

In answering this question, the optimists would point to the improvements in governance and macroeconomic policy in developing countries and to the still not-fully exploited potential of economic globalization to foster new industries in the poor regions of the world through outsourcing and technology transfer. Pessimists would fret about the drag that rich countries exert on the world economy, the threats to globalization, and the obstacles that late industrializers have to surmount given competition from China and other established export champions. The weights that one places on these diverse considerations—and many others—would depend on one's views as to the ultimate drivers of economic growth in lagging countries. Extrapolation is tempting, but not necessarily a good guide to where we are headed.

We can also turn around the question about the sustainability of growth and pose it in a different form: what kind of changes in the institutional framework within countries and globally would most facilitate rapid growth and convergence? This is a normative, rather than positive, question about the needed policies. But answering it requires yet again a view on what drives growth. The more clearly articulated that view is, the more transparent the policy implications are.

The objective in this article is to provide a longer-term perspective on economic growth so we can better understand its key drivers, as well as the constraints that act on it. An analytical framework is developed that is motivated by the empirical evidence and embeds the conventional approaches to economic growth. While orthodox in many ways, the framework also highlights a somewhat different strategic emphasis that provides a better account of the heterogeneity with respect to growth performance around the developing world.

Two key dynamics are behind growth. First, there is the development of fundamental capabilities in the form of human capital and institutions. Long-term growth ultimately depends on the accumulation of these capabilities—everything from education and health to improved regulatory frameworks and better governance. But fundamental capabilities are multidimensional, have high set-up costs, and exhibit complementarities. Therefore, investments in them tend to yield paltry growth payoffs until a sufficiently broad range of capabilities has already been accumulated—that is, until relatively late in the development process. Growth based on the accumulation of fundamental capabilities is a long-drawn-out affair.

Second, there is the dynamic of structural transformation, which refers to the birth and expansion of new (higher-productivity) industries and the transfer of labor from traditional or lower-productivity activities to modern ones. With the exception of natural-resource bonanzas, extraordinarily high growth rates are almost always the result of rapid structural transformation, industrialization in particular. Growth miracles are enabled by the fact that industrialization can take place in the presence of a low level of fundamental capabilities: poor economies can experience structural transformation even when skills are low and institutions weak. This helps explains the rapid take-off of East Asian countries in the postwar period, from Taiwan in the late 1950s to China in the late 1970s.

The policies needed to accumulate fundamental capabilities and those required to foster structural change naturally overlap, but they are distinct. The first entail a much broader range of investments in skills, education, administrative capacity, and governance, while the second can take the form of narrower, targeted remedies. Without some semblance of macroeconomic stability and property rights protection, new industries cannot emerge. But one does not need to attain Sweden's level in institutional quality in order to be able to compete with Swedish producers on world markets in many manufactures. Furthermore, as discussed below, fostering new industries often requires second-best, unconventional policies that are in tension with fundamentals. When successful, heterodox policies work precisely because they compensate for weakness in those fundamentals.

As an economy develops, the dualism between modern and traditional sectors disappears and economic activities become more complex across the board. Correspondingly, these two drivers merge, along with the sets of policies that underpin them. Fundamentals become the dominant force over structural transformation. Put differently, if strong fundamentals do not eventually come into play, growth driven by structural transformation runs out of steam and falters.

The article begins by describing the consequences of recent growth performance on the global income distribution. The salient facts that emerge from the analysis are that growth in developing countries (especially China) has been a boon to the "average citizen" of the world and has created a new global middle class. Next, it turns to economic history and highlights the role of differential patterns of industrialization in shaping the world economy's great divergence between a rich core and a poor periphery. This is followed by a section that summarizes the growth record to date in the form of six empirical regularities, or "stylized facts." Key among these is the presence of unconditional labor-productivity convergence in manufacturing industries. The next section interprets the policy experience of successful economies in light of this empirical background. The rest of the article discusses the policy implications and the prognosis for the future.

HOW IS THE "AVERAGE" PERSON DOING? GROWTH AND THE GLOBAL INCOME DISTRIBUTION

Let us define the phrase "average individual" as the person in the middle of the global income distribution—that is, the individual who receives the median level of income in the global economy. One way of gauging the extent of global inequality is to compare the income of the average individual to average global income (i.e., global gross domestic product per capita). Were income distributed evenly, median and average incomes would coincide. The more unequal is the world economy, the larger the gap between the two. As Table 1 shows, the average median-income ratio is huge for the world as a whole, roughly twice what we observe in the world's most unequal societies (such as Brazil). Global inequality is much higher than within-country inequality.

The good news is that this ratio has come down significantly since the 1980s, driven by the much more rapid increase in median income than in average income. In 1988, the world's median income stood at $846 (in 2005 purchas-

TABLE 1   Median and Average Incomes

		Median income	Average income($)	Ratio
World	1988	846	3,523	4.16
	2005	1,209	3,946	3.26
	increase	42.9%	12.0%	
United States	1988	12,327	14,819	1.20
	2005	15,664	20,001	1.28
	increase	27.1%	35.0%	
China	1988	310	361	1.16
	2005	1,013	1,303	1.29
	increase	226.8%	260.9%	
Brazil	1988	1,901	4,030	2.12
	2005	2,107	3,890	1.85
	increase	10.8%	–3.5%	

NOTE: See text for source. All dollar amounts in 2005 PPP$.

ing power parity–adjusted dollars). By 2005, this figure had risen to $1,209, an increase of 43 percent over the course of less than two decades. The rise in average world incomes over the same period was only 12 percent (from $3,523 to $3,946). Correspondingly, global inequality fell substantially, at least when measured by this indicator. As Table 1 shows, this happened even though within-country inequality rose in most large economies such as the United States and China (but not Brazil).

Since the 1980s, China has turned itself from a poor country, where the bulk of its population stood below the global median, into a middle-income country, where median income has caught up with the global median (Table 1). Today, China's income distribution is centered at the middle of the global income distribution. The result is that the global economy now has a much larger middle class, with Chinese households making up a large part of it.

The impact that Chinese economic growth has had on the global distribution of income reflects an important feature of global inequality. Depending on the measure used and time period, between 75 and 80 percent of global income inequality is accounted for by inequality across countries—that is, differences in per-capita incomes between countries. Inequality within countries is responsible for a quarter or less of global inequality. That is why rapid growth in China has greatly expanded the world's middle class even though China's income distribution has deteriorated noticeably. Thanks to differential patterns of economic growth in different parts of the world, it is increasingly the country in which one is born that determines one's economic fortunes.

To drive the point home, I often ask people to consider whether it is better to be rich in a poor country or poor in a rich country. To clarify the question,

I spell out what I mean by "rich" and "poor." I tell them that they should think of a rich person as someone in the top 10 percent of a country's income distribution, while a poor person is in the bottom 10 percent. Similarly, a rich country is in the top decile of all countries ranked by average income per person, while a poor country is in the bottom decile of that list. Which would they prefer?

Most have little hesitation in responding that they would prefer to be rich in a poor country—which is the wrong answer. The correct answer is "poor in a rich country"—and it is not even close. The average poor person in a rich country, defined along the lines above, in fact earns three times more than the average rich person in the poor country (as always, adjusted for PPP across countries). Disparities in other aspects of well-being, such as infant mortality, go the same way, too. The poor in a rich country have it much, much better than the rich in the poor country.

Poor countries, of course, have their own superrich, people who drive Mercedes luxury cars and live in mansions with large household staffs. But what my audience typically overlooks is that these super-rich families represent a minute share of the population in a poor country—no larger perhaps than 0.01 percent of the total population. When we travel down the income distribution scale to include the full top 10 percent of a typical poor country, we reach income levels that are a fraction of what most poor people in rich countries make. Disparities in income (as well as health and other indicators of well-being) are much larger across countries than they are within them. The country in which you are born largely determines your life possibilities. . . .

Hence recent evidence on the global distribution of income allows us to reach the following three conclusions. First, the middle of the global income distribution has filled out in recent decades, largely thanks to China's rise. Second, differences across average incomes of countries remain the dominant force behind global inequality. Third, aggregate economic growth in the poorest countries is the most powerful vehicle for reducing global inequality. The more rapid growth of poor countries since the 1990s is the key to the recent decline in global inequality.

GROWTH OVER THE LONG TERM: INDUSTRIALIZATION AND THE GREAT DIVERGENCE

At the dawn of the Industrial Revolution, the gap between the richest and poorest parts of the world economy stood at a ratio of roughly 2:1. Hence the between-country component of global inequality was tiny. Today the income gap between the richest and poorest economies of the world has risen to more than 80:1. What happened in between is that parts of the world economy— Western Europe, the United States, Japan, and a few others—took off while the rest grew very slowly, when at all, and often lost ground after temporary spurts. . . .

There is no better prism through which to view this divergence than the experience with industrialization in different parts of the world. Table 2 provides some interesting data from Paul Bairoch's seminal work (Bairoch 1982). In Table 2 the level of industrial output per capita in Britain in 1900 is fixed at 100, so we can easily make comparisons across regions and over time. At the onset of the Industrial Revolution in 1760, this number stood at 10 in Britain and at 8 for today's developed countries. There was virtually no difference between them and what later came to be called developing countries. In fact, China's level of industrialization was comparable to that of Western Europe.

Beginning in the nineteenth century, the numbers began to diverge in a striking fashion. Britain's industrial output per capita went from 10 in 1750 to 64 in 1860 and to 115 on the eve of World War I. Developed countries as a whole followed a similar, if less steep, trajectory. But what is really striking is not just that the gap between them and the countries in Latin America and Asia (save for Japan) opened wide. It is also that today's developing countries typically experienced deindustrialization. China's industry shrank from 8 in 1750 to 3 in 1913. India's went from 7 to 2 over the same period. Industrial output failed to keep up with population growth.

The culprit was the global division of labor that the first era of globalization fostered during the nineteenth century. Cheap manufactures from Europe and later the United States, particularly cotton textiles, flooded the markets of peripheral regions. The latter in turn specialized in commodities and natural resources. In the Ottoman empire, for example, textile imports shot up to capture nearly 75 percent of the home market by the 1870s, up from a mere

TABLE 2 Industrialization before World War I (per capita levels of industrialization, UK = 100 in 1900)

	1750	1800	1830	1860	1880	1900	1913
Developed countries	8	8	11	16	24	35	55
United Kingdom	10	16	25	64	87	100	115
United States	4	9	14	21	38	69	126
Germany	8	8	9	15	25	52	85
Japan	7	7	7	7	9	12	20
Developing countries	7	6	6	4	3	2	2
China	8	6	6	4	4	3	3
India	7	6	6	3	2	1	2
Brazil	n.a.	n.a.	n.a.	4	4	5	7
Mexico	n.a.	n.a.	n.a.	5	4	5	7

SOURCE: Bairoch (1982).

3 percent in the 1820s. This global division of labor was imposed not just by markets but also by the forces of informal and formal empire: European powers, and later the United States, prevailed on India, China, Japan, and the Ottoman empire to open their markets, while their navies ensured security for merchants and financiers.

The parts of the world that proved receptive to the forces of the Industrial Revolution shared two advantages. They had a large enough stock of relatively educated and skilled workers who could fill up and run the new factories. They also had sufficiently good institutions—well-functioning legal systems, stable politics, and restraints on expropriations by the state—to generate incentives for private investment and market expansion. With these preconditions, much of continental Europe was ready to absorb the new production techniques developed and applied in Britain.

Elsewhere, industrialization depended on "importing" skills and institutions. Intercontinental labor mobility was a tremendous advantage here. Where Europeans settled in large numbers, they brought with them both the skills and the drive for more representative, market-friendly institutions that would promote economic activity alongside their interests. The consequences were disastrous for the native populations, who perished in large numbers courtesy of European aggression and germs. But the regions of the world . . . called "Western offshoots"—the United States, Canada, Australia, and New Zealand—were able to acquire the necessary prerequisites thanks to large immigration. Supported also by sizable capital flows from Europe, these economies would eventually become part of the industrial "core."

Colonization's impact on other parts of the world was quite different. When Europeans encountered inhospitable conditions that precluded their settlement in large numbers, or began to exploit natural resources that required armies of manual workers, they set up institutions that were quite different from those in the Western offshoots. These purely "extractive" institutions were designed to get the raw materials to the core as cheaply as possible. They entailed vast inequalities in wealth and power with a narrow elite, typically white and European, ruling over a vast number of natives or slaves. Colonies built on the extractive model did little to protect general property rights, support market development, or stimulate other kinds of economic activity. The plantation-based economies in the Caribbean and the mineral economies of Africa were typical examples. Studies by economists and economic historians have established that this early experience with institutional development—or lack thereof—produced a debilitating effect on economies in Africa and Latin America that is still felt today.

Once the lines were clearly drawn between industrializing and commodity-producing countries, there were strong economic dynamics that reinforced the demarcation. Commodity-based economies faced little incentive or opportunity to diversify. As transport costs fell during the nineteenth century and growth in the industrial core fed demand, these economies experienced commodity booms. This was very good for the small number of people who reaped the windfall from the mines and plantations that produced these commodities, but not very good for manufacturing industries that were squeezed as a result. International trade worked just as in textbook models: profits rose in economic activities in which countries had comparative advantage but fell elsewhere.

International trade induced industrial countries to keep investing in skills, technology, and other drivers of economic growth. It also encouraged families to have fewer, better educated children, in light of the high returns to skills that modern manufacturing industries brought. These effects were reversed in the developing countries of the periphery. Specialization in primary commodities did not encourage skill accumulation and delayed the reduction in fertility and population growth. Birthrates remained high in the developing world well into the twentieth century, unlike in the industrialized countries, which experienced sharp declines in fertility toward the end of the nineteenth century. . . . Commodity-exporting countries gave up productivity in exchange for population.

The long-term consequences of this division of labor are what developing countries are still trying to break free of. That escape is possible was shown by the experience of the first non-Western country to industrialize before 1914: Japan.

In the middle of the nineteenth century, Japan looked no different than other economies of the periphery. It exported primarily raw materials—raw silk, yarn, tea, fish—in exchange for manufactures. This commerce had boomed in the aftermath of the opening to free trade imposed by Commodore Matthew Perry in 1854. Left to its own devices, the economy would have likely followed the same path as so many others in the periphery. But Japan had an indigenous group of well-educated and patriotic businessmen and merchants and, even more important, a government, following the Meiji Restoration of 1868, that was single-mindedly focused on economic (and political) modernization. The government was little moved by the laissez-faire ideas prevailing among Western policy elites at the time. Japanese officials made clear that the state had a significant role to play in developing the economy.

The reforms introduced by the Meiji bureaucrats were aimed at creating the infrastructure of a modern national economy: a unified currency, railroads, public education, banking laws, and other legislation. Considerable effort also went into what today would be called industrial policy—state initiatives targeted at promoting new industries. The Japanese government built and ran state-owned plants in a wide range of industries, including cotton textiles and shipbuilding. Even though many of these enterprises ended as failures, they produced important demonstration effects and trained many skilled artisans and managers who would subsequently ply their trade in private establishments. State enterprises were eventually privatized, enabling the private sector to build on the foundations established by the state. The government also paid to employ foreign technicians and technology in manufacturing industries and financed training abroad for Japanese students. In addition, as Japan regained tariff autonomy from international treaties, the government raised import tariffs on many industrial products to encourage domestic production. These efforts paid off most remarkably in cotton textiles, which by 1914 Japan had established as a world-class industry that was able to displace British exports not just from the Japanese markets but from neighboring Asian markets as well.

Japan's militarist and expansionist policies in the run-up to World War II tarred these accomplishments, but its achievements on the economic front demonstrated that an alternative path was available. It was possible to steer an economy away from its natural specialization in raw materials. Economic growth was achievable, even if a country started at the wrong end of the international division of labor, if you combined the efforts of a determined government with the energies of a vibrant private sector.

The Japanese experience would become a model for other countries in East and Southeast Asia. While specific policies differed, these emulators would rely on the same model of export-oriented industrialization, achieved through a combination of private-sector entrepreneurship with government inducements and cajoling. (The sole exception, where government intervention in industry remained minimal, was Hong Kong.) More on these growth strategies below.

SIX STYLIZED FACTS OF ECONOMIC GROWTH

The success of Japan and other Asian growth miracles has produced a seemingly unending debate. Are these countries examples of successful state-directed industrialization, or are they examples of what reliance on markets and globalization can produce? Framed this way, the question generates more heat than light. What works in practice is a judicious combination of markets and government encouragement, rather than a choice of one at the expense of the other.

But why is such a combination needed, what exactly does "judicious" mean, and how do we operationalize it? To answer these questions, it is helpful to start with some basic stylized facts associated with economic growth. In this section, I document six stylized facts that are particularly relevant to the policy context.

Stylized Fact 1: Growth Has Increased Over Time

When the Industrial Revolution took hold of Britain and other early industrializers, the pickup in the growth rate of economic activity and overall productivity was so gradual as to be virtually imperceptible. To this day, we are unable to establish the timing of the Industrial Revolution or the onset of modern economic growth with any precision. A clear break in the time series simply does not exist. Economic historians estimate that total factor productivity expanded at an annual rate of 0.5 percent in the century after 1780. This is clearly better than the near-zero rate of technological progress in earlier centuries, but it is a fraction of what industrial economies would experience later in the second half of the twentieth century.

. . . Before World War II, the most successful period was 1870–1913, the Gold Standard period, during which the world economy expanded at an annual average rate of more than 1 percent per capita. This rate is dwarfed by the post-1950 expansion, which registered global growth at nearly 3 percent per annum until the mid-1970s. Even though growth slowed down somewhat after the oil shock of the 1970s, it was still far superior to anything experienced before World War II.

What stands out particularly sharply . . . is the stupendous and historically unprecedented growth rate experienced by the growth champions of the postwar period. These were Japan in 1950–1973, South Korea in 1973–1990, and China since 1990. These East Asian tigers, along with a few more of their neighbors, grew at 7–8 percent per annum in per capita terms, experiencing more rapid convergence with the living standards of the West than anything seen to date. These growth miracles were based on rapid industrialization and exports of manufactures. Clearly, the postwar global economy presented huge rewards to those lagging countries that got their policies right.

Stylized Fact 2: Convergence Has Been the Exception Rather Than the Rule

As economic historians and contemporary growth theorists have both argued, there are advantages to economic backwardness. Technologies that advanced countries have already developed can be imported and adapted; the wheel does not have to be reinvented. Global markets allow small economies to specialize in what they are good at, and they are a source of cheap intermediate inputs and of capital goods. Global financial markets can relax domestic saving constraints and finance investments that would otherwise not take place. Yet most developing countries have not been able to exploit such advantages. The experience of East Asian growth champions is very much the exception to the rule.

Contrary to theoretical expectations, there is no tendency for poor economies to grow more rapidly than richer economies. The experience of the past decade, reviewed above, is not at all representative of the historical record. Over any sufficiently long time horizon, the growth rate of economies is basically uncorrelated with their initial level of productivity or distance to the technological frontier. This means that a middle-income or rich economy is as likely to experience rapid growth as a poor economy.

In the literature on growth empirics, this result is known as the absence of "unconditional" convergence. It stands in contrast to "conditional" convergence, which is a well-established regularity in cross-country data. That is, when growth rates are conditioned on a small set of variables such as human capital, investment, institutional quality, exposure to trade, and macroeconomic stability, the growth residuals are systematically and negatively correlated with initial levels of gross domestic product per capita. Put differently, there is economic convergence, but only among the subset of countries that attain these conditioning variables.

The conditional convergence result would appear at first sight to be quite a useful one, potentially unlocking the secrets of economic growth. Unfortunately, the conditioning variables that are typically included in growth regressions are usually endogenous variables themselves, and they tell us little about what specific policies to pursue. For example, it may be helpful to know that greater levels of investment and human capital or better institutions are growth enhancing. But the result leaves unclear how these ends are to be achieved. Is human capital increased by building more schools, reducing teacher absenteeism, or providing better information to parents? Is private investment boosted by reducing red tape or providing tax incentives? Is governance enhanced by adopting legal and institutional blueprints from abroad or by engineering local solutions? From a policy standpoint, it is these questions that must be ultimately answered. . . .

Stylized Fact 3: Economic Development Goes Hand-in-Hand with Productive Diversification

Poor economies are not shrunk versions of rich economies; they are structurally different. This key insight of old-fashioned development economics is often forgotten when modern growth theory is applied to developing economies. Developing countries are characterized by large structural gaps in productivity between traditional and new economic activities. Hence the essence of development is structural change: it entails moving workers from traditional, low-productivity activities to modern, high-productivity activities that are quite different in terms of location, organization, and technological characteristics. Rapidly growing countries are those that are better at removing the bottlenecks that impede this transformation.

One can document this structural transformation in a number of different ways. Economies progressively become less specialized and more diversified as they get richer. Poor economies produce a relatively narrow range of commodities and services; as they grow, the range of economic activities expands. Note also that past a certain point, diversification ceases, and there are hints of greater specialization at high levels of income. But the turning point comes quite late in the development process, roughly at the income level of a country such as Ireland.

This does stand in some tension with approaches that emphasize the role of trade and comparative advantage in spurring economic development. After all, the central insight of classical trade theory is that countries gain from trade by specializing in product lines they are comparatively good at. Comparative advantage–based specialization may therefore seem to be a potent avenue for growth—and is often presented as such in policy discussions that emphasize the benefits of globalization. Whatever the benefits of trade, specialization is not the route to riches; quite the contrary.

Stylized Fact 4: Historically, Industrialization and Manufactured Exports Have Been the Most Reliable Levers for Rapid and Sustained Growth

I noted previously that the growth miracles of Japan, South Korea, and China were all based on rapid industrialization. The point generalizes to other successful cases of catch-up, too. With the exception of a few small countries that have benefited from natural resource windfalls (and have managed not to squander them), virtually all countries that have sustained high growth rates over decades have done so on the back of manufacturing. Industrialization is how Britain and other early emulators entered modern economic growth. It is also what has enabled successful latecomers to catch up.

I define "very high growth" as per-capita growth of 4.5 percent per annum or higher. Growth is said be "sustained" if such a rate has been maintained for at least three decades. Naturally there are not many such instances—less than thirty, in fact. But the composition of such "growth miracles" is telling.

First, virtually all growth miracles took place in more recent times, since 1950. There were only three instances before 1950: Australia and New Zealand, two Western offshoots that benefited from extensive resource-boom–led immigration waves during the nineteenth century, and Venezuela, which experienced an oil boom in the first half of the twentieth century. Since 1950, by contrast, there have been twenty-four distinct instances of growth miracles. This is consistent with the increase in growth rates over time noted previously as stylized fact 1.

Second, most of the post-1950 growth miracles were rapid industrializers. These came in two clusters. The first were a set of countries like Greece, Italy, Portugal, and Spain that were on the periphery of Western Europe and benefited first from European reconstruction in the immediate aftermath of World War II and subsequently from the European integration process. For the most part, these growth episodes ran their course by the late 1970s. The only exception is Ireland, which was a late bloomer and experienced its boom after the 1970s.

The second cluster comprises the well-known East and Southeast Asian tigers, countries such as Japan, South Korea, Taiwan, Singapore, Hong Kong, Malaysia, and China. Unlike the first cluster, these did not share (at least initially) a geographic advantage. But the example of prewar Japanese industrialization, as well as its resumption during the 1950s, provided an important demonstration effect in the region. South Korea's strategy was directly influenced by those of Japan and China (by the precedents of Hong Kong and Taiwan). Southeast Asian countries such as Malaysia and Indonesia explicitly targeted industrialization after observing the successes of the so-called gang of four (South Korea, Taiwan, Hong Kong, and Singapore). Almost all of these economies built highly competitive manufacturing industries and experienced very rapid penetration of export markets in manufactures.

The third set of post-1950 growth miracles comprises countries such as Saudi Arabia, Iraq, and Botswana, which benefited from sustained booms in natural resources (e.g., oil and diamonds). These are reminiscent of the few pre-1950 cases.

Stylized Fact 5: Manufacturing Industries Are "Special" in That They Tend to Exhibit Unconditional Convergence

I noted previously in stylized fact 2 that there is no tendency for developing economies to converge toward the productivity levels that prevail in rich economies. The modern, industrial parts of those economies seem to be quite different, however. When one looks at formal manufacturing industries, one uncovers a surprisingly strong convergence relationship. Industries that start farther away from the frontier in terms of labor productivity have experienced significantly faster productivity growth.

This is a remarkable finding. It does not denigrate the role of good policies or favorable external circumstances. The rate of convergence considering such factors is even more rapid, meaning that countries with better institutions and policies will experience faster rates of productivity growth in manufacturing. In particular, countries with better trade links and at higher levels of financial development likely provide a better context for manufacturing convergence. But it does suggest that formal manufacturing industries are natural "escalator" industries that tend to propel an economy forward, even in the presence of bad governance, lousy policies, and a disadvantageous context. (The countries included in my data range from Ethiopia, Malawi, and Madagascar at the low end to Japan and the United States at the high end.) Productivity convergence seems to be considerably easier to achieve in this part of the economy than in others such as traditional agriculture or most services. Presumably, at least some of the cause relates to the tradable nature of manufacturing industries and the relative ease of technology transfer across borders. At the same time, manufacturing convergence does not seem to have picked up speed in more recent decades under greater globalization and wider use of outsourcing. The data indicate that rates of convergence in the late 1960s and 1970s are statistically indistinguishable from those we have seen more recently since the 1990s.

This finding raises a puzzle. If manufacturing exhibits unconditional convergence, why is this not enough to generate aggregate convergence? The formal manufacturing sector tends to be quite small in low-income countries, employing less than 5 percent of the labor force in the poorest among them. Still, one would expect convergence to aggregate up to the national level, as labor and other resources move from technologically stagnant parts of the economy to the escalator industries.

The difficulty is that the requisite structural transformation is not automatic. It is a process that is fraught with both government failures and market failures. The expansion of formal manufacturing is blocked in practice by both government policies (such as entry barriers or high taxes on formal enterprises) and market imperfections (such as coordination problems and learning externalities), both of which push the return to investment in modern industries below the social return. The relative weights of these factors depend on the country and the context.

So even though manufacturing productivity tends to converge almost everywhere, what distinguishes successful countries from others is their ability to expand manufacturing employment and output rapidly. Successful developing economies undergo both manufacturing convergence and rapid industrialization. Underperforming economies make do with the former.

Stylized Fact 6: The Most Successful Economies Have Not Been the Ones with the Least State Intervention

Consider the economic policies of four key developing countries: China, India, Brazil, and Mexico. Among these, the Asian ones have performed significantly better than the Latin American ones over the last couple of decades. As the Heritage Index ratings make clear, the Asian ones are also characterized by significantly greater degrees of government intervention—whether in international trade, international finance, or domestic markets. The point generalizes to other countries, too. It is difficult to find a strong correlation, in either direction, between standard measures of government activism (such as tax rates or indices of market restrictions) and rates of economic growth. It is easy to conclude that extreme controls of the central planning type that suffocate the private sector are bad for growth. But for virtually the entire universe of countries that lie in between central planning and laissez-faire, less intervention is not necessarily good for performance.

I now provide an interpretation that is informed by these stylized facts and try to make sense of success and failure around the world against this empirical background.

THE STRATEGY OF REFORM

Let us go back to the obstacles that confront structural transformation. As mentioned above, these take the form of both government and market failures. The relevant government failures are well known: excessive regulation and red tape, high taxes, corruption, restrictive labor laws, financial repression, insecure property rights, poor contract enforcement, and macroeconomic instability. All these stifle entrepreneurship, especially in modern economic activities that tend to rely heavily on the institutional environment. Efforts to fix these problems lie at the core of the "orthodox" development agenda, as in the Washington Consensus and its successors.

A reform agenda that focuses on eliminating these government failures would seem to be the most obvious and direct way of unleashing desirable structural change. In practice, however, it suffers from three problems.

First, it contains a blind spot with respect to market failures. New industries can fail to get off the ground not just because they face high taxes or excessive red tape, but also because markets work too poorly in low-income environments to reward entrepreneurs with the full social value of their investments. The two most important constraints typically are coordination failures and demonstration effects. Coordination failures occur when scale economies preclude complementary investments that would otherwise be profitable. Building, say, a successful processed food business requires significant investments both upstream (to ensure a steady high-quality supply of raw materials that satisfy health and sanitary standards) and downstream (to ensure an efficient, timely transport and logistics network that links the operation to foreign markets). Any part of the chain will lack profitability in the absence of the other parts. Demonstration effects in turn refer to unremunerated learning spillovers. For example, any potential investor in an entirely new line of economic activity has to consider the risks of failure. If he goes bankrupt, he bears the full cost. But if he succeeds, he sets a model for other entrepreneurs to follow. In other words, much of the gain from new industries is public, while the losses remain private. This acts like a tax on new industries. Standard welfare economics justifies the use of subsidies and other government interventions in such instances.

Second, the standard approach presumes too much from reformist governments. As Washington Consensus enthusiasts discovered following the disappointing results in Latin America over the 1990s, the list of government failures that need to be fixed is neither short nor well defined. It turned out not to be enough to reduce subsidies, formal trade barriers, and state ownership. Many economists and policymakers rationalized the failures by calling for a second and eventually third generation of reforms in institutions—everything from more "flexible" labor markets to less corruption, from better courts to better governance. Apparently, standard policy reforms did not produce lasting effects if the background institutional conditions were poor. Sound policies needed to be embedded in solid institutions.

So the orthodox reform agenda became increasingly open-ended. At times it seemed as if the to-do list was designed to ensure that the policy advisers would never be proved wrong: if performance lagged despite extensive reforms, the government could always be faulted for having fallen short and not having to undertake even more reforms. . . .

That many analysts were led down this path is the result of the inherently complementary nature of most of the orthodox reforms. In order to succeed in one, you need to have undertaken many of the others at the same time. For example, trade liberalization would not work if fiscal institutions were not in place to make up for lost trade revenue, capital markets did not allocate finance to expanding sectors, customs officials were not competent and honest enough, labor-market institutions did not work properly to reduce transitional unemployment, and so on.

To see this in its starkest form, consider what a conventional reform agenda would have looked like in China in 1978—an economy that was highly distorted as a result of central planning. An analyst would have easily figured that the right place to start reform was in the countryside, where the vast majority of the people lived. The analyst, if thoughtful enough, would also realize that each reform, when applied in the conventional form, would require the support of others to become effective. Low agricultural productivity required price reform, which in turn required property reform to become effective. Price reform in agriculture would necessitate tax reform, since controlled prices were an important source of government revenue. It would also require higher wages in urban areas, as food prices rose. State enterprises would have to be allowed some autonomy to respond to price and wage changes. But since state enterprises were monopolies, any price autonomy would have to be matched by competition-enhancing policies such as trade liberalization. A rise in imports, in turn, would force enterprise restructuring, necessitating better finance and social safety nets for displaced workers.

Which brings us to the third, and most subtle, point. The standard approach overlooks the contribution of unorthodox shortcuts. In reality, few if any countries have grown fast because of across-the-board institutional reforms of the type just discussed. Successful economic transitions are marked by the sequential relaxation of one "binding constraint" after another, using policy tools that are tailored to local circumstances.

This means not only that high growth is feasible in institutional environments that look quite distorted, but also that policy remedies can look quite unorthodox by the standards of the conventional rule book. China provides the most telling illustration of both of these principles, but East Asian countries have all followed similar approaches. Two-track reform, the household responsibility system, and township and village enterprises were some of the innovations that the Chinese used to short-circuit institutional complementarities noted above.

Return now to the challenge of stimulating new industries. The list of potential culprits is likely to be quite long, running the full gamut of government and market failures. The advantage of operating significantly below potential, however, is that one does not need to get everything right in order to have a big impact. A remedy that is sufficiently well targeted can produce a large investment response. However, a scattershot approach that tries to fix as many problems as possible may not be effective if it ends up missing the real targets. If high cost of credit is the greatest obstacle to investment, for example, reducing the regulatory burden in product markets is unlikely to help much. Conversely, if investment is held back mainly by poor contract enforcement, reducing the cost of credit will be like pushing on a string.

Next consider how a particular constraint should be relaxed. Suppose entrepreneurship is hampered by low private returns, which may be the result in turn of a high-risk or poor institutional environment. The most direct remedy would be to target the relevant distortions and remove them at the source. But this may be impractical for both economic and political reasons. Economically, we may not be able to identify the relevant distortions sufficiently closely. Politically, we may not want to step on some powerful toes. An alternative strategy that is often more feasible is to raise entrepreneurs' profits in other ways, through subsidies or other instruments, so as to compensate them for the costs they incur on account of the irremovable distortions.

Most successful outward-oriented industrialization efforts have in fact been the product of such second-best strategies. South Korea and Taiwan directly subsidized exports. Singapore subsidized foreign investors. China created special economic zones and subsidized its exporters both directly and indirectly through an undervalued exchange rate. Mauritius relied on an export-processing zone. In none of these cases did import liberalization and across-the-board institutional reform play a significant causal role in setting off the transition to high growth.

When successful, such heterodox second-best strategies have the virtue that they can cut a path around important economic or political-economy obstacles. For example, China's special economic zones created new enterprises and export opportunities at the margin, without pulling the rug from underneath the highly protected and less efficient state enterprises. The conventional remedy of across-the-board import liberalization would have exposed these enterprises to a quite severe shock, resulting in employment losses and social and political problems in urban areas. Similarly, two-track price reform in agriculture insulated government revenues from the adverse effects of incentive reform by providing price incentives at the margin.

The bottom line is that successful growth-promoting reforms are pragmatic and opportunistic. Industrialization in particular is often stimulated by unconventional policies that compensate entrepreneurs and investors for the high taxes imposed on them by the poor market and institutional environment. In these second-best environments, more intervention can sometimes be better than less. The most effective way to counter market or government failures can be to compensate for such failures indirectly, rather than attempting to eliminate them.

PROGNOSIS

The framework outlined above shows how fundamental improvements in capabilities, defined as both skills and institutional development, and narrower policies targeted at rapid structural change, industrialization in particular, interact to produce sustainable, longer-term growth. In the long run, convergence with wealthy economies requires the accumulation of human capital and the acquisition of high-quality institutions. But the quickest route for getting there is to deploy policies that help build modern industries that employ an increasing share of the economy's labor resources. The policies of the latter type overlap with those needed to build up fundamental capabilities; but they are not one and the same, and often they may diverge significantly. An excessive focus on "fundamentals" may be adverse to growth if it distracts policymakers from resorting to the (often unconventional) policies of structural transformation required to get modern industries off the ground. Similarly, an excessive focus on industrialization may set the economy up for an eventual downfall if the requisite skills and institutions are not built up over time.

In principle, this broad recipe can continue to serve developing countries well in the future. In particular, it can allow the world's poorest nations in Africa to embark on Asian-style structural transformation and rapid growth. But a number of considerations suggest that developing countries will face stronger headwinds in the decades ahead.

First, the global economy is likely to be significantly less buoyant than in recent decades. The world's richest economies—the United States, Europe, and Japan—are hobbled by high levels of public debt, which typically results in low growth and defensive economic policies. The eurozone, in particular, faces an existential crisis, and even if it manages to stay together, its problems will continue to dampen the region's animal spirits. Policymakers in these rich countries will remain preoccupied with domestic challenges and will be unlikely to exhibit much global leadership.

The rules of the game for developing countries have already become stricter. The World Trade Organization (WTO) prohibits a range of industrial policies (subsidies, local-content requirements, copying of patented products) that Asian countries have deployed to good effect in decades past to foster structural transformation. For example, both China and India used local content requirements to force foreign investors to develop efficient domestic first-tier suppliers—a strategy that would be illegal today. Fortunately, these WTO restrictions do not apply to the poorest developing countries (which are still allowed a free ride).

We can expect further pressures to narrow policy space in developing countries as trade becomes more politicized in the advanced countries as a result of their economic difficulties. Subsidy schemes that have so far operated under the radar screen are more likely to be litigated in the WTO and retaliated against. With or without the acquiescence of the WTO, Europe and the United States will exhibit greater willingness to shield their industries from import surges. Developing countries that undervalue their currencies through intervention in foreign-currency markets or controls on capital inflows are likely to be branded "currency manipulators." Strategies aimed at maintaining competitive currencies—again, an East Asian hallmark—have so far evaded global discipline. But for some years there have been efforts to render International Monetary Fund oversight over currency values more effective, and there is growing discussion about treating currency undervaluation as an export subsidy in the WTO sense. Even if these multilateral efforts do not bear fruit, domestic politics will push the U.S. government toward unilateral action against governments (such as China) that are perceived to be taking unfair advantage of global trade.

We need to draw a distinction here between the smaller developing countries and the larger ones (such as China, Brazil, and India). The former are likely to enjoy significantly greater policy space than the latter. It is hard to imagine policymakers in Washington, DC, or Brussels getting worked up over the industrial policies of Ethiopia or El Salvador. This means that the vast majority of the world's developing countries—and almost all of those in sub-Saharan Africa—will remain relatively free of external encumbrances that restrict the scope of structural transformation policies. That is the good news. The bad news is that large and "systemically important economies" such as India and China continue to house a substantial portion of the world's poor. In 2008, the latest year for which we have estimates, 62 percent of the poor earning less than $2/day lived in China and South Asia, and only 23 percent in sub-Saharan Africa (Chen and Ravallion 2012). The continued growth of these populous countries remains a crucially important factor in global poverty reduction.

A second important source of headwinds relates to changes that are happening within manufacturing industries. As I mentioned previously, technological changes are rendering manufacturing more capital- and skill-intensive. This reduces the employment-elasticity of industrialization and lowers the capacity of manufacturing to absorb large amounts of unskilled labor from the countryside and informal workers. Global supply chains may facilitate entry into manufacturing for low-cost countries that are able to attract foreign investment. But they also reduce linkages with the rest of the economy and the potential for the development of local upstream suppliers. The ease with which global companies sitting at the apex of the production chains can switch suppliers gives these industries a fleeting character: here today, gone tomorrow.

In all these ways, many manufacturing industries are, in effect, becoming more like natural resource enclaves: skill- and capital-intensive, disengaged from the domestic economy, and transitory. A potentially compensating trend is that some service industries may be acquiring manufacturing-like properties. Certain service sectors such as food and clothing retail services are becoming adept at absorbing technologies from abroad (e.g., hypermarkets), employ relatively unskilled workers, and have significant linkages with the domestic economy. If such service activities are also subject to absolute productivity convergence, as it seems plausible, they, too, could act as the escalator industries of the future.

Other factors will disfavor manufacturing industries. New entrants into standardized manufacturing activities face much greater global competition today than South Korea and Taiwan faced in the 1960s and 1970s or China faced in the 1990s. Even though its production costs have been rising, China itself poses a formidable competitive challenge to any producer attempting to make inroads on global markets. Almost all Asian manufacturing superstars started with protected home markets. This gave them a home base on which to build experience and ensured domestic profits to subsidize forays on world markets. Most African manufacturers today face an onslaught of cheap imports from China and other Asian exporters, which makes it difficult for them to survive on their home turf, let alone cross-subsidize their international activities. The burdens placed on government policy to incubate and develop domestic manufacturing firms are correspondingly heavier.

Finally, environmental concerns will play a much larger role than they did in the past and will make it more costly to develop traditional "dirty industries" such as steel, paper, and chemicals. Comparative advantage and economic logic dictate that such industries migrate to poorer nations. But producers everywhere will be under pressure to utilize greener technologies that generate less pollution and greenhouse gas emissions. To the extent that environmental concerns raise the technological requirements of running these industries, they will diminish the comparative advantage of developing nations. The capital and skill requirements of green technologies are also higher. There will be the usual exhortations to the effect that these new technologies should be subsidized and made available to poor countries. But whether this will happen in practice is an open question.

POLICY IMPLICATIONS

These considerations suggest that we are entering a phase of the world economy in which East Asian–style growth rates will be difficult to sustain for the East Asian countries themselves and hard to attain for the next generation of emulators. The future of growth is quite unlikely to look like its recent past. It may well be that we will look at the six decades after the end of World War II as a very special period, an experience not replicated either before or since. The rate of convergence between poor and rich countries is likely to come down considerably from the levels we have seen during the past two decades. Developing countries will probably still grow faster than the advanced economies, but this will be due in large part to the decline of growth in the latter.

Ultimately, growth depends primarily on what happens at home. Even if the world economy provides more headwinds than tailwinds, desirable policies will continue to share features that have served successful countries well in the past. These include: a stable macroeconomic framework; incentives for economic restructuring and diversification (both market led and government provided); social policies to address inequality and exclusion; continued investments in human capital and skills; and a strengthening of regulatory, legal, and political institutions over time. Countries that do their homework along these dimensions will do better than those that do not.

Beyond these generalities, however, the main policy implication is that we will require future growth strategies that differ in their emphasis, even if not their main outlines. In particular, reliance on domestic (or in certain cases, regional) markets and resources will need to substitute at the margin for reliance on foreign markets, foreign finance, and foreign investment. The upgrading of the home market will in turn necessitate greater emphasis on income distribution and the health of the middle class as part and parcel of a growth strategy. In other words, social policy and growth strategy will become complements to a much greater extent.

Globally, it will not make sense to pursue the extensive harmonization and coordination of policies in finance and trade that ultimately are neither sustainable nor, in view of the heterogeneity of needs and preferences around the world, desirable. International institutions will do better to accommodate the inevitable reduction of the pace of globalization (or, perhaps, some deglobalization) than to shoehorn countries into ill-fitting rules. Industrialized countries will need to carve out some policy space to rework their social bargains, just as developing countries need policy space to restructure their economies. We need a new settlement between advanced countries and large emerging markets in which the latter no longer see themselves as free riders on the policies of the former.

. . . The global economy suffers from a shortfall between the demand and supply of adequate global governance. It is possible that some of this shortfall can be addressed by reforms and new forms of representations; by individual citizens and nations acting in ways that are more conscious of the global consequences of their decisions; by the transnational expansion of networks of activists and regulators; and by reforming the governance of multilateral economic institutions themselves. But as I have emphasized here, at best these changes will take place in an environment with strong centrifugal forces, characterized by increasing number of actors and greater diversity of interests. If these forces are managed well, they need not endanger economic globalization per se. But if we fail to take them into account, we are more likely to undermine support for an open global economy than to strengthen it.

Ultimately, a healthy world economy needs to rest on healthy national economies and societies. Global rules that restrict domestic policy space too much are counterproductive insofar as they narrow the scope for growth- and equity-producing policies. They thus undermine the support for and legitimacy of an open global economy. The challenge is to design an architecture that respects the domestic priorities of individual nations, while ensuring that major cross-border spillovers and global public goods are addressed.

REFERENCES

Bairoch, Paul. 1982. "International Industrialization Levels from 1750 to 1980." *Journal of European Economic History* 11: 269–310.

Chen, Shaohua, and Martin Ravallion. 2012. "An Update to the World Bank's Estimates of Consumption Poverty in the Developing World." World Bank, http://sitesources .worldbank.org/INTPOVCALNET/Resources/Global_Poverty_Update_2012_02-29 -12.pdf.

28

History Lessons: Institutions, Factor Endowments, and Paths of Development in the New World

KENNETH L. SOKOLOFF AND STANLEY L. ENGERMAN

In this reading, Kenneth L. Sokoloff and Stanley L. Engerman argue for the importance of domestic political institutions as determinants of economic growth. Their objective is to understand why some former colonies in the Americas have grown so much more than others, producing the wide disparity in economic development seen in the Western Hemisphere today. The authors begin by showing that English colonies in the Caribbean (such as Barbados) and many Spanish colonies (such as Mexico and Peru) were initially just as well-off as, or even richer than, northern colonies like the present-day United States or Canada. To explain the subsequent differences in development, Sokoloff and Engerman develop an argument that runs from initial factor endowments (in soil and climatic conditions, as well as land, labor, and capital) to the development of domestic institutions to long-term growth rates. In areas like the Caribbean and Brazil, soils and climate were suited to valuable plantation crops, such as sugar, which stimulated the importation of slaves. This created a large, poor, and disenfranchised segment of the population. In other places, like Peru, large indigenous populations and ample silver ore deposits combined with inequitable land tenure systems to produce a similar outcome: highly unequal societies. Sugar and silver made these colonies wealthy in their early histories, but economic and political inequality impeded the development of domestic institutions necessary for modern economic growth. By contrast, colonies in the northeastern United States and eastern Canada had soils suited for wheat and other grains that required smallholder production. The authors contend that this led to settlement by European immigrants working relatively small farms. These colonies developed more egalitarian societies and political institutions, which provided better protection of property rights and thereby generated more investment and growth.

INTRODUCTION

As Europeans established colonies in the New World of North and South America during the sixteenth, seventeenth, and eighteenth centuries, most knowledgeable observers regarded the North American mainland to be of relatively marginal economic interest, when compared with the extraordinary opportunities available in the Caribbean and Latin America. Voltaire, for example, considered the conflict in North America between the French and the British during the Seven Years' War (1756–63) to be madness and characterized the two countries as "fighting over a few acres of snow." The victorious British were later to engage in a lively public debate over which territory should be taken from the French as reparations—the Caribbean island of Guadeloupe (with a land area of 563 square miles) or Canada. Several centuries later, however, we know that the U.S. and Canadian economies ultimately proved far more successful than the other economies of the hemisphere. The puzzle, therefore, is how and why the areas that were favored by the forecasters of that era, and the destinations of the vast majority of migrants to the Americas through 1800, fell behind economically. . . .

These differentials in paths of development have long been of central concern to scholars of Latin America and have recently attracted more attention from economic historians and economists more generally (North, 1988; Coatsworth, 1998; Acemoglu, Johnson and Robinson, 2000). Although conventional economic factors have certainly not been ignored, the explanations offered for the contrasting records in growth have most often focused on institutions and highlighted the variation across societies in conditions relevant to growth such as the security of property rights, prevalence of corruption, structures of the financial sector, investment in public infrastructure and social capital, and the inclination to work hard or be entrepreneurial. But ascribing differences in development to differences in institutions raises the challenge of explaining where the differences in institutions come from. Those who have addressed this formidable problem have typically emphasized the importance of presumed exogenous differences in religion or national heritage. Douglass North (1988), for example, is one of many who have attributed the relative success of the United States and Canada to British institutions being more conducive to growth than those of Spain and other European colonizers. Others, like John Coatsworth (1998), are skeptical of such generalizations, and suggest that they may obscure the insight that can be gained by examining the extreme diversity of experiences observed across the Americas, even across societies with the same national heritage.

Indeed, . . . the relationship between national heritage and economic performance is weaker than popularly thought. During the colonial period, the economies with the highest per capita incomes were those in the Caribbean, and it made little difference whether they were of Spanish, British, or French origin. The case for the superiority of British institutions is usually based on the records of the United States and Canada, but the majority of the New World societies established by the British—including Barbados, Jamaica, Belize, Guyana, and the lesser-known Puritan colony on Providence Island—were like their other neighbors in not beginning to industrialize until much later. Having been part of the British Empire was far from a guarantee of economic growth. Likewise, there was considerable diversity across the economies of Spanish America. This is most evident in the contrasts between the experiences of the nations of the southern cone and those with large populations of

Native American descent, such as Mexico or Peru. It is the former class of countries, including Argentina, that of all the other economies of the New World most closely resemble the United States and Canada in experience over time.

With the evidence of wide disparities even among economies of the same European heritage, scholars have begun to reexamine alternative sources of differences. Though not denying the significance of national heritage, nor of idiosyncratic conditions that are unique to individual countries, they have begun to explore the possibility that initial conditions, or factor endowments broadly conceived, could have had profound and enduring impacts on long-run paths of institutional and economic development in the New World. Economists traditionally emphasize the pervasive influence of factor endowment, so the qualitative thrust of this approach may not be entirely novel. What is new, however, is the specific focus on how the extremely different environments in which the Europeans established their colonies may have led to societies with very different degrees of inequality, and on how these differences might have persisted over time and affected the course of development through their impact on the institutions that evolved. In particular, while essentially all the economies established in the New World began with an abundance of land and natural resources relative to labor, and thus high living standards on average, other aspects of their factor endowments varied in ways that meant that the great majority were characterized virtually from the outset by extreme inequality in wealth, human capital, and political power. From this perspective, the colonies that came to compose the United States and Canada stand out as somewhat deviant cases.

FROM FACTOR ENDOWMENTS TO INEQUALITY

The "discovery" and exploration of the Americas by Europeans was part of a grand, long-term effort to exploit the economic opportunities in underpopulated or underdefended territories around the world. European nations competed for claims and set about extracting material and other advantages through the pursuit of transitory enterprises like expeditions as well as by the establishment of more permanent settlements. At both the levels of national governments and private agents, adaptation or innovation of institutional forms was stimulated by formidable problems of organization raised by the radically novel environments, as well as by the difficulties of effecting the massive and historically unprecedented intercontinental flows of labor and capital. Common to all of the colonies was a high marginal product of labor, as evidenced by the historically unprecedented numbers of migrants who traversed the Atlantic from Europe and Africa despite high costs of transportation.

Well over 60 percent of the more than 6 million individuals who migrated to the New World from 1500 through the end of the eighteenth century were Africans brought over involuntarily as slaves. With their prices set in competitive international markets, slaves ultimately flowed to those locations where they were most productive. There were no serious national or cultural barriers to owning or using them; slaves were welcomed in the colonies of all the major European powers. The fraction of migrants who were slaves grew continuously, from roughly 20 percent prior to 1580 to nearly 75 percent between 1700 and 1760. The prominence of slaves, as well as the increase over time in the proportion of migrants going to the colonies of Portugal, France, and the Netherlands, and the continued quantitative dominance in the destinations of migrants to British America of colonies in the West Indies and on the southern mainland, reflects the increasing specialization by the New World over the colonial period in the production of sugar, coffee, and other staple crops for world markets. These colonies attracted heavy inflows of labor (especially slaves) because their soils and climates made them extraordinarily well-suited for growing these lucrative commodities, and because of the substantial economies of scale in producing such crops on large slave plantations (Fogel, 1989). Indeed, there are few examples of significant colonies which were not so specialized: only the Spanish settlements on the mainlands of North and South America (some of which had concentrations of labor in silver or other mines) and the New England, Middle Atlantic, and Canadian settlements of Britain and France. It was not coincidental that these were also the colonies that relied least on slaves for their labor force.

The economies that specialized in the production of sugar and other highly valued crops associated with extensive use of slaves had the highest per capita (including slaves) incomes in the New World. Most, including Barbados, Cuba, and Jamaica, were in the West Indies, but some (mainly Brazil) were in South America. They specialized in these crops early in their histories, and through the persistent working of technological advantage and international markets in slaves, their economies came to be dominated by large slave plantations and their populations by slaves of African descent. The greater efficiency of the very large plantations, and the overwhelming fraction of the populations that came to be black and slave, made the distributions of wealth and human capital extremely unequal. Even among the free population, there was greater inequality in such economies than in those on the North American mainland.

Although the basis for the predominance of an elite class in such colonies may have been the enormous advantages in sugar production available to those able to assemble a large company of slaves, as well as the extreme disparities in human capital between blacks and whites (both before and after emancipation), the long-run success and stability of the members of this elite were also facilitated by their disproportionate political influence. Together with the legally codified inequality intrinsic to slavery, the greater inequality in wealth contributed to the evolution of institutions that protected the privileges of the elites and restricted opportunities for the broad mass of the population to participate fully in the commercial economy even after the abolition of slavery.

The importance of factor endowments is also evident in a second category of New World colonies that can be thought of as Spanish America, although it also included some islands in the Caribbean. Spain focused its attention on, and designed their New World policies around conditions in, colonies such as Mexico and Peru, whose factor endowments were characterized by rich mineral resources and by substantial numbers of natives surviving contact with the European colonizers. Building on preconquest social organizations, whereby Indian elites extracted tribute from the general population, the Spanish authorities adopted the approach of distributing enormous grants of land, often including claims to a stream of income from the native labor residing in the vicinity, and of mineral resources among a privileged few. The resulting large-scale estates and mines, established early in the histories of these colonies, endured even where the principal production activities were lacking in economies of scale. Although small-scale production was typical of grain agriculture during this era, their essentially non-tradeable property rights to tribute from rather sedentary groups of natives (tied to locations by community property rights in land) gave large landholders the means and the motive to operate at a large scale.

Although the processes are not well understood, it is evident that large-scale agriculture remained dominant in Spanish America . . . and that the distribution of wealth remained highly unequal over time. Elite families generally acted as local representatives of the Spanish government in the countryside during the colonial period and maintained their status long after independence. The persistence and stability of elites, as well as of inequality generally, were also certainly aided by the restrictive immigration policies applied by Spain to her colonies, and by laws throughout Spanish America requiring that a citizen (a status entailing the right to vote and other privileges) own a substantial amount of land (qualifications that were modified in post-independence constitutions to require literacy and a specified economic standing). For different reasons, therefore, Spanish America was like the colonies specializing in the production of crops like sugar in generating an economic structure in which wealth, human capital, and political power were distributed very unequally, and where the elites were drawn from a relatively small group that was of European descent and racially distinct from the bulk of the population.

As in the colonial sugar economies, the economic structures that evolved in this second class of colonies were greatly influenced by the factor endowments, viewed in broad terms. The fabulously valuable mineral resources and abundance of labor with low amounts of human capital were certainly major contributors to the extremely unequal distributions of wealth and income that came to prevail in these economies. Moreover, without the extensive supply of native labor, it is unlikely that Spain could have maintained its policies of tight restrictions on European migration to its colonies and of generous awards of property and tribute to the earliest settlers. The colonists in Spanish America endorsed formidable requirements for obtaining permission to go to the New World—a policy that limited the flow of migrants and helped to preserve the political and economic advantages enjoyed by those of European descent who had already made the move. In 1800, less than 20 percent of the population in Spanish colonies such as Mexico, Peru, and Chile was composed of whites; it would not be until the major new inflows from Europe late in the nineteenth century that Latin American countries such as Argentina and Chile would attain the predominantly European character they have today.

The final category of New World colonies were those located in the northern part of the North American mainland—chiefly those that became the United States, but including Canada as well. These economies were not endowed with substantial populations of natives able to provide labor, nor with climates and soils that gave them a comparative advantage in the production of crops characterized by major economies of using slave labor. For these reasons, their development, especially north of the Chesapeake, was based on laborers of European descent who had relatively high and similar levels of human capital. Compared to either of the other two categories of New World colonies, this class had rather homogenous populations. Correspondingly equal distributions of wealth were also encouraged by the limited advantages to large producers in the production of grains and hays predominant in regions such as the Middle Atlantic and New England. With abundant land and low capital requirements, the great majority of adult men were able to operate as independent proprietors. Conditions were somewhat different in the southern colonies, where crops such as tobacco and rice did exhibit some limited scale economies; cotton, which was grown predominantly on large slave plantations, was not a quantitatively important crop until the nineteenth century. But even here, the size of the slave plantations, as well as the degree of inequality in these colonies, were quite modest by the standards of Brazil or the sugar islands of the Caribbean.

THE ROLE OF INSTITUTIONS IN THE PERSISTENCE OF INEQUALITY

There is strong evidence that various features of the factor endowments of these three categories of New World economies—including soils, climates, and the size or density of the native population—predisposed them toward paths of development associated with different degrees of inequality in wealth, human capital, and political power. Although these conditions might reasonably be treated as exogenous at the beginning of European colonization, it is clear that such an assumption becomes increasingly tenuous as one moves later in time after settlement. Particularly given that both Latin America and many of the economies of the first category, such as Haiti and Jamaica, are known today as generally the most unequal in the world, we suggest that the initial conditions had lingering effects, not only because certain fundamental characteristics of New World economies were difficult to change, but also because government policies and other institutions tended to reproduce them. Specifically, in those societies that began with extreme inequality, elites were better able to establish a legal framework that insured them disproportionate shares of political power, and to use that greater influence to establish rules, laws, and other government policies that advantaged members of the elite relative to nonmembers—contributing to persistence over time of the high degree of inequality. In societies that began with greater equality or homogeneity among the population, however, efforts by elites to institutionalize an unequal distribution of political power were relatively unsuccessful, and the rules, laws, and other government policies that came to be adopted, therefore, tended to provide more equal treatment and opportunities to members of the population.

Land policy provides an illustration of how institutions may have fostered persistence in the extent of inequality in New World economies over time. Since the governments of each colony or nation were regarded as the owners of the public lands, they set those policies which influenced the pace of settlement as well as the distribution of wealth, by controlling its availability, setting prices, establishing minimum or maximum acreages, and designing tax systems. We have already mentioned the highly concentrated pattern of landownership produced and perpetuated by land policies in most of Spanish America. In the United States, where there were never major obstacles to acquiring land, the terms of land acquisition became even easier over the course of [the] nineteenth century. Similar changes were sought around the mid-nineteenth century in both Argentina and Brazil, as a means to encourage immigration, but these steps were less successful than in the United States and Canada in getting land to smallholders. The major crops produced in the expansion of the United States and Canada were grains, which permitted relatively small farms given the technology of the times and may help explain why such a policy of smallholding was implemented and was effective. But as the example of Argentina indicates, small-scale production of wheat was possible even with ownership of land in large units, maintaining a greater degree of overall inequality in wealth and political power.

The contrast between the United States and Canada, with their practices of offering small units of land for disposal and maintaining open immigration, and the rest of the Americas, where land and labor policies led to large land-holdings and great inequality, seems to extend across a wide spectrum of institutions and other government interventions. In the areas of law and administration pertaining to the establishment of corporations, the regulation of financial institutions, the granting of property rights in intellectual capital (patents), industrial policies, as well as the provision of access to minerals and other natural resources on government-owned land, New World societies with greater inequality tended to adopt policies that were more selective in the offering of opportunities. Of course, members of wealthy elites almost always enjoy privileged positions, but these societies were relatively extreme in the degree to which their institutions advantaged elites. Moreover, this contrast across New World societies with respect to the differences in the breadth of the respective populations having effective access to opportunities for economic and social advancement seems much more systematic than has been generally recognized.

Perhaps the most straightforward way of subjecting to an empirical test our hypothesis that elites in societies which began with greater inequality evolved more power to influence the choice of legal and economic institutions is to look at how broadly the franchise was extended and what fractions of respective populations actually voted in elections. Since most societies in the Americas were nominally democracies by the middle of the nineteenth century, this sort of information has a direct bearing on the extent to which elites—based largely on wealth, human capital, and gender—held disproportionate political power in their respective countries. . . . Although it was common in all countries to reserve the right to vote to adult males until the twentieth century, the United States and Canada were the clear leaders in doing away with restrictions based on wealth or literacy, and in attaining secrecy in balloting. . . .

. . . But meaningful extension of the franchise occurred much later in Latin America. Although a number of Latin countries relaxed restrictions based on landholding or wealth during the nineteenth century, they almost always chose to rely on a literacy qualification; as late as 1900, none had a secret ballot and only Argentina was without a wealth or literacy requirement. As a result, through 1940 the United States and Canada routinely had proportions voting that were 50 to 100 percent higher than their most progressive neighbors to the South (Argentina, Uruguay, and Costa Rica—countries notable as well for their relative equality and small shares of the population that were not of European descent), three times higher than in Mexico, and up to five to ten times higher than in countries such as Brazil, Bolivia, Ecuador, and Chile. . . .

Our conjecture is that these differences across societies in the distribution of political power may have contributed to persistence in the relative degrees of inequality through the effects on institutional development. The institution of public primary schools, which was the principal vehicle for high rates of literacy attainment and an important contributor to human capital formation, is interesting to examine in this regard. Nearly all of the New World economies were sufficiently prosperous by the beginning of the nineteenth century to establish a widespread network of primary schools. However, although many countries (through their national governments) expressed support for such efforts, few actually made investments on a scale sufficient to serve the general population before the twentieth century. The exceptional societies in terms of leadership were the United States and Canada. Virtually from the time of settlement, these North Americans seem generally to have been convinced of the value of mobilizing the resources to provide their children with a basic education. Especially in New England, schools were frequently organized and funded at the village or town level. It is likely that the United States already had the most literate population in the world by 1800, but the "common school movement" that got under way in the 1820s (following closely after the movement for the extension of the franchise) put the country on an accelerated path of investment in education institutions. Between 1825 and 1850, nearly every state in the American west or north that had not already done so enacted a law strongly encouraging localities to establish "free schools" open to all children and supported by general taxes. Although the movement made slower progress in the south, which had greater inequality and population heterogeneity than the north, schooling had spread sufficiently by the middle of the nineteenth century that over 40 percent of the school-age population was enrolled, and more than 90 percent of white adults were literate. . . . Schools were also widespread in early nineteenth-century Canada, and even though it lagged the United States by several decades in establishing tax-supported schools with universal access, its literacy rates were nearly as high.

The rest of the hemisphere trailed far behind the United States and Canada in primary schooling and in attaining literacy. Despite enormous wealth, the British colonies (with the exception of Barbados) were very slow to organize schooling institutions that served broad segments of the population. Indeed, it was evidently not until the British Colonial Office took an interest in the promotion of schooling late in the nineteenth century that significant steps were taken in this direction. Similarly, even the most progressive Latin American countries—like Argentina, Uruguay, and Costa Rica—were more than 75 years behind the United States and Canada. Major investments in primary schooling did not generally occur in any Latin American country until the national governments provided the funds; in contrast to the pattern in North America, local and state governments in Latin America were generally not willing or able to fund them on their own. As a consequence, most of these societies did not achieve high levels of literacy until well into the twentieth century.

CONCLUSIONS

Many scholars have been concerned with why the United States and Canada have developed so differently and were so much more successful than other economies of the Americas. All of the New World societies enjoyed high levels of product per capita early in their histories. The divergence in paths can be traced back to the achievement of sustained economic growth by the United States and Canada during the late eighteenth and early nineteenth centuries, while the others did not manage to attain this goal until late in the nineteenth or in the twentieth century. Although many explanations have been proposed, the substantial differences in the degree of inequality in wealth, human capital, and political power, which were initially rooted in the factor endowments of the respective colonies but persisted over time, seem highly relevant.

These early differences in the extent of inequality across New World economies may have been preserved by the types of economic institutions that evolved and by the effects of those institutions on how broadly access to economic opportunities was shared. This path of institutional development may in turn have affected growth. Where there was extreme inequality, and institutions advantaged elites and limited the access of much of the population to economic opportunities, members of elites were better able to maintain their elite status over time, but at the cost of society not realizing the full economic potential of disadvantaged groups. Although the examples we have discussed— landownership, the extension of the franchise and investment in public schools—do not prove the general point, they are suggestive of a pattern whereby institutions in New World societies with greater inequality advantaged members of the elite through many other types of government policies as well, including those concerned with access to public lands and natural resources, the establishment and use of financial institutions, and property rights in technological information. Overall, where there existed elites who were sharply differentiated from the rest of the population on the basis of wealth, human capital, and political influence, they seem to have used their standing to restrict competition. Although one could imagine that extreme inequality could take generations to dissipate in even a free and even-handed society, such biases in the paths of institutional development likely go far in explaining the persistence of inequality over the long run in Latin America and elsewhere in the New World.

REFERENCES

Acemoglu, Daron, Simon Johnson and James A. Robinson. 2000. "The Colonial Origins of Comparative Development: An Empirical Investigation." Working paper, Massachusetts Institute of Technology and University of California, Berkeley.

Coatsworth, John H. 1998. "Economic and Institutional Trajectories in Nineteenth-Century Latin America." In *Latin America and the World Economy Since 1800*, John H. Coatsworth and Alan M. Taylor, eds. Cambridge, MA: Harvard University Press.

Fogel, Robert William. 1989. *Without Consent or Contract.* New York: W. W. Norton.

North, Douglass C. 1988. "Institutions, Economic Growth and Freedom: An Historical Introduction." In *Freedom, Democracy and Economic Welfare*, Michael A. Walker, ed. Vancouver: Fraser Institute.

VIII

CURRENT PROBLEMS
IN INTERNATIONAL
POLITICAL ECONOMY

In the new millennium, the international economy is ever more global in scope and orientation. In the 1970s, analysts worried that America's economic decline would lead to a new bout of protectionism and economic closure. In the 1980s, scholars trumpeted the Japanese model of state-led economic growth and feared the consequences of the international debt crisis. Today, policy makers and analysts alike are concerned with the consequences of a global market. Although less fearful that the international economy will collapse into a new round of beggar-thy-neighbor policies, analysts and individual citizens today worry more about untrammeled markets degrading the environment, displacing the nation-state as the primary locus of political activity, and undermining the social welfare state, which had been the foundation of the postwar international economic order in the developed world.

As people become increasingly aware of the effects of environmental degradation—both globally, as with climate change, and locally, as with species preservation—pressures build for the imposition of greater governmental regulations to control pollution and manage scarce natural resources. But these pressures have increased at different rates in different countries, creating difficult problems of international policy coordination. Jeffrey A. Frankel (Reading 29) examines how efforts to promote trade affect the environment through the channel of economic growth, and explores how countries with different preferences and policies on the environment can best manage their interactions so as to promote environmental quality. He also suggests that domestic institutions that protect private property rights and enfranchise everyday citizens can have important environmental benefits.

Rising concerns about the environment, along with concerns about sweatshop conditions in developing countries, may also be undermining public support for free trade in the United States. Sean D. Ehrlich (Reading 30) explores American public opinion and finds that concern for environmental protection and labor standards abroad is generating a new form of opposition to free trade that is distinct from traditional protectionist pressures that are driven by self-interest. Ehrlich sees this "fair trade" movement as a threat to the post-war compromise that conjoined free trade with compensatory welfare and educational benefits for the losers precisely because it is not self-interested.

Robert O. Keohane and David G. Victor (Reading 31) explore the international interactions required to address climate change, a problem that cannot be mitigated by the actions of any single nation or group of nations acting alone. Climate change is a global public goods problem, which means it requires a truly global solution. Such deep international cooperation hinges on repeated interactions and a structure of institutions that provide incentives for all parties to make their respective contributions to the collective effort.

Like climate change mitigation, international financial stability is a global public good. An integrated and stable international financial system benefits all nations but also creates strong incentives to free ride. In the aftermath of two major financial meltdowns in the 2000s—the Global Financial Crisis that originated in the United States and the subsequent Eurozone Debt Crisis—nations have tried to overcome the free-rider problem and improve the international financial architecture. Jeffry A. Frieden (Reading 32) takes stock of these interactions and evaluates post-crises efforts to improve lender-of-last-resort facilities, harmonize financial regulations, and coordinate national macroeconomic policies.

Outsourcing may comprise another threat to an open world economy. As improvements in technology and communications have made it easier for companies to move their operations overseas, outsourcing has become a major political issue. Average people see outsourcing as the business practice of moving jobs overseas. For decades, this practice was limited to low-skilled jobs in the manufacturing sector, but relatively high-skilled jobs in the service sector are increasingly vulnerable. Edward D. Mansfield and Diana C. Mutz (Reading 33) seek to understand how everyday citizens form attitudes about outsourcing. They find little evidence that interests play a role, as measured by the vulnerability of a respondent's occupation or industry to outsourcing, but they find that nationalism and ethnocentrism are key drivers of attitudes toward outsourcing. Whether such nativist public sentiment actually influences U.S. policy remains an open question.

29

Globalization and the Environment

JEFFREY A. FRANKEL

In this reading, Jeffrey A. Frankel surveys the economics of environmental degradation and explores how countries with different preferences and policies on the environment can best manage their interactions to improve environmental outcomes without damaging trade relations. He argues that trade liberalization helps the environment through the channel of economic growth—the so-called Environmental Kuznets Curve. He also shows that domestic institutions that protect private property rights and empower everyday citizens in the democratic process can have important environmental benefits.

At the ministerial meeting of the World Trade Organization in Seattle in November 1999, when anti-globalization protesters launched the first of their big demonstrations, some wore turtle costumes. These demonstrators were concerned that international trade in shrimp was harming sea turtles by ensnaring them in nets. They felt that a WTO panel had, in the name of free trade, negated the ability of the United States to protect the turtles, simultaneously undermining the international environment and national sovereignty. Subsequently, anti-globalization protests became common at meetings of multinational organizations.

Perhaps no aspect of globalization worries the critics more than its implications for the environment. The concern is understandable. It is widely (if not universally) accepted that the direct effects of globalization on the economy are positive, as measured by Gross Domestic Product. Concerns rise more with regard to "noneconomic" effects of globalization. Of these, some, such as labor rights, might be considered to be a subject properly of national sovereignty, with each nation bearing the responsibility of deciding to what extent it wishes to protect its own labor force, on the basis of its own values, capabilities, and politics. When we turn to influences on the environment, however, the case for countries sticking their noses into each other's business is stronger. We all share a planet.

Pollution and other forms of environmental degradation are the classic instance of what economists call an externality: the condition under which individuals and firms, and sometimes even individual countries, lack the incentive to restrain their pollution, because under a market system the costs are borne primarily by others. The phrase "tragedy of the commons" was originally coined in the context of a village's shared pasture land, which would inevitably be overgrazed if each farmer were allowed free and unrestricted use. It captures the idea that we will foul our shared air and water supplies and deplete our natural resources unless somehow we are individually faced with the costs of our actions.

A central question for this chapter is whether globalization helps or hurts in achieving the best trade-off between environmental and economic goals. Do international trade and investment allow countries to achieve more economic growth for any given level of environmental quality? Or do they undermine environmental quality for any given rate of economic growth? Globalization is a complex trend, encompassing many forces and many effects. It would be surprising if all of them were always unfavorable to the environment, or all of them favorable. The highest priority should be to determine ways in which globalization can be successfully harnessed to protect the environment rather than to degrade it.

One point to be emphasized here is that it is an illusion to think that environmental issues could be effectively addressed if each country were insulated against incursions into its national sovereignty at the hands of international trade or the WTO. Increasingly, people living in one country want to protect the air, water, forests, and animals not just in their *own* countries, but also in *other* countries as well. To do so international cooperation is required. National sovereignty is the obstacle to such efforts, not the ally. Multilateral institutions are a potential ally, not the obstacle.

In the course of this chapter, we encounter three ways in which globalization can be a means of environmental improvement. So the author hopes to convince the reader, at any rate. Each has a component that is new.

First is the exercise of *consumer power*. There is the beginning of a worldwide trend toward labeling, codes of corporate conduct, and other ways that environmentally conscious consumers can use their purchasing power to give expression and weight to their wishes. These tools would not exist without international trade. American citizens would have few ways to dissuade Mexican fishermen from using dolphin-unfriendly nets if Americans did not import tuna to begin with. The attraction of labeling is that it suits a decentralized world, where we have both national sovereignty and consumer sovereignty. Nevertheless, labeling cannot be a completely laissez-faire affair. For it to work, there need to be some rules or standards. Otherwise, any producer could inaccurately label its product as environmentally pure, and any country could unfairly put a pejorative label on imports from rival producers. This consideration leads to the second respect in which globalization can be a means of environmental improvement.

International environmental issues require international cooperation, a system in which countries interact under a set of *multilateral rules* determined in multilateral negotiations and monitored by multilateral institutions. This is just as true in the case of environmental objectives, which are increasingly cross-border, as of other objectives. It is true that, in the past, the economic objectives of international trade have been pursued more effectively by the GATT and other multilateral organizations than have environmental objectives. But multilateral institutions can be made a means of environmental protection. This will sound like pie-in-the-sky to the many who have been taken in by the mantra that recent WTO panel decisions have overruled legislative efforts to protect the environment. But the WTO has actually moved importantly in the environmentalists' direction in recent years.

The front lines of multilateral governance currently concern—not illusory alternatives of an all-powerful WTO versus none at all—but rather questions about how reasonably to balance both economic and environmental objectives. One question under debate is whether countries are to be allowed to adopt laws that may be trade-restricting, but that have as their objective influencing other countries' processes and production methods (PPMs), such as their fishermen's use of nets. While the issue is still controversial, the WTO has moved clearly in the direction of answering this question in the affirmative, that is, asserting in panel decisions countries' ability to adopt such laws. The only "catch" is that the measures cannot be unnecessarily unilateral or discriminatory. The environmentalist community has almost entirely failed to notice this major favorable development, because of confusion over the latter qualification. But not only is the qualification what a reasonable person would want, it is secondary to the primary issue of countries' rights under the trading system to implement such laws. By ignoring their victory on the main issue—the legitimacy of addressing PPMs—environmentalists risk losing the opportunity to consolidate it. Some players, particularly poor countries, would love to deny the precedent set in these panel decisions, and to return to a system where other countries cannot restrict trade in pursuit of others.

Third, countries can learn from others' experiences. There has recently accumulated *statistical evidence* on how globalization and growth tend to affect environmental objectives on average, even without multilateral institutions. Looking for patterns in the data across countries in recent decades can help us answer some important questions. Increased international trade turns out to have been beneficial for some environmental measures, such as SO_2 pollution. There is little evidence to support the contrary fear that international competition in practice works to lower environmental standards overall. Rather, globalization can aid the process whereby economic growth enables people to demand higher environmental quality. To be sure, effective government regulation is probably required if this demand is ever to be translated into actual improvement; the environment cannot take care of itself. But the statistical evidence says that high-income countries do indeed eventually tend to use some of their wealth to clean up the environment, on average, for measures such as SO_2 pollution. For the increasingly important category of global environmental externalities, however, such as emission of greenhouse gases, regulation at the national level is not enough. An international agreement is necessary.

These three new reasons to think that globalization can be beneficial for the environment—consumer power, multilateralism, and cross-country statistical evidence—are very different in nature. But in each case what is striking is how little the facts correspond to the suspicions of critics that turning back the clock on globalization would somehow allow them to achieve environmental goals. The rise in globalization, with the attempts at international environmental accord and quasi-judicial oversight, is less a threat to the environment than an ally. It is unfettered national sovereignty that poses the larger threat.

This chapter will try to lay out the key conceptual points concerning the relationship of economic globalization and the environment, and to summarize the available empirical evidence, with an emphasis on what is new. We begin by clarifying some basic issues, such as defining objectives, before going on to consider the impact of globalization.

OBJECTIVES

It is important to begin a consideration of these issues by making clear that both economic income and environmental quality are worthy objectives. Individuals may disagree on the weight that should be placed on one objective or another. But we should not let such disagreements lead to deadlocked political outcomes in which the economy and the environment are both worse off than necessary. Can globalization be made to improve the environment that comes with a given level of income in market-measured terms? Many seem to believe that globalization necessarily makes things worse. If Mexico grows rapidly, is an increase in pollution inevitable? Is it likely, on average? If that growth arises from globalization, rather than from domestic sources, does that make environmental damage more likely? Less likely? Are there policies that can simultaneously promote *both* economic growth and an improved environment? These are the questions of interest.

Two Objectives: GDP and the Environment

An extreme version of environmental activism would argue that we should turn back the clock on industrialization—that it is worth deliberately impoverishing ourselves—if that is what it takes to save the environment. If the human species still consisted of a few million hunter-gatherers, man-made pollution would be close to zero. Thomas Malthus, writing in the early nineteenth century, predicted that geometric growth in population and in the economy would eventually and inevitably run into the natural resource limits of the carrying capacity of the planet. In the 1960s, the Club of Rome picked up where Malthus had left off, warning that environmental disaster was coming soon. Some adherents to this school might favor the deliberate reversal of industrialization—reducing market-measured income below current levels in order to save the environment.

But environmental concerns have become more mainstream since the 1960s. We have all had time to think about it. Most people believe that both a clean environment and economic growth are desirable, that we can have a combination of both, and it is a matter of finding the best tradeoff. Indeed, that is one possible interpretation of the popular phrase "sustainable development."

To evaluate the costs and benefits of globalization with regard to the environment, it is important to be precise conceptually, for example to make the distinction between effects on the environment that come *via* rapid economic growth and those that come *for a given level* of economic output.

We have a single concept, GDP, that attempts to measure the aggregate value of goods and services that are sold in the marketplace, and that does a relatively good job of it. Measurement of environmental quality is much less well advanced. There are many different aspects of the environment that we care about, and it is hard to know how to combine them into a single overall measure. It would be harder still to agree on how to combine such a measure with GDP to get a measure of overall welfare. Proponents of so-called *green GDP accounting* have tried to do exactly that, but so far the enterprise is very incomplete. For the time being, the best we can do is look at a variety of separate measures capturing various aspects of the environment.

A Classification of Environmental Objectives

For the purpose of this chapter, it is useful to array different aspects of the environment according to the extent to which damage is localized around specific sources, as opposed to spilling out over a geographically more extensive area.

The first category of environmental damage is pollution that is *internal* to the household or firm. Perhaps 80 percent (by population) of world exposure to particulates is indoor pollution in poor countries—smoke from indoor cooking fires—which need not involve any externality. There may be a role for dissemination of information regarding long-term health impacts that are not immediately evident. Nevertheless, what households in such countries primarily lack are the economic resources to afford stoves that run on cleaner fuels. In the case of internal pollution, higher incomes directly allow the solution of the problem.

Some other categories of environmental damage pose potential externalities, but could be internalized by assigning property rights. If a company has clear title to a depletable natural resource such as an oil well, it has some incentive to keep some of the oil for the future, rather than pumping it all today. The biggest problems arise when the legal system fails to enforce clear divisions of property rights. Tropical forest land that anyone can enter to chop down trees will be rapidly over-logged. Many poor countries lack the institutional and economic resources to enforce laws protecting such resources. Often corrupt arms of the government themselves collude in the plundering. Another example is the dumping of waste. If someone agreed to be paid to let his land be used as a waste disposal site, voluntarily and without hidden adverse effects, economics says that there would not necessarily be anything wrong with the arrangement. Waste has to go somewhere. But the situation would be different if the government of a poor undemocratic country were to agree to be paid to accept waste that then hurt the environment and health of residents who lacked the information or political clout to participate in the benefits.

A second category, *national externalities,* includes most kinds of air pollution and water pollution, the latter a particularly great health hazard in the third world. The pollution is external to the individual firm or household, and often external to the state or province as well, but most of the damage is felt within the country in question. Intervention by the government is necessary to control such pollution. There is no reason why each national government cannot undertake the necessary regulation on its own, though the adequacy of economic resources to pay the costs of the regulation is again an issue.

A third category is *international externalities.* Increasingly, as we will see, environmental problems cross national boundaries. Acid rain is an example. In these cases, some cooperation among countries is necessary. The strongest examples are purely *global externalities*: chemicals that deplete the stratospheric ozone layer, greenhouse gases that lead to global climate change, and habitat destruction that impairs biological diversity. Individual countries should not expect to be able to do much about global externalities on their own. The distinctions among internal pollution, national externalities, and global externalities will turn out to be important.

The Relationship between Economic Production and the Environment

Scholars often catalog three intermediating variables or channels of influence that can determine the aggregate economic impacts of trade or growth on the environment.

1. The *scale* of economic activity: for physical reasons, more output means more pollution, other things equal. But other things are usually not equal.
2. The *composition* of economic activity: trade and growth can shift the composition of output, for example, among the agricultural, manufacturing, and service sectors. Because environmental damage per unit of output varies across these sectors, the aggregate can shift.
3. The *techniques* of economic activity: often the same commodity can be produced through a variety of different techniques, some cleaner than others. Electric power, for example, can be generated by a very wide range of fuels and techniques. To the extent trade or growth involve the adoption of cleaner techniques, pollution per unit of GDP will fall.

The positive effects of international trade and investment on GDP are already moderately well established, both theoretically and empirically. The relationship between GDP and the environment is not quite as well understood, and is certainly less of a constant relationship. The relationship is rarely monotonic: sometimes a country's growth is first bad for the environment and later good. The reason is the three conflicting forces that were just noted. On the one hand, when GDP increases, the greater scale of production leads directly to more pollution and other environmental degradation. On the other hand, there tend to be favorable shifts in the composition of output and in the techniques of production. The question is whether the latter two effects can outweigh the first.

The Environmental Kuznets Curve

A look at data across countries or across time allows some rough generalization as to the usual outcome of these conflicting effects. For some important environmental measures, a U-shaped relationship appears: at relatively low levels of income per capita, growth leads to greater environmental damage, until it levels off at an intermediate level of income, after which further growth leads to improvements in the environment. This empirical relationship is known as the Environmental Kuznets Curve. The label is by analogy with the original Kuznets Curve, which was a U-shaped relationship between average income and inequality. The World Bank (1992) and Grossman and Krueger (1993, 1995) brought to public attention this statistical finding for a cross section of countries. Grossman and Krueger (1995) estimated that SO_2 pollution peaked when a country's income was about \$5,000–\$6,000 per capita (in 1985 dollars). Most developing countries have not yet reached this threshold.

For countries where a long enough time series of data is available, there is also some evidence that the same U-shaped relationship can hold across time. The air in London was far more polluted in the 1950s than it is today. (The infamous "pea soup" fogs were from pollution.) The same pattern has held in Tokyo, Los Angeles, and other cities. A similar pattern holds typically with respect to deforestation in rich countries: the percentage of U.S. land that was forested fell in the eighteenth century and first half of the nineteenth century, but rose in the twentieth century.

The idea behind the Environmental Kuznets Curve is that growth is bad for air and water pollution at the initial stages of industrialization, but later on reduces pollution, as countries become rich enough to pay to clean up their environments. The dominant theoretical explanation is that production technology makes some pollution inevitable, but that demand for environmental quality rises with income. The standard rationale is thus that, at higher levels of income per capita, growth raises the public's demand for environmental quality, which can translate into environmental regulation. Environmental regulation, if effective, then translates into a cleaner environment. It operates largely through the techniques channel, encouraging or requiring the use of cleaner production techniques for given products, although regulation might also have a composition effect: raising the price of polluting goods and services relative to clean ones and thus encouraging consumers to buy more of the latter.

It would be inaccurate to portray the Environmental Kuznets Curve as demonstrating—or even claiming—that if countries promote growth, the environment will eventually take care of itself. Only if pollution is largely confined within the home or within the firm does that Panglossian view necessarily apply. Most pollution, such as SO_2, NO_x, etc., is external to the home or firm. For such externalities, higher income and a popular desire to clean up the environment are not enough. There must also be effective government regulation, which usually requires a democratic system to translate the popular will into action (something that was missing in the Soviet Union, for example), as well as the rule of law and reasonably intelligent mechanisms of regulation. The empirical evidence confirms that the participation of well-functioning democratic governments is an important part of the process. That is at the national level. The requirements for dealing with cross-border externalities are greater still.

Another possible explanation for the pattern of the Environmental Kuznets Curve is that it works naturally via the composition of output. In theory, the pattern could result from the usual stages of economic development: the transition from an agrarian economy to manufacturing, and then from manufacturing to services. Services tend to generate less pollution than heavy manufacturing. This explanation is less likely than the conventional view to require the mechanism of effective government regulation. If the Kuznets Curve in practice resulted solely from this composition effect, however, then high incomes should lead to a better environment even when externalities arise at the international level, which is not the case. No Kuznets Curve has yet appeared for carbon dioxide, for example. Even though emissions per unit of GDP do tend to fall, this is not enough to reduce overall emissions, in the absence of a multilateral effort.

REGULATION

It will help if we clarify one more fundamental set of issues before we turn to the main subject, the role of globalization per se.

It is logical to expect environmental regulation to cost something, to have a negative effect on measured productivity and income per capita. "There is no free lunch," Milton Friedman famously said. Most tangible good things in life cost something, and for many kinds of regulation, if effective, people will readily agree that the cost is worth paying. Cost-benefit tests and cost-minimization strategies are economists' tools for trying to make sure that policies deliver the best environment for a given economic cost, or the lowest economic cost for a given environmental goal. Taxes on energy, for example, particularly on hydrocarbon fuels, are quite an efficient mode of environmental regulation (if the revenue is "recycled" efficiently). Fuel efficiency standards are somewhat less efficient. (Differentiated CAFE standards for vehicles, for example, probably encouraged the birth of the SUV craze.) And crude "command and control" methods are less efficient still. (Government mandates regarding what specific technologies firms must use, for example, deny firms the flexibility to find better ways to achieve a given goal.) Some environmental regulations, when legislated or implemented poorly, can impose very large and unnecessary economic costs on firms, as well as on workers and consumers.

Occasionally there are policy measures that have both environmental and economic benefits. Usually these "win-win" ideas constitute the elimination of some previously existing distortion in public policy. Many countries have historically subsidized the use of coal. The United States subsidizes mining and cattle grazing on federal land, and sometimes logging and oil drilling as well, not to mention water use. Other countries have substantial subsidies for ocean fishing. Elimination of such subsidies would improve the environment and save money at the same time—not just for the federal budget, but for people's real income in the aggregate as well. Admittedly the economists' approach—taxing gasoline or making ranchers pay for grazing rights—is often extremely unpopular politically.

Another idea that would have economic and environmental benefits simultaneously would be to remove all barriers against international trade in environmental equipment and services, such as those involved in renewable energy generation, smokestack scrubbing, or waste treatment facilities. There would again be a double payoff: the growth-enhancing effect of elimination of barriers to exports (in a sector where the United States is likely to be able to develop a comparative advantage), together with the environment-enhancing effect of facilitating imports of the inputs that go into environmental protection. A precedent is the removal of barriers to the imports of fuel-efficient cars from Japan, which was a clear case of simultaneously promoting free trade and clean air.

A different school of thought claims that opportunities for saving money while simultaneously saving the environment are common rather than rare. The *Porter Hypothesis* holds that a tightening of environmental regulation stimulates technological innovation and thereby has positive effects on both the economy and the environment—for example, saving money by saving energy. The analytical rationale for this view is not always made clear. (Is the claim that a change in regulation, regardless in what direction, stimulates innovation, or is there something special about environmental regulation? Is there something special about the energy sector?) Its proponents cite a number of real-world examples where a new environmental initiative turned out to be profitable for a given firm or industry. Such cases surely exist, but there is little reason to think that a link between regulation and productivity growth holds as a matter of generality. The hypothesis is perhaps better understood as making a point regarding "first mover advantage." That is, if the world is in the future to be moving in a particular direction, such as toward more environmentally friendly energy sources, then a country that innovates new products and new technologies of this sort before others do will be in a position to sell the fruits to the latecomers.

EFFECTS OF OPENNESS TO TRADE

The central topic of this chapter is the implications of trade for the environment. Some effects come via economic growth, and some come even for a given level of income. In both cases, the effects can be either beneficial or detrimental. Probably the strongest effects of trade are the first sort, via income. Much like saving and investment, technological progress, and other sources of growth, trade tends to raise income. As we have seen, higher income in turn has an effect on some environmental measures that is initially adverse but, according to the Environmental Kuznets Curve, eventually turns favorable.

What about effects of trade that do not operate via economic growth? They can be classified in three categories: systemwide effects that are adverse, systemwide effects that are beneficial, and effects that vary across countries depending on local "comparative advantage." We consider each in turn.

Race to the Bottom

The *"race to the bottom"* hypothesis is perhaps the strongest basis for fearing that international trade and investment specifically (rather than industrialization generally) will put downward pressure on countries' environmental standards and thus damage the environment across the global system. Leaders of industry, and of the unions whose members are employed in industry, are always concerned about competition from abroad. When domestic regulation raises their costs, they fear that they will lose competitiveness against firms in other countries. They warn of a loss of sales, employment, and investment to foreign competitors. Thus domestic producers often sound the competitiveness alarm as a way of applying political pressure on their governments to minimize the burden of regulation.

To some, the phrase "race to the bottom" connotes that the equilibrium will be a world of little or no regulation. Others emphasize that, in practice, it is not necessarily a matter of globalization leading to environmental standards that literally decline over time, but rather retarding the gradual raising of environmental standards that would otherwise occur. Either way, the concern is that, to the extent that countries are open to international trade and investment, environmental standards will be lower than they would otherwise be. But how important is this in practice? Some economists' research suggests that environmental regulation is not one of the more important determinants of firms' ability to compete internationally. When deciding where to locate, multinational firms seem to pay more attention to such issues as labor costs and market access than to the stringency of local environmental regulation.

Once again, it is important to distinguish (1) the fear that globalization will lead to a race to the bottom in regulatory standards, from (2) fears that the environment will be damaged by the very process of industrialization and economic growth itself. Opening of national economies to international trade and investment could play a role in both cases, but the two possible channels are very different. In the first case, the race to the bottom hypothesis, the claim is that openness undermines environmental standards even for a given path of economic growth. This would be a damning conclusion from the standpoint of globalization, because it would imply that by limiting trade and investment in some way, we might be able to attain a better environment for any given level of GDP. In the second case, the implication would be that openness only affects the environment in the way that investment, or education, or productivity growth, or any other source of growth affects the environment, by moving the economy along the Environmental Kuznets Curve. Trying to restrict trade and investment would be a less attractive strategy in this case, because it would amount to deliberate self-impoverishment.

Gains from Trade

While the possibility that exposure to international competition might have an adverse effect on environmental regulation is familiar, less widely recognized and more surprising is the possibility of effects in the beneficial direction, which we will call the *gains from trade hypothesis*. Trade allows countries to attain more of what they want, which includes environmental goods in addition to market-measured output.

How could openness have a positive effect on environmental quality, once we set aside the possibility of accelerating progress down the beneficial slope of the Environmental Kuznets Curve? A first possibility concerns technological and managerial innovation. Openness encourages ongoing innovation. It then seems possible that openness could encourage innovation beneficial to environmental improvement as well as economic progress. A second possibility is an international ratcheting up of environmental standards. The largest political jurisdiction can set the pace for others. Within the United States, it is called the "California effect." When the largest state sets high standards for auto pollution control equipment, for example, the end result may be similar standards in other states as well. The United States can play the same role globally.

Multinational corporations (MNCs) are often the vehicle for these effects. They tend to bring clean state-of-the-art production techniques from high-standard countries of origin, to host countries where they are not yet known, for several reasons:

> First, many companies find that the efficiency of having a single set of management practices, pollution control technologies, and training programmes geared to a common set of standards outweighs any cost advantage that might be obtained by scaling back on environmental investments at overseas facilities. Second, multinational enterprises often operate on a large scale, and recognise that their visibility makes them especially attractive targets for local enforcement officials. . . . Third, the prospect of liability for failing to meet standards often motivates better environmental performance. (Esty and Gentry 1997: 161)

The claim is not that all multinational corporations apply the highest environmental standards when operating in other countries, but rather that the standards tend on average to be higher than if the host country were undertaking the same activity on its own. Corporate codes of conduct, as under the UN Global Compact promoted by Kofi Annan, offer a new way that residents of some countries. Formal international cooperation among governments is another way that interdependence can lead to higher environmental standards rather than lower.

Furthermore, because trade offers consumers the opportunity to consume goods of greater variety, it allows countries to attain higher levels of welfare (for any given level of domestically produced output), which, as before, will raise the demand for environmental quality. Again, if the appropriate institutions are in place, this demand for higher environmental quality will translate into effective regulation and the desired reduction in pollution.

Attempts to Evaluate the Overall Effects of Trade on the Environment

If a set of countries opens up to trade, is it on average likely to have a positive or negative effect on the environment (for a given level of income)? Which tend in practice to dominate, the unfavorable "race to the bottom" effects or the favorable "gains from trade" effects? Econometrics can help answer the question.

Statistically, some measures of environmental quality are positively correlated with the level of trade. . . . But the causality is complex, running in many directions simultaneously. One would not want to claim that trade leads to a cleaner environment, if in reality they are both responding to some other third factor, such as economic growth or democracy.

Eiras and Schaeffer (2001:4) find: "In countries with an open economy, the average environmental sustainability score is more than 30 percent higher than the scores of countries with moderately open economies, and almost twice as high as those of countries with closed economies." Does this mean that trade is good for the environment? Not necessarily. It might be a result of the Porter hypothesis—environmental regulation stimulates productivity—together with the positive effect of income on trade. Or it might be because democracy leads to higher levels of environmental regulation, and democracy is causally intertwined with income and trade. As noted, democracy raises the demand for environmental regulation. . . . But there remain other possible third factors.

A number of studies have sought to isolate the independent effect of openness. Lucas et al. (1992), study the toxic intensity implied by the composition of manufacturing output in a sample of 80 countries, and find that a high degree of trade-distorting policies increased pollution in rapidly growing countries. The implication is that trade liberalization now is good for the environment. Harbaugh, Levinson, and Wilson (2000) report in passing a beneficial effect of trade on the environment, after controlling for income. Dean (2002) finds a detrimental direct of liberalization for a given level of income, via the terms of trade, though this is outweighed by a beneficial indirect effect via income.

Antweiler, Copeland, and Taylor (2001) and Copeland and Taylor (2001, 2003a) represent an extensive body of empirical research explicitly focused on the effects of trade on the environment. They conclude that trade liberalization that raises the scale of economic activity by 1 percent works to raise SO_2 concentrations by .25 to .5 percent via the scale channel, but that the accompanying technique channel reduces concentrations by 1.25 to 1.5 percent, so that the overall effect is beneficial. But none of these studies makes allowance for the problem that trade may be the *result* of other factors rather than the cause. Antweiler et al. point out this potential weakness.

Frankel and Rose (2003) attempt to disentangle the various causal relationships. The study focuses on exogenous variation in trade across countries, attributable to factors such as geographical location. It finds effects on several measures of air pollution (particularly SO_2 and NO_x concentrations), for a given level of income, that are more good than bad. This suggests that the "gains from trade" effects may be at least as powerful as the "race to the bottom" effect. The findings are not so optimistic for other measures of environmental quality, however, particularly emissions of CO_2.

Differential Effects Arising from Comparative Advantage

So far we have only considered effects that could be expected to hold for the average country, to the extent that it is open to international trade and investment. What if the environment improves in some open countries and worsens in others? An oft-expressed concern is that, to the extent that countries are open to international trade and investment, some will specialize in producing dirty products, and export them to other countries. Such countries could be said to exploit a comparative advantage in pollution. The prediction is that the environment will be damaged more in this set of countries, as compared to what would happen without trade. The environment will be *cleaner* in the second set of countries, those that specialize in clean production and instead import the dirty products from the other countries. Leaving aside the possibility of a race to the bottom effect, the worldwide environment on average might even benefit somewhat, just as aggregate output should benefit, because of the gains from trade. But not everyone would approve of such a bargain.

What determines whether a given country is expected to be in the set of economies specializing in clean or dirty environmental production? There are several possible determinants of comparative advantage.

ENDOWMENTS AND COMPARATIVE ADVANTAGE. First, trade patterns could be determined by endowments of capital and labor, as in the standard neoclassical theory of trade, attributed to Heckscher, Ohlin, and Samuelson. Assume manufacturing is more polluting than alternative economic activities, such as services. (If the alternative sector, say agriculture, is instead just as polluting as manufacturing, then trade has no overall implications for the environment.) Since manufacturing is capital intensive, the country with the high capital/labor ratio—say Japan—will specialize in the dirty manufactured goods, while countries with low capital/labor ratios—say China—will specialize in cleaner goods.

For example, Grossman and Krueger predicted that NAFTA might reduce overall pollution in Mexico and raise it in the United States and Canada, because of the composition effect: Mexico has a comparative advantage in agriculture and labor-intensive manufacturing, which are relatively cleaner, versus the northern comparative advantage in more capital intensive sectors. This composition effect runs in the opposite direction from the usual worry, that trade would turn Mexico into a pollution haven as a result of high demand for environmental quality in the United States. That theory is discussed in the next section.

Second, comparative advantage could be determined by endowments of natural resources. A country with abundant hardwood forests will tend to export them if given the opportunity to do so. Here there cannot be much doubt that trade is indeed likely to damage the environment of such countries. True, in theory, if clear property rights can be allocated and enforced, someone will have the proper incentive to conserve these natural resources for the future. In practice, it seldom works this way. Poor miners and farmers cannot be kept out of large tracts of primitive forest. And even if there were clear property rights over the natural resources, private firms would not have the correct incentives to constrain external side effects of logging and mining, such as air and water pollution, soil erosion, loss of species, and so on. Government regulation is called for, but is often stymied by the problems of inadequate resources, at best, and corruption, at worst.

POLLUTION HAVENS.   Third, comparative advantage could be deliberately created by differences in environmental regulation itself. This is the pollution haven hypothesis. The motivation for varying levels of regulation could be differences in demand for environmental quality, arising, for example, from differences in income per capita. Or the motivation could be differences in the supply of environmental quality, arising, for example, from differences in population density.

Many object to an "eco dumping" system according to which economic integration results in some countries exporting pollution to others, even if the overall global level of pollution does not rise. They find distasteful the idea that the impersonal market system would deliberately allocate environmental damage to an "underdeveloped" country. A Chief Economist of the World Bank once signed his name to an internal memo with economists' language that read (in the summary sentence of its most inflammatory passage) "Just between you and me, shouldn't the World Bank be encouraging *more* migration of the dirty industries to the LDCs?" After the memo was leaked, public perceptions of the young Larry Summers were damaged for years.

There is some empirical evidence, but not very much, to support the hypothesis that countries that have a particularly high demand for environmental quality—the rich countries—currently specialize in products that can be produced cleanly, and let the poor countries produce and sell the products that require pollution. For the case of SO_2, the evidence appears to be, if anything, that trade leads to a reallocation of pollution from the poor country to the rich country, rather than the other way around. This is consistent with the finding of Antweiler, Copeland, and Taylor (2001) that trade has a significantly less favorable effect on SO_2 emissions in rich countries than in poor countries. Their explanation is that rich countries have higher capital/labor ratios, capital-intensive industries are more polluting, and this factor-based pollution-haven effect dominates the income-based pollution-haven effect.

Is the Majority of U.S. Trade and FDI with Low-Standard Countries?

To listen to some American discussion of globalization, one would think that the typical partner in U.S. trade and investment is a poor country with low environmental or labor standards. If so, it would help explain the fear that opening to international trade and investment in general puts downward pressure on U.S. standards. In fact, less than half of U.S. trade and investment takes place with partners who have lower wages and lower incomes than we do. Our most important partners have long been Canada, Japan, and the European Union (though Mexico has now become important as well). These trading partners often regard the United States as the low-standard country rather than the opposite.

DOES ECONOMIC GLOBALIZATION CONFLICT WITH ENVIRONMENTAL REGULATION?

There is a popular sense that globalization is a powerful force undermining environmental regulation. This can be the case in some circumstances. The "race to the bottom" phenomenon can potentially put downward pressure on the regulatory standards of countries that compete internationally in trade and investment. But, as an argument against globalization, it leaves much out.

First is the point that, for most of us, environmental quality is one goal, but not the only goal. As already noted, we care also about income, and trade is one means of promoting economic growth. The goals often need to be balanced against each other.

Environmental concerns can be an excuse for protectionism. If policymakers give in to protectionist arguments and erect trade barriers, we will enjoy less growth in trade and income. We will not even necessarily end up with a better environment. Import-competing corporations (or their workers), in sectors that may themselves not be particularly friendly to the environment, some-times seek to erect or retain barriers to imports in the name of environmental protection, when in reality it is their own pocketbooks they are trying to protect. In other words, environmentalism is an excuse for protectionism.

Often, the problem is less sinister, but more complex. To see how the political economy works, let us begin with the point that most policy debates are settled as the outcome of a complicated mix of multiple countervailing arguments and domestic interest groups on both sides. Most of the major viewpoints are in some way represented "at the table" in the federal government decisionmaking process. In the case of environmental measures, there are often representatives of adversely affected industry groups sitting across the table from the environmentalists, and they have an effect on the final political outcome. But when the commodity in question happens to be produced by firms in foreign countries, then that point of view largely disappears from the table around which the decision is made. If the issue is big enough, the State Department may weigh in to explain the potential costs facing foreign countries. But, understandably, the foreigners receive less weight in the policy process than would the identical firms if they were American. The result is that the environmental policies that are adopted on average can discriminate against foreign firms relative to domestic firms, without anyone ever deliberately having supported a measure out of protectionist intent.

One possible example is the strong opposition in Europe to Genetically Modified Organisms (GMOs). A Biosafety Agreement was negotiated in Montreal, January 29, 2000, in which the United States felt it had to agree to label grain shipments that might in part be bio-engineered, and to allow countries to block imports of GMOs. In some ways, these negotiations might serve as a useful model for compromise in other areas. But why have Europeans decided that they want to keep out genetically modified varieties of corn, despite the emergence of little or no scientific evidence against them as of yet, where American consumers are far less agitated? Is it because Europeans are predisposed to have higher standards for environmental issues? Perhaps. An important part of the explanation, however, is that Monsanto and other U.S. technology companies, and U.S. farmers, are the ones who developed the technology and produce the stuff, not European companies or European farmers. Thus it is American producers, not Europeans, who stand to lose from the European squeamishness. European agriculture need not consciously launch a campaign against GMOs. All that the European movement needed was an absence around the table of producers who would be adversely affected by a ban. But the result is to reduce trade, hurt American producers, and benefit European farmers.

Whatever the source of different perceptions across countries, it is important to have a set of internationally agreed rules to govern trade, and if possible a mechanism for settling disputes that arise. That is the role of the WTO. The need for such an institution does not vanish when environmental issues are a part of the dispute. Certainly if one cares at all about trade and growth, then one cannot automatically sign on to each and every campaign seeking to block trade on environmental grounds. But even if one cares solely about the environment, claims need to be evaluated through some sort of neutral process. One can be easily misled; corporations make dubious claims to environmental motivations in, for example, seeking federal support of "Clean Coal" research or ethanol production. Most of the time, there is no substitute for investigating the details and merits of the case in question. One should not presume that an interest group's claims are right just because that group happens to be of one's own nationality. . . .

Environmental Concerns Cross National Borders

Even those who do not care about trade at all should appreciate the need for some international agreements and institutions. The reason is the increasing importance of major sources of environmental damage that cross national borders, and that would do so even if there were no such thing as international trade. Some externalities have long spilled over from each country to its immediate neighbors—such as SO_2 pollution, which is responsible for acid rain, or water pollution, which flows downriver. They can be addressed by negotiations between the two countries involved (e.g., United States and Canada). An increasing number of environmental externalities are truly global, however. The best examples are greenhouse gases. A ton of carbon dioxide creates the same global warming potential regardless where in the world it is emitted. Other good examples of direct global externalities are stratospheric ozone depletion, depletion of ocean fish stocks, and threats to biodiversity.

Even localized environmental damage, such as deforestation, is increasingly seen as a valid object of international concern. A distinction is traditional between trade measures that target specific undesirable products, such as asbestos, and those that target *Processes and Production Methods* (PPMs), such as the use of prison labor in the manufacture of the commodity in question. It is clear that a country concerned about its own health or environment has the right to tax or ban products that it regards as harmful, so long as it does not discriminate against foreign producers. Indeed, such bans are less liable to become a vehicle for surreptitious protectionism than are attempts to pass judgment on other countries' production methods that are unrelated to the physical attributes of the product itself. But is it legitimate for importing countries also to discriminate according to how a given product was produced? Some ask what business is it of others whether the producing country wants to use its own prison labor, or cut down its own forests, or pollute its own environment?

Often an international externality can be easily identified. Forests absorb carbon dioxide (a process called sequestration, or creating carbon sinks), so logging contributes to global climate change. An endangered species may contain a unique genetic element that someday could be useful to international scientists. Desertification can lead to social instability and political conflict, which can in turn produce problems for international security. Thus environmental damage in one country can have indirect effects on others.

But foreign residents increasingly care about localized environmental damage as well, even when they live far away and even when there is no evident link to their interests. The idea of "non-use value" is that many people place value on keeping, for example, a river canyon unspoiled, even if they know they will never see it. While the methodology of estimating the value according to what people say they would pay ("contingent valuation") is fraught with problems, the basic principle of non-use value is now widely accepted. This means that citizens in one country may have a stake in whether another country dams up a gorge, kills its wildlife, or pollutes its air and water.

Reversing Globalization Would Not End the Tension of Regulation vs. Sovereignty

Thus, for an increasingly important set of environmental issues, the idea that individual countries could properly address the issues if left on their own is myth. If countries do not cooperate through multilateral institutions, each will be tempted to free ride on the efforts of others, and little will get done. Globalization and multilateral institutions are not the obstacle—and the appeal of national sovereignty is not an ally—in international efforts to protect the environment. Rather, environmentalists need global agreements and global agencies if they are going to get other countries to do the things they want them to do. It is the appeal of national sovereignty that is the obstacle.

The mistake of blaming all ills on globalization and multilateral institutions such as the WTO has yielded some very strange bedfellows. Environmentally concerned protestors have been treating labor unions and poor countries as comrades in arms, proud of the fact that a disparate set of groups have supposedly been brought together by a shared opposition to globalization. But in fact, some of these groups are on the other side of the environmental issue. U.S. labor unions are strong opponents of the Kyoto Protocol on Global Climate Change. Poor countries tend to be strong opponents of international environmental agreements in general. Both groups cite national sovereignty in support of their positions. It is particularly puzzling that some environmentalists see pro-sovereignty supporters as natural allies, when so many environmental problems in fact need to be addressed by means of multilateral institutions that in fact infringe on national sovereignty.

If labor unions and environmentalists can come together on an issue, that is fine. *But they have to agree on that issue.* They should share something more than an emotional antipathy to some particular multilateral institution: they should want the institution to move in the same direction, not opposite directions. They don't have to get into fine details, if they don't want to. But if, for example, one group thinks that the proper response to globalization is that the multilateral institutions should exercise less invasion of national sovereignty in the pursuit of environmental regulation and the other thinks the institutions should exercise more invasion of national sovereignty in that pursuit, then they are in truth hardly allies.

INTERNATIONAL AGREEMENTS AND INSTITUTIONS

Those who live in the world of international trade negotiations tell those who live in the environmentalist world along the lines that their concerns may be valid, but that they should address them by their own, separate, negotiations, and their own multilateral agencies.

Multilateral Environmental Organizations

The one multilateral organization dedicated to environmental issues in general, the United Nations Environmental Program, is universally considered small and weak, even by the standards of UN agencies. Some may favor beefing it up. Many feel that it is not fixable, that—to begin with—it would have to be based somewhere like Geneva in order to be taken seriously, not in Nairobi as now. On these grounds, some have proposed a new, powerful, multilateral World Environment Organization. Daniel Esty (1994) has proposed that it be called the Global Environmental Organization, providing the appropriate acronym GEO. But the source of the problem is not some accident of bureaucratic design history or geography. The problem, rather, is that there is very little support among the world's governments for a powerful multilateral agency in the area of the environment. They fear infringement on their sovereignty.

One can say that in concentrating their fire on the WTO, environmental activists are adopting a strategy of taking the multilateral trading system hostage. They envy the relative success of the WTO system. They are aware that international environmental treaties, even if successfully negotiated and ratified, may be toothless. The agreements made at Rio de Janeiro in 1992 are an example. The activists would ideally like to adopt trade sanctions as a means of enforcement, as does the WTO itself.

Such proposals do not explain attempts to take globalization hostage more broadly, for example by demonstrations at WTO ministerial meetings. There is nothing in the WTO to block multilateral environmental treaties from adopting penalties against relevant trade with nonmembers. Indeed, the Montreal Protocol on stratospheric ozone depletion has such trade controls, ran into no problems under international trade rules, and is generally considered to have been successful in achieving its goals. Admittedly there is strong resistance in other cases. Most governments do not favor international environmental agreements that are so aggressive as to include trade sanctions. Again, the failure does not mean that globalization and global institutions like the WTO are the problem. More likely it is the other way around: globalization is the ally, and national sovereignty is the obstacle.

Bilateral and Regional FTAs

Regional and bilateral agreements, such as the European Union or the Australia-New Zealand Closer Economic Relationship, have incorporated environmental components more often than have multilateral agreements. Whether because of cultural homogeneity or the small numbers involved, a group consisting of a few neighbors is usually readier to contemplate the sort of "deep integration" required for harmonization of environmental standards than are negotiators in groups with more than 100 diverse members, such as the WTO.

In the public debate over the North American Free Trade Agreement, one of the most prominent concerns of opponents was the pollution that had already accompanied industrialization in northern Mexico, particularly among the *maquilladoras* along the border, which in turn was a result of the ability to trade with the United States. The final agreement departed from previous U.S. trade agreements, or those in most other parts of the world, by taking into account environmental concerns, at least in a small way. The preamble includes environmentally friendly language, such as a stipulation that the NAFTA goals are to be pursued "in a manner consistent with environmental protection and conservation." Chapter 7B allows the member countries to continue adopting sanitary and phyto-sanitary standards. Chapter 9 allows countries to set whatever environmental standards they want, provided only that they do not discriminate or discourage trade unnecessarily.

Nevertheless, environmental groups were unhappy with the subsequent outcome. Proposed side-agreements, for example, to establish a bank to finance environmental clean-up along the border, received a lot of attention during Bill Clinton's presidential campaign and during the subsequent NAFTA ratification campaign. Follow-up after the NAFTA went into effect in 1994, however, was disappointing.

Meanwhile, provisions under Chapter 11, which governs direct investment, have turned out to be important. On the one hand, the text reads "the Parties recognize that it is inappropriate to encourage investment by relaxing domestic health, safety or environmental measures." On the other hand, protection of the rights of investors has confirmed some environmentalists' fears, particularly a case brought by a Canadian company called Metalclad under the dispute settlement mechanism. Under a clause that forbids a signatory from taking measures "tantamount to nationalization or expropriation" of firms from other member countries, Metalclad in August 2000 won a judgment from a NAFTA tribunal against a local Mexican regulators' attempt to close its hazardous waste disposal plant without compensation. The finding that Mexican regulation had denied a foreign firm fair and equitable treatment was potentially an important precedent under the NAFTA. But it would be strange, even from a pro-business viewpoint, if an American or Canadian firm were extensively protected against regulatory "takings" in Mexico when it would not be protected in its country of origin.

The NAFTA experience reinforced environmentalists' concerns with trade agreements. They urged the U.S. government to bring environmental issues inside trade negotiations, for example, forbidding parties in trade agreements from relaxing environmental regulation in order to seek competitive advantage. A preferential trading arrangement negotiated by the United States at the end of the Clinton Administration, the Jordan-U.S. free trade agreement, incorporated such environmental provisions directly in the text, rather than as a side agreement, a precedent that was hoped to establish a "template" or precedent for future agreements. In addition, an Executive Order now requires that the government prepare an "environmental impact statement" whenever negotiating new trade agreements in the future, to guard against possible inadvertent side-effects adverse to the environment. . . .

The WTO and Some Panel Cases

In the postwar period, the vehicle for conducting the multilateral negotiations that succeeded in bringing down trade barriers in many countries was the General Agreement on Tariffs and Trade. An important outcome of the Uruguay Round of negotiations was the replacement of the GATT organization with a real agency, the World Trade Organization, which came into existence in 1995. One reason why the change was important is that the new institution featured a dispute settlement mechanism, whose findings were to be binding on the member countries. Previously, a party that did not like the ruling of a GATT panel could reject it.

Why do so many environmentalists apparently feel that the still-young WTO is a hostile power? Allegations concern lack of democratic accountability and negative effects on the environment. It is difficult to see how these allegations could apply to the process of setting WTO rules themselves. Regarding the alleged lack of democracy, the GATT and WTO are in principle one-country one-vote bodies that make decisions by consensus. Clearly in practice, some countries—particularly the United States—matter far more than others. But consider what it would mean to make this process more democratic. It would presumably mean giving less weight to U.S. views and more to the views, for example, of India, the world's most populous democracy. But, given India's preferences and its aversion to "eco-imperialism," this would clearly mean giving *less* attention in the WTO to environmental goals, not more.

The allegation that the GATT and WTO are hostile to environmental measures could conceivably arise from the core provisions of the GATT, which prohibit a member country from discriminating against the exports of another, in favor of "like products" made either by a third country (that is the Most Favored Nation provision of Article I) or by domestic producers (the national treatment provision of Article III). But Article XX allows for exceptions to the nondiscrimination principle for environmental reasons (among others), provided that the measures in question are not "a means of arbitrary or unjustifiable discrimination" or a "disguised restriction on international trade."

Moreover, umbrella clauses allow countries to take actions to protect human, animal or plant life or health, and to conserve exhaustible natural resources.

Under the GATT, there was ambiguity of interpretation as to what was to happen when Article XX conflicted with the nondiscrimination articles. To clarify the matter, language was added to the preamble to the articles agreed to at Marrakech that established the WTO specifying that its objectives were not limited to promoting trade but included also optimal use of the world's resources, sustainable development, and environmental protection. Environmental objectives are also recognized specifically in the WTO agreements dealing with product standards, food safety, intellectual property protection, etc.

The protests are in a sense a puzzle. It would be easy to understand a political campaign in favor of the WTO taking a more aggressive pro-environment stance. But how does one explain the common view in the protest movement that the WTO currently is actively harmful to the environment?

When members of the protest movement identify specifics, they usually mention the rulings of WTO panels under the dispute settlement mechanism. The panels are quasi-judicial tribunals, whose job is to rule in disputes whether parties are abiding by the rules that they have already agreed to. Like most judicial proceedings, the panels themselves are not intended to be democratic. The rulings to date do not show a pattern of having been dominated by any particular country or interest group. There have been three or four fairly prominent WTO panel rulings that concern the environment in some way. Most within the environmentalist and NGO community have at some point acquired the belief that these rulings told the United States, or other defendant country, that their attempts to protect the environment must be repealed. The mystery is why this impression is so widespread, because it has little basis in fact.

The four WTO cases that will be briefly reviewed here are Canadian asbestos, Venezuelan reformulated gasoline, U.S. hormone-fed beef, and Asian shrimp and turtles. We will also touch on the Mexican tuna-dolphin case. Each of the cases involves an environmental measure that the producer plaintiff alleged to have trade-distorting effects. The complaints were not based, however, on the allegation that the goal of the measure was not valid, or that protectionism was the original motivation of the measure. In most of the cases, the allegation was that discrimination against foreigners was an incidental, and unnecessary, feature of the environmental measure.

CANADIAN ASBESTOS. One case is considered a clear win for the environmentalists. The WTO Appellate Body in 2001 upheld a French ban on asbestos products, against a challenge by Canada, which had been exporting to France. This ruling made real the WTO claim that its charter gives priority to health, safety, and environmental requirements, in that for such purposes GATT Article XX explicitly allows exceptions to the Most Favored Nation and national treatment rules.

VENEZUELAN REFORMULATED GASOLINE. In the reformulated gasoline case, Venezuela successfully claimed that U.S. law violated national treatment, i.e., discriminated in favor of domestic producers (with regard to whether refineries were allowed to use individual composition baselines when measuring pollution reduction). The case was unusual in that the intent to discriminate had at the time of passage been made explicit by U.S. administration officials seeking to please a domestic interest group. If the WTO had ruled in the U.S. favor, it would have been saying that it was fine for a country to discriminate needlessly and explicitly against foreign producers so long as the law came under an environmental label. Those who oppose this panel decision provide ready-made ammunition for the viewpoint that environmental activism is a false disguise worn by protectionist interests.

The United States was not blocked in implementing its targets, under the Clean Air Act, as commonly charged. Rather, the offending regulation was easily changed so as to be nondiscriminatory and thus to be permissible under the rules agreed to by members of the WTO. This case sent precisely the right message to the world's governments, that environmental measures should not and need not discriminate against foreign producers.

HORMONE-FED BEEF. What happens if the commodity in question is produced entirely, or almost entirely, by foreign producers, so that it cannot be conclusively demonstrated whether a ban, or other penalty, is or is not discriminatory? The WTO has attempted to maintain the rule that such measures are fine so long as a scientific study has supported the claimed environmental or health benefits of the measure. In the hormone-fed beef case, the WTO ruled against an EU ban on beef raised with growth hormones because the EU conspicuously failed to produce a science-based risk assessment showing that it might be dangerous. It thus resembles the case of the EU moratorium on GMOs.

These are genuinely difficult cases. On the one hand, where popular beliefs regarding a scientific question vary widely, a useful role for a multilateral institution could be to rule on the scientific merits. Or at least a useful role could be, as under the current WTO procedures, to rule on whether the country seeking to impose the regulation has carried out internally a reasonable study of the scientific merits. This logic suggests overruling the EU bans. On the other hand, the world may not be ready for even this mild level of loss of national sovereignty. If a nation's intent is to protect its health or environment, even if the measure has little scientific basis and even if its primary burden would fall on foreign producers, perhaps ensuring that the ban does not unnecessarily discriminate among producing countries is the best that can be done.

Despite the WTO ruling on hormone-fed beef, the Europeans did not cancel the ban. Their strategy, which they justify with the name "precautionary principle," is to continue to study the matter before allowing the product in. The precautionary principle, as the Europeans apply it, says to prohibit new technologies that have not yet been proven safe, even if there is no evidence that they are dangerous. At a minimum, it seems that they should be forced to allow imports of American beef subject to labeling requirements, as in the Montreal agreement on GMOs. Let the consumer decide.

SHRIMP-TURTLE.   Perceptions regarding the WTO panel ruling on a dispute about shrimp imports and the protection of sea turtles probably vary more widely than on any other case. The perception among many environmentalists is that the panel ruling struck down a U.S. law to protect sea turtles that are caught in the nets of shrimp fishermen in the Indian Ocean. (The provision was pursuant to the U.S. Endangered Species Act.) In reality, the dispute resembled the gasoline case in the respect that the ban on imports from countries without adequate regulatory regimes in place was unnecessarily selective and restrictive. The WTO panel and appellate body decided that the U.S. application of the law, in a complex variety of ways, was arbitrarily and unjustifiably discriminatory against the four plaintiff countries (Asian shrimp suppliers). The United States had unilaterally and inflexibly banned shrimp imports from countries that did not have in place for all production a specific turtle-protection regime of its own liking, one that mandated Turtle Excluder Devices.

The case could in fact be considered a victory for the environmentalists, in that the WTO panel and the appeals body in 1998 explicitly stated that the United States could pursue the protection of endangered sea turtles against foreign fishermen. The United States subsequently allowed more flexibility in its regulation, and made good-faith efforts to negotiate an agreement with the Asian producers, which is what it should have done in the first place. The WTO panel and appellate body in 2001 found the new U.S. regime to be WTO-compliant. The case set a precedent in clarifying support for the principle that the WTO rules allow countries to pass judgment on other countries' Processes and Production Methods, even if it means using trade controls to do so, provided only that the measures are not unnecessarily discriminatory.

TUNA-DOLPHIN.   In an earlier attempt to protect another large flippered sea animal, the United States (under the Marine Mammal Protection Act) had banned imports of tuna from countries that allowed the fishermen to use nets that also caught dolphins. Mexico brought a case before the GATT, as this predated the WTO, and the GATT panel ruled against the U.S. law. Its report was never adopted. The parties instead in effect worked out their differences bilaterally, "out of court." The case could be considered a setback for trade-sensitive environmental measures, at least unilateral ones, but a setback that was to prove temporary. That the GATT ruling in the tuna case did not affirm the right of the United States to use trade bans to protect the dolphins shows how much the environmentalist cause has progressed under the WTO, in the subsequent gasoline, shrimp-turtle, and asbestos cases.

A system for labeling tuna in the U.S. market as either "dolphin safe" or not was later found consistent with the GATT. The American consumer response turned out to be sufficiently great to accomplish the desired purpose. Since 1990, the major companies have sold only the dolphin-safe kind of tuna. The moral is not that the goal of protecting the dolphins was accomplished despite globalization in its GATT incarnation, but rather that *globalization was instrumental in the protection of the dolphins*. The goal could not have been accomplished without international trade, because American citizens would have had no effective way of putting pressure on Mexico. Leaving the U.S. government free to regulate its own fishermen would not have helped.

Multilateral Environmental Agreements

When it comes to global externalities such as endangered species, stratospheric ozone depletion, and global climate change, it is particularly clear that the problem cannot be addressed by a system where each country pursues environmental measures on its own. Multilateral negotiations, agreements, and institutions are required. Furthermore, the point is not simply that global regulatory measures are needed to combat the effects of economic globalization. If countries had industrialized in isolation, without any international trade or investment among them, they would still be emitting greenhouse gases, and we would still need a globally coordinated response.

Multilateral environmental agreements (MEAs), even if they involve trade-restricting measures, are viewed more favorably under the international rules than unilateral environmental measures. Leaving aside the Law of the Sea, the Basel Convention on Hazardous Wastes, and a large number of relatively more minor agreements, three MEAs merit particular mention.

The Convention on International Trade in Endangered Species (CITES) was negotiated in 1973. Although it lacks the teeth that many would like, it was notable as a precedent establishing that MEAs are compatible with the GATT even if they restrict trade. An interesting issue relevant for species protection is whether a plan of using animals to support the economic livelihood of local residents can be a more sustainable form of protection than attempts to leave them untouched altogether.

The Montreal Protocol on Substances that Deplete the Ozone Layer is the most successful example of an MEA, as it has resulted in the phasing out of most use of CFCs (Chlorofluorocarbons) and other ozone-depleting chemicals. The success of this agreement is partly attributable to the enforcement role played by trade penalties: the protocol prohibits trade in controlled substances with countries that do not participate. This created the necessary incentive to push those developing countries that otherwise might have been reluctant into joining. If substantial numbers of countries had nevertheless remained outside the protocol, the trade controls would have also accomplished the second objective—minimizing *leakage*, that is, the migration of production of banned substances to nonparticipating countries. One reason why the protocol succeeded was there were a relatively small number of producers. It also helped that there turned out to be good substitutes for the banned substances, though that was not known until the ban was tried. One might say it also helped establish the principle that PPM-targeted measures were not necessarily incompatible with the GATT: the agreement threatened nonparticipants not only with a ban on trade in ozone-depleting chemicals themselves, but also a potential ban on trade in goods manufactured with such chemicals in the sense that governments were required to determine the feasibility of such a ban. But it never went further than that.

The Kyoto Protocol on Global Climate Change, negotiated in 1997, is the most ambitious attempt at a multilateral environment agreement to date. This is not the place to discuss the Kyoto Protocol at length. The task of addressing Climate Change while satisfying the political constraints of the various factions (particularly, the United States, EU, and developing countries) was an inherently impossible task. Most economists emphasize that the agreement as it was written at Kyoto would impose large economic costs on the United States and other countries, while making only a minor dent in the problem. The Clinton Administration's interpretation of the protocol insisted on so-called flexibility mechanisms, such as international trading of emission permits, to bring the economic costs down to a modest range. This interpretation was rejected by the Europeans at the Hague in November 2000. Without the flexibility mechanisms, the United States would be out of the protocol, even if the subsequent administration had been more environmentally friendly than it was. (Ironically, now that European and other countries are trying to go ahead without the United States, they are finding that they cannot manage without such trading mechanisms.)

Even most of those who for one reason or another do not believe that Kyoto was a useful step, however, should acknowledge that multilateral agreements will be necessary if the problem of Global Climate Change is to be tackled. The Bush administration has yet to face up to this. The point for present purposes is that a system in which each country insists, based on an appeal to national sovereignty, that it be left to formulate environmental policies on its own, would be a world in which global externalities like greenhouse gas emissions would not be effectively addressed.

SUMMARY OF CONCLUSIONS

The relationship between globalization and the environment is too complex to sum up in a single judgment—whether "good" or "bad." In many respects, global trade and investment operate like other sources of economic growth. They tend to raise income as measured in the marketplace. On the one hand, the higher scale of output can mean more pollution, deforestation, and other kinds of environmental damage. On the other hand, changes in the composition and techniques of economic activity can lower the damage relative to income. Although it is not possible to generalize universally about the net effect of these channels, it is possible to put forward general answers to some major questions.

- A key question is whether openness to international trade undermines national attempts at environmental regulation, through a "race to the bottom" effect. This no doubt happens sometimes. But there is little statistical evidence, across countries, that the unfavorable effects on average outweigh favorable "gains from trade" effects on measures of pollution, such as SO_2 concentrations. If anything, the answer seems to be that favorable effects dominate.
- Perceptions that WTO panel rulings have interfered with the ability of individual countries to pursue environmental goals are poorly informed. In cases such as Canadian asbestos, Venezuelan gasoline, and Asian shrimp, the rulings have confirmed that countries can enact environmental measures, even if they affect trade and even if they concern others' Processes and Production Methods (PPMs), provided the measures do not unnecessarily discriminate among producer countries.
- People care both about the environment and the economy. As their real income rises, their demand for environmental quality rises. Under the right conditions, this can translate into environmental progress. The right conditions include democracy, effective regulation, and externalities that are largely confined within national borders and are therefore amenable to national regulation.
- Increasingly, however, environmental problems do in fact spill across national borders. The strongest examples are pure global externalities such as global climate change and ozone depletion. Economic growth alone will not address such problems, in a system where each country acts individually, due to the free rider problem. International institutions are required. This would be equally true in the absence of international trade. Indeed, trade offers a handle whereby citizens of one country can exercise a role in environmental problems of other countries that they would otherwise not have. Consumer labeling campaigns and corporate codes of conduct are examples.
- Many aspects of the environment that might have been considered purely domestic matters in the past, or that foreign residents might not even have known about, are increasingly of concern to those living in other countries. This again means that multilateral institutions are needed to address the issues, and expressions of national sovereignty are the obstacle, not the other way around. Indeed, if one broadens the definition of globalization, beyond international trade and investment, to include the globalization of ideas and of NGO activities, then one can see the international environmental movement as itself an example of globalization.

REFERENCES

Antweiler, Werner, Brian Copeland, and M. Scott Taylor. 2001. "Is Free Trade Good for the Environment?" *NBER Working Paper* No. 6707. *American Economic Review* 91, no. 4 (September): 877–908.

Copeland, Brian, and M. Scott Taylor. 2001. "International Trade and the Environment: A Framework for Analysis." *NBER Working Paper* No. 8540, Oct.

———. 2003. *Trade and the Environment: Theory and Evidence*. Princeton: Princeton University Press.

Dean, Judy. 2002. "Does Trade Liberalization Harm the Environment? A New Test." *Canadian Journal of Economics* 35, no. 4 (November): 819–42.

Eiras, Ana, and Brett Schaefer. 2001. "Trade: The Best Way to Protect the Environment." *Backgrounder*, The Heritage Foundation no. 1480, September 27.

Esty, Daniel. 1994. *Greening the GATT: Trade, Environment, and the Future*. Washington, DC: Institute for International Economics.

Esty, Daniel, and Bradford Gentry. 1997. "Foreign Investment, Globalisation, and the Environment." In *Globalization and the Environment*, ed. Tom Jones. Paris: Organization for Economic Cooperation and Development.

Frankel, Jeffrey, and Andrew Rose. 2003. "Is Trade Good or Bad for the Environment? Sorting Out the Causality." RWP03–038, Kennedy School of Government, Harvard University, September. Revised version of NBER Working Paper 9201. Forthcoming, *Review of Economics and Statistics*.

Grossman, Gene, and Alan Krueger. 1993. "Environmental Impacts of a North American Free Trade Agreement." In *The U.S.-Mexico Free Trade Agreement*, ed. Peter Garber. Cambridge: MIT Press.

———. 1995. "Economic Growth and the Environment." *Quarterly Journal of Economics* 110, no. 2 (May): 353–77.

Harbaugh, William, Arik Levinson, and David Wilson. 2000. "Reexamining the Empirical Evidence for an Environmental Kuznets Curve." *NBER Working Paper* No. 7711, May.

Lucas, Robert E.B., David Wheeler, and Hememala Hettige. 1992. "Economic Development, Environmental Regulation and the International Migration of Toxic Industrial Pollution: 1960–1988." In *International Trade and the Environment*, ed. Patrick Low. World Bank Discussion Papers no. 159. Washington, DC: The World Bank.

World Bank. 1992. *Development and the Environment*. World Development Report.

30

The Fair Trade Challenge to Embedded Liberalism
SEAN D. EHRLICH

Many Americans profess to be opposed to international trade for reasons that have little to do with their own narrow interests—global environmental concerns and objections to sweatshop working conditions in developing countries are often given as reasons to be critical of globalization. Sean D. Ehrlich examines the fair trade movement and finds that it is not just a cover for protectionist self-interest. Rather, the left-wing Americans that hold these views tend to be legitimately concerned with globalization's impact on the environment and on labor standards in poor countries. Ehrlich concludes that, since this movement is not self-interested, it poses a threat to the postwar compromise that conjoined free trade with compensatory welfare benefits extended to the people that are harmed by globalization.

The past decade has seen a veritable explosion of research on public opinion on trade policy in both political science and economics. The earliest work in this research agenda investigated whether the determinants of trade policy preferences were in line with economic theories of the individual-level effects of trade and were frequently used to test Stolper-Samuelson models of trade against Ricardo—Viner models to determine whether trade policy preferences were determined by class or industry cleavages. A recent branch of this research agenda, such as Hays, Ehrlich, and Peinhardt (2005) and Mayda, O'Rourke, and Sinnott (2007), has begun to examine how policymakers can manage public opinion toward trade, investigating the role of compensation policies on preference formation in line with Ruggie's (1982) Embedded Liberalism Thesis, which argues that policymakers can increase support for trade by compensating those who may be harmed by trade.

Following the neoliberal economic trade theories that inspired them, these studies have almost universally studied trade policy preferences unidimensionally: respondents are assumed to either support free trade or oppose it. More specifically, the research either assumes that opposition to trade is based on employment-related factors or builds this opposition directly into the trade policy question. In fact, one of the most common questions that researchers analyze to determine trade policy preferences is as follows: "How much do you agree or disagree with each of the following statements? (Respondent's country) should limit the imports of foreign products in order to protect its national economy." This research tends to thus categorize respondents into one of two categories: either they support free trade or they support protection, with "free trade" defined as trade without government barriers and "protection" defined as support for erecting barriers to trade. Given the survey questions asked and the research questions driving the research, it is typically asserted or assumed that the reason for these barriers is to protect domestic jobs from import competition. All opposition to trade is therefore conflated into a single category of protectionism, a term that has gained pejorative connotations given the dominance of neoliberal economic theory suggesting that protection hurts a country's aggregate welfare.

This article argues that this conflation oversimplifies trade policy preferences: one can oppose, or be uncomfortable with, free trade for reasons other than personal employment concerns, and one may wish to erect barriers to trade for reasons other than protecting jobs or the national economy. This possibility has particularly strong implications for the Embedded Liberalism literature in that the compensation policies discussed in this literature are designed to increase support for trade by diminishing the negative employment effects of trade. If opposition to trade is generated by other sources, these compensation policies should be ineffective in increasing support for trade. This is of particular concern because of the increased prominence in policy debates of "fair traders," individuals who express opposition or discomfort with free trade because of the potential negative effects of trade on labor or environmental conditions. In other words, the fair trade debate raises the possibility that trade policy preferences are multidimensional: one can express opposition to trade without being a protectionist and one can express opposition to protection without supporting barrier-free trade.

Most economic analyses of fair trade have assumed away this problem by arguing that fair traders are really "protectionists in disguise," that is, they desire limits to trade to protect their jobs but because neoliberal economic theory has supposedly discredited protection, they need to offer alternative arguments for why they oppose trade. This article argues the opposite: that a significant portion of fair traders are expressing sincere beliefs that trade should be somehow limited or regulated (whether by government or the market) in order to prevent harm to foreign workers or the environment and that fair traders are, to a large extent, fundamentally different from protectionists. If this is true, then previous public opinion research has likely overstated the support for free trade and has drawn overbroad conclusions about who is likely to oppose trade. Furthermore, this has important implications for what policies can be used to manage public support for trade, suggesting that there are limits to how many opponents of trade can be influenced by the compensation policies of embedded liberalism. . . .

To make this case, the article is organized as follows: first, in the next section, the article more precisely defines the terms "free trade," "protection," and "fair trade." Second, the article summarizes the literature on trade policy preference formation, highlighting how the literature tends to dichotomize preferences and the implications of this dichotomization, especially for Embedded Liberalism. Third, the article presents a multidimensional theory of trade policy preference formation and derives hypotheses about who we would expect to support fair trade as a sincere expression of concern for labor and the environment and who we would expect to support it if it is protectionism in disguise. The fourth section introduces the data and methods used to test these hypotheses with the results of these tests presented in the fifth section. The final section concludes by discussing the implications of these findings both for academic and policy debates.

FREE TRADE, PROTECTIONISM, AND FAIR TRADE

This article defines free trade as support for trade with as few restrictions as possible. This is a relatively straightforward definition although it acknowledges that some restrictions have been viewed as allowable even by the most doctrinaire free trader. For instance, the United States bars trade in nuclear material without this being viewed generally as a violation of free trade principles. I define protectionism as expressing concerns about the effects of trade on the domestic economy and wanting to take action to ameliorate those effects; I define fair trade as expressing concerns about the effects of trade on the environment or labor standards and wanting to take action to ameliorate those effects. These two definitions are less straightforward and more controversial, so I provide elaboration and justification below.

These definitions have two important elements that require elaboration. The first is the focus on the motivation behind the concerns, which I posit is the main difference between protectionism and (the current incarnation of) fair trade. Protectionism is concerned with "protecting" the domestic economy from harm: most analyses focus on the number of jobs or the average income of those jobs and average profits from investments, but one can broaden this to include concerns about domestic labor and environmental standards within those jobs. Fair trade, as defined here, focuses on concerns for labor and environmental standards in a country's trading partner. This distinction will be further discussed below.

The second crucial element is that concerns about trade are married to a desire to ameliorate these negative effects. However, the type of action taken is left intentionally vague. In protectionism, the most obvious actions are public policies that limit imports, such as tariffs and quotas, and these policies are the usual frames for analyses of trade policy preferences. In addition, though, other public policies can be used, such as tax breaks or direct subsidies for potentially affected industries, to give them an advantage over foreign competition. Private action is also possible, such as "Buy American" campaigns. In fair trade, the potential actions are more nebulous, in part because of the novelty of the claims and the lack of straightforward attention given to them by academics and policymakers. The actions could include public policies such as limiting imports that do not meet standards, although these policies may run afoul of WTO rules and may be of limited value in raising standards abroad; they could also include private actions, such as labeling and certification systems. The analysis here examines both these public and private strategies given the limited amount of academic attention to either that would provide a baseline for expectations about which fair trade actions are popular and/or effective. Looking at the three definitions together, they have two crucial implications that the rest of this article explores and tests: first, the definitions imply that fair trade public policies and "private" labeling strategies are essentially the same; second, they imply that protectionism and fair trade are different. The rest of this section explores these two implications in turn.

Concerns about the effects of trade on domestic economies have always been expressed and have been one of the leading justifications for restrictions to trade. Fair trade concerns, at least as defined in this article, are of more recent vintage. Although the term "fair trade" has been used for decades to denote circumstances where critics believe trade partners are playing by different rules than the home country, recently, the terminology of fair trade has been largely re-appropriated to focus on the effects of trade on the environment and labor conditions, frequently with a specific, and fairly novel, focus on foreign environmental and labor conditions. The most visible expression of these fair trade concerns is probably the labeling of products that meet "fair trade standards," such as coffee at Starbucks. Other agricultural products, handcrafted goods, and textiles also often fall under this fair trade labeling rubric. In 2002, an international non-governmental organization called the Fair Trade Labeling Organizations International (FLO) created a fair trade label for products meeting certain standards. FLO claims that more than one billion Euro worth of products carrying this label were sold in 2005.

Fair trade is more than just labeling, though, and also includes calls for changes in government policy, as can be seen, in part, by examining the policy proposals of those who support fair trade labeling. For instance, Global Exchange, a prominent progressive advocacy group and leading critic of the WTO, promotes fair trade as an alternative to neoliberal globalization and runs a "Fair Trade Store," but also advocates opposition to additional free trade agreements and opposition to continuing the WTO, both public policy positions. Tucker and Wallach (2009) argue that fair traders oppose extension of fast-track authority, and Wallach (2004) argues that the WTO should be reformed to make it more hospitable to environmental and labor concerns or the United States should withdraw from the WTO. The reforms suggested by Wallach and others include the creation of environmental or social dumping provision that would enable countries to raise tariffs on trading partners with low standards. Finally, there have been calls for domestic legislation to ban or limit imports of products made with poor standards, including the successful implementation in the United States of the 2000 Trade and Development Act that included requirements that trade partners adhere to international standards for child labor. Each of these public policy proposals is ostensibly designed to improve standards abroad or, at least, limit domestic complicity with the poor standards, although critics of these policies, such as the economists discussed below, often argue that the policies will be ineffective at improving standards or that the real motives of the policies' supporters are to protect domestic jobs.

Support for labeling products that meet high standards (and the willingness to pay extra for these products) and support for policies that limit imports of products that fail to meet these standards are certainly different. Although many activists support both, there is no necessary logical connection between the two, and it is possible to support one without supporting the other. This article defines fair trade as encompassing both because it argues that the same underlying concerns motivate both, that is, concern for the effects of trade on labor and environmental standards abroad, so that there should be significant overlap between supporters of each. This is an empirically testable assertion and the survey data described below provides the opportunity to test this assertion by including questions asking respondents about both policy and labeling opinions.

Equally important, and even more controversial, as this conflation of fair trade labeling and fair trade policy is the distinction this article draws between fair trade and protectionism. While the literature on trade policy preferences discussed below tends to unintentionally conflate all opposition to free trade with protectionism, economists who have examined fair trade have tended to intentionally and explicitly conflate fair trade and protectionism. In fact, it is common for this part of the literature to refer to fair trade as nothing more than "protectionism in disguise." . . .

In sum, the standard economic literature on the topic suggests that protectionists use fair trade rhetoric because protectionism has been discredited. Thus, those seeking protectionism must disguise their motives behind more palatable concerns for foreign labor and environmental standards. On the other hand, this article argues that protectionism and fair trade are distinct preference dimensions: one can support fair trade without supporting protection and vice versa, and support for fair trade is (at least by some) sincere. This distinction between fair trade and protectionism is also a testable hypothesis and is, in fact, the major goat of this article. The next section will lay out a theoretical framework for determining whether support for fair trade and protection are different and whether support for fair trade product labeling and fair trade policies that limit trade are properly considered part of the same preference dimension. . . .

A TWO-DIMENSIONAL THEORY OF TRADE POLICY PREFERENCES

As described above, most theories of trade policy preferences assume a single dimension ranging from protectionist to free trade with an individual's location on that dimension determined by the anticipated effect of increased trade on their employment prospects and expected income. If increased trade is expected to reduce employment or income, the individual is more likely to support protection; if increased trade is expected to increase employment or income, the individual is more likely to support free trade. This article argues that this dimension does exist but that another dimension also exists, namely whether an individual has concerns about trade's anticipated effects on the environment and the rights of foreign workers, that is, the fair trade dimension. Combining these two policy dimensions (and assuming, for simplicity, a dichotomization of both dimensions) yields four different trade policy orientations, summarized in Figure 1, as opposed to the two orientations of free trade and protectionism typically assumed. The people in Cell I oppose both protection and fair trade and can be described as free traders. Those in Cell III support fair trade but oppose protection and are, thus, fair traders. Those in Cell II support protection but oppose fair trade; in this article, I refer to them as economic protectionists. Those in Cell IV support both protection and fair trade and are referred to here as general protectionists.

The prevailing economic view on fair trade suggests that the sincere preferences of all individuals fall in either Cells I or IV: if fair trade and protection are the same, then no one should support (oppose) one without supporting (opposing) the other. On the other hand, this view suggests that the revealed preferences of individuals may be different: some people may not want to admit to being protectionist and will disguise their true preferences by admitting to being fair traders. In this view, people should fall into Cells I and III, although some people may be willing to admit their protectionist preferences, so Cell IV should also be represented. However, Cell II should be empty as there is no reason to support protection but oppose fair trade in this view.

FIGURE 1 Trade Policy Orientations

	Oppose Protection	Support Protection
Oppose Fair Trade	**I** Free Traders	**II** Economic Protectionists
Support Fair Trade	**III** Fair Traders	**IV** General Protectionists

The argument of this article—that supporting fair trade can be a sincere preference distinct from supporting protection—suggests two differences from this traditional view. First, people's sincere and revealed preferences should both fall in all four cells as it is possible to sincerely support both fair trade and protection independent of supporting the other policy. Also, it is possible to believe in no limits on trade and thus fall in Cell I, and it is possible to oppose trade so that any limits would be preferable, or to oppose trade both on protectionist and fair trade grounds. No cell should be empty, therefore, as opposed to the traditional view in which one or two cells are empty.

Second, the two views provide different explanations for why people would be in the cell supporting fair trade. The traditional view suggests that the people in this cell would be those who support economic protection (although they provide no explanation to differentiate between chose who fall in this cell and those who fall in the general protection cell). This article's view suggests that the people in this cell would be those who support environmentalism and workers' rights. The forces that tend to explain support for protectionism and environmental and labor standards vary, providing the crucial leverage needed to test the two views against each other.

If fair trade is nothing but protectionism in disguise, then we should expect the same type of people who support protection to also support fair trade, that is, people would fall in the "Fair Trade" cell if they had the attributes usually associated with support for protection described above. In particular, we would expect those who work in export industries and those with high levels of skill and capital to oppose fair trade and those who work in import-competing industries and those with low levels of skill and capital to support fair trade. Unfortunately, the data set used in this study does not include a variable for industry of employment, so the effect of industry on support for fair trade cannot be tested. Variables for skill and capital are included, though, so we can test the effect of factor endowment. Typically, skill is indirectly measured by either education level—assuming that education imparts job-related skills—or by income—assuming that increased skills increases demand for the worker and, thus, the worker's income. Income can also be seen as a proxy for capital. According to economic theory, if fair trade is protectionism in disguise, we should expect low-skilled workers, whether measured by education or income, to support fair trade and high-skilled workers and owners of capital to oppose it. In addition, as discussed in the section above, if fair trade is the same as protectionism, then we should expect women, the old, the married, the unemployed, and the liberal to support fair trade.

If, on the other hand, support for fair trade is a sincere expression of belief in the value of environmental and labor rights, then the people who support fair trade should have the same characteristics as those who support environmental protection, high labor standards, and human rights. Support for these positions, for instance, could all be considered elements of postmaterialism where people express greater concern for quality-of-life issues, such as environmental protection, individual freedom, and self-expression, rather than economic and physical security issues, such as economic growth. Post-materialists are expected to be young, highly educated, and wealthy and to have liberal ideologies. Also, economic security is often a pre-requisite for expressing postmaterialist values; thus, the unemployed should be less likely to be postmaterialist, and the single should be more likely to as well, as they are less likely to have dependents to support and, thus, have a lower threshold for security. Women have also been found to be less postmaterialist, although, as with the gender difference on trade policy, the reason for this is not entirely clear. Overall, these characteristics of post-materialists are the exact opposite of the characteristics of protectionists. In addition, union members might be expected to be more supportive of fair trade, especially as collective bargaining rights are often considered a core element of labor standards. On the other hand, unionized workers often support protection as they view free trade as a threat to their jobs.

Figure 2 summarizes the expectations about which factors influence choosing protection and choosing fair trade (assuming the latter choice is sincere). If fair trade is protectionism in disguise or the equivalent to protectionism, then the factors in the left-most columns should not only explain why respondents support protectionism, but why they support fair trade as well. Thus, Figure 2 lists the predictions of what characteristics fair traders should have, depending on whether they are sincere or protectionists in disguise.

If fair trade is sincere and distinct, then there are four possible policy orientations, as shown in Figure 1. What prediction can we make about why respondents fall into any one of the four categories? Many of the predictors for why someone would support fair trade are the same as why someone would support free trade. For instance, economic theory predicts that people with higher levels of education and income should be more likely to support free trade, as they will benefit from it economically. This article suggests that those with higher levels of education and income should also be more likely to support fair trade, as they are more likely to be postmaterialist. These two effects might cancel out, and we might expect these variables to have *no* influence when distinguishing between a free trader and a fair trader. However, we would expect fair traders to be more educated and have higher incomes than protectionists (both general and economic). In other words, the factors listed in Figure 2 under sincere preferences should explain why respondents choose fair trade instead of one of the variants of protectionism. What might explain the difference between fair traders and free traders? Only two variables have different predicted effects for support for these two orientations: conservatism and union membership. We should, thus, expect fair traders to be less conservative and more likely to be a union member than free traders. Finally, we might expect economic protectionists to be more conservative and less likely to be a union member than are general protectionists, for similar reasons.

FIGURE 2   Factors Affecting Support for Trade Policy Dimension

Support for Protection		Support for Fair Trade	
+	−	+	−
Union	Income	Income	Conservatism
Unemployed	Education	Education	Unemployed
Age	Conservatism	Union	Age
Female			Female
Married			Married

DATA AND METHODS

To test the argument that fair trade support is sincere, we need public opinion data asking questions about fair trade support. The Cooperative Congressional Election Study of 2006 included such questions as part of a larger battery of questions asked of 1,000 respondents before and after the November 2006 elections in the United States. The questions were specifically designed to test the hypotheses offered here.

Two types of questions about fair trade policy were included in the survey. The first set asked questions about the respondents' support for protectionism and fair trade policies. The fair trade question is listed below:

(1) How much do you agree or disagree with each of the following statements? The United States should limit the imports of foreign products made with low labor standards in order to protect the rights of foreign workers.
  1 Strongly Agree
  2 Agree
  3 Neither agree nor disagree
  4 Disagree
  5 Strongly Disagree

The protectionism question is modeled on a standard question about support for free trade vs. protectionism included in many previous surveys and is listed below:

(2) How much do you agree or disagree with each of the following statements? The United States should limit the imports of foreign products in order to protect the U.S. national economy.
  1 Strongly Agree
  2 Agree
  3 Neither agree nor disagree
  4 Disagree
  5 Strongly Disagree

These two policy questions are used to construct the four policy orientations discussed above. If a respondent agreed (answered 1 or 2) with both questions, they are coded as general protectionists. If they agreed with only one question, they are coded as fair traders or economic protectionists, depending on the question with which they agreed. If they agreed with neither (answered 3, 4, or 5), they are coded as free traders. The coding of the 3's, those who neither agree nor disagree with the statements, is arbitrary, but the results presented below are robust to coding the 3's as supporting, instead of opposing, fair trade or protection. . . .

The survey also included numerous demographic questions, allowing for a detailed examination of the expectations discussed above. The analyses below include the following independent variables. *Income* is an ordinal variable measuring family income, ranging from 1 (less than $10,000) to 14 (more than $150,000). *Education* is an ordinal variable measuring educational attainment, ranging from 1 (for no high school) to 6 (for postgraduate degree). *Ideology* is a five-point scale equal to 5 if the respondent is very conservative, 3 if the respondent is moderate, and 1 if the respondent is very liberal. *Unemployment* is a dummy variable measuring whether the respondent is currently unemployed (out of a job and seeking work) or not. *Union* is equal to 1 if the respondent is a current union member and 0 if not. *Age* measures the age of the respondent in years. *Gender* equals 1 if the respondent is female and 0 if the respondent is male. *Married* equals 1 if the respondent is currently married and 0 otherwise. . . .

To evaluate the expectations described above in the policy orientation analysis, we need to know what attributes influence the probability of a respondent falling into one of the four unordered categories relative to each of the other categories. As such, the analysis below will use multinomial probit that estimates the effect of independent variables on the probability a respondent will choose each alternative category over the baseline category. Three of the four categories will be used as the baseline in turn in order to estimate the probability of choosing every category against all of the others. . . .

RESULTS

The results of the analyses strongly confirm the basic argument of this article that a sizable portion of those supporting fair trade are expressing sincere policy positions rather than just being protectionists (in disguise or not). The first piece of evidence to support this contention is an examination of how many people fall in each of the four policy orientations. The standard economic view of fair trade as synonymous with protection would suggest that Cell II and possibly Cell III should be empty. Figure 3 reveals that this is incorrect: there are roughly equal numbers of free traders, fair traders, and general protectionists, and a sizable (though much smaller) number of economic protectionists.

On its own, this evidence may not be particularly compelling. However, the multinomial probit results, presented in Table 1, also strongly support the view that fair trade preferences are sincere expressions of support for labor standards. Looking first at what explains why people choose the other policy orientations instead of free trade, which is listed in Column 1 of the table, the first crucial point is that the factors influencing why people are protectionists (either general or economic) are mostly what trade theory and previous public opinion studies have suggested: higher income respondents are less likely to be protectionists of either flavor, with conservatives less likely and union members and women more likely to be general protectionists. The one anomalous finding here is that women are less likely to be economic protectionists than free traders, which goes against previous findings. Only one factor helps explain why respondents are fair traders rather than free traders, but this factor is in the direction expected by the sincere preferences perspective: the more conservative you are, the less likely you are to support fair trade.

The fair trade orientation is the baseline in Column 2, which demonstrates that factors influencing why respondents fall into the protectionist orientations instead of fair trade are what we would expect from the sincere preferences perspective. Most importantly, the skill variables behave as expected: respondents with higher incomes and education levels are more likely to be fair traders and less likely to be protectionists of either flavor, although the education variable is insignificant for economic protectionists. In addition, as expected, conservatives are more likely to choose one of the protectionist orientations, although this is only significant for economic protectionists. Women are also more likely to be general protectionists but less likely to be economic protectionists than fair traders, continuing the inconsistent results on gender.

Finally, Column 3 lists general protectionists as the baseline and allows us to see why economic and general protectionists differ. As expected, union members are less likely to choose economic protectionism, suggesting that union members want to protect their jobs but also care about promoting labor standards. Also as expected, conservatives are more likely to be economic protectionists than general protectionists. Unexpectedly, gender is significant, with women less likely to be economic protectionists. As found in previous

FIGURE 3 Supporters of Each Orientation

I Free Traders 31.4% (N = 307)	II Economic Protectionists 7.6% (N = 74)
III Fair Traders 30.3% (N = 297)	IV General Protectionists 30.7% (N = 301)

TABLE 1   Multinomial Probit Results about Determinants of Trade Policy Orientation

	Free trade		Fair trade		General protectionist	
	Coefficient	SE	Coefficient	SE	Coefficient	SE
Free trade						
Income	—	—	−0.013	0.025	0.052*	0.026
Education	—	—	−0.022	0.057	0.094	0.057
Female	—	—	−0.044	0.15	−0.324*	0.152
Married	—	—	0.085	0.171	−0.14	0.173
Union	—	—	−0.189	0.272	−0.594*	0.264
Unemployed	—	—	−0.692	0.44	0.128	0.377
Conservative	—	—	0.432**	0.08	0.331**	0.08
Age	—	—	0.006	0.005	0.003	0.005
Fair trade						
Income	0.013	0.025	—	—	0.065*	0.025
Education	0.022	0.057	—	—	0.116*	0.056
Female	0.044	0.15	—	—	−0.28***	0.15
Married	−0.085	0.171	—	—	−0.225	0.169
Union	0.189	0.272	—	—	−0.405	0.248
Unemployed	−0.692	0.44	—	—	−0.564	0.434
Conservative	−0.432**	0.08	—	—	−0.101	0.078
Age	−0.006	0.005	—	—	−0.003	0.005
Economic protection						
Income	−0.093**	0.034	−0.106**	0.034	−0.041	0.35
Education	−0.04	0.077	−0.062	0.077	0.053	0.077
Female	−0.363***	0.205	−0.406*	0.206	−0.687**	0.205
Married	−0.175	0.231	−0.09	0.231	−0.315	0.232
Union	−0.633	0.528	−0.822	0.525	−1.227*	0.519
Unemployed	−0.18	0.498	0.512	0.542	−0.052	0.493
Conservative	0.042	0.11	0.473**	0.111	0.372**	0.11
Age	−0.011	0.007	−0.005	0.007	−0.008	0.007
General protection						
Income	−0.052*	0.026	−0.065*	0.025	—	—
Education	−0.094	0.057	−0.116*	0.056	—	—
Female	0.324*	0.152	0.28***	0.15	—	—
Married	0.14	0.173	0.225	0.169	—	—
Union	0.594*	0.264	0.405	0.248	—	—
Unemployed	−0.128	0.377	0.564	0.434	—	—
Conservative	−0.331**	0.08	0.101	0.078	—	—
Age	−0.003	0.005	0.003	0.005	—	—
N	741		741		741	
Chi-squared	96.39		96.39		96.39	
Log-likelihood	−893.809		−893.809		−893.809	

(NOTES: $*p<.1$; $**p<.05$; $***p<.01$; Constant not reported.)

studies of public opinion on trade policy, gender is consistently a significant predictor, although it is not obvious why women are most likely to fall in the general protectionist category and least likely to fall in the economic protectionist category.[1]

The substantive size of these effects can be seen by examining the predicted probabilities, shown in Table 2, of an individual choosing each of the four orientations, varying one variable at a time while holding all the other variables at their median or, for dummy variables, their mode, with different columns for men and women. The table shows the effects of the three most important variables found above—education, income, and ideology—showing the predicted probabilities at the sample minimum, median, and maximum, as well as the values one standard deviation above and below the median. The effect of gender can best be seen by examining the differences between men and women when holding all the other variables at their median or mode (this will be the case when any of the three listed variables are held at their median): women are 10% more likely to be general protectionists than men (36% vs. 26%) but 4.5% less likely to be economic protectionists (8–3.5%). Women are also slightly less likely to be fair traders (32% for women vs. 34% for men) and free traders (30% vs. 33%).

The effects of the other variables are about the same for men as for women, although they start at different baselines. Looking first at education, one can see that raising the level of education decreases the probability of choosing general protectionism while increasing the probability of choosing both fair and free trade and having very little effect on choosing economic protectionism. Men with some college education are 29% likely to choose general protectionism, 32% likely to choose fair trade, and 31% likely to choose free trade. A two standard deviation increase in the level of education—to having a four-year degree—decreases the probability of choosing general protectionism by about 5% while increasing the probability of choosing fair trade and free trade 4% and 2%, respectively.

Income has a similar effect, although increasing income levels also decreases the probability of choosing economic protectionism in addition to choosing general protectionism. Moving from one standard deviation below the median ($30,00–$39,999) to one standard deviation above the median ($80,000–$99,999) decreases the probability of being either type of protectionist by more than 5% each (30–24% for general protectionists and 11.5–6% for economic protectionists). The same change in income increases the chances of

---

1. All of these results are robust to different specifications that, for instance, drop all the control variables other than ideology, education, and income or that include only education or income and not both. The only major change is that in those comparisons where income is significant and education is not, education becomes significant when income is excluded. This is true for the general protectionists compared to free traders and economic protectionists compared to both free and fair traders.

TABLE 2 Predicted Probabilities of Trade Policy Orientations

	Male				Female			
	General protection	Economic protection	Fair trade	Free trade	General protection	Economic protection	Fair trade	Free trade
Education								
No HS (Min)	0.345	0.087	0.281	0.287	0.452	0.038	0.26	0.25
Some College	0.29	0.083	0.319	0.308	0.39	0.037	0.3	0.273
2-Year Degree (Median)	0.264	0.081	0.338	0.317	0.36	0.036	0.32	0.284
4-Year Degree	0.239	0.078	0.357	0.326	0.33	0.035	0.341	0.294
Postgraduate (Max)	0.215	0.076	0.375	0.334	0.302	0.034	0.361	0.303
Income								
<$10,000 (Min)	0.347	0.189	0.223	0.241	0.471	0.1	0.215	0.218
$30,000–39,999	0.298	0.115	0.296	0.292	0.404	0.054	0.281	0.261
$60,000–$69,999 (Median)	0.264	0.081	0.338	0.317	0.36	0.036	0.32	0.284
$80,000–$99,999	0.241	0.063	0.365	0.332	0.33	0.027	0.346	0.297
>$150,000 (Max)	0.206	0.041	0.404	0.35	0.285	0.017	0.384	0.314
Ideology								
Very Liberal (Min)	0.315	0.027	0.506	0.152	0.403	0.001	0.46	0.127
Liberal	0.296	0.049	0.426	0.229	0.389	0.02	0.394	0.197
Moderate (Median)	0.264	0.081	0.338	0.317	0.36	0.036	0.32	0.284
Conservative	0.221	0.121	0.249	0.409	0.316	0.06	0.244	0.38
Very Conservative (Max)	0.173	0.164	0.169	0.493	0.262	0.089	0.173	0.476

being a fair trader by about 7% (30–36.5%) and the chances of being a free trader by 4% (29–33%). These effects of both education and income highlight the point made above that economic theories of income effects are not the sole driving force for policy orientation: if they were, then increasing education and income should not only decrease the probability of being a protectionist but should also decrease the probability of being a fair trader.

Both education and income have the same pattern of effects on both fair trade and free trade orientations. Ideology, though, strongly distinguishes between these two orientations (as it does between the two protectionist orientations). Liberals have a 43% probability of being fair traders and a 23% probability of being free traders, while this flips for conservatives, who have a 41% probability of being free traders and a 25% probability of being fair traders. In addition, liberals have a 30% probability of being general protectionists but only a 5% probability of being economic protectionists, while conservatives have a 22% probability of being general protectionists and a 12% probability of being economic protectionists. Taking all of these factors together, one can simplify who falls into each policy orientation as follows: rich, educated liberals are fair traders, while rich, educated conservatives are free traders; poor, uneducated liberals are general protectionists, while poor, uneducated conservatives are economic protectionists. That education and income differentiate fair traders from protectionists while only ideology distinguishes fair traders and free traders is highly consistent with the predictions of the sincere preferences view of fair trade and not consistent with the conventional economic view. . . .

CONCLUSIONS

The results of this article strongly support the view that fair trade is, at least partially, a reflection of sincere support for environmental protection and labor standards among the public. Other fair traders may be motivated by economic self-interest, as most previous analyses have suggested, but this is by no means the dominant reason to support fair trade. What are the implications of this finding?

Most important is its implications for the compromise of embedded liberalism. If the theory of embedded liberalism is correct that the postwar free trade consensus has been maintained by increasing the size of the welfare state in order to compensate those who lose their jobs or take on increased risk because of free trade, then the above findings suggest that these compensatory policies may be increasingly less effective in maintaining public support for trade as the fair trade movement grows or increases in prominence. If new opposition to free trade is being generated by sincere concerns for environmental protection and labor standards abroad, then the standard technique of increasing unemployment insurance or job-retraining programs is unlikely to be able to address these concerns and maintain support for free trade. In short, without new policy tools, the fair trade movement may pose a more serious threat to free trade than previous movements opposed to free trade. Although this is only indirectly demonstrated in this article, future research will directly examine whether fair trade support can be diminished through compensation mechanisms.

The fair trade threat to free trade is likely to be exacerbated if the sincere fair traders see their concerns hijacked by traditional protectionists. Scholars sympathetic to the moral concerns of fair trade . . . still fear that interest groups like labor unions may be able to use fair trade to achieve their protectionist ends. By wrapping up their calls for protection in complaints about labor rights abuses, labor unions may be able to increase the number of people who support their demands. The results presented here suggest that this strategy may be profitable: there is a large pool of people who support fair trade who would oppose traditional protectionism. If protectionists can win over these people by marketing their protectionism as a tool to achieve fair trade, they may be able to craft a large enough constituency to get their measures enacted. The results presented here do not demonstrate one way or another whether this strategy would be successful, but it does suggest that . . . fears are legitimate, as the conditions exist that would make success possible. Future research is needed, however, to determine whether protectionist interest groups are willing or able to exploit this demand.

What policy tools might be able to address fair trade concerns? Any answers provided here would have to be purely speculative, of course. One approach attempted by the U.S. government has been to attach labor or environmental side agreements to trade agreements, as was done with NAFTA. Pro-environmental and labor groups have, in general, been disappointed with these agreements, and some environmental groups that supported NAFTA after President Clinton negotiated the side agreements have since switched to opposing new preferential trade agreements (PTAs). On the other hand, Hafner-Burton (2005) demonstrates that PTAs with hard enforcement provisions for human rights abuses are able to improve human rights conditions, while PTAs with only soft enforcement provisions are not effective. The NAFTA side agreement's enforcement mechanisms were quite soft in response to Mexican and Canadian opposition to harder mechanisms. What may be needed, then, are stronger side agreements. Whether the experience with NAFTA's side agreements has soured activist groups in the United States on the entire process and what public opinion on the topic might be are not known given the current state of the research, but this is one potentially effective measure that would be compatible with existing WTO rules.

Finally, the research presented here suggests that the entire literature on trade policy preferences in both political science and economics needs to be expanded. Models of trade policy tend to view policy options as residing on a single continuum from complete free trade to absolute protection, or autarchy. This article's research suggests that we need to move beyond free trade and protection: there is at least one other dimension to the trade policy debate that partially, but not entirely, overlaps with the free trade/protection dimension. One can oppose free trade without supporting protection and oppose protection without supporting free trade. Existing theories about trade policy are ill-equipped to explain when and why this will be the case or what the results of fair trade support will be. As the fair trade movement possibly grows, these theories will become increasingly incapable of predicting and explaining trade policy outcomes. Before we can devise new theories or revise the old ones, though, we need to more fully understand what this new movement is, who supports it, and what their demands are, a process this article will hopefully start.

REFERENCES

Hafner-Burton, Emile M. (2005). Trading Human Rights: How Preferential Trade Agreements Influence Government Repression. *International Organization* 59 (3): 593–629.

Hays, Jude C., Sean D. Enrlich, and Caint Plinhardt. (2005). Government Spending and Public Support for Trade in the OECD. *International Organization* 59 (2): 473–94.

Mayda, Anna M., Kevin H. O'Rourke, and Richard Sinnott. (2007). Risk, Government and Globalizaiton: International Survey Evidence. IUS Discussion Paper No. 218. Available at SSRN: http://ssrn.com/abstract=980939.

Ruggie, John G. (1982). International Regimes, Transactions, and Change: Embedded Liberalism in the Postwar Economic Order. *International Organization* 36 (2): 195–231.

Tucker, Todd, and Lori Wallach. (2009). *The Rise and Fall of Fast Track Authority.* Washington, DC: Public Citizen.

Wallach, Lori. (2004). *Whose Trade Organization? A Comprehensive Guide to the WTO.* New York: New Press.

31

Cooperation and Discord in Global Climate Policy

ROBERT O. KEOHANE AND DAVID G. VICTOR

The optimism of the Environmental Kuznets Curve does not apply to the problem of climate change: as countries get richer, they just keep emitting more and more carbon dioxide. Robert O. Keohane and David G. Victor explain that climate change is a global public goods problem plagued by strong incentives to free ride. They explore the nature of the international interactions and the institutions that will be required to make meaningful progress on climate change. Given the free-rider problem, they argue that progress requires deep international cooperation based on repeated interactions, as well as institutions that provide incentives for all nations to honor their individual contributions to the collective effort.

Over the past three decades, scientific understanding of the climate problem has radically improved, and since the late 1980s there have been continuous diplomatic talks as well as numerous formal agreements on the topic. Central to the diplomatic process have been the 1992 United Nations Framework Convention on Climate Change (UNFCCC) and its Conference of the Parties (COP), which takes place annually. The COP generates many decisions and periodically adopts new accords, such as the 1997 Kyoto Protocol and the recent agreements in Paris in December 2015. Although there is much optimism about the new Paris accords, so far the UNFCCC has had little real impact on emissions.[1] There has been lots of "climate talk" and little "climate action."

In other words, climate politics displays the "organized hypocrisy" that characterizes so much of international relation. To help explain the weakness of multilateral cooperation—and to identify strategies for making cooperation more effective—we turn to literature on international coordination and cooperation, largely from the discipline of political science, with contributions also from economists.

Climate change politics, as currently structured, is not conducive to much cooperation. The structure of the problem—the patterns of interests and incentives for action or inaction facing states—is malign. Because the pollutants that cause climate change mix across national borders in the atmosphere and because the economic effects of controlling those emissions are felt throughout the global economy, actions to protect the climate inherently involve the provision of a global public good.[2] That is, a safe climate system is advantageous to everyone on the planet (to different degrees), but no party can be excluded from these benefits regardless of its own actions. Public goods are typically underprovided in the absence of a governing authority, because each actor has an incentive to free-ride—to gain a beneficial climate while failing to pay its share. The problem of free-riding is worsened by the fact that leaders of states think that cutting emissions will make energy more expensive, adversely affecting national economic competitiveness.

Global public goods are most easily provided when a single dominant country, or a small group, takes the lead. In climate change, however, no such group can readily solve the problem. The two largest emitters—China (23%) and the United States (12%)—together account for only about one-third of world net emissions of warming gases. Global public goods can emerge, as well, when a global governing authority is already in place. Yet no such authority exists, although the Paris process may, in time, yield one. Thus, by the underlying structure of the problem itself, most states have strong incentives to avoid costly unilateral action, to wait for others to act and to negotiate for self-interested advantages. Breaking this gridlock requires building international institutions that help to promote collaboration.

Collaboration is the most encompassing concept to describe joint international action to achieve mutual gains. Collaboration can take many forms along a continuum from coordination to cooperation. In situations of coordination, agreements are self-enforcing, that is, once an agreement has been made, the parties do not have incentives to defect from it. For instance, once everyone in the United States understands that Americans drive on the right-hand side of the road, no rational driver has an incentive to drive on the left, and vice versa for drivers in the United Kingdom. Cooperation, by contrast, is

TABLE 1 Prospects for Coordination and Cooperation under Four Different Conditions

	Potential joint gains are high	Potential joint gains are low
Agreements are not self-enforcing (cooperation is required for collaboration)	Possible cooperation with high rewards, but with dangers of defection that rise with the depth of cooperation.	Little incentive to seek to cooperate, although shallowness of cooperation limits dangers of defection.
Agreements are self-enforcing (coordination is sufficient for collaboration)	Likely coordination, with limited but realizable gains, often leaving potential gains "on the table"	Easy coordination, limited by the low level of potential gains.

not self-enforcing. In the famous game of "Prisoners' Dilemma," for instance, each player has an incentive to confess, implicating his partner in crime in return for a lighter sentence. The deep coordination needed between states to provide public goods has a similar structure. We develop a simple framework, revolving around Table 1, which helps to explain the observed combination of persistent negotiations with disappointing outcomes in terms of real impacts on emissions that can stop global climate change. Put differently, Table 1 describes the political structure of efforts to collaborate to solve common problems such as global climate change. Making progress on solutions will require both understanding and manipulation of these political structures.

STRUCTURE

The two most important variables that affect prospects for collaboration are shown in Table 1. As shown in the columns, larger prospective joint gains generate incentives for joint action. The second variable concerns whether collaboration is self-enforcing. When agreements are not self-enforcing, coordination is insufficient because parties have incentives to defect in order to gain an advantage for themselves. Additional incentives such as penalties or rewards for good behavior are required to induce cooperation, so collaboration is more reliable when agreements are self-enforcing. However, agreements with the greatest potential for joint gains often cannot be structured in a self-enforcing way—thus creating for policy makers a tradeoff between greater potential gains and an increased likelihood of achieving at least some collaboration. Although self-enforcing cooperation is more reliable, it may also be shallow.

The most important and interesting cases are in the left-hand column of Table 1, where the potential joint gains are high. In the upper-left quadrant are the crucial situations where there are large potential gains from cooperation but strong incentives for parties to shirk from doing their share. Deep mitigation of warming emissions is a good example. As the gains from joint action on this public good rise, so does the temptation to defect. Effective action on mitigation of climate change requires policies and institutions that reduce that temptation.

In this upper-left quadrant, cooperation can emerge, but does so typically as the result of participants devising institutions that create patterns of reciprocity. Engaged in repeated interactions in which payoffs grow over long periods of time, participants have incentives to continue to cooperate to induce their partners to do so as well. Much of the huge success with international trade cooperation follows this logic. Despite the immediate incentives for individual countries to violate trade agreements, the World Trade Organization (WTO) and other trade institutions have helped focus political leaders on the need to preserve the long-term benefits of an open global trading system. The WTO works largely because trade is essentially bilateral, facilitating the use of reciprocity: if one state violates its commitments, the victims of its action can be authorized to retaliate.[3]

In the lower-left quadrant of Table 1, coordination is sufficient to achieve joint gains. Often, diplomats shift problems from the difficult cooperation box, in which incentives to defect are high, to the much easier coordination box, which has low incentives to defect. Over the 60 years of international diplomacy on trade, for example, international agreements began by focusing on the highest tariffs, the reduction of which was clearly in the self-interest of countries and thus self-enforcing. As confidence grew, it became feasible to construct the WTO, with binding rules, adjudication and enforcement mechanisms. The 1987 Montreal Protocol on Substances that Deplete the Ozone Layer began as a prime example of successful coordination, in which countries adopted national policies offering benefits to the United States and the European Union (EU) that exceeded the cost by a wide margin. Deeper cooperation followed later. However, this strategy of shifting hard problems to an easier structure comes with risks if collaboration remains shallow, enabling the parties to capture only a portion of the potential gains that could, in principle, be available.

As noted above, collaboration can also emerge when a single participant or small group finds it worthwhile to bear the expense. Many alliances, for example, provide a public good of security for a set of countries. In the hegemonic variant, the biggest partner (the "hegemon") pays most of the cost. In the club variant, a relatively small number of members share the cost. For decades, the North Atlantic Treaty Organization alliance and the U.S.–Japan security alliance have operated in this way, sharing costs but with the United States paying the predominant share. This is essentially a situation of coordination in which incentives to defect are low. Such situations are quite stable but tend to be organized around the interests of the hegemon.

The right-hand column of Table 1 is somewhat less interesting, but parallel. The November 2014 U.S.–China bilateral agreement on emissions and cooperative research exemplifies easy coordination (lower-right quadrant). The United States and China announced individual as well as joint efforts to address a global problem, limiting themselves to efforts that aligned with their self-interest and initially providing small joint gains. Many initiatives announced in Paris—such as those on innovation, protection of forests, and regulation of potent short-lived climate pollutants—can also be seen as examples of relatively easy coordination. When such easy but shallow coordination is unsatisfactory to participants, they have incentives to press for deeper cooperation. Here, as elsewhere, cooperation derives not from harmony but from discovering areas of discord where additional collaboration—moving west and northwest on Table 1—would provide additional gains. Insofar as this logic applies, cooperation could arise from such coordination within small groups of countries, and other actors dissatisfied with the status quo. It seems clear, for instance, that the U.S.–China accord of November 2014 was important in generating incentives for other countries to make meaningful pledges of action as part of the Paris process.

In the upper-right quadrant, cooperation is difficult and potential joint gains are low. Efforts to create an international cooperative regime for managing deep-sea mining are an example: as countries learned that such activities would be less profitable than originally imagined, efforts to generate cooperation on this heated topic faded away.

The situations in Table 1 are stylized, omitting an important feature of all negotiations: domestic politics. Attempts at international collaboration engage interest groups within countries that can favor (or oppose) it. One lesson from the highly successful accords on international trade is that successful multilateral institutions create interest groups that favor collaboration. Liberal trade institutions strengthen exporters. In turn, exporters pressure and work with sympathetic government agencies that also seek liberal policy reforms—an alliance that was on display, for example, when domestic political forces within China mobilized to favor that country joining the WTO. In almost every major area of international collaboration, domestic interest groups play essential roles in this way—allowing early steps toward coordination to create stronger internal political forces that beget deeper cooperation. For example, global financial institutions provide openings for banks to help shape regulatory rules; and human rights institutions provide leverage for civil society groups seeking to improve domestic human rights performance. This topic is ripe for further investigation in the study of climate change.[4] Under what conditions do domestic civil society groups working on climate change gain leverage from participation in international institutions, and could different institutions mobilize stronger interest groups within countries to favor international collaboration? Will the credibility of international accords, such as those adopted in Paris, help form political interest groups working across borders to strengthen national policies in ways that make deeper cooperation possible? Under what conditions might successful international collaboration also create backlashes that bedevil further efforts to deepen cooperation?

The distinction between shallow coordination and deep cooperation helps to explain why there has been massive diplomatic activity on climate change but little progress on the difficult task of cutting emissions. The coordination–cooperation distinction also suggests how progress could be made on climate change. If the toughest problems are tackled first, deadlock is likely to result. Examples include the failed effort by governments to reach agreement on a meaningful new treaty at the Copenhagen conference in 2009 to replace the original Kyoto Protocol. Too many issues with too many fissures of disagreement were packaged into an accord that required too many countries to consent before it could become law. It is crucial to move from shallow coordination towards deeper cooperation, while at the same time creating the conditions for favourable political coalitions within countries. Much of the enthusiasm around the larger role for "bottom-up" cooperation on climate change, as was on display in Paris, is rooted in this idea of building cooperation by working on smaller, easier problems and in smaller groups where progress is feasible. Effective cooperation requires focusing on areas where agreement is feasible and then working with reciprocity-based strategies that are known to promote deeper collaboration over time.

Our analysis also has implications for the construction of appropriate climate policy institutions. Deep cooperation hinges on repeated interactions and on incentives for parties to make their contribution to the collective effort. Much research on international cooperation therefore focuses on the roles of institutions; that is, persistent and connected sets of formal and informal rules, coupled with related organizations. Institutions establish focal points for coordination, reduce uncertainty about the behavior of other states, and reduce the costs of making and enforcing agreements. Properly constituted, they influence practices and discourses within states, helping government officials and interest groups favoring cooperation to exert more leverage over government policies and the behavior of firms. Institutions also disproportionately reflect the preferences of powerful states, a reality that needs to be taken into account. Poorly constituted or badly functioning institutions may inhibit collaboration, as their rules and practices are difficult to alter. For instance, in the UNFCCC, disagreements dating back to the earliest days of that institution prevented it from developing any formal rules (other than consensus) for making even the most trivial decisions. Effective policies to promote cooperation on climate change mitigation will require appropriate institutions. . . .

It is tempting to imagine that once general agreement has been reached on the nature of the climate change problem—for example, agreement that warming should be stopped at 1.5 or 2°C, as was visibly codified in Paris— appropriate institutions will emerge and that optimal mitigation strategies discovered by economic analysis will somehow follow suit. One of the central insights from political science is that optimal institutions often don't emerge, even when there are large potential gains to be had. Rather, strategies are needed to create those institutions. We now turn to conditions for institutional development, looking first at the underlying preferences of governments and other essential players, and then at the strategies for building effective collaboration.

PREFERENCES

Whether governments will agree to cooperate by investing in institutions depends on their preferences. The major countries vary in population, affluence, technology, and vulnerability to climate impacts—factors that, among others, affect how much they are willing to pay to address global climate change. They also vary in their capacity to design and implement the policies that could alter emissions trajectories. Such diversity in circumstances leads to huge variations in the preferences of countries.

Yet empirical research on national preferences has been plagued by the fact that governments often avoid making their real preferences clear. The combination of general promises about acting on climate change with an unwillingness to pay substantially to achieve nominal goals leads, as noted above, to organized hypocrisy.

The negotiating process that was established in preparation for the Paris COP may make it much easier to observe reliably what countries seek. This process is based on countries submitting pledges—"intended nationally determined contributions" (INDCs)—specifying proposed policy measures, especially in the period up to 2030. The INDCs offer nearly complete coverage, as 184 countries had submitted an INDC by the time the Paris conference opened in November 2015. When governments formally join the Paris Agreement, they will have the opportunity to offer new pledges—known more simply as Nationally Determined Contributions.

As with an earlier system of "national communications" under the UNFCCC, INDCs vary in the extent to which they contain misleading promises and politically motivated information. So far, the aggregate contribution of the INDCs to keeping climate change to the 2°C limit is small, with emissions continuing to rise to 2030 even if all intended measures are implemented. Nonetheless, they are a first step in building a system that creates incentives to reveal more reliably their actual and proposed contributions to global emission cuts. Indeed, the mere existence of these pledges has prompted an array of nongovernmental organizations and other analysts to assess their content, fill in the missing pieces and evaluate which of the pledged actions are plausible.

For political scientists, these pledges can reveal a lot about national preferences that, previously, were impossible to observe systematically. Research on this topic should begin with a system of categories based on what countries might be trying to achieve with their pledges. We offer a preliminary list of motivations for action in Box 1, which shows that countries are motivated by many different factors when they make national climate pledges.

Applying the categories in Box 1, we can see the great variation among countries in incentives to take climate action. China, the biggest emitter, follows the logic of points 2 and 3. Its INDC and underlying policies emphasize the overlap between national pollution control, energy security objectives and global emissions controls, and it is also aiming to build new export industries in clean energy. It shares the objective of building new export industries with the United States, as revealed in the November 2014 bilateral agreement. In addition, both countries have reputational incentives (point 5) to be perceived as global leaders, albeit not at an excessive cost. In their INDCs and other related policy statements, Brazil and Indonesia—the most forested nations on Earth—have emphasized national public goods (point 2) and side-payments (point 4). Some countries remain largely uninterested in collaboration unless it aligns perfectly with local interests. Saudi Arabia's seven-page INDC, submitted long after other countries had already issued their pledges, simply

BOX 1 The Range of Interests Reflected in National Pledges

(1) **Create the global public good of reduced climate change.** It might be thought that most countries seek to contribute to a global public good. But only a small fraction of world emissions—perhaps one-quarter or less—comes from jurisdictions such as the EU and some regions in the United States (for example, California and the northeast)—that are primarily motivated by global public goods. For the rest, other logics drive preferences.

(2) **Create local or national public goods that happen to address, as well, the global public good of climate change.** An example is provided by measures to reduce emissions of soot, or black carbon, which both cause local health problems and contribute to global warming. One of the important advances in climate science over the past decade has been to understand how these "co-benefits" are linked to global climate change. However, most climate science has analyzed these links by starting with policies aimed at slowing global warming and showing the local or national co-benefits. A political analysis would emphasize the local benefits, as these often drive policy decisions.

(3) **Generate competitive economic benefits, such as the creation of new industries—solar, wind, batteries.** Governments will be more interested in emission regulations at home and abroad inso-far as they believe that they have competitive advantage, real or potential, in zero-carbon industries, such as solar and wind power. But they may, at the same time, persist in high-emissions activities, especially where vested interests—for instance, in coal power—are strong, so their search for economic benefits can be beneficial or harmful from the standpoint of mitigating climate change.

(4) **Bargain for side payments, such as requests for money to help pay the cost of controlling emissions and adapting to climate change.** This motivation is likely to be especially strong for relatively poor developing countries, particularly those countries likely to bear significant costs as they prepare for and adapt to rising sea levels, more extreme weather and other effects of global climate change.

(5) **Create reputational benefits.** Governments have stakes in a wide variety of issues, and may find it advantageous to be seen as leaders in providing global public goods. According to J. S. Nye, doing so may enhance their "soft power."[5] For other states, as climate pledges become the norm, it could be important not to be stigmatized as a non-cooperator, which could hurt the state with respect to issues in which it has clear interests.

describes what Saudi Arabia is already planning, highlighting the country's vulnerability not just to climate change but also to curtailment of the sale of carbon-based fuels.

Only a small fraction of world emissions—perhaps one-quarter or less— comes from countries such as the members of the EU and plausibly the United States that are adopting policies mainly for the purpose of providing global public goods (point 1 in Box 1). This helps explain why making progress on climate change requires looking more broadly at other preferences, and why international cooperation on climate change has such complex motivations behind it. Nonetheless, most world emissions come from countries that favor at least some degree of action on climate change, for whatever reasons; so genuine cooperation is imaginable. That is, one could envisage a situation in which the world moved to the upper-left quadrant of Table 1. Furthermore, effective domestic political mobilization and transnational networking could move the preferences of some states further towards additional costly action.

Yet, as interests in serious action on climate change are not universally shared, and many laggard countries are resistant to domestic and transnational pressure, institutions such as the UNFCCC that require near-universal consensus are likely to make only modest progress. Even states that would conditionally be willing to do more are unlikely to offer ambitious policies, insofar as such policies would make sense for them only in the context of an ambitious agreement in which all major polluters participated. Such an agreement is not in prospect and bold demands for such a regime to be created are not credible. In the language used above, the current collection of INDCs reflects shallow coordination: not negligible, but not nearly ambitious enough to stop the build-up of warming gases in the atmosphere. Without new incentives for action, climate change collaboration is firmly stuck now in the lower-left quadrant of Table 1. What could be done to make more progress in ways that reflect the diversity in national preferences and capabilities?

STRATEGIES TOWARDS DEEP COOPERATION

Given the political structure of the climate change problem and the preferences of governments, our next step . . . concerns the strategies that could lead beyond shallow coordination to deeper and more effective collective action. We can view these strategies as attempts to activate causal mechanisms that align with state preferences, reinforcing preferences for effective action, such as through the use of reciprocity, and transforming preferences over time so that countries and other political units favor deeper collaboration.

We now consider six strategies that have been tried in some form. We begin with those that are most comprehensive or intrusive and could therefore have the highest impact—but are difficult to implement—and move towards those at the other end of the impact—likelihood continuum.

- Universal agreements with legally binding targets and timetables (for example, Kyoto). Every state has to fit within the same framework, which ensures that the preferences of some states will not be closely met. As noted above, this strategy of ambitious cooperation falls into the top-left quadrant of Table 1, implying high potential rewards but correspondingly high dangers of defection. Accordingly, efforts to create successors to the Kyoto Protocol have either led to deadlock (Copenhagen) or very low levels of formal participation (Doha).

- Climate clubs. Such clubs would allow cooperation to emerge in small groups, gradually deepening and expanding to cover other countries, either excluding non-members from the benefits that they produce or forcing these non-members to pay for the benefits they receive. Trade sanctions against non-participants are the obvious coercive means, but they are costly to impose. In seeking to solve cooperation problems by punishing defection, the club strategy therefore generates a different cooperation problem—how to induce participants to pay the costs of sanctions. This cooperation problem may or may not be easier to resolve than the original problem of providing the public good of emissions control.

- Coordinated research to invent new technologies that create energy sources that are cheaper than high-carbon fossil fuels. The Montreal Protocol generated new technological changes, which sharply reduced the cost of change and made it easier to achieve progressively tougher targets. Successful technological innovation would have enormous consequences on emissions, suggesting that an active effort to coordinate innovation policies on climate could alter the preference of countries for cooperation in the future. How such a program could be organized remains an area of future work.

- Pledge and review, as in the current Paris process. Each country makes a pledge to reduce emissions, which is reviewed by its peers or through some centralized process. Pledge and review is comprehensive, although one should expect coordination at only a relatively low level to result, unless the review mechanisms are highly effective and designed to engender deeper cooperation and links between countries as they tighten and refocus their pledges on areas of joint gain. . . . By giving scope to states to define their policy actions, pledge and review is politically easier to enact than either binding targets and timetables or a coercive climate club. Optimally, pledge and review would be coupled with a set of institutions designed to promote experimentation so that societies can learn what works. Such approaches require a diversity of experiments, periodic deliberation and penalties for parties that fail to make a contribution. For example, palm oil producers have made substantial progress in cutting deforestation under the threat of losing access to the lucrative EU market for palm oil.

- ■ Coordinated national actions with substantial benefits for the states taking action. The U.S.–China agreement of November 2014 . . . provides an example. Chinese climate efforts will include efforts to cut soot, which causes massive local harm to public health and is also a strong global warming agent. The problem, however, is that these actions are rational for governments to adopt anyway and thus, by themselves, may not engender further collaboration. Analytically, a central challenge in analyzing pledges such as the INDCs is to assess the business as usual (BAU) level of emissions that would occur in the absence of policy and to credit or respond to efforts that cut emissions below BAU. . . .
- ■ Universal agreements on the basis of the lowest common denominator (for example, UNFCCC process agreements). Although feasible, such agreements for minimal coordination lead to few actions beyond what countries would have done anyway.

Strategies two to five probably hold out the most promise. No single negotiating process will deliver a desirable outcome; instead, a diversity of strategies will yield a patchwork of different, partially linked rules and organizations, which we call "regime complexes."[6] . . . The result could be a combination of climate clubs, coordinated research efforts, pledge and review with associated experimentalist processes, and coordination of national policies designed in part to deal with strictly national or local problems. For years, this complex and decentralized outcome has been seen as something to be feared, but our analysis of coordination and cooperation suggests that it could be essential. States should cooperate where cooperation is possible, often on the basis of voluntary groupings; coordinate on issues where cooperation is too difficult or where universal participation is desirable; and probe experimentally to seek to expand the boundaries of feasible cooperation. As no single path is likely to be globally effective on its own, a multiplicity of actions should be taken. . . .

INCREMENTAL CHANGE

Occasionally, world politics is characterized by disruptive change—change that creates new patterns of strategic interaction. For climate, the most plausible disruptions are probably those rooted in technology, such as new cost-effective methods for generating electricity with low or zero emissions. Already, the world has seen how quickly electricity production in the United States has changed as natural gas became cheaper than coal in some markets. Interest groups are emerging around new zero-emission technologies, such as renewables and nuclear. Strong interest groups may yet emerge, as well, for negative emission technologies, as they are vital to deep cuts in net global emissions; at present, however, those technologies are still immature and hypothetical.

Yet those who want effective action on climate change cannot count on technological innovation to appear autonomously and to solve climate problems.

Serious international cooperation will have to emerge incrementally. The fundamental logic of global public goods makes it difficult for countries to create deep cooperation quickly. However, shallow coordination can create vital conditions for deeper cooperation, such as reliable systems for emissions accounting and reporting. And coordination can build confidence, lengthening the time horizons of the players and putting a greater collective focus on the joint gains from deeper cooperation. It can facilitate a dynamic of positive reciprocity, in which greater credibility and confidence facilitate further cooperation. Incremental progress towards cooperation can therefore occur.

But such progress requires those who seek effective action to understand the structures of the problems they are trying to solve and to seek to engage on relatively favorable terrain. Understanding the sources of state preferences—and how they change through persuasion and incentives—can inform more effective cooperation. Strategies based on real preferences, and appropriate incentives, work better than lecturing leaders on their scientific ignorance or simply hoping that good science will ensure that politicians will do the right thing.

Proceeding by small steps to build confidence and generate paterns of reciprocity is not a timid, second-best strategy. Instead, it is essential, because in world politics authority is divided, national preferences vary and there is pervasive suspicion that states seek self-interested gains at the expense of others. Rather than seeking to force policies and institutions into a single, integrated mould—a bold, grand bargain—supporters of effective climate policy must figure out how to operate effectively in a polycentric global system. Success is by no means guaranteed, but incremental policy change that takes polycentrism seriously is at least consistent with the political realities of world politics.

NOTES

1. Victor, D. G. 2011. *Global Warming Gridlock*. Cambridge Univ. Press.

2. Sandler, T. 2004. *Global Collective Action*. Cambridge Univ. Press.

3. Axelrod, R. & R. O. Keohane. 1985. Achieving cooperation under anarchy: strategies and institutions. *World Politics* (38): 226–54.

4. Bang, G. & A. Underdal, eds. 2015. *The Domestic Politics of Global Climate Change: Key Actors in International Climate Cooperation*. Edward Elgar.

5. Nye, J. S. 2004. *Soft Power: The Means to Success in World Politics*. Public Affairs.

6. Keohane, R. O. & D. G. Victor. 2011. The regime complex for climate change. *Perspectives on Politics* (9): 7–23.

32

The Governance of International Finance

JEFFRY A. FRIEDEN

Preventing international financial crises, and reducing their costs once they occur, is just as much a global public good as preventing global warming. Jeffry A. Frieden explains that, because international financial stability benefits all nations, whether they contribute to it or not, it creates strong free-rider incentives. Frieden examines the international interactions that followed the Global Financial Crisis and the Eurozone Crisis and aimed to improve the stability of the international financial system. While the free-rider problem still remains, Frieden finds modest improvements in three areas: lender-of-last-resort facilities, harmonization of financial regulations, and the coordination of macroeconomic policies.

INTRODUCTION

International finance is at the cutting edge of contemporary international economic integration. Today's global financial markets are of enormous size and can move huge quantities of money around the world with extraordinary speed and massive effect. Their impact was demonstrated with a vengeance during the Great Financial Crisis (GFC) that began at the end of 2007, during which financial markets transmitted economic impulses—many of them highly damaging—from country to country in a matter of days or weeks.

The great economic and political prominence of international financial markets has given rise to extensive discussion of the need to regulate, monitor, or otherwise control their impact on national economies and polities. Indeed, the ranks of those who believe that some form of governance of global finance is desirable are clearly growing. However, even among the more fervent believers in global financial governance, it is not clear how this might be accomplished in a world in which policies are still made almost entirely by nation-states.

In this article, I evaluate the state of attempts to provide some financial oversight at the international level that comes close to what exists at the national level. I start below with a summary of the normative argument for international financial governance. The following section provides a brief overview of what has been done to supply something approaching global public goods in this arena. Finally, I move on to analytical approaches to understanding what has been done, and might be done, in global financial governance.

NORMATIVE ARGUMENTS FOR GLOBAL FINANCIAL GOVERNANCE

Analysts and policy makers make a variety of arguments for some form of international governance of global financial affairs. In this context, governance implies the provision of government-like functions at a level above that of the nation-state. The normative basis for these arguments, then, must be analogous to the rationale for the government provision of public goods at the national level: because of market failures, things for which there is demand are undersupplied by private actors.

One typical form of argumentation is by analogy. As financial markets grew from being local to being national, there was a need for national public goods involved in overseeing these markets. This led all governments to provide national financial regulation and supervision (discussed below). Financial markets are now global, which means that overseeing the international financial markets must require global public goods. This is the character of many arguments for global financial governance.

An argument for global governance, however, requires that such global public goods cannot adequately be supplied by national governments. In other words, to build a case for a truly global governance of international financial relations, it is not enough to show that the goods in question would be undersupplied by the private sector (a justification that would suffice at the national level). For global governance to be justifiable, national governments must be unable, or unwilling, to oversee their financial affairs on their own so as to provide the desired international outcome. In other words, the argument for global governance requires demonstration that not only private actors but also national governments are insufficiently willing or able to provide something that is globally desirable. To take an analogy, in pure welfare terms international trade liberalization does not in itself require global governance inasmuch as it is in the national interest to liberalize unilaterally: enough of the positive effects of trade liberalization are internalized within the liberalizing country that it has an incentive to undertake the liberalization.

This then means that the argument for global governance must inherently involve political economy considerations. Unlike at the national level, where government provision is justifiable because private supply is insufficient to satisfy demand, at the international level global provision would be justified only if national governments did not have incentives to supply the good—and the incentives to governments are inherently political. Therefore, a normative argument for the global governance of international finance, as of anything else, requires that supporters show that national governments are either technically unable or politically unmotivated to provide the necessary and relevant policies. In this context, we can identify the sorts of interventions that are most commonly, and justifiably, presented as the kinds of global public goods that the global governance of international finance could or should provide.

The overarching public good at stake in this realm is financial stability. Financial markets provide important benefits to society, both domestically and internationally, by moving funds from where they are less needed to where they can be used more productively. However, they are also subject to periodic crises with substantial economic costs. Domestically, national governments have long recognized that systemic stability is unlikely to be provided sufficiently by private actors, and they have intervened in a variety of ways to reduce the threat of financial instability.

A similar logic holds internationally. Financial crises that begin in one country or group of countries are often transmitted to the rest of the world, causing contagious international financial crises. Here, the political economy argument for this sort of global public good is clear. Each national government may act to protect its own financial institutions and system, but it stops there. Measures taken to stabilize the international financial system could benefit all countries and all participants; however, no single country has an incentive to undertake the great costs of providing this stability, because no country fully internalizes the externalities. Indeed, if left to their own devices, individual governments may have incentives to encourage behavior by their own financial institutions that might give them a competitive edge but endanger international financial stability—such as engaging in risky lending or secretive banking practices. The fact that countries do not fully internalize both positive and negative externalities in this realm provides a clear and cogent argument for the global provision of global financial governance.

There are many ways of attempting to provide financial stability. Below I examine those that have been most prominent in discussions of the governance of international financial markets.

Lender-of-Last-Resort Facilities

At least since the middle 1800s, it has been understood that financial markets are subject to "panics" or "bank runs," in which doubts about the solvency of financial institutions can lead market participants to withdraw funds. These panics can be self-reinforcing, causing otherwise healthy institutions to fail solely due to a potentially misplaced loss of confidence. Such bank runs can also be contagious and snowball into full-blown financial crises with serious costs to society, which means that there are strong welfare arguments for avoiding them. As a result, virtually every government has agreed, in one way or another, to act as an implicit or explicit lender of last resort. This means that it stands ready to provide liquidity to the financial market to keep otherwise solvent financial institutions from being bankrupted by a contagious loss of confidence. This is not an unproblematic policy: the line between insolvency and illiquidity can be unclear, as is the best way for the government to intervene. However, the basic principle is well established: governments need to stand ready to intervene in an emergency to supply funds to financial markets to avoid a descent into panic.

International financial markets are, it turns out, exquisitely susceptible to these sorts of panics. In the international financial system, which is populated by large financial institutions rather than small depositors, panic typically takes the form of a loss of confidence in the ability of other financial institutions to fulfill contracts, even for very short-term (such as overnight) arrangements. The financial components of the crisis that began in 2007 are the modern equivalent of a bank run: with intermediation taking place in markets rather than through banks, the panic that developed was about the inability of markets to reliably allow contracts to be completed and serviced. Extraordinary levels of uncertainty made it difficult or impossible even for the largest financial institutions to borrow on the interbank market, which is necessary for them to carry on everyday business.

Today's international financial system is subject to the threat of panics, which means that lender-of-last-resort facilities are desirable. The modern system performs a function that is analogous to that of a traditional national banking system: maturity transformation with fractional reserves, underpinned by a very short-term interbank market.[1] To some extent national governments have addressed the international lender of last resort problem by working out arrangements that require home country authorities to provide these facilities to their financial institutions even when they are operating internationally. However, these arrangements have many weaknesses and vulnerabilities, such as the fact that the commitments involve many different currencies, and most observers agree that some manner of international lender-of-last-resort facilities would be desirable.

As in the general case, the political economy case for an international lender of last resort is strong. Such facilities are complex and can be costly to provide in a credible way. Although each national government has powerful reasons to establish lender-of-last-resort facilities domestically to protect its own financial institutions and system, the benefits largely stop at the water's edge. No one government can internalize the full benefits of providing liquidity to the international financial system, which makes the normative case for global provision a powerful one.

Regulatory Harmonization

Financial regulation is a central component of national efforts to provide financial stability. In fact, it can be seen as the counterpart of policies to backstop the financial system, such as the lender of last resort: if governments are providing some sort of insurance to financial markets, they need to attempt

---

1. "Maturity transformation" refers to the process whereby financial institutions borrow at short term (i.e., from depositors) and lend at long term (i.e., to mortgage holders). A fractional reserve system is one where banks have only a fraction of the money necessary to cover their liabilities (such as to depositors) available upon demand, on the principle that only a fraction of these liabilities are expected to be called at any given time.

to limit moral hazard and adverse selection. But experience has shown that a financial system with inconsistent or discordant regulatory components, whether regionally or functionally, can create serious problems. Major regulatory differences give financial institutions incentives to engage in regulatory arbitrage, designing their operations so as to find the most permissive regulations for each segment of their business.

At the international level, major regulatory differences and private-sector regulatory arbitrage can lead to an accumulation of under-regulated activities. This in turn creates the potential for very large international financial institutions to manipulate regulations so as to put many national regulators and financial systems at risk. It might also lead to regulatory competition with a harmful race to the bottom. And because financial crises in one major financial market are typically transmitted to other markets, lax regulation in one country can cause contagious crises throughout the world.

Just as it is desirable for national financial systems to avoid regulatory fragmentation and contagious financial crises, there is a normative argument for regulatory harmonization at the international level. As with lender-of-last-resort facilities, the argument takes into account the political economy of the issue. Individual national governments do not fully internalize the benefits of tighter regulation, and they may even realize significant costs if business flees for looser jurisdictions. This means that national governments, like private firms, may not have sufficient incentives to provide adequate global regulatory consistency or rigor on their own. The case for some form of global governance, even if only for cooperative arrangements among national authorities, is strong.

This sort of regulatory harmonization can take different forms. Regulators can agree to impose common rules for capital adequacy, that is, how much capital banks have to hold in compared to their outstanding assets (loans and investments). This is meant to impose common standards of prudence on financial institutions. A related measure is to harmonize the treatment of shadow banking activities, that is, the activities of financial institutions that are typically outside of the normal reach of banking regulators. Harmonization can also provide common standards for how national financial authorities are expected to intervene in the case of major bank failures.

Other Sources of Financial Stability

A range of other policies may also stabilize a financial system. Especially in the aftermath of the GFC, there has been much discussion of interventions to either limit the likelihood of financial instability or reduce its effects.

One set of policies that has attracted a great deal of attention is macroprudential regulation. This approach takes financial regulation to a higher level, requiring regulators to supervise financial institutions and to consider their impact on the entire financial system. This could lead regulators to influence the pace and direction of lending, focusing not simply on the solvency of individual banks but rather on the broader systemic impact of their behavior. Moreover, assessing the macroeconomic impact of individual banks' activities is a complex and potentially controversial task: no bank wants to be denied profit opportunities solely due to nebulous systemic considerations. Nonetheless, the experience of recent financial crises has led many national regulators to take systemic factors much more seriously. Again, the normative case for some form of macroprudential regulation at the global level—or at the least for coordination of national macroprudential policies—is strong. Although national regulators have incentives to take nationally systemic effects seriously, they have no strong reasons to think about the global financial system. Again, the positive externalities are not internalized, and national regulators are unlikely to pay due attention to potential internationally systemic implications of their banks' activities.

Another policy dimension that has generated much discussion recently is the control of cross-border capital flows to limit their impact on domestic, and potentially international, financial conditions. Indeed, the International Monetary Fund (IMF) has indicated that it regards the judicious use of such capital controls as a reasonable response to the threat of financial instability: national authorities might limit inflows to avoid excessive borrowing, and in time of crisis they might limit outflows to avoid currency runs or other destabilizing financial movements. Once more, inasmuch as national financial crises can be contagious, there is a normative basis for some global provision, or at least coordination, of policies to control capital movements. A national government that does not take global effects into consideration could encourage foreign borrowing even if it risks an eventual crisis, especially if many of the costs of the crisis are borne by foreigners (creditors or other countries infected by panic). In this context, policies to limit capital movements would best be designed with global factors in mind, in ways no national government would be inclined to do.

Macroeconomic Policy Coordination

Divergences in macroeconomic policies are at the root of many financial difficulties. This is especially the case today, in a world with enormous capital markets and rapid capital flows: minor differences in macroeconomic conditions can lead to large financial flows that increase those divergences and exacerbate boom-and-bust cycles, which carry substantial social costs. The normative case for macroeconomic policy coordination has been contested: a traditional view would be that responsible macroeconomic policies are unilaterally desirable and their positive effects are fully realized by the country that pursues them, so that the incentives for such policies would be strong enough not to require any international coordination. However, recent trends have strengthened the argument for coordination, given that uncoordinated national macroeconomic policies could lead to the sorts of regional and global crises that have beset so much of the world over the past 20 years. . . . As with the other policies discussed above, there are strong political economy grounds to justify something other than purely national action: inasmuch as one country's macroeconomic policies can impose externalities on other countries, there is an argument for a supranational effort to internalize the externalities.

If we accept that financial stability is a public good, and further accept that policies to provide it at the national level create cross-border externalities that are not fully internalized, there is a normative case for providing the global public good of financial stability at a level above that of the nation-state. This global governance might, however, take many forms. The form most similar to national-level government is probably provision by a supranational institution, followed by closely coordinated provision by a coalition of national governments. Global governance could conceivably take the form of provision of the public good by one government, if enough of the benefits were realized by its home country—or if others could somehow compensate it for the job. The governance function could be provided by nongovernmental organizations, such as private, usually corporate, regulatory or standardization bodies.

The form taken by global governance is likely to depend both on the issue area and on the agents involved. One perspective, familiar from the literature on federalism (including the European literature on subsidiarity), emphasizes that the governance structure should reflect the distribution of externalities. So if most of the positive, or negative, effects are realized by one, or a few, nations, they are more likely both to provide the governance and to benefit disproportionately from it. A similar consideration could explain why a highly motivated NGO, or a group of corporations, might have powerful enough incentives to undertake the difficult task of creating a global institution to provide some of these government-like functions. . . .

It should be noted that even if analysis provides criteria within which some form of international financial governance constitutes a global public good, it does not necessarily follow that this governance is distributionally neutral. Because the definition of global public goods refers largely to nations and governments, it is perfectly conceivable that some such governance policies and structures could impose net costs on groups or individuals within countries. Moreover, there are many different and distributionally varied ways in which public goods can be supplied. I return to this in much more detail when discussing positive analyses of global governance.

Despite the strong normative argument for international financial governance, we might still doubt that national governments will agree on whether or how to work together to provide global public goods. In a world of independent nation-states, cooperation to provide public goods may be the exception rather than the rule. However, the past 25 years or so provide some surprising evidence of an increasing tendency toward the provision of such global public goods in the financial realm. In the next section, I summarize some of these developments; in the following section, I turn to how we might explain them.

DEVELOPMENTS IN GLOBAL FINANCIAL GOVERNANCE

The international financial system was hit by a series of financial crises in the 1990s, the most prominent of which were the Mexican crisis of 1994 and the East Asian crisis of 1997–1998. In each case, there was substantial contagion within the respective region, and even outside it. Again in each case, there was enough serious concern about the implications for the international financial system that the IMF and the national governments of the major financial centers stepped in to provide hundreds of billions of dollars to bail out the troubled debtor nations and supervise the restructuring of hundreds of billions of dollars in private credit. The Mexican and East Asian events were followed in short order by similar, if more isolated, crises in Russia, Turkey, and Argentina.

In the aftermath of these crises, policy makers and observers began serious discussions of what was at the time usually called the international financial architecture. They increasingly shared the belief that financial instability in one country or region could cause serious global problems and required a more explicitly cooperative global response. Depending on the forum and the protagonists, discussions included financial regulation, macroeconomic policies, and adjustment measures.

Several institutional developments reflected the expressed desire for more international consultation and cooperation on financial issues. One was the broadening of the Group of Seven (G7) industrial countries with the creation of the Group of Twenty (G20), which includes some of the largest developing nations. A second was the extension of the mandate of the IMF to include monitoring member states' financial stability and its international implications. This included asking the IMF to issue an annual Global Financial Stability Report and later to focus its surveillance obligations on what was called a Multilateral Consultation on Global Imbalances. Finally, member states expanded the role of the Bank for International Settlements (BIS, of which more below) and established a new Financial Stability Forum to bring together central bankers, finance ministers, and other international financial policy makers to discuss common problems. . . .

Despite these innovations, the most significant progress toward global financial governance came under the auspices of the BIS and its Basel Committee on Banking Supervision. This committee was originally made up of regulatory and monetary authorities from 13 principal industrial countries (the G7 plus Belgium, Luxembourg, the Netherlands, Spain, Sweden, and Switzerland). The committee began meeting in the aftermath of the first modern panic-like event, when in 1974 the failure of two mid-sized banks, one German and one American, practically froze the international interbank market. After a series of agreements to avoid a recurrence of the problem, eventually in 1988 the committee adopted a formal set of harmonized regulatory principles, which came to be called the Basel Accord (and eventually Basel I). The principles were implemented by the committee members by 1992. This was an unprecedented step toward cooperation among national bank supervisors, and it reflected the growing belief that there were clear systemic externalities that could not be addressed without explicit collaboration—an early step toward financial governance at the international level. Over the next decade or so, many other countries claimed to have conformed to the Basel regulatory framework. Starting in the late 1990s, the committee began a substantial revision and enhancement of the standards, eventually leading to a second agreement in 2004 called Basel II. But the implementation of Basel II was interrupted by the eruption of the GFC in 2007.

The GFC provoked a dramatic increase in international attempts to address global financial issues. The crisis graphically demonstrated the depth, breadth, and speed with which financial instability could spread around the world. As financial markets reached near-panic in October 2008, emergency plans were made for an unprecedented meeting of the leaders of the G20 countries. The G20 had been expanded in 1999 to include about a dozen emerging markets (including Brazil, Russia, India, China, South Africa, and Mexico), but its meetings had only been among finance ministers and similar policy makers. The Washington Summit of November 14–15, 2008, brought together the heads of government or state of the G20 members. Among other agreements, the summit, followed about five months later by another one in London, committed members to a coordinated macroeconomic response to the crisis. Although the principal macroeconomic coordination that ensued involved only the major central banks—especially the Federal Reserve, European Central Bank, Bank of England, Bank of Japan, and Bank of Canada—the very high level of representation at the G20 meetings and the inclusion of major emerging markets in the deliberations were significant.

The G20 has become the focus of many of the measures aiming to provide some degree of global financial governance. It has expanded the Financial Stability Forum, now rebranded the Financial Stability Board (FSB), to include the major emerging markets, and it has overseen substantive discussions over regulatory harmonization as well as attempts to resolve such complex issues as the regulatory and moral hazard problems associated with systemically important financial institutions.

Closely related to the G20's efforts have been the redoubled attempts by the BIS's Basel Committee on Banking Supervision to address the flaws in Basel II that were revealed by the GFC. The committee developed a new, significantly more encompassing, Basel Accord by the end of 2010. There have been substantial revisions since then, and Basel III is unlikely to be fully implemented by major financial centers before 2020. Nonetheless, there has definitely been substantial movement toward greater coordination among national regulators and toward the harmonization of regulatory and supervisory standards among the major financial centers.

Meanwhile, central bankers have continued to cooperate at levels that had not been seen before the crisis. This cooperation has developed more or less in tandem with an expansion of the IMF's role, especially through substantial increases in the funds available for crisis lending and emergency liquidity provision. In a variety of ways, the IMF, clearly with the approval of its principal members, is moving in the direction of acting as something like an international lender of last resort. The funds it has available are insufficient to play this role fully, but it can be argued that, in concert with the involvement of national governments, the major national and supranational players in the international financial system take seriously the need for a global lender of last resort and have worked toward that goal. . . .

In summary, over the past decade the G20's Financial Stability Board and related institutions, the BIS, the IMF, and the major financial centers have progressed toward providing an international financial governance infrastructure at the global level that resembles national financial management. There are the beginnings of international-lender-of-last-resort facilities, of globally harmonized financial supervision and regulation to accompany these facilities, and of systematic collaboration among national authorities and supranational institutions. Even optimists would admit that the progress has been slow, difficult, and partial, and that much remains to be done. But even pessimists would probably accept that there has been more movement in this direction than they had anticipated a decade ago. . . .

ANALYZING INTERNATIONAL FINANCIAL GOVERNANCE

We would like to understand the forces that have constrained or enabled the creation of institutions and policies associated with international financial governance. Of course, an understanding of these forces is strongly affected by the theoretical tools used by scholars to analyze the politics of international financial relations. It is to an overview of the different analytical perspectives that I now turn. These perspectives are not necessarily mutually exclusive, but they do tend to focus on different potential sources of government actions. . . .

The most simple-minded approach—which is so simple-minded as to not be represented in the scholarly literature—explains governance developments on social welfare grounds, based on the promotion of global efficiency. This is what might be called a functionalist view, in the sense that governance functions grow out of the inherent demand for them. The analytical problem, of course, is that there is no agent, public or private, with a clear incentive to intervene solely in the interests of global social welfare. However, this baseline is important, and in fact somewhat contested.

Although it is common to claim that international financial initiatives are undertaken in the interests of all, as noted above, it is perfectly plausible that such initiatives may have strong distributive effects. These may involve the uneven allocation of costs and benefits among countries: creditor nations may be able to force debtor nations into bearing a disproportionate share of the burden of adjusting to the aftermath of irresponsible lending, or large countries may be able to constrain small countries to conform to standards that harm them and their private sectors. Even if these initiatives are arrived at voluntarily among member governments, which implies that they benefit all *governments*, there may still be domestic distributive effects within countries. For example, a government might have no compunctions about forcing taxpayers to shoulder the full expense of reckless lending by national financial institutions.

In all these cases, even though there may be social benefits to the financial stability that is enhanced by the policies in question, for individual countries or individuals within countries these benefits may be outweighed by their costs. In other words, both among countries and within countries, there is no guarantee that the governance structures will deliver Pareto improvements. And even where the policies are Pareto improving, there are typically many ways in which they can be structured, with different distributional implications. . . .

Analytically, the fact that these global public goods may not be distributionally neutral—whether the distributional features are international or domestic—provides a mechanism to explain how and why they might be supplied in a world without global government. Again, there is an analogy to the provision of public goods at the national level. Leaving aside political entrepreneurship, which has only weak parallels at the international level, a common explanation for the provision of public goods is that they are promoted by concentrated groups that stand to benefit disproportionately from them. This could be because the public good in question has differential benefits, with much more significant effects on some groups than others (bankers versus farmers, for example). It could also be because the public good comes bundled with private benefits that accrue to a concentrated group. . . .

At the international level, one could imagine that a global public good might have particularly significant benefits for some country or small group of countries; that it might have particularly significant benefits for concentrated groups within countries; or that it might be closely associated with private benefits to some countries or groups within countries. The existence of concentrated benefits to domestic groups could provide incentives for a government to pursue the global public good; the existence of concentrated benefits to one country or group of countries could similarly provide them with incentives to undertake the efforts necessary to supply the global public good.

For all these reasons, even scholars who accept the broad desirability of some form of international financial governance look for distributional features of their evolution that explain why such global public goods might be promoted by governments, potentially at significant national cost. One approach emphasizes the extent to which particularly large and important financial centers internalize the benefits of financial stability, which may give their governments incentives enough to play a major role in working toward global governance agreements and structures. In this picture, the disproportional size of a country can give it a disproportional interest in resolving some of the problems that arise in the absence of public goods in the international financial arena.

This approach, then, focuses on the willingness of the governments of the largest financial powers to lead the way in expanding global financial governance, and, typically, on the ability of these governments to use their power to cajole or persuade other governments to follow their lead. In somewhat different ways, for example, . . . Kapstein (1994), Posner (2009), and Simmons (2001) ascribe financial regulatory harmonization to the willingness and ability of countries (or, in the case of the European Union, groups of countries) to use their bargaining power and influence to create a context to which smaller actors are forced to respond, usually by complying with the patterns set by the dominant actors.

The fact that dominant governments can strong-arm others into accepting their version of the public good in question—be it financial regulation, lender-of-last-resort facilities, or something else—does not rule out the possibility that the outcome actually improves the welfare of all governments that sign onto the regime. Although the point is often implicit, it is probably the case that most scholars in this tradition think of the eventual provision of some form of international financial governance as an improvement over its absence. Inasmuch as Pareto improvements come in many distributionally relevant varieties, and the bargaining power of the larger states gives them outsized influence on outcomes, the international governance structures that emerge are likely to be disproportionately favorable to the largest countries. One example is the role of the IMF in resolving debt crises: although it is probably in the interest of debtor and creditor nations alike to have some mechanism to deal with such crises, Copelovitch (2010) argues that the IMF's behavior is powerfully affected by the influence of the largest creditor nations, and Stone (2011) is even more insistent that formal and informal rules bias international financial institutions heavily toward the interest of the largest states.

A further step away from functionalist logic is to question whether in fact the governance structures improve welfare for all. The most consistent variant of this argument is to note that the agreements to provide this sort of global public good are made by national governments, and that there is little guarantee that a government will be acting in the national interest, however defined. More specifically, national governments may be "captured" in the global financial realm by powerful domestic special interests that want to see international financial agreements bent in their favor, even if this works against the interests of their countrymen. One common argument to this effect is that the shape of global financial cooperation is strongly affected, and perhaps distorted, by the particularistic interests of powerful and internationally engaged private financial institutions. In this sense, what looks to some like global financial governance might also be described as the solidification of a global financial cartel, organized so as to extract resources from those outside the cartel; borrowers and taxpayers, in particular.

For these reasons, many scholars begin their analysis of international financial policies, cooperation, and governance with the concentrated interests of nationally based economic groups, particularly financial institutions. Then they can build up to governments that may or may not have national interests in mind, but that bias their policy orientations toward the concerns of these powerful groups (Singer 2007). Returning to the example of the IMF in crisis resolution, Copelovitch (2010) argues that it was not just the interests of the largest countries that were most strongly reflected in IMF policies, but more specifically the interests of the large private financial institutions of these largest countries. At an even more differentiated level, Broz (2008) shows that support for the actions and institutions of global financial governance are contingent on their domestic distributional impact: the behavior of American legislators in making decisions on these matters is strongly influenced by the economic interests of their constituents.

These first two modes of analysis have a lot in common and are not mutually exclusive. They both tend to assume that international financial cooperation improves global welfare, but they both temper this view with the observation that the results are likely to be strongly biased by power differentials among countries and among groups within countries. Both approaches rely primarily upon the behavior of national states, although they accept that government policy depends on domestic as well as international considerations. Both focus on the economic interests of private actors and/or their reflection in the preferences of national governments.

Many scholars deemphasize economic interests, the actions of governments, or both. "Ideational" approaches to the making of foreign policy have their reflection in the international financial realm, as elsewhere. These analyses tend to emphasize the changing nature of common understandings of the problems faced in international financial relations and of how they might be addressed (Chwieroth 2010). Clearly, policy makers and others are influenced by the state of knowledge, or opinion, about these issues. If ideas converge within an epistemic community of experts or technocrats, or within a community of policy makers, this convergence can lead to policy outcomes that might otherwise be unimaginable. The evolution of the views of the IMF in the aftermath of the Asian financial crisis of 1997–1998, and of the more recent GFC, leads some observers to posit that this sort of ideational change can create conditions for a higher degree of global financial governance—whether under the auspices of the IMF or otherwise.

An ideas-based explanation of the management of international financial relations has resonated with many scholars, especially those who are particularly critical of mainstream neoliberal policy prescriptions. One of the more famous variants of this view comes from Washington-based economist John Williamson, who dubbed the IMF–World Bank–U.S. Treasury view of how developing countries should manage their economies the "Washington Consensus" (Williamson 1989). In Williamson's view, a nearly religious attitude toward development policy had biased the recommendations coming from the IMF and the World Bank in ways that were not warranted by theory or evidence. More recently, both scholars and observers, including many politicians, have attacked governmental responses to the GFC, especially in Europe, for an attachment to austerity that they regard as both ideologically motivated and genuinely unwarranted (Blyth 2013 is the canonical statement).

Rather than centering on national politicians who respond to political pressures, a related perspective focuses on international or domestic bureaucrats who respond both to these sorts of ideational factors and to more technocratic considerations. An emphasis on technocratic bureaucracies is especially plausible in the international financial realm, where the problems and potential solutions are technically complex and well beyond the understanding of most citizens and many politicians. This provides an opportunity for experienced and well-informed officials of national governments, international organizations, or even nongovernmental organizations to create strong networks that can affect both national and supranational policies (Bach & Newman 2010, Lall 2015). These transnational networks can be particularly powerful if they are able to garner support from individual governments or groups of governments, including those not normally in the inner corridors of international financial power (Gallagher 2014).

Idea-centered and technocrat-centered approaches are often blended. Indeed, some of the influential analyses focus on how ideologically committed technocrats in international institutions guide the course of institutional engagement and policy. At the same time, it is common to suggest that many of these technocratic and ideological biases are motivated by distributionally relevant considerations, for example, in favor of the corporate sector (Blyth 2013 combines aspects of all three).

Developments in international financial politics in the aftermath of the GFC provide an opportunity to see how different perspectives might analyze the course of global financial governance. Some would emphasize the interaction of the major states, especially within the G7, each concerned with nationally specific conditions. This emphasis on interstate strategic interaction could be augmented by seeing how the management group was expanded to the G20—although the extent to which this expansion affected outcomes would be contested.

Related scholarship would emphasize how bargaining among the principal national governments over how to confront the crisis was, and is, strongly constrained by the domestic conditions faced by each of the major players. Foremost among these constraints are the interests and influence of major private financial institutions that operate internationally. The domestic politics of financial regulation and monetary policy is now tightly interwoven with international financial developments, especially in the leading financial centers. There is undoubtedly plenty of evidence for the influence of powerful private-sector players and of national policy makers over the developments in international financial governance since 2008.

Evidence for the importance of changing ideas about the appropriate policies for today's international financial system is also likely to be strong. It is not surprising that an unprecedented level of financial integration and technological change, along with the most serious financial crisis since the 1930s, should give rise to a rethinking of the precepts that have guided policy making. At this point, much of what we know—or think we know—about international finance is up for discussion, and the pathways these discussions take have had, and will have, an impact on policy makers at both the national and the international levels.

Finally, there is little question that the GFC has highlighted the centrality of technically trained policy makers in both national and international institutions. To a great extent, the principal global response to the crisis has been managed by the world's principal central banks, and although central bankers are hardly impervious to political pressure, much of what they have done has been guided by their technocratic training and expertise. At the same time, the crisis has certainly enhanced the role of international institutions in the financial realm. The IMF and the BIS have both played major parts in discussions of how the world may move forward in the aftermath of the crisis.

In short, all of the factors identified by scholars as relevant to the making of international financial governance can be seen as having affected the course of the world's financial order since 2008. This is hardly surprising: there are good theoretical and empirical reasons for the significance of all of these factors. What remains to be argued is whether one or more of the approaches described here outperforms the others in explaining the course of international financial events.

My summary of recent experience, undoubtedly colored by my own theoretical prejudices, is that we can understand most of the policy reaction to the GFC as a combination of domestic politics and interstate bargaining. Certainly the theoretical novelty of the panic of 2008 and the unprecedented nature of the Eurozone crisis have provided some space for policy entrepreneurship among international bureaucracies and for new ideas. But one of the striking features of the political economy of the crisis is just how similar it looks to previous financial and debt crises (Chinn & Frieden 2011). There has been massive conflict over how the burden of adjustment should be distributed, both among and within countries. The intersection of intercountry bargaining and domestic political conflicts has been particularly prominent in the Eurozone crisis. Although there have been ideas in conflict, and technocrats in the mix, it is hard to escape the conclusion that the cold hard cash at stake, both domestically and internationally, has been the main determinant of the political economy of the crisis.

CONCLUSION

International financial markets today are extraordinarily large and wield enormous influence over the course of global economic and political affairs. In the wake of the most damaging financial crisis in the last 75 years, it is no wonder that everyone, from policy makers and journalists to scholars, is interested to know if a higher level of international financial governance might avoid a repetition of the past decade's disasters. In a way, current discussions are reminiscent of the debates that took place in the aftermath of previous financial crises and bank panics at the national level, most of which led to an expansion of national financial regulation and supervision.

There are in fact good normative arguments for the development of international mechanisms to limit the damage international financial markets can cause and to enhance their benefits. At the domestic level, financial markets create positive externalities when they work well and negative externalities when they do not, and this creates a demand for management that is undersupplied by the private actors themselves—hence justifying the government's provision of the public goods associated with financial stability. At the international level, no single government has sufficient incentive to supply these global public goods, so their provision would depend on the joint decisions of multiple governments. But whatever the normative and theoretical argument for global public goods, the realities of international and domestic politics make their supply in practice problematic.

Nonetheless, there has unquestionably been movement toward greater global financial governance over the past 25 years, and this movement is in the direction of providing something akin to global public goods in the financial area. This development has taken the form of greater cooperation among the major financial centers, increased harmonization of financial regulations among countries, a more significant role for international financial institutions, and other measures that supply some part of what is typically associated with financial stability at the domestic level.

Scholars have adduced several factors to help explain both progress and obstacles in the path of international financial governance. The realities of collaboration among independent, self-interested nation-states may stand in the way, although if some countries expect to benefit disproportionately from international financial stability they may be more likely to work hard to contribute to it. By the same token, inasmuch as powerful groups—especially private financial institutions—anticipate private benefits from greater international financial governance, they will be inclined to pressure their governments to work in that direction. At the same time, trends in the intellectual understanding of international financial problems and of how they might most effectively be addressed can affect the ways in which national and international policy makers confront the problems they face. This is especially true when the policy makers are united by common technical training and by long experiences of working together either at the national level or in international financial institutions.

The international financial system is likely to continue to grow and to expand its influence over both the global economy and the economies of countries. It is just as likely to continue to be subject to periodic tensions and pressures, and at times these tensions will almost certainly erupt into full-blown financial crises. Crises have always been endemic to financial markets, and we have no reason to believe that the near future will be different from the past. National governments have gradually developed ways to limit, though not eliminate, the damage caused by these financial stresses at the domestic level. The evidence of the past several decades is that the world's major governments, along with the major international financial institutions, are moving gradually and haltingly in the direction of managing international financial affairs more comprehensively at the global level. This does not necessarily mean that the results of these efforts will be some magical resolution of global problems, or even that they will make most people and most countries better off. But there are prospects for progress in addressing the potential costs of international financial integration and enhancing its positive effects. It is important to understand these prospects and the obstacles to their realization.

REFERENCES

Bach, D., A. Newman 2010. Transgovernmental networks and domestic policy convergence: Evidence from insider trading regulation. *Int. Organ.* 64: 505–28.

Blyth, M. 2013. *Austerity: The History of a Dangerous Idea.* Oxford, UK: Oxford University Press.

Broz, J. L. 2008. Congressional voting on funding the international financial institutions. *Review of International Organizations* 3, no. 4: 351–74.

Chinn, M., J. Frieden. 2011. *Lost Decades: The Making of America's Debt Crisis and the Long Recovery.* New York: W. W. Norton.

Chwieroth, J. 2010. *Capital Ideas: The IMF and the Rise of Financial Liberalization.* Princeton, NJ: Princeton University Press.

Copelovitch, M. 2010. *The International Monetary Fund in the Global Economy: Banks, Bonds, and Bailouts.* Cambridge, UK: Cambridge University Press.

Gallagher, K. 2014. *Ruling Capital: Emerging Markets and the Re-regulation of Cross-Border Finance.* Ithaca, NY: Cornell University Press.

Kapstein, E. B. 1994. *Governing the Global Economy: International Finance and the State.* Cambridge, MA: Harvard University Press.

Lall, R. 2015. Timing as a source of regulatory influence: A technical elite network analysis of global finance. *Regulation and Governance* 9, no. 2: 125–43.

Posner, E. 2009. Making rules for global finance: Transatlantic regulatory cooperation at the turn of the millennium. *International Organization* 63, no. 4: 665–99.

Simmons, B. 2001. The international politics of harmonization: The case of capital market regulation. *International Organization* 553: 589–620.

Singer, D. 2007. *Regulating Capital: Setting Standards for the International Financial System.* Ithaca, NY: Cornell University Press.

Stone, R. 2011. *Controlling Institutions: International Organizations and the Global Economy.* Cambridge, UK: Cambridge University Press.

Williamson, J. 1989. What Washington means by policy reform. In *Latin American Readjustment: How Much Has Happened*, ed. J. Williamson, 7–40. Washington, DC: Inst. Int. Econ.

33

US versus Them: Mass Attitudes toward Offshore Outsourcing

EDWARD D. MANSFIELD AND DIANA C. MUTZ

Attitudes toward globalization can be shaped by both economic self-interest and noneconomic factors like nationalism and ethnocentrism. A large part of the literature seeks to ascertain the relative importance of these contending forces by way of public opinion data. In this reading, Edward D. Mansfield and Diana C. Mutz explore the sources of everyday Americans' attitudes toward outsourcing, which citizens understand to mean when companies move jobs overseas. They find that nationalism and ethnocentrism are key drivers of citizens' attitudes toward outsourcing. By contrast, they find little evidence to support the argument that respondent self-interest plays a role, as measured by the vulnerability of an individual's occupation or industry to outsourcing. The open question is whether public opinion plays any role in shaping U.S. outsourcing policy, which remains largely unrestricted.

The movement of jobs overseas has caused mounting anxiety in the United States over the past decade. Variously referred to as "outsourcing," "offshoring," or "offshore outsourcing," this phenomenon first started to arouse concern in the U.S. at the turn of the twenty-first century, when the conclusion of an economic downturn was followed by a tepid recovery in the U.S. labor market. As China, India, and the post-Communist states took steps to increase their engagement with the global economy, an extra 1.3 billion workers joined the global workforce, nearly doubling its size and raising fears that U.S. firms would relocate jobs overseas to cut labor costs. This issue rose to prominence during the 2004 presidential election, when Senator John Kerry accused President George W. Bush of promoting outsourcing and lambasted "Benedict Arnold CEOs" for moving jobs abroad. Since then, this issue has continued to stimulate widespread public interest. A burgeoning literature on the economics of outsourcing and offshoring has emerged, but few studies have addressed the politics of this phenomenon. We aim to help fill this gap in the literature by providing an understanding of the origins of American attitudes toward outsourcing.

We begin by addressing differences in terminology among academics, policymakers, and the mass public. In popular discourse and the relatively few studies of mass opinion, the practice of moving jobs overseas has been referred to as "outsourcing, meaning when American businesses hire workers in other parts of the world in order to save money." Economists are more likely to use the term "offshoring" to refer to the same phenomenon, and politicians fall somewhere in between in their attempt to communicate with both popular and technical audiences, calling it "offshore outsourcing" or some other combination of terms. We thus use these terms interchangeably throughout this article.

Economists have argued that outsourcing is another form of international trade. As such, it should have the same sort of distributional consequences as foreign commerce. A growing number of studies have analyzed whether mass attitudes about trade and other aspects of globalization fall along the factoral or sectoral lines emphasized by various political economy models. Based on a representative national survey of Americans, however, we find little evidence that either an individual's industry of employment or her occupation explains attitudes toward outsourcing. Instead, such attitudes tend to be shaped by ethnocentrism and antiforeign sentiment. Individuals who believe the U.S. should take an isolationist stance on international affairs more generally, who feel a sense of national superiority, or who feel that members of other ethnic and racial groups are less praiseworthy than their own racial or ethnic group, tend to have particularly hostile reactions to outsourcing. In addition, opinions about outsourcing are shaped in important ways by how people understand the term and what kind of cues they receive from outside sources such as unions and political parties. Taken together, the results of our study strongly suggest that attitudes are shaped less by the economic consequences of this phenomenon than by what offshoring implies about heightened interaction with and dependence on out-groups, foreign firms, and foreign people.

DEFINING OUTSOURCING

The terms outsourcing and offshoring are frequently used synonymously in public discourse and sometimes in academic studies. Strictly speaking, however, outsourcing refers to whether or not the production process takes place entirely within a given firm, whereas offshoring refers to whether the production process is entirely domestic or includes foreign components. Outsourcing can be either domestic or foreign; it occurs whenever one firm contracts with another firm for goods or services included in the production process. "Foreign outsourcing," "international outsourcing," and "offshore outsourcing" refer to the movement of part of the production process both outside the firm and overseas. Offshoring occurs when part of the production process is moved abroad, regardless of whether the relocated process is handled within or outside the firm.

However, as interest in the effects of international trade on the U.S. labor market grew during the first years of the twenty-first century, Jagdish Bhagwati, Arvind Panagariya, and T. N. Srinivasan point out that "outsourcing took on a different meaning. It referred now to a specific segment of the growing international trade in services." Although these scholars consider this new meaning to be the proper definition of outsourcing, they also acknowledge that public debate over this phenomenon has been muddled as the definition has become ever more elastic. In their words, "when many politicians, journalists and even some economists start discussing 'outsourcing,' they soon leap beyond purchases of offshore arm's-length services to include, without analytical clarity, phenomena such as offshore purchases of manufactured components and even direct foreign investment by firms."[1]

In this study, we use the terms outsourcing and offshoring interchangeably to describe the decision by a firm to locate part of the production process abroad and therefore shift some jobs overseas. When asking survey respondents about their opinions and perceptions, however, we use "outsourcing" since it is the most popular and widely recognized term for this phenomenon in popular political discourse.

Regardless of the public understanding of this term, economists emphasize that outsourcing is similar to international trade. By and large, they agree that the practice heightens national welfare by promoting a more efficient allocation of resources, thereby raising national income and increasing productivity. In congressional testimony and a widely covered press conference surrounding the 2004 *Economic Report of the President*, N. Gregory Mankiw, chair of President George W. Bush's Council of Economic Advisers, stated that "outsourcing is just a new way of doing international trade. More things are tradable than were tradable in the past and that's a good thing."[2] Mankiw's comments equating outsourcing with trade precipitated a political firestorm, but his views on this topic are widely shared among economists.

Below we turn to a discussion of the three leading models used to explain public attitudes toward trade and that, by extension, might explain attitudes toward outsourcing. It is unclear whether opinions on outsourcing and trade will dovetail. But in light of the dearth of research on attitudes toward outsourcing and the similarities that many observers draw between trade and outsourcing, studies of attitudes toward trade provide a logical point of departure for our analysis.

Self-Interest

Various studies argue that attitudes about international trade are driven by its distributional implications. Some individuals gain economically from overseas commerce, whereas others lose. These studies maintain that the former tend to be more supportive of open trade than the latter. In the same vein, outsourcing's distributional consequences may shape mass opinion about this phenomenon.

Analyses of these distributional consequences often emphasize that the U.S. has an abundance of high-skilled labor and a scarcity of low-skilled labor

1. Bhagwati, Panagariya, and Srinivasan 2004, 93–94.
2. Weisman 2004, A6.

relative to the rest of the world. As a result, low-skilled labor is more expensive in the U.S. than abroad and U.S. firms have an incentive to outsource tasks involving such labor to generate cost savings. This action, in turn, drives down the demand for low-skilled U.S. workers, thereby reducing their wages. Conversely, high-skilled labor is cheaper in the U.S. than elsewhere, which increases the demand for such workers and bids up their wages. The heightened demand is likely to stem from U.S. firms that need highly skilled workers as well as from foreign firms that "insource" high-skill jobs to the U.S. to take advantage of the lower labor costs. This simple comparative advantage account suggests that the distributional implications of outsourcing should fall along the lines predicted by a Stolper-Samuelson approach: highly skilled workers in the U.S. should favor outsourcing whereas less-skilled workers should oppose it.

However, evidence has been inconclusive as to whether the distributional consequences are as theorized. Some economists argue that the distributional impact of outsourcing varies across industries and occupations, implying that workers' attitudes toward this phenomenon may be shaped by mechanisms other than comparative advantage. Research on manufacturing industries has furnished considerable support for the comparative advantage approach. Robert Feenstra and Gordon Hansen, for example, found that outsourcing increased the real wages of skilled American manufacturing workers by 1–2 percent during the 1980s, a significant rise.[3] Similarly, J. Bradford Jensen and Lori Kletzer conclude that skilled workers in U.S. manufacturing industries have excellent employment prospects, but that the prospects for low-skill, low-wage U.S. manufacturing workers are far bleaker because these jobs have a high likelihood of moving offshore.[4]

Whereas outsourcing in manufacturing seems to accord with a comparative advantage approach, outsourcing in services does not. Recent improvements in technology and communications have enhanced the ability to conduct international trade in services, rendering it increasingly feasible to outsource a wide range of service jobs. Some of them require extensive skills (for example, computer programming or accounting); others do not (for example, telemarketing). Alan Blinder therefore concludes that "the dividing line between the jobs that produce services that are suitable for electronic delivery (and are thus threatened by offshoring) and those that do not does not correspond to traditional distinctions between high-end and low-end work."[5] Instead, he argues that the potential for outsourcing a job depends on how much face-to-face contact is required, or more specifically, whether "the work can be delivered to a remote location . . . [a]nd if so, how severely is the quality degraded."[6]

---

3. Feenstra and Hansen 1999.
4. Jensen and Kletzer 2008.
5. Blinder 2006, 199.
6. Blinder 2009a, 36.

Based on these criteria, Blinder concludes that roughly 22–29 percent of the U.S. workforce—amounting to 30–40 million jobs—is *potentially* offshorable.[7] Even if Blinder's projections are correct, they only pertain to jobs that *could be* outsourced—not those that have been or will be—and they do not account for jobs that are likely to be insourced to the U.S., especially in high-skill service occupations. Nonetheless, economists foresee considerable churning in the U.S. labor market as a result of outsourcing, leading to increased job displacement, reduced job security and bargaining power for workers, and downward pressure on benefits and wages. In fact, Blinder estimates that workers in the most offshorable jobs are paid 13 percent less than would otherwise be expected.[8] Kletzer and Richard Freeman argue that workers displaced due to outsourcing tend to suffer a considerable loss (roughly 13–20 percent) in earnings once they are reemployed.[9] Thus, individuals employed in offshorable occupations might be especially hostile to this phenomenon due to its economic implications for them.

Information

The type of information to which citizens are exposed may also play a crucial role in shaping preferences toward trade and outsourcing. Beyond the objective economic self-interest of individuals, attitudes toward these phenomena may be based on information about their effects on the country as a whole, or a lack thereof in the case of partial or inaccurate information. For example, collective or so-called "sociotropic" economic considerations are based on the *perceptions* that individuals have of how others are affected by economic policies. As Michael Hiscox and his colleagues have emphasized, those without any formal economics training may arrive at conclusions about the impact of outsourcing or trade that are at odds with the conventional arguments of economists.[10] For example, they suggest that women are more protectionist than men because females do not take economics courses as frequently as males. Likewise, recent research indicates that the content of media coverage about trade has a considerable influence on public attitudes about foreign commerce. More generally, if people form opinions about trade and outsourcing based on the particular information to which they are exposed, their views may not reflect individual or collective economic self-interest.

By relaying information about outsourcing and trade, political parties and unions may contribute to perceptions about them. Although the cues emanating from political parties in the U.S. have not always been particularly clear on these issues, Democratic politicians have been more likely to publicly oppose outsourcing and free trade, whereas Republicans have been more likely to

7. Blinder 2009a; Blinder 2009b.
8. Blinder 2009a.
9. Kletzer 2004; Freeman 2009.
10. Burgoon and Hiscox 2004; Hainmueller and Hiscox 2006.

favor them, with many notable exceptions. But unlike trade policies, one would be hard pressed to find any politician publicly supporting outsourcing these days.

Unions in the United States have been consistently and outspokenly hostile to outsourcing and trade. Most major unions oppose outsourcing and promote such views among their rank and file. The AFL-CIO Web site, for example, contains four pages designed to dispel "corporate myths" about the benefits of outsourcing. In addition, a recent study cosponsored by the AFL-CIO attacks outsourcing with even greater vigor, claiming that the phenomenon poses a threat to U.S. national security, creates unnecessary health risks when the production of food is shifted overseas, and jeopardizes the "traditional way of life" for working Americans. Thus, both political parties and unions may provide information cues that shape opinions on outsourcing.

Out-Group Attitudes

In addition to models emphasizing personal economic self-interest and the informational basis of attitudes toward globalization, another school of thought highlights that such attitudes may be influenced by the views individuals hold of other countries or types of people. For example, if views on outsourcing are formed on the same basis as views about trade, they may be guided by whether people favor active involvement of the U.S. in international affairs. In a landmark study, Raymond Bauer, Ithiel de Sola Pool, and Anthony Dexter argue that protectionist attitudes toward trade in the U.S. were driven in part by attitudes toward whether the U.S. should engage with other countries, regardless of the policy or economic implications.[11] In other words, Americans form opinions about trade based on their views about involvement in international affairs more generally, rather than economic affairs in particular. Consistent with this argument, a recent study finds that individuals with more interventionist preferences have a much higher opinion of free trade than individuals with more isolationist preferences, even though measures of interventionism (whether the U.S. should intervene to prevent human rights abuses abroad, cooperate with foreign countries to solve global problems, and so forth) do not address economic relations between countries. People who advocate an interventionist foreign policy may also be more likely to support engaging with foreign firms and foreign governments. If so, anti-interventionism and hostility to outsourcing are likely to coincide with their opposition to involvement in all things foreign.

Critics of outsourcing also have made nationalist appeals. Over forty years ago, the economist Harry Johnson argued that economic protectionism in many countries stemmed from a sense of national superiority.[12] Recent survey research confirms that Americans who hold strong nationalist views are

11. Bauer, Pool, and Dexter 1963, 96–99.
12. Johnson 1965, 183.

much more hostile to trade than their counterparts who are less nationalist. To the extent that trade and outsourcing attitudes have similar origins, a sense of national superiority may affect attitudes toward outsourcing as well. To the extent that one believes American workers perform better than foreign workers, nationalism naturally leads one to oppose outsourcing.

Finally, if attitudes toward outsourcing are driven by the same forces as attitudes toward trade, then they also may be guided by ethnocentrism—that is, the tendency to think less of those who are racially or ethnically different from one's own in-group. Although the feelings that whites have toward blacks and Hispanics (or vice versa) are completely superfluous to economic considerations and have nothing to do with national boundaries, domestic ethnocentrism may extend to whole countries that are different from one's own. In the case of all three factors addressed in this section—active involvement in international affairs, nationalism, and domestic ethnocentrism—the driving force is not outsourcing's economic effect on the individual or the collective.

PUBLIC PERCEPTIONS OF WHAT CONSTITUTES OUTSOURCING

To analyze influences on public attitudes toward outsourcing, we rely on a representative national survey we conducted in 2007 as well as an experiment embedded within a second representative national survey that we conducted in 2009. The initial survey included a probability sample of 2,085 working or temporarily unemployed Americans and was conducted via the Internet or Web TV by Knowledge Networks. The Knowledge Networks sample is a random probability sample recruited using address-based sampling combined with random-digit dialing. All Americans were eligible for inclusion, regardless of whether they had Internet access. In order to strengthen our conclusions regarding the effect of some key independent variables analyzed in 2007, a population-based survey experiment was commissioned in 2009. We use that experiment to systematically manipulate certain variables, allowing us to establish their causal impact within the context of a representative population sample.

The data drawn from these two surveys allow us to address three key questions pertaining to outsourcing. First, how does the American public understand what constitutes outsourcing? Second, are Americans' attitudes toward outsourcing essentially the same as their attitudes toward trade? Third, how well do each of the three models we have outlined (self-interest, information, and out-group attitudes) account for variation in American attitudes toward outsourcing? We begin with the survey results and then turn to the population-based survey experiment to confirm some of the causal inferences suggested by the initial findings.

This study focuses on the attitudes of Americans because the U.S. has been the dominant country in the global economy for over half a century. As a result of this dominance, social scientists have expressed particular interest in explaining the attitudes of Americans, whose views are likely to influence U.S. economic policy. Moreover, most of the empirical work on outsourcing has focused on the U.S. primarily because the practice has been a much larger political issue in the U.S. than elsewhere.

Nonetheless, very little is known about how Americans think about out-sourcing. For example, because even economists and other experts disagree about what constitutes outsourcing, it is unclear how the mass public defines it. To address this initial issue, we asked each survey respondent to indicate which of the following six scenarios they considered to be examples of outsourcing.

1. A U.S. car company purchases seat fabric from a company in another state rather than make it themselves.
2. A car company in another country decides to build a manufacturing plant in the United States.
3. A U.S. car company purchases the services of a company in another country to handle their customer service calls.
4. A U.S. car company purchases door handles for their cars from a company located in another country.
5. A U.S. car company purchases the services of a company in another country to design door handles for their cars and the designs are sent via internet to the U.S.
6. A U.S. car company decides to build a manufacturing plant outside the United States.

Respondents were free to indicate that all of these scenarios were instances of outsourcing, that some were and others were not, or that none of them were outsourcing. Given the widespread attention that overseas call centers have received in public discussion of outsourcing, it comes as no surprise that 90 percent of our survey respondents considered scenario 3 to be outsourc-ing. In addition, 80 percent viewed purchasing door handles from a foreign country as outsourcing, over 72 percent considered foreign-designed door handles to be outsourcing, and 70 percent thought that locating a manufac-turing plant outside of the U.S. was outsourcing.

However, only about one-third of the respondents considered purchasing seat fabric across state lines to be outsourcing. This percentage is the lowest among the six scenarios, a finding that strongly suggests that the mass public thinks that outsourcing involves shifting economic activity overseas, since it is the only scenario that refers to a completely domestic process. Furthermore, less than half the respondents identified building a plant within the U.S. as out-sourcing, probably because the activity involves shifting production from a foreign country into the U.S., rather than from the U.S. to somewhere abroad.

Fully two-thirds of our survey respondents believed that at least four of these six scenarios constitute outsourcing. Over 14 percent thought that all six were outsourcing; fewer than 4 percent thought that none of them were. Consequently, despite the fact that all respondents in our survey were asked the same exact questions about their attitudes toward outsourcing, they answered slightly different questions based on their understanding of the term. Likewise, when expressing support or opposition to outsourcing policies, they may have somewhat different understandings in mind.

Not all six scenarios would ordinarily be considered outsourcing by economists, but situations similar to each of them have been described as outsourcing in public discourse. The first scenario is an example of domestic outsourcing, although many economists and other observers use "outsourcing" to refer to the movement of part of the production process outside of the firm and overseas, not simply outside of the firm alone. The third, fourth, and fifth scenarios are examples of offshore outsourcing. The second and sixth scenarios are examples of foreign direct investment (FDI), which Bhagwati explicitly argues is not outsourcing. At the same time, however, he points out that journalists, politicians— including Senator Kerry during the 2004 presidential campaign—and some economists have confused FDI and outsourcing. As such, it is easy to understand why the mass public would confuse these phenomena as well.

A STATISTICAL MODEL OF OUTSOURCING ATTITUDES

In order to assess the contributions of variables within the three models we have outlined, we constructed measures of attitudes toward outsourcing from two survey questions:

1. Recently, some American companies have been hiring workers in other countries to replace workers in the U.S. who are paid higher wages. An example of this is people who take customer service telephone calls. Do you think the government should encourage or discourage this or stay out of this matter?
2. Some say that outsourcing jobs is bad and should be discouraged by the government. Others say that outsourcing saves companies money and allows them to sell goods more cheaply, so the government should encourage it. Which of the following statements comes closest to your view?

The first item was scored on a five-point scale, based on whether respondents felt that the government should discourage outsourcing a lot or a little, stay out of this matter, or encourage outsourcing a lot or a little. The second item was scored on a three-point scale, where the highest score was assigned to respondents who believed that the government should encourage outsourcing, the lowest score was assigned to those who believed the government should discourage outsourcing, and the middle score was assigned to individuals who felt that the government should stay out of this matter. Responses to these two items were highly correlated (Spearman's $\rho = .60$, $p < .001$), strongly suggesting that the two questions are tapping the same underlying concept.

Using these items, we constructed two dependent variables. The first was the mean of the two scores. Because they have a different number of categories, we first converted the items to z-scores so that each one was weighted equally in the index. Combining the two items has various advantages, chief among them being that the dependent variable is a more reliable measure and is less prone to problems associated with idiosyncratic wording or measurement error than if we analyzed each item separately. The second dependent variable indicated whether a respondent consistently favored or opposed outsourcing. This categorical variable equals 3 if, for both of these items, a respondent believed the government should encourage outsourcing; 1 if, for both items, he or she believed the government should oppose it; and 2 if the respondent did not express a consistent view.

By employing multi-item indexes for all of the key concepts in this study, we facilitate assessments of reliability and avoid the possibility that results stem from the peculiarities of one particular survey item, an inevitable risk with single-item indicators. Throughout the following empirical analysis, we address the robustness of our results by examining both dependent variables. The results are uniformly similar. . . .

Our key independent variables fall into the three broad categories outlined above: (1) indicators of economic vulnerability suggested by theories of economic self-interest; (2) indicators that reflect variability in information affecting respondents' understanding of outsourcing and its effect; and (3) indicators tapping attitudes toward other types of people, other countries, and active involvement in the affairs of other countries.

Self-Interest

To analyze personal economic vulnerability, we include measures of a respondent's skill level and occupation. Economic studies typically use the average annual wage for an individual's occupation to measure skill, a tack that has been followed in much of the research on attitudes toward foreign economic policy. In this study, we tap skill by calculating the *Occupational Wage* in 2006 for each job reported by respondents in our sample (expressed in tens of thousands of U.S. dollars). We asked the respondents to choose what best described their current (or most recent) occupation from a list of twenty-eight categories listed on the survey.

Using this information, we created a set of variables designed to measure the extent to which a respondent's occupation or industry of employment is susceptible to outsourcing. . . . To begin, we simply coded whether a respondent worked in a U.S. industry in which final products face import competition. Respondents were asked to choose the industry in which they work or most recently worked based on the three-digit North American Industrial Classification System (NAICS) categories. For each industry represented in our sample, i, we constructed a measure of *Import Orientation*, which is defined as (M_i / Y_i), where M_i is sector i's total imports and Y_i is this sector's total output. Because the distribution of this variable is highly skewed, we rely on its natural logarithm. In addition, we include a variable derived from Blinder's measure of whether an occupation is potentially offshorable, based largely on the degree to which the job requires face-to-face contact with customers (*Offshorable*).

We also include dummy variables indicating whether each respondent works in *Manufacturing*, the *Service* sector, or elsewhere. Various economists argue that high-skilled individuals in the manufacturing sector have gained from outsourcing while low-skilled manufacturing workers have suffered. There is also some evidence that highly skilled workers in service occupations will gain from outsourcing. We use these variables in combination with the measures of skill discussed above to determine whether attitudes toward outsourcing depend on these distributional consequences. However, because *Import Orientation* and *Manufacturing* are highly correlated, we analyze them separately rather than in combination.

The key advantage of the indicators discussed above is that they are not self-reported by the respondents, and thus pose no risk of endogeneity with respect to attitudes toward outsourcing. Nonetheless, they may not capture all possible ways in which one's personal economic self-interest could be influenced by outsourcing. Thus, we also asked respondents, "Have you or has anyone in your family been positively or negatively affected by outsourcing?" Answers were coded as 1 for negatively affected by outsourcing, 2 for not affected, or 3 for positively affected to create the variable *Perceived Effect of Outsourcing on Self*.

On the one hand, it is seldom easy for an individual to accurately assess whether and in what direction outsourcing has affected his or her well-being, if at all. On the other hand, as Freeman suggests, "Most Americans judge economic reality from what they observe in their lives, not from debates among economists or what journalists write. The reality includes job losses and threats of job losses due to offshoring and trade."[13] Freeman makes several related points. Personal experience forms the basis of self-interest, although it may be difficult to know with accuracy whether and in what direction one has been affected by outsourcing. People might assume they have been adversely affected when they have not been, or they may have been adversely affected but not be aware of it. Regardless of accuracy, people will nonetheless form subjective judgments of how this policy has affected them. This judgment may reflect a sound assessment of the economic impact on the individual or fears about future job losses.

13. Freeman 2009, 67.

While these subjective assessments of personal benefit or loss therefore may be indicators of personal economic self-interest, they may also reflect the information individuals have been exposed to. If people come to believe that they are being positively or negatively affected by outsourcing because an information source tells them as much, they are being influenced by information rather than experience. We address the ambiguities of interpreting this measure in our discussion of the results. Beyond difficulties in determining whether it represents the impact of self-interest or of information, perceived assessments of personal gain or loss from outsourcing are also potentially endogenous with respect to outsourcing attitudes. For example, those who oppose outsourcing as a policy may, as a result, be more likely to claim adverse personal effects, even in the absence of any concrete personal experience. We include this variable in our analyses despite these difficulties of interpretation because doing so yields a more fully specified model. Accounting for both objective and subjective measures of self-interest also provides a more conservative test of the importance of other factors included in our analysis.

In order to more fully specify our models, we also include a variable indicating whether the respondent was currently unemployed or laid off, since the immediacy of such an experience might make one more likely to blame a policy like outsourcing. Finally, we include a measure of local unemployment (by the respondent's zip code) because people living in areas marked by extensive job loss could experience indirect effects by virtue of falling housing markets or the closing of local stores and businesses due to economic downturns.

Information

Based on previous work, there is reason to expect that variations in the information people have received about outsourcing affect their perceptions of its impact as well as their understanding of what constitutes outsourcing. In particular, it is important whether people think of outsourcing purely in terms of interactions with foreign nations as opposed to defining it in a broader way that incorporates domestic outsourcing. To the extent that outsourcing is perceived to be about shifting part of the production process outside the firm, even if it is just next door, this practice should be seen as less threatening. To the extent that it is defined as offshore outsourcing and incorporates economic interactions with other countries, it is likely to be viewed in terms of "us versus them" and should trigger greater hostility.

To test this idea, we use responses to the six potential outsourcing scenarios discussed above to create two independent variables: (1) the number of scenarios involving a foreign country that a respondent considers to be outsourcing (*Foreign Definition*) and (2) whether the respondent considers the domestic item (scenario 1) to be outsourcing (*Domestic Definition*). We expect that the broader the range of foreign economic activities that someone defines as outsourcing, the more he or she is likely to oppose it. In contrast, a definition that incorporates domestic economic activity should prompt less opposition.

In addition to variance in individual definitions of the term, some studies suggest that a formal understanding of economics plays a role in views about outsourcing. Economists frequently maintain that critics of outsourcing rely on faulty economic logic. Individuals with more formal exposure to economics may, as a result, have a better appreciation of the associated gains from this phenomenon and hence a more favorable view of outsourcing than other individuals. To address the effects of economic knowledge, we include two items: (1) whether the respondent has ever taken an economics course and (2) whether the respondent thinks that economists believe free trade is good or bad for the economy. The second item is included to determine whether the respondent has an understanding of the basic principles of international economics as usually taught, regardless of previous enrollment in an economics course. Two dummy variables were created based on these items. The first, *Economics Class*, is coded as 1 if a respondent has taken an economics class and 0 otherwise. The second, *Economists' View of Trade*, is coded as 1 if a respondent understands that economists believe that free trade is good for the economy and 0 otherwise.

A final source of information with implications for attitudes toward outsourcing stems from important groups to which individuals may belong. The group identifications most relevant to views on outsourcing are political parties and unions. Thus, our models also include measures of party identification (with one variable indicating whether respondents describe themselves as Democrats and another for Republicans, with the reference category representing those without a partisan affiliation or who just lean Democrat or Republican) and membership in a union.

Out-Group Attitudes

Beyond self-interest and the sources of information that may affect preferences on outsourcing, we also address three features of attitudes toward other countries and types of people that proved important in previous empirical studies of attitudes regarding trade. The first index, *Active Involvement*, is composed of five items widely used to tap the extent to which respondents believe the U.S. should pursue an activist stance on international affairs outside the economic realm. These previously validated items address whether the U.S. should intervene in the affairs of other countries to prevent human rights abuses abroad, cooperate with foreign countries to solve global problems, and so forth. Here, as in previous studies, they form a highly reliable scale. We expect that people who think the U.S. should get involved in the affairs of other countries will be more likely to support outsourcing.

A second index, *Nationalism*, draws on three questions previously used to assess whether respondents believe that the U.S. is culturally superior to other countries. What we refer to as nationalism is similar to what other scholars have dubbed "patriotism" or "national superiority" in referring to a sense of positive national identity coupled with thinking less of people from outside one's national borders.

A third index, *Ethnocentrism*, taps levels of prejudice toward those of a different race or ethnicity. Ethnocentrism scales are designed to measure the "Commonplace inclination to divide the world into in-groups and out-groups, the former characterized by virtuosity and talent, the latter by corruption and mediocrity." By asking an individual about some positive and some negative human characteristics with reference to their racial in-group as well as to some out-groups, we can gauge the extent to which the person employs an in-group/out-group mode of thinking. To construct these measures, we employ the same domestic racial and ethnic in-groups and out-groups as previous studies (blacks, whites, and Hispanics), asking respondents to rate each of the groups separately in a randomized order on three characteristics (hardworking–lazy, efficient–wasteful, and trustworthy–untrustworthy). Consistent with previous studies, the two out-group scores are averaged and then subtracted from the in-group rating. Because people systematically evaluate their in-group more favorably than out-groups, the ethnocentrism scores are overwhelmingly positive, with higher scores indicating even higher ratings of the in-group relative to the out-group. All three indicators—*Active Involvement, Nationalism*, and *Ethnocentrism*—are standardized with a mean of zero and coded such that larger positive (negative) values of these variables reflect views that are more (less) interventionist, nationalistic, and ethnocentric, respectively.

Finally, because our data are cross-sectional, we include as control variables age, gender, race, and income. Education is also included as a control variable using a series of three dummy variables indicating whether the person graduated from a technical school or a two-year college (*2-Year College*), graduated from a four-year college (*4-Year College*), or holds a graduate degree (*Graduate School*). Those who did not receive any formal education beyond high school serve as the reference category. Although education has been used as an alternative measure of skill in some studies and, at times, as a proxy for economic knowledge, our study already includes more precise measures of economic knowledge and skill level, thus leaving the meaning of any remaining impact theoretically ambiguous.

We use an ordered logit specification to analyze the categorical and ordered dependent variable. All tests of statistical significance are based on robust standard errors, which account for any heteroskedasticity in the data and help take into account the highly skewed distribution of our dependent variables.

SURVEY RESULTS

To begin, it is useful to address whether, in the American mind, outsourcing is essentially the same as trade. While economists argue that outsourcing is simply a form of international trade, the mass public perceives the two very differently. In our survey, we asked respondents a set of questions about whether they support or oppose international trade and other aspects of globalization. We then constructed a categorical variable indicating whether respondents consistently support trade, oppose trade, or have mixed attitudes. The correlation between this variable and our categorical measure of outsourcing is weak (Spearman's $\rho = .28$, $p < .001$). . . . While more than half of the respondents have mixed or inconsistent attitudes about trade, almost two-thirds of them consistently oppose outsourcing and fewer than two percent consistently support it. Indeed, outsourcing appears to have very few advocates among the mass public, and people tend to have highly consistent views on this issue.

Having established that outsourcing is not trade by another name in the eyes of most Americans, we turn to an assessment of the extent to which outsourcing attitudes stem from personal economic self-interest. In Table 1, we begin by estimating a model that includes gender, race, age, family income, and all of the indicators corresponding to self-interest. Notably, there are no strong effects of *Personally Unemployed*, *Occupational Wage*, *Import Orientation*, *Income*, *Manufacturing*, and *Service*. For each of these variables, the corresponding regression coefficient is small and far from statistically significant. More importantly, and most surprisingly, there is little evidence that the offshorability of an individual's occupation or industry of employment has any bearing on his or her attitudes toward outsourcing. . . .

The one exception to these overwhelmingly null findings is the impact of an individual's subjective perception of the extent to which he or she has been positively or negatively influenced by outsourcing. The estimated coefficients of *Perceived Effect of Outsourcing on Self* are statistically significant, indicating that respondents who feel that outsourcing has helped them and their family hold far more favorable views of this phenomenon than individuals who feel they have been harmed by it. Because many more feel negatively as opposed to positively affected by outsourcing (25 percent versus 8 percent, respectively), the net effect of this consideration is to lower support for outsourcing.

As discussed above, this result could be interpreted at face value as an indicator of self-interest's influence on attitudes toward outsourcing. Alternatively, this finding might provide evidence that information shapes these attitudes if perceptions of outsourcing's effects on a respondent stem from the information he or she has been exposed to. We return to this issue in our discussion of information-based models. But a third possibility is that this relationship represents a mere rationalization of pre-existing attitudes toward outsourcing and thus is not a causal influence on policy preferences at all. Nonetheless, in order to provide a conservative test of the contribution of information-based indicators and out-group attitudes, we keep this variable in the model despite its ambiguous interpretation. Interestingly, the correlation between *Perceived Effect of Outsourcing on Self* on the one hand, and each of the objective measures of outsourcing's impact on the individual on the other, hovers around zero and never approaches statistical significance. This suggests that perceiving one's self as having been influenced by outsourcing and actually having been influenced by it are very different things. The lack of relationship with

TABLE 1 Effects of Economic Self-Interest on Support for Outsourcing

	Model 1	Model 2	Model 3	Model 4
Male	0.298*	0.244*	0.322**	0.269*
	(0.117)	(0.120)	(0.121)	(0.124)
Race	0.281*	0.233+	0.273*	0.225+
	(0.132)	(0.134)	(0.132)	(0.133)
Age	−0.008+	−0.009+	−0.008+	−0.009+
	(0.005)	(0.005)	(0.005)	(0.005)
Income	−0.041	−0.027	−0.041	−0.027
	(0.035)	(0.036)	(0.035)	(0.036)
Personally Unemployed	0.043	0.048	0.011	0.014
	(0.284)	(0.276)	(0.283)	(0.275)
2-Year College	0.064	0.163	0.042	0.139
	(0.146)	(0.148)	(0.146)	(0.148)
4-Year College	0.501**	0.602***	0.471**	0.573***
	(0.163)	(0.167)	(0.165)	(0.169)
Graduate School	0.820***	0.876***	0.775***	0.828***
	(0.216)	(0.218)	(0.224)	(0.226)
Occupational Wage (in $10K)	−0.007	−0.017	−0.006	−0.016
	(0.035)	(0.037)	(0.035)	(0.036)
Import Orientation	−0.003	−0.004		
	(0.023)	(0.024)		
Perceived Effect of Outsourcing on Self		0.818***		0.813***
		(0.119)		(0.119)

Manufacturing			0.090	0.115
			(0.212)	(0.211)
Service			0.134	0.147
			(0.145)	(0.149)
cut1	0.430	1.940***	0.508$^+$	2.013***
	(0.300)	(0.376)	(0.291)	(0.372)
cut2	3.622***	5.197***	3.705***	5.274***
	(0.388)	(0.440)	(0.375)	(0.431)
Pseudo log likelihood	−1536.238	−1492.675	−1540.315	−1497.233
N	2060	2060	2068	2068

Entries are ordered logit estimates with robust standard errors in parentheses. Two-tailed tests of statistical significance are conducted for all coefficient estimates. Statistical significance is indicated as follows: $^+p<.10$, $^*p<.05$, $^{**}p<.01$, $^{***}p<.001$.

any of the objective indicators also suggests that self-perceptions are more a function of information than of outsourcing's economic impact on an individual.

In terms of demographics, as in the case of attitudes toward trade, there is a gender gap in attitudes toward outsourcing, with women more hostile to this phenomenon than men. There is also a racial gap, in that minorities express greater support for outsourcing than whites. Further, respondents with more education have a more favorable view of outsourcing than those who are less educated, even after including variables that more accurately take into account occupation and skill level.

If not personal economic susceptibility to outsourcing's impact, then to what extent do factors associated with variability in information about outsourcing or noneconomic factors explain mass attitudes? To examine this question, Table 2 includes the key variables from Table 1, plus indicators of information-based considerations and preference for active international involvement, nationalism, and ethnocentrism. The evidence suggests that people form opinions based in part on their understanding of what constitutes outsourcing and on the cues in their information environment about whether one should support or oppose it. For example, the larger the number of scenarios involving a foreign country that individuals consider to be outsourcing, the more hostile they are to this phenomenon, as illustrated by the coefficient estimates of *Foreign Definition*, which are negative and statistically significant. This finding may reflect a tendency to blame outsourcing for a wider range of problems if it is defined as encompassing a broader array of overseas activities. In contrast, however, the coefficient estimates of *Domestic Definition* are positive and significant; respondents who identify outsourcing as a domestic practice have a more favorable view of it than respondents who do not consider domestic activity to be outsourcing.

In addition, Democrats are significantly more opposed to outsourcing than unaffiliated individuals are, while Republicans and nonpartisans do not differ in their views. These results are unsurprising, given the pro-labor stance that many Democrats adopt, the pro-business stance of many Republicans, and the criticism that Senator Kerry and then–Senator Barack Obama leveled at companies engaging in this practice during the 2004 and 2008 presidential elections.

It is also unsurprising that union members tend to oppose outsourcing given the kinds of information cues that they receive. Based on the results shown in Table 2, model 6, these individuals are roughly 35 percent less likely to consistently favor outsourcing than respondents who lack a union affiliation (and this difference is statistically significant at the .05 level). One explanation for this finding is that outsourcing places downward pressure on wages and reduces job security in many of the lower skilled occupations and industries that tend to be unionized. However, we have already accounted for skill level and whether the industry of employment is threatened by trade, which suggests that union membership is not simply another indicator of self-interest. Moreover, most union members work in nontradable sectors, such as primary, secondary, and higher education. There is no reason why outsourcing would harm these individuals.

An understanding of economists' views about trade improves an individual's opinion about outsourcing. The estimated coefficients of *Economists' View of Trade* are positive and statistically significant. Moreover, the effects of economic knowledge are substantially large and beyond those of education. Respondents who understand that economists consider free trade to be beneficial are 40 percent more likely to consistently support outsourcing than other individuals (a difference that is statistically significant at the .05 level). Simply taking an economics course, however, has little bearing on these attitudes. These results suggest that, consistent with the views of some economists, part of the opposition to outsourcing stems from a lack of economic knowledge. However, given the cross-sectional nature of the survey, it is also possible this relationship is more of a rationalization and projection of existing outsourcing preferences than an indicator of how knowledge affects preferences.

A number of studies of attitudes toward international trade conclude that Americans with more formal education tend to hold more favorable attitudes about free trade because highly skilled individuals benefit from trade, while lower skilled individuals do not. Jens Hainmueller and Hiscox challenge this interpretation, maintaining that a college education affects trade opinions by exposing people to theories about the benefits of trade.[14] Our results indicate that economic knowledge does improve attitudes toward outsourcing, though we find no effects from occupational wages. But importantly, the inclusion of these indicators does not account for the more general influence of education. Including *Economists' View of Trade* and *Economics Class* in our model has no bearing on the size or significance of the coefficients associated with education.

Finally, and perhaps most importantly, attitudes about outsourcing are not entirely about economics. They are shaped in powerful ways by one's sense of obligation to those in other countries and one's attitudes toward out-groups. As shown in Table 2, models 5 and 6, the estimated coefficients of *Ethnocentrism*, *Nationalism*, and *Active Involvement* indicate little support for outsourcing among people who believe the U.S. is superior to other countries, those who hold anti-interventionist views about U.S. involvement in the affairs of other countries, and those who exhibit prejudice toward groups unlike themselves. The effects of these factors are relatively large and independent of variables associated with self-interest and information. A change from the least globally interventionist attitudes registered by respondents to the polar opposite

14. Hainmueller and Hiscox 2006.

TABLE 2 Effects of Self-Interest, Information, and Noneconomic Factors on Support for Outsourcing

	Model 1	Model 2	Model 3	Model 4	Model 5	Model 6
Male	0.298*	0.273*	0.281*	0.228*	0.304*	0.264*
	(0.117)	(0.116)	(0.123)	(0.121)	(0.123)	(0.132)
Race	0.282*	0.293*	0.184	0.350*	0.207	0.228
	(0.132)	(0.131)	(0.145)	(0.140)	(0.149)	(0.175)
Age	-0.008*	-0.008	-0.009*	-0.005	-0.005	-0.003
	(0.005)	(0.005)	(0.005)	(0.005)	(0.005)	(0.005)
Income	-0.041	-0.041	-0.041	-0.043	-0.057	-0.070*
	(0.035)	(0.035)	(0.037)	(0.038)	(0.037)	(0.041)
Personally Unemployed			0.030			-0.192
			(0.285)			(0.308)
2-Year College	0.062	0.046	0.159	0.143	-0.106	0.050
	(0.144)	(0.143)	(0.149)	(0.155)	(0.153)	(0.171)
4-Year College	0.499**	0.502**	0.646***	0.597***	0.265	0.506*
	(0.162)	(0.156)	(0.168)	(0.178)	(0.169)	(0.203)
Graduate School	0.819***	0.805***	0.943***	0.872***	0.344	0.578*
	(0.216)	(0.200)	(0.221)	(0.217)	(0.230)	(0.262)
Occupational Wage (in $10K)	-0.007		-0.024			-0.017
	(0.035)		(0.037)			(0.039)
Import Orientation	-0.003		-0.008			-0.002
	(0.023)		(0.024)			(0.024)
Perceived Effect of Outsourcing on Self			0.846***			0.816***
			(0.121)			(0.128)
Local Unemployment			-0.463			-0.091
			(3.282)			(3.586)
Foreign Definition				-0.219***		-0.276***
				(0.051)		(0.053)

Domestic Definition				0.487***		0.499***
				(0.125)		(0.133)
Economists' View of Trade				0.395**		0.360*
				(0.131)		(0.142)
Economics Class				-0.223		-0.129
				(0.146)		(0.159)
Democrat				-0.356*		-0.449**
				(0.143)		(0.156)
Republican				0.035		0.049
				(0.145)		(0.164)
Union Membership				-0.452*		-0.435*
				(0.198)		(0.220)
Nationalism					-0.157*	-0.188*
					(0.069)	(0.076)
Active Involvement					0.402***	0.342***
					(0.065)	(0.070)
Ethnocentrism					-0.125+	-0.129+
					(0.066)	(0.072)
Offshorable			0.002			0.002
			(0.003)			(0.003)
cut1	0.423	0.439+	1.969***	-0.103	0.334	1.111*
	(0.294)	(0.254)	(0.408)	(0.318)	(0.282)	(0.494)
cut2	3.614***	3.641***	5.193***	3.167***	3.707***	4.640***
	(0.383)	(0.343)	(0.469)	(0.373)	(0.387)	(0.558)
Pseudo log likelihood	-1536.256	-1554.099	-1451.014	-1478.118	-1335.755	-1194.759
N	2060	2085	2013	2043	1890	1814

Entries are ordered logit estimates with robust standard errors in parentheses. Two-tailed tests of statistical significance are conducted for all coefficient estimates. Statistical significance is indicated as follows: $^{+}p<.10$, $^{*}p<.05$, $^{**}p<.01$, $^{***}p<.001$.

increases the predicted probability of consistently supporting outsourcing roughly five times. A shift from the least ethnocentric views to the most ethnocentric views increases the predicted value of consistently opposing outsourcing by over 50 percent as well. And a switch from the least nationalistic attitudes expressed to the most nationalistic increases this predicted probability by roughly 25 percent.

Not only do *Active Involvement*, *Nationalism*, and *Ethnocentrism* bear on preferences about outsourcing, they also dampen the effects of education. After including them in the model, the estimated coefficients of *4-Year College* and *Graduate School* become substantially smaller (compare models 2 and 5 in Table 2 and in Table A2). Equally, the strength of the relationship between outsourcing attitudes and both *4-Year College* and *Graduate School* becomes attenuated.

If one were to tally results for our efforts to capture the effects of self-interest, information-based, and out-group attitudes models, self-interest easily receives the least support with only one variable out of nine achieving statistical significance as a predictor. Even that one variable, *Perceived Effect of Outsourcing on Self*, is difficult to interpret since it may reflect rationalization on the part of respondents or the information to which they are exposed. Information-based cues and considerations, however, generate significant findings for five out of seven variables. Contrary to what certain political economy models suggest, attitudes toward outsourcing are not driven exclusively by economics. Active involvement, nationalism, and ethnocentrism have strong and sizable effects on opinions about outsourcing, even after controlling for the effects of demographics, self-interest, and information-based considerations.

It may not seem surprising that factors such as racism and opposition to humanitarian aid to other countries affect how people feel about outsourcing; interventionism draws on feelings Americans have toward foreign countries, and those in other countries are sometimes (though not always) of different races. But when one considers that neither trade nor outsourcing require any kind of immediate contact between ordinary Americans and foreigners, it becomes more difficult to understand why racism or opposition to humanitarian aid promote opposition to the idea that low-wage jobs that lower the costs of goods for Americans may be performed by foreign people in foreign places.

Overall, our survey results yield three important findings. First, Americans have strong, consistent, and primarily negative views of outsourcing, even though they may disagree on what precisely constitutes outsourcing. Americans vary substantially in their subjective understanding of this phenomenon and individuals' subjective understanding of what defines outsourcing and how they have been influenced by it has important implications for their attitudes toward this practice. Second, although attitudes toward outsourcing and trade are loosely related, as would be expected, they are neither marked by the same distribution nor characterized by equal intensity. Third, these attitudes are not a function of the vulnerability that respondents experience as a result of their occupation and the industry in which they work. Instead, the informational cues that they receive about this policy's economic effects, along with their attitudes toward the "other," play the most important roles in forming views toward outsourcing. Interestingly, this pattern remains consistent whether it is an attitude toward intervention in the affairs of another country (as in active involvement), a relative assessment of other countries (as in nationalism), or an attitude toward a racial out-group relative to one's own in-group (as in ethnocentrism). People who do not like out-groups also dislike outsourcing.

OUTSOURCING EXPERIMENT

As noted above, some of the relationships observed in our survey are subject to alternative interpretations. Ideally, we would confirm the causal nature of the significant relationships documented in Tables 1 and 2 by experimentally manipulating each of these independent variables. However, not all of these concepts can be altered in short-term or even longer-term studies. Ethnocentrism, for example, is believed to be particularly intransigent. Nonetheless, we used an experiment to confirm two of the key causal relationships and to better understand the impact of people's understanding of and response to the term "outsourcing."

Toward that end, we designed a population-based survey experiment (2009) systematically manipulating three independent factors—nationalism, whether the word outsourcing was used when asking respondents about this practice, and the respondent's definition of outsourcing—in order to assess their impact on attitudes toward outsourcing. Together, these experimental treatments form a $2 \times 2 \times 2$ factorial design, with eight total conditions to which respondents were randomly assigned with equal probabilities.

To assess the causal impact of nationalism, the first factor, we assigned respondents to receive an experimental treatment promoting either lower or higher levels of national superiority. Respondents read one of two statements designed either to encourage or discourage feelings of national superiority before they were asked the questions about outsourcing. Neither manipulation mentioned anything about trade or outsourcing. Instead, the statements emphasized pride in "American traditions of hard work, decency, honesty, and innovation" or shame regarding "a system that rewards greed and dishonesty over hard work and decency." Manipulation checks using the same index as in the survey confirmed that these statements did, in fact, significantly alter levels of nationalism. The mean level of *Nationalism* was significantly greater in the high national superiority condition than in the low superiority condition (Analysis of Variance [ANOVA] mean comparison, $F = 7.63$, $p < .01$).

Given that the term outsourcing conveys a broad range of meaning to respondents, we wanted to assess how much baggage the word itself conveyed compared to asking people about the practice without reference to the term itself. Consequently, the second experimental factor altered the wording of the questions addressing attitudes toward outsourcing so that the substance of the items was the same, but the word itself was not mentioned. Based on our survey findings of strong views but limited understanding or agreement on what the issue actually is, we suspected that attitudes toward outsourcing were highly symbolic in nature. In other words, people may have a strong knee-jerk reaction to the term that is not necessarily rooted in thoughts about its substance or consequences.

In our original survey, two of the three opinion items included the term outsourcing, and one included the most widely recognized example of outsourcing—telephone call centers. Thus, from those survey data it is impossible to tell how much of the opposition was driven by the term's symbolic value. We altered the questions in the experiment by systematically including or excluding the term in a factor completely orthogonal to *Nationalism*. Minor alterations to our measures either included or excluded the term as shown in brackets below:

1. Some people think that it is a bad thing when a company in the U.S. purchases services from a foreign company in order to save money, rather than producing these services itself. Others think that [outsourcing/this] is a good thing because it allows the company to save money. Do you generally favor or oppose this practice [of outsourcing]?
2. Recently, some American companies have been [outsourcing, that is,] hiring workers in other countries to replace workers in the U.S. who are paid higher wages. An example of this is people who take customer service telephone calls. Do you think the government should encourage or discourage [outsourcing/this practice] or stay out of this matter?
3. Some say that having jobs done by people in other countries is a bad idea and should be discouraged by the government. Others say that [this/outsourcing] saves companies money and allows them to sell goods more cheaply, so the government should encourage it. Which of the following statements comes closest to your views about what government should do?

These three items created a highly reliable index of attitudes toward outsourcing that served as our dependent variable, *Opinion toward Outsourcing* (Cronbach's alpha = .85).

Finally, the third factor attempted to manipulate the respondents' definitions of this practice by informing them in the course of the question about the types of activities included within the definition. Our manipulation check indicated that we did not successfully alter the breadth of people's definitions as intended. While we were not able to alter respondents' ideas about what constitutes outsourcing, the extent of endorsement of foreign definitions and domestic definitions remained very powerful predictors of attitudes.

Respondents comprised a representative national sample of just under 2,000 currently working or previously working Americans, using the same specifications for qualification as the 2007 survey. For the two successfully manipulated experimental factors, *Nationalism* and *Mention of Outsourcing*, our hypothesis was that the term outsourcing, as opposed to the practice itself, would serve as a symbol that, together with high levels of nationalism, would trigger stronger opposition to outsourcing. In other words, people view it as patriotic to oppose outsourcing, and under conditions of strong nationalism, one is considered a "Benedict Arnold" if one supports it. The term itself stimulates a form of economic jingoism, whereby nationalistic sentiment seems consistent with expressing this anti-out-group policy preference. In statistical terms, we expected an interaction effect between the presence of the term outsourcing and high levels of nationalism, such that in combination this would encourage opposition to outsourcing.

An analysis of variance including the two orthogonal experimental factors (*Low/High Nationalism* and *Mention of Outsourcing*) suggested that neither main effect was statistically significant, but the anticipated interaction was as predicted ($F = 8.94$, $p < .01$). As shown in Figure 1, perceived national superiority significantly reduced support for the practice of outsourcing, but only when the term outsourcing was used in the question ($F = 4.01$, $p < .05$). When the same question was asked without mentioning the term, the level of support for the policy was the same regardless of the national superiority condition to which a respondent was assigned ($F = .99$, $p = .32$). Although the upward slope of the dashed line looks somewhat similar to the downward slope of the solid one, the greater variance in estimates of means when the policy is not explicitly called outsourcing renders it statistically indistinguishable from no change whatsoever. In other words, if we do not explicitly call it outsourcing, people do not know what they think about the policy. The pattern observed in our survey data reflects the negative impact shown in the solid line in Figure 2. But importantly, the same pattern does not occur in the absence of the term outsourcing.

Overall, these results make it clear that nationalism does indeed play a causal role in influencing attitudes toward outsourcing. Inducing higher levels of nationalism has a substantial impact on opinions about outsourcing. But when we asked about outsourcing without mentioning the word itself, nationalism did not cause the same negative reaction. In contrast, the term itself, combined with feelings of national superiority, triggers negative out-group, or more aptly, out-country, attitudes.

Using our manipulation check index for nationalism, we further examined the possibility that the term outsourcing might trigger higher levels of nationalistic sentiment, but we did not find this to be the case. The mention of outsourcing did not trigger higher levels of national superiority, whereas the national superiority manipulation did. Based on these findings, we suggest

FIGURE 1 Support for Outsourcing by Nationalism and Mention of Outsourcing[a]

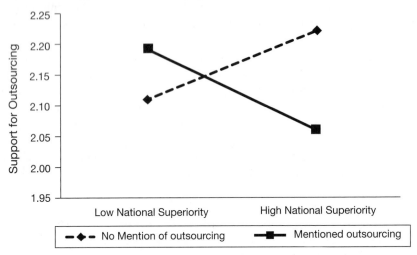

[a] The interaction between mention of outsourcing and nationalism is statistically significant ($F = 8.94$, $p < .01$), while the main effects are not. The solid line represents a statistically significant decline with higher levels of nationalism when the term outsourcing is mentioned. Despite appearances, the broken line does not increase significantly. The 95 percent confidence intervals for the means are as follows (lower bound, upper bound): (1) no mention of outsourcing×low national superiority (2.031, 2.189); (2) no mention of outsourcing×high national superiority (2.134, 2.299); (3) mentioned outsourcing×low national superiority (2.114, 2.274); (4) mentioned outsourcing×high national superiority (1.977, 2.135).

that it is the term outsourcing and whatever symbolic baggage it carries more than the substance of this issue that spurs negative out-group anxiety among those who feel most positively about their nation.

CONCLUSION

Most economists agree that outsourcing generates benefits for countries as a whole. Like international trade, outsourcing helps to allocate factors of production efficiently and enhance the economic welfare of countries. But like trade, outsourcing also has distributional consequences: some segments of society will gain as a result of this phenomenon, while other segments lose. These losses are likely to include both jobs and income. Although most estimates suggest that outsourcing has produced little actual job loss to date, there is widespread fear that this practice will or already has harmed many American workers. Consequently, while outsourcing yields economic benefits, it also creates economic and political costs.

Indeed, Blinder concludes that "offshoring may be one of the biggest political issues in economics over the next generation."[15] Nonetheless, the politics of outsourcing are poorly understood. Little has been known about public attitudes toward outsourcing, except that American workers are concerned about it and perceive that it already has had vast effects. Moreover, Americans tend to view outsourcing in terms of in-group/out-group dynamics. For many individuals, the "out" in outsourcing seems to refer to the out-group, that is, any group other than the one in which he or she claims membership. If one's own nation is considered to be superior to others, then attitudes toward outsourcing will be more negative. The less people think of out-groups relative to their own in-group, the more they oppose outsourcing—*even when those out-groups are racial and ethnic minorities within their own country*. Likewise, those who do not want to engage with foreign countries are especially hostile to outsourcing. Opposition to outsourcing appears to be part of a broader worldview that defines people as "us" or "them."

Nearly half a century ago, various distinguished observers advanced the argument that nationalism and isolationism shape foreign economic policy. This view has fallen out of favor more recently, supplanted by models that emphasize the material self-interest of countries and people. The newer models go a long way toward explaining trade policy, especially at the national and international level, but they have little traction in explaining the foreign policy attitudes of the mass public.

Our results have important implications for understanding public opposition to outsourcing. Attitudes toward this policy are obviously part of a broader worldview that focuses on taking care of one's own—via isolationist foreign policy or support for people of the same race and ethnicity. If outsourcing is economically beneficial and policymakers want to generate public support for this practice, they need to do a better job of framing the issue. Outsourcing by another name would, indeed, be more palatable to the public. Our findings suggest that the term used for this policy is not without consequence. Indeed, support for outsourcing is un-American to many. Further, the term outsourcing may have been terminologically doomed from the start in the eyes of the mass public. After all, trading implies that all parties obtain some benefit from a transaction while outsourcing demands an in-group that is opposed to the out-group—an "us" in opposition to "them." In order to call a practice outsourcing, a line must be drawn that distinguishes who is in and who is outside the group of concern. Interestingly, this is not always the country, or even the state. Recently some roofing companies in Pennsylvania claim to have lost substantial amounts of business to outsourcing. In this case, the complaints were directed at the Amish within their own state (and city) because Amish

15. Blinder 2009a, 43.

roofers were consistently underbidding them. Because the term outsourcing requires people to divide the world into insiders and outsiders, those prone to making such distinctions are especially likely to oppose this practice, regardless of how they might be affected economically.

Policymakers have gone to great lengths at times to suggest that outsourcing is not the same as trade, even when by most economists' accounts they are much the same. Is the underlying fear that the extremely negative attitudes toward outsourcing will taint the more evenly divided views of trade? Indeed, trade opinions might suffer, but advocates of outsourcing might also improve support for it by associating it with trade, or at least by linking it to a policy that suggests some inherent benefits for both the in-group and the out-group.

In addition, these results point to the delicate balance involved in promoting positive "in-country" views among the populace without denigrating attitudes toward others. Notably, our experiment was done at the height of economic malaise, with strong negative feelings toward the U.S. among its own citizenry. And yet, perceptions of national superiority were nonetheless both manipulable and effective in promoting opposition to outsourcing. Although many have linked economic decline to perceptions of personal economic threat, much of the hostility toward outsourcing stems from concerns that U.S. workers are at risk of losing jobs to "others," not just that they are vulnerable to job loss.

REFERENCES

Bauer, Raymond Augustine, Ithiel de Sola Pool, and Lewis Anthony Dexter. 1963. *American Business and Public Policy: The Politics of Foreign Trade*. New York, N.Y.: Atherton Press.

Bhagwati, Jagdish, Arvind Panagariya, and T. N. Srinivasan. 2004. "The Muddles over Outsourcing." *The Journal of Economic Perspectives* 18, no. 4 (Fall): 93–114.

Blinder, Alan S. 2006. "Offshoring: The Next Industrial Revolution?" *Foreign Affairs* 85, no. 2 (March/April): 113–28.

———. 2009a. "Offshoring: Big Deal, or Business as Usual?" In *Offshoring of American Jobs: What Response from US Economic Policy?* ed., Benjamin M. Friedman, Cambridge, Mass.: MIT Press: 19–59.

———. 2009b. "How Many US Jobs Might Be Offshorable?" *World Economics* 10, no. 2 (April–June): 41–78.

Burgoon, Brian, and Michael J. Hiscox. 2004. "The Mysterious Case of Female Protectionism: Gender Bias in the Attitudes and Politics of International Trade." Paper presented at the annual meeting of the American Political Science Association, Chicago, Ill., September 2–5.

Feenstra, Robert C., and Gordon H. Hanson. 1999. "The Impact of Outsourcing and High-Technology Capital on Wages: Estimates for the United States, 1979–1990." *Quarterly Journal of Economics* 114, no. 3 (August): 907–40.

Freeman, Richard B. 2009. "Comments." In *Off-shoring of American Jobs: What Response from US Economic Policy?* ed., Benjamin M. Friedman, Cambridge, Mass.: MIT Press: 61–71.